Business
BASICS

A study guide for degree students

LAW

PUBLISHING

Second edition June 1997

ISBN 0 7517 2117 4
(previous edition 0 7517 2071 2)

British Library Cataloguing-in-Publication Data

A catalogue record for this book
is available from the British Library

Published by
BPP Publishing Limited
Aldine House, Aldine Place
London W12 8AW

BPP Publishing would like to thank the following:

Jacqueline Hayes and *Angela Clark* for authorial input

Genesys Editorial for editorial input

Our thanks are also due to the Institute of
Chartered Secretaries and Administrators, for
permission to reproduce examination questions in
this text. The suggested solutions have been
prepared by BPP Publishing

Printed in Great Britain by

Contents

PREFACE

BUSINESS BASICS are targeted specifically at the needs of:

- students taking business studies degrees;
- students taking business-related modules of other degrees;
- students on courses at a comparable level;
- others requiring business information at this level.

This *Law* text has been written with two key goals in mind.

- To present a substantial and useful body of knowledge on law at degree level. This is not just a set of revision notes – it explains the subject in detail and does not assume prior knowledge.
- To make learning and revision as easy as possible. Therefore

  each chapter:

  - starts with an introduction and clear objectives;
  - contains numerous activities;
  - includes a chapter roundup summarising the points made;
  - ends with a quick quiz

  and at the back of the book you will find:

  - multiple choice questions and solutions;
  - exam-style questions and solutions.

The philosophy of the series is thus to combine techniques which actively promote learning with a no-nonsense, systematic approach to the necessary factual content of the course.

BPP Publishing have for many years been the leading providers of targeted texts for professional qualifications. We know that our customers need to study effectively in order to pass their exams, and that they cannot afford to waste time. They expect clear, concise and highly-focused study material. As university and college education becomes more market driven, students rightly demand the same high standards of efficiency in their learning material. The BUSINESS BASICS series meets those demands.

BPP Publishing
June 1997

Titles in this series

Accounting
Law
Information Technology
Economics
Marketing
Human Resource Management
Organisational Behaviour
Quantitative Methods

You may order other titles in the series using the form at the end of this text. If you would like to send in your comments on this book, please turn to the review form following the order form.

HOW TO USE THIS STUDY GUIDE

This book can simply be read straight through from beginning to end, but you will get far more out of it if you keep a pen and paper to hand. The most effective form of learning is *active learning*, and we have therefore filled the text with activities for you to try as you go along. We have also provided objectives, a chapter roundup and a quick quiz for each chapter. Here is a suggested approach to enable you to get the most out of this book.

(a) Select a chapter to study, and read the introduction and objectives in the box at the start of the chapter.

(b) Next read the chapter roundup at the end of the chapter (before the quick quiz and the solutions to activities). Do not expect this brief summary to mean too much at this stage, but see whether you can relate some of the points made in it to some of the objectives.

(c) Next read the chapter itself. Do attempt each activity as you come to it. You will derive the greatest benefit from the activities if you write down your solutions before checking them against the solutions at the end of the chapter.

(d) As you read, make use of the 'notes' column to add your own comments, references to other material and so on. Do try to formulate your own views. In business, many things are matters of interpretation and there is often scope for alternative views. The more you engage in a dialogue with the book, the more you will get out of your study.

(e) When you reach the end of the chapter, read the chapter roundup again. Then go back to the objectives at the start of the chapter, and ask yourself whether you have achieved them.

(f) Finally, consolidate your knowledge by writing down your answers to the quick quiz. You can check your answers by going back to the text. The very act of going back and searching the text for relevant details will further improve your grasp of the subject.

(g) You can then try the multiple choice questions at the end of the book and the exam level question, to which you are referred at the end of the chapter. Alternatively, you could wait to do these until you have started your revision – it's up to you.

Further reading

While we are confident that the BUSINESS BASICS books offer excellent range and depth of subject coverage, we are aware that you will be encouraged to follow up particular points in books other than your main textbook, in order to get alternative points of view and more detail on key topics. We recommend the following books as a starting point for your further reading on Law.

Cheshire Fifoot and Furmston, *Law of Contract*, 12th edition 1991, Butterworths

Cooke, J, *The Law of Tort*, 2nd edition 1995, Pitman

Gower, *Principles of Modern Company Law*, 5th edition 1992, Sweet & Maxwell

Griffin, Stephen, *Company Law: Fundamental Principles*, 2nd edition 1996, Pitman

Harvey and Parry, *The Law of Consumer Protection and Fair Trading*, 4th edition 1996, Butterworths

Hicks and Goo, *Cases and Material on Company Law*, 1st edition 1994, Blackstone

Mayson, French and Ryan, *On Company Law*, 14th edition 1997, Blackstone Press

Shaw, J, *Law of the European Union*, 2nd edition 1996, MacMillan

Singleton, E.S., *Introduction to Competition Law*, edition 1992, Pitman

Smith and Bailey, *The Modern English Legal System*, 2nd edition 1991, Sweet & Maxwell

Smith and Keenan, *Company Law for Students*, 10th edition 1996, Pitman

Smith and Keenan, *English Law*, 10th edition 1992, Pitman

Chapter 1

THE NATURE AND SOURCES OF ENGLISH LAW

Introduction

English law consists of a practical body of rules and procedures which are created by the state and which provide resolutions to ordinary problems. Much of English law is created by the legislature, that is to say Parliament, and is therefore contained in acts of Parliament (or statutes). Where this is not so, legal principles can be found in case law, which consists of the decisions laid down by judges in individual cases, or in customary practices.

English law is classified into criminal law and civil Law and this distinction is reflected throughout the legal system.

This chapter provides an outline of the development of English law and explains the sources of English law. EC law, which has an increasingly important impact in the UK, is the subject of a separate chapter.

Your objectives

After completing this chapter you should:

(a) understand the nature of law;

(b) know the main sources of law;

(c) understand the relationship between common law and equity;

(d) know how to refer to cases, and how cases are reported;

(e) be able to distinguish between *ratio decidendi* and *obiter dicta*;

(f) know which courts can create binding precedents, and which courts are so bound;

(g) be able to assess the advantages and disadvantages of the system of precedent;

(h) understand the concept of Parliamentary sovereignty;

(i) know the stages a bill passes through before it becomes an act of Parliament;

(j) understand the need for delegated legislation;

(k) know the subsidiary sources of law;

(l) know the canons and general principles of statutory interpretation and the statutory sources of help in interpretation.

1   THE NATURE OF LAW

The law is not static but changes and develops, reflecting the values and institutions of each era. Any study of English law as it now is (for the time being) requires a brief explanation of the process of historical development which has made it what it is. Until Parliament was reformed in the nineteenth century the main purpose and effect of English law was to define and safeguard rights of property and to uphold public order. Since that time there has been an increasing flow of new laws designed, for example, to deal with social problems and to develop the national economy. Many old laws have been repealed; for instance, a broken promise of marriage was formerly actionable by the jilted woman as a breach of contract, but this is no longer so.

Although English law has many features which are common to other national legal systems, it also has some distinctive features of its own. It differs from the law of many Western European countries (and also Scotland) in having absorbed only a small amount of Roman law. Secondly, English law is case law made by decisions of the courts to a much greater extent than the law of many other countries.

1.1   Continuity

England was last conquered in 1066. Since then no major changes have been imposed on the legal system, and so there is a progression in the development of the law over a long period. Principles of English law do not become inoperative through the lapse of time. Thus in *R v Casement 1917*, the Treason Act 1351 was consulted. This does not just apply to Acts of Parliament, but also to case law. The outcome of *Pinnel's case 1602* is still important today.

1.2   The system of precedent

The doctrine of precedent means that a judge is bound to apply decisions from earlier cases to the facts of the case before him, provided certain conditions are satisfied.

1.3   Common law and equity

The earliest element of the legal system to develop was the common law, a harsh system incorporating rigid rules applied by royal courts after the Norman conquest. Equity was developed several hundred years later as a system of law applied by the Chancellor where for some reason justice did not appear to be done under common law principles. The rules of equity were more flexible, based on the principles of equality and good conscience.

1.4   Codification

Definition

Codification: the replacement of common law rules by statute which embodies those rules.

Consolidation: the passing of an act of Parliament to 'tidy up the law'.

On occasion, the law in a particular area may be *codified*; the relevant rules as derived from existing legislation and from case law may be set out anew in a single codifying statute. Case law is law made in the courts. Legislation, or statute, is made by Parliament, the supreme law-making body in the United Kingdom. Codification should not be confused with consolidation, which is a process of bringing together statutory provisions (not case law) on a particular topic.

In some countries most of the law has been codified, or reduced to written codes which contain the whole of the law in a particular area. This is not generally the case in England. Examples of codification which has taken place are the Bills of Exchange Act 1882 and the Sale of Goods Act 1893 (the latter being subsequently *consolidated* into the Sale of Goods Act 1979). The resource required to codify key areas of the law is now thought to be too great to allow it; it is unlikely, for example, that the law of contract will be codified, although certain areas of criminal law may be addressed in the foreseeable future.

1.5 The courts

The courts have to be organised to accommodate the working of the legal system. There are four main functional aspects of the court system which underlie its structure.

(a) *Civil and criminal law* differ so much in substance and procedure that they are best administered in separate courts. However, there is no clear division into criminal courts and civil courts, although certain courts may have jurisdiction primarily in one area.

(b) *Local courts* allow the vast bulk of small legal proceedings to be decentralised. But important civil cases, in which large sums of money are at stake, begin in the High Court in London.

(c) Although the courts form a single system (as a result of the Judicature Acts 1873-1875), there is some *specialisation* both within the High Court (split into three divisions) and in other courts with separate functions.

(d) There is a system of *review by appeal* to higher courts. However, there is no clear division between courts of first instance and appeal courts; some courts function as both.

2   SOURCES OF ENGLISH LAW

The term 'sources of law' is used in several different senses.

(a) The *historical sources* are common law and equity.

(b) The *legal sources* are the means by which the law is currently brought into existence. There are four legal sources. The two most important today are case law (or judicial precedent) and legislation (or statute law). Custom is of little practical importance as a source of law, but is still classified as a current source. The impact of EC law, the fourth current source of law, is increasing and is the subject of a separate chapter.

(c) The *subsidiary sources* are not currently responsible for the direct creation of law. They include law merchant, roman law and canon law.

3   HISTORICAL SOURCES OF LAW

As noted earlier in this chapter, English law has developed in an unbroken progression over a period of some 900 years. English law's historical sources are those procedures, rules and ways of thinking which have given rise to today's current sources of law. A legal problem may be decided on the rules of the legal sources, but these in turn (particularly judicial precedent) have been derived from the historical sources of common law and equity.

3.1 Common law

Definition

Common Law: the body of legal rules developed by the common law courts and now embodied in legal decisions.

At the time of the Norman Conquest in 1066 there was no system of law common to the whole country. Rules of local custom were applied by local manorial courts. To improve the system, the King sent royal commissioners on tour (circuit) to different parts of the realm to deal with crimes and civil disputes. These commissioners, who often heard their cases with the assistance of a local jury, at first applied the local customary law of the neighbourhood. On their return from circuit the commissioners sat in the royal courts at Westminster to try cases there. In time the commissioners developed rules of law, selected from the differing local customs which they had encountered, as a common law (*ius commune*) which they applied uniformly in all trials (before the King's courts) throughout the kingdom.

Definitions

Plaintiff: the person who complains or brings an action asking the court for relief.

Defendant: the person against whom a civil action is brought or who is prosecuted for a criminal offence.

Writ: a written command issued under the King's authority.

To commence an action before any of these courts, the plaintiff obtained from the main royal office, the Chancery, an order (a writ) issued under the King's authority and addressed to the Sheriff of the county in which the defendant resided, by which the Sheriff was required to ensure that the defendant appeared for the trial. The writ specified the ground of complaint and gave a brief summary of the facts on which the plaintiff required judgment. Writs could only be issued in one of the established forms, which were grounds of action. If there were no appropriate writ it was not possible to have one of a new type in order to bring a grievance before the royal courts. This principle was slightly relaxed in 1285 but the common law system, based on the availability of standard writs, was still very rigid and hence an inadequate means of providing justice.

The procedure of common law courts was also unsatisfactory. A *plaintiff* might lose his case owing to a minor technicality of wording or be frustrated by specious defences, deliberate delay or corruption, or find himself unable to enforce a judgment given in his favour because there was no suitable common law remedy.

Activity 1

D agrees to purchase a Picasso painting, which is an original, from S for £200,000. They sign a contractual document but S later refuses to hand over the painting to D. What remedy would be available to D?

3.2 Equity

Definition

Equity: a source of English law consisting of those rules which emerged from the Court of Chancery.

Citizens who could not obtain redress for grievances in the common law courts petitioned the King to obtain relief by direct royal intervention. These petitions came before the King in Council and by custom were referred to the principal civil minister, the Chancellor. In dealing with each petition his concern was to establish the truth of the matter and then to impose a just solution without undue regard for technicalities or procedural points.

Because the principles on which the Chancellor decided points were based on *fair* dealing between two individuals as equals, these principles became known as equity. The system of equity, developed and administered by the Court of Chancery, was not an alternative to the common law, but a method of adding to and improving on the common law. This interaction of common law and equity produced three major changes.

(a) *New rights*. Equity recognised and protected rights for which the common law gave no safeguards. If, for example, Sam transferred property to the legal ownership of Tom to pay the income of the property to Ben (in modern law Tom is a trustee for Ben), the common law simply recognised that Tom was the owner of the property and ignored Tom's obligations to Ben. Equity recognised that Tom was the owner of the property at common law but insisted, as a matter of justice and good conscience, that Tom must comply with the terms of the trust imposed by Sam (the settlor) and pay the income to Ben (the beneficiary).

(b) *Better procedure*. Equity could be more effective than common law in bringing a disputed matter to a decision.

(c) *Better remedies*. The standard common law remedy for the successful plaintiff was the award of monetary compensation, damages, for his loss. Equity was able to order the defendant to do what he had agreed to do (*specific performance*), to abstain from wrongdoing (*injunction*), to alter a document so that it reflected the parties' true intentions (*rectification*) or to restore the pre-contract status quo (*rescission*).

Definitions

Specific performance: an equitable remedy in which the court orders the defendant to perform his side of a contract.

Injunction: an equitable remedy in which the court orders the other party to a contract to observe negative restrictions.

Rectification: an equitable remedy in which the court can order a document to be altered so that it reflects the parties' true intentions.

Rescission: an equitable remedy through which a contract is cancelled or rejected and the parties are restored to their pre-contract condition, as if it had never been entered into.

The development of equity was based on a number of *equitable maxims* (or principles).

These are still applied today if an equitable remedy is sought. The following are examples.

(a) *He who comes to equity must come with clean hands*. To be fairly treated, the plaintiff must have acted fairly himself. For example, in the case *D and C Builders v Rees 1966* the defendant could not plead a defence of equitable estoppel because she had tried to take advantage of the plaintiff's financial difficulties.

(b) *Equality is equity*. The law attempts to play fair and redress the balance; hence what is available to one person must be available to another. As an example, equity does not allow the remedy of specific performance to be granted against a minor, and it does not allow a minor to benefit from the remedy either.

(c) *Equity looks at the intent, not the form*. However a person may try to pretend that he is doing something in the correct form, equity will look at what he is actually trying to achieve. For example, if an agreed damages clause in a contract is not a genuine estimate of likely loss, equity will treat the clause as a penalty clause.

3.3 The relationship between common law and equity

In theory, equity accepted common law rights but insisted that they should be exercised in a just fashion. The practical effect was nonetheless that a decision of the Court of Chancery often reversed or conflicted with common law rules. At one stage, the Court of Chancery went so far as to issue orders by which litigants were forbidden to bring an action at common law to enforce strict common law rights. The rivalry between Chancery and common law courts was resolved in 1615 by a decision of the King (in the *Earl of Oxford's Case*) that where common law and equity conflict, equity must prevail.

Equity was not in its origins a consistent code of law: it was simply disconnected intervention in legal disputes. Each Chancellor (and the Chancery judges acting under his authority) applied a personal and sometimes arbitrary standard of what he considered fair. Equity, it was said, varied with the length of the individual Chancellor's foot. From the sixteenth century onwards, however, the Chancellor and his deputies were usually recruited from the legal profession trained in common law. Under common law influence, equity became a consistent body of doctrine and at least as technical as the common law.

Thus the common law, administered in royal courts, was supplemented and sometimes overruled by principles of equity administered in the Court of Chancery. A plaintiff who began proceedings in one set of courts might after years of expensive litigation find that for some technical reason, he could not obtain the desired result but must abandon his case and begin again in the other courts. This dual court system was ended by the Judicature Acts 1873–1875, which amalgamated the English courts. It is now possible to rely on any principle of common law or equity in any court of law. In case of conflict, equity still prevails over common law.

Although the courts have been amalgamated, common law and equity remain distinct. Where common law applies it tends to be automatic in its effect. Equity recognises the common law, as it always did. It sometimes offers an alternative solution, but the court has discretion as to whether or not it will grant an equitable remedy in lieu of a common law one.

If, for example, breach of contract is proved, the plaintiff will at least get common law damages as compensation for his loss automatically; in certain circumstances the court may, at its discretion, provide an alternative remedy of equity. It may, for instance, order the defendant to perform the contract rather than allow him to buy his way out of his contractual obligations by paying damages. The discretionary nature of equitable remedies means that a person who wins an action will not necessarily get the remedy he wants.

Miller v Jackson 1977
The Court of Appeal held that a cricket club had committed both negligence and nuisance by allowing cricket balls to be struck out of the ground into the plaintiff's adjoining premises. However, the court refused to grant the injunction that the plaintiff had sought. It awarded damages instead on the grounds that the interest of the public in being able to play and watch cricket on a ground where it had been played for over 70 years should prevail over the hardship of a few individual householders who had only recently purchased their homes.

Activity 2

Consider whether the recognition of trusts illustrates the principle that equity prevails over common law.

4 CASE LAW

As noted above, the development of common law and equity has led to one of the main legal sources of law, case law, and informs much of the other main source, legislation.

4.1 Judicial precedent

Both common law and equity are the product of decisions in the courts. They are judge-made law but based on a principle of consistency. Once a matter of principle has been decided (by one of the higher courts) it becomes a *precedent*. In any later case to which that principle is relevant the same principle should (subject to certain exceptions) be applied. This doctrine of consistency, following precedent, is expressed in the maxim *stare decisis*, 'to stand by a decision'.

Definition

Stare decisis: 'to stand by the decision'. The maxim on which judicial precedent is based.

Judges inevitably create law. Sometimes an Act of Parliament will deliberately vest a wide discretion in the judiciary. In other cases there may be no statutory provision and no existing precedent relevant to the particular dispute. Even so, the doctrine of judicial precedent is based on the view that it is not the function of a judge to make law, but to decide cases in accordance with existing rules.

It is generally accepted that consistency is an important feature of a good decision-making process. Similar cases should be treated in the same way. However, the passage of time, or changing circumstances, may cause a case to offer a solution which no longer appears just. One of the main functions of the higher courts is to give an authoritative decision on disputed questions of law. A court's decision is expected to be consistent (or at least not unjustifiably inconsistent) with previous decisions and to provide an opinion which the parties, and others, can use to direct their future relationships. This is the basis of the system of judicial precedent.

Judicial precedent depends on the following.

(a) There must be adequate and reliable reports of earlier decisions.

(b) There must be rules for extracting from an earlier decision on one set of facts the legal principle to be applied in reaching a decision on a different set of facts.

    (i)   The principle must be a proposition of law.

    (ii) It must form part of the *ratio decidendi* of the case.

    (iii) The material facts of each case must be the same.

(c) Precedents must be classified into those which are binding and those which are merely persuasive. This depends primarily on the respective status of the preceding court and the later one.

4.2   Law reports

Until the mid-nineteenth century law reports – reports of decided cases – were notes made by practising lawyers. Later on, reports were published without official authorisation by professional law reporters. In modern times there are major series of law reports on general law published weekly and then bound as annual volumes. In addition there are other special series of reports, for example, of tax cases, commercial cases and industrial relations cases. At a hearing in court, the barrister who cites a case as a precedent will read aloud from the reported judgment.

Every case has a title, usually (in a civil case) in the form *Brown v Smith*, that is Brown (plaintiff) versus Smith (defendant). In the event of an appeal the plaintiff's name is still shown first, whether he or she is the appellant or the respondent. Some cases are cited (for technical reasons of procedure) by reference to the subject matter, such as *Re Enterprises Limited* (a company case) or *Re Black's Settlement* (a trust case) ('re' means 'about'); or in shipping cases by the name of the ship, for example, *The Wagon Mound*. In a full citation the title of the case is followed by abbreviated particulars of the volume of the law reports in which the case is reported, for example, *Best v Samuel Fox & Co Ltd (1952)* 2 All ER 394 (The report is at p 394 of Vol. 2 of the All England Reports for 1952). The same case may be reported in more than one series of law reports and sometimes under different names.

As regards content, a full law report includes the following.

(a) The names of the parties.

(b) The court in which the case was decided.

(c) The judge or judges.

(d) The date of the hearing.

(e) A summary (*head note*) of the points of law established by the case.

(f) A list of the earlier cases cited as precedents at the hearing.

(g) The previous history of the litigation.

(h) The facts.

(i) The names of counsel and their arguments.

(j) The verbatim text of the judgment (or judgments if more than one).

(k) The order of the court.

(l) Whether leave to appeal was granted.

(m) The solicitors.

(n) The reporting barrister.

It is only decisions of the higher courts, that is the High Court, the Court of Appeal and the Judicial Committee of the House of Lords, which are included in the general law reports. Only the important cases are included in the law reports, though certain libraries hold copies of judgments in unreported cases.

Activity 3

You find a case called *Donoghue v Stevenson 1932* referred to in a textbook on the English legal system. What can you conclude about the case?

4.3   Proposition of law

A decision must be based on a proposition of *law* before it can be considered as a precedent. It may not be a decision on a question of *fact*. The distinction is not straightforward. An issue is a finding of fact where it depends on the credibility of direct evidence or on deductions drawn from circumstantial evidence. For example, a judge may, from the direct facts of weather conditions and the length of skidmarks, infer that a driver has been negligent. This finding of fact is not binding and so a judge in a later case involving the same conditions and facts need not be bound by the earlier decision.

4.4 *Ratio decidendi* and *obiter dicta*

Definition

Ratio decidendi: the reason for a decision.

Obiter dicta: statements made by a judge 'by the way'.

A judgment will start with a description of the facts of the case and probably a review of earlier precedents and possible alternative theories. The judge will then make statements of law applicable to the legal problems raised by the material facts. Provided these statements are the basis for the decision, they are known as the *ratio decidendi* of the case. The *ratio decidendi* (reason for deciding) is the vital element which binds future judges. If a judge's statements of legal principle do not form the basis of the decision, or if his statements are not based on the existing material facts but on hypothetical facts, they are known as *obiter dicta* (said by the way). A later court may respect such statements, but it is not bound to follow them. They are only of *persuasive* authority.

> *Rondel v Worsley 1969*
> The House of Lords stated an opinion that a barrister could be held liable for negligence when not acting as an advocate, and that a solicitor would be immune from action when acting as an advocate. Since the case actually concerned the liability of a barrister when acting as an advocate these opinions were *obiter dicta*.

It is not always easy to identify the *ratio decidendi*. The same judgment may appear to contain contradictory views of the law in different passages. In decisions of appeal courts, where there are three or even five separate judgments, the members of the court may reach the same conclusion but give different reasons. The *ratio* may also be mingled with *obiter* statements. Many judges help by indicating in their speeches which comments are *ratio* and which are *obiter*.

Activity 4

A case hinges upon whether clementines are oranges. The judgment contains the remark 'clementines are oranges, just as peanuts are nuts'. How does this remark illustrate the distinction between *ratio decidendi* and *obiter dicta*?

4.5 Distinguishing the facts

Although there may arguably be a finite number of legal principles to consider when deciding a case, there are necessarily an infinite variety of facts which may be presented. Apart from identifying the *ratio decidendi* of an earlier case, it is also necessary to consider how far the facts of the previous and the latest case are similar. Facts are never identical. If the differences appear significant the court may 'distinguish' the earlier case on the facts and thereby avoid following it as a precedent.

Business Basics: Law

4.6   The status of courts

A court's status has a significant effect on whether its decisions are binding, persuasive or disregarded.

(a) The Judicial Committee of the House of Lords stands at the apex of the judicial system. Its decisions are binding on all other English courts. The House of Lords generally regards itself as bound by its own earlier decisions but, since the issue of a Practice Statement in 1966, it reserves the right to depart from its own precedents in exceptional cases.

(b) The Court of Appeal's decisions are binding on all English courts except the House of Lords. It is bound by its own previous decisions and by those of the House of Lords: *Young v Bristol Aeroplane Co 1944*. However, the Criminal Division may deviate from its own previous decisions where to follow a decision would cause injustice to the appellant; the need for justice exceeds the desire for certainty where human liberty is at stake: *R v Gould 1986*.

(c) A single High Court judge is bound by decisions of higher courts but not by a decision of another High Court judge sitting alone (though he would treat it as strong persuasive authority). When two or more High Court judges sit together as a Divisional Court, their decisions are binding on any other Divisional Court (and on a single High Court judge sitting alone).

(d) Lower courts (the Crown Court, county courts and magistrates' courts) do not make precedents, and their decisions are not usually reported. They are bound by decisions of the higher courts.

(e) If, in a case before the House of Lords there is a dispute about a point of European Community (EC) law, it must be referred to the Court of Justice (of the EC) for a ruling. English courts are also required to take account of principles laid down by the Court of Justice in so far as these are relevant. The Court of Justice does not, however, create or follow precedents as such.

Apart from binding precedents as described above, reported decisions of any court (even if lower in status) may be treated as *persuasive* precedents: they may be (but need not be) followed in a later case. Reported decisions of the Judicial Committee of the Privy Council (which is a court of appeal from certain Commonwealth countries), of higher courts of Commonwealth countries which have a common law legal tradition and of courts of the United States of America may be cited as persuasive precedents. With persuasive precedents much depends on the personal reputation of the judge whose earlier decision is cited.

Overruling a precedent

A court of higher status is not only free to disregard the decision of a court of lower status in an earlier case. It may also deprive it of authority and expressly overrule it. This does not affect the outcome as regards the defendant and plaintiff in the earlier decision; it only affects the precedents to be applied in later cases.

Reversing a decision

A case in, for example, the High Court may be taken on appeal to the Court of Appeal. If the latter court reverses the former decision, that first decision cannot be a precedent, and the reversing decision becomes a precedent. However, if the original decision had been reached by following a precedent, then reversing that decision overrules the precedent which formed the *ratio*.

4.7   Avoidance of a binding precedent

Even if a precedent appears to be binding, a court may decline to follow it:

(a) by distinguishing the facts (as described above);

(b) by declaring the *ratio decidendi* obscure, particularly when a decision by three or five judges gives as many *rationes decidendi*;

(c) by declaring that the previous decision was made *per incuriam*, that is without taking account of some essential point of law, such as an important precedent;

(d) by declaring the precedent to be in conflict with a fundamental principle of law, for example where a court has failed to apply the doctrine of privity of contract: *Beswick v Beswick 1968*;

(e) by declaring the precedent to be too wide. For example, the duty of care to third parties found in *Donoghue v Stevenson 1932* has since been considerably refined;

(f) because the earlier decision has been subsequently overruled by another court or by statute.

Activity 5

A brings an action against B and the case is finally settled in favour of B in the Court of Appeal. Fifteen years later C brings an action against D on similar but slightly different facts and the case of *A v B* is the only relevant precedent. If *C v D* reaches the House of Lords, consider whether the case of *A v B* is binding.

4.8   The advantages and disadvantages of precedent

Many of the strengths of judicial precedent also indicate some of its weaknesses. Generally the arguments revolve around the principles of consistency, clarity, flexibility and detail.

Consistency. The whole point of following binding precedent is that the law is decided fairly and predictably. In theory therefore it should be possible to avoid litigation because the result is a foregone conclusion. However, judges are often forced to make illogical distinctions to avoid an unfair result which, combined with the wealth of reported cases, serves to complicate the law.

Clarity. Following only the reasoning in *ratio* statements should lead to statements of principle for general application. In practice, however, the same judgment may be found to contain propositions which appear inconsistent with each other or with the precedent which the court purports to follow.

Flexibility. The real strength of the system lies in its ability to change with changing circumstances since it arises directly out of the actions of society. The counter argument is that the doctrine limits judges' discretion and they may be unable to avoid deciding in line with a precedent which produces an unfair result. Often the deficiency may only be remedied by passing a statute to correct the law's failings.

Detail. Precedents state how the law applies to facts, and it should be flexible enough to allow for details to be different, so that the law is all-encompassing. However, judges often distinguish cases on facts to avoid following a precedent. The wealth of detail is also a drawback in that it produces a vast body of reports which must be taken into account; again, though, statute can help by codifying rules developed in case law.

Practicality. Case law is based on the experience of actual cases brought before the courts, not on logic or theory. This is an advantage as against legislation, which is sometimes found wanting when tested. There is currently debate about the adequacies and possible need for revision of a number of statutes, for example the Consumer Credit Act 1974 and the Criminal Justice Act 1991.

The most famous (adverse) description of case law is that made by Jeremy Bentham, when he called it 'dog's law'. Precedent follows the event, just as beating a dog follows the dog disobeying his master: before the dog transgressed, the offence did not exist. It can be answered, however, that a thing can only be prevented when it is seen to be harmful, and that this is only usually seen when harm has already been done.

5 LEGISLATION

Legislation is enacted by Parliament. Until the UK entered the European Community (the EC) in 1973 the UK Parliament was completely sovereign: its law-making powers were unfettered.

Parliamentary sovereignty means that:

(a) Parliament is able to make the law as it sees fit. It may repeal earlier statutes, overrule case law developed in the courts or make new law on subjects which have not been regulated by law before. Thus the War Damage Act 1965, removing rights to compensation from the Crown, reversed the decision of the House of Lords in *Burmah Oil v Lord Advocate 1965*.

(b) no Parliament can legislate so as to prevent a future Parliament changing the law:

> *Vauxhall Estates v Liverpool Corporation 1932*
> If compensation for compulsory purchase were assessed under an Act of 1919 the plaintiffs would receive £2,370, whereas if it were assessed under an Act of 1925 they would only receive £1,133. The Act of 1919 provided that any Act inconsistent with it would have no effect.

> *Held:* this provision did not apply to subsequent Acts because a Parliament cannot bind its successors. In addition the 1925 Act by implication repealed the 1919 Act so far as it was inconsistent with it. The plaintiffs therefore received £1,133.

(c) judges are bound to apply the relevant statute law however distasteful to them it may be. But judges have to *interpret* statute law, and they may find a meaning in a statutory rule which those members of Parliament who promoted the statute did not intend.

In practice, Parliament usually follows certain conventions which limit its freedom. It does not usually enact statutes which alter the law with retrospective effect or deprive citizens of their property without compensation.

Parliamentary procedure

A proposal for legislation is originally aired in public in a Government green paper. After comments are received a white paper is produced, which sets out the aim of the legislation. It is then put forward in draft form as a bill, and may be introduced into either the House of Commons or the House of Lords, the two Houses of Parliament. When the bill has passed through one House it must then go through the same stages in the other House.

In each House the successive stages of dealing with the bill are as follows.

(a) *First reading*: publication and introduction into the agenda: no debate.

(b) *Second reading*: debate on the general merits of the bill but no amendments at this stage.

(c) *Committee stage*: the bill is examined by a standing committee of about 20 members, representing the main parties and including some members at least who specialise in the relevant subject. The bill is examined section by section and may be amended. If the bill is very important all or part of the committee stage may be taken by the House as a whole sitting as a committee.

(d) *Report stage*: the bill as amended in committee is reported to the full House for approval. If the Government has undertaken in committee to reconsider various points it often puts forward its final amendments at this stage.

(e) *Third reading*: this is the final approval stage at which only verbal amendments may be made.

When it has passed through both Houses it is submitted for the Royal Assent which in practice is given on the Queen's behalf by a committee of the Lord Chancellor and two other peers. It then becomes an act of Parliament (or statute). It comes into effect at the start of the day on which Royal Assent is given, or (if the act itself so provides) at some other time or on a commencement date set by statutory instrument.

Most bills are public bills of general application, whether introduced by the Government or by a private member. They are referred to as Government bills or private members' bills respectively. An example of the latter is the Abortion Act 1967, sponsored by David Steel MP. A private bill (not the same as a private member's bill) has a restricted application: for example, a local authority may promote a private bill to give it special powers within its own area. Private bills undergo a different form of examination at the committee stage.

If the House of Commons and the House of Lords disagree over the same bill, the House of Lords may delay the passing of the bill for a maximum of one year (except for financial measures, such as the annual Finance Act). It may veto any bill which tries to extend the life of Parliament beyond five years, and it may veto any private bill.

Activity 6

Many countries have a bill of rights, which cannot be changed by normal legislative procedures. What aspect of Parliamentary sovereignty would make it difficult to give a bill of rights for the UK such a secure position?

6 DELEGATED LEGISLATION

Definition

Delegated legislation: rules of law made by subordinate bodies to whom the power to do so has been given by statute.

To save time in Parliament it is usual to set out the main principles in the body of an act as numbered sections and to relegate the details to schedules (at the end of the act) which need not be debated, though they are visible and take effect as part of the act. But even with this device there is a great deal which cannot conveniently be included in acts. It may, for example, be necessary, after an act has been passed, for the Government to consult interested parties and then produce regulations, having the force of the law, to implement the act, to fix commencement dates to bring the act into operation or to prescribe printed forms for use in connection with it. To provide for these and other matters a modern act usually contains a section by which power is given to a minister, or a public body such as a local authority, to make subordinate or delegated legislation for specified purposes only.

Delegated legislation appears in various forms. Ministerial powers are exercised by *statutory instrument* (including emergency powers of the Crown exercised by Orders in Council). Local authorities are given statutory powers to make *bye-laws*, which apply within a specific locality.

Definition

Bye-law: a type of delegated legislation made by local authorities.

6.1 Advantages and disadvantages

This procedure is unavoidable for various reasons.

(a) Parliament has no time to examine these matters of detail.

(b) Much of the content of delegated legislation is technical and is better worked out in consultation with professional, commercial or industrial groups outside Parliament.

(c) If new or altered regulations are required later, they can be issued in a much shorter time than is needed to pass an amending act.

The disadvantages of delegated legislation are that Parliament loses control of the law-making process and that a huge mass of detailed law appears piecemeal each year. It is difficult for persons who may be affected by it to keep abreast of the changes. Yet ignorance of the law is not accepted as an excuse for infringing it.

6.2 Control

Parliament does exercise some control over delegated legislation by restricting and defining the power to make rules and by keeping the making of new delegated legislation under review. Some statutory instruments do not take effect until approved by affirmative resolution of Parliament. Most other statutory instruments must be laid before Parliament for 40 days before they take effect. During that period members may propose a negative resolution to veto a statutory instrument to which they object.

There are standing scrutiny committees of both houses whose duty it is to examine statutory instruments with a view to raising objections if necessary, usually on the grounds that the instrument is obscure, expensive or retrospective.

As explained above, the power to make delegated legislation is defined by the Act which confers the power. A statutory instrument may be challenged in the courts on the ground that it is *ultra vires*, that is that it exceeds the prescribed limits, or on the ground that it has been made without due compliance with the correct procedure. If the objection is valid the court declares the statutory instrument to be void.

Definition

Ultra vires: beyond their powers. In company law this term is used in connection with transactions which are outside the scope of the objects clause and therefore, in principle, unenforceable.

Activity 7

An act of Parliament gives the Chancellor of the Exchequer power to fix the rate of tax on land values by statutory instrument. The Chancellor issues a statutory instrument extending the tax to the values of shareholdings. Consider whether the statutory instrument could be challenged.

7 THE INTERPRETATION OF STATUTES

Statutes, including delegated legislation, are expressed in general terms. For example, a Finance Act may impose a new tax on transactions described as a category; it does not expressly impose a tax of a specified amount on a particular transaction by a particular person. If a dispute arises as to whether or how a statute applies to particular acts or events, the courts must interpret the statute and decide whether or not it applies to a given case.

In the statutory interpretation the court is concerned with what the statute itself provides. It is not required to take account of what may have been said in parliamentary discussion as reported in *Hansard* and it may only consider statements by a Government spokesman explaining the intended effect of the bill when the statements are clear and the legislation is ambiguous or obscure, or leads to absurdity. A report of a committee or commission recommending legislation is not to be used as a guide to the interpretation of a statute.

7.1 Canons of Statutory Interpretation

Unless the statute contains express words to the contrary it is presumed that the following presumptions, or 'canons' of statutory interpretation apply, although any of them may be rebutted by contrary evidence. In practice a statute usually deals expressly with these matters (other than (e)) to remove any possible doubt.

(a) A statute does not alter the existing law nor repeal other statutes.

(b) If a statute deprives a person of his property, say by nationalisation, he is to be compensated for its value.

(c) A statute does not have retrospective effect to a date earlier than its becoming law. Some legislation is made specifically retrospective, for example the War Crimes Act 1991.

(d) A statute does not bind the Crown. In some areas, where the Crown's potential liability is great, it is expressly bound. Examples include the Equal Pay Act 1970 and the Occupier's Liability Acts.

(e) Any point on which the statute leaves a gap or omission is outside the scope of the statute.

(f) A statute has effect only in the UK; it does not have extraterritorial effect.

(g) A statute cannot impose criminal liability without proof of guilty mind or intention (*mens rea*). Some modern statutes rebut this presumption by imposing *strict liabilit* that is liability even without any intention to commit a crime.

(h) A statute does not run counter to international law and should be interpreted so as to give effect to international obligations.

Activity 8

A statute given Royal Assent on 15 July 1993 provides that it shall come into force on 1 January 1993 and that another statute given Royal Assent on 14 April 1993 shall be repealed. Is either of these provisions invalid?

Since judges are called upon to interpret statutes, a system has been developed to guide them. This consists of statutory assistance and a set of general principles.

7.2 Statutory assistance

Statutory assistance consists of:

(a) the Interpretation Act 1978, which defines certain terms frequently found in legislation;

(b) intrinsic aids, as contained in the Queen's Printers' copy of the statute as follows:

    (i)   interpretation sections of acts, defining various terms;

    (ii) preambles or long titles to acts, which often direct the judge as to the act's intentions and objects;

    (iii) sidenotes (summary notes in the margin) which may be used to give a general interpretation of the sections to which they are attached.

7.3   Rules of statutory interpretation

In interpreting the words of a statute the courts use the following general principles.

(a) *The literal rule:* words should be given their ordinary grammatical sense. Normally a word should be construed in the same literal sense wherever it appears throughout the statute. The courts will use standard dictionaries to aid them in their interpretation.

(b) *The golden rule:* a statute should be construed to avoid a manifest absurdity or contradiction within itself.

> *Re Sigsworth 1935*
> The golden rule was applied to prevent a murderer from inheriting on the intestacy of his victim although he was, as her son, her only heir on a literal interpretation of the Administration of Estates Act 1925.

(c) *The mischief rule:* if the words used are ambiguous and the statute discloses (perhaps in its preamble) its purpose, the court will adopt the meaning which is likely to give effect to that purpose (that is, to take account of the mischief or weakness which the statute is intended to remedy).

> *Gardiner v Sevenoaks RDC 1950*
> The purpose of an Act was to provide for the safe storage of flammable cinematograph film wherever it might be stored on 'premises'. A notice was served on G who stored film in a cave, requiring him to comply with the safety rules. G argued that 'premises' did not include a cave.
>
> *Held:* the purpose of the Act was to secure the safety of persons working in all places where film was stored. Insofar as film was stored in a cave, the word 'premises' included the cave.

(d) *The contextual rule:* a word should be construed in its context. It is permissible to look at the statute as a whole to discover the meaning of a word in it.

(e) *The ejusdem generis rule:* statutes often list a number of specific things and end the list with more general words. In that case the general words are to be limited in their meaning to other things of the same kind (*Ejusdem generis*) as the specific items which precede them.

> *Evans v Cross 1938*
> E was charged with driving his car in such a way as to 'ignore a traffic sign'. He had undoubtedly crossed to the wrong side of a white line painted down the middle of the road. 'Traffic sign' was defined in the Act as 'all signals, warning signposts, direction posts, signs or other devices'. Unless, therefore, a white line was an 'other device', E had not ignored a 'traffic sign' and had not committed the offence charged.
>
> *Held:* 'other devices' must be limited in its meaning to signs of the sorts mentioned in the list which preceded it. Thus restricted it did not include a painted line, which was quite different.

(f) *Expressio unius est exclusio alterius:* to express one thing is by implication to exclude anything else. For example, a statutory rule on 'sheep' does not include goats.

(g) *In pari materia:* if the statute forms part of a series which deals with similar subject matter, the court may look to the interpretation of previous statutes on the assumption that Parliament intended the same thing.

The courts have been paying more attention to what Parliament intended in recent times. This is partly an extension of the mischief rule. In October 1988, for example, the Attorney-General issued a statement interpreting the word 'obtain' in the Company Securities (Insider Dealing) Act 1985. This was in order that the courts should apply the law for the purpose for which it was enacted by Parliament. A more purposive approach is also being taken because so many international and EC regulations have to be interpreted by the courts.

Re Attorney-General's Reference (No 1) 1988
The accused had received unsolicited information from a merchant banker telling him of a forthcoming merger. He knew that this was price-sensitive information and instructed his broker to buy shares in one of the companies, later netting a profit of £3,000. The Act sets out the offence of 'knowingly obtaining' such information. His defence was that he had obtained it passively, not actively.

Held: both the Court of Appeal and the House of Lords rejected this interpretation on the grounds that the effect of the legislation would be lessened if it were followed.

The House of Lords has decided that it is permissible for the courts to refer to reports, by certain bodies, which led to the statute in question: *Davis v Johnson 1978.* For example, reports by the Law Commission or by committees appointed by the Government may be used, as described in a judgment by Lord Diplock, 'to identify the mischief which the legislation is intended to remedy but not for the purpose of construing the enacting words.'

It is open to the UK courts to decide that a British statute should be interpreted according to British court rules. EC directives need not be taken into account: *Duke v GEC Reliance Systems Ltd 1988.*

Activity 9

A statute applies to 'lions, tigers, leopards and other felines'. Is it likely to apply to domestic cats?

8 CUSTOM

In early mediaeval times the courts created law by enforcing selected customs. Custom is now of little importance as a source of law, but it is still classified as a legal source of law.

Definition

Custom: unwritten law which formed the basis of common law.

In disputes over claims to customary rights, such as a right to use the land of another or to remove things from it, the alleged custom may be established subject to certain conditions. It must have existed since *time immemorial,* in theory since 1189 AD. It usually suffices to show that the custom has existed without interruption as far back as records (if any) go. It must have been enjoyed *openly as of right.* If it has only been enjoyed secretly, by force or with permission of a landowner, it is not a custom for legal purposes.

In determining the implied terms of a contract, the court may take account of local or trade customs which the parties intended should be part of their contract.

Hutton v Warren 1836
The parties were landlord and tenant of a farm. The landlord gave notice to the tenant to quit. Disputes arose as to the tenant's obligation to continue to cultivate the farm until the notice expired and as to his entitlement to allowances for work done and seed supplied.

Held: these matters were to be resolved according to local custom which had been incorporated in the contract.

9 SUBSIDIARY SOURCES OF LAW

A number of subsidiary sources have had some influence on the law's development, and are still recognisable today.

9.1 The law merchant

In mediaeval times, traders (often from overseas) submitted their disputes to courts at main ports, fairs and markets which applied mercantile custom. The law of negotiable instruments was brought to England as a commercial practice recognised by bankers and traders in Northern Italy, Germany and elsewhere in late mediaeval times. The work of these courts was absorbed (with the law merchant) into common law in the seventeenth century.

9.2 Roman law

Although it is the basis of most continental systems of law, Roman law is of little importance as a source of English law. Its influence was mainly felt in the ecclesiastical courts and in the rules relating to the requirements of a valid will. A soldier's privileged will (an informal will) is an example of a current law which has Roman origins.

9.3 Canon law

Like the courts of the law merchant, the ecclesiastical courts were independent of the common law courts. They mainly dealt with offences against morality, such as adultery and slander. They also had jurisdiction over the law of succession. They kept their jurisdiction until 1857, when the Divorce Court and the Probate Court were established. Their jurisdiction is now confined to church matters.

9.4 Codes of practice

In recent years some statutes have provided for codes of practice to be drawn up to supplement the law. These codes are usually prepared by appropriate bodies as guides to recommended practice, for example codes on picketing at a factory gate in the course of an industrial dispute or dealings between traders and their consumer customers. Such codes are not law and it is not unlawful to disregard them. But in any legal proceedings the court may take account of compliance with or disregard of a code of practice in deciding whether, for instance, a person has behaved reasonably (if that is a legal obligation imposed on him in general terms, as it is, for instance, in the unfair dismissal rules of employment law).

Chapter roundup

- Laws are rules enforced by the State. English law is largely case law, with little Roman law.

- The sources of law are the historical sources, the legal sources and the subsidiary sources.

- Common law developed after the Norman Conquest, but became too rigid to give just results in many cases.

- Equity gave more discretion to do justice than common law, and new rights and remedies, but fair dealing was expected from litigants expecting to be treated fairly themselves.

- Common law and equity remain separate, although both are applied in all courts. Equity prevails over common law.

- Case law is the application of reported cases to later cases. Several series of law reports are published.

- Decided cases can fix the law for the purposes of future cases heard before certain courts, through the doctrine of precedent.

- The binding element in an earlier decision is the *ratio decidendi*, not the *obiter dicta*.

- The House of Lords binds all courts except itself. The Court of Appeal and a Divisional Court of the High Court bind themselves and all lower courts.

- A court can avoid following a precedent on several grounds.

- Statute law is made by Parliament, which, subject to the UK's membership of the European Community, has unfettered legislative powers.

- A bill goes through two readings, a committee stage, a report stage and a third reading in each House of Parliament before receiving the Royal Assent.

- Much detailed legislation is delegated to Government departments exercising powers conferred by Acts of Parliament.

- Statutes need to be interpreted to determine their application to different cases. There are canons of statutory interpretation, concerned with a statute's scope and its impact on the law and on persons, and there are also rules of statutory interpretation, concerned with the detailed interpretation of the words of a statute. There are also some statutory aids to interpretation.

- Custom may be a source of law, so long as the custom in question satisfies certain criteria.

- The subsidiary sources of law are the law merchant, Roman law, canon law and codes of practice.

Quick quiz

1 How was the common law first developed?
2 Give some examples of equitable maxims.
3 Can a successful plaintiff be certain of obtaining a desired equitable remedy?
4 What are the normal contents of a report of a case?
5 Can *obiter dicta* in a case have any influence on the outcome of subsequent cases?
6 When may the Court of Appeal deviate from its own previous decisions?

7   What does it mean to say that a court's decision was taken *per incuriam*?

8   What is meant by Parliamentary sovereignty?

9   Why is delegated legislation essential?

10 List the canons of statutory interpretation.

11 What is the mischief rule?

12 How may a code of practice influence the outcome of a court case?

Solutions to activities

1   The plaintiff (D) could seek an equitable order of specific performance requiring the defendant (S) to honour the contract by proceeding with the sale. This would be more appropriate than the common law remedy of damages.

2   Common law would only recognise trustees' rights as legal owners of the trust property, whereas equity (which prevails) would make those rights subject to any beneficiaries' interests.

3   The name of the case tells you that it is a civil case and that Donoghue is the plaintiff, while Stevenson is the defendant.

4   'Clementines are oranges' is the *ratio decidendi*. 'Peanuts are nuts' is an *obiter dictum*.

5   The House of Lords in *C v D* could disregard the Court of Appeal decision in *A v B* or even over-rule it. Alternatively the case *A v B* might be distinguished on its facts.

6   No Parliament can bind its successors.

7   It would be *ultra vires*.

8   Both provisions are valid.

9   No: the *ejusdem generis* rule applies.

Further question practice

Now try the following practice questions at the end of this text

Multiple choice questions: **1 to 5**

Exam style question: **1**

Chapter 2

THE ENGLISH LEGAL SYSTEM

Introduction

There are a number of key distinctions between civil and criminal proceedings. Criminal actions are brought by the State. The accused, if found guilty, is convicted and punished. Some crimes (such as murder) have a victim while others, (for example, speeding) can be committed without causing loss to any particular person.

Civil law regulates disputes over the rights and obligations of persons dealing with each other. The State has no direct role and it is up to the persons involved to settle the matter in the courts if they so wish.

In this chapter, we describe the court system. We have included both criminal and civil courts, as some courts fulfil both roles, but it is more important that you understand the role of the civil courts, particularly the county court and the High Court which are of greatest practical relevance.

The publicity afforded to court cases, nearly all of which are open to reporters and the public, and the fact that even cases of local interest may be reported in the regional press – precisely in the area where a company operates – means that many companies prefer not to become involved in court proceedings. There are other options open to them, sometimes described collectively as *alternative dispute resolution*. We will examine court procedure and alternative means of resolving disputes in Chapter 4.

Your objectives

After completing this chapter you should:

(a) understand the difference between civil and criminal liability;

(b) know the system of courts, and the appeals available;

(c) know the jurisdiction of each of the courts;

(d) know the different divisions of the High Court;

(e) understand the structure of the legal profession.

1 CIVIL AND CRIMINAL LIABILITY

The distinction between criminal and civil liability is central to the legal system and to the way in which the court system is structured. The objectives of each category of the law, although closely connected, are different.

1.1 Criminal law

A crime is conduct prohibited by the law. The State (in the form of the Crown Prosecution Service) is the usual prosecutor in a criminal case because it is the community as a whole which suffers as a result of the law being broken. However, private individuals may also prosecute (although this is rare). Persons guilty of crimes are punished by fines or imprisonment.

In a criminal trial, the burden of proof to convict the accused rests with the prosecution, which must prove its case *beyond reasonable doubt*. A criminal case might be referred to as *R v Granger 1993*. The prosecution is brought in the name of the Crown (R signifying Regina, or the Queen). Granger is the name of the accused or defendant.

1.2 Civil proceedings

Civil law exists to regulate disputes over the rights and obligations of persons dealing with each other. The State has no role in a dispute over, for instance, a breach of contract. It is up to the persons involved to settle the matter in the courts if they so wish. The general purpose of such a course of action is to impose a settlement, sometimes using financial *compensation* in the form of the legal remedy of damages, sometimes using equitable remedies such as injunctions or other orders. There is no concept of punishment.

In civil proceedings, the case must be proved on the *balance of probability*. The party bearing the burden of proof is not required to produce absolute proof, nor prove the issue beyond reasonable doubt. He must convince the court that it is more probable than not that his assertions are true.

Terminology is different from that in criminal cases; the *plaintiff* sues the *defendant*, and the burden of proof may shift between the two.

The main areas of civil liability are contract and tort. Both are forms of relationship between persons.

(a) A *contract* is a legally binding agreement, breach of which infringes one person's legal right given by the contract to have it performed.

(b) A *tort* is a wrong committed by one person against another (such as a libel), infringing general rights given by the law. Hence for there to be liability there need not have been any pre-existing personal relationship before the tort was committed.

Definition

Standard of proof: the extent to which the court must be satisfied by the evidence presented.

Activity 1

Why does the standard of proof in criminal trials not have to be beyond *all* doubt?

2 THE STRUCTURE OF THE LEGAL SYSTEM

The courts have to be organised to accommodate the working of the law. The English court system is quite complex. It has four basic levels.

(a) The House of Lords;

(b) The Court of Appeal;

(c) The High Court (including the Crown Court);

(d) The inferior courts (including county courts and magistrates' courts).

Within this structure there is neither a clear division into criminal courts and civil courts nor a division into courts of first instance and appeal courts. The Queen's Bench Division of the High Court provides an example of this. It hears civil cases *and* criminal cases, and in its civil jurisdiction it operates as a court of first instance *and* as a court hearing appeals from the county courts. However, the vast majority of cases are heard in the magistrates' courts or the county courts.

A court of first instance is the court where the case is originally heard in full. The appeal court is the court to which an appeal is made against the ruling or the sentence.

Definition

Appeal: a request to a higher court by a person dissatisfied with the decision of a lower court that the previous decision be reviewed.

If an appellate court finds in favour of the appellant the original decision is *reversed*. This is different from *overruling* which happens when a higher court finds a lower court's precedent to be wrong. Although the precedent is overruled and hence not followed again, the overruling has no effect on the actual outcome of the original case.

Activity 2

A sues B in the High Court, and judgment is given in favour of A. B then appeals to the Court of Appeal. If A later appeals to the House of Lords, what may we conclude about the judgment given in the Court of Appeal?

The diagram which follows sets out the English Civil Court structure.

Figure 2.1 Civil Court Structure

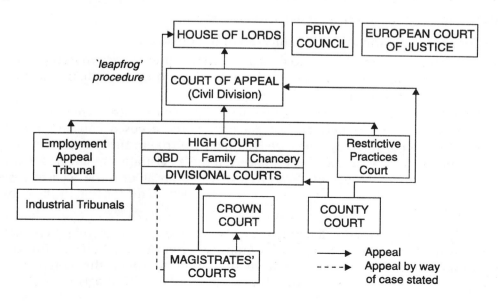

The diagram which follows sets out the English Criminal Court structure. As can be seen from these diagrams, some courts deal only with civil cases and some only with criminal cases. Most, however, can deal with both.

Figure 2.2 Criminal Court Structure

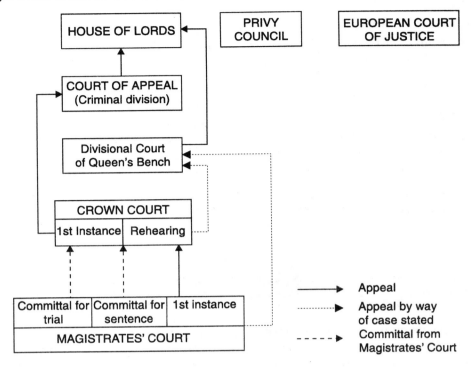

3   MAGISTRATES' COURTS

Magistrates' courts are the inferior criminal courts. In addition, they exercise certain family law, administrative law and minor civil functions.

3.1   Criminal jurisdiction

Magistrates' courts deal with *criminal* cases as follows.

(a) They try summarily (without a jury) all minor offences.

(b) They conduct committal proceedings, which are preliminary investigations of the prosecution case, when the offence is triable only on indictment (in the Crown Court with a jury).

(c) Certain offences are 'triable either way'. This means that they are triable summarily or on indictment with a jury. If the accused consents and the magistrates consider that the case is suitable for trial in the magistrates' court, then they may try such a case summarily. If the magistrates are satisfied that the prosecution has enough evidence to justify a full trial, or if the accused insists on his rights to trial by jury, they commit the defendant for trial in the Crown Court.

The maximum penalties which magistrates may impose on a defendant convicted summarily of a criminal offence are six months' imprisonment and/or a fine of up to £5,000. The magistrates also have discretion to order the defendant to compensate his victim up to £5,000. If in a summary trial the magistrates consider that their sentencing powers are inadequate they may convict and commit the defendant to the Crown Court for sentence. They may also make community service, restitution, supervision and probation orders. Other miscellaneous sentences include binding over to keep the peace (a fine being payable in the event of a breach), disqualification from driving and endorsement of a driving licence.

3.2 Civil jurisdiction

Magistrates' *civil* jurisdiction includes various types of licensing and the enforcement of local authority rates and the council tax. The magistrates' courts also have an important role to play in the law relating to children; they are the first tier in what is in effect a Family Court in which specially trained magistrates and judges apply uniform procedures across the magistrates' court, county court and High Court.

3.3 Appeals

A convicted defendant has a general right to a rehearing by a Crown Court. Either the defendant or the prosecution may appeal on a point of law only by way of 'case stated' to a Divisional Court of the Queen's Bench Division. A 'case stated' appeal is based on the idea not that magistrates (or the Crown Court) have wrongly decided the facts but that they have wrongly interpreted the law. The magistrates produce written reasons for the way in which they decided the case. These, together with the facts, are considered by the Divisional Court to ensure that the law was correctly applied. If not then the case may be sent back to the lower court with instructions as to how it should be decided. On family matters, appeals are to a divisional court of the Family Division of the High Court.

3.4 Staffing

Magistrates' courts are mostly staffed by lay magistrates who are not legally qualified and sit part-time. They are appointed on the Lord Chancellor's advice and are assisted by salaried, legally qualified clerks who must be solicitors or barristers of at least five years' standing. Stipendiary magistrates sit in large towns and are salaried. They must be solicitors or barristers of at least seven years' standing. Lay magistrates sit two or three to a court; Stipendiary magistrates sit alone.

Activity 3

C is being prosecuted for an offence which is triable either way. He elects to be tried summarily. Consider whether this will ensure that he will not be sentenced to more than six months' imprisonment. Give reasons for your answer.

4 COUNTY COURTS

County courts have *civil* jurisdiction only but deal with almost every kind of civil case arising within the local areas for which the courts are established. The practical importance of the county courts is that they deal with the majority of the country's civil litigation. Over one and a half million actions are commenced each year (about one million are for debt), although only about 5% result in trials since most actions are discontinued or settled out of court before the trial stage is reached.

4.1 Jurisdiction

County courts are involved in:

(a) contract and tort claims (see below);

(b) equitable matters concerning trusts, mortgages and partnership dissolution, but only up to £30,000 unless the parties waive the limit;

(c) disputes concerning land where the capital value of the land is less than £30,000;

(d) family cases;

(e) probate matters where the estate of the deceased is estimated to be less than £30,000;

(f) miscellaneous matters as set out in various statutes, for example, the Consumer Credit Act 1974 (no limit on jurisdiction);

(g) some bankruptcy, company winding up and admiralty cases; and

(h) small claims.

The High Court and County Court Jurisdiction Order 1991 made new arrangements for the distribution of proceedings between the High Court and county courts. Criteria are laid down for where proceedings are to be commenced and tried and where judgments are to be enforced. In particular, actions in respect of *personal injuries* are to be commenced in a county court unless the claim is worth £50,000 or more.

Actions in contract and tort worth less than £25,000 must normally be tried in a county court and those worth £50,000 or more must normally be tried in the High Court, with those in between going either way, subject to:

(a) the 'financial substance' of the action;

(b) whether questions of public interest are raised;

(c) the complexity of the facts, the legal issues, the procedures or the remedies involved; and

(d) whether transfer is likely to result in a more speedy trial.

These criteria may also be used to transfer an action worth less than £25,000 to the High Court or an action worth over £50,000 to a county court.

4.2 Small claims procedure

Definitions

Small claim: a claim not exceeding £1,000 which may brought within the quicker, cheaper and more informal arbitration procedure within the county court.

Arbitration: a means of settling disputes outside the courts.

To assist litigants who decide to conduct their cases in person the court may, if the amount involved does not exceed £1,000 or if the parties agree, refer a case to an arbitrator to hear and decide informally in a small claims court. The arbitrator is usually the district judge but may be another person chosen by the parties. The arbitrator's award is recorded as a county court judgment. This is a cheaper and quicker way of settling small claims in an informal atmosphere, and is often used in consumer cases, motor accident and personal injury claims, employment, tenancy, travel and debt disputes.

4.3 Appeals

From the county court there is a right of appeal direct to the Civil Division of the Court of Appeal.

4.4 Staffing

A circuit judge usually presides in a county court. He or she is a barrister of at least ten years' standing. A recorder, a part-time appointment in the Crown Court, is a solicitor or barrister of at least ten years' standing, and may be appointed as a circuit judge if he has three years' experience as a recorder. A district judge, who must be a solicitor or barrister of at least seven years' standing, assists the circuit judge; the district judge may also hear small claims, or any other claims with the consent of the parties. The circuit judge normally sits alone, although in a limited number of civil cases (fraud, libel, slander) there may be a jury of eight persons.

Activity 4

P sues D for breach of contract, asking for and obtaining damages of £10,000. In which court would the case be heard?

---

5 THE CROWN COURT

The Crown Court is theoretically a single court forming part of the Supreme Court, but in fact it comprises local courts in large towns and also the Central Criminal Court (the Old Bailey in the City of London). It tries all serious (indictable) offences with a jury and hears appeals and deals with committals for sentencing from magistrates' courts. It also deals with a few types of civil cases, being appeals from the magistrates' court on matters of betting, gaming and licensing.

From the Crown Court there is a right of appeal on criminal matters to the Criminal Division of the Court of Appeal. An appeal by way of 'case stated' on a point of law may also be made to a Divisional Court of the Queen's Bench division.

A circuit judge, a recorder or a High Court judge may sit in the Crown Court. Sometimes lay magistrates also sit. Very serious offences, such as murder and treason, may only be heard by a High Court judge in the Crown Court. All prosecutions for indictable offences are heard by a judge with a jury of 12 persons.

6 THE HIGH COURT

The High Court is organised into three divisions: Queen's Bench, Chancery and Family. Except where other special courts have exclusive jurisdiction, the High Court can deal with any civil matter.

In hearing a case for the first time (*at first instance*) a High Court judge sits alone. A *Divisional Court* of two or more High Court judges sits to hear appeals from magistrates (and from Crown Courts in respect of civil matters tried in those courts).

The Queen's Bench division

The Queen's Bench division (QBD) deals mainly with common law matters such as actions based on contract or tort. It is the largest of the three divisions. It includes a separate Admiralty Court to deal with shipping matters such as charterparties, salvage and collisions at sea. There is also within the QBD the Commercial Court which specialises in commercial cases, such as insurance claims. The Commercial Court offers a rather simpler trial procedure to meet business needs. Judges of the Commercial Court may also sit as arbitrators.

Supervisory role

A Divisional Court of the QBD has a supervisory role over other courts. It may issue a writ of *habeas corpus*, which is an order for the release of a person wrongfully detained, and also prerogative orders against inferior courts, tribunals and other bodies such as local authorities, insofar as they have a duty to exercise a discretion fairly. There are three types of prerogative order.

(a) *Mandamus* requires a court or other body to carry out a public duty. For example, a tribunal may be ordered to hear an appeal which it has wrongly refused to hear, or a local authority may be ordered to produce its accounts for inspection by a council tax payer.

(b) *Prohibition* prevents a court or tribunal from exceeding its jurisdiction (*before* it has done so).

(c) *Certiorari* orders a court or tribunal which has taken action to submit the record of its proceedings to the High Court for review. The High Court may then quash the decision but cannot substitute its own decision (as it can under the ordinary appeal procedure).

Application may be made for all these three remedies, together with an injunction, under a single claim for judicial review. Leave for an application for judicial review is made to a single judge, following which application is made to the QBD. A person making such an application must have the appropriate *locus standi*, that is a sufficient interest in the matter to which the application relates.

The Chancery division

This division deals with traditional equity matters such as:

(a) trusts and mortgages;

(b) revenue matters;

(c) bankruptcy (though outside London this is a county court subject);

(d) disputed wills and the administration of estates of deceased persons;

(e) partnership and company matters.

There is a separate Companies Court within the division which deals with liquidations and other company proceedings, and a Patents Court established under the Patents Act 1977.

The Family division

This division deals with the same matters of family law as the magistrates' and county courts, except that magistrates' courts have no jurisdiction on divorce.

6.1 Appeals

Appeals in *civil cases* may be made to the Court of Appeal (Civil Division) or to the House of Lords, under what is known as the 'leapfrog' procedure. For the leapfrog procedure to be followed, all parties must give their consent to it, and the case must involve a point of law of general public importance. The House of Lords must also give their leave to this.

Appeals in *criminal cases* are made direct to the House of Lords where the case has reached the High Court on appeal from a magistrates' court or from the Crown Court.

6.2 Staffing

The High Court is staffed by puisne (pronounced 'puny') judges, who must be barristers of at least ten years' standing. A judge's name is written as Smith J (plural JJ), and pronounced 'Mr Justice Smith'. The Queen's Bench division is presided over by the Lord Chief Justice. The Chancery division is presided over (nominally) by the Lord Chancellor. The Family division has its own President.

Activity 5

A local authority decides not to provide education for children of school age. What action could be taken by:
(a) a parent of a child affected?
(b) someone from a different part of the country who thinks that the law should always be enforced?

---

7 THE RESTRICTIVE PRACTICES COURT

The Restrictive Practices Court is not part of the High Court but has the same status, and appeals from it go to the Court of Appeal. It investigates the merits of agreements registered under the Restrictive Trade Practices Act 1976 and agreements falling under the Resale Prices Act 1976. In these functions it is required to have regard to EC law. It is also concerned with proceedings to prohibit practices deemed prejudicial to consumers under the Fair Trading Act 1973.

8 THE EMPLOYMENT APPEAL TRIBUNAL (EAT)

The Employment Appeal Tribunal is a court of equal status with the High Court. It hears appeals from industrial tribunals mainly on employment matters (such as unfair dismissal, redundancy pay or sex discrimination). There is a right of appeal from the EAT to the Court of Appeal.

9 THE COURT OF APPEAL

The Civil Division of the Court of Appeal hears appeals from county courts, the High Court, the Restrictive Practices Court, the Employment Appeal Tribunal and various other special tribunals such as the Lands Tribunal. It does not conduct a complete rehearing but reviews the record of the evidence in the lower court and the legal arguments put before it. It may uphold or reverse the earlier decision or order a new trial.

The Criminal Division of the Court of Appeal hears appeals from Crown Courts. It may also be invited to review a criminal case by the Home Secretary or to consider a point of law at the request of the Attorney General. Its powers and procedures are very similar to those of the Civil Division.

Lords Justices of Appeal are promoted from the High Court. A Lord Justice's name is written Green LJ (plural LJJ) and pronounced 'Lord Justice Green'. Three judges normally sit together. In the Criminal Division, the Lord Chief Justice presides. Both he and judges of the High Court may be selected to sit along with Civil Division judges. In the Civil Division the Master of the Rolls presides, but he may also sit in the Criminal Division. A majority decision is sufficient and dissenting judgments are expressed.

10 THE JUDICIAL COMMITTEE OF THE HOUSE OF LORDS

Apart from the limited jurisdiction of the Court of Justice (of the EC), the Judicial Committee of the House of Lords is the highest court of appeal of the English, Scottish and Northern Irish legal system. It hears appeals from both the civil and the criminal divisions of the Court of Appeal (and in certain circumstances directly from the High Court).

Judges are promoted from the Court of Appeal to be members of the Judicial Committee of the House of Lords. They are known as Lords of Appeal in Ordinary, or Law Lords. Five judges normally sit together, though there may be only three. Majority decisions are sufficient and dissenting judgments are expressed.

11 THE JUDICIAL COMMITTEE OF THE PRIVY COUNCIL (JCPC)

About 25 countries of the Commonwealth still retain a right of appeal from their national courts to the Queen's Privy Council. Canada and India abolished appeals in 1949 and Australia in 1986. The Judicial Committee is (with a slightly different membership) in effect the same body as the Judicial Committee of the House of Lords. It also deals with appeals from the English ecclesiastical court.

Activity 6

In what circumstances might it be appropriate for the Court of Appeal to order a new trial, rather than simply reviewing the earlier proceedings in a lower court and upholding or reversing the earlier decision?

12 THE LEGAL PROFESSION

The legal profession is divided into two mutually exclusive groups, barristers and solicitors. The two groups have some shared arrangements for basic training but, before qualifying, the recruit must take his advanced training in one or the other branch exclusively. It is not possible to be a member of both, though individuals may transfer from one to the other.

12.1 Solicitors

Solicitors are the general practitioners of the legal profession and provide many services to their clients which do not involve them in court proceedings. Generally solicitors may only appear as advocates for their clients before magistrates' and county courts. In most other court proceedings the solicitor prepares the case and retains one or more counsel (barristers) to appear in court as advocates for his client, although it is sometimes possible for clients to brief barristers without the intervention of solicitors. The individual conduct and collective affairs of solicitors are subject to regulation (partly on a statutory basis) by the Law Society. It is common for solicitors to practise as partners in a firm, but they may not carry on business through companies.

The Lord Chancellor has recently announced that solicitors can be granted extended rights of audience. Solicitors (those in private practice and not, for the time being, employed solicitors) can therefore apply for the grant of higher court qualifications, either in civil proceedings, allowing them to appear additionally in the High Court, or in criminal proceedings, allowing them to appear additionally in the Crown Court, or in both. Applicants must demonstrate experience of advocacy, pass a test of evidence and procedure and complete an advocacy training course.

12.2 Barristers

Barristers are members of one of the four Inns of Court, the Inner Temple, the Middle Temple, Gray's Inn and Lincoln's Inn, and obtain their admission to the bar (to practise in the courts) after taking examinations set by the Council of Legal Education and satisfying certain other conditions. They are required to complete a year's pupillage in professional training in the chambers of a practising barrister (in London or a provincial city). Although groups of barristers share the occupation of chambers (and the services of a clerk of chambers and his assistants), they are not allowed to enter into partnership.

Definition

Inns of Court: professional institutions which intending barrisers must join and which have the exclusive privilege of conferring the status of barrister.

Barristers are specialists in advocacy in court, but much of their working time is spent in chambers conducting conferences with instructing solicitors and their clients. There is also a great deal of paperwork, for example drafting legal documents and opinions. Barristers are consultants who usually (but not always) deal with lay clients only through solicitors. The Bar Council has approved proposals which allow direct access by certain professionals (such as accountants and engineers).

Definition

Council's opinion: the advice of a barrister on a specialised or difficult point of law which may be obtained by a solicitor before advising his or her clients on whether or not to proceed with their action.

There are advantages and disadvantages to the division of the legal profession into two branches. The present system gives the public greater access to barristers than a fused system would. Under fusion barristers would probably join the larger legal firms. The present system, by keeping advocacy in the hands of specialists, also means that judges hear clear arguments in trials. Those who argue in favour of fusion would point to duplication of effort, unnecessary division of responsibility, the high cost of paying more than one expert and the overlaps which already exist, particularly in the field of advocacy.

Business Basics: Law

12.3 LEGAL EXECUTIVES

Finally, mention should be made of the legal executives who are employed by firms of solicitors to do professional work. Some may be qualified as members of the Institute of Legal Executives, though this is not obligatory. A legal executive is usually a specialist in one type of work only, such as litigation, conveyancing or trust administration.

Activity 7

If a non-lawyer requires the services of a barrister in order to argue a case in court, what useful work can a solicitor do before a barrister is instructed?

Chapter roundup

- Crimes offend against society as a whole, and criminals are prosecuted, usually by the State.
- Civil proceedings are brought by the person who has suffered loss, the aim being compensation.
- The courts are structured in a system which allows for appeals.
- Magistrates' courts deal mainly with minor crimes, although they have some civil jurisdiction.
- County courts only have civil jurisdiction, and do not generally deal with cases where very large amounts are at stake.
- The Crown Court deals with serious crimes.
- The High Court deals with substantial civil cases. It has three divisions, the Queen's Bench division, the Chancery division and the Family division. It also has a supervisory jurisdiction over other courts and authorities.
- The Court of Appeal hears appeals from lower courts. It has both a civil division and a criminal division.
- The Judicial Committee of the House of Lords is the final appellate court.
- Other courts include the Restrictive Practices Court, the Employment Appeal Tribunal and the Judicial Committee of the Privy Council.
- The legal profession is divided into solicitors and barristers. Solicitors deal with members of the public directly, and have only limited advocacy rights. Barristers generally deal with members of the public through solicitors, and can act as advocates in all courts.

Quick quiz

1 How does the standard of proof differ between civil and criminal proceedings?
2 Which courts comprise the Supreme Court?
3 What is the difference between summary trial and trial on indictment?
4 What civil jurisdiction do magistrates' courts have?
5 List the types of case which may be dealt with in a county court.
6 Who may hear a case in the Crown Court?
7 What are the three types of prerogative order which may be issued by the Queen's Bench division of the High Court?
8 What matters are dealt with by the Chancery division of the High Court?
9 What matters are dealt with by the Restrictive Practices Court?
10 From which courts does an appeal lie to the Court of Appeal?
11 Which body regulates the conduct of solicitors?
12 What sorts of work do barristers do apart from advocacy?

Solutions to activities

1 Nothing can be proved beyond all doubt.
2 In the Court of Appeal judgment was given in favour of B.
3 This will not ensure a lower sentence because he may be convicted in a Magistrates' court and then committed to the Crown Court for sentencing.
4 The case would probably be heard in a county court.
5 A parent could seek a *mandamus* order. Someone from another part of the country would have no *locus standi* and could do nothing.
6 When there is new evidence (perhaps from new witnesses) to consider.
7 A solicitor can ensure that the client has an adequate case, and can compile evidence and ensure that the facts are presented to the barrister in an orderly fashion.

Further question practice

Now try the following practice questions at the end of this text

Multiple choice questions: **6 to 9**

Exam style question: **2**

Chapter 3

EUROPEAN COMMUNITY LAW

Introduction

The European Union exists to promote free trade and competition, economic integration and the harmonisation of law between the fifteen member states.

There were six original signatories to the Treaty of Rome in 1957: Belgium, France, Germany, Italy, Luxembourg and The Netherlands. Subsequently the United Kingdom, Eire and Denmark joined in 1973, Greece in 1981 and Spain and Portugal in 1986. Membership of the EU was extended to Austria, Sweden and Finland from 1 January 1995. (Norway failed to deposit their instrument of ratification following a negative vote in a referendum in November 1994, and so remain outside the EU.)

There are actually three communities which make up the EU: the European Community (formerly the European Economic Community), the European Coal and Steel Community and the European Atomic Energy Community. For legal purposes it is the European Community (EC) which is the most important.

The Treaty of Rome is the legal foundation for the powers of EU institutions. The original treaty has been amended, most notably by the Treaty on European Union (the Maastricht treaty) which came into force on 1 November 1993.

Since this date, the EC has not ceased to exist, but has been subsumed within the European Union. The term European Union should be used to refer to the whole European organisation consisting of the three original communities and the Maastricht areas of co-operation such as politics, single currency, foreign affairs, defence and conventions.

Your objectives

After completing this chapter you should:

(a) understand the composition and role of the European Community (the EC);

(b) know the names and functions of the law-making EU institutions;

(c) understand the role of the Court of Justice, and how it hears cases;

(d) know what general principles of law are applied by the Court of Justice;

(e) understand the notions of direct applicability and direct effect of EC law;

(f) know how treaty provisions, regulations and directives differ;

(g) know how EC law can be enforced in national courts;

(h) appreciate the supremacy of EC law over national law.

1 THE EUROPEAN UNION

The EU generates much law, mainly on economic and social matters such as competition between businesses, working conditions and the free movement of people within the European Union. The legislative process is independent of national legislatures, such as the United Kingdom Parliament, although it is controlled by government ministers from the member states. EC law can be enforced through the national courts in the member states and through the Court of Justice. If EC law conflicts with national law, EC law takes priority. EC law should thus be seen as a separate system of law, independent of national systems and overriding them where necessary.

In this chapter, we will have to consider the institutions of the EU, the member states, natural persons (human beings) and legal persons (for example companies, which are recognised as separate legal entities in their own right). For simplicity, we will refer to member states as 'states' and to natural and legal persons as 'persons'.

2 THE LAW-MAKING INSTITUTIONS OF THE EC

EC law is generated by three institutions working together. These are the Council of the European Union, the Commission and the Parliament.

2.1 The Council of the European Union

The Council of the EU comprises one government minister from each state. The ministers who attend meetings vary with the subjects to be discussed. Thus agriculture ministers would attend a meeting to discuss farming matters, and foreign affairs ministers would attend to discuss responses to a war being waged outside the EC. The Council considers proposed legislation submitted to it by the Commission, and may decide to adopt it. It also gives the Commission the necessary powers to implement legislation. The Council is the closest of the three law-making institutions to the governments of the states, because it comprises ministers from those governments. It has more power in the EC legislative process than the other two institutions: it can block legislation which it does not approve of, and it can ensure that legislation which it wants is put forward. It normally takes decisions by 'qualified majority vote': larger states have more votes than smaller states, but the five largest states cannot win a vote against the other seven states combined.

2.2 The Commission

The Commission comprises 20 commissioners, one or two nominated by each state. Once the members of the Commission have been nominated, the Commission as a whole is subject to approval by the Parliament. The Parliament can also at any time insist that the whole Commission resign and be replaced by a new Commission (again nominated by the states). The commissioners act in the interests of the EC as a whole, and do not put forward the views of the states which nominated them. The Commission proposes new laws for consideration, and it also ensures that existing EC law is applied. It can impose fines on persons. If a state is not fulfilling its obligations under EC law, the Commission can take the case to the Court of Justice, which can require compliance with EC law, and impose a fine on the state if it still fails to comply.

2.3   The Parliament of the European Community

The Parliament (often referred to as the European Parliament) is directly elected by the citizens of the states. Its role is largely advisory. It cannot make law in the way in which the UK Parliament can. The Commission must submit all its proposals for legislation to the Parliament as well as to the Council of the EU. The Parliament can propose amendments, but if the Council does not approve of an amendment it can override the Parliament by a unanimous vote.

Activity 1

The Council of Ministers wishes to pass a new EC law.
(a) Could a single state prevent its being passed, assuming that no amendments had been proposed?
(b) Could a single state prevent its being passed in its unamended form if an amendment had been proposed by the Parliament?

3   THE COURT OF JUSTICE OF THE EUROPEAN COMMUNITY

The Court of Justice (CJ), often referred to as the European Court of Justice, is the court which hears legal actions connected with EC law. There is no long hierarchy of courts allowing for several appeals as there is in the UK, but some actions may be heard by the Court of First Instance (see later in this chapter), with the possibility of an appeal to the CJ.

The procedure of the CJ is in the continental tradition, so its proceedings are inquisitorial rather than adversarial: that is, the court takes an active part in trying to find out what happened and what should be done. In an English court, the court leaves it to the parties to an action to come up with evidence and legal arguments, and then decides between the parties. The CJ has 15 judges and nine advocates-general, all of whom are appointed by states but are independent of the states which appointed them. There are extensive written stages, in which evidence and arguments are exchanged, before a court hearing takes place. At a hearing, the parties can put their cases but the court is also given the opinion of an advocate-general on the case. He or she is impartial, and offers reasoned submissions. A single majority judgment is given, and the views of dissenting judges are not published.

The CJ's jurisdiction is limited to that set out in the EC treaties. This is as follows.

(a) It can hear disputes between states or between the Commission and a state relating to matters covered by an EC treaty.

(b) It can consider the legality of acts or omissions of the Council, the Commission or the Parliament, and it can declare that any of these institutions has violated the EC treaties. An action may be brought by a state, by the Council or by the Commission. In addition, the Parliament may bring an action in order to protect its prerogatives.

(c) It can hear appeals by persons, for example against fines imposed by the Commission for breaches of EC law.

(d) It can interpret EC law when asked to do so by a court in a state. This is called giving a preliminary ruling. The final court of appeal in each state (the House of Lords in the UK) must refer such questions of interpretation to the CJ. Lower courts may do so. Such a reference to the CJ is made merely to establish the meaning of EC law. The case is still decided by the relevant national courts.

(e) It can, at the request of the Council or of the Commission, give an advisory opinion on whether their proposals are compatible with existing EC law.

The CJ cannot interpret, apply, enforce, repeal or annul legislation or administrative acts of states, and it cannot pronounce on their validity under national law. The CJ applies the following general principles of law, which have been evolved in cases.

(a) The protection of fundamental human rights.

(b) Equality (for example, in cases of discrimination on the ground of gender or religion).

(c) The protection of legitimate expectations. Thus a farmer who had temporarily given up his right to sell milk was allowed to enforce the restoration of that right to him at the end of the agreed period, because he could legitimately expect that it would be restored *(Mulder v Minister of Agriculture and Fisheries 1989)*.

(d) Proportionality. Administrative measures, such as penalties, should not be excessive.

(e) Legal certainty. Earlier decisions of the CJ are normally followed, so that people can be reasonably confident of what the law is in an area which the CJ has considered in the past. However, the CJ is not legally bound by its own previous decisions.

3.1 The Court of First Instance

The Court of First Instance is attached to the CJ. It has 15 judges and no advocates-general. It can hear certain cases which would otherwise go to the CJ. There is a right of appeal from its decisions to the CJ, but only on a matter of law.

Activity 2

A builder bought some land, and built a house for his own use on it. Under EC law, value added tax is chargeable when business assets are applied for private use. Could either or both of the following questions be referred to the Court of Justice by a national court?
(a) Is this a case of business assets being applied for private use?
(b) How much was the land worth? (Assume that there is no doubt as to the correct method of valuation.)

4 TYPES OF EC LAW

EC law may be made in several ways. Although all EC law is supreme over the law of states, the way in which it is made is important for two reasons.

(a) It affects the way in which the EC law comes into force in states. In some cases it comes into force without any further action. Such law is said to be directly applicable. In other cases it only comes into force when national legislation is enacted in states.

(b) It affects the types of rights and obligations which arise under the EC law. States may acquire rights, or persons may acquire rights which they may enforce against states or against each other. EC law which itself creates rights which persons may enforce is said to have direct effect. Such rights must be protected by the courts in the states; there is no need to go to the CJ to take legal action on the basis that EC legislation has direct effect. If the rights are against other persons, the law has horizontal effect. If the rights are against states, the law has vertical effect.

The two main categories of EC law are primary legislation, which is given in the EC treaties, and secondary legislation, which is given in regulations, directives and decisions. EC institutions may also issue recommendations and opinions, but these have no binding force.

4.1 The EC treaties

The EC treaties are self-executing, that is they do not require any other legal backing in order to become law in the states. They become law on their ratification by the states. Treaties are therefore directly applicable. The normal procedure is for the heads of governments to indicate their agreement to a treaty by signing it, but that agreement needs to be ratified by national governments acting with their parliaments' authorities.

Each EC treaty is divided into numbered articles. Most articles of EC treaties have direct effect. Whether this is horizontal effect or vertical effect depends on the nature of the article. Thus articles granting individuals the right to live and work in any state have vertical effect, because such a right would be enforced against a state where an individual wished to live or work. Articles intended to ensure free competition, on the other hand, would be more likely to have horizontal effect, because they would be enforced against persons engaging in anti-competitive trade practices.

Some treaty articles do not have direct effect. This may be because they state that further legislation is required, or because they give states discretionary power on their application. In the latter case, their effect is subject to the exercise of that discretion.

The direct effect of treaty articles has been upheld by the Court of Justice in several cases. In an early case, *Van Gend en Loos v Nederlandse Tariefcommissie 1963*, it appeared to be important that the treaty article in question should contain a clear negative prohibition (in that case a prohibition on imposing new customs duties or increasing existing duties). In some other cases in the 1960s, notably *Costa v Ente Nazionale per l'Energia Elettrica 1964*, this prohibition rule was affirmed, but in later cases it has not been applied and treaty articles have been held to have direct effect even if they do not contain negative prohibitions. Thus an article requiring states to ensure that nationals of other states should (if suitably qualified) be able to practise their professions was held to have direct effect in *Reyners v Belgium 1974*. The horizontal effect of treaty articles was illustrated in *Robert Bosch GmbH v de Geus 1962*, which concerned a sole agency agreement for the distribution of Bosch products in the Netherlands.

4.2 EC Regulations

Regulations of the EC are directly applicable in all states, and they also have direct effect. This effect may be either horizontal or vertical, depending on the content of the regulation. Regulations are also generally applicable. This means that they apply to all persons meeting certain criteria, rather than to named persons. For example, a regulation might be expressed to apply to all businesses with annual turnovers exceeding 5bn ecus (European currency units). It would not be expressed to apply to X plc and Y AG, even if those companies happened to be the only businesses with annual turnovers exceeding 5bn ecus.

A regulation is binding in its entirety, and takes priority over any conflicting national law.

> *Leonisio v Italian Ministry of Agriculture and Forestry 1972*
> Signora Leonisio was entitled, under a regulation, to a premium from the Italian state because she had slaughtered some cattle. The Italian state claimed that it did not have to pay the premium because it had not gone through the budgetary procedures needed under Italian law for such payments to be made.

Held: the premium must be paid. Italian national law could not be used to defeat the regulation.

EC Commission v United Kingdom (Re Tachographs) 1979
A regulation concerning tachographs in vehicles required states to enact national legislation. The UK did not incorporate the whole of the regulation in the UK legislation.

Held: states must not implement regulations in an incomplete or selective way. The UK had therefore not fulfilled its EC obligations.

4.3   EC Directives

Directives of the EC are not directly applicable. They are binding on the states to which they are addressed, but only as to the result to be achieved. That is, they set out specific aims (such as allowing companies to have only one shareholder), but they leave it to states to alter national law so as to achieve those aims within a specified period.

A directive may have vertical direct effect, so as to give persons a remedy if a state fails to implement a directive. Legal action may only be taken against the state or its emanations, and it is limited so as not to interfere with any discretion the state may be given under the directive in how to implement it. The state may not take action against persons on the basis of an unimplemented directive.

Marshall v Southampton and South-West Hampshire Area Health Authority 1986
A female employee was required to retire at a younger age than a male employee would have been, on the basis that the UK state pension age was 60 for women and 65 for men.

Held: this policy of different retirement ages for men and women breached a directive on equal treatment of men and women. The employee could rely on the directive against her employer, which was an emanation of the state.

A local authority was held to be an emanation of the state in *R v London Boroughs Transport Committee 1990*. In *Foster and others v British Gas plc 1988*, it was held that British Gas (pre-privatisation) was an emanation of the state, because it was under state control and had powers greater than those which would normally apply in relations between individuals.

A directive cannot have direct horizontal effect, giving persons rights against each other, but a similar effect has been achieved by requiring that national law be interpreted in conformity with directives.

Marleasing SA v La Commercial Internacional De Alimentacion SA 1992
A directive which had not been implemented in Spain set out all the grounds on which the incorporation of a company could be declared void. Spanish law included another ground. The case hinged on whether that extra ground could be used.

Held: Spanish law must be interpreted so as to make it consistent with EC law. The extra ground could not be used, and the rights of the persons involved in the case were to be decided accordingly.

4.4   EC Decisions

Decisions of the EC are addressed to particular states or persons, and are binding on the addressees. They are issued by the Commission to enforce the application of EC law.

Activity 3

If a state refused to change its national law in order to implement a directive, what would it have to do in order not to continue in breach of its treaty obligations?

5   THE SUPREMACY OF EC LAW

EC law overrides national law when the two conflict, and national parliaments have surrendered some of their sovereignty to EC institutions. In this final section, we will look at the way in which this supremacy of EC law is achieved.

For the UK to reach the position in which directly applicable EC law alters UK law without UK legislation, the UK Parliament had to surrender some of its sovereignty using its existing procedures. This was achieved by the European Communities Act 1972, which allows EC law to alter UK law without further UK legislation.

The supremacy of EC law over national law is to be enforced by the national courts. National legislatures have given law-making powers to EC institutions, but they cannot be prevented from passing laws which contradict EC law. If they do so, it is the duty of the national courts to enforce the EC law and override the national law. This rule was stated clearly in *Simmenthal SpA v Commission 1979*. The House of Lords applied this rule in the *Factortame case*.

> *Factortame Ltd v Secretary of State for Transport (No 2) 1991*
> Under a British statute, 75% of directors and shareholders in companies operating British-registered fishing vessels had to be British. A UK company controlled by Spanish nationals claimed that this law was incompatible with EC law forbidding discrimination against nationals of other EC states.
>
> *Held:* the supremacy of EC law had to be ensured. The House of Lords therefore temporarily suspended the UK statute while the interpretation of the EC law was considered by the CJ. Thus the House of Lords directly overrode the will of the UK Parliament.

6   INTERPRETATION OF EC LAW

EC legislation is drafted in a different way from UK legislation. The legislation states the broad principles and leaves the judges to develop the detail and thereby assist the objectives of legislation. English techniques of interpretation are not well-suited to be applied to EC legislation. Additionally, EC legislation is deemed equally valid in any language in which it is originally published. The exact meaning of words used inevitably varies between versions. There is no intention that lawyers should be able to 'shop around' to find the version most favourable to their case.

Lord Denning, in *HP Bulmer Ltd v J Bollinger SA 1974*, has said the following.

The draftsmen of our statutes have striven to express themselves with the utmost exactness. They have tried to foresee all possible circumstances that may arise and to provide for them. They have sacrificed style and simplicity. They have foregone brevity ... How different is this treaty! It lays down general principles. It expresses aims and purposes ... It uses words and phrases without defining what they mean ... It is the European way.

The English courts should therefore try to follow the approach of European courts when interpreting the legislation. To do otherwise would create differences in the way in which the law is interpreted and applied in different member states.

In *Iberion (UK) Ltd v BPB Industries plc and Another 1996* it was held that the courts should not interpret rules of procedure in a way that risked that they and institutions of the European Union would arrive at inconsistent results on EU competition issues.

In the matter of interpreting UK statutes, it is open to the UK courts to decide that a British statute should be interpreted according to British court rules. The interpretation of EC directives need not be taken into account: *Duke v GEC Reliance Systems Ltd 1988*.

Chapter roundup

- The EU is an association of 15 states. EC law generally concerns economic and social matters. The EC has now been subsumed within the European Union, which includes the Maastricht areas of co-operation.

- There are three law-making EC institutions. The Council of the EU has the final say on new law. The Commission proposes new law and enforces existing EC law. The Parliament's role is largely advisory.

- The Court of Justice hears legal actions. It can hear disputes involving EC institutions and disputes between states. It also interprets EC law when asked to do so by national courts. It applies certain general legal principles.

- EC law may be directly applicable. It may also have direct effect, horizontal and/or vertical.

- Treaties and regulations are generally directly applicable and have direct effect. Directives are not directly applicable, but require national legislation to bring them into force. They may however have direct effect in favour of persons against the state or its emanations.

- EC law is supreme over national law. This supremacy is enforced by the national courts.

Quick quiz

1 List the members of the EU.
2 How is the Commission appointed?
3 Can the Parliament make law?
4 To what extent does the Court of Justice follow its earlier decisions?
5 What is the role of the Court of First Instance?
6 When does an article of an EC treaty not have direct effect?
7 To what extent are directives binding on states?
8 What was the significance of the Factortame case?

Solutions to activities

1 (a) No: only a qualified majority vote would be needed.

   (b) Yes: unanimity is required to override an amendment proposed by the Parliament.

2 (a) Yes: this is a question of the interpretation of EC law.

   (b) No.

3 It would have to leave the EU.

Further question practice

Now try the following practice questions at the end of this text

Multiple choice questions:	**10 to 13**
Exam style question:	**3**

Chapter 4

THE SETTLEMENT OF DISPUTES

Introduction

Most of this text is concerned with the principles relating to business law. It is important to have a clear grasp of this underlying theory because it forms the basis for deciding which party to a dispute is entitled to succeed in his claim. But there are numerous *practical* points which affect the outcome of commercial disputes. Settlements are often arrived at not as a result of the relative merits of the parties' cases, but from negotiations within, or outside, the framework of litigation.

Business people tend to regard commercial disputes as being just one more test of the managerial and negotiating skills which they bring to bear on other aspects of their work. Knowledge of legal principles is important because it can indicate the strength of a negotiating position. But the legal merits of a case may never be put to the test and settlements out of court are common.

In this chapter we will look at some of the practical and procedural aspects of business law. We will begin by describing the stages in litigation and then proceed to discuss the process of arbitration. Note that we are considering civil, not criminal, law: the object is to obtain a remedy, not to inflict a punishment.

Your objectives

After completing this chapter you should:

(a) understand why litigation is not always advisable;

(b) know how judgment may be obtained without a trial;

(c) know the stages in an action in the High Court;

(d) know the stages in an action in a county court;

(e) understand the need for injunctions;

(f) understand the nature of *Mareva* injunctions and *Anton Pillar* orders;

(g) be aware of the advantages and disadvantages of arbitration;

(h) know the main terms implied in an arbitration agreement;

(i) be able to outline the stages in arbitration, and the powers of an arbitrator;

(j) know the extent to which courts may become involved in cases subject to arbitration;

(k) be aware of the extent of legal aid;

(l) know the main tribunals available to settle disputes, and their jurisdictions.

1 LITIGATION

The object of litigation is firstly to obtain judgment from the court in favour of the person seeking it, and secondly to make sure that it is enforced.

The system of litigation in England is *adversarial*. This means that the parties to a dispute put forward their cases and the court adjudicates on the matters presented to it. It is not the business of the court to look beyond the evidence presented so as to find other evidence which might be relevant. One criticism which has been made of the adversarial system is that important evidence may not be taken into account. It can happen, for example, that a piece of evidence is known to only one of the parties in dispute, and is not brought forward by him because it tells against his case.

Even when litigation is decided on, legal theory is only one aspect of the problem and there may be practical difficulties to overcome.

(a) If a plaintiff is successful, he will usually want to obtain financial compensation. Before commencing litigation he should be convinced that the defendant has sufficient assets to make it worthwhile. There is no point in seeking recompense from someone with no resources.

(b) Even if the party at fault is financially sound, he may resist the judgment of the court, perhaps by transferring his assets outside the jurisdiction of the court.

(c) An injured party may feel that he has a strong legal case and still refrain from action. This might be because he cannot afford the risk of losing (with its associated costs), or because a court case might damage his reputation or otherwise harm his long-term interests.

Commercial disputes involving large sums are usually heard in the High Court, either in the Queen's Bench division or in the Chancery division. Each of these divisions has specialist courts within it: for example, the Commercial Court is a part of the Queen's Bench division. Actions in both divisions are usually heard by a judge, but judges in the Chancery division may delegate to solicitors acting as *Masters*. Actions in the Queen's Bench division may also be heard by Masters, but the similarity of title conceals an important difference in function. Queen's Bench Masters are barristers exercising independent jurisdiction rather than acting merely as delegates of a judge.

Activity 1

P wishes to sue D, a person with whom he has regular business dealings, for breach of contract. The damages sought would be £3,000, and the total legal costs (mostly borne by the loser) would be about £800. P could only seek damages, and not any equitable remedy, because of the maxim that he who comes to equity must come with clean hands. D's easily realisable assets are worth about £3,000. What factors should P consider before deciding whether to take legal action?

1.1 Obtaining judgment

There are some circumstances in which judgment may be given without trial. The most important are judgment in default, summary judgment and judgment on admissions.

Judgment in *default* may be given if the defendant fails to meet the specified time limits either in announcing his intention to contest the case or in presenting his defence.

Summary judgment is available when it appears that the defendant has no proper defence and is going through the motions of contesting the case merely to cause delay and trouble to the plaintiff.

Judgment *on admissions* may occur where a defendant admits some part of the plaintiff's claim, but disputes the rest. It is then open to the plaintiff to apply for any judgment that he may be entitled to on the basis of the admission, without waiting for resolution of any other points that may still be in dispute.

1.2 A contested action in the High Court

The stages in a contested High Court action are as follows. The stages before the trial itself are referred to as the *interlocutory* stages.

(a) The issue and service of a writ.

(b) The return of an acknowledgement of service.

(c) The pleadings.

(d) The close of pleadings and discovery.

(e) The summons for directions.

(f) The trial.

A *writ* must first be served on the defendant. As a minimum this must state the ground of action and the relief sought; the plaintiff may wish in addition to set out his statement of claim (see below). The writ must be accompanied by a form of *acknowledgement of service*. If he wishes to contest the plaintiff's claim, the defendant must return this form to the court within 14 days. If he fails to do so, he makes himself liable to judgment in default.

The *pleadings* define the issues which will eventually be brought before the court. Neither party will be allowed to bring before the court any grounds of claim or defence which he has not already adduced in his pleadings, and for this reason the drafting of pleadings must be done with great care. The exchange of pleadings is begun by the plaintiff who serves a *statement of claim* on the defendant. This must be done within a prescribed time, and similar time limits apply to the submission of a defence by the defendant. Once the pleadings have been completed, *discovery* takes place. Each party must disclose to the other all relevant documents which are or have been in his possession.

The final step before the trial is a *summons for directions* by which the parties may seek directions for further discovery, amendment of pleadings or any other tidying up that may be necessary.

Finally, the *trial* itself takes place. After opening speeches by counsel for both parties, the witnesses are brought forward to be examined and cross-examined. The proceedings conclude with closing speeches by counsel and the judge's delivery of his judgment. In general, costs will be awarded to the successful party, but he will rarely be fully reimbursed for all his costs.

Activity 2

How do the interlocutory stages help to ensure that as many cases as possible are settled before trial?

1.3 A contested action in the county court

County court procedure is similar, but somewhat simpler and less expensive than a High Court action. The plaintiff applies to the county court office, setting out the nature of his claim and particulars of the defendant, who must normally reside or carry on business within the county court district. The registrar issues a summons which, among other things, specifies a *return day*. The summons and particulars of the plaintiff's claim must be served on the defendant personally or at his address, or by post, not less than 21 days before the return day. The defendant may, within 14 days of receiving the summons, pay into court the whole amount claimed, or as much as he agrees is due, plus costs, or file a defence setting out his rejection of the plaintiff's claim. Alternatively he may appear on the return day to dispute the claim or to admit the claim and ask for time to pay.

The final stage before trial of a defended case is a *pre-trial review* by the court registrar (following enactment of the Courts and Legal Services Act 1990 a district judge will preside). He may make various appropriate orders according to the circumstances. Unless the action is disposed of by his order, the registrar fixes a date for the hearing if the case is in his opinion ready for trial. The trial will be conducted in the same manner as a trial in the High Court. There is not usually a jury but there are exceptions in, for example, actions for malicious prosecution or false imprisonment and some personal injury cases.

2 INTERLOCUTORY MATTERS

In many cases, the eventual award of damages in court may be an inadequate remedy for a plaintiff. The courts have developed other procedures which may assist him, some of which are used between the commencement of proceedings and the trial. One of the most commonly applied for is an *injunction*.

Definition

Injunction is an order restraining a defendant from committing some act before the trial comes to be heard.

A plaintiff may apply to the court for an injunction, which is an equitable remedy preventing breach of duties or infringement of intellectual property rights. It is common for the plaintiff to apply *Injunction* is an order restraining a defendant from committing some act before the trial comes to be heard *Injunction* is an order restraining a defendant from committing some act before the trial comes to be heard *ex parte* in the first instance, that is without giving notice to the defendant. If the judge is convinced by the case he makes out, he will grant an *interim* injunction for a short period during which the defendant will be formally notified, and allowed to make representations. Alternatively, the court may make an *interlocutory* injunction, which applies until the full hearing of the case; it is for a determined period, whereas an interim injunction may be varied between hearings.

Because the plaintiff may not be ultimately successful in the trial, he must give an undertaking to pay damages to the defendant if he fails in his case. This is to compensate the defendant for the prejudice caused by an injunction.

2.1 Mareva injunctions

A recent development in this field is the *Mareva* injunction. A successful plaintiff may be unable to enforce judgment if the defendant's assets have been transferred outside the jurisdiction of the court or otherwise dissipated. If the plaintiff can convince the court that he has a good case and that there is a danger of the defendant's assets being exported or dissipated, he may be awarded an injunction which restricts the defendant's dealing with the assets at all, either at home or by taking them abroad.

The *Mareva* injunction is named from the case of *Mareva Compania Naviera SA v International Bulkcarriers SA 1975*, but it has now been given statutory effect by s 37 Supreme Court Act 1981. The terms which the court will impose in granting such an injunction may vary, but they will not be so restrictive as to prevent the defendant from the ordinary running of his business, from paying ordinary business debts or having an ordinary way of life. The injunction is designed to prevent the defendant's assets from being exported or dissipated; it does not attempt to give the plaintiff any charge over the assets or to place the plaintiff in a preferential position compared with other creditors who may have claims on the assets.

The court will not grant a *Mareva* injunction unless:

(a) there is a 'good arguable case' on the part of the plaintiff;

(b) the court has jurisdiction over the case, and the defendant has available assets within that jurisdiction;

(c) there exists a genuine risk that if the injunction is not granted then:

   (i)   the assets will be removed or dissipated; or

   (ii) the defendant will not satisfy the plaintiff's claim; and

(d) the balance of convenience is in favour of the injunction.

2.2   Anton Pillar orders

A procedural aid for plaintiffs who suspect that their products (usually tape, film, video or computer goods) are being copied is the *Anton Pillar* order, named after the case of *Anton Pillar KG v Manufacturing Processes Ltd 1976*. In this case a German manufacturer feared that his English agent would pass on details of a new range of computer equipment to a competitor. The German company applied for an *ex parte* injunction authorising its solicitor to enter the agent's premises in order to inspect, and if necessary remove, the relevant documents.

The great benefit of the *Anton Pillar* order is that it is granted *ex parte*, that is on the application of the plaintiff alone and without reference to the defendant. Ordinary *inter partes* injunctions are often inadequate because with notice of the plaintiff's intentions the defendant has the opportunity to destroy the evidence. An *Anton Pillar* order can be applied for before either issue or service of a writ. As well as admitting the plaintiff to premises, the order often also requires the defendant to reveal the names and addresses of anybody else engaged in the copying scheme. In addition, the plaintiff may obtain an injunction restraining him from warning those persons.

2.3   Quia timet injunction

A *quia timet* injunction may be granted to restrain the commission of a threatened infringement. For example, the defendant might be erecting a building which, if completed, would infringe the plaintiff's right to light.

Activity 3

X is planning to emigrate and to move all of his assets abroad. Y, who is opposed to this plan for personal reasons, brings an action against X which is unlikely to succeed, and then asks for a *Mareva* injunction in order to delay X in moving his assets abroad. Is Y's plan likely to succeed?

---

3 COMMERCIAL ARBITRATION

Arbitration is an alternative to litigation in commercial disputes. As a process, it has much more in common with a business person's other commercial activities than does litigation. It is often preferred for that reason. However, arbitration only exists within the framework of law, and the court's jurisdiction cannot be ousted.

Some of the advantages of arbitration are as follows.

(a) The proceedings are less formal and more flexible than litigation.

(b) In some cases, arbitration may be quicker and cheaper than litigation, although since the parties must often bear the arbitrator's costs and remuneration directly, this is not always so.

(c) The parties can select an arbitrator in whom they have confidence.

(d) The person chosen is likely to be familiar with the commercial activities of the parties.

(e) The hearing is usually in private, so avoiding publicity.

(f) The atmosphere of an arbitration is more friendly than that of a court action. This is a point of some importance if the parties intend to continue their commercial dealings with each other.

Nevertheless, arbitration suffers from some disadvantages compared with litigation.

(a) Plaintiff and defendant are bound to observe certain time limits in litigation, and so an arbitration procedure may provide more scope for deliberate time-wasting by a defendant.

(b) A judge has power to grant interim relief (such as an injunction) or curtail proceedings by means of a summary judgment. An arbitrator's powers are less extensive.

(c) Judges exercise their profession after many years of training in the process of weighing evidence and interpreting law. Arbitrators may be unqualified in such matters, and hence their decisions may be subjective.

In England, arbitration is regulated by the Arbitration Acts 1950, 1975 and 1979 and the Consumer Arbitration Agreements Act 1988. The 1950 Act is the principal Act.

The Consumer Arbitration Agreements Act 1988 regulates the extent to which a consumer is bound by a clause in a contract requiring disputes to be referred to arbitration. Such a clause may not be enforced against a party entering into the agreement as a consumer (if the cause of action is within the county court's jurisdiction) unless the consumer gives written consent *after* differences arise. Except where the dispute could qualify as a 'small claim' the court may order that it should go to arbitration where it is satisfied that the consumer's interest will not be damaged.

3.1 Arbitration agreements and procedure

Disputes are most likely to be referred to arbitration under the terms of an *arbitration agreement* An arbitration agreement is defined in s 32 Arbitration Act 1950 as 'a written agreement to submit present or future differences to arbitration, whether an arbitrator is named therein or not'. Although an arbitration agreement may by made orally, the Arbitration Acts only apply to written agreements. The definition includes not only *executory agreements* (agreements that disputes will be referred to arbitration) but also agreements to submit disputes to arbitration after they have arisen.

Certain provisions are implied into an arbitration agreement unless a contrary intention is expressed.

(a) The parties to the agreement must submit to being examined on oath by the arbitrator and must produce all relevant documents which may be called for.

(b) The award made by the arbitrator is final and binding on the parties.

(c) The arbitrator can normally offer specific performance of a contract.

(d) An interim award may be made.

The procedure for an arbitration may sometimes be similar to that of a court action. The usual first step is to arrange a meeting between the arbitrator and the parties, and from there to move on to pleadings and discovery. The hearing itself may well be similar to a trial, though less formal. But there are important differences between the two processes. For example, an arbitrator is not normally bound by the rules of evidence and procedure that would apply in a court.

An arbitrator's powers in the interlocutory stages of an arbitration are less than those of a judge in an action. For example, he has no power to enter summary judgment or to penalise either party for failure to comply with his orders. However, the High Court is able to make interlocutory orders for an arbitration in much the same way as for an action. Since enactment of the Arbitration Act 1979 the arbitrator's own position has been strengthened: if either party fails to comply with his orders he may apply to the High Court for power to act, in effect, as a judge might do.

Activity 4

Why should it be harder for a consumer to become bound by an arbitration clause in a contract than for a business person to become bound by one?

3.2 The involvement of the courts

The main object of the Arbitration Act 1979 was to limit the right of parties to an arbitration to apply to a court in the event of disagreement over the outcome of arbitration. The Act:

(a) limits the right to refer a preliminary point of law to the High Court;

(b) limits the right of appeal on a point of law;

(c) requires the arbitrator in certain cases to state reasons for his awards; and

(d) allows for the right of appeal to be expressly excluded by agreement between the parties.

The referral of preliminary points of law

Although a party to arbitration proceedings may apply to the court for settlement of a preliminary point of law before full arbitration proceedings are commenced, this is only allowed if the arbitrator agrees, both parties agree or the leave of the court is obtained.

The court will only grant leave to refer a preliminary point of law if the point of law to be clarified is capable, on clarification, of settling the parties' entire dispute (*Universal Petroleum Co Ltd v Handels und Transport Gesellschaft GmbH 1987*) and also significant cost savings are anticipated as a result of the referral.

The right of appeal on a point of law

Provided either both parties agree to an appeal or the court gives leave an appeal may be made to the court on a point of law. Leave is not given lightly by the court, and is limited to cases where the point is of general public importance. In addition the arbitrator's decision must not be *prima facie* wrong in law: *The Antasios 1984*.

The reasons for an arbitrator's award

With the court's leave, application may be made to the court for an order to obtain detailed reasons for the arbitrator's decision. Again the court is sparing in granting such orders.

Exclusion of the right of appeal

Although generally the law resists attempts to limit access to judicial review, parties in an arbitration may make an 'exclusion agreement' which prevents the parties from appealing on a point of law or referring preliminary points of law.

In domestic cases (where both parties reside in the UK) and in international cases relating to insurance or shipping matters, the exclusion agreement is only valid if it is entered into *after* the arbitration proceedings have begun. In other international cases it is valid even if entered into *before* such proceedings.

An exclusion agreement should not be confused with:

(a) a *Scott v Avery* clause, which makes it a condition precedent to court proceedings that arbitration proceedings should have commenced first; and

(b) an *Atlantic Shipping* clause which requires that, unless arbitration proceedings are commenced within a certain time period, the right of recourse to the courts is lost.

Both these types of clause have been upheld in the courts, since they do not totally oust the court's jurisdiction.

Activity 5

To what extent would the advantages of arbitration be lost if it were easier to get the court to intervene?

---

4   LEGAL AID

Legal aid is a payment out of state funds to provide legal advice or representation, by either solicitors or barristers, for people who would otherwise be unable to afford it. The grant of legal aid in both civil and criminal matters is governed by the Legal Aid Act 1988 and the regulations passed under it and under earlier legislation. It is administered by the Legal Aid Board.

In *criminal cases*, application for aid is made to the court of trial. The applicant must submit a written statement as to his means and the court must be satisfied that it is desirable in the interests of justice for legal aid to be given, and that the applicant's means are such that he needs assistance to meet the costs of the case. When assessing the 'interests of justice' the clerk of the court will consider whether there is a serious risk that the accused will lose his liberty, job or reputation. If there is such a risk, legal aid is more likely to be granted. Nevertheless, there is concern that these criteria are not being applied consistently.

In *civil proceedings*, legal aid is only available to persons of very limited means. A person must satisfy a means test both on disposable income and disposable capital. He must also satisfy a merits test: has he a good arguable case with which, if he were paying his own costs, a solicitor would advise him to proceed? Two types of help are available.

(a) *Legal advice and assistance.* Under this scheme solicitors can undertake work falling short of court appearances. There is a relatively low limit on the value of this work, but it may be extended with the consent of the local area office of the Legal Aid Board.

(b) *Legal aid.* This is available for nearly all civil court hearings (except defamation). It is administered by local Legal Aid Board offices. Depending upon his financial position, the applicant for legal aid may receive legal services free of charge or he may be required to make some contribution to the total cost.

5 ADMINISTRATIVE TRIBUNALS

Definition

Administrative tribunals: specialised courts established by statute to deal with disputes between government agencies and individuals or between two individuals in a simpler and less formal way than is possible in a court of law.

Some of the more important administrative tribunals are listed below.

(a) *Social security tribunals* An individual who is refused a social security benefit may have his claim referred to a local tribunal consisting of a chairman (usually a lawyer) and two members from panels representative of employers and of employees. Either party may appeal from the decision of the tribunal to a National Insurance Commissioner who is a barrister or solicitor of at least ten years' standing. On a point of law there is a further right of appeal to the High Court.

(b) *The Land Tribunal* This tribunal deals with disputes over the value of property, for example for compulsory purchase purposes. An experienced lawyer and a qualified valuation expert usually preside.

(c) *Rent tribunals* These assess rents of certain furnished dwellings. County courts assess rents of unfurnished dwellings.

(d) *ACAS* The Advisory, Conciliation and Arbitration Service as various functions including conciliation in disputes between employer and employee before such disputes go to an industrial tribunal.

(e) *Industrial tribunals* These have membership similar to that of social security tribunals. They deal mainly with claims for compensation for unfair dismissal, redundancy pay, equal pay and sex discrimination. There is a right of appeal to the Employment Appeal Tribunal (EAT).

(f) *Administrative enquiries* Some statutes, such as the town and country planning legislation, provide that objectors may put their case at a public enquiry conducted by an *inspector* (professionally qualified expert) appointed by a minister. The inspector makes a report to the minister who takes the final decision.

Administrative tribunals offer a quicker and less expensive method of resolving a dispute than the court. But they may make mistakes of law or fail to convince interested parties that a fair and impartial hearing has been given.

The working of this system of administrative tribunals is supervised by a Council on Tribunals. In many instances, especially industrial tribunals, there is a statutory right to appeal from a tribunal to a court on points of law. The High Court may also make prerogative orders to prevent or remedy errors and injustices. At the appeal stage (but not usually in the proceedings before the lower tribunal) the applicant may be able to obtain legal aid.

5.1 Domestic tribunals

Within some professions, trade associations and trade unions, there are *domestic tribunals* which deal with charges of professional misconduct or breach of membership obligations. Some of these domestic tribunals are established by statute, for example the Solicitors' Disciplinary Tribunal and the disciplinary panel of the General Medical Council. Others are created merely by contract between the members of the relevant body who, on becoming members, agree to submit to a code of rules, including disciplinary procedures. This is the position in, for example, trades unions. If a domestic tribunal is established by law there is often a statutory right of appeal. The High Court may make prerogative orders to remedy misconduct by a domestic tribunal where there is no other relief available.

Activity 6

A group of employees who are being made redundant are in dispute with their employer. Name two bodies other than the courts which might be involved in settling the dispute.

Chapter roundup

- A negotiated settlement may be preferable to litigation, in order to avoid legal costs or publicity, or to ensure that the compensation sought is actually received.
- Judgment may be obtained without trial, by obtaining judgment in default, summary judgment or judgment on admissions.
- Before a High Court action reaches trial, there are several interlocutory stages, in which each party learns about the other party's case. The parties thus have the opportunity to reach an agreement, but if the case does go to trial it is already clear what the issues are.
- County court procedure is simpler than High Court procedure.
- Injunctions may be sought to govern the actions of the parties prior to trial. A *Mareva* injunction prevents assets from being taken outside the jurisdiction of the court, and an *Anton Pillar* order prevents illicit copies of goods from being destroyed.
- Arbitration offers an alternative to litigation in the settlement of commercial disputes. Contracts may incorporate arbitration agreements just in case disputes arise.
- Even if arbitration is used, the courts may still become involved in settling preliminary points of law or in hearing appeals on points of law.
- Legal aid is available to make legal advice and representation available to those without means, but it is very limited.
- Administrative tribunals deal with particular types of dispute more cheaply and quickly than the courts could.

Quick quiz

1 What does it mean to say that the system of litigation in England is adversarial?
2 What are the stages in a contested action in the High Court?

3   What are the stages in a contested action in a county court?

4   To what extent will the terms of a *Mareva* injunction be limited so as not to be too restrictive?

5   What are the main disadvantages of arbitration compared with litigation?

6   What conditions must be satisfied for a court to hear an appeal from an arbitration on a point of law?

7   List six administrative tribunals, and state the types of case which they deal with.

Solutions to activities

1   (a) Will P end up having to pay his own legal costs (and perhaps D's, if they reduce the £3,000 available)?

(b) Will D be put out of business?

(c) Even if D remains in business, will he refuse to have further dealings with P?

2   When the parties disclose their cases, it may become clear that one has a much stronger case than the other, so that a settlement would be sensible.

3   No: a *Mareva* injunction will only be granted if the plaintiff has a good arguable case.

4   An arbitration clause is likely to be stipulated by the seller of goods to a consumer, and the consumer must either accept it or not buy the goods. A consumer may also not understand its significance.

5   Someone doing badly in an arbitration would try to get the decision reversed by the courts, thus leading to delay and further expense.

6   ACAS and an industrial tribunal.

Further question practice

Now try the following practice questions at the end of this text

Multiple choice questions: **14 and 15**

Exam style question: **4**

Chapter 5

FORMATION OF CONTRACT

Introduction

Chapters 5 to 8 deal with contract law. A contract is an agreement which legally binds the parties to it. Consider the contracts that you may have entered into as an individual, when buying a house for example, or starting work. Similarly, a business will enter into contracts when it deals with property or takes on new staff.

Most contracts do not have to be in writing. Consider what happens when you go shopping. Clearly, in most cases, the retailer and purchaser do not draw up and sign a written contract, and yet a contract is formed. This is an important point.

However restrictions on the individual's freedom to make contracts have been developed to protect the disadvantaged, particularly in their dealings with large or monopolistic organisations. An example is the Sale of Goods Act 1979, which implies certain terms into contracts for the the sale of goods, which cannot be excluded in consumer sales. A seller is bound by these terms even though he has never agreed to them, or may never have even thought of them.

Your objectives

After completing this chapter you should:

(a) understand the nature of a contract;

(b) appreciate the circumstances in which legal relations are or are not intended;

(c) know what constitutes a valid offer, and how it may be terminated;

(d) know how an offer may be accepted, and how acceptance may be communicated;

(e) understand the circumstances in which contracts may arise without offer and acceptance;

(f) understand the need for consideration, and know the three types of consideration;

(g) appreciate the rules on adequacy and sufficiency of consideration;

(h) know the uses of promissory estoppel;

(i) understand the doctrine of privity of contract.

1 MODERN CONTRACT LAW

A contract is an agreement which legally binds the parties. A party to a contract is bound because he has agreed to be bound. The underlying theory, then, is that a contract is the outcome of 'consenting minds'. However, this is in itself misleading; no court can discover the *intent* of a party to a contract. Parties are not judged by what is in their minds, but by what they have said, written or done. It is often said that English law adopts an objective test of agreement.

Contracts are sometimes referred to as *enforceable agreements*. This too is somewhat misleading. English law will not usually allow one party to force the other to fulfil his part of the bargain. He will usually be restricted to the remedy of damages.

1.1 Factors affecting the modern contract

Modern contract law is strongly influenced by the events of the nineteenth century, and many principles are still based on the outcomes of important cases decided over one hundred years ago. However, a number of developments in the twentieth century should be brought into consideration in any study of modern contract law.

(a) *Inequality of bargaining power.* It is almost invariably the case that the two parties to a contract bring with them differing levels of bargaining power. Many contracts are made between experts and ordinary consumers. It may be said that there is a stronger party and a weaker party in many cases. This inequality of bargaining power does not of itself invalidate a contract. If a stronger party and a weaker party wish to enter into a contract with each other, there is no reason for the law to intervene and prevent this. The law will intervene only where the former takes *unfair* advantage of his position.

(b) *The standard form contract.* Mass production and nationalisation have led to the standard form contract. This is a standard document prepared by many large organisations and setting out the terms on which they contract with their customers. The individual must usually take it or leave it: he does not really 'agree' to it. For example, a customer has to accept his supply of electricity on the electricity board's terms. He is not likely to succeed in negotiating special terms, unless he represents a large consumer of electricity, such as a factory.

(c) *Consumer protection.* During the second half of the twentieth century there has been a surge of interest in consumer matters. In 1961, the Molony Committee on Consumer Protection reported a 'growing tendency for manufacturers to appeal directly to the public by forceful national advertising'. This new method of doing business arrived together with the further influence of 'the development of a mass market for extremely complex mechanical and electrical goods ... [whose] performance cannot in some cases be accurately established by a short trial; ... inherent faults may only come to light when the article breaks down after a period of use'. These developments were identified as leading to a greater need for consumer protection. The consumer could no longer rely on his own judgment when buying sophisticated goods or services. Consumer interests are now served by, *inter alia*, consumer protection agencies, which include government departments (the Office of Fair Trading) and independent bodies (the Consumers' Association), and by legislation. Public policy sometimes requires that the freedom of contract should be modified. For example, the Consumer Credit Act 1974 (CCA) and the Unfair Contract Terms Act 1977 (UCTA) both regulate the extent to which contracts can contain certain terms.

1.2 Essential elements of a contract

The essential elements of a contract are that:

(a) the parties *intend to create legal relations* between themselves;

(b) it is an agreement made by *offer and acceptance*; and

(c) it is a bargain by which the obligations assumed by each party are supported by *consideration* (value) given by the other. However, a gratuitous promise is binding if made by deed.

2 THE INTENTION TO CREATE LEGAL RELATIONS

An agreement is not a binding contract unless the parties intend thereby to create legal relations. Where there is no express statement as to whether or not legal relations are intended (as may be said to be true of the majority of contracts), the courts apply one of two presumptions:

(a) *Social, domestic and family arrangements* are not usually intended by the parties involved to be binding;

(b) *Commercial agreements* are usually intended to be legally binding.

2.1 Domestic arrangements

In most agreements no intention is expressly stated. If it is a domestic agreement between husband and wife, relatives or friends it is presumed that there is no intention to create legal relations unless the circumstances point to the opposite conclusion. However, where agreements between husband and wife or other relatives relate to property matters the courts are very ready to impute an intention to create legal relations.

Balfour v Balfour 1919
The husband was employed in Ceylon. He and his wife returned to the UK on leave but it was agreed that for health reasons she would not return to Ceylon with him. He promised to pay her £30 a month as maintenance. Later the marriage ended in divorce and the wife sued for the monthly allowance which the husband no longer paid.

Held: an informal agreement of indefinite duration made between husband and wife (whose marriage had not then broken up) was not intended to be legally binding.

Merritt v Merritt 1970
The husband had left the matrimonial home, which was owned in the joint name of husband and wife, to live with another woman. The spouses met and held a discussion in the husband's car in the course of which he agreed to pay her £40 a month out of which she agreed to keep up the mortgage payments on the house. The wife refused to leave the car until the husband signed a note of these agreed terms and an undertaking to transfer the house into her sole name when the mortgage had been paid off. The wife paid off the mortgage but the husband refused to transfer the house to her.

Held: in the circumstances, an intention to create legal relations was to be inferred and the wife could sue for breach of contract.

Domestic arrangements extend to those between people who are not related but who have a close relationship of some form. The nature of the agreement itself may lead to the conclusion that legal relations were intended.

Simpkins v Pays 1955
The defendant, her granddaughter and the plaintiff, a paying boarder, took part together in a weekly competition organised by a Sunday newspaper. The arrangements were informal and the entries were made in the grandmother's name. One week they won £750 but the paying boarder was denied a third share by the other two.

Held: there was a 'mutuality in the arrangements between the parties', amounting to a joint enterprise. As such it was not a 'friendly adventure' as the defendant claimed, but a contract.

2.2   Commercial agreements

When businessmen enter into commercial agreements it is presumed that there is an intention to enter into legal relations unless this is expressly disclaimed or the circumstances displace that presumption. Any express statement by the parties of their intention not to make a binding contract is conclusive.

Rose and Frank v J R Crompton & Bros 1923
A commercial agreement by which the defendants (a British manufacturer) appointed the plaintiffs to be their distributor in the USA expressly stated that it was 'not subject to legal jurisdiction' in either country. The defendants terminated the agreement without giving notice as required, and refused to deliver goods ordered by the plaintiffs, although they had accepted these orders when placed.

Held: the general agreement was not legally binding, but the orders for goods were separate and binding contracts. The claim for damages for breach of the agreement failed, but the claim for damages for non-delivery of goods ordered succeeded.

Edwards v Skyways Ltd 1964
In negotiations over the terms for making an employee redundant, the employer undertook to make an *ex gratia* payment to him.

Held: although the defendants argued that the use of the phrase *ex gratia* showed no intention to create legal relations, this was a commercial arrangement and the burden of refuting the presumption of legal relations had not been discharged by them.

Procedural agreements between employers and trade unions for the settlement of disputes are not by their nature intended to give rise to legal relations in spite of their elaborate and very legal contents: *s 179 Trade Union and Labour Relations (Consolidation) Act 1992.*

Activity 1

A widow tells her adult son that he can stay at her house temporarily so long as he does his share of domestic chores. Consider whether there is likely to be a contract under which accommodation is supplied in return for housework. Give reasons for your answer.

3   OFFER AND ACCEPTANCE

Definitions

Offer: an express or implied statement of the terms on which the maker is willing to be contractually bound.

Acceptance: a positive act by a person accepting an offer so as to bring a contract into effect.

3.1   Offer

An offer is a definite promise to be bound on specific terms. However, if an apparently vague offer can be made certain by reference to the parties' previous dealing or the customs of the trade, then it will be regarded as certain.

Gunthing v Lynn 1831
The offeror offered to pay a further sum for a horse if it was 'lucky'.

Held: the offer was too vague and no contract could be formed by any purported acceptance.

Hillas & Co Ltd v Arcos Ltd 1932
The plaintiffs agreed to purchase from the defendants '22,000 standards of softwood goods of fair specification over the season 1930'. The agreement contained an option to buy a further 100,000 standards in 1931, without terms as to the kind or size of timber being specified. The 1930 transaction took place in spite of the vague specification used, but the sellers sought to prevent the buyers from exercising the option. They refused to supply any wood in 1931, saying that the agreement was too vague to bind the parties.

Held: the missing terms of the agreement could be ascertained by reference to previous transactions between the parties.

A definite offer does not have to be made to a particular person. It may be made to a class of persons or to the world at large. (The principles in defences (c) and (d) raised in the case below will be considered further later.)

Carlill v Carbolic Smoke Ball Co 1893
The manufacturers of a patent medicine published an advertisement by which they undertook to pay '£100 reward ... to any person who contracts ... influenza ... after having used the smoke ball three times daily for two weeks'. The advertisement added that £1,000 had been deposited at a bank 'showing our sincerity in this matter'. The plaintiff read the advertisement, purchased the smoke ball and used it as directed. She contracted influenza and claimed her £100 reward. In their defence the manufacturers argued a number of defences.

(a)   The offer was so vague that it could not form the basis of a contract as no time limit was specified.

(b)   It was not an offer which could be accepted since it was offered to the whole world.

(c)   The plaintiff had not communicated to them her acceptance of the offer.

(d)   The plaintiff had not supplied any consideration.

(e)   The offer was a mere sales 'puff' not intended to create legal relations.

Held: the court considered each defence as follows.

(a)   The smoke ball must protect the user during the period of use. The offer was not vague.

(b)   Such an offer was possible, by comparison with reward cases.

(c) Communication was not necessary, again a comparison was drawn with reward cases.

(d) The act of sniffing the smoke ball was consideration (the purchase price was consideration for a contract with the retailer).

(e) The deposit of £1,000 indicated an intention to create legal relations.

Activity 2

A manufacturer of vitamin pills states in an advertisement that the regular use of its product is likely to improve the user's health, but says nothing more. A user notices no improvement in his health, and wonders whether he can sue for breach of contract on the basis of *Carlill's* case. What are the significant differences from that case which would mean that there would be no basis for an action for breach of contract (although there might be other grounds of action)?

Definition

Invitation to treat: an indication that a person is prepared to receive offers with a view to entering into a binding contract.

An offer must be distinguished from the mere *supply of information* and from an *invitation to treat* (that is, negotiate). Only an offer in the proper sense (made with the intention that it shall become binding when accepted) may be accepted so as to form a binding contract.

Harvey v Facey 1893
The plaintiff telegraphed to the defendant 'Will you sell us Bumper Hall Pen? Telegraph lowest cash price.' The defendant replied 'Lowest price for Bumper Hall Pen £900.' The plaintiff telegraphed to accept what he regarded as an offer; the defendant made no further reply.

Held: The defendant's telegram was merely a statement of his minimum price if a sale were to be agreed. It was not an offer which the plaintiff could accept. No contract had been made.

To display goods in a shop window or on the open shelves of a self service shop (with a price tag), or to advertise goods for sale is to invite customers to make offers to purchase. The shopkeeper or advertiser makes an 'invitation to treat', not an offer to sell.

Fisher v Bell 1961
A shopkeeper was prosecuted for offering for sale an offensive weapon by exhibiting a flick knife in his shop window.

Held: the display of an article with a price on it in a shop window is merely an invitation to treat. It is not an offer for sale.

Pharmaceutical Society of Great Britain v Boots Cash Chemists (Southern) 1952
Certain drugs may only be sold 'under the supervision of a registered pharmacist.' It was alleged that this rule had been broken by Boots who put supplies of these drugs on open shelves in a self service shop. Boots, however, contended that there was no sale until a customer brought the goods which he had selected to the cash desk at the exit and offered to buy them. A registered pharmacist was stationed at this point.

Held: Boots were correct in their analysis of the situation. The court commented that if it were true that a customer accepted an offer to sell by removing goods from the shelf he could not then change his mind and put them back; it would be breach of contract. Plainly neither Boots nor their customers intended such a result.

Partridge v Crittenden 1968

Mr Partridge placed an advertisement in *Cage and Aviary Birds* magazine's 'classified' columns containing the words 'Bramblefinch cocks, bramblefinch hens, 25s [£1.25] each'. One person who purchased a bird in response to the advertisement reported Partridge to the RSPCA, who brought a prosecution against him for offering for sale a brambling in contravention of the Protection of Birds Act 1953. The justices, satisfied that the bird in question was a wild bird which had been trapped, convicted Partridge. He appealed to the Court of Appeal.

Held: the conviction was quashed. Although there had been a sale in contravention of the Act, the prosecution could not rely on the offence of 'offering for sale', as the advertisement constituted an invitation to treat.

Activity 3

The following conversation takes place between A and B.

A: 'Would you be interested in buying my car?'
B: 'Yes, but I would only give you £800 for it.'
A: 'I would want £850 at least.'
B: 'Very well, I accept your offer to sell the car to me for £850.'

Consider whether A is bound to sell the car to B for £850. Give reasons for your answer.

3.2   Acceptance

Acceptance may be by express words or (as in *Carlill's* case) by action. It may also be implied by conduct.

Brogden v Metropolitan Railway Co 1877

For many years B supplied coal to M. He suggested that they should enter into a written agreement, and M's agent sent a draft to him for consideration. B added the name of an arbitrator in a space left for the purpose and, having marked it 'approved', returned the amended draft to M's agent. M's agent took no further action on it. B continued to supply coal to M and the parties applied the terms of the draft agreement to their dealings, but never signed a final copy of it. B later denied that there was any agreement between him and M.

Held: the return of the draft was not an acceptance of the offer, but the subsequent conduct of the parties was only explicable on the assumption that they both agreed to its terms. The draft agreement became the contract between the parties as soon as M ordered and B supplied coal after the return of the draft to the agent.

There must, however, be some act on the part of the offeree to indicate his acceptance. Mere passive inaction is not acceptance.

Felthouse v Bindley 1862

The plaintiff wrote to his nephew offering to buy the nephew's horse for £30.15s [£30.75], adding 'If I hear no more about him, I consider the horse mine at that price'. The nephew intended to accept his uncle's offer but did not reply. He instructed the defendant, an auctioneer, in whose possession the horse was at the time, not to sell the horse by auction. Owing to a misunderstanding the horse was sold to someone else. The uncle sued the auctioneer in conversion (a tort alleging wrongful disposal of another's property).

Held: the action failed. There could be no acceptance by silence in these circumstances – the offeror cannot impose acceptance merely because the offeree does not reject the offer. The plaintiff had no title to the horse and could not sue in conversion.

Acceptance must be unqualified agreement to the terms of the offer. Acceptance which purports to introduce any new terms is a counter-offer. A counter-offer is a final rejection of the original offer. A counter-offer may, however, be accepted by the original offeror; this will have the effect of creating a binding contract.

> *Hyde v Wrench 1840*
> The defendant offered to sell property to the plaintiff for £1,000 on 6 June. Two days later, the plaintiff made a counter-offer of £950 which the defendant rejected on 27 June. The plaintiff then informed the defendant on 29 June that he accepted the original offer of £1,000.
>
> *Held:* the original offer of £1,000 had been terminated by the counter-offer of £950 made on 8 June; it could not therefore be revived by the plaintiff changing his mind and tendering a subsequent acceptance.
>
> *Butler Machine Tool Co. v Ex-cell-O Corp (England) 1979*
> The plaintiffs offered to sell tools to the defendants. Their quotation included details of their standard terms and conditions of sale. The defendant 'accepted' the offer, enclosing their own standard terms. The plaintiffs acknowledged acceptance by returning a tear-off slip from the order form.
>
> *Held:* the defendants' order was really a counter-offer. The plaintiffs had accepted this by returning the tear-off slip.

Acceptance 'subject to contract'

It is possible to respond to an offer without accepting or rejecting it by a request for information (for example, a request as to whether other terms would be acceptable: *Stevenson v McLean 1880*) or by acceptance 'subject to contract'. Acceptance subject to contract is neither acceptance nor rejection by counter-offer. It means that the offeree is agreeable to the terms of the offer but proposes that the parties should negotiate a formal (usually written) contract on the basis of the offer. Neither party is bound until the formal contract is signed.

Activity 4

When the two parties to a contract for a sale of goods each put forward their own standard conditions of sale or purchase, in respect of what matters would the two sets of conditions be likely to differ?

3.3 Acceptance of tender

A 'tender' is a term often used in commercial dealings.

Definition

Tender: an estimate submitted in response to a prior request.

When a person tenders for a contract, he is making an offer to the person who has advertised a contract as being available. An invitation for tenders does not amount to an offer to contract with the person quoting the best price, except where the person inviting tenders makes it clear that he is in fact making an offer, for example by the use of words such as 'we confirm that if the offer made by you is the highest offer received by us we bind ourselves to accept such offer': *Harvela Investments Ltd v Royal Trust Co of Canada Ltd 1985*.

There are two distinct types of tender.

(a) A tender to perform one task, such as building a new hospital, is an offer which can be accepted. Acceptance of the tender creates a legal obligation.

(b) A tender to supply or perform a series of things, such as the supply of vegetables daily to a restaurant, is not accepted until an order is placed. It is a standing offer. Acceptance of the tender does not create a binding contract. Each order placed by the offeree is an individual act of acceptance creating a separate contract. He is not bound to place any orders unless he has expressly undertaken to do so.

Communication of acceptance

The general rule is that acceptance must be communicated to the offeror and is not effective until this has been done.

> *Entores v Miles Far Eastern Corporation 1955*
> The offeror sent an offer by telex to the offeree's agent in Amsterdam and the latter sent an acceptance by telex. The plaintiffs alleged breach of contract and wished to serve a writ. The legal issue was whether the contract had been made in London (within the jurisdiction of the English court) or abroad (outside it).
>
> *Held:* the acceptance took effect (and the contract was made) when the telex message was printed out on the offeror's terminal in London. A writ could therefore be issued.

But the offeror may by his offer dispense with communication of acceptance. For example, the offer to Mrs Carlill merely required that she should buy and use the smoke ball. This was sufficient acceptance, although not reported to the manufacturer.

The offeror may call for acceptance by specified means. Unless he stipulates that this is the only method of acceptance which suffices, the offeree may accept by some other means (if it is equally advantageous to the offeror).

> *Yates Building Co v R J Pulleyn & Sons (York) 1975*
> The offer called for acceptance by registered or recorded delivery letter. The offeree sent an ordinary letter which arrived without delay.
>
> *Held:* the offeror had suffered no disadvantage and had not stipulated that acceptance must be made in this way only. The acceptance was valid.

In *Tinn v Hoffman 1873* it was said that a telegram or even an oral message could be sufficient acceptance of an offer inviting acceptance 'by return of post'.

The postal rule

The offeror may expressly or by implication indicate that he expects acceptance by letter sent through the post. The *postal rule* states that, where the use of the post is within the contemplation of both the parties, the acceptance is complete and effective as soon as a letter (if it is correctly addressed and stamped and actually put in the post) is posted, even though it may be delayed or lost altogether in the post.

> *Adams v Lindsell 1818*
> L made an offer by letter to A on 2 September 1817 requiring an answer 'in course of post'. The letter of offer was misdirected and somewhat delayed in the post, reaching A on 5 September. A posted a letter of acceptance immediately: this reached L on 9 September. But L assumed that the absence of a reply within the expected period (that is by 7 September) indicated non-acceptance and sold the goods to another buyer on 8 September.
>
> *Held:* the acceptance was made 'in course of post' (no time limit was imposed) and effective when posted. The contract was made on 5 September, when the letter of acceptance was posted.

The intention to use the post for communication of acceptance may be deduced from the circumstances (for example, if the offer is made by post), without express statement to that effect.

Household Fire and Carriage Accident Insurance Co v Grant 1879
G handed a letter of application for shares to the company's agent in Swansea with the intention that it should be posted (as it was) to the company in London. The company posted an acceptance (a letter of allotment) which was lost in the post and never arrived. G was called upon to pay the amounts outstanding on his shares.

Held: G had to pay. The contract between him and the company had been formed when the letter of allotment was posted, regardless of the fact that it was lost in the post.

Under the postal rule, the offeror may be unaware that a contract has been made by acceptance of his offer. If that possibility is clearly inconsistent with the nature of the transaction (and of course if the offeror so stipulates), the rule (complete acceptance by posting) is excluded and the letter of acceptance takes effect only when received.

Activity 5

With the usual rules on acceptance by post, the offeror does not know that the offer has been accepted until a day or two after acceptance: he is therefore legally bound without knowing that he is. Although this is unsatisfactory, why would it be equally unsatisfactory to rule that acceptance takes place when the offeror receives the letter of acceptance?

3.4 Termination of an offer

An offer may only be accepted (so as to form a contract) while the offer is still open. An offer is terminated in any of the following circumstances.

Lapse of time

An offer may be expressed to last for a *specified time*. It then expires at the end of that time. If however, there is no express time limit it expires after a *reasonable time*. What is reasonable depends on the circumstances of the case, on what is usual and to be expected.

Ramsgate Victoria Hotel Co v Montefiore 1866
M applied to the company for shares in June and paid a deposit to the company's bank. At the end of November the company sent him an acceptance by issue of a letter of allotment and requested payment of the balance due. M contended that his offer had expired and could no longer be accepted.

Held: M's offer was for a reasonable time only and five months was much more than that. It was an excessive interval. The offer had lapsed.

Revocation

The offeror may *revoke* his offer revocation at any time before acceptance. If he undertakes that his offer shall remain open for acceptance for a specified time he may nonetheless revoke it within that time unless by a separate contract (an option agreement) he has bound himself to keep it open for the whole of the specified time.

Routledge v Grant 1828
G offered to buy R's house, requiring acceptance within six weeks. Within the six weeks G withdrew his offer.

Held: G could revoke his offer at any time before acceptance, even though the time limit had not expired. The plaintiff could only have held him to his offer if there had been a separate option agreement (for which consideration must be given).

Revocation may be by express statement or by an act of the offeror indicating that he no longer regards the offer as in force. But however he revokes it, his revocation does not take effect (and the offer continues to be available for acceptance) until the revocation is communicated to the offeree. This raises two important points. Firstly, posting a letter is *not* a sufficient act of revocation. Secondly, revocation may be communicated either by the offeror or by any third party who is a sufficiently reliable informant.

Byrne v Van Tienhoven 1880
The offeror was in Cardiff: the offeree in New York. The sequence of events was as follows.

1 October   Letter of offer posted in Cardiff.

8 October   Letter of revocation of offer posted in Cardiff.

11 October   Letter of offer received in New York and telegram of acceptance sent.

15 October   Letter confirming acceptance posted in New York.

20 October   Letter of revocation received in New York. The offeree had meanwhile re-sold the contract goods.

Held: the letter of revocation could not take effect until received (20 October); it could not revoke the contract made by acceptance of the offer on 11 October. Simply posting a letter does not revoke the offer until it is received.

Dickinson v Dodds 1876
A, on 10 June, wrote to B to offer property for sale at £800, adding 'This offer to be left open until Friday 12 June, 9.00 am.' On Thursday 11 June B delivered a letter of acceptance to an address at which A was no longer residing so that A did not receive it. A later sold the property to another buyer. C, who had been an intermediary between A and B, informed B that A had sold to someone else. On Friday 12 June, before 9.00 am, C delivered to A a duplicate of B's letter of acceptance.

Held: A was free to revoke his offer and had done so by sale to a third party; B could not accept the offer after he had learnt from a reliable informant (C) of A's revocation of the offer to B. The purported acceptance was too late.

Rejection

As noted earlier, an offer may be *rejected* outright or by a counter-offer made by the offeree.

Death

Death of the offeree terminates the offer. Death of the offeror terminates the offer unless the offeree accepts it in ignorance of the offeror's death, and the offer is not of a personal nature.

Activity 6

X offers to sell some rare books to Y. Before Y has decided whether to accept the offer, she hears from X's solicitor (whom Y knows acts in that capacity) that X has withdrawn the offer. Y then tries to accept the offer, on the ground that revocation was not communicated by X himself. Must X sell the books to Y?
Why is this the case?

3.5 Agreement without offer and acceptance

Offer and acceptance are merely a means of establishing the fact of agreement. But it is doubtful whether an agreement effected by any other means suffices to make a contract. This view is supported by the House of Lords decision in *Gibson v Manchester City Council 1979*, when the House overruled the Court of Appeal, disagreeing with Lord Denning who had said 'there is no need to look for strict offer and acceptance. You should look at the correspondence as a whole and at the conduct of the parties.' In general therefore offer and acceptance are essential to make a contract. Problems may however arise in reward cases, with cross-offers and with collateral contracts.

Reward cases

If A offers a *reward* to anyone who finds and returns his lost property and B, in ignorance of the offer, does in fact return it to him, is B entitled to the promised reward? There is agreement by conduct, but B is not accepting A's offer since he is unaware of it. There is no contract by which A is obliged to pay the reward to B: *R v Clarke 1927*.

Acceptance may be valid if the offer of reward was in the plaintiff's mind when he acted, even if the offer was not the sole reason for the acceptance being made.

> *Williams v Carwardine 1833*
> A reward was offered to bring criminals to book. W, an accomplice in the crime, supplied the information. Although she had knowledge of the reward she was moved primarily by remorse at her own part in the crime.
>
> Held: as the information was given with knowledge, the acceptance was related to the offer, despite the fact that remorse was the prime motive.

Cross-offers

If, after an inconclusive discussion, X writes to offer to buy property from Y and Y at the same time writes to offer to sell the property to X on the same terms, these *cross-offers* establish agreement, but neither offer has been accepted. It has been held (*Tinn v Hoffman 1873*) that cross-offers cannot constitute a contract, although this was only a majority decision and may still be challenged.

Collateral contracts

A collateral contract, although not expressly entered into by the parties to it, arises when a statement which is not part of the principal contract is nevertheless part of another contract related to the same subject matter. This means that a person not party to the principal contract can, if a collateral contract exists, sue on the collateral contract.

> *Shanklin Pier v Detel Products 1951*
> D gave assurances to S, the owner of a pier, that paint manufactured by D would be satisfactory and durable if used in repainting S's pier. S, in his contract with T for the repainting of the pier, specified that T should use D's paint. The paint proved very unsatisfactory and the remedial work cost £4,127. The plaintiffs sued D for breach of undertaking. The defendants argued that there was no contract between the plaintiffs and themselves.
>
> *Held:* although S could not sue D on the contract of sale of the paint, to which he was not a party, the contract between S and T requiring the use of D's paint (to be purchased and supplied by T) was the consideration for a contract between S and D, by which D guaranteed that D's paint was of the quality described.

Activity 7

Mary contracts with Peter to do some computer programming for him. Peter asks Mary to subcontract some of the work to Jane, whom Peter believes (on the strength of Jane's assurance) to be a competent programmer. Jane proves to be unable to do the work she has agreed to do. Who may sue Jane, and on what grounds?

4 CONSIDERATION

Definition

Consideration: that which is given, promised or done by a party to a contract.

A promise given in a contract is only binding on the promisor if it is supported by consideration or if the promise is in the form of a deed. A contract not made by deed is a *simple contract*. In such a contract, the law looks for an element of *bargain*: a contractual promise is one which is not purely gratuitous. Consideration is what the promisee must give in exchange for the promise to him.

The accepted full length definition of consideration (given in *Currie v Misa 1875*) states that consideration is either an advantage to the promisor or a detriment incurred by the promisee. A better definition adopted by the House of Lords in *Dunlop v Selfridge 1915* is as follows.

'An act or forbearance of one party, or the promise thereof, is the price for which the promise of the other is bought, and the promise thus given for value is enforceable'.

Activity 8

P and Q are neighbours. P undertakes not to sell part of his garden to a developer in return for a promise by Q to pay £1,000 to P. Q then claims that, because P has not actually given Q anything but has merely refrained from action, Q's promise to pay £1,000 is not supported by consideration and is not binding.
Consider whether Q is correct, and why.

4.1 Executory, executed and past consideration

It is sometimes said that consideration may be executed or executory, but it cannot be past. *Executed* consideration is an act in return for a promise. The consideration for the promise is an executed, or performed, act. If, for example, A offers a reward for the return of lost property, his promise becomes binding when B performs the act of returning A's property to him. A is not bound to pay anything to anyone until the prescribed act is done.

Executory consideration is a promise given for a promise. The consideration in support of each promise is the other promise, not a performed act. If, for example, a customer orders goods which a shopkeeper undertakes to obtain from the manufacturer, the shopkeeper promises to supply the goods and the customer promises to accept and pay for them. Neither has yet done anything, but each has given a promise to obtain the promise of the other. It would be breach of contract if either withdrew without the consent of the other.

Anything which has already been done *before* a promise is given in return is *past* consideration which as a general rule is not sufficient to make the promise binding. In such a case the promisor may by his promise recognise a moral obligation, but he is not obtaining anything in exchange for his promise (as he already has it before the promise is made).

Re McArdle 1951

Under a will the testator's children were entitled to a house at their mother's death. In the mother's lifetime one of the children and his wife lived in the house with the mother. The wife made improvements to the house. The children later agreed in writing to repay to the wife the sum of £488 which she had spent on the improvements, but at the mother's death they refused to do so.

Held: at the time of the promise the improvements were past consideration and so the promise was not binding.

In three cases past consideration for a promise does suffice to make the promise binding.

(a) Past consideration is sufficient to create liability on a bill of exchange (such as a cheque) under s 27 Bills of Exchange Act 1882. Most cheques are issued to pay existing debts.

(b) After six (or in some cases 12) years the right to sue for recovery of a debt becomes statute-barred by the Limitation Act 1980. If, after that period, the debtor makes written acknowledgement of the creditor's claim, it again becomes enforceable at law. The debt, although past consideration, suffices.

(c) When a request is made for a service this request may imply a promise to pay for it. If, after the service has been rendered, the person who made the request promises a specific reward, this is treated as fixing the amount to be paid under the previous implied promise rather than as a new promise.

Activity 9

In *Roscorla v Thomas 1842*, the plaintiff contracted to buy a horse from the defendant. After the contract was made, the defendant told the plaintiff that the horse was 'sound and free from vice'. It later turned out to be vicious, so the plaintiff sued on the warranty. What was the nature of the consideration for the promise that the horse was sound, and why did the plaintiff fail?

4.2 Adequacy and sufficiency of consideration

There are two overlapping rules. Consideration need not be *adequate*, that is equal in value to the consideration received in return (there is no remedy in law for someone who simply makes a bad bargain), but consideration must be *sufficient*, that is capable in law of being regarded as consideration.

The courts will not enquire into the adequacy of consideration. It is presumed that each party is capable of serving his own interests, and the courts will not seek to weigh up the comparative value of the promises or acts exchanged.

Thomas v Thomas 1842

By his will the plaintiff's husband expressed the wish that his widow should have the use of his house during her life. The defendants, his executors, allowed the widow to occupy the house (a) in accordance with her husband's wishes and (b) in return for her undertaking to pay a rent of £1 per annum. They later said that their promise to let her occupy the house was not supported by consideration.

Held: compliance with the husband's wishes was not valuable consideration (no economic value attached to it), but the nominal rent was sufficient consideration, even though inadequate as a rent.

Consideration is sufficient if it has some identifiable value. The value may however be nominal, such as 50p in consideration of a promise worth £1 million, or it may be very subjective. The law only requires an element of bargain, not that it shall be a good bargain.

Chappell & Co v Nestlé Co 1960
As a sales promotion scheme, the defendant offered to supply a record of the dance tune *Rockin' Shoes* to anyone who sent in a postal order for 1s.6d [7½p] and three wrappers from 6d [2½p] bars of chocolate made by them. The plaintiffs owned the copyright of the popular tune to the record. They sued for infringement of copyright. In the ensuing dispute over royalties the issue was whether the wrappers, which were thrown away when received, were part of the consideration for the promise to supply the record (which the defendants obtained in bulk for 4d each from the recording company). The defendants offered to pay a royalty based on the price of 1s.6d per record, but the plaintiffs rejected this, claiming that the wrappers also represented part of the consideration.

Held: the defendants had required that wrappers be sent (for obvious commercial reasons). It was immaterial that the wrappers when received were of no economic value to them. The wrappers were part of the consideration as they had commercial value.

As stated earlier, forbearance or the promise of it may be sufficient consideration if it has some value or amounts to giving up something of value. A promise not to pursue a genuine but disputed claim may be consideration. Even forbearance without any promise may suffice: *Alliance Bank v Broom 1864*. But a promise not to perform an act which the promisor had no intention of performing anyway does not suffice as consideration: *Arrale v Costain Engineering 1976*; nor does waiver of a claim known to be hopeless, or abstention from pressing a purely moral claim: *White v Bluett 1853*.

4.3 Performance of existing contractual duties

Performance of an existing obligation imposed by statute, such as to appear as a witness when called upon in a lawsuit, is no consideration for a promise of reward: *Collins v Godfrey 1836*. But if some extra service is given that is sufficient consideration.

Glasbrook Bros v Glamorgan CC 1925
At a time of industrial unrest, colliery owners, rejecting the view of the police that a mobile force was enough, asked for and agreed to pay for a special stationary police guard on the mine. Later they repudiated liability saying that the police had done no more than perform their public duty of maintaining order.

Held: the police had done more than perform their general duties. The *extra* services given, beyond what the police in their discretion considered necessary, were consideration for the promise to pay.

If there is already a contract between A and B, and B promises additional reward to A if he (A) will perform the contract, there is no consideration to make that promise binding; A assumes no extra obligation and B obtains no extra rights or benefits.

Stilk v Myrick 1809
Two members of the crew of a ship deserted in a foreign port. The master was unable to recruit substitutes and promised the rest of the crew that they should

share the wages of the deserters if they would complete the voyage home. The shipowners however repudiated the promise.

Held: in performing their existing contractual duties the crew gave no consideration for the promise of extra pay and the promise was not binding.

However, if a plaintiff does more than perform an existing contractual duty, this may amount to consideration.

Hartley v Ponsonby 1857
17 men out of a crew of 36 deserted. The remainder were promised an extra £40 each to work the ship to Bombay. The plaintiff, one of the remaining crew-members, sued to recover this amount.

Held: the large number of desertions made the voyage exceptionally hazardous, and this had the effect of discharging the original contract. The plaintiff had therefore been left free to enter into a new contract, under which his promise to complete the voyage formed consideration for the promise to pay an additional £40.

The courts appear to be taking a slightly different line recently on the payment of additional consideration. The line seems to be that the principles of consideration will not be applied if the dispute before the court can be dealt with on an alternative basis.

Williams v Roffey Bros & Nicholls (Contractors) Ltd 1990
W agreed to refurbish a block of flats for R at a fixed price of £20,000. The work ran late and so R, concerned that the job might not be finished on time and that they would in that event have to pay money under a penalty clause in another contract, agreed to pay W an extra £10,300 to ensure the work was completed on time. R later refused to pay the extra amount.

Held: the fact that there was no apparent consideration for R's promise was not held to be important, and in the court's view both R and W derived benefit from the promise. The telling point was that R's promise had not been extracted by duress or fraud: it was therefore binding.

Re Selectmove 1994
A company which was the subject of a winding-up order offered to settle its outstanding debts by instalment. An Inland Revenue inspector agreed to this proposal. The company tried to enforce it.

Held: despite the verdict in *Williams v Roffey Bros & Nicholls*, the court followed *Foakes v Beer* (discussed next) in holding that an agreement to pay in instalments is unenforceable. Even though the creditor might obtain some practical benefit, this is not adequate consideration to render the agreement legally binding.

Activity 10

A contracted with B to repair B's roof for £500. B then said that he would pay A an extra £200 to do the work which he was already obliged to do, even though there was no risk that A would otherwise do the work late or to an unsatisfactory standard.
Could this promise of extra money be made legally binding without any other change in the terms agreed between A and B, and, if so, how?

4.4 Waiver of existing rights

Definition

> *Waiver:* a promise to give up a claim or right, such as a landlord's right to receive notice.

If X owes £100 to Y but Y agrees to accept a lesser sum, say £80, in full settlement of Y's claim, that is a promise by Y to waive his entitlement to the balance of £20. The promise, like any other, should be supported by consideration. In other words, payment on the day that a debt is due of less than the full amount of the debt is not adequate consideration for a promise to release the balance.

> *Foakes v Beer 1884*
> B obtained judgment against F for the sum of £2,091 with interest. By a written agreement B agreed to accept payment by instalments of the sum of £2,091, no mention being made of the interest. Later B claimed the interest, claiming that the agreement was not supported by consideration.
>
> *Held:* B was entitled to the debt with interest. No consideration had been given by F for waiver of any part of B's rights against him.

There are, however, exceptions to the rule that the debtor (X) must give consideration if the waiver is to be binding.

(a) If X arranges with a number of creditors that they will each accept part payment in full settlement, that is a bargain between the creditors. X has given no consideration but he can hold the creditors individually to the agreed terms: *Wood v Robarts 1818*

(b) If a third party (Z) offers part payment and Y agrees to release X from Y's claim to the balance, Y has received consideration from Z against whom he had no previous claim: *Welby v Drake 1825*.

(c) If X offers and Y accepts anything to which Y is not already entitled (for example goods instead of cash, or payment before the due date) the extra thing will be sufficient consideration for the waiver: *Pinnel's case 1602*.

(d) The principle of *promissory estoppel* may prevent Y from retracting his promise with retrospective effect.

Promissory estoppel

If a creditor (Y) makes a promise (unsupported by consideration) to the debtor (X) that Y will not insist on the full discharge of the debt (or other obligation), and *the promise is made with the intention that X should act on it and he does so* (by more than just making part payment), Y is estopped (prohibited) from retracting his promise, unless X can be restored to his original position. This last point will prevent Y from retracting his waiver with retrospective effect, though it may allow him to insist on his full rights in the future.

> *Central London Property Trust v High Trees House 1947*
> In 1939, Y let a block of flats to X at an annual rent of £2,500. It was difficult to let the individual flats in wartime. Y agreed in writing to accept a reduced annual rent of £1,250. No time limit was set on the arrangement but it was clearly related to wartime conditions. The reduced rent was paid from 1940 to 1945 and X sublet flats during the period on the basis of its expected liability to pay rent under the head lease at £1,250 only. In 1945 the flats were fully let. Y made a test claim for rent at the full annual rate of £2,500 for the final two quarters of 1945.
>
> *Held:* Y was entitled to the full annual rent of £2,500 for the period for which this was claimed; the agreement to reduce the rent was a temporary expedient

only. Denning J was of the opinion that had Y sought arrears for the earlier period (1940-45), he would have failed because the 1940 agreement would have served to defeat the claim.

The precise scope of promissory estoppel is still uncertain (though the principle is now well established) but two limitations are clear.

(a) *It only applies to a promise of waiver which is entirely voluntary.*

> *D and C Builders v Rees 1966*
> X owed £482 to Y (a small firm of builders). Y, which was in acute financial difficulties, reluctantly agreed to accept £300 in full settlement (in order to obtain the money quickly). X had been aware of and had exploited Y's difficulties ('he was held to ransom' said Lord Denning). The builder later claimed the balance.
>
> *Held:* the debt must be paid in full. Promissory estoppel only applies to a promise voluntarily given. In this important case it was also held that payment by cheque (instead of in cash) is normal and gives no extra advantage which could be treated as consideration for the waiver under the rule in *Pinnel's* case.

(b) *It applies only to a waiver of existing rights.* A promise which creates new obligations is not binding unless supported by consideration in the usual way. The principle is 'a shield not a sword'.

> *Combe v Combe 1951*
> A wife obtained a divorce decree nisi against her husband. He then promised her that he would make maintenance payments. The wife did not apply to the court for an order for maintenance but this forbearance was not at the husband's request. The decree was made absolute; the husband paid no maintenance; the wife sued him on his promise. In the High Court the wife obtained judgment on the basis of promissory estoppel.
>
> *Held:* (in the Court of Appeal) promissory estoppel 'does not create new causes of action where none existed before. It only prevents a party from insisting on his strict legal rights when it would be unjust to allow him to enforce them'. The wife's claim failed.

Activity 11

C pays her daughter D a monthly allowance of £200. In January, C promises to increase this to £400 a month from April. On the strength of this promise, D incurs various financial obligations in March. C then changes her mind, and does not increase the allowance. Why would D be unable to rely on the doctrine of promissory estoppel to enforce the promised increase?

---

5   PRIVITY OF CONTRACT

Definition

Privity of contract: the relation between two contracting parties which allows either to sue the other for breach of contract.

The principle of *privity of contract* has two overlapping aspects: consideration must move from the promisee, and only the parties to a contract can enforce it.

5.1 Consideration must move from the promisee

As consideration is the price of a promise, the price must be paid by the person who seeks to enforce the promise (the promisee). If for example, A promises B that (for a consideration provided by B) A will confer a benefit on C, then C cannot as a general rule enforce A's promise since C has given no consideration for it.

Tweddle v Atkinson 1861
T married the daughter of G. On the occasion of the marriage T's father and G exchanged promises that they would each pay a sum of money to T. The agreement between the two fathers expressly provided that T should have enforceable rights against them. G died without making the promised payment and T sued G's executor (A) for the specified amount.

Held: T had provided no consideration for G's promise. In spite of the express terms of the agreement, T had no enforceable rights under it.

It is not essential that the promisor should receive any benefit from the promisee. In *Tweddle's* case each father as promisee gave consideration by his promise to the other but T was to be the beneficiary of each promise. Each father could have sued the other on his promise but his claim would have been for damages and he would have recovered nothing since he himself suffered no loss.

5.2 Only the parties to a contract may enforce it

As a general rule, only a person who is a party to a contract has enforceable rights or obligations under it.

Dunlop v Selfridge 1915
D, a tyre manufacturer, supplied tyres to X, a distributor, on terms that X would not re-sell the tyres at less than the prescribed retail price. If X sold the tyres wholesale to trade customers, X must impose a similar condition on those buyers to observe minimum retail prices (such clauses were legal at the time though prohibited since 1964 by the Resale Prices Act). X resold tyres on these conditions to S, the Oxford Street store. Under the terms of the contract between X and S, S was to pay to D a sum of £5 per tyre if it sold tyres to customers below the minimum retail price. S sold tyres to two customers at less than the minimum price. D sued to recover £5 per tyre.

Held: D could not recover damages under a contract (between X and S) to which D was not a party. This is the leading case (decided in the House of Lords) on privity of contract.

A party to a contract who imposes a condition or obtains a promise of a benefit for a third party can usually enforce it. Damages cannot be recovered on the third party's behalf unless the contracting party is suing as agent or trustee, since a plaintiff can only recover damages for a loss he has suffered. Thus only nominal damages can be given if the contract was only for a third party's benefit. Other remedies may be sought however.

Beswick v Beswick 1968
P transferred his business to the defendant, his nephew, in consideration for a pension and, after his death, a weekly annuity to P's widow. Only one annuity payment was made. The widow, as her husband's administratrix, sued for an order of specific performance.

Held: as her husband's representative, the widow was successful in enforcing the contract for a third party's (her) benefit. The House of Lords held that she would not have succeeded if she had only been the intended recipient.

There is some inconsistency in the case law, but the general tenor is that a seller of goods cannot impose conditions which pass with the goods to a third party even if the latter buys with knowledge of the conditions. There are, however, special rules of the law of property which enable a person to impose restrictions on land to pass with the land from one owner to the next.

There are a number of real or apparent exceptions to the general rule of privity of contract.

(a) In a contract between A and B by which B is to confer a benefit on C, A may constitute himself a trustee for C. C as beneficiary may then enforce the contract against B.

(b) The benefit of a contract may be transferred by assignment, or by negotiation of a bill of exchange.

(c) There are statutory exceptions which permit a person injured in a road accident to claim against the motorist's insurers, and which permit husband and wife to insure his or her own life for the benefit of the other under a trust which the beneficiary can enforce: Road Traffic Act 1972; Married Women's Property Act 1882.

(d) An undisclosed principal may adopt a contract made for him by an agent.

Activity 12

Civil law, unlike criminal law, mainly deals with matters which are of no general interest to the community. How is this fact related to the doctrine of privity of contract?

Chapter roundup

- A contract is a legally binding agreement between the parties. A contract only arises if there is an intention to create legal relations. Such an intention is assumed to be present in business agreements and absent in domestic arrangements, but either presumption may be rebutted.

- Not every suggestion that a transaction be entered into is an offer. The display of goods in a shop, for example, is an invitation to treat.

- Acceptance may be by express words or action, or it may be implied by conduct. Mere inaction is not sufficient for acceptance. Where there is a standing offer, each acceptance creates a separate contract.

- Acceptance needs to be communicated to the offeror. Acceptance by post generally takes effect when the letter of acceptance is posted, but in some cases only when the letter is received by the offeror.

- An offer may lapse or be revoked, or it may be rejected by the offeree. A counter-offer amounts to a rejection.

- There are special rules for reward cases (the claimant must have been aware of the offer of a reward), for cross-offers (there is no contract) and for collateral contracts.

- Consideration, which may be either executory or executed but not past, is required when a contract is not made by deed.

- Consideration must be sufficient (have some value), but it need not be adequate (have a value similar to the value of what is given in return). A promise to perform existing obligations is not in general sufficient consideration.

> ## Chapter roundup *continued*
>
> - Waivers of existing rights mostly need to be supported by consideration, but there are some exceptions involving third parties, and promissory estoppel may apply.
> - Consideration must move from the promisee, and in general only a party to a contract may enforce it. These rules make up the doctrine of privity of contract.

Quick quiz

1 When may it be misleading to presume that a contract is the outcome of consenting minds?

2 Give three essential elements of a binding agreement.

3 How do the courts deduce the intention of the parties (to create legal relations or not to do so) from the terms of a domestic or family agreement?

4 What sorts of domestic agreement are the courts willing to interpret as legally binding?

5 What is the effect of a statement in a business agreement that it is not intended to create legal relations?

6 When is a commercial agreement never intended to create legal relations?

7 Do any of the following constitute an offer which becomes a contract if accepted?

(a) A statement of the price of goods

(b) An advertisement

(c) A display of goods

8 Can an offer be accepted by doing nothing if the offer so provides?

9 What is the effect of acceptance 'subject to contract'?

10 What is the effect of accepting a tender?

11 What is the effect of posting a letter accepting an offer made by letter to the offeree?

12 How is an offer terminated?

13 When is revocation of an offer effective?

14 May a contract be formed without offer and acceptance?

15 What is a collateral contract?

16 In what circumstances is something which is done before a promise is made sufficient consideration to make the promise binding?

17 If, in return for a promise, the promisee hands over something which no longer has any value, has he given sufficient consideration to make the promise binding?

18 Is acceptance of part payment of an existing debt binding on the person who accepts it or may he still claim the unpaid balance?

19 Explain the doctrine of promissory estoppel and indicate the limitations placed upon it.

20 Is it possible for a person to enforce a contract if he is not a party to it?

Solutions to activities

1 No: legal relations are unlikely to be assumed because it is a family arrangement.

2 The claim is vague and there is no offer of any particular reward or compensation.

3 No: 'I would want £850 at least' is an invitation to continue to treat. It is not a definite offer to contract at that price.

4 Delivery arrangements, responsibility for damage in transit, time for payment and the right to reject the goods. You may well have thought of other examples.

5 With the alternative suggested, the acceptor would not know for a day or two whether or not he had succeeded in accepting the offer.

6 No: X's revocation of his offer has been effectively communicated as X's solicitor is a reliable third party.

7 Mary may sue Jane for straightforward breach of contract. Peter may sue Jane on the contract under which she assured him of her skills, his contract with Mary being consideration. The latter being a collateral contract.

8 No: forbearance (as by P) can be consideration.

9 The plaintiff failed because the consideration for the promise (the plaintiff's purchase of the horse) was past consideration.

10 Yes: the promise would have to be by deed.

11 Promissory estoppel does not create new causes of action where none existed before. D never had any right to the increased allowance.

12 In general, only the parties to a contract are affected by it, so only they may sue on it.

Further question practice

Now try the following practice questions at the end of this text

Multiple choice questions: **16 to 20**

Exam style question: **5**

Chapter 6

TERMS OF CONTRACT

Introduction

As a general principle the parties may by their offer and acceptance include in their contract whatever terms they like, but certain legal rules apply and the law may modify these express terms in various ways.

(a) The terms must be sufficiently complete and precise to produce an agreement which can be binding. If they are vague there may be no contract.

(b) Statements made in the pre-contract negotiations may become *terms* of the contract or remain as *representations* to which different rules attach.

(c) The terms of the contract are usually classified as *conditions* or as *warranties* according to their importance.

(d) In addition to the express terms of the agreement, additional terms may be implied by law.

(e) Terms which exclude or restrict liability for breach of contract (*exemption or exclusion clauses*) are restricted in their effect or overridden by common law and statutory rules.

Your objectives

After completing this chapter you should:

(a) understand the effects of incompleteness in the terms of a contract;

(b) know the limitations on the use of oral evidence for contract terms;

(c) understand the distinction between representations and contract terms;

(d) understand the concepts of condition, warranty and innominate term;

(e) know how terms may be implied into a contract;

(f) know which contracts must be in specified forms;

(g) know the limitations on the effectiveness of exclusion clauses;

(h) appreciate how exclusion clauses may fail to be effectively incorporated into a contract;

(i) know how exclusion clauses are interpreted;

(j) know the main provisions of the Unfair Contract Terms Act 1977.

1 INCOMPLETE CONTRACTS

A legally binding agreement must be complete in its term otherwise there is no contract since the parties are still at the stage of negotiating the necessary terms.

> *Scammell v Ouston 1941*
> An agreement for the purchase of a van provided that the unpaid balance of the price should be paid over two years 'on hire purchase terms'.
>
> *Held:* there was no agreement since it was uncertain what terms of payment were intended. Hire purchase terms vary as to intervals between payments, interest charges to be added, and so on.

It is always possible for the parties to leave an essential term to be settled by specified means outside the contract. For example, it may be agreed to sell at the ruling open market price (if there is a market) on the day of delivery, or to invite an arbitrator to determine a fair price. The price may even be determined by the course of dealing between the parties: *Hillas & Co Ltd v Arcos Ltd 1932*.

If the parties use meaningless but non-essential words, for example by use of standard printed conditions some of which are inappropriate, such phrases may be disregarded: *Nicolene v Simmonds 1953*.

If however the parties expressly agree to defer some essential term for later negotiation there is no binding agreement. This is described as 'an agreement to agree' which is void, as the parties may subsequently fail to agree.

Activity 1

A contract contains a term which states that the price shall be £50,000 unless the parties agree otherwise within seven days of the contract's being signed.
Does this invalidate the contract? Give reasons for your answer.

1.1 Oral evidence relating to contracts in writing

The general rule is that if a contract is or includes a written document, oral evidence may not be given to 'add to, vary or contradict' the document. There are the following exceptions to the rule.

(a) Oral evidence may be given of trade practice or custom.

(b) Evidence may be given to show that the parties agreed orally that their written consent should not take effect until a *condition precedent* had been satisfied.

(c) Oral evidence may be given as an addition to a written contract if it can be shown that the document, such as printed conditions of sale, was not intended to comprise all the agreed terms. But the presumption is that a contract document is the entire contract until the contrary is proved.

> *SS Ardennes 1951*
> A printed bill of lading (for shipment of a cargo of oranges) provided that the ship might go 'by any route ... directly or indirectly' to London. The shipowners' agent had given an oral undertaking that the vessel would sail directly from Spain to London.
>
> *Held:* evidence might be given of the oral undertaking as a term overriding the bill of lading.

(d) Oral evidence may be adduced to correct a written agreement which contains a mistake.

2 REPRESENTATIONS AND CONTRACT TERMS

If something said in pre-contract negotiations proves to be untrue, the party misled can only claim for breach of contract if the statement became a term of the contract. Otherwise his remedy is for misrepresentation only (explained in the next chapter). Even if the statement is not repeated or referred to in making the contract it may be treated as a contract term. But such factors as a significant interval of time between statement and contract or the use of a written contract making no reference to the statement suggest that it is not a term of the contract. If, however, the party who makes the statement speaks with special knowledge of the subject it is more likely to be treated as a contract term.

Bannerman v White 1861

In negotiations for the sale of hops the buyer emphasised that it was essential to him that the hops should not have been treated with sulphur. The seller replied explicitly that no sulphur had been used. It was later discovered that a small proportion of the hops (bought in by the seller from another grower) had been treated with sulphur. The buyer refused to pay the price.

Held: the representation as to the absence of sulphur was intended to be a term of the contract.

Oscar Chess v Williams 1959

A private motorist negotiated the sale of an old car to motor dealers in part exchange for a new car. The seller stated (as the registration book showed) that his car was a 1948 model and the dealer valued it at £280. In fact it was a 1939 model worth only £175 (the registration book had been altered by a previous owner).

Held: the statement was a mere representation. The seller was not an expert and the buyer had better means of discovering the truth.

3 CONDITIONS AND WARRANTIES

The terms of the contract are usually classified by their relative importance as *conditions* or *warranties*.

Definition

Condition: a term which is vital to the contract, going to the root of the contract.

Warranty: a less important term. It does not go to the root of the contract, but is subsidiary to the main purpose of the agreement.

Non-observance of a condition will affect the main purpose of the agreement. Breach of a condition entitles the party not in breach to treat the contract as discharged. Breach of a warranty only entitles the injured party to claim damages.

Poussard v Spiers 1876

Madame Poussard agreed to sing in an opera throughout a series of performances. Owing to illness she was unable to appear on the opening night or on the next few days. The producer engaged a substitute who insisted that she should be engaged for the whole run. When Mme Poussard had recovered the producer declined to accept her services for the remaining performances.

Held: failure to sing on the opening night was a breach of condition which entitled the producer to treat the contract for the remaining performances as discharged.

Bettini v Gye 1876

An opera singer was engaged for a series of performances under a contract by which he had to be in London for rehearsals six days before the opening performance. Owing to illness he did not arrive until the third day before the opening. The defendant refused to accept his services, treating the contract as discharged.

Held: the rehearsal clause was subsidiary to the main purpose of the contract. Breach of the clause must be treated as breach of warranty, so the producer was bound to accept the singer's services. He had no right to treat the contract as discharged and must compensate the plaintiff, though he could claim damages (if he could prove any loss) for failure to arrive in time for six days' rehearsals.

Schuler v Wickham Machine Tool Sales 1973

The plaintiffs entered into a four-year contract with the defendants giving them the sole right to sell panel presses in England. A clause of the contract provided that it should be a condition of the agreement that the defendants' representative should visit six named firms each week to solicit orders. The defendants' representative failed on a few occasions to do so and the plaintiffs claimed to be entitled to repudiate the agreement on the basis that a single failure was a breach of condition giving them an absolute right to treat the contract as at an end.

Held: such minor breaches by the defendants did not entitle the plaintiffs to repudiate. The House of Lords construed the clause on the basis that it was so unreasonable that the parties could not have intended it as a condition (giving the plaintiffs a right of repudiation) but rather as a warranty. Thus the plaintiffs were themselves in breach of contract leaving the defendants with a claim for damages against them.

Determining whether a contractual term is a condition or a warranty is clearly very important. Classification depends on the following issues.

(a) Statute often identifies implied terms specifically as conditions or warranties. Such identification must be followed by the courts. An example is the Sale of Goods Act 1979.

(b) Case law may also define particular clauses as conditions, for example a clause as to the date of 'expected readiness' of a ship let to a charterer: *The Mihalis Angelos 1971*

(c) Where statute or case law does not shed any light, the court will consider the intention of the parties *at the time the contract was made* as to whether a broken term was to be a condition or a warranty: *Bunge Corporation v Tradax SA 1981*.

3.1 Innominate terms

Where the term broken was not clearly intended to be a condition, and neither statute nor case law define it as such, it cannot necessarily be assumed that the term is a warranty. Instead, the contract must be interpreted; only if it is clear that in no circumstances did the parties intend the contract to be terminated by breach of that particular term can it be classed as a warranty. Such intention may be express or be implied from surrounding circumstances. Where it is not clear what the effect of breach of the term was intended to be, it will be classified by the court as innominate, intermediate or indeterminate (the three are synonymous).

The consequence of a term being classified as innominate is that the court must decide what is the actual effect of its breach. If the nature and effect of the breach is such as to deprive the injured party of substantially the whole benefit which it was intended he should obtain under the contract then it will be treated as a breached condition, so that the injured party may terminate the contract and claim damages.

Hong Kong Fir Shipping Co Ltd v Kawasaki Kisa Kaisha Ltd 1962
The defendants chartered a ship from the plaintiffs for a period of 24 months. A term in the contract stated that the plaintiffs would provide a ship which was 'in every way fitted for ordinary cargo service'. They were in breach of this term since the ship required a competent engine room crew which they did not provide. Because of the engine's age and the crew's lack of competence the ship's first voyage was delayed for five weeks and further repairs were required at the end of it, resulting in the loss of a further 15 weeks. The defendants purported to terminate the contract so the plaintiffs sued for beach of contract on the grounds that the defendant had no right to terminate; the defendants claimed that the plaintiffs were in breach of a contractual condition.

Held: the term was innominate and could not automatically be construed as either a condition or a warranty. The obligation of 'seaworthiness' embodied in many charter party agreements was too complex to be fitted into one of the two categories. The term would be construed in the light of the actual consequences of the actual breach. The ship was still available for 17 out of 24 months. The consequences of the breach were not so serious that the defendants could be justified in terminating the contract as a result. The defendants were in breach of contract for terminating it when they did.

Activity 2

A company contracts for the purchase of 200 mobile telephones 'immediately suitable for use in the UK'. Assume that this term is innominate. How would the court classify it if:

(a) the telephones supplied required tuning to particular frequencies, a task taking two minutes for each one?

(b) use of the telephones supplied was illegal in the UK, and they could not be modified to make their use legal?

How did you arrive at that conclusion?

---

4 IMPLIED TERMS

Additional terms of a contract may be implied by law.

4.1 Contractual terms implied by custom

The parties may be considered to enter into a contract subject to a custom or practice of their trade. For example, when a farm is let to a tenant it may be an implied term that local farming custom on husbandry and tenant rights shall apply: *Hutton v Warren 1836*. But any express term overrides a term which might be implied by custom.

Les Affreteurs v Walford 1919
A charter of a ship provided expressly for a 3% commission payment to be made on signing the charter. There was a trade custom that it should only be paid at a later stage. The ship was requisitioned by the French government before the charterparty began, and so no hire was earned.

Held: an express term prevails over a term otherwise implied by custom. The commission was payable on hire.

4.2 Contractual terms implied by statute

Terms may be implied by statute. In some cases the statute permits the parties to contract out of the statutory terms (thus the terms of partnership implied by the Partnership Act 1890 may be excluded). In other cases the statutory terms are obligatory. The protection given by the Sale of Goods Act 1979 to a consumer who buys goods from a trader cannot be taken away from him.

4.3 Contractual terms implied by the courts

Terms may be implied if the court concludes that the parties intended these terms to apply and did not mention them because they were taken for granted or because they were inadvertently omitted. The court may then supply a further term to prevent the failure of the agreement and to implement the manifest intention of the parties. The contract is given 'business efficacy'. In such cases the 'officious bystander' test is applied; if an officious bystander had intervened to remind the parties that in formulating their contract they had failed to mention a particular point they would have replied 'of course ... we did not trouble to say that; it is too clear'.

The Moorcock 1889
The owners of a wharf agreed that a ship should be moored alongside to unload its cargo. It was well known to both wharfingers and shipowners that at low tide the ship would ground on the mud at the bottom. At low tide the ship rested on a ridge concealed beneath the mud and suffered damage.

Held: it was an implied term, though not expressed, that the ground alongside the wharf (which did not belong to the wharfingers) was safe at low tide since both parties knew that the ship must rest on it.

Terms will not be implied to contradict the express terms of the contract (see *Les Affreteurs* case above) nor to provide for events which the parties did not contemplate in their negotiations.

Activity 3

A qualified accountant undertakes to prepare a client's tax return. The accountant then finds that the tax return form has been redesigned, and that his computer system cannot cope with the new design. Consider whether he could claim that there was no term in the contract stating that he should be able to prepare a return in the new form, and that he is therefore not obliged to do so.

---

5 THE REQUIRED FORM OF A CONTRACT

As a general rule a contract may be made in any form-in writing, by word of mouth or even by implication from conduct.

To the general rule there are some exceptions.

(a) *Contracts by deed.* Some rights and obligations, such as a *transfer of title to land*, or a lease of land for a period of three years or more, or a promise not supported by consideration (such as a covenant to make annual payments to a charity) must be in the form of a deed. A deed used to be referred to as a contract under seal, but under s 1 Law of Property (Miscellaneous Provisions) Act 1989 an individual need not seal a deed. It is a written document (on paper, parchment or other substance) which has been signed by the person executing it (and sealed if created by a corporate body with a common seal) and is expressed on its face to be a deed. Signature must be witnessed. To be validly executed by an individual, the document must be delivered to the other party by the individual or his agent. A contract by deed is binding even though no consideration is given or received.

(b) *Contracts in writing*. Some types of contract (mainly commercial) are required to be in the form of a written document, usually signed by at least one of the parties. This category includes *bills of exchange, hire purchase agreements* and *agreements relating to land*. A contract for the sale of land must be distinguished from the actual document which transfers the title to that land, that is the conveyance (*unregistered land*) or transfer (*registered land*). The contract promises to transfer title at a future date (usually four weeks hence) and must be in writing. The conveyance or transfer must be by deed and will therefore also be in writing. A contract promising to grant a lease must be in writing but the lease itself, if it is for three years or more, must be by deed.

(c) *Contracts which must be evidenced in writing*. Certain types of contract may be made orally but are not enforceable in a court of law unless there is written evidence of their terms. The important contract falling under this head is that of *guarantee*.

Activity 4

A agrees to transfer his house to B in 28 days time at a price of £100,000. Both parties sign the contract, but neither signature is witnessed. Is the contract binding? Why?

---

6   EXCLUSION CLAUSES

If the parties negotiate their contract from positions of more or less equal bargaining strength and expertise, neither the courts nor Parliament have usually interfered. But there has been strong criticism of the use of exclusion (or exemption) clauses in contracts made between manufacturers or sellers of goods or services and private citizens as consumers. In such cases there may be great inequality. The seller puts forward standard conditions of sale which the buyer may not understand and must accept if he wishes to buy. In those conditions the seller may try to exclude or limit his liability for failure to perform as promised for breach of contract or negligence, or he may try to offer a 'guarantee' which in fact reduces the buyer's rights.

Definition

Exclusion clause: a clause in a contract by which one of the parties purports to exclude or restrict liability.

The main limitations on exclusion clauses are now contained in the Unfair Contract Terms Act 1977 which applies to clauses excluding or restricting liability in contract or tort.

An exclusion clause which is not void by statute may still be ineffectual. The courts have generally sought to protect the consumer from the harsher effects of exclusion clauses in two ways.

(a) An exclusion clause must be properly *incorporated* into a contract before it has any legal effect.

(b) Exclusion clauses are *interpreted* strictly; this may prevent the application of the clause.

7 THE INCORPORATION OF EXCLUSION CLAUSES

Uncertainty often arises over which terms have actually been incorporated into a contract. It is not enough for one party to claim that he possesses a set of draft terms; it must be shown that any such terms were incorporated into the agreement between the parties when the agreement was formed. These rules apply to any contract and not just to exclusion clauses, although it is convenient to discuss them here, as many do concern exclusion clauses.

(a) The document containing notice of the exclusion clause must be an integral part of the contract.

(b) If the document is an integral part of the contract, a term may not usually be disputed if it is included in a document which a party has signed.

(c) The term cannot be part of the contract unless put forward *before* the contract is made.

(d) It is not a binding term unless the person whose rights it restricts was made sufficiently aware of it at the time of agreeing to it.

(e) Onerous terms must be sufficiently highlighted.

7.1 Contractual documents

The courts will not treat an exclusion clause as a term of the contract unless the party affected by it was sufficiently informed of it when he accepted it. It must be shown that this document is an integral part of the contract and is one which could be expected to contain terms.

Chapelton v Barry UDC 1940
There was a pile of deck chairs and a notice stating 'Hire of chairs 2d (1p) per session of 3 hours'. The plaintiff took two chairs, paid for them and received two tickets which he put in his pocket. One of the chairs collapsed and he was injured. The defendant council relied on a notice on the back of the tickets by which it disclaimed liability for injury.

Held: the notice advertising chairs for hire gave no warning of limiting conditions and it was not reasonable to communicate them on a receipt. The disclaimer of liability was not binding on the plaintiff.

Thompson v LMS Railway 1930
An elderly lady who could not read asked her niece to buy her a railway excursion ticket on which was printed 'Excursion: for conditions see back'. On the back it was stated that the ticket was issued subject to conditions contained in the company's timetables. These conditions excluded liability for injury.

Held: the conditions had been adequately communicated and therefore had been accepted.

In the *Chapelton* case, the ticket was a mere receipt; in the *Thompson* case, it should have been obvious to a reasonable person that the ticket had contractual effect, as tickets of that kind generally contain contract terms.

7.2 Signed contracts

If a person signs a document containing a clause restricting his rights he is held to have agreed to the restriction even if he had not read the document. But this is not so if the party who puts forward the document for signature gives a misleading explanation of its legal effect.

L'Estrange v Graucob 1934

A sold to B, a shopkeeper, a slot machine under conditions which excluded B's normal rights under the Sale of Goods Act 1893. B signed the document without reading the relevant condition.

Held: the conditions were binding on B since she had signed them. It was not material that A had given her no information of their terms nor called her attention to them. (Under the law as it now stands, some rights under the Sale of Goods Act 1979, which replaced the 1893 Act, may not be excluded.)

Curtis v Chemical Cleaning Co 1951

X took her wedding dress to be cleaned. She was asked to sign a receipt on which there were conditions by which the cleaners disclaimed liability for damage however it might arise. Before signing X enquired what was the effect of the document and was told that it restricted the cleaner's liability in certain ways and in particular placed on X the risk of damage to beads and sequins on the dress. The dress was badly stained in the course of cleaning.

Held: the cleaners could not rely on their disclaimer since they had misled X as to the effect of the document which she signed. She was entitled to assume that she was running the risk of damage to beads and sequins only.

Activity 5

A contract between P and Q includes a clause excluding P's liability in certain circumstances. When Q enquires as to the meaning of this clause, P replies that he does not wish to provide an oral interpretation, but that Q must read the clause for herself. Q reads the clause and signs the contract. P later seeks to rely on the exclusion clause, and Q claims that P should have interpreted the clause for her. The clause itself is not misleadingly phrased. Consider whether Q is likely to be able to prevent P from relying on the clause.

7.3   Prior information on terms

Many contracts are entered into without the parties signing a document. In such cases, exclusion clauses may be stated on notices or tickets. However, since the terms of the contract are fixed at the moment of acceptance of the offer, an exclusion clause cannot be introduced thereafter (except by mutual consent). Each party must be aware of an exclusion clause *at the time of entering into the agreement* if it is to be binding.

Olley v Marlborough Court 1949

A husband and wife arrived at a hotel and paid for a room in advance. On reaching their bedroom they saw a notice on the wall by which the hotel disclaimed liability for loss of valuables unless handed to the management for safe-keeping. The wife locked the room and handed the key in at the reception desk. A thief obtained the key and stole the wife's furs from the bedroom.

Held: the hotel could not rely on the notice disclaiming liability since the contract had been made previously (when the room was booked and paid for) and the disclaimer was too late.

Complications can arise when it is difficult to determine at exactly what point in time the contract is formed so as to determine whether or not a term is validly included.

Thornton v Shoe Lane Parking Ltd 1971

X saw a sign saying 'Parking' outside the defendant's car park. He drove up to the unattended machine and was automatically given a ticket. He had seen a sign disclaiming liability for damage to cars before obtaining the ticket and when he received the ticket he saw that it contained words which he did not read. In fact these made the contract subject to conditions which, if he had looked hard enough in the car park, also excluded liability for injury. When he returned to collect his car (which had been stacked in a special machine) there was an accident in which he was badly injured.

Held: the contract was formed before he got the ticket (the offer was the 'Parking' sign; acceptance was parking his car so as to receive a ticket) so reference on the ticket to conditions was too late for the conditions to be included as contractual terms. (Note that since UCTA 1977 the personal injury clause would be void anyway.)

7.4   Previous dealings

An exception to the rule that there must be prior notice of the clause is where the parties have had consistent dealings with each other in the past, and the documents used then contained similar clauses: *J Spurling Ltd v Bradshaw 1956.*

If the parties have had previous dealings (not on a consistent basis) then the person to be bound by the exclusion clause may be sufficiently aware of it (as a proposed condition) at the time of making the latest contract. For this purpose it is necessary to show in a consumer contract that he actually knew of the condition; it is not sufficient that he might have become aware of it.

Hollier v Rambler Motors 1972
On three or four occasions over a period of five years H had had repairs done at a garage. On each occasion he had signed a form by which the garage disclaimed liability for damage caused by fire to customers' cars. On the latest occasion, however, he did not sign the form. The car was damaged by fire caused by negligence of garage employees. The garage contended that the disclaimer had by course of dealing become an established term of any contract made between them and H.

Held: the garage was liable. There was no evidence to show that H knew of and agreed to the condition as a continuing term of his contracts with the garage.

But in a commercial contract it is sufficient to show that, by a previous course of dealings, the other party has constructive if not actual notice of the term: *British Crane Hire Corporation Ltd v Ipswich Plant Hire 1974.*

Activity 6

Customers of a self service shop take goods from the shelves and then walk down a corridor to a till. A conspicuous notice is hung across this corridor incorporating an exclusion clause into contracts for the purchase of goods from the shop. Could a customer claim that the exclusion clause was invalid because he had selected goods before seeing the notice?
Why is this so?

7.5   Onerous terms

Where a term is particularly unusual and onerous it should be highlighted so that the attention of the other party is drawn to it when the contract is being formed. Failure to do so may mean that it does not become incorporated into the contract.

Interfoto Picture Library Ltd v Stiletto Visual Programmes Ltd 1988
Forty-seven photographic transparencies were delivered to the defendant

together with a delivery note with conditions on the back. Included in small type was a clause stating that for every day late each transparency was held a 'holding fee' of £5 plus VAT would be charged. They were returned 14 days late. The plaintiffs sued for the full amount of £3,782.50.

Held: the term was onerous and had not been sufficiently brought to the attention of the defendant. The court reduced the fee to 50p per transparency per day (one tenth of the contractual figure) to reflect more fairly the loss caused to the plaintiffs by the delay.

8   THE INTERPRETATION OF EXCLUSION CLAUSES

In deciding what an exclusion clause means, the courts interpret any ambiguity against the person at fault who relies on the exclusion. This is known as the *contra proferentem* rule (against the person relying on it). Liability can only be excluded or restricted by clear words. In particular, if the clause gives exclusion in unspecific terms it is unlikely to be interpreted as covering negligence on the part of the person relying on it unless that is the only reasonable interpretation.

Hollier v Rambler Motors 1972
The facts are as given above. The garage disputed liability for fire damage to the plaintiff's car on the basis of a contractual term which stated that the company was not liable for damage caused by fire to customers' cars on the premises.

Held: as shown above, the term was not *incorporated* into the contract; as a matter of *interpretation* the disclaimer of liability could be interpreted to apply (a) only to accidental fire damage or (b) to fire damage caused in any way including negligence. It should therefore be interpreted against the garage in the narrower sense of (a) so that it did not give exemption from fire damage due to negligence.

Alderslade v Hendon Laundry 1945
The conditions of contracts made by a laundry with its customers excluded liability for loss of or damage to customers' clothing in the possession of the laundry. By its negligence the laundry lost A's handkerchief.

Held: the exclusion clause would have no meaning unless it covered loss due to negligence. It did therefore cover loss by negligence.

When construing an exclusion clause the court will also consider the *main purpose rule*. By this, the court presumes that the clause was not intended to defeat the main purpose of the contract, although of course the presumption may be rebutted. In order to rebut the presumption the party relying on the clause must show that its wording is sufficiently precise and relevant. In the context of a clause in a supplier's standard term contract which allows the supplier to render performance in a substantially different manner, the main purpose rule is supplemented by s 3 UCTA 1977 which provides that such a term must be reasonable.

Fundamental breach

There used to be some doubt on how far an exclusion clause could exclude liability in a case where the breach of contract was a failure to perform the contract altogether (a fundamental breach). In the case given below the House of Lords overruled some earlier decisions of the Court of Appeal and so the legal position is now reasonably clear.

Photo Productions v Securicor Transport 1980

Securicor agreed to guard the plaintiffs' factory under a contract by which Securicor were excluded from liability for damage caused by any of their employees. One of the Securicor guards deliberately started a small fire which got out of hand and destroyed the factory and contents, worth about £615,000. It was contended (on the authority of earlier decisions of the Court of Appeal) that Securicor had entirely failed to perform their contract since they had not guarded the factory and so they could not rely on any exclusion clause in the contract.

Held: there is no principle that total failure to perform a contract deprives the party at fault of any exclusion from liability provided by the contract. It is a question of interpretation of the exclusion clause whether it is widely enough expressed to cover total failure to perform. In this case the exclusion clause was wide enough to cover the damage which had happened. (As the fire occurred before the UCTA came into force in 1977 the Act could not apply here. But if it had done it would have been necessary to consider whether the exclusion clause was reasonable.)

Activity 7

A road haulage company's standard conditions exclude liability for delays caused by factors beyond the company's control. Would this exclusion be interpreted to cover a delay due to a driver choosing to use minor roads because he found motorway driving boring, given that it is the company's policy never to interfere with drivers' choices of routes? Why?

9   THE UNFAIR CONTRACT TERMS ACT 1977 (UCTA)

Before we consider the specific term of UCTA, it is necessary to describe how its scope is restricted.

(a) In general the Act only applies to clauses inserted into agreements by *commercial concerns or businesses*. In principle private persons may restrict liability as much as they wish.

(b) The Act does not apply to certain contracts, for example contracts relating to the creation or transfer of patents, contracts of insurance, contracts relating to the creation or transfer of interests in land and contracts relating to company formation or securities transactions.

The Act uses two techniques for controlling exclusion clauses: some types of clauses are void, whereas others are subject to a *test of reasonableness*. The main provisions of the Act are as follows.

Avoidance of liability for negligence (s 2)

A person acting in the course of a business cannot, by reference to any contract term, restrict his liability for death or personal injury resulting from negligence. In the case of other loss or damage, a person cannot restrict his liability for negligence unless the term is reasonable. 'Negligence' covers breach of contractual obligations of skill and care, the common law duty of skill and care and the common duty of occupiers of premises under the Occupiers' Liability Acts 1957 and 1984.

Avoidance of liability for breach of contract (s 3)

The person who imposes the standard term, or who deals with the consumer, cannot *unless the term is reasonable*:

(a) restrict liability for his own breach or fundamental breach; or

(b) claim to be entitled to render substantially different performance or no performance at all.

Unreasonable indemnity clauses (s 4)

A clause whereby one party undertakes to indemnify the other for liability incurred in the other's performance of the contract is void if the party giving the indemnity is a consumer, unless it is reasonable.

Sale and supply of goods (ss 6-7)

A consumer contract for the sale of goods, hire purchase, supply of work or materials or exchange of goods cannot exclude or restrict liability for breach of the conditions relating to description, quality, fitness for the purpose for which sold and sample implied by the Sale of Goods Act 1979 and the Supply of Goods and Services Act 1982. In a non-consumer contract these implied conditions may be excluded if the exclusion clause is *reasonable*. The implied condition as to title cannot be excluded in any contract.

Activity 8

A contract for the sale of a washing machine to a consumer contains the following clause: 'The seller undertakes to repair any defects arising within the first 12 months free of charge, and the buyer shall accordingly not be permitted to return the machine if it does not work at the time of sale'. A consumer would normally have a statutory right to return the machine if it did not work at the time of sale. Consider whether this right has effectively been excluded by the clause.

The statutory definition of consumer (s 12)

A person deals as a consumer if:

(a) he neither makes the contract in the course of a business, nor holds himself out as doing so; and

(b) the other party does make the contract in the course of a business; and

(c) the goods are of a type ordinarily supplied for private use or consumption.

Where a business engages in an activity which is merely incidental to the business, the activity will not be in the course of the business unless it is an integral part of it and it will not be an integral part of it unless it is carried on with a degree of regularity.

> *R & B Customs Brokers Ltd v United Dominions Trust Ltd 1988*
> The plaintiffs, a company owned by Mr and Mrs Bell and operating as a shipping broker, bought a second-hand Colt Shogun. The car was to be used partly for business and partly for private use.
>
> *Held:* this was a consumer sale, since the company was not in the business of buying cars.

9.1 The statutory test of reasonableness (s 11)

The term must be fair and reasonable having regard to all the circumstances which were, or which ought to have been, known to the parties when the contract was made. The burden of proving reasonableness lies on the person seeking to rely on the clause. Statutory guidelines have been included in the Act to assist in the determination of reasonableness although the court has discretion to take account of all factors. For example, for the purposes of ss 6 and 7, the court will consider the following.

(a) The relative strength of the parties' bargaining positions and in particular whether the customer could have satisfied his requirements from another source.

(b) Whether any inducement (such as a reduced price) was offered to the customer to persuade him to accept a limitation of his rights and whether any other person would have made a similar contract with him without that limitation.

(c) Whether the customer knew or ought to have known of the existence and extent of the exclusion clause (having regard, where appropriate, to trade custom or previous dealings between the parties).

(d) If failure to comply with a condition (for example, failure to give notice of a defect within a short period) excludes or restricts the customer's rights, whether it was reasonable to expect when the contract was made that compliance with the condition would be practicable.

(e) Whether the goods were made, processed or adapted to the special order of the customer.

Activity 9

A contract under which a consumer buys a 20 volume encyclopaedia contains a clause excluding liability for defects not notified within a week of delivery. Two weeks after delivery, the buyer finds that several pages which should have been printed are blank. Will the seller be able to rely on the exclusion clause?
What is the reason for your answer?

9.2 The Unfair Terms in Consumer Contracts Regulations 1994 (UTCCR)

These regulations, which came into effect on 1 July 1995, implement an EC directive on unfair contract terms. UCTA 1977 continues to apply. Companies supplying goods and services to consumers and non-consumers will have to have regard to both laws, as no consolidation has yet taken place. There are now three layers of relevant legislation.

(a) The common law, which applies to all contracts, regardless of whether or not one party is a consumer;

(b) UCTA 1977, which applies to all contracts and which has specific provisions for consumer contracts;

(c) The Regulations, which only apply to consumer contracts and to terms which have not been individually negotiated.

The new regulations apply to contracts for the supply of goods or services.

(a) They apply to terms in consumer contracts. A consumer is defined as 'a natural person who, in making a contract to which these regulations apply, is acting for purposes which are outside his business'.

(b) They apply to contractual terms which have not been individually negotiated, that is they have been drafted in advance and the consumer has not been able to influence their substance.

(c) There are a number of exceptions, including contracts relating to family law or to the incorporation or organisation of companies and partnerships and employment contracts.

A key aspect of the regulations is the definition of an unfair term. This is:

'any term which contrary to the requirement of good faith causes a significant imbalance in the parties' rights and obligations under the contract to the detriment of the consumer.'

In making an assessment of good faith, the courts will have regard to the following. (The first three of these are very similar to UCTA terms on reasonableness.)

(a) The strength of the bargaining positions of the parties;

(b) Whether the consumer had an inducement to agree to the term;

(c) Whether the goods or services were sold or supplied to the special order of the consumer;

(d) The extent to which the seller or supplier has dealt fairly and equitably with the consumer.

The effect of the regulations is to render certain terms in consumer contracts unfair, for example:

(a) excluding or limiting liability of the seller when the consumer dies or is injured, where this results from an act or omission of the seller (UCTA 1977 covers only *negligent* acts or omissions);

(b) excluding or limiting liability where there is partial or incomplete performance of a contract by the seller (as in UCTA 1977); and

(c) making a contract binding on the consumer where the seller can still avoid performing the contract.

Terms should be written in plain, intelligible language; where they are unclear, they will be construed against the seller.

Two forms of redress are available. The second is an interesting one.

(a) A consumer who has concluded a contract containing an unfair term can ask the court to find that the unfair term should not be binding. The remainder of the contract will remain valid if it can continue in existence without the unfair term.

(b) A complaint, for example by an individual, a consumer group or a trading standards department can be made to the Director General of Fair Trading who is empowered to seek injunctions against unfair terms. He can bring an action against sellers and suppliers, manufacturers, franchisors and trade associations.

Chapter roundup

- If a purported contract omits an essential term, and gives no means for settling that term, there is no contract.
- Oral evidence may only be adduced to assist in the interpretation of a written contract in certain limited circumstances.
- Statements made in the course of negotiations may not become terms of a contract at all. They may only amount to representations.
- A condition is a term which is vital to a contract, and its breach allows the party not in breach to treat the contract as discharged. Breach of a warranty, on the other hand, only entitles the injured party to damages.
- Innominate terms can only be classified as conditions or warranties once the effects of their breach can be assessed.
- Some terms may be implied by law whereas others are so obvious that they are implied under the officious bystander test.
- Transfers of land and gratuitous promises must be by deed. Bills of exchange, hire purchase agreements and contracts for the sale of land must be in writing. Contracts of guarantee must be evidenced in writing.
- Exclusion clauses are not automatically illegal, but some such clauses are ruled out to prevent abuses of economic power by one party.
- Exclusion clauses must be properly incorporated into a contract at or before the time of acceptance, and must not be presented in a misleading manner.
- Exclusion clauses are interpreted strictly, against the person seeking to rely on them.
- The Unfair Contract Terms Act 1977 makes certain exclusion clauses void, and others void unless they are reasonable.
- The UTCCR 1994 defines what is meant by an unfair term.

Quick quiz

1   When may oral evidence add to a written contract?
2   What is the difference between a representation and a contract term?
3   What is the difference between a condition and a warranty?
4   Explain the significance of an innominate term.
5   In what circumstances may additional terms, not expressed in the contract, nonetheless be implied as part of it?
6   What contracts relating to an interest in land may still be enforceable even if they are only evidenced in writing?
7   When will a court treat an exclusion clause as void because the affected party was not properly informed?
8   What effect does the fact that parties have had previous dealings have on an exclusion clause?
9   If there is ambiguity in an exclusion clause, how does the court interpret the clause?
10 What is the main purpose rule?
11 When may liability for negligence never be excluded?
12 What tests are applied to determine the reasonableness of an exclusion clause?
13 How does UCTA 1977 define a consumer?

Solutions to activities

1   No: if there is no agreement, a definite price (£50,000) is automatically fixed.

2   (a) A warranty

(b) A condition

In the latter situation the buyer is being deprived of the whole benefit of the contract.

3   No: it is an implied term that a qualified accountant can prepare a tax return in any form required by the Inland Revenue.

4   Yes: the contract (as opposed to the transfer) need not be in the form of a deed, so a witness is not required.

5   No: Q has not been misled.

6   No: the exclusion clause was notified before the contract was made at the till.

7   No: the company could choose to control its drivers' choices of routes.

8   No: a consumer contract cannot exclude the term that goods are fit for their purpose.

9   No: it is not reasonable to expect a consumer to find all printing defects in a 20 volume work within the first two weeks of use.

Further question practice

Now try the following practice questions at the end of this text

Multiple choice questions: **21 to 25**

Exam style question: **6**

Chapter 7

VITIATING FACTORS

Introduction

Even if the essential elements can be shown, a contract may not necessarily be valid. The validity of a contract may also be affected by any of the following factors.

(a) As we saw in the last chapter, the parties may in general enter into a contract on whatever *terms* they choose. But a contract can only be enforced if it is sufficiently complete in its terms. Some terms which the parties do not express may be implied and some terms which the parties do express are overridden.

(b) We also saw how some contracts must be made in a particular *form*.

(c) Some persons have only restricted *capacity* to enter into contracts and are not bound by agreements made outside those limits.

(d) A *misrepresentation* or *mistake* made by one party to the contract may affect the validity of the contract.

(e) A person induced to enter into a contract by *duress* or *undue influence* is entitled to avoid the contract at common law.

(f) The courts will not enforce a contract which is deemed to be *illegal* or contrary to public policy.

Your objectives

After completing this chapter you should:

(a) know how contractual capacity may be limited;

(b) know the types of operative mistake and their effect on a purported contract;

(c) be aware of the remedies in cases of mistake;

(d) understand the nature of a representation, and what may constitute a misrepresentation;

(e) know the types of misrepresentation, and the available remedies;

(f) appreciate the nature and effect of duress;

(g) understand how undue influence may arise, and the remedies available;

(h) know the main types of void and illegal contracts, and the consequences for the parties.

1 VITIATED CONTRACTS

A contract which does not satisfy the relevant tests may be either void, voidable or unenforceable.

Definitions

Void contract: a contract which has no legal effect.

Voidable contract: a contract which is capable of being rendered void at the option of one of the parties, but is valid until the option is exercised.

Unenforceable contract: a contract which is not actionable in a court.

A *void* contract is not a contract at all. The parties are not bound by it and if they transfer property under it they can sometimes (unless it is also an illegal contract) recover their goods even from a third party. A *voidable* contract is a contract which one party may avoid, that is terminate at his option. Property transferred before avoidance is usually irrecoverable from a third party.

An *unenforceable* contract is a valid contract and property transferred under it cannot be recovered even from the other party to the contract. But if either party refuses to perform or to complete his part of the performance of the contract, the other party cannot compel him to do so. A contract is usually unenforceable when the required evidence of its terms, for example, written evidence of a contract relating to land, is not available.

2 CONTRACTUAL CAPACITY

Definition

Capacity: the ability or power of a person to enter into legal relationships or carry out legal acts.

It is a prerequisite for forming a binding agreement that both parties should have the capacity to enter into it. In certain circumstances certain types of person do not have that capacity, namely minors, persons suffering from mental incapacity and companies.

2.1 Minors

The legal capacity of minors (persons under the age of 18) is determined by the Minors' Contracts Act 1987. A contract between a minor and another party may be of one of three types.

(a) A *valid* contract is binding in the usual way.

(b) A *voidable* contract is binding unless and until the minor rescinds the contract.

(c) An *unenforceable* contract is unenforceable against the minor unless he ratifies (adopts) it; but the other party is bound.

Valid contracts of a minor

Two sorts of contract are valid and binding on a minor.

(a) Contracts for the supply of goods or services which are *necessaries*.

(b) A *service contract* for the minor's benefit.

If goods or services which are necessaries are delivered to a minor under a contract made by him, he is bound to pay a reasonable price (not the contract price if that is excessive) for them: s 3 Sale of Goods Act 1979. Necessaries are goods suitable to the condition in life of the minor and to his actual requirements at the time of sale and delivery. Services may also be necessaries.

Suitability is measured by the living standards of the minor. Things which are in ordinary use may be necessaries even though they are luxurious in quality, if that is what the minor ordinarily uses. Food, clothing, professional advice and even a gold watch have been held to be necessaries. However, in some cases it is clear that a broad definition of necessaries has been adopted, not for the benefit of the minor, but to protect traders who gave credit to young people from wealthy families. It has been said that an item of 'mere luxury' cannot be a necessary, for example a racehorse, but that a luxurious item of utility such as an expensive car may be a necessary. Expensive items bought as gifts are not usually necessaries, but an engagement ring to a fiancée can be.

The second test is whether the minor requires the goods for the personal *needs* of himself (or his wife or child if any). Goods required for use in a trade are not necessaries, nor are goods of any kind if the minor is already well supplied with them and so does not need any more.

Nash v Inman 1908

N was a Savile Row tailor who had solicited orders from I, a Cambridge undergraduate of extravagant tastes. N sued I on bills totalling £145 for clothes, including eleven fancy waistcoats, supplied over a period of nine months. It was conceded that the clothes were suitable for I but it was shown that he was already amply supplied with such clothing.

Held: the clothes were not necessaries since, although quite suitable for his use, the minor had no need of them. It was immaterial that N was unaware that I was already well supplied.

Mercantile Union Guarantee Corporation v Ball 1937

A minor obtained a lorry on hire purchase terms for use in his road haulage business.

Held: this was not a contract for necessaries since the lorry was required for business, not personal use. Under the hire purchase contract the owner could recover the lorry as still his property, but could not enforce payment of the hire purchase instalments.

If a minor uses borrowed money to pay for necessaries the lender can stand in the shoes of the supplier who has been paid with the lender's money, and the lender may recover so much of his loan as corresponds to a reasonable price for the necessaries.

A *service contract* for the minor's benefit is the other type of contract binding on a minor.

Doyle v White City Stadium 1935

D, who was a minor, obtained a licence to compete as a professional boxer. Under his licence (which was treated as a contract of apprenticeship or vocation) he agreed to be bound by rules under which the British Boxing Board of Control could withhold his prize money if he was disqualified for a foul blow (as in fact happened). He asserted that the licence was a void contract since it was not for his benefit.

Held: the licence enabled him to pursue a lucrative occupation. Despite the penal clause, it was beneficial as a whole.

Apart from the test of benefit, the contract must relate to education or training, or to some occupation or vocation.

Chaplin v Leslie Frewin (Publishers) Ltd 1966

The plaintiff, a son of Charlie Chaplin, was a minor. He contracted with the defendants to give them, for an advance of £600, exclusive rights to his autobiography *I couldn't smoke the grass on my father's lawn.* He later claimed that the completed work, written by two journalists based on information furnished by him, contained libellous matter and attributed to him views which he did not hold. He sought to repudiate the contract.

Held: the contract was binding; it was on the whole, beneficial to him as it would enable him to make a start as an author.

Voidable contracts of a minor

A minor may enter into a contract by which he acquires an interest of a continuing nature. Such contracts are voidable by the minor during his minority and within a reasonable time after attaining his majority. Until he rescinds (avoids) the contract it is binding. If he rescinds it before his majority, he may withdraw his rescission within a reasonable time afterwards. If he rescinds it, he is relieved of any future obligations. There are four categories of these voidable contracts.

(a) Contracts concerning land, for example leases;

(b) Purchases of shares in a company;

(c) Partnership agreements;

(d) Marriage settlements.

A contract of this type does not require any kind of ratification by the minor on his majority. It remains binding unless he repudiates it within a *reasonable time.*

> *Edwards v Carter 1893*
> A marriage settlement was made under which the father of the husband-to-be agreed to pay £1,500 per annum to the trustees. The husband-to-be, who was a minor at the time of the settlement, executed a deed under which all property which he might receive under his father's will would also be vested in the trustees. He attained his majority one month later; three and a half years later his father died. A year after this, he repudiated the agreement, arguing that when he signed the agreement he did not realise the extent of his obligations and that he could only reach a decision once he knew the details of the will.
>
> *Held:* the repudiation was too late and was ineffective.

The effect of repudiation is to relieve the minor (or former minor) of any contractual obligations arising after the repudiation. There are conflicting decisions as to whether repudiation relieves the minor of obligations which arose *before* the repudiation. (For example, if a minor repudiates a lease of land, is he liable for rent which has already fallen due?)

Unenforceable contracts of a minor

All other contracts entered into by a minor are described as unenforceable: the minor is not bound (though he may ratify the contract after his majority) but the other party is bound. If he is to be bound the minor must ratify the contract within a reasonable time after his majority. Once ratified the contract is valid and is enforceable both by and against the ex-minor.

Activity 1

A minor makes a contract for the purchase of food for his own consumption. He eats all the food without over-eating. The food includes luxurious items such as quails' eggs. The actual price for the items supplied is £130, but a reasonable price would be £90 and the minor could have obtained a comparable amount of nutrition by spending £50 on more ordinary types of food. The minor borrows £130 to pay for the goods, but then refuses to repay the lender. Consider how much the lender may recover.

2.2 Mental incapacity

If a person who is temporarily insane, under the influence of drugs or drunk enters into a contract, it is binding on him unless he is at the time incapable of understanding the nature of the contract and the other party knows or ought to know of his disability.

When necessaries are supplied (not as a gift but with the intention of obtaining payment) to a person under such disability, he must pay a reasonable price for them in any event (s 3 Sale of Goods Act 1979). The rules are similar to those applicable to minors.

2.3 Companies

Companies and other artificial legal persons such as local authorities do not have unlimited contractual capacity. Often they are limited in what they can do by their constitutions, which only give them certain powers. Actions done outside those powers are said to be *ultra vires*. *Ultra vires* contracts are void, so neither party can enforce their terms.

The *ultra vires* rule as it applies to companies is now of very limited effect following the Companies Act 1989.

3 MISTAKE

The general rule is that a party to a contract is not discharged from his obligations because he is mistaken as to the terms of the contract or the relevant circumstances. The terms of the contract are established by offer and acceptance; what the parties may think or intend should not override those terms or render the contract void. There are, however, limited categories of *operative mistake* which render the contract void. Only a mistake of fact can render a contract void: a mistake of law cannot have this effect.

Definitions

Operative mistake may be classified as follows.

- *Common mistake:* there is complete agreement between the parties but both are equally mistaken as to some fundamental point.
- *Mutual mistake:* the parties are at cross-purposes but each believes that the other agrees with him and does not realise that there is a misunderstanding.
- *Unilateral mistake:* one party is mistaken and the other is aware of this fact.

3.1 Common mistake

If the parties make a contract relating to subject matter which unknown to both of them does not exist (*res extincta*), there is no contract between them.

> *Couturier v Hastie 1852*
> A contract was made in London for the sale of a cargo of corn thought to have been shipped from Salonika. Unknown to the parties the cargo had meanwhile been sold by the master of the ship at Tunis since it had begun to rot. The London purchaser repudiated the contract and the agent who had sold the corn to him was sued (as a *del credere* agent he had indemnified his principal against any losses arising from such a repudiation).
>
> Held: the claim against the agent failed. The corn was not really in existence when the contract was made; the contract pre-supposed that it existed but, as it

related to non-existent subject matter the contract was void.

Galloway v Galloway 1914
A man and a woman entered into a separation agreement relating to their apparent status as husband and wife. Neither then knew that their marriage was null and void.

Held: the contract related to non-existent subject matter (the marriage) and was void.

The rule on non-existent subject matter *res extincta* has been extended to the infrequent cases where a person buys what already belongs to him (*res sua*). In such cases the contract cannot be performed because there is nothing to buy.

Cochrane v Willis 1865
Under a family settlement A would inherit property on the death of his brother B. B had become bankrupt in Calcutta and, to save the property from sale to a third party, A agreed with B's trustee in bankruptcy in England to purchase the property from B's bankrupt estate. Unknown to A and B's trustee, B had already died in Calcutta and so the property had passed to A by inheritance before he bought it.

Held: the contract was void and A was not liable to pay the agreed contract price.

Activity 2

A rogue claims that a new island has just been formed in the Atlantic Ocean by a volcanic eruption, and that he owns the sea bed and therefore the island. He sells the alleged island to a dupe, although no such island exists. Consider whether this is a case of common mistake. Give reasons for your answer.

The leading case on both parties being equally mistaken on some fundamental point (a decision of the House of Lords) left open the question as to whether common mistake could be extended any further.

Bell v Lever Bros 1932
L, the controlling shareholder of a Nigerian Company appointed B to be its managing director for five years. Before five years had elapsed, B became redundant owing to a merger and L negotiated with B for the cancellation of his service agreement on payment to B of £30,000. Later L discovered that, while serving as managing director, B had used inside information to trade in cocoa on his own account. This was serious misconduct for which B might have been summarily dismissed. B was said to have forgotten the significance of his past conduct in negotiating the cancellation of his service agreement and it was treated as a case of common mistake, not unilateral mistake. L's claim to recover £30,000 from B was that there had been a common mistake as to an essential quality of the subject matter, since the service agreement for which L had paid £30,000 was in fact valueless to B since he could have been dismissed without compensation.

Held: L's claim must fail. It was not a case of non-existent subject matter. If L's claim was correct in its theoretical basis there was not here a sufficiently fundamental mistake as to the 'quality' of the subject matter. Modern opinion is inclined to interpret the decision to mean that no mistake as to mere 'quality' of the subject matter can ever make the contract void for mistake (but equitable relief is sometimes given).

But common mistake resulting in a contract being void *ab initio* was upheld in the following case (decided in the High Court), in which the principles were clearly analysed.

Associated Japanese Bank (International) v Credit du Nord SA 1988

A rogue, B, entered into a sale and leaseback agreement with the plaintiff to fund the purchase of four machines, identified by serial numbers. The defendant guaranteed the transaction as a leasing agreement. The plaintiff advanced £1m to B, who made one quarterly repayment before being arrested for fraud, and adjudged bankrupt. The machines did not exist, and so the plaintiff sued to enforce the guarantee. The defendant claimed the contract was void for common or mutual mistake since the non-existence of the machines made the subject of the contract essentially different.

Held:

(a)   the law exists to uphold rather than destroy agreements;

(b)   the law on mistake as to quality exists to cope with unexpected and exceptional circumstances;

(c)   in order to be 'operative' a mistake must be shared by the parties and relate to facts as they existed at the time of the agreement;

(d)   the subject-matter of the contract must be rendered essentially and radically different to that which the parties believed to exist; and

(e)   a party must have reasonable grounds for believing a common mistake for it to be operative.

The non-existence of the machines in the principal contract (the lease) on which the secondary contract (the guarantee) relied was so fundamental as to render the subject matter 'essentially different'. Hence there was common mistake: the guarantee was void and could not be enforced.

3.2   Mutual mistake

If the parties are at cross purposes without either realising it, the terms of the contract usually resolve the misunderstanding in favour of one or the other.

Tamplin v James 1880

J went to an auction to bid for a public house. J believed that the property for sale included a field which had been occupied by the publican. But the sale particulars, which J did not inspect, made it clear that the field was not included. J was the successful bidder but when he realised his mistake refused to proceed with the purchase. The auctioneer had been unaware of J's mistake.

Held: J was bound to pay the price which he had bid for the property described in the particulars of sale. The contract was quite clear and his mistake did not invalidate it.

The parties may, however, have failed to reach any agreement at all if the terms of the contract fail to identify the subject matter. Such a mistake renders the contract void.

Raffles v Wichelhaus 1864

A and B agreed in London on the sale from A to B of a cargo of cotton to arrive 'Ex Peerless from Bombay'. There were in fact two ships named *Peerless* with a cargo of cotton from Bombay; one sailed in October and the other in December. B intended the contract to refer to the October sailing and A to the December one.

Held: as a preliminary point B could show that there was an ambiguity and that he intended to refer to the October shipment. If the case had gone further (there is no record that it did) the contract would have been void.

If the subject matter is adequately identified, a misunderstanding concerning its *qualities* does not make the contract void. If each party is unaware that the other intends subject matter of a different quality (and has not contributed to the misunderstanding by lack of precision on his side), he may perform his side of the contract according to his intention although the other party was expecting something different.

Smith v Hughes 1871
Oats were bought by sample. The buyer believed that they were old oats. The seller (who was unaware of the buyer's impression) was selling new oats which are less valuable. On discovering that they were new oats the buyer refused to complete the sale.

Held: the contract was for the sale of 'oats' and the buyer's mistake as to a quality (old or new oats) did not render the contract void. The seller was entitled to deliver and to receive payment for his oats.

Activity 3

X owned two racehorses, Mercury and Hermes. Y offered to buy one of the horses, but after a contract was made it transpired that Y thought he was to buy Mercury, and X thought he was to sell Hermes. Would this be a case of mutual mistake if the contract referred to:
(a) Hermes, but Y had not read the contract carefully?
(b) X's racehorse, with no name being given?

3.3   Unilateral mistake

A unilateral mistake is usually (but not invariably) the result of misrepresentation by one party. The party misled is entitled to rescind the contract for misrepresentation but it may then be too late to recover the goods. Title to the goods passes to the dishonest party under a contract which is voidable and he may re-sell them to an innocent third party who is entitled to retain them (since the rogue still had title at the time of the re-sale to him). If, on the other hand, the contract is void for mistake at the outset, no title passes to the dishonest party and it may be possible for the party misled to recover his goods. The difference between a voidable and a void contract determines which of two innocent persons is to bear the loss caused by fraud.

Most of the case law on this type of mistake is concerned with mistake of identity. A contract is only void for mistake by the seller about the buyer's identity if the seller intended to sell to someone different from the actual buyer. If that is the position the seller never intends to sell to the actual buyer and the contract with him is void. In any other case the contract is valid when made, though it may later be rescinded since it may be voidable for misrepresentation.

The parties may negotiate the contract by correspondence without meeting face to face. If the buyer fraudulently adopts the identity of another person known to the seller with whom the seller intends to make the contract, the sale to the actual buyer is void.

Cundy v Lindsay 1878
Blenkarn, a dishonest person, wrote to C from '37 Wood St, Cheapside' to order goods and signed the letter so that his name appeared to be 'Blenkiron & Co', a respectable firm known to C, with their offices at 123 Wood St. The goods were consigned to Blenkiron & Co at 37 Wood St and Blenkarn re-sold the goods to L. C sued L for conversion to recover the value of the goods (for which L had already paid Blenkarn in good faith).

Held: C intended to sell only to B & Co and no title passed to Blenkarn. The mistake over the Wood St address was reasonable. L was liable to C for the value of the goods.

But if the buyer fraudulently adopts the alias of a non-existent person who could not have been known to the seller, the contract is only voidable for misrepresentation.

King's Norton Metal Co v Edridge Merrett & Co 1897

K received an order for goods from 'Hallam & Co', an alias assumed by a rogue called Wallis. The letterhead indicated that H & Co had substantial premises and overseas branches. K had not previously dealt with or heard of H & Co. On receiving the goods (consigned to H & Co) W re-sold them to EM and K sued EM for the value of the goods.

Held: K intended to sell to the writer of the letter, who was W trading as H & Co. The misdescription of H & Co as a substantial firm induced a mistake as to the quality of creditworthiness, not as to identity. W acquired title to the goods and EM in turn acquired title before the contract between K and W was rescinded by K. EM was not accountable for the value of the goods.

Face to face transactions

When the parties meet face to face it is generally inferred that the seller intends to sell to the person whom he meets. The latter may mislead the seller as to the buyer's creditworthiness by assuming a false identity. But even if he takes the identity of a real person about whom the seller makes enquiries, there is no mistake of identity which renders the contract void. It is merely voidable for misrepresentation and the loss falls on the seller. (The decision in *Ingram v Little 1961* described below has been criticised and would appear to be an exceptional one.)

Phillips v Brooks 1919

A rogue entered a jeweller's shop, selected various items which he wished to buy and proposed to pay by cheque. The jeweller replied that delivery must be delayed until the cheque had been cleared. The rogue then said that he was Sir George Bullough, a well known person, and the jeweller checked that the real Sir George Bullough lived at the address given by the rogue. The rogue then asked to take a ring away with him and the jeweller accepted his cheque and allowed him to have it. The rogue pledged the ring to the defendant, a pawnbroker, who was sued by the jeweller to recover the ring.

Held: the action must fail. The jeweller had intended to contract with the person in the shop. There was no mistake of identity which made the contract void but only a mistake as to the creditworthiness of the buyer. Good title had passed to the rogue until the contract was avoided.

Ingram v Little 1961

A rogue calling himself Hutchinson offered £717 to buy a car advertised for sale by the plaintiffs. They accepted, but called the deal off when he proposed payment by cheque. He then told them that he was P G M Hutchinson and that he lived at Stanstead House, Caterham. One of the plaintiffs checked this in a telephone directory and, reassured, accepted the cheque and let him take the car. The cheque bounced and the rogue sold the car to the defendants.

Held: the plaintiffs intended to sell only to PGMH; the rogue was incapable of entering into a contract with them and the contract was void for mistake.

Lewis v Averay 1971

Lewis agreed to sell his car to a rogue who gave the impression that he was the actor Richard Greene. The rogue paid with a dud cheque signed in the name R A Green and was allowed to take the car and documents when he produced a pass for Pinewood Studios with an official stamp.

Held: Lewis had contracted to sell the car to the rogue. The contract might be voidable for fraud but it was not void for mistake. Perusal of a pass was insufficient to demonstrate that he only wished to contract with RG, the actor.

Activity 4

A rogue telephones a supplier to place an order for goods. He claims to represent a respectable firm with which the supplier has had previous dealings, and he arranges to collect the goods in person later the same day. The cost is to be charged to the firm's account with the supplier. The rogue meets the supplier when he comes to collect the goods. Consider whether the contract would be void due to a unilateral mistake. Give reasons for your answer.

3.4   Mistakes over documents – *non est factum*

The law recognises the problems of a blind or illiterate person who signs a document which he cannot read. If it is not what he supposes he may be able to repudiate it as not his deed (*non est factum*). The relief is not now restricted to the blind or illiterate, but will not ordinarily be given to a person who merely failed to read what it was within his capacity to read and understand.

In the *Saunders* case described below the House of Lords reviewed earlier case law and laid down conditions which must be satisfied in repudiating a signed document as *non est factum*: there must be a fundamental difference between the legal effect of the document signed and that which the person who signed it believed it to have, and the mistake must have been made without carelessness on the part of the person who signs.

Saunders v Anglia Building Society 1971 (also known as Gallie v Lee 1971)
Mrs Gallie, a widow of 78, agreed to help her nephew, Parkin, to raise money on the security of her house provided that she might continue to live in it until her death. Parkin did not wish to appear in the transaction himself since he feared that his wife, from whom he was separated, would then enforce against him her claim for maintenance. Parkin therefore arranged that Lee, a solicitor's clerk, should prepare the mortgage. As a first step Lee produced a document which was in fact a transfer of the house on sale to Lee. However, Lee told Mrs Gallie that the document was a deed of gift to Parkin and she signed it at a time when her spectacles were broken and she could not read. Lee then mortgaged the house as his property to a building society. Lee paid nothing to Mrs Gallie or to Parkin. Mrs Gallie sought to repudiate the document as *non est factum*.

Held: Mrs Gallie knew that she was transferring her house and her act in signing the document during a temporary inability to read amounted to carelessness. The claim to repudiate the transfer failed.

Lloyds Bank plc v Waterhouse 1990
The bank obtained a guarantee from a father as security for a loan to his son to buy a farm. It also took a charge over the farm. The father did not read the guarantee because he was illiterate (which he did not tell the bank) but he did enquire of the bank about the guarantee's terms. As a result he believed that he was guaranteeing only the loan for the farm. In fact he signed a guarantee securing all the son's indebtedness to the bank. The son defaulted and the bank called on the father's guarantee for that amount of the son's debts which was not repaid following the farm's sale.

Held: the father had made adequate attempts to discover his liability by questioning the bank's employees (he was not careless). They had caused him to believe he was signing something other than he believed. This was a case of both *non est factum* and negligent misrepresentation.

In a case where the signature to a document is obtained by fraud the person who signs can rescind the contract between himself and the fraudster (as in the

Waterhouse case above). The defence of *non est factum* need only be raised when an honest third party has acquired rights on the document and therefore rescission is not available.

3.5 Equitable reliefs for mistake

Rescission, explained in the next section, is an equitable remedy which is available when the contract is voidable. A different type of relief, *rectification,* may be claimed when the document does not correctly express the common intention of the parties. A party who applies for rectification must show that:

(a) the parties had a 'common intention', though it need not have become a binding agreement, and they retained that common intention at the time of signing the document; and

(b) the document does not correctly express their common intention.

It is also possible occasionally to obtain other equitable relief for mistake if it does not render the contract void. No general principle can be deduced from the cases except that such relief is only likely to be given to relieve unfairness. For example, *equity* will sometimes impose a compromise on the parties.

> *Solle v Butcher 1950*
> Extensive improvements were made to what had been a flat at a controlled rent. Both landlord and tenant believed (common mistake) that the flat had therefore ceased to be subject to rent control. It was let at a rent of £250 a year. The original controlled rent was £140 a year but if the landlord had served a notice on the tenant in time he could have had the controlled rent increased to almost £250 a year on account of the improvements. After the period for claiming increased rent had expired it was discovered that the flat was still subject to rent control. The tenant sought to recover the excess rent and the landlord to rescind the lease.
>
> *Held:* the tenant should have the choice between a surrender of the lease and accepting a new lease at a controlled rent increased to make allowance for the landlord's improvements.

Activity 5

In what ways does the remedy of rectification differ from the defence of *non est factum*?

4 MISREPRESENTATION

A statement made in the course of negotiations may become a term of the contract. If it is a term of the contract and proves to be untrue, the party who has been misinformed may claim damages for breach of contract. If, however, the statement does not become a term of the contract and it is untrue, the party misled may be able to treat it as a misrepresentation and rescind (cancel) the contract, or in some cases, recover damages. *The contract is voidable for misrepresentation.*

Definition

A *misrepresentation* is:

- a statement of fact which is untrue;
- made by one party to the other before the contract is made;
- which is an inducement to the party misled actually to enter into the contract.

4.1 Representation

In order to analyse whether a statement may be a misrepresentation, it is first of all necessary to decide whether it could have been a representation at all.

(a) A statement of fact is a representation.

(b) A statement of law, intention, opinion or mere sales talk is not a representation.

(c) Silence is not usually a representation.

Statement of opinion

A statement of opinion or intention is a statement that the opinion or intention exists, but not that it is a correct opinion or an intention which will be realised. In deciding whether a statement is a statement of fact or of opinion, the extent of the speaker's knowledge as much as the words he uses determines the category to which the statement belongs.

Bisset v Wilkinson 1927
A vendor of land which both parties knew had not previously been grazed by sheep stated that it would support about 2,000 sheep. This proved to be untrue.

Held: in the circumstances this was an honest statement of opinion as to the capacity of the farm, not a statement of fact.

Smith v Land and House Property Corporation 1884
A vendor of property described it as 'let to F (a most desirable tenant) at a rent of £400 per annum for 27½ years thus offering a first class investment'. In fact F had only paid part of the rent due in the previous six months by instalments after the due date and he had failed altogether to pay the most recent quarter's rent.

Held: the description of F as a 'desirable tenant' was not a mere opinion but an implied assertion that nothing had occurred which could make F an undesirable tenant. As a statement of fact this was untrue.

Statement of intention

A statement of intention, or a statement as to future conduct, is not actionable. An affirmation of the truth of a fact (a representation) is different from a promise to do something in the future. If a person enters into a contract or takes steps relying on a representation, the fact that the representation is false entitles him to remedies at law. However, if he sues on a statement of intention – a promise – he must show that that promise forms part of a valid contract if he is to gain any remedy.

Maddison v Alderson 1883.
The plaintiff had been the defendant's housekeeper for ten years. She had received no wages in this period. She announced that she wished to leave and get married. She alleged that the defendant had promised that, if she stayed with him, he would leave her in his will a life interest in his farm. She agreed to remain with him until he died. He left a will which included this promise, but because it had not been witnessed it was void. She claimed that the promise to make a will in her favour was a representation.

Held: 'the doctrine of estoppel by representation is applicable only to representations as to some state of facts alleged to be at the time actually in existence, and not to promises *de futuro* which, if binding at all, must be binding as contracts'

Statement of the law

A statement of the law is not a representation and hence no remedy is available if it is untrue. However, most representations on law are statements of the speaker's opinion of what the law is; if he does not in fact hold this opinion then there is a misrepresentation of his state of mind and hence a remedy may be available.

Activity 6

P sells a car to Q. Which of the following statements by P to Q could be misrepresentations?
(a) 'The car can do 120 mph.'
(b) 'I have enjoyed driving the car.'
(c) 'You should get the brakes checked before you agree to buy the car.'

Silence

As a general rule neither party is under any duty to disclose what he knows. If he keeps silent that is not a representation. But there is a duty to disclose information in the following cases.

(a) What is said must be complete enough to avoid giving a misleading impression. A half truth can be false.

R v Kylsant 1931
When inviting the public to subscribe for its shares, a company stated that it had paid a regular dividend throughout the years of the depression. This clearly implied that the company had made a profit during those years. This was not the case since the dividends had been paid out of the accumulated profits of the pre-depression years.

Held: the silence as to the source of the dividends was a misrepresentation since it distorted the true statement that dividends had been paid.

(b) There is a duty to correct an earlier statement which was true when made but which may become untrue before the contract is completed: *With v O'Flanagan 1936*.

(c) In contracts of 'utmost good faith' (*uberrimae fidei*) there is a duty to disclose the material facts which one knows. Contracts of insurance fall into this category.

The person to whom a representation is made is entitled to rely on it without investigation, even if he is invited to make enquiries.

Redgrave v Hurd 1881
R told H that the income of his business was £300 per annum and produced to H papers which disclosed an income of £200 per annum. H queried the figure of £300 and R produced additional papers which R stated showed how the additional £100 per annum was obtained. H did not examine these papers which in fact showed only a very small amount of additional income. H entered into the contract but later discovered the true facts and he refused to complete the contract.

Held: H relied on R's statement and not on his own investigation. H had no duty to investigate the accuracy of R's statement and might rescind the contract.

4.2 Statement made by one party to another

Although in general a misrepresentation must have been made by the misrepresentor to the misrepresentee, there are two exceptions to the rule.

(a) A misrepresentation can be made to the public in general, as where an advertisement contains a misleading representation.

(b) The misrepresentation need not be made directly on a one-to-one basis. It is sufficient that the misrepresentor knows that the misrepresentation would be passed on to the relevant person.

Pilmore v Hood 1873

H fraudulently misrepresented the turnover of his pub so as to sell it to X. X had insufficient funds and so repeated the representations, with H's knowledge, to P. On the basis of this P purchased the pub.

Held: H was liable for fraudulent misrepresentation even though he had not himself misrepresented the facts to P.

4.3   Inducement to enter into the contract

If the plaintiff was not aware of the misrepresentation, his action will fail.

Horsfall v Thomas 1862

H made a gun to be sold to T and, in making it, concealed a defect in the breech by inserting a metal plug. T bought the gun without inspecting it. The gun exploded and T claimed that he had been misled into purchasing it by a misrepresentation (the metal plug) that it was sound.

Held: T had not inspected the gun at the time of purchase. Therefore the metal plug could not have been a misleading inducement because he was unaware of it, and did not rely on it when he entered into the contract.

Since to be actionable a representation must have induced the person to enter into the contract, it follows that he must have known of its existence, allowed it to affect his judgment and been unaware of its untruth.

Activity 7

R sells some farmland to S. Before the contract is made, R states that the land is good for grazing. In fact it is good for grazing sheep, but not cattle. R also suggests that S might like to get an independent opinion on the quality of the land. Has R made a misrepresentation to S?

4.4   Types of misrepresentation

Misrepresentation is classified (for the purpose of determining what remedies are available) as:

(a) *fraudulent misrepresentation*: a statement made with knowledge that it is untrue, or without believing it to be true, or recklessly careless whether it be true or false;

(b) *negligent misrepresentation*: a statement made in the belief that it is true but without reasonable grounds for that belief;

(c) *innocent misrepresentation*: a statement made in the belief that it is true and with reasonable grounds for that belief.

Fraudulent misrepresentation requires an absence of honest belief.

Derry v Peek 1889

D and other directors of a company published a prospectus inviting the public to apply for shares. The prospectus stated that the company (formed under a special Act of Parliament) had statutory powers to operate trams in Plymouth, drawn by horses or driven by steam power. The Act required that the company should obtain a licence from the Board of Trade for the operation of steam trams. The directors assumed that the licence would be granted whenever they might apply for it, but it was later refused.

Held: the directors honestly believed that the statement made was true and so this was not a fraudulent misrepresentation. The false representation was not made knowingly, without belief in its truth or recklessly, and so the directors escaped liability.

Negligent misrepresentation may be at common law (involving breach of a duty of care owed) or under the statutory protection of the Misrepresentation Act 1967 (when the defendant must disprove his negligence). Under the Act no duty of care need be shown.

In 1963 the House of Lords reached an important decision by which it held that in certain instances an action in tort for negligent misstatement might be possible.

Hedley Byrne & Co Ltd v Heller & Partners Ltd 1963
The plaintiffs were advertising agents acting for a new client E. If E defaulted on payment, the plaintiffs would themselves be liable. They checked E's financial position by asking their bank to make enquiries of E's bank (the defendants). Relying on the replies they placed orders and suffered substantial losses when E went into liquidation.

Held: the action failed because the defendants were able to rely on a disclaimer. However, had it not been for this, an action for negligence would have succeeded. Liability for negligent statements depends upon the existence of a 'special relationship'; the defendants knew what the information was to be used for.

At the same time as case law on negligent misrepresentation was developing as outlined above, the Law Reform Committee recommended that damages should be given for negligent misrepresentation. Their recommendations resulted in the Misrepresentation Act 1967. Under s 2(1) of the Act, where a person has entered into a contract after a misrepresentation has been made to him by another party to the contract and has as a result suffered loss, then, if the person making the misrepresentation would be liable to damages if the misrepresentation had been made fraudulently, he will be liable to damages notwithstanding that the misrepresentation was not made fraudulently. He will escape liability if he can prove that he had reasonable grounds to believe, and did believe, up to the time the contract was made, that the facts represented were true.

This puts the burden of proof on the person making the representation. He will be deemed negligent and liable to pay damages unless he can disprove negligence. This suggests that it may be more advantageous for a plaintiff to bring a claim under the Act than at common law.

Howard Marine and Dredging Co Ltd v A Ogden & Sons (Excavations) Ltd 1978
The defendants required two barges for use in an excavation contract. During negotiations with the plaintiffs, the plaintiff's marine manager stated that the payload of two suitable barges was 1,600 tonnes. This was based on figures given by Lloyds Register, which turned out to be in error. The payload was only 1,055 tonnes. The defendants stopped paying the hire charges and were sued. They counterclaimed for damages at common law and under the Misrepresentation Act 1967.

Held: the court was unable to decide on whether there was a duty of care (in the common law action), but the plaintiffs had not discharged the burden of proof under the Act, as shipping documents in their possession disclosed the real capacity.

Following the creation of the two categories of negligent misrepresentation, an *innocent misrepresentation* is any misrepresentation made without fault. (Before this, an innocent misrepresentation was any non-fraudulent misrepresentation.)

4.5   Remedies for misrepresentation

In a case of *fraudulent* misrepresentation the party misled may, under common law, rescind the contract (since it is voidable), refuse to perform his part of it and/or recover damages for any loss by a common law action for deceit (which is a tort).

In a case of *negligent* misrepresentation the party misled may, under equitable principles, rescind the contract and refuse to perform his part under it. In order to gain a remedy, the plaintiff must show that the misrepresentation was in breach of a duty of care which arose out of a special relationship.

> *Esso Petroleum Co Ltd v Mardon 1976*
> E negligently told M that a filling station, the tenancy for which they were negotiating, had an annual turnover of 200,000 gallons. This induced M to take the tenancy, but in fact the turnover never rose to more than 86,000 gallons.
>
> *Held:* E owed a special duty of care and was in breach. Damages were awarded to M.

In a case of *innocent* misrepresentation the party misled may also, in equity, rescind the contract and refuse to perform his part of it. He is not ordinarily entitled to claim damages for any additional loss.

Under the *Misrepresentation Act 1967* a victim of negligent misrepresentation can claim *damages* for any actual loss caused by the misrepresentation. It is then up to the party who made the statement to prove, if he can, that he had reasonable grounds for making it and that it was not in fact negligent. As noted above, this placing of the burden of proof on the maker of the statement makes an action under the Act easier for the victim to win than an action at common law.

Under s 2(2) of the Act the court may in the case of non-fraudulent (negligent or innocent) misrepresentation award damages instead of rescission. This may be a fairer solution in some cases. But damages may only be awarded instead of rescission if the right to rescind has not been lost.

Activity 8

X negotiates to sell some paper to Y. X tells Y that the paper is suitable for colour printing, whereas in fact it is only suitable for black and white printing. In making the statement to Y, X relies on statements made to him by the (reputable) paper merchant who supplied the paper to him, and on the independent opinion of a printer who had inspected the paper. However, two days before the contract is made (but after X makes his statement to Y), the printer tells X that he made a mistake and that the paper is not suitable for colour printing. Could X's misrepresentation to Y be treated as negligent?

Loss of the right to rescind

The principle of rescission is that the parties should be restored to their position as it was before the contract was made. The right to rescind is lost in any of the following circumstances.

(a) If the party misled *affirms the contract* after discovering the true facts he may not afterwards rescind. For this purpose it is not necessary that he should expressly affirm the contract. Intention to affirm may be implied from conduct indicating that the party is treating the contract as still in operation. In a number of cases concerned with untrue prospectuses, subscribers have lost the right to rescind by continuing to exercise their rights as shareholders even though they did not realise that this would be the effect. Mere inaction over a period of time may also be treated as affirmation.

> *Long v Lloyd 1958*
> The plaintiff bought a lorry for £750 after the defendant had described it as being in first class condition. On the plaintiff's first business journey, the dynamo failed, an oil seal leaked, a wheel cracked and the vehicle returned only five miles to the gallon. The plaintiff told the defendant of the

problems; the latter agreed to pay half the cost of the dynamo but denied knowledge of any other problems. On the next business journey the lorry broke down and was declared by an expert to be unroadworthy. The plaintiff sought to rescind the contract.

Held: acceptance of a financial contribution, together with the embarking upon the second journey, constituted affirmation of the contract.

(b) If the parties can no longer be restored to substantially the pre-contract position, the right to rescind is lost.

> *Clarke v Dickson 1858*
> The contract related to a business which at the time of the misrepresentation was carried on by a partnership. It was later reorganised as a company and the plaintiff's interest was with his consent converted into shares. He later sought to rescind.
>
> *Held:* the conversion of the plaintiff's interest in the partnership into shares in the company was an irreversible change which precluded restoration to the original position. The right to rescind had been lost.

(c) If the rights of third parties, such as creditors of an insolvent company, would be prejudiced by rescission, it is too late to rescind: *White v Garden 1851*.

(d) Lapse of time may bar rescission where the misrepresentation is innocent: *Leaf v International Galleries 1950*. Where misrepresentation is fraudulent, lapse of time does not, by itself, bar rescission because time only begins to run from the discovery of the truth.

4.6 Contracts *uberrimae fidei*

The general rule is that a party to a contract has no duty to disclose what he knows which may affect the willingness of the other party to enter into the contract, either spontaneously or in answer to questions. Three types of contract carry a duty of utmost good faith (*uberrimae fidei*), which means that failure to disclose material facts gives rise to a right for relief. The types are:

(a) contracts of insurance;

(b) contracts preliminary to family arrangements, such as land settlements; and

(c) contracts where there is a fiduciary relationship, such as exists between solicitor and client, or partner and partner.

Activity 9

Is it reasonable that when a contract of insurance is proposed to an insurer, the onus is on the proposer to disclose all relevant facts?

---

5 DURESS

A person who has been induced to enter into a contract by duress or undue influence is entitled to avoid it at common law: the contract is *voidable* at his option, because he has not given his genuine consent to its terms.

Duress is fundamentally a threat. This may be of physical violence, imprisonment, damage to goods or business, or even breach of a contract.

In older cases it has been held that threatened seizure of goods or property is not duress as it should be limited to threats of physical harm or imprisonment. But in some recent decisions the courts have set aside contracts made under 'economic duress'.

The Atlantic Baron 1979
The parties had reached agreement on the purchase price of a ship. There was then a currency devaluation and the vendor claimed a 10% increase in price. The purchaser refused to pay. The vendor then stated that if the extra was not paid he would terminate the contract and amicable business relations would not continue. The purchaser then agreed to pay the increased price.

Held: the threat to terminate the contract and discontinue amicable business relations amounted to economic duress. The contract was therefore voidable.

Atlas Express Ltd v Kafco (Exporters and Distributors) Ltd 1989
K had a big order to fulfil with W for a supply of baskets. K negotiated with A that deliveries should be made at £7.50 each. This was confirmed by telex. Later A decided that £7.50 was not enough and drew up an updated 'agreement'. A's driver arrived at K's depot with the update and said that he would not collect goods unless K signed the update. K protested but was unable to speak to someone in charge at A. Being bound to supply to W, K signed under protest and continued to pay only the original agreed amount.

Held: A could not enforce the higher payment since consent had been obtained by economic duress: K would have suffered dire consequences if it had been unable to supply W.

___

Activity 10

A indicates to B that she would probably supply microcomputers of a specified type to B at £1,200 each. When A and B meet to agree a contract, A says that the price per computer will be £1,300, and says that unless B accepts this price he will have to go elsewhere. Both A and B know that the lowest price available elsewhere is £1,400. Why is this not a case of economic duress?

___

6   UNDUE INFLUENCE

A contract (or a gift) is *voidable* if the party who made the contract or gift did so under the undue influence of another person (usually the other party to the transaction). This is an equitable relief.

To succeed in a claim for undue influence, it must be shown that:

(a) a relationship of trust and confidence existed (in some cases this is assumed);

(b) the weaker party did not exercise free judgment in making the contract;

(c) the resulting contract is to the manifest disadvantage of the weaker party and the obvious benefit of the stronger; and

(d) the weaker party has sought to avoid the contract as soon as the undue influence ceased to affect him or her.

6.1   Relationship of trust and confidence

When the parties stand in certain relationships the law assumes that one has undue influence over the other. These relationships include the following in which the stronger party is mentioned first. This is not an exhaustive list.

(a) Parent and minor child (*sometimes* even if the child is an adult)

(b) Guardian and ward

(c) Trustee and beneficiary under the trust

The following relationships are not assumed to be ones in which undue influence is exerted, although this assumption may of course be rebutted: bank and customer; husband and wife; employer and employee.

The courts will look at all the facts in ascertaining whether in a particular case undue influence has in fact been exercised.

> *Williams v Bayley 1866*
>
> A bank official told an elderly man that the bank might prosecute his son for forgery, and to avoid such action the father mortgaged property to the bank.
>
> *Held:* there is no presumption of undue influence in the relation of bank and customer but it could be proved to exist (as was in this case) by the relevant facts.

It is perfectly possible for a relationship to exist where one person places trust and confidence in another without a resulting contract being voidable for undue influence. It is only where the stronger person steps outside a fair and businesslike relationship and obtains a benefit from the abuse of trust that undue influence arises: *National Westminster Bank v Morgan 1985*.

6.2   Free judgement

If it appears that there is undue influence, the party who is deemed to have the influence may resist the attempt to set aside the contract by showing that the weaker party did in fact exercise free judgement in making the contract.

> *Lloyds Bank v Bundy 1975*
>
> On facts very like those of *Williams v Bayley* above (except that the son was in financial difficulty and the bank required additional security for its loan to him) a customer gave the bank a charge over his house.
>
> *Held:* the bank could not itself give independent financial advice to a customer on a matter in which the bank was interested as a creditor. Since the bank had not arranged for the customer to have independent advice the charge in favour of the bank would be set aside.

> *Barclays Bank v O'Brien 1993*
>
> O was persuaded by her husband to mortgage the family home as security for his present and future business debts. He had misled her into believing that the liability would be no more than £60,000. In fact the documents she signed allowed the bank to claim up to £154,000. The bank representative did not ensure that O was aware of this. When the bank attempted to foreclose O refused to leave the house and the bank sought to enforce the charge against her.
>
> *Held:* The defendant would only be liable for £60,000 and the bank's request for possession of the property was dismissed. The bank had a duty to take all reasonable steps to ensure that potential liability is fully understood, particularly when taking a married persons security for a spouse's business debt.

However, there may be undue influence even where the defendant tries to rebut the presumption by showing that the plaintiff has refused independent advice.

> *Goldsworthy v Brickell 1987*
>
> G, an 85 year old man, entered into an agreement to give tenancy of a farm to B, who had been helping him run it. The terms were highly favourable to B, but G had rejected opportunities to consult a solicitor. G sought for the agreement to be rescinded.

Held: although there had been no domination (see Morgan's case below), the fact that the agreement's terms were clearly unfair and that G placed trust in B meant that the presumption could not be rebutted by showing that free exercise of judgement was allowed. G could rescind.

Activity 11

A religious adviser suggests to a disciple that he should give half of his property to a religious order. The adviser points out that the disciple should seek independent advice, and recommends that he consult another adviser who is a member of the same order. The disciple does so consult, but goes ahead with the gift by deed. Advise the disciple.

6.3   Manifest disadvantage

A transaction will not be set aside on the ground of undue influence unless it can be shown that the transaction is to the manifest disadvantage of the person subjected to undue influence. The case below also demonstrates that a presumption of undue influence will not arise merely because a confidential relationship exists, provided that the person in whom confidence is placed keeps within the boundaries of a normal business relationship.

National Westminster Bank v Morgan 1985
A wife (W) signed a re-mortgage of the family home (owned jointly with her husband H) in favour of the bank, to prevent the original mortgagee from continuing with proceedings to repossess the home. The bank manager told her in good faith, but incorrectly, that the mortgage only secured liabilities in respect of the home. In fact, it covered all H's debts to the bank. W signed the mortgage at home, in the presence of the manager, and without taking independent advice. H and W fell into arrears with the payments and soon afterwards H died. At the time of his death, nothing was owed to the bank in respect of H's business liabilities. The bank sought possession, but W contended that she had only signed the mortgage because of undue influence from the bank and, therefore, it should be set aside.

Held: the manager had not crossed the line between explaining an ordinary business transaction and entering into a relationship in which he had a dominant influence. Furthermore, the transaction was not unfair to W. Therefore, the bank was not under a duty to ensure that W took independent advice. The order for possession was granted.

CIBC Mortgages v Pitt 1993
A wife signed an application for a loan from the plaintiffs using the house as security as a result of pressure placed on her by her husband. He wished to use the money to buy shares on the stock market but the plaintiffs were told that the money was to be used for paying off the existing mortgage and buying a holiday home. When the stock market crashed in 1987 the husband was no longer able to keep up the mortgage repayments and the plaintiff applied for possession of the matrimonial home. The wife contested the application on the grounds that she had been induced to sign the charge through undue influence on the part of the husband.

Held: A claimant who proved (as in this case) actual undue influence was not under the further burden of proving that the transaction was manifestly disadvantageous. The undue influence of the husband, however, did not affect the validity of the transaction with the plaintiffs because the husband was not acting as agent and the plaintiff had no actual or constructive notice of the undue influence.

Loss of the right to rescind

As seen earlier, the right to rescind for undue influence is lost if there is delay in taking action after the influence has ceased to have effect.

Allcard v Skinner 1887

Under the influence of a clergyman, A entered a Protestant convent and in compliance with a vow of poverty transferred property worth about £7,000 to the order. After ten years A left the order and became a Roman Catholic. Six years later she demanded the return of the unexpended balance of her gift.

Held: it was a clear case of undue influence since, among other things, the rules of the order forbade its members to seek advice from any outsider. But A's delay of six years after leaving the order in making her claim debarred her from setting aside the gift and recovering her property. (This is an example of the equitable doctrine of 'laches' or delay.)

Activity 12

A has undue influence over B. A would very much like to live in B's house, so A persuades B to sell the house to him for £80,000 when its open market value is £10,000 less. B then regrets selling the house, which she was very fond of. Could B have the transaction set aside on the ground of undue influence?

7 VOID AND ILLEGAL CONTRACTS

Some types of contract cannot be enforced in a court of law because they are unlawful in themselves or disapproved as contrary to public policy. The following categories may be distinguished.

(a) Contracts *void by statute*, including restrictive trading agreements and resale price maintenance agreements.

(b) Contracts *void at common law on the grounds of public policy*, of which the most important are contracts in restraint of trade.

(c) Contracts *illegal, void and prohibited by statute*, for example cartel agreements.

(d) Contracts *illegal and void at common law as contrary to public morals or the interests of the state*, including agreements to commit a crime or tort (such as assault or defrauding the Revenue), contracts to promote sexual immorality and contracts to promote corruption in public life.

All such contracts are *void* and neither party can enforce them. In general, money paid or property transferred under a contract which is merely void may be recovered. If the void part can be separated from the other terms without rendering the agreement meaningless, then the remainder may be valid. But if the contract is also illegal the courts will not (subject to some exceptions) assist a party to recover his money or property.

7.1 Effect of illegal contracts

If the contract is obviously illegal in its inception or if the contract appears to be legal but both parties intend to accomplish an illegal purpose by it, neither has an enforceable right at law against the other.

Pearce v Brooks 1866

The plaintiffs, who were coachbuilders, let a carriage described as 'of a somewhat intriguing nature' to a prostitute. They knew that she was a prostitute and the jury found (although they denied it) that they also knew that she intended to parade along the streets in the carriage as a means of soliciting clients and would pay for the carriage out of her immoral earnings. She failed to pay the agreed amount and they sued to recover it.

Held: although the letting of a carriage is not obviously unlawful, to do so to facilitate known immoral purposes is an illegal contract which will not be enforced.

If one party in performing a contract does an act prohibited by statute, the act only may be illegal or the whole contract may be illegal. It depends on whether or not the statute was intended to prohibit the whole contract from being formed.

Archbolds v Spanglett 1961
S contracted to carry whisky belonging to A in a van which was not licensed to carry goods which did not belong to him. In carrying the whisky S therefore committed a crime. The whisky was stolen on the journey and A sued for damages. S pleaded the illegality as his defence.

Held: the defence failed because:

(a) the statute in question did not prohibit the contract expressly or by implication; and

(b) A did not know that S did not have the correct licence.

Activity 13

J runs an illegal radio station. K, who runs a local business and who is aware of the illegality of the radio station, arranges to have some advertisements broadcast. K pays J in advance, but the advertisements are broadcast at the wrong time of day and have little effect. K wishes to sue J. Consider whether K can sue J.

7.2   Contracts in restraint of trade

Any restriction on a person's normal freedom to carry on a trade, business or profession in such a way and with such persons as he chooses is a restraint of trade. A restraint of trade is treated as contrary to public policy and therefore void unless it can be justified under the principles explained below. If a restraint is void the remainder of the contract by which the restraint is imposed is usually valid and binding: it is merely the restraint which is struck out as invalid.

The objection to a restraint of trade is that it denies to a community useful services which would otherwise be available. On the other hand, it is recognised that a restraint may be needed to protect legitimate interests. A restraint of trade may therefore be justified and be enforceable if:

(a) the person who imposes it has a legitimate interest to protect;

(b) the restraint is reasonable between the parties as a protection of that interest; and

(c) it is also reasonable from the standpoint of the community.

In principle any restraint of trade may be subject to scrutiny by reference to the tests set out in the previous paragraph. But where the parties have agreed upon it in the normal course of business and on the basis of equal bargaining strength, it is accepted that the restraint is justifiable and valid without detailed examination. In practice the doctrine of restraint of trade is applicable primarily to restrictions on *employees* and restrictions *on vendors of businesses.*

Restrictions on employees

An employer may (in consideration of the payment of wages) insist that the employee's services shall be given only to him while the employment continues. But any restraint imposed on the employee's freedom to take up other employment (or to carry on business on his own account) *after* leaving the employer's service is void unless it can be justified. Such a restraint, if reasonable in its extent, may be valid if it is imposed to prevent the employee from making use of the trade secrets or trade connections (business goodwill) of the employer, since these are interests which the employer is entitled to protect.

An employee who has access to *trade secrets* such as manufacturing processes or even financial and commercial information which is confidential, may be restricted to prevent his using such information after leaving his present job: *Forster & Sons v Suggett 1918.*

In contrast to trade secrets the employer has no right to restrain an employee from exercising a *personal skill* acquired in the employer's service: *Morris v Saxelby 1916.*

If the employer imposes the restraint to protect his connection with his customers or clients, he must show that the employee had something more than a routine contact with them. The restraint is only valid if the nature of the employee's duties gives him an intimate knowledge of the affairs or requirements of customers such that, if he leaves to take up other work, they might follow him because of his knowledge (as distinct from his personal skill).

Fitch v Dewes 1921
D was successively an articled clerk and a managing clerk in the employment of F, a solicitor practising at Tamworth. D undertook never to practise as a solicitor (after leaving F) within seven miles of Tamworth.

Held: the restraint was valid since D's knowledge of the affairs of F's clients should not be used to the detriment of F. (In modern practice a restriction unlimited in time would probably be treated as excessive.)

S W Strange v Mann 1965
A bookmaker employed M to conduct business, mainly by telephone, with his clients. M's contract of service restricted his freedom to take similar employment.

Held: the contact between M and his employer's clients was too remote to give him the required influence over them. The restraint was void.

Activity 14

A computer programmer is employed by a computer manufacturer. In the course of her work she acquires a detailed knowledge of the workings of the computers produced by her employer, including some features not known to other manufacturers. In learning these features, she acquires new programming skills which could be applied to a wide range of computers. She has said that she would accept the incorporation into her contract of a restriction on her future employment, in consideration of an increase in her holiday entitlement. Try to draft a restriction which would distinguish between her personal skill and her knowledge of trade secrets, and which would only restrict her use of the latter.

If the employer can show that the restraint is imposed to protect his legitimate interest he must next show that it is reasonable between the parties, and that it is no more than is necessary to protect his interest. Many restraints have been held void because they prohibited the employee from working in a wider area than the catchment area of the employer's business, or restricted him for an excessively long time.

If the restraint is too wide the entire restriction is usually void and not merely the excess which is unreasonable. The court will not rewrite an excessive restraint by limiting it to that part which might be reasonable.

> *Office Angels Ltd v Rainer-Thomas and O'Connor 1991*
> The defendants' contracts of employment included clauses stating that, for a period of six months after leaving the plaintiff's employ, they would neither solicit clients of the business nor engage in similar business within a radius of three kilometres of the branch in the City of London. The defendants left and set up their own business in a nearby location. An injunction was obtained preventing this in the High Court. The defendants appealed.
>
> *Held:* the restraint on the poaching of clients was reasonable, but the area of restraint was not. The *whole* restraint clause was void.

An employer who is in breach of the main contract may no longer be allowed to enforce a restraint clause in it.

> *Briggs v Oates 1990*
> The employer who was a solicitor wrongfully dismissed an employee. He then sought to enforce a restraint clause in the contract against the employee.
>
> *Held:* Having breached and repudiated the contract the employer could not now claim the benefit of the restraint clause. His ex-employee was therefore free to set up immediately in practice nearby.

The blue pencil rule

In some cases however, the court has concluded that the parties did not intend by the words used to adopt as wide a restraint as the words might impose and have struck out the words which are too wide. This is the 'blue pencil' rule of simple deletion.

> *Home Counties Dairies v Skilton 1970*
> A milk roundsman's contract of employment prohibited him, for one year after leaving his employment, from selling *milk or dairy produce* to customers of the employer to whom the roundsman had supplied his employer's goods during the final six months of his employment.
>
> *Held:* the words 'or dairy produce' were excessive since they would prevent the employee from engaging in a different trade, such as a grocery shop. As the object of the restraint was to protect the employer's connection with customers who purchased their milk, the restraint would be upheld in respect of milk supplied only.

Activity 15

An employer imposes a restraint on employees' future employment which is stated to apply 'throughout the UK for 20 years after the termination of employment, but if this is held to be excessive the restraint shall apply over whatever area and period the court shall deem to be reasonable'. Why is this tactic unlikely to succeed?

Restraints on vendors of businesses

A purchaser of the goodwill of a business obviously has a right to protect what he has bought by imposing restrictions to prevent the vendor doing business with his old customers or clients. But the restraint must protect the business sold and it must not be excessive.

Nordenfelt v Maxim Nordenfelt Guns and Ammunition Co Ltd 1894
N had developed a new firing mechanism for guns and carried on, among other things, a business manufacturing these guns and their ammunition. When he sold the assets and goodwill of the business he entered into an agreement, later duplicated when the business merged with another, that he would not engage directly or indirectly in a wide number of gun-related activities or any other competing business for 25 years except on its behalf.

Held: the covenant as it related to guns was valid but the term as to competition was void since it went much further than could reasonably be required to protect the business.

British Reinforced Concrete Engineering Co v Schelff 1921
S carried on a small local business of making one type of road reinforcement. He sold his business to BC which carried on business throughout the UK in making a range of road reinforcements. S undertook not to compete with BC in the sale or manufacture of road reinforcements.

Held: the restraint was void since it was widely drawn to protect BC from any competition by S. In buying the business of S, BC was only entitled to protect what they bought: a local business making one type of product and not the entire range produced by BC in the UK.

Allied Dunbar (Frank Weisinger) Ltd v Frank Weisinger 1987
The defendant had sold his business to A for a sum which included £386,000 as consideration for F, a financial consultant who had built up his successful business from scratch, not to be employed in a similar capacity for two years.

Held: the restraint was valid since it was agreed after equal negotiation, had been paid for and reasonable in itself.

Activity 16

F bought G's supermarket, with G accepting a restraint on carrying on 'any comparable retail business' in the locality within the following year. Would this be likely to prevent G from opening a bookshop nearby within six months?

Chapter roundup

- Contracts made by a minor are binding on the minor if they are for the supply of necessaries, or if they are service contracts which are for the minor's benefit. Other contracts made by a minor are either voidable or unenforceable. The contractual capacity of the mentally incapacitated and of companies is also limited.

- Not all mistakes render a contract void. The three classes of operative mistake are common mistake (both parties have the same – wrong – understanding), mutual mistake and unilateral mistake.

- Common mistake may arise when the subject matter of the contract does not exist. Mutual mistake sufficient to render a contract void may arise when the subject matter is not identified, but a mistake as to quality is not normally sufficient to render a contract void. Unilateral mistake may arise when one party is mistaken as to the identity of the other party.

- The defence of *non est factum* may be raised when someone has signed a document which he could not read, but not when he has merely not troubled to read it.

> ## Chapter roundup *continued*
>
> - The main remedies for mistake are rescission and rectification, but other equitable remedies may also be available.
> - A misrepresentation is a false statement of fact which induced the party to whom it was made to enter into the contract. Silence is only a misrepresentation in special cases.
> - Misrepresentation may be fraudulent, negligent or innocent. In all cases rescission may be available, but this is only available in equity unless the misrepresentation is fraudulent. Damages may also be claimed except in the case of innocent misrepresentation. However, where the misrepresentation was not fraudulent, the court may award damages instead of rescission. In any case, the right to rescission is easily lost.
> - A contract entered into under duress, whether physical threats or economic duress, is voidable.
> - Contracts entered into under undue influence are voidable in equity. Several family and professional relationships give rise to a presumption of undue influence, but a contract will only be set aside if it is to the manifest disadvantage of the person influenced. The right to rescind can be lost.
> - Certain contracts are void, and of these some are illegal.
> - If a contract includes a term which is in restraint of trade, that term is liable to be struck out unless the party imposing it has a legitimate interest to protect and the term is reasonable.
> - Restraints on employees may limit their use of trade secrets, but not their use of personal skills. Restraints must be appropriately limited in geographical scope and in duration. Restraints on the vendors of businesses must protect the business sold and must not be excessive.

Quick quiz

1 How may a minor's different general contractual liabilities be classified?

2 In what circumstances may a minor be bound to pay for goods?

3 In what circumstances may a minor be bound by a contract of apprenticeship or vocation?

4 When is a person who is insane or drunk not bound by a contract which he enters into?

5 Explain the difference between common, mutual and unilateral mistake.

6 Give examples of contracts rendered void by common mistake.

7 In what circumstances does a contract become void for mistake by one party over the identity of the other?

8 What is a misrepresentation and how does it differ from a statement of opinion?

9 When may silence be construed as misrepresentation?

10 What are the three different kinds of misrepresentation?

11 What are the remedies available to a party who has been misled by negligent misrepresentation by the other party to the contract?

12 In what circumstances may a party misled by misrepresentation be unable to rescind the contract?

13 What types of contract are *uberrimae fidei*?

14 Distinguish between duress and undue influence.

15 How is undue influence established?

16 Which contracts are (a) void and (b) illegal?

17 What is a restraint of trade?

18 What must be shown in order to validate a restraint of trade?

19 Illustrate the types of circumstance in which an employee may be subject to a valid restraint on his freedom to take other employment.

Solutions to activities

1   The lender may recover £90 on the basis that the minor had borrowed the money to pay for necessaries (that is food) and the lender may stand in the shoes of the supplier and recover as much of the loan as corresponds to a reasonable price.

2   An example of a common mistake is where both parties make some mistake as to the existence of the subject matter for the contract. Here there is no common mistake because the rogue knew that the subject matter did not exist.

3   (a) No: the subject matter was adequately identified.

    (b) Yes.

4   The contract would be void due to a unilateral mistake despite the face-to-face contact. The contract was made on the telephone, before the rogue met the supplier. As the supplier believes the rogue is a respectable firm with whom he has had previous dealings and with whom he intends to make the contract, the contract is void.

5   *Non est factum* applies when the person pleading it never intended to enter into the contract, and may only be raised when an honest third party has acquired rights. Rectification applies when the parties did intend to contract, but a document fails to express their common intention.

6   (a) and (b). Both are statements of fact.

7   Yes.

8   Yes: when the contract was made, X had lost his reasonable grounds for believing that his representation was true.

9   It may be argued to be reasonable because the insurer has no way of knowing the full range of potentially relevant facts.

10 There was no pre-existing contract in which B was trapped, and B was still being offered a bargain.

11 The disciple could claim that the contract is voidable because he was under the undue influence of another. The presumption of undue influence could not be rebutted because the second piece of advice was clearly not independent of the first.

12 No: B has not suffered manifest disadvantage.

13 The whole contract was illegal, and K knew of the illegality.

14 One possible answer would be as follows.

    'The employee shall not disclose confidential information about the workings of the employer's computers, and shall not use programming techniques relating only to computers of similar design, but she shall not be prevented from using programming techniques of more general application.'

15 The court will not rewrite an excessive restraint.

16 No: a bookshop is not likely to compete with a supermarket to any significant degree, even though some supermarkets sell a few books.

Further question practice

Now try the following practice questions at the end of this text

Multiple choice questions: **26 to 29**

Exam style question: **7**

Chapter 8

DISCHARGE OF CONTRACT

Introduction

A party who is subject to the obligations of a contract may be discharged from those obligations in one of four ways. The agreement is then at an end. The four ways are performance, agreement, breach and frustration. After a discussion of these, we look at remedies for breach of contract

A party has a number of remedies when the other party is in breach of contract. Damages are a form of compensation for loss caused by the breach. An action for the price may be commenced where the breach is failure to pay. A *quantum meruit* is payment to the plaintiff for the value of what he has done. Specific performance, an equitable remedy, is a court order to the defendant to perform the contract. An injunction is a court order for the other party to observe negative restrictions.

Damages and action for the price are common law remedies and are most frequently sought when a remedy is needed for breach of contract, since they arise as of right. A *quantum meruit* claim is categorised as a claim in quasi-contract. (You do not, at this stage, need to know the technicalities of quasi-contract.) The other types of remedy are equitable remedies which are only appropriate in specialised circumstances.

Your objectives

After completing this chapter you should:

(a) know what is necessary for a contract to be discharged by performance;

(b) understand how a contract may be discharged by an agreement which is binding on the parties;

(c) know the types of repudiatory breach of contract, and how anticipatory breach may arise;

(d) understand the effects of termination and affirmation;

(e) understand the circumstances in which frustration arises and when it cannot be pleaded;

(f) know the position of the parties following frustration;

(g) know which losses may give rise to damages, and how damages are computed;

(h) be able to distinguish between liquidated damages and penalty clauses;

(i) understand the limitations on action for the price;

(j) know the uses of *quantum meruit*, specific performance, injunction and rescission;

(k) know how actions for breach of contract may be limited by the passage of time.

1   DISCHARGE BY PERFORMANCE

This is the normal method of discharge. Each party fulfils or performs his contractual obligations and the agreement is then ended. As a general rule contractual obligations are discharged only by complete and exact performance. *Partial* performance does not usually suffice, nor does incorrect performance.

> *Cutter v Powell 1795*
> The defendant employed C as second mate of a ship sailing from Jamaica to Liverpool at a wage for the complete voyage of 30 guineas [£31.50]. The voyage began on 2 August, and C died at sea on 20 September, when the ship was still 19 days from Liverpool. C's widow sued for a proportionate part of the agreed sum.
>
> *Held:* C was entitled to nothing unless he completed the voyage.

> *Bolton v Mahadeva 1972*
> The plaintiff agreed to install a central heating system in the defendant's home for £800. The work was defective: the system did not heat adequately and it gave off fumes. The defendant refused to pay for it.
>
> *Held:* the plaintiff could recover nothing.

In each of these cases the defendant might appear to have profited to an undue degree, since he obtained part of what the plaintiff contracted to deliver without himself having to pay anything. Although these cases can be justified on their facts, the courts have developed a number of exceptions to the rule to ensure that the interests of both parties are protected.

Substantial performance

The doctrine of substantial performance may be applied, especially in contracts for building work and the like. If the building contractor has completed the essential work and in doing so has completed a very large part of it, he may claim the contract price less a deduction for the minor work outstanding. This may also be regarded as a deduction of damages for breach of warranty when the contract price is paid.

> *Hoenig v Isaacs 1952*
> The defendant employed the plaintiff to decorate and furnish his flat at a total price of £750. There were defects in the furniture which could be put right at a cost of £56. The defendant argued that the plaintiff was only entitled to reasonable remuneration.
>
> *Held:* the defendant must pay the balance owing of the total price of £750 less an allowance of £56, as the plaintiff had substantially completed the contract.

> *Sumpter v Hedges 1898*
> The plaintiff undertook to erect buildings on the land of the defendant for a price of £565. He partially erected the buildings, then abandoned the work when it was only completed to the value of £333. The defendant completed the work using materials left on his land. The plaintiff sued for the value of his materials used by the defendant and for the value of his work.
>
> *Held:* the defendant must pay for the materials since he had elected to use them but he had no obligation to pay the unpaid balance of the charges for work done by the plaintiff before abandoning it. It was not a case of substantial performance of the contract.

Partial performance

The promisee may accept partial performance and must then pay for it. For example, A orders a dozen bottles of beer from B; B delivers ten which is all he has in stock. A may reject the ten bottles but if he accepts them he must pay for ten bottles at the appropriate rate. The principle here is that although the promisor has only partially fulfilled his contractual obligations, it may sometimes be possible to infer the existence of a fresh agreement by which it is agreed that payment will be made for work already done or goods already supplied. Mere performance by the promisor is not enough; it must be open to the promisee either to accept or reject the benefit of the contract. Thus in *Bolton v Mahadeva*, above, this could not apply once the heating system had been installed.

1.1   Prevention of performance

The promisee may prevent performance. In that case the offer (*tender*) of performance is sufficient discharge. For example, if the buyer will not accept delivery of the contract goods and the seller sues for breach of contract, the seller need only show that he tendered performance by offering to deliver.

If one party is prevented by the other from performing the contract completely he may sue for damages for breach of contract, or alternatively bring a *quantum meruit* action to claim for the amount of work done: *Planché v Colburn 1831*.

Activity 1

Why could the doctrine of partial performance not be applied in *Cutter v Powell*?

1.2   Time of performance

If one party fails to perform at the *agreed time* he may perform the contract later – the contract continues in force, inless prompt performance is an essential condition ('time is of the essence'). In that case the injured party may refuse late performance and treat the contract as discharged by breach. Where time is not of the essence the injured party may claim damages for any loss or expense caused by the delay but must accept late performance.

If the parties expressly agree that time is of the essence and so prompt performance is to be a condition, that is conclusive and late performance does not discharge obligations. If they make no such express stipulation the following rules apply.

(a) In a commercial contract, time of performance (other than the time of payment) is usually treated as an essential condition.

Elmdore v Keech 1969
An advertisement was to be published within 120 days of delivery. Publication was 11 days late.

Held: the party who had supplied the advertisement was entitled to refuse to pay for it. Time was of the essence.

(b) In a contract for the sale of land (unless it fluctuates in value or is required for business use) equity may permit the plaintiff to have an order for specific performance even if he is late.

(c) If time was not originally of the essence, either party may make it so by serving on the other (after the time for performance has arrived) a notice to complete within a reasonable time.

Charles Rickards Ltd v Oppenheim 1950
The contract was to build a Rolls-Royce chassis by 20 March. When this period expired without delivery the purchaser agreed to wait another three months. As the chassis had still not been built by 29 June, he served a notice requiring completion by 25 July at the latest; if this were not done he would cancel the

order. He did cancel it but the makers tendered delivery three months after he had done so.

Held: although the purchaser had at first waived his rights (by the three month extension) he could, by serving reasonable notice to complete, make time of the essence and treat the contract as discharged if there was no performance within the period of the notice. He had done so and was justified in refusing delivery.

(d) As long as the time given for performance is not unreasonably short, the injured party may treat any failure to meet the new date as a repudiation of contract terms: *Behzadi v Shaftesbury Hotels Ltd 1991.*

Severable contracts

The contract may provide for performance by instalments with separate payment for each of them (a *divisible* or *severable* contract).

Taylor v Laird 1856
The plaintiff agreed to captain a ship up the River Niger at a rate of £50 per month. He abandoned the job before it was completed. He claimed his pay for the months completed.

Held: he was entitled to £50 for each complete month. Effectively this was a contract that provided for performance and payment in monthly instalments.

Activity 2

In a contract for B to build an extension to A's house, time is not originally of the essence but it becomes clear that B is running seriously behind schedule. When B has only done half of the work, A serves a notice to complete the work within three days. B fails to do so. Consider whether this will entitle A to terminate the contract.

---

2   DISCHARGE BY AGREEMENT

A contract may include provision for its own discharge by imposing a *condition precedent*, which prevents the contract from coming into operation unless the condition is satisfied: *Aberfoyle Plantations Ltd v Cheng 1960.* Alternatively, it may impose a *condition subsequent* by which the contract is discharged on the later happening of an event; a simple example of the latter is provision for termination by notice given by one party to the other.

In any other case the parties may agree to cancel the contract before it has been completely performed on both sides. But the agreement to cancel is itself a new contract for which consideration must be given (unless it is a contract for release by deed).

If there are unperformed obligations of the original contract on both sides (that is, it is an executory contract), each party provides consideration for his own release by agreeing to release the other (*bilateral* discharge). Each party surrenders something of value.

But if one party has completely performed his obligations, his agreement to release the other from his obligations (*unilateral discharge*) requires consideration, such as payment of a cancellation fee. This is called *accord and satisfaction*.

If the parties enter into a new contract to replace the unperformed contract, the new contract provides any necessary consideration. This is called *novation* of the old contract.

3 BREACH OF CONTRACT

A party is said to be in breach of contract where, *without lawful excuse*, he does not perform his contractual obligations precisely. This may be because he refuses to perform them, he fails to perform them, he incapacitates himself from performing them or he performs them defectively.

Breach of contract gives rise to a secondary obligation to pay the other party damages but, unless breach is treated as repudiation, the primary obligation to perform the contract's terms remains.

A person has a lawful excuse not to perform primary contractual obligations (that is, what he promised to do under his side of the bargain) in the following situations.

(a) Where performance is impossible.

(b) Where he has tendered performance but this has been rejected.

(c) Where the other party has made it impossible for him to perform.

(d) Where the contract has been discharged through frustration.

3.1 Repudiatory breach

A repudiatory breach is a serious actual breach of contract. It does not automatically discharge the contract. The injured party has a choice.

(a) He can elect to treat the contract as repudiated by the other, recover damages and treat himself as being discharged from his primary obligations under the contract. This is termination of the contract for repudiatory breach, or

(b) he can elect to affirm the contract.

Types of repudiatory breach

Repudiatory breach giving rise to a right either to terminate or to affirm arises in the following circumstances.

(a) *Refusal to perform (renunciation).* One party renounces his contractual obligations by showing that he has no intention to perform them nor to be otherwise bound by the contract. Such refusal may be express or implied.

(b) *Failure to perform an entire obligation.* An entire obligation is one where complete and precise performance of it is a precondition of the other party's performance. As noted earlier, partial performance alone is not usually sufficient. Thus a contractual condition is often an entire obligation, so failure to perform the acts required by a condition can amount to a repudiatory breach.

(c) *Incapacitation.* Where a party, by his own act or default, prevents himself from performing his contractual obligations he is treated as if he refused to perform them. For instance, where A sells a thing to C even though he promised to sell it to B he is in repudiatory breach of his contract with B.

Genuine mistakes, even to one party's detriment will not necessarily repudiate a contract. This was the decision in *Vaswani Motors (Sales and Services) Ltd 1996.* A seller of a motor vehicle, acting in good faith, mistakenly demanded a higher price than that specified in the contract. However, the buyer could not evade his responsibilities under the contract, since he could have offered to pay the original price.

Activity 3

J contracts to sell a painting to K, and K contracts to sell it to L. However, when the time comes for the contract between J and K to be completed, K refuses to pay for the painting so J will not let him have it. Which two types of repudiatory breach arise in relation to the two contracts?

Termination for repudiatory breach

As noted above, the innocent party in a case of repudiatory breach may elect to accept the contract as terminated or discharged by breach, thereby discharging himself from any further obligation to perform. Alternatively, he may affirm the contract. If he decides to terminate for repudiatory breach the innocent party must notify the other of his decision. This may be by way of refusal to accept defects in performance, to accept further performance or to perform his own obligations. The effects of such termination are as follows for the innocent party.

(a) He is not bound by his future or continuing contractual obligations, and cannot be sued on them.

(b) He need not accept nor pay for further performance.

(c) He can refuse to pay for partial or defective performance already received.

(d) He can reclaim money paid to a defaulter if he rejects defective performance.

(e) He is *not* discharged from the contractual obligations which were due at the time of termination.

The innocent party can also claim damages from the defaulter for:

(a) losses sustained by him in respect of unperformed contractual obligations due at the time of default (the defaulter is in theory still bound); and

(b) losses sustained by him in relation to contractual obligations which were due in the future.

Finally an innocent party who began to perform his contractual obligations but who was prevented from completing them by the defaulter can claim reasonable remuneration on a *quantum meruit* basis.

Affirmation after repudiatory breach

If a person is aware of the other party's repudiatory breach and of his right to terminate the contract as a result but still decides to treat the contract as being in existence he is said to have affirmed the contract. Such a decision should be a conscious or active one; it is not deemed to have been made purely by virtue of the fact that a person retains defective goods while he or she decides what to do.

The effect of affirmation is that the contract remains fully in force, so each party is bound to perform existing and future obligations and may sue to enforce them. If the election is unconditional – 'I shall keep the goods despite their defects' – it may not be revoked. If it is conditional – 'I will keep the defective goods provided they are mended free of charge' – and the condition is not satisfied, the contract may then be terminated.

Activity 4

G and H make a contract under which H is to redecorate G's lounge. After stripping the old wallpaper, H declares (without any reason) that he will not do any more work. G then notifies H that he is terminating the contract for repudiatory breach. G has already paid H £50, but refuses to pay any more. H claims a further £200 for the work done. Advise G as to the legal position.

3.2 Anticipatory breach

A party may break a condition of the contract merely by declaring in advance that he will not perform it when the time for performance arrives, or by some other action which makes future performance impossible. The other party may treat this as *anticipatory breach* and can choose between treating the contract as discharged forthwith and allowing it to continue until there is an actual breach.

The risk is that, in the latter case, the party guilty of anticipatory breach may subsequently change his mind and perform the contract after all. If the contract is allowed to continue in this way the parties may be discharged from their obligations without liability by some other cause which occurs later.

Hochster v De La Tour 1853
T engaged H as a courier to accompany him on a European tour commencing on 1 June. On 11 May T wrote to H to say that he no longer required his services. On 22 May H commenced legal proceedings for anticipatory breach of contract. T objected that there was no actionable breach until 1 June.

Held: H was entitled to sue as soon as the anticipatory breach occurred on 11 May.

Avery v Bowden 1855
There was a contract to charter a ship to load grain at Odessa within a period of 45 days. The ship arrived at Odessa and the charterer told the master that he did not propose to load a cargo. The master remained at Odessa hoping the charterer would change his mind-that is, he did not there and then treat the contract as discharged by the charterer's anticipatory breach. Before the 45 days for loading cargo had expired the outbreak of the Crimean war discharged the contract by frustration.

Held: the shipowner, through the master, had waived his right to sue for anticipatory breach (with a claim for damages). The contract continued and had been discharged later by frustration (the outbreak of war) without liability for either party.

If the innocent party elects to treat the contract as still in force despite the other party's anticipatory breach, the former may continue with his preparations for performance and recover the agreed price for his services. But any claim for damages will be assessed on the basis of what the plaintiff has really lost.

The Mihalis Angelos 1971
There was a charter of a ship to be 'ready to load at Haiphong' (in Vietnam) on 1 July 1965. The charterers had the option to cancel if the ship was not ready to load by 20 July. On 17 July the charterers repudiated the contract believing (wrongly) that they were entitled to do so. The shipowners accepted the repudiation and claimed damages. On 17 July the ship was still in Hong Kong and could not have reached Haiphong by 20 July.

Held: the shipowners were entitled only to nominal damages since they would have been unable to perform the contract and the charterers could have cancelled it without liability on 20 July.

Activity 5

X contracts to sell a computer to Y. Ten days before the date for delivery and payment, Y tells X that he does not intend to go ahead with the purchase. Does X need to deliver the computer immediately in order to secure his legal position against Y?

4   DISCHARGE BY FRUSTRATION

If it is impossible to perform the contract when it is made, there is usually no contract at all: it is void and each party is released from performing any obligation after the frustrating event. In addition, the parties are free to negotiate 'escape clauses' or *force majeure* clauses covering impossibility which arises after the contract has been made. If they fail to do so, they are, as a general rule, in breach of contract if they find themselves unable to do what they have agreed to do Thus if a shipowner agrees to load his ship with guano at a certain place in West Africa, he is liable in damages even if no guano is obtainable: *Hills v Sughrue 1846*.

> *Paradine v Jane 1647*
> A tenant who as being sued for rent pleaded that he had been dispossessed of the land for the previous three years by the King's enemies.
>
> *Held:* his plea failed. 'Where a party by his own contract creates a duty or charge upon himself, he is bound to make it good, notwithstanding any accident by inevitable necessity, because he might have provided against it by his contract.'

The rigour of this principle is modified by the doctrine that in certain circumstances a contract may be discharged by frustration (also referred to as subsequent impossibility). If it appears that the parties assumed that certain underlying conditions would continue, the contract may be frustrated if their assumption proves to be false. An alternative theory of the doctrine of frustration is that the parties should be discharged from their contract if altered circumstances render the contract fundamentally different in its nature from the original contract made by the parties. This alternative avoids imputing to the parties assumptions which in fact never occurred to them. They simply did not foresee what would happen. Frustration does not render a contract void *ab initio*, rather it discharges it automatically as to the future. Contracts have been discharged by frustration in the following circumstances.

(a) Destruction of the subject matter. This case was the origin of the doctrine of frustration.

> *Taylor v Caldwell 1863*
> A hall was let for a series of concerts on specified dates. Before the date of the first concert the hall was destroyed by fire. The concert organiser sued the owner of the hall for damages for failure to let him have the use of the hall as agreed.
>
> *Held:* destruction of the subject matter rendered the contract impossible to perform and discharged the contract.

(b) Personal incapacity to perform a contract of personal service. Other instances of frustration in this category are where the person dies, is called up for military service or is interned in wartime.

> *Condor v Barron Knights 1966*
> C, aged 16, contracted to perform as drummer in a pop group. His duties, when the group had work, were to play on every night of the week. He fell ill and his doctor advised that he should restrict his performances to four nights a week. The group terminated his contract.
>
> *Held:* a contract of personal service is based on the assumption that the employee's health will permit him to perform his duties. If that is not so the contract is discharged by frustration.

> *F C Shepherd & Co Ltd v Jerrom 1986*
> J entered into a contract of apprenticeship with S & Co. Subsequently he was sentenced to a period of borstal training following a conviction for conspiring to assault and to cause affray. He served 39 weeks. The employers told J's father that they were not prepared to take J back.
>
> *Held:* the contract has been discharged by frustration.

(c) Government intervention or supervening illegality

Re Shipton, Anderson & Co etc 1915
The contract was for the sale of wheat stored in a Liverpool warehouse. It was requisitioned by the government under emergency wartime powers.

Held: it was no longer lawful for the seller to deliver the wheat. The contract had been discharged by frustration.

(d) Non-occurrence of an event if it is the sole purpose of the contract. Two contrasting examples of this application of the doctrine are provided by the so-called 'coronation cases'.

Krell v Henry 1903
A room overlooking the route of the coronation procession of Edward VII was let for the day of the coronation for the purpose of viewing the procession. The coronation was postponed owing to the illness of the King. The owner of the room sued for the agreed fee, which was payable on the day of the coronation.

Held: the contract was made for the sole purpose of viewing the procession. As that event did not occur the contract was frustrated.

Herne Bay Steamship Co v Hutton 1903
A steamboat was hired for two days to carry passengers round the naval review at Spithead and for a day's cruise round the fleet. The review had been arranged as part of the coronation celebrations. The review was cancelled owing to the King's illness but the steamboat could have taken passengers for a trip round the assembled fleet, which remained at Spithead.

Held: the royal review of the fleet was not the sole occasion of the contract and the contract was not discharged. The owner of the steamboat was entitled to the agreed hire charge less what he had earned from the normal use of the vessel over the two day period.

(e) Interruption which prevents performance of the contract in the form intended by the parties

Jackson v Union Marine Insurance Co 1874
There was a contract for a charter of a ship to proceed immediately to load cargo for San Francisco. Off the coast of Wales the ship went ashore and could not be refloated for a month. Thereafter she would need repairs to make her fit for the voyage. Meanwhile the charterers hired another vessel.

Held: the interruption had put an end to the contract in the commercial sense: it was no longer possible to perform the contract intended. The contract was discharged by frustration. There are numerous other interruption cases. In deciding whether it is a case of frustration the test applied is whether the interruption takes away from the agreed duration of the contract so much of it as to alter the fundamental nature of the contract insofar as it can be performed at all; contrast the *Tsakiroglou* case in the next paragraph.

In some cases, the parties may make express provision for certain contingencies. However if the effect of the contingency is to frustrate the essential object of the contract, the contract will nevertheless be discharged.

Jackson v Union Marine Insurance Co 1874
The parties contracted in November 1871 for a charter of a ship to proceed immediately from Liverpool to Newport, 'damages and accidents of navigation excepted', to load cargo for San Francisco. Having sailed on 2 January, the ship went ashore off the coast of Wales on 3 January and could not be refloated for a month. Thereafter she needed repairs in Liverpool to make her fit for the voyage; these were still in progress in August. Meanwhile the charterers hired another vessel. The plaintiff claimed on his policy of insurance.

Held: the interruption had put an end to the contract in the commercial sense. It was no longer possible to perform the contract intended. The contract was discharged by frustration. The plaintiff had no claim against the charterer and could claim from the defendants.

Gamerco SA v ICM/Fair Warning (Agency) Ltd 1995
Gamerco SA, pop concert promoters, agreed to promote a concert to be held by the defendant group at a stadium in Spain. However, the stadium was found by engineers to be unsafe and the authorities banned its use and revoked the plaintiffs' permit to hold the concert. No alternative site was available and the concert was cancelled.

Held: The contract was frustrated because the stadium was unsafe, a circumstance beyond the control of Gamerco SA.

Activity 6

A small company of coal merchants has contracts to supply householders. The main lorry driver of the company dies suddenly, and the remaining staff cannot manage to deal with all the orders placed. A householder whose order is not fulfilled sues for breach of contract. Consider whether or not the company can plead discharge by frustration.

A contract is *not* discharged by frustration in the following circumstances.

(a) If an alternative mode of performance is still possible.

> *Tsakiroglou & Co v Noblee and Thorl GmbH 1962*
> There was a contract for the sale of 300 tons of Sudan groundnuts to be delivered to Hamburg. The normal and intended method of shipment from Port Sudan (on the Red Sea coast) was by a ship routed through the Suez Canal to Hamburg. Before shipment the Suez Canal was closed; the sellers refused to ship the cargo arguing that it was an implied term that shipment should be via Suez or, alternatively, that shipment via the Cape of Good Hope would make the contract 'commercially and fundamentally' different, so that it was discharged by frustration.
>
> *Held:* both arguments failed. There was no evidence to support the implied term argument nor was the use of a different (and more expensive) route an alteration of the fundamental nature of the contract sufficient to discharge it by frustration.

(b) If performance suddenly becomes more expensive.

> *Davis Contractors v Fareham UDC 1956*
> DC agreed to build 78 houses at a price of £94,000 in eight months. Labour shortages caused the work to take 22 months and cost £115,000. DC wished to claim frustration so that they could then claim for their work on a *quantum meruit* basis.
>
> *Held:* hardship, material loss or inconvenience did not amount to frustration; the obligation must change such that the thing undertaken would, if performed, be a different thing from that contracted for.

(c) If one party has accepted the risk that he will be unable to perform.

> *Budgett & Co v Binnington & Co 1891*
> A bill of lading provided that if the consignee could not unload his cargo within ten days, demurrage (compensation) would be payable. A strike prevented the unloading during the ten days.
>
> *Held:* the consignee had accepted the risk and must pay the demurrage as agreed.

(d) If one party has induced frustration by his own choice between alternatives.

Maritime National Fish v Ocean Trawlers 1935
There was a contract for the hire of a trawler for use in otter trawling. The hirers had four other trawlers of their own. They applied to the Canadian government for the necessary licences for five trawlers but were granted only three licences. They nominated three of their own trawlers for the licences and argued that the contract for the hire of a fifth trawler had been frustrated since it could not lawfully be used.

Held: the impossibility of performing the hire contract was the result of a choice made by the hirers: the trawler on hire could have been nominated for one of the three licences. This was not a case for discharge by frustration.

4.1 The Law Reform (Frustrated Contracts) Act 1943

Where a contract is frustrated, the common law provides that the loss shall lie where it falls; money paid before frustration cannot be recovered and money payable at the time of frustration remains payable, unless there is a complete failure of consideration. The consequences of this can be harsh.

Chandler v Webster 1904
The defendant agreed to let the plaintiff have a room for £141.15s [£141.75] for the purpose of viewing the coronation procession of Edward VII. The contract provided that the money was payable immediately. The coronation was postponed owing to the illness of the King. The plaintiff sued for the return of his £100 and the defendant counterclaimed for the unpaid amount of £41.15s.

Held: the obligation to pay rent had fallen due before the frustrating event. The plaintiff's action failed and the defendant's claim was upheld.

This case can be contrasted with *Krell v Henry 1903*, where the contract stipulated that payment was due on the day of the procession. The common law provides that the loss shall lie where it falls; money paid before frustration cannot be recovered and money payable at the time of frustration remains payable. Only in 1942 was the doctrine modified, so that, where there is a complete failure of consideration, the contract can be held void *ab initio: Fibrosa v Fairbairn 1942*.

In most cases the rights and liabilities of parties to a contract discharged by frustration are now regulated by the Law Reform (Frustrated Contracts) Act 1943 as follows.

(a) Any money paid under the contract by one party to the other is (subject to rule (b) below) to be repaid. Any sums due for payment under the contract then or later cease to be payable.

(b) A party who is liable under rule (a) to repay money received (or whose entitlement to payments already accrued is due for payment at the time of frustration is cancelled), may at the discretion of the court be allowed to set off (or to recover) out of those sums the whole or part of his expenses incurred in performing the contract up to the time when it is discharged by frustration. But he cannot recover from the other party his expenses insofar as they exceed sums paid or due to be paid to him at the time of discharge.

(c) If either party has obtained a valuable benefit (other than payment of money) under the contract before it is discharged, the court may in its discretion order him to pay to the other party all or part of that value. If, for example, one party has delivered to the other some of the goods to be supplied under the contract, the latter may be ordered to pay the amount of their value to him.

Activity 7

A contract between F and G is frustrated, and the Law Reform (Frustrated Contracts) Act 1943 applies. At the time of frustration, G has paid F £600 and F has incurred expenses of £270. G has not so far received any valuable benefit. Had the contract not been frustrated, F would have incurred further expenses of £430 and G would have paid F a further £500, giving F a profit of £400. If the court exercises its discretion in favour of F, what final settlement between F and G will be made?

5 DAMAGES

Definition

Damages: the sum claimed or awarded in a civil action in compensation for the loss or injury suffered by the plaintiff.

Damages are a common law remedy and are primarily intended to restore the party who has suffered loss to the same position he would have been in if the contract had been performed. They are *not* meant to be a punishment, which is a criminal, not a civil, measure. In addition, they should not allow the party to whom they are awarded to profit, nor to achieve a better result: the law will not make up for a bad bargain.

In a claim for damages the first issue is *remoteness of damage*: how far down the sequence of cause and effect should the consequences of breach be traced before they become so indirect that they should be ignored? Secondly, the court must decide how much money (the *measure of damages*) to award in respect of the breach and its relevant consequences.

5.1 Remoteness of damage

Under the rule in *Hadley v Baxendale* (below) damages may only be awarded in respect of loss as follows.

(a) (i) The loss must arise naturally, according to the usual course of things, from the breach; or

   (ii) the loss must arise in a manner which the parties, in making the contract, may reasonably be supposed to have contemplated as the probable result of the breach of it.

(b) A loss outside the natural course of events will only be compensated if the exceptional circumstances which cause the loss are within the defendant's knowledge, actual or constructive, when he made the contract.

Hadley v Baxendale 1854

H owned a mill at Gloucester which came to a standstill because the main driving shaft had broken. H made a contract with B, a carrier, for the transport of the broken shaft to the makers at Greenwich to serve as a pattern for making a new shaft. Delivery was to be made at Greenwich the following day. Owing to neglect by B delivery was delayed and the mill was out of action for a longer period than would have resulted if there had been no delay. B did not know that the mill would be idle during this interval. He was merely aware that he had to transport a broken mill shaft from H's mill. H claimed for loss of profits of the mill during the period of delay.

Held: although the failure of the carrier to perform the contract promptly was the direct cause of the stoppage of the mill for an unnecessarily long time, the claim must fail, since B did not know that the mill would be idle until the new shaft was delivered (part (b) of the rule did not apply) and it was not a natural consequence of delay in transport of a broken shaft that the mill would be out of action meanwhile (part (a) of the rule did not apply). The importance of the shaft was not obvious; the miller might have had a spare.

Victoria Laundry (Windsor) v Newman Industries 1949

N contracted to sell a large boiler to V 'for immediate use' in V's business of launderers and dyers. Owing to an accident in dismantling the boiler at its previous site delivery was delayed by a period of four months. V claimed damages for (i) normal loss of profits (£16 per week) for the period of delay and (ii) loss of abnormal profits (£262 per week) from losing 'highly lucrative' dyeing contracts to be undertaken if the boiler had been delivered on time.

Held: damages for loss of normal profits were recoverable since in the circumstances failure to deliver major industrial equipment ordered for immediate use would be expected to prevent operation of the plant: it was a natural consequence covered by the first head of the rule. The claim for loss of special profits fell under the second head of the rule; it failed because N had no knowledge of the dyeing contracts and the abnormal profits which they would yield.

The *Victoria Laundry* judgment was confirmed (but slightly reformulated) by the House of Lords in the *Heron* case (below). It has also been established in the *Parsons* case (below) that if the type of loss caused is not too remote the defendant may be liable for consequences which are much more serious in extent than could reasonably be contemplated.

The Heron II 1969

There was a contract for the shipment of a bulk cargo of sugar from the Black Sea to Basra in Iraq. K, the shipowner, was aware that C were sugar merchants but he did not know that C intended to sell the cargo as soon as it reached Basra. The ship arrived nine days late and in that time the price of sugar on the market in Basra had fallen. C claimed damages for the loss due to the fall in market value of the cargo over the period of delay.

Held: the claim succeeded. It is common knowledge that market values of commodities fluctuate so that delay might cause loss. It was sufficiently obvious that a bulk cargo of sugar owned by merchants was destined for sale to which the market value would be relevant.

H Parsons (Livestock) v Uttley Ingham 1978

There was a contract for the supply and installation at a pig farm of a large storage hopper to hold pig foods. Owing to negligence of the supplier the ventilation cowl, sealed during transit to the farm, was left closed. The pig food went mouldy. Young pigs contracted a rare disease from which they died. The pig farmer claimed damages for (i) the value of the dead pigs and (ii) loss of profits from selling the pigs when mature.

Held: illness of the pigs was to be expected as a natural consequence (the first half of the rule applied). Since illness was to be expected, death from illness (although not a normal consequence) was not too remote.

Activity 8

Draft a clause which could have been included in the contract in Hadley v Baxendale 1854 in order to enable Hadley to recover damages for loss of profits during any delay.

5.2 The measure of damages

As a general rule the amount awarded as damages is the amount needed to put the plaintiff in the position he would have achieved if the contract had been performed. If, for example, there is failure to deliver goods at a contract price of £100 per ton and at the due time for delivery similar goods are obtainable at £110 per ton, damages are calculated at the rate of £10 per ton (s 51 (3) Sale of Goods Act 1979). This is sometimes referred to as protecting the *expectation* interest of the plaintiff. A plaintiff may alternatively seek to have his *reliance* interest protected; this refers to the position he would have been in had he *not* relied on the contract. Because they compensate for wasted expenditure, damages for reliance loss cannot be awarded if they would put the plaintiff in a better position than he would have attained under protection of his expectation interest.

> *C & P Haulage v Middleton 1983*
>
> The plaintiffs granted to the defendant a six month renewable licence to occupy premises as an engineering workshop. He incurred expenditure in doing up the premises, although the contract provided that he could not remove any fixtures he installed. He was ejected in breach of the licence agreement ten weeks before the end of a six month term. He was allowed by the local council to use his own garage as a temporary workshop. He sued for damages.
>
> *Held:* the defendant could only recover nominal damages. He could not recover the cost of equipping the premises (as reliance loss) as he would not have been able to do so if the contract had been lawfully terminated.

More complicated questions of assessing damages can arise. The general principle is to compensate for actual financial loss.

> *Thompson Ltd v Robinson (Gunmakers) Ltd 1955*
>
> The defendants contracted to buy a Vanguard car from the plaintiffs. They refused to take delivery and the plaintiffs sued for loss of profit on the transaction. There was at the time a considerable excess of supply of such cars over demand for them and the plaintiffs were unable to sell the car.
>
> Held: the market price rule, which the defendants argued should be applied, was inappropriate in the current market. The seller had lost a sale and was entitled to the profit which would have resulted from the purchase.

> *Charter v Sullivan 1957*
>
> The facts were the same as in the previous case, except that the sellers were able to sell every car obtained from the manufacturers.
>
> *Held:* only nominal damages were payable.

Non-financial loss

At one time damages could not be recovered for any *non-financial loss* arising from breach of contract. In some recent cases, however, damages have been recovered for mental distress where that is the main result of the breach. It is uncertain how far the courts will develop this concept.

Mitigation of loss

In assessing the amount of damages it is assumed that the plaintiff will take any reasonable steps to reduce or *mitigate* his loss.

> *Payzu v Saunders 1919*
>
> There was a contract for the supply of goods to be delivered and paid for by instalments. The purchaser failed to pay for the first instalment when due, one month after delivery. The seller declined to make further deliveries unless the buyer paid cash in advance. The buyer refused to accept delivery on those terms. The price of the goods rose and he sued for breach of contract.

Held: the seller was in breach of contract, as he had no right to repudiate the original contract. But the buyer should have mitigated his loss by accepting the seller's offer of delivery against cash payment. Damages were limited to the amount of the buyer's assumed loss if he had paid in advance, which was interest over the period of pre-payment. 'In commercial contracts, it is generally reasonable to accept an offer from the party in default.'

The injured party is not, however, required to take discreditable or risky measures to reduce his loss since these are not 'reasonable': *Pilkington v Wood 1953*. Moreover in a case of anticipatory breach, if the injured party elects to treat the contract as still in being he may continue with his own performance of it, even though in doing so he increases the loss for which, when actual breach occurs, he will recover damages.

Liquidated damages and penalty clauses

To avoid complicated calculations of loss or disputes over the amount the parties may include in their contract a formula (*liquidated damages*) for determining the damages payable for breach. In construction contracts, for example, it is usual to provide that if the building contractor is in breach of contract by late completion a deduction is to be made from the contract price (1% per week subject to a maximum of 10% in all is a typical example). The formula will be enforced by the courts if it is 'a genuine pre-estimate of loss' (without enquiring whether the actual loss is greater or smaller).

> *Dunlop Pneumatic Tyre Co Ltd v New Garage & Motor Co 1915*
> The contract for sale of tyres to a garage imposed a minimum retail price (resale price maintenance was then legal). The contract provided that £5 per tyre should be paid by the buyer if he re-sold at less than the prescribed retail price or in four other possible cases of breach of contract. He did sell at a lower price and argued that £5 per tyre was a penalty and not a genuine pre-estimate of loss.

> *Held:* as a general rule when a fixed amount is to be paid as damages for breaches of different kinds, some more serious in their consequences than others, that is not a genuine pre-estimate of loss and so it is void as a penalty. But the general rule is merely a presumption which does not always determine the result. In this case the formula was an honest attempt to agree on liquidated damages and would be upheld, even though the consequences of the breach were such as to make precise pre-estimation almost impossible.

A contractual term designed as a penalty clause to discourage breach is void and not enforceable. The court will disregard it and require the injured party to prove the amount of his loss.

Activity 9

Under a contract between C and D, D must pay C damages of £100 if a particular type of breach occurs. This amount is a reasonable estimate of the loss which C would suffer. The breach occurs, and C's actual loss is £200. How much must D pay C?

---

6 ACTION FOR THE PRICE

If the breach of contract arises out of one party's failure to pay the contractually agreed price due under the contract, the creditor should bring an action to recover that sum.

This is a fairly straightforward procedure but is subject to two specific limitations. The first is that an action for the price under a contract for the sale of goods may only be brought if property has passed to the buyer, unless the price has been agreed to be payable on a specific date (s 49 Sale of Goods Act 1979). Secondly, whilst the injured party may recover an agreed sum due *at the time* of an anticipatory breach whether or not he continues the contract then, sums which become due *after* the anticipatory breach may not be recovered unless he affirms the contract: that is, he carries on with his side of the bargain. Even where he does affirm the contract, he will be unable to recover the price if:

(a) the other party withholds its co-operation so that he cannot continue with his side in order to make the price due; or

(b) the injured party had no other reason or 'legitimate interest' in continuing his obligations than to claim damages. Such a legitimate interest may be obligations which have arisen to third parties.

These points were decided in *White & Carter (Councils) v McGregor 1961*, where the party who affirmed the contract succeeded in an action for the price.

7 QUANTUM MERUIT

In particular situations, a claim may be made on a *quantum meruit* basis as an alternative to an action for damages for breach of contract. A *quantum meriut* claim is treated as a claim in quasi-contract. In some circumstances where there is no contract the law seeks to achieve a just result by treating the persons concerned as if (*quasi* means 'as if') they had entered into a contract on the appropriate terms.

The phrase *quantum meruit* literally means 'how much it is worth'. It is a measure of the value of contractual work which has been performed. The aim of such an award is to restore the plaintiff to the position he would have been in *if the contract had never been made*. It is a restitutory award. (By contrast, an award of damages aims to put the plaintiff in the position he would have been in *if the contract had been performed*. It is a compensatory award.)

Quantum meruit is likely to be sought where one party has already performed part of his obligations and the other party then repudiates the contract (repudiatory breach). Provided the injured party elects to treat the contract as terminated, he may claim a reasonable amount for the work done. In most cases, a quantum meruit claim is needed because the other party has unjustifiably prevented performance.

> *Planché v Colburn 1831*
> P agreed to write a book on costumes and armour for C's 'Juvenile Library' series. He was to receive £100 on completion. He did some research and wrote part of the book, but then C abandoned the series, preventing P's completion.
>
> *Held:* P could recover £50 as reasonable remuneration for the work done on a *quantum meruit* basis.

8 EQUITABLE REMEDIES

8.1 Specific performance

The court may in its discretion order the defendant to perform his part of the contract instead of letting him 'buy himself out of it' by paying damages for breach.

Specific performance will only be ordered in a case where the common law remedy of damages is inadequate. An order will be made for specific performance of a contract for the sale of land since the plaintiff may need the land for a particular purpose and would not be adequately compensated by damages for the loss of his bargain. He could not obtain another piece of land which is identical. For this reason specific performance of a contract for sale of goods is unlikely to be ordered unless the goods are unique and therefore no substitute could be obtained.

The order will not be made if it would require performance over a period of time and the court could not ensure that the defendant did comply fully with the order. Therefore specific performance is not ordered for contracts of employment or personal service nor usually for building contracts. By contrast, a contract for the sale of land requires only that the vendor should execute and deliver a transfer and other documents, so the order is readily enforceable.

Only contracts where consideration has passed may be remedied by an order for specific performance, since it is an equitable remedy and equity will not assist a volunteer; that is, it will not provide a remedy for someone who has given nothing.

Specific performance will be refused unless the plaintiff on his side has behaved fairly and the *principle of mutuality* is satisfied. This principle has two aspects, positive and negative.

(a) As the purchaser of land may obtain an order for specific performance the same remedy is available to the vendor, even though for him damages might be an adequate remedy.

(b) If the plaintiff could not be ordered to perform the contract, for example, if he is a minor, the defendant will not be ordered to do so.

Activity 10

Would specific performance of a contract for the sale of the Mona Lisa be likely to be ordered against the buyer?

8.2 Injunction

An injunction is (in this context) also a discretionary court order, requiring the defendant to observe a negative restriction of a contract. An injunction may be made even to enforce a contract of personal service for which specific performance would be refused.

Warner Bros v Nelson 1937
N (the film star Bette Davis) agreed to work for a year for WB (film producers) and not during the year not to work for any other film or stage producer nor 'to engage in any other occupation' without the consent of WB. N came to England during the year to work for a British film producer. WB sued for an injunction to restrain N from this work and N resisted arguing that if the restriction were enforced she must either work for WB (indirectly it would be an order for specific performance of a contract for personal service which should not be made) or abandon her livelihood.

Held: the court would not make an injunction if it would have the result suggested by N. But WB merely asked for an injunction to restrain N from working for a British film producer. This was one part of the restriction accepted by N under her contract and it was fair to hold her to it to that extent. But the court would not have enforced the 'any other occupation' restraint. Moreover, an English court would only have made an injunction restraining N from breaking her contract by taking other work in England.

An injunction is an equitable remedy limited to enforcement of contract terms which are in substance negative restraints. It is immaterial that the restraint, if negative in substance, is not so expressed.

> *Metropolitan Electric Supply Co v Ginder 1901*
> G contracted to take all the electricity which he required from MES. MES sued for an injunction to restrain G from obtaining electricity from another supplier.
>
> *Held:* the contract term (electricity only from MES) implied a negative restriction (no supplies from any other source) and to that extent it could be enforced by injunction.

But there must be a clear negative implication. An injunction would not be made merely to restrain the defendant from acts inconsistent with his positive obligations. *Whitwood Chemical Co v Hardman 1891.*

Because the plaintiff may not be ultimately successful in the case, he must give an undertaking to pay damages to the defendant if he fails. This is to compensate the defendant for the prejudice caused by an interlocutory injunction.

8.3 Rescission

Strictly speaking the equitable right to rescind an agreement is not a remedy for breach of contract: it is a *right* which exists in certain circumstances, such as where a contract is voidable for misrepresentation, duress or undue influence.

Rescinding a contract means that it is cancelled or rejected and the parties are restored to their pre-contract condition, as if it had never been entered into.

Activity 11

J will need 3,000 litres of liquid fertiliser over the next 12 months. He therefore contracts with K to purchase at least 2,500 litres over that period, at an agreed price which is less than the normal price because of the quantity involved. J then negotiates to buy 1,000 litres from L, so that he would only require 2,000 litres from K. K finds out about this before J makes a contract with L. Would K be able to obtain an injunction to ensure that J buys at least 2,500 litres from him? Why?

9 LIMITATION TO ACTIONS FOR BREACH OF CONTRACT

The right to sue for breach of contract becomes statute-barred after six years from the date on which the cause of action accrued, which is usually the date of the breach, not the date on which damage is suffered: s 5 Limitation Act 1980. The period is 12 years if the contract is by deed: s 8 Limitation Act 1980.

In two situations the six year period begins not at the date of the breach but later.

(a) If the plaintiff is a minor or under some other contractual disability (for example unsound mind) at the time of the breach of contract, the six year period begins to run only when his disability ceases or he dies, whichever is the earlier. If it has once begun to run it is not suspended by a subsequent disability: s 28.

(b) If the defendant or his agent conceals the right of action by fraud (which here denotes any conduct judged to be unfair by equitable standards) or if the action is for relief from the results of a mistake, the six year period begins to run only when the plaintiff discovered or could by reasonable diligence have discovered the fraud, concealment or mistake: s 32.

Where the claim can only be for the equitable reliefs of specific performance or injunction, the Limitation Act 1980 does not apply. Instead, the claim may be limited by the equitable doctrine of delay or 'laches'.

The limitation period may be extended if a debt, or any other certain monetary amount, is either acknowledged at any time or is paid in part before the original six (or 12) years has expired: s 29. Hence if a debt accrues on 1 January 1989, the original limitation period expires on 31 December 1994. But if part payment is received on 1 January 1993, the debt is reinstated and does not then become 'statute barred' until 31 December 1998. The following conditions apply.

(a) *Acknowledgement.* The claim must be acknowledged as existing, not just as possible, but it need not be quantified. The acknowledgement must be in writing, signed by the debtor and addressed to the creditor: s 30.

(b) *Part payment.* To be effective, the part payment must be identifiable with the particular debt, not just a payment on a running account.

Activity 12

R owes S £100. The debt is incurred on 1 July 1986, but S does not press R for payment and R forgets about the debt. On 1 July 1993, S reviews his records and discovers that the debt has never been paid. He writes to R asking for payment of 'the £500 you owe me'. R then remembers that in fact only £100 is owed, and he drafts a letter pointing out S's error. Should he send the letter?

Chapter roundup

- Complete and exact performance or tender thereof is generally required to discharge a contract by performance. If time is not of the essence, it may be made so by giving reasonable notice. In some cases, part payment may be recovered for incomplete performance.

- Contracts may be discharged by agreement, and each party normally gives consideration for being released from his obligations by releasing the other party.

- Repudiatory breach may be by refusal to perform, by failure to perform an entire obligation or by incapacitation. The party not in breach may treat the contract as repudiated, or may affirm the contract.

- In cases of anticipatory breach, the party not in breach may sue immediately or may wait to see whether the other party performs his obligations after all.

- A contract may be discharged by frustration when certain underlying conditions are no longer satisfied. However, changes not rendering performance impossible, or arising from one party's choices, do not discharge a contract by frustration.

- Losses will only be compensated by damages if they arise in the usual course of things or are within the reasonable contemplation of the parties. Damages are calculated so as to put the plaintiff in the position he would have been in if the contract had been performed. Liquidated damages will be enforced, but not penalty clauses.

- An action for the price is used when one party does not pay money due under the contract. Such an action is limited in its effects in cases of anticipatory breach.

Chapter roundup *continued*

- In cases of partial performance, damages may be claimed on a *quantum meruit* basis. The aim of an award is to put the plaintiff in the position he would have been in if the contract had never been made, so the profit he would have made is lost.

- Specific performance forces one party to perform his obligations under the contract. It will only be awarded when its enforcement is practicable. Like injunction, it is an equitable remedy. An injunction will only be granted to enforce an essentially negative restriction in a contract.

- Actions for breach of contract must normally be brought within six years of the breach occurring, although there are exceptions.

Quick quiz

1   In what ways may a party to a contract be discharged from his obligations under it?

2   Is it a condition of a contract that it shall be performed at the appointed time?

3   In what circumstances may a party who has not completed the performance of his part of a contract be entitled to payment for what he has done?

4   How should money paid be applied to debts?

5   When must the principle of 'accord and satisfaction' be applied?

6   What types of repudiatory breach are there?

7   What are the effects of an innocent party's termination of a contract for repudiatory breach? What happens if the innocent party decides to affirm such a contract?

8   What are the alternatives open to an innocent party if the other party declares in advance that he will not perform his obligations?

9   Give three examples of circumstances by which a contract may be frustrated and one example of subsequent impossibility which does not frustrate and so discharge a contract.

10 What are the rules on payments to be made when a contract is discharged by frustration?

11 State the two heads of the rule in *Hadley v Baxendale*.

12 What is the principle by which the court generally determines the amount payable as damages for breach of contract?

13 What is the duty to mitigate loss and on whom does it fall?

14 What is the difference between liquidated damages and a penalty for non-performance?

15 When may an injured party fail in an action for the price?

16 What is the purpose of a *quantum meruit* claim?

17 In what circumstances may the plaintiff obtain an order from the court requiring the defendant to perform his part of the contract?

18 On what principles will the court sometimes order the defendant not to commit a breach of contract?

19 What is meant by limitation? What are the limitation periods?

20 How may a limitation period be extended?

Solutions to activities

1 Partial performance can only be accepted by the promisee when he has a choice of acceptance or rejection. In *Cutter v Powell*, performance consisted of Cutter's services as second mate. Once he had provided those services, they could not be returned by the shipowners after his death.

2 A is not entitled to terminate the contract because, although A has served a notice on B to complete the work, he has not given B reasonable time to do so.

3 K refuses to perform his contract with J, and K incapacitates himself in relation to his contract with L.

4 G has terminated the contract for repudiatory breach and has given H notice of this. As the innocent party, G may refuse to pay for the defective performance already received and may reclaim the £50 already paid to H.

5 No: X may allow the contract to continue and see whether there is actual breach on the completion date.

6 The company could not plead frustration on the basis of personal incapacity because it would have been possible to hire another lorry driver. Unlike a singer, a lorry driver is not an artist hired for his unique talents.

7 F will repay £(600 – 270) = £330 to G.

8 'If the broken shaft is not delivered to Greenwich on the next day after collection from Hadley, then Baxendale shall pay Hadley the sum of £10 for each day's delay, being the lost profits from the mill's being out of action.'

9 £100.

10 Yes, because it would be enforced against the seller.

11 K would not be able to obtain an injunction because an injunction will only be granted to enforce a negative restraint.

12 No: if he does so, he will have acknowledged the debt in writing and it will cease to be statute barred.

Further question practice

Now try the following practice questions at the end of this text

Multiple choice questions: **30 to 33**

Exam style question: **8**

Chapter 9

AGENCY

Introduction

Additional legal rules apply to certain specific types of contract. Agency has important business applications, particularly for those acting on behalf of companies or partnerships. In this chapter we examine how the agency relationship arises and how the agent's authority is acquired and defined. We will also consider the effect of an agency contract on third parties and see how the contract may be terminated.

Agency can be defined as a relationship which exists between two legal persons, the principal and the agent, in which the function of the agent is to form a contract between his principal and a third party. Agency is a very important feature of modern commercial life.

Agents are employed by principals to perform tasks which the principals cannot or do not wish to perform themselves, typically because the principal does not have the time or expertise to carry out the task. If businessmen did not employ the services of factors, brokers, estate agents, *del credere* agents, bankers and auctioneers, they would be weighed down by the need to make contracts with or dispose of property to third parties and would probably achieve very little else.

Your objectives

After completing this chapter you should:

(a) understand how a relationship of agency may be created, both explicitly and by implication;

(b) know the duties and rights of an agent;

(c) be aware of the different types of authority an agent may have;

(d) know the liabilities of principals and agents to third parties;

(e) understand the position of an agent acting for an undisclosed principal;

(f) know how an agency relationship may be terminated;

(g) understand the positions of certain special types of agent.

1 THE CREATION OF AGENCY

The relationship of principal and agent is usually created by mutual consent. The consent need not generally be formal nor expressed in a written document. It is usually an express agreement even if informal. For example, P may ask A to take P's shoes to be repaired. P and A thereby expressly agree that A is to be P's agent in making a contract between P and T, the shoe repairer.

1.1 Agency by consent

An agent by consent authorised to carry out a certain task or act in a certain capacity is said to have *actual authority*. Consent may be express or implied.

1.2 Express agency

Usually an agent is expressly appointed by the principal to undertake certain transactions. Very often the appointment is oral, but in commercial transactions it is usual to appoint an agent in writing, so that the terms and extent of the relationship are set down to avoid misunderstanding. If the agent is to make a contract for his principal in the form of a deed, the agent must be formally appointed by a document called a power of attorney.

1.3 Implied agency

Two persons may by their relationship or their conduct towards each other *imply* an agreement between them that one is the agent of the other. If, for example, an employee's duties include making contracts for his employer, say by ordering goods on his account, the employee is, by implied agreement, the agent of the employer for this purpose. An agent authorised in this way is said to have *implied authority*.

This implied authority may fall into one of three categories.

(a) It may be *incidental* authority. This is the implied authority to do whatever is necessarily or normally incidental to the agent's activities.

(b) It may be *customary* authority. This relates to the authority of agents operating in a particular market or business, such that they have the authority which an agent operating in that market or business usually has.

(c) It may be *usual* authority. This is similar to customary authority, and confers upon an agent who occupies a particular position or engages in a particular trade the authority to act in a manner usual to persons in that position or trade.

1.4 Agency by ratification

If A makes a contract on behalf of P at a time when A has no authority from P, the contract may later be ratified by P and then has retrospective effect to the time when A made the contract. The principle of retrospective effect imposes the following conditions on agency by ratification.

(a) P must exist and have capacity to enter into the contract when it is made. For this reason a company cannot ratify a contract made on its behalf before the company is formed.

> *Kelner v Baxter 1866*
> The promoters of a company to be formed to carry on a hotel business obtained stock in trade for the company from the plaintiff. The company which was formed three weeks later took over and sold the stock but failed to pay for it. The plaintiff sued the promoters who argued that they were merely agents of the company which had ratified the contract.

Held: the company could not by ratification bind itself retrospectively to a contract made before it existed. The promoters were liable for breach of warranty of authority and must pay.

(b) In making the contract, the agent must reveal that he is acting as agent. If there is an *undisclosed* principal, the undisclosed principal will be unable to ratify.

> *Keighley Maxsted & Co v Durant 1900*
>
> An agent was authorised to buy wheat at 45s 3d [£2.26] per quarter from D. D would not sell for less than 45s 6d [£2.27] and the agent bought at that price without disclosing that he was buying for a principal, KM. KM later purported to ratify the contract but failed to pay the agreed price. D sued KM on the contract.
>
> *Held:* where there is no immediate contract because the agent lacks authority, an undisclosed principal cannot adopt and ratify the contract.

(c) The principal must be capable of being ascertained, or identified, at the time when the authorised act was done (*Watson v Swann 1862*) if he is to be allowed to ratify the act afterwards.

(d) The principal must have the legal capacity to make the contract himself, both at the time the act was carried out and at the time of the purported ratification: *Boston Deep Sea Fishing & Ice Co Ltd v Farnham 1957*.

The principal may only ratify if:

(a) he does so within a reasonable time after the agent has made the contract for him;

(b) he ratifies the whole contract and not merely parts of it;

(c) he communicates a sufficiently clear intention to ratify (either by express words or by conduct) such as refusing to return goods purchased for him by an agent who lacked authority (mere passive inactivity does not amount to ratification);

(d) he is either fully informed of the terms of the contract or is prepared to ratify whatever the agent may have agreed to on his behalf.

Ratification relieves the agent of any liability for breach of warranty of authority and entitles him to claim from the principal any agreed remuneration for making the contract.

The principle of ratification does pose one particular problem. Let us imagine that A purports to act as P's agent. T offers to buy goods from A, who accepts this offer. The question may arise as to whether or not T can revoke his offer before P ratifies the acceptance. Under the law of contract, an offer may be revoked at any time up to acceptance. However, once P ratifies her agent's actions, the ratification has retrospective effect. P is of course free to decide whether or not to ratify.

This situation may appear strange: the third party is bound as soon as the agent acts, while the principal is not bound unless and until he ratifies: *Bolton Partners v Lambert 1889*. (This rule appears somewhat unjust to the third party, and certain limitations have been developed.)

Activity 1

D buys some coal, stating that he is acting as agent for M although she has not appointed him as her agent. The coal merchant lets D have two sacks of grade A coal at slightly below the market price because as part of the same contract he takes three sacks of grade B coal at slightly above the market price. When M learns of what has happened, she tells the coal merchant that she will accept and pay for the grade A coal but not the grade B coal. Advise the coal merchant as to his legal position.

Business Basics: Law

1.5   Agency of necessity

By operation of law a principal may be bound by a contract made on his behalf but without his consent. This rule is of very restricted application and is generally confined to carriers of goods by sea or land. The principle applies when the following conditions apply.

(a) The agent must have no practical way of contacting the principal to obtain the principal's instructions: *Springer v Great Western Railway 1921*.

(b) While the goods are in A's possession some emergency arises in which action must be taken to protect the goods: *Prager v Blatspiel, Stamp and Heacock Ltd 1924*. Cases usually involve perishable goods or starving animals.

(c) The agent must act *bona fide* in the interests of the principal.

Definition

Bona fide: 'in good faith'.

Sachs v Miklos 1948

M agreed to store furniture which belonged to S. After a considerable time had elapsed M needed the storage space for his own use. He tried to contact S to get the furniture removed but was unable to trace S. M then sold the furniture. S sued M for conversion and M pleaded agency of necessity in making the sale.

Held: there was no agency of necessity since no emergency had arisen and M had sold the furniture for his own convenience. If M's house had been destroyed by fire and the furniture left in the open M would then have been justified in selling it.

(d) The action taken by the agent must have been reasonable and prudent in the circumstances.

Great Northern Railway v Swaffield 1874

S delivered a horse to a railway company for transport to another station but failed to collect it on arrival as agreed. The railway company claimed from S the cost of feeding and stabling the horse arguing that if it had delivered the horse to a stable that would have been a contract made under agency of necessity and S would be bound to pay.

Held: the railway company's claim would be upheld for the reasons given.

1.6   Agency by estoppel

Definition

Estoppel: if a person, by his words or conduct, leads another to believe that a certain state of affairs exists, and that other alters his or her position to his or her detriment in reliance on that belief, the first person is estopped (prevented) from later claiming that a different state of affairs exited.

If P leads T to believe that A is P's agent, and T deals with Adam on that basis, P is bound by the contract with T which A has made on his behalf. This situation may arise:

(a) when A, who dealt with T as P's authorised agent, continues to do so after his authority as agent of P has been terminated but T is unaware of the termination;

(b) when A, to P's knowledge, enters into transactions with T as if A were P's agent and P fails to inform T that A is not P's agent.

(c) When A, who dealt with T as P's authorised agent, acts beyond the scope of the authority actually conferred upon him by P but T, is unaware of it.

Agency by estoppel can only arise where the conduct of the apparent *principal* creates it. Agency does not arise by estoppel if it is the putative agent who holds himself out as agent, not the putative principal: *Armagas v Mundogas, The Ocean Frost 1986.*

Activity 2

Why is agency of necessity now unlikely to arise when goods are transported within Western Europe on behalf of a major company based in London?

---

2   THE DUTIES OF AN AGENT

When an agent agrees to perform services for his principal for reward there is a contract between them. But even if the agent undertakes his duties without reward he has certain obligations to his principal. The agent's duties are listed below.

(a) *Performance.* The agent who agrees to act as agent for reward has a contractual obligation to perform his agreed task. An unpaid agent is not bound to carry out his agreed duties, because there is no consideration. Any agent may refuse to perform an illegal act.

> *Turpin v Bilton 1843*
> A broker agreed to arrange insurance of his principal's ships but failed to do so. A ship was lost at sea.
>
> *Held:* the broker was liable to make good the loss.

(b) *Skill.* A paid agent undertakes to maintain the standard of skill and care to be expected of a person in his profession. For example, an accountant has a duty to his client to show the skill and care of a competent accountant. An unpaid agent if he acts as agent (which he need not do) must show the skill and care which people ordinarily use in managing their own affairs.

(c) *Obedience.* The agent must act strictly in accordance with his principal's instructions insofar as these are lawful and reasonable. Even if he believes disobedience to be in his principal's best interests, he may not disobey instructions. Only if he is asked to commit an illegal act may he do so.

> *Bertram, Armstrong & Co v Godfray 1830*
> An agent was instructed to sell shares at a particular price. He delayed, hoping the price would rise.
>
> *Held:* he was liable for the ensuing loss.

(d) *Personal performance.* The agent is presumably selected because of his personal qualities and owes a duty to perform his task himself and not to delegate it to another. But he may delegate in a few special circumstances, if delegation is necessary. Thus a solicitor acting for a client would be obliged to instruct a stockbroker to buy or sell securities on the Stock Exchange.

(e) *Accountability.* An agent must both provide full information to his principal of his agency transactions and account to him for all moneys arising from them.

(f) *No conflict of interest.* The agent owes to his principal a duty not to put himself in a situation where his own interests conflict with those of the principal; for example, he must not sell his own property to the principal, even if the sale is at a fair price.

Armstrong v Jackson 1917
A client instructed his stockbroker to buy for him 600 shares of X Ltd. The broker sold to his client 600 shares which he himself owned.

Held: the sale was made in breach of the broker's duty and would be set aside.

(g) *Confidence.* The agent must keep in confidence what he knows of his principal's affairs even after the agency relationship has ceased.

(h) *Any benefit* must be handed over to the principal unless he agrees that the agent may retain it. Although an agent is entitled to his agreed remuneration, he must account to the principal for any other benefits. If he accepts from the other party any commission or reward as an inducement to make the contract with him, that is a bribe and the contract is fraudulent. The agent may be dismissed.

Boston Deep Sea Fishing & Ice Co v Ansell 1888
A, who was managing director of the plaintiff company, accepted commissions from suppliers on orders which he placed with them for goods supplied to the company. He was dismissed and the company sued to recover the commissions from him.

Held: the company was justified in dismissing A and he must account to it for the commissions.

Even if the agent has acted honestly throughout and substantial benefits have accrued to the principal, the agent may not keep any benefit: *Boardman v Phipps 1967*.

The principal who discovers that his agent has accepted a bribe may:

(a) dismiss the agent;

(b) recover the amount of the bribe from him (as in *Ansell's* case);

(c) refuse to pay him his agreed remuneration, and recover amounts already paid;

(d) repudiate the contract with the third party;

(e) sue both the agent and the third party who paid the bribe to recover damages for any loss. He may not recover any more than this so he may not, for instance, recover both the bribe from the agent and compensation from the third party so as to make a profit: *Mahesan v Malaysian Government Officers' Co-operative Housing Society Ltd 1978*;

(f) seek prosecution of the agent under the Prevention of Corruption Act 1916.

Activity 3

P appoints A as his agent, and pays A £100 for his services. P requires A to buy some explosives and to deliver them to a certain address, allegedly so that they can be used in mining. A discovers that they are actually to be used in a bank robbery. Must A carry out P's instructions, given that P has provided consideration?

3 THE RIGHTS OF AN AGENT

The agent is entitled to be *repaid his expenses* and to be *indemnified* by his principal against losses and liabilities: *Hichens, Harrison, Woolston & Co v Jackson & Sons 1943*. These rights are limited to acts of the agent done properly within the limits of his authority. If he acts in an unauthorised manner or negligently he loses his entitlement. He may recover expenses properly paid even if he was not legally bound to pay: for example, a solicitor who pays counsel's fees (which the counsel cannot recover at law) may reclaim this expense from his client.

The agent is also entitled to be paid any agreed *remuneration* for his services by his principal. The amount may have been expressly agreed or it may be implied, for example by trade or professional practice. If it is agreed that the agent is to be remunerated but the amount has not been fixed, the agent is entitled to a reasonable amount: *Way v Latilla 1937*. However, a right to remuneration is not implied in every agreement.

Estate agents

There is a considerable body of case law on the claims of estate agents for their agreed remuneration although the property has not been sold or has been sold to a purchaser not introduced by the agent. Unless the contract states very clearly a contrary intention, the courts are inclined to hold that the parties intended commission to be paid only out of the proceeds of an actual sale to a purchaser introduced by the agent. The following matters in particular have been considered.

(a) The principal is entitled to withdraw from the transaction: there is no implied term that he will not prevent the agent from earning his commission: *Luxor (Eastbourne) v Cooper 1943*.

(b) The principal may agree to pay a fee to the agent if he is able 'to find a purchaser' or 'find a person willing and able to purchase'. If a purchaser introduced by the agent then enters into a binding contract to purchase, the agent has earned his fee. If however, the purchaser whom he introduces merely makes a conditional offer to purchase, for example 'subject to contract' or 'subject to survey', the agent has not found a purchaser in the strict sense.

> *Christie, Owen and Davies v Rapacioli 1974*
> The purchaser made an offer and later paid a deposit and signed his copy of the contract. The vendors then withdrew. The agent claimed his fee for having introduced 'a person ready, able and willing to purchase'.
>
> *Held:* on these facts the agent had earned his fee.

Activity 4

A stockbroker buys shares on behalf of a client with whom he has no other connection, but, owing to an oversight, no prior agreement was made about the stockbroker's fees. Consider whether the stockbroker would be able to claim a fee, and if so how it might be computed.

---

4 THE AUTHORITY OF AN AGENT

A contract made by an agent is binding on the principal and the other party only if the agent was acting within the limits of his authority. We must distinguish actual from apparent authority.

4.1 Actual authority

The *actual authority* of an agent is the authority which the principal agrees he shall have. As we have seen the actual authority may be either *express* (explicitly given) or *implied*.

The basis of *implied incidental authority* is that the principal, by appointing an agent to act in a particular capacity, gives him authority to make those contracts which are a necessary or normal incident of the agent's activities. It may cover such things as the authority to advertise when given express authority to sell goods.

Implied customary authority is that which an agent operating in a particular market or business usually has: *Dingle v Hare 1859*.

Implied usual authority is that which an agent who occupies a particular position or engages in a particular trade usually has: *Howard v Sheward 1866*.

Between principal and agent the latter's express authority is paramount; the agent cannot contravene the principal's express instructions by claiming that he had implied authority to act in the way he did. But as far as third parties are concerned, they are entitled to assume that the agent has implied usual authority unless they know to the contrary.

> *Watteau v Fenwick 1893*
> The owner of a hotel (F) employed the previous owner H to manage it. F forbade H to buy cigars on credit but H did buy cigars from W. W sued F who argued that he was not bound by the contract, since H had no actual authority to make it, and that W believed that H still owned the hotel.
>
> *Held:* it was within the usual authority of a manager of a hotel to buy cigars on credit and F was bound by the contract (although W did not even know that H was the agent of F) since his restriction of usual authority had not been communicated.

4.2   Apparent authority

The apparent (or ostensible) authority of an agent is that which his principal represents to other persons (with whom the agent deals) that he has given to the agent. As a result an agent with limited express or implied authority can be held in practice to have a more extensive authority.

Apparent authority is not restricted to what is usual and incidental. The principal may expressly or by his conduct confer on the agent any amount of exceptional apparent authority. For example, a partner has considerable but limited implied authority merely by virtue of being a partner. If, however, the other partners allow him to exercise a greater authority than is implied, they represent that he has it and they are bound by the contracts which he makes within the limits of this apparent authority.

For apparent authority to be created so as to bind the principal where the third party acted on it the following conditions must be met.

(a) There must be representations or holding out by the principal or by an agent acting on his behalf (*not* by the agent claiming apparent authority: *Armagas v Mundogas, The Ocean Frost 1986*).

(b) The representation must be one of fact.

(c) The representation must be made to the third party.

(d) The third party must rely on that representation.

Activity 5

P authorises A to buy 400 personal computers on his behalf, but instructs A confidentially not to pay more than £2,000 for any one computer. A becomes well known among computer dealers in the area as a buyer of computers for P. A buys one computer for £3,000. Must P pay for the computer?

5   LIABILITY OF THE PARTIES

A principal is generally liable to the third party for contracts formed by his agent within the latter's actual or apparent authority. He must therefore perform his side of the bargain.

5.1   Liability of principal for agent's fraud, torts or misrepresentations

Although apparent authority does not in itself create an agency relationship (though agency by estoppel is similar) it does mean that the alleged principal is bound even if the acts are entered into for the agent's own purposes or are fraudulent. This also applies to fraudulent acts carried out by the agent within his *actual* authority.

The principle of vicarious liability for torts is well established in employment law. It states that an employer is liable for the torts of his employee where the torts are committed in the course of his employment. Vicarious liability also applies to principals where there is no employment relationship but where the agent is acting within the limits of his or her apparent authority. Hence a principal is liable for misrepresentation and the torts of deceit, negligence and so on which are committed by an agent acting within his apparent authority. In such a case the principal can claim an indemnity from his agent if he has had to compensate a third party: *Lister v Romford Ice and Cold Storage Co Ltd 1957*.

5.2   Liability of the agent

An agent contracting for his principal within his actual and/or apparent authority generally has no liability on the contract and is not entitled to enforce it. However, the agent will be personally liable and can enforce it:

(a) when he intended to undertake personal liability, as where he signs a contract as party to it without signifying that he is an agent. In particular, he will be liable on a cheque which he signs without indicating his agency status: s 26 Bills of Exchange Act 1882. Thus a director should sign cheques 'K Black, for and on behalf of XYZ Ltd';

(b) where the principal was undisclosed (see below);

(c) where it is usual business practice or trade custom for an agent to be liable and entitled; for example, an advertising agent is liable to the media for contracts made on its client's behalf;

(d) where the agent is acting on his own behalf even though he purports to act for a principal (as in *Kelner v Baxter 1866*, where the agents thought they were acting on behalf of a company principal which was not yet in existence). This applies to any cases of agents acting for fictitious or non-existent principals;

(e) where the agent contracts by deed without having a power of attorney from the principal.

It is possible for there to be joint liability of agent and principal. This is usually the case where there is an undisclosed principal.

5.3   Breach of warranty of authority

An agent who exceeds his apparent authority will generally have no liability to his principal, since the latter will not be bound by the unauthorised contract made for him. But the agent will be liable in such a case to the third party for breach of warranty of authority.

If A purports to enter into a contract with X on behalf of P, A warrants to X that P exists and has capacity to enter into the contract, and that A has authority from P to make the contract for him. If any of these implied statements proves to be untrue, then (unless P ratifies the contract) X may claim damages from A for his loss, provided that X was unaware that A had no authority to make the contract. A is liable even though he was himself unaware that he lacked authority, for example because P had died.

Activity 6

J purports to act as an agent for D, even though D has not asked her to do so and does not wish her to do so. G is aware of these facts, although D has not told him of the position. J buys some goods from G 'as agent for D', but fails to pay for them. D also fails to pay for the goods. Why can G not sue J for breach of warranty of authority?

6 AGENTS ACTING FOR UNDISCLOSED PRINCIPALS

In normal circumstances, the agent discloses to the other party that he (the agent) is acting for a principal whose identity is also *disclosed*. If he discloses that he acts for an unnamed principal, the position is the same (an *unnamed* principal is a disclosed principal).

However, if a person enters into a contract apparently on his own account as principal but in fact as agent on behalf of a principal, the doctrine of the *undisclosed principal* determines the position of the parties.

The undisclosed principal will usually intervene and enforce the contract on his own behalf against the other party since it is really his contract, not the agent's. Until such time as the principal takes this action, the agent himself may sue the third party (since he is treated as the other party to the contract).

The undisclosed principal's right to intervene in a contract made by his agent is limited to those contracts which the agent was authorised to make as agent. The principal cannot ratify an unauthorised act or seek to take over the agent's contract without the third party's consent: *Keighley, Maxsted & Co v Durant 1900*. The undisclosed principal is also prevented from taking over a contract:

(a) where the contract terms are such that agency is *implicitly* denied:

> *Humble v Hunter 1848*
> The principal (P) authorised his agent (A) to charter out his ship. A contracted with a third party for the charter of the vessel, describing himself as 'owner' of it.
>
> *Held:* the principal could not enforce the contract against the third party because the agent had implied that he was the owner and hence the principal. P's ownership contradicted the contract's terms;

(b) where the contract terms are such that agency is expressly denied: *United Kingdom Mutual SS Insurance Association v Nevill 1887*.

(c) where the agent, when making the contract, expressly denies that a principal is involved (this is misrepresentation);

(d) where the *identity* of the parties is material to the third party, that is, where the third party wants to contract with the agent and would not contract at all if he knew of the identity of the principal.

> *Said v Butt 1920*
> A theatre critic, S, had a disagreement with the manager of a particular theatre and had been banned from attending there. He wanted to see the first night of a new play at the theatre and so asked Pollock, whom the

manager did not know to be connected with S, to obtain a ticket for him. S was refused admission on the ticket and sued for breach of contract.

Held: S's identity was of great importance to the theatre and it would not have contracted with Pollock if it had known that S was his undisclosed principal. S could not enforce the contract.

Activity 7

X plc requires some tax advice. The managing director asks N, a highly respected specialist, to prepare a report for the company. She agrees to do so, but does not mention that she is in fact acting as agent for P, securing tax advice work for him. The managing director of X plc, on discovering this, refuses to accept P's services. Advise P as to whether he could enforce the contract against the company. Give reasons for your answer.

7 TERMINATION OF AGENCY

Agency is terminated by *act of the parties* in the following ways.

(a) If an agent is employed for a particular transaction, such as sale of a house, he ceases to be an agent when the transaction is completed. In the same way, agency for a fixed period ends with the expiry of the period.

(b) Either party may give notice to the other or they may mutually agree to terminate the agency. But certain types of agency are irrevocable.

   (i) Where the agent has 'authority coupled with an interest' and the agency has been created to protect his interests, for instance, where a debtor appoints his creditor as agent to sell the debtor's property and recover the debt from the proceeds, the principal cannot terminate the agency.

   (ii) Where the agent has begun to perform his duties and has incurred liability the principal cannot terminate the agency: *Read v Anderson 1884.*

   (iii) Statute declares some agencies to be irrevocable, such as powers of attorney for a limited period expressed to be irrevocable, and powers of attorney under the Enduring Powers of Attorney Act 1985.

Agency is terminated by *operation of law* (with some exceptions for irrevocable agencies) by:

(a) the death of principal or agent;

(b) the insanity of principal or agent (though the law here is obscure);

(c) the bankruptcy of the principal, and also the bankruptcy of the agent if, as is likely, it renders him incapable of performing his duties;

(d) frustration, for example by the agency becoming unlawful because the principal has become an enemy alien.

At first, the termination of agency only affects the principal and agent, as it brings the actual authority of the agent to an end. Third parties who knew of the agency are entitled to enforce (against the principal) any later contracts made by the former agent until they are actually or constructively informed that the agency has been terminated.

For example, when a partner retires from a firm he remains an apparent member and liable on contracts of the firm made after his retirement with persons who knew him to be a partner, when he was one, until notice of his retirement has been given to those persons. Therefore, a retiring partner should advertise his retirement generally and ensure that existing suppliers and customers are actually informed of his retirement. General advertisement ensures that persons who first dealt with the firm *after* the partner's retirement cannot claim that the partner was still *apparently* a member.

Activity 8

A buyer of land gives his solicitor power of attorney to sign both the contract to buy the land and a mortgage deed needed to obtain funds for the purchase. Why would the solicitor be likely to insist on an irrevocable power of attorney?

8   SPECIAL TYPES OF AGENT

8.1   Del credere agents

A *del credere* agent undertakes (in return for extra commission) responsibility for due payment of the contract price by persons whom he introduces to his principal. He undertakes that a buyer will pay for goods delivered to him but not that he will accept the goods. It is a form of financial support which is convenient where the other party's creditworthiness is unknown to the principal. A factor who sells goods on credit terms, or an advertising agent who obtains orders (for advertisements to be published in the media) may assume this liability.

8.2   Factors or mercantile agents

A *factor* (also called a 'mercantile agent') is a person whose ordinary business is to sell goods, or consign them for sale, or to buy goods, or to raise money on the security of goods: Factors Act 1889. His principal gives him implied authority to enter into such transactions and usually gives him possession of the goods. A simple example is a motor dealer to whom the owner of a vehicle delivers the vehicle (and registration book) with authority to sell it.

A factor when in possession of goods has wider authority than an ordinary agent. When an ordinary agent has possession of goods for sale, his apparent authority is no greater than the actual authority given to him by the principal. But a factor in possession of goods, or documents of title to goods, with the consent of the owner may sell, pledge or otherwise dispose of them so as to bind the owner (in excess of the actual authority given by him) provided that the factor acts in the ordinary course of his business and the other party acts in good faith and is unaware that the agent is exceeding his authority: s 2 Factors Act 1889.

The purpose of the rule is to protect persons who deal with factors in ignorance of their lack of actual authority. However, the rule only applies when the goods (or documents of title) are voluntarily delivered to the factor for some purpose incidental to his business (of sale, purchase or pledging). The principal is bound even though the factor then sells or pledges without authority.

Lloyds Bank Ltd v Bank of America National Trust 1938
A mercantile agent deposited commercial documents with a bank as a pledge. Later the bank allowed him to recover the documents under a 'trust receipt': he was authorised to deal with the documents but undertook to hold the proceeds in trust for the bank. He then fraudulently pledged them to another bank. Both banks claimed the documents.

Held: for the purpose of applying the rule, the first bank must be regarded as the 'owner'. It had given the factor possession with a view to a sale, a disposition in the course of his business. The second bank (which had been unaware of the fraud) therefore had good title.

Activity 9

F, a factor, and G, his accomplice, agree to act as follows. F will obtain possession of goods belonging to H, with H's consent. F will then sell the goods to G at below their market value. When H finds out what has happened, F will disappear with the proceeds and G will be left with good title to goods which he has obtained cheaply. Why will this scheme not succeed?

8.3 Brokers

There are many kinds of broker in different trades. Any broker is essentially a middleman or intermediary who arranges contracts in return for commission or brokerage. He does not usually have possession of the goods and (unlike a factor) does not deal in his own name. When a contract has been arranged he sends a 'bought note' to the buyer and a 'sold note' to the seller which evidences the existence and terms of the contract.

If a broker, even innocently, makes a contract for the sale of goods by a person who has no right to sell, the broker is liable for the tort of conversion.

> *Hollins v Fowler 1875*
> The subject matter was cotton purchased through a broker from a seller who had no title. The broker merely received a commission.
>
> *Held:* the true owner could recover, as damages from the broker, the full value of the cotton.

A *confirming house* is an intermediary between a foreign buyer and a UK exporter. The exporter may know nothing of the buyer or his credit rating. The buyer employs the confirming house as guarantor and it assumes responsibility for payment of the price when the goods are shipped. It may also attend to the export formalities (customs declarations, and so on) and arrange for the goods to be shipped.

An *insurance broker* is an agent of an insurer who arranges contracts of insurance with the other party who wishes to be insured. However, in some contexts (for example, when the broker assists a car owner to complete a proposal form) he is also treated as the agent of the insured. Insurance, especially marine insurance, has complicated rules applicable to the relationships between the insurer, the broker and the insured.

8.4 Auctioneers

An auctioneer is an agent who is authorised to sell property at auction, usually in a room or place to which the public has access. He is the agent of the vendor. An auctioneer should sell only for cash (though he may accept payment by cheque). He may receive a deposit in part payment but may only pay it over to the vendor if the purchaser consents or if he defaults on the contract.

An auctioneer warrants that he has authority to sell to the highest bidder unless he announces that the seller has set a 'reserve price' (that is he will withdraw the property if a certain price is not reached. He does not of course disclose what that price is. If the seller has set a reserve price and the auctioneer fails to say so, then the property must be sold to the highest bidder (and the vendor as principal will recover the deficiency from the auctioneer).

An auctioneer, like a broker, is liable in conversion to the true owner if he sells property on behalf of a principal who has no right to sell.

8.5 Bankers

The duties owed by a bank to its customer are similar to those owed by an agent, but the banker-customer contract is not one of agency in the normal run of things, such as in the operation of a current account. However, banks often do act as agents for their customers: examples are where they undertake to arrange dealings in shares or where they offer advice on investments such as life assurance and pensions.

Activity 10

The tort of conversion is any action in connection with goods which denies or is inconsistent with the true owner's title to the goods. Explain how the actions of brokers and auctioneers noted above as amounting to conversion fit this definition.

9 COMMERCIAL AGENTS

The Commercial Agents (Council Directive) Regulations 1993 were introduced as a result of a European directive. They came into effect on 1 January 1994. A commercial agent is a self-employed independent agent who has authority to negotiate the sale or purchase of goods on behalf of a principal. The Regulations therefore do not apply to employees, directors or partners but are aimed rather at long term selling agents paid by commission or fee.

The regulations harmonise the legal relationship between commercial agents and principals in three main areas: the duties owed, remuneration and termination of the agency.

(a) *Duties*. In general the agent must act dutifully and in good faith, complying with instructions and keeping the principal informed of all necessary developments. In return the principal must also act dutifully by providing the agent with all the necessary information regarding business transactions.

(b) *Remuneration*. The agent is entitled to remuneration that commercial agents customarily receive or, where there is no customary practice, a reasonable remuneration. The agent is also entitled to commission arising from a transaction that the agent has arranged or from a repeat order from a customer previously secured. This entitlement extends to transactions made after the agency has been terminated if that transaction arises mainly from the work of the agent and is within a reasonable time. Where a transaction is not completed due to the fault of the agent, any commission is lost.

(c) *Termination*. The principal must give the agent at least one month's notice for the first year, two months for the second year and three months for the third and subsequent years. The agent is entitled to compensation if the principal ends the agency early unless the agent is in fundamental breach. Compensation must also be given if the agency ends because of the agent's age, illness or death.

The requirements under these regulations may not be excluded or altered by the agency agreement.

Chapter roundup

- An agency relationship may be created expressly, or it may be implied.
- A principal may, subject to certain conditions, ratify a contract made by an agent acting without authority.
- Agency of necessity may arise in an emergency. Agency may also arise by statute, and a principal may be estopped from denying that someone is his agent.
- An agent must in general perform his duties personally, and with an appropriate degree of skill. He is entitled to his agreed remuneration, but not to any other benefits.
- An agent also has a right to be paid his expenses and to be indemnified for losses and liabilities. There is case law on the right of estate agents to their fees.
- An agent's actual authority may be express or implied, and implied authority may be incidental or usual (customary). Apparent authority is the authority which third parties are led to believe the agent has.
- A principal is liable on contracts made by his agent within the agent's actual or apparent authority, and for the agent's misrepresentations and torts within his apparent authority. The agent is only personally liable on contracts in certain special circumstances, but he may be liable to third parties for breach of warranty of authority.
- Where an agency relationship is not disclosed, a third party may hold either the agent or the principal liable on a contract. An undisclosed principal's right to take over a contract may be limited.
- An agency may be terminated by the conclusion of the relevant transaction, by notice (although some types of agency are irrevocable) or by operation of law. Third parties need to be informed to ensure that the termination is effective.
- Special rules apply to *del credere* agents, to factors (mercantile agents), to brokers, to auctioneers and to bankers.
- The position of commercial agents is now regulated by The Commercial Agents (Council Directive) Regulations 1993. These Regulations clarify the position between principal and agent with regard to duties, remuneration and termination of the agency agreement.

Quick quiz

1 How may an agency relationship be created?
2 Under what conditions may a person ratify a contract made without his authority but on his behalf?
3 In what circumstances may one person be an agent of necessity for another?
4 When may agency by estoppel arise?
5 What duties does an agent owe to his principal? What are the agent's rights?
6 Distinguish actual and apparent authority of an agent.
7 What is breach of warranty of authority?
8 When may an agent be liable under a contract made for a disclosed principal?
9 When is an undisclosed principal prevented from taking over a contract?
10 How may agency be terminated?

11 When has a factor wider powers than an ordinary agent?

12 Why would a buyer employ a confirming house?

13 How may an auctioneer's authority be limited?

14 Explain the rules relating to commercial agents with regard to remuneration and commission.

Solutions to activities

1   The coal merchant can prevent M from accepting only the grade A coal on the grounds that if she ratifies the contact she must ratify the whole contract and not just part of it.

2   The carrier of the goods will usually be able to communicate with the owner.

3   No: any agent may refuse to perform an illegal act (such as facilitating a bank robbery).

4   The stockbroker could claim a fee, the usual scale of fees being applied.

5   Yes: A has apparent authority to buy computers, and the limitation to £2,000 per computer has not been publicised.

6   G was aware of J's lack of authority.

7   As an undisclosed principal P may have a right to intervene and enforce the contract against the company. In this case, however, the identity of the parties is material to the company in that they intended to contract with N (because of her skill) and not P. This may prevent P from being able to enforce the contract.

8   The solicitor must ensure that funds will be available to complete the contract, and would not want to exchange contracts and then have his power to sign the mortgage deed revoked.

9   G will not get good title because he will not have bought the goods from F in good faith.

10 If a broker or auctioneer sells goods on behalf of a principal with no right to sell, he is purporting to pass title to the buyer, which denies the true owner's title.

Further question practice

Now try the following practice questions at the end of this text

Multiple choice questions: 34 to 37

Exam style question: 9

Chapter 10

SALE OF GOODS

Introduction

The law relating to contracts for the sale of goods was originally codified into the Sale of Goods Act 1893. The law is currently contained in the Sale of Goods Act 1979, a consolidating Act. One of the main functions of the legislation is to codify the terms implied into contracts of sale. These have evolved largely from case law. Some are conditions and some are warranties. The Sale of Goods Act 1979 has been amended by the Sale and Supply of Goods Act 1994.

Two other statutes are of particular relevance to this area of the law. The Unfair Contract Terms Act 1977 restricts the use of contract terms which exclude the conditions of the 1979 Act. The Supply of Goods and Services Act 1982 for the most part extends the terms of the 1979 Act to contracts where the supply of services is the major part, such as contracts of repair.

We first examine the terms implied into contracts for the sale of goods and then look at transfer of property and possession. Determining at what stage property passes from seller to buyer is important for two reasons.

(a) Risk of accidental loss or damage is, as a general rule, borne by the owner, so risk passes with ownership in a sale of goods.

(b) The rights of the parties against each other, and the rights of either party's creditors if one of them becomes insolvent, are also affected.

As with any other contract, a contract for the sale of goods may be breached. In addition to the usual common law remedies (damages and action for the price) the parties have rights peculiar to this type of contract. The remedies which are against goods are described as 'real remedies', all others are called 'personal remedies'.

Statutory references in this chapter are to the Sale of Goods Act 1979 unless otherwise noted.

Your objectives

After completing this chapter you should:

(a) know what constitutes a sale of goods;

(b) be able to define existing, future, specific and ascertained goods;

(c) know how the price for goods may be fixed;

(d) know what terms are implied by the Sale of Goods Act 1979 (as amended);

(e) know when time is of the essence;

(f) appreciate the significance of the seller's title and the consequences of defective , title;

(g) know what is meant by the description of goods, and the implied conditions in a sale by sample;

(h) know what is meant by satisfactory quality and by fitness for purpose;

(i)   know when property and risk pass to the buyer;

(j)   understand the rule *nemo dat quod non habet* and the exceptions to it;

(k)   be aware of the rules on delivery;

(l)   be aware of the limits on the buyer's right to reject the goods;

(m) know what remedies the parties may have against each other;

(n)   appreciate the effect of the Supply of Goods and Services Act 1982.

1   DEFINITION OF A CONTRACT FOR THE 'SALE OF GOODS'

Definition

Contract for the sale of goods: 'a contract by which the seller transfers, or agrees to transfer, the property in goods to a buyer for a money consideration, called the price' s 2 (1).

Sale includes both an immediate sale, such as purchase of goods in a shop, and an agreement by which the seller is to transfer ownership (in this context called 'property') in goods to the buyer at a future date.

2   TYPES OF GOODS

The rules on sale of goods make the following distinctions.

(a) *Existing goods* are those which exist and are owned by the seller at the time when the contract is made. *Future goods* are those which do not exist or which the seller does not yet own when he contracts to sell them. The main point of this distinction is that property (the ownership of the goods) cannot usually pass from seller to buyer unless, or until, the goods *exist* as specific or ascertained goods.

(b) *Specific goods* are those which are identified as the goods to be sold at the time when the contract is made, such as 'my Ford Escort, registration no H123 ABC'. Goods which are not specific are *unascertained* and become *ascertained goods* when they are subsequently identified as the goods to be sold under the contract.

2.1   Goods which have perished

In a contract for sale of specific goods there are rules laid down regarding the contract's status if the goods are perishable.

(a) If, unknown to the seller, the goods have perished at the time when the contract is made, the contract is void: s 6.

(b) If the goods perish after the contract is made, without fault of either party and before the risk passes to the buyer, the contract is avoided: s 7.

In addition to simple destruction, goods may 'perish' when they deteriorate to such an extent as to lose their commercial identity. The case law is concerned mainly with rotting of produce; it is a question of degree as to when they perish.

H R & S Sainsbury v Street 1972
S agreed to sell a 275 ton crop of barley to be grown on his farm to H. Due to general adverse conditions, his crop failed and only 140 tons were yielded.

These he sold at a higher price to a third party.

Held: although 135 tons of produce had perished so that the contract in that respect was frustrated, S should have offered the remainder to the plaintiff. Hence the contract as a whole had not been avoided.

Activity 1

A agrees to sell a car to B on hire purchase. B must pay regular hire charges for two years, and at the end of that period B will have an option to buy the car on payment of a further sum. Consider whether there is a contract for the sale of goods within the meaning of the Sale of Goods Act 1979.

---

3   THE PRICE

The definition states that there should be 'a money consideration, called the price'. This means that an exchange (barter) for other goods does not give rise to a sale of goods. However, provided some money changes hands, as with a trade-in arrangement for a car, there is a contract for the sale of goods even though goods are also given. But there can be complications regarding 'money consideration'.

Esso v Commissioners of Customs & Excise 1976
With every four gallons of petrol purchased from its filling stations, Esso promised to give away a free coin depicting a member of England's 1966 World Cup squad. Customs & Excise argued that this constituted a sale of goods and that therefore Esso had to pay purchase tax (now abolished) on all the World Cup coins it bought and gave away.

Held: there was a valid contract in respect of the World Cup coins, in that Esso had offered to give them away and any customer who purchased four gallons of petrol thereby accepted that offer and could enforce the contract. However, it was accepted that it was not a contract of sale, since the customer gave not a money consideration in return but a separate contract (for the purchase of petrol). There were two contracts, the one for the coins being a collateral contract to the one for the sale of petrol. The collateral contract was not one for the sale of goods.

Activity 2

If, in the case of *Esso v Commissioners of Customs & Excise 1976*, Esso had not offered a free coin with every four gallons of petrol but had instead offered 'four gallons of petrol and one World Cup coin for £2', would there have been a collateral contract for the coins?

The price may be fixed by the contract or in a manner set out in the contract, such as the ruling market price on the day of delivery, or by the course of dealing between the parties. If there is no agreed price, a reasonable price must be paid: s 8.

Foley v Classique Coaches 1934
A bus company agreed to purchase its petrol from F 'at a price to be agreed in writing from time to time'; any dispute between the parties was to be submitted to arbitration. For three years the bus company purchased its petrol from F at the current price but there was no formal agreement on price. The bus company then repudiated the agreement arguing that it was incomplete since it was an agreement to agree on the price.

Held: in view of the course of dealing between the parties and the arbitration clause there was an agreement that a reasonable price (at any given time) should be paid. The agreement was therefore enforceable.

4 TERMS IMPLIED BY THE SALE OF GOODS ACT 1979

One of the main functions of the Sale of Goods Act 1979 is to codify the terms implied into contracts of sale. As noted in Chapter 6, these have largely evolved from case law. Much depends on whether an implied term is a condition or a warranty, and on whether one party to the contract is dealing as a consumer.

The Sale of Goods Act 1979 states that conditions and warranties are both terms of the contract, unlike a representation, which is a statement of fact made by one party which induces the other party to enter into the contract. A *condition* is a central or important term of the contract. It is so essential to the contract that its non-fulfilment 'may give rise to a right to treat the contract as repudiated': s 11(3). A *warranty* is 'an agreement with reference to goods which are the subject of a contract of sale, but collateral to the main purpose of such contract, the breach of which gives rise to a claim for damages but not a right to reject the goods and treat the contract as repudiated': s 61.

A sale of goods may be subject to statutory rules on:

(a) the effect of delay in performance (s 10);

(b) title, or the seller's right to sell the goods (s 12);

(c) the description of the goods (s 13);

(d) sale by sample (s 15);

(e) the quality of the goods (s 14);

(f) the fitness of the goods for the purpose for which they are supplied (s 14).

In addition, the Unfair Contract Terms Act 1977 prohibits or restricts the possibility of modifying these statutory rules (other than those on time) by the use of exclusion clauses as follows.

(a) It is not possible to exclude or restrict:

    (i) the statutory terms on the seller's title (s 12) in any circumstances;

    (ii) the statutory terms relating to contract description or sample, quality or fitness for a purpose (ss 13-15) when the *buyer is dealing as a consumer*; that is when he is not buying in the course of a business but the seller is selling in the course of a business: ss 6 and 12 UCTA 1977.

(b) In a contract under which the buyer is not dealing as a consumer, that is when seller and buyer are both engaging in the transaction in the course of business, the terms of ss 13-15 may be excluded or restricted, but only if the exclusion or restriction satisfies the *statutory requirement of reasonableness*.

5 TIME OF PERFORMANCE (S 10)

Whether time of performance is of the essence depends on the terms of the contract. If it is, then breach of it is breach of a condition, which entitles the injured party to treat the contract as discharged. In commercial contracts for the supply of goods for business use, it will readily be assumed that time is of the essence even where there is no express term to that effect. Often one party is given a period of time within which to perform his obligation, say for delivery of goods. That party is not in breach until the whole period has elapsed without performance.

The contract may stipulate that the party should use his 'best endeavours' to perform his side by a certain time. If he fails to make that date, he must perform his obligations within a reasonable time. (Under s 29, similar reasonableness is required if no date is set by the contract.) In any case, time of performance stipulates a 'reasonable hour' for obligations to be performed: this is a question of fact. Hence it is not reasonable to offer delivery of perishable goods to a factory on the Friday evening before a two week shutdown of which the seller is aware.

Time for *payment* is not of the essence unless a different intention appears from the contract. For example A, a manufacturer, orders components from B and B fails to deliver by the agreed date. A can treat the contract as discharged and refuse to accept late delivery by B. But if B delivers a first instalment on time and A pays the price a week after the agreed date, B could not (under a continuing contract) refuse to make further deliveries, and treat the contract as discharged. If, however, A failed to pay altogether, that is not a delay in payment but rather a breach of an essential condition that the price is payable in exchange for the goods (unless otherwise agreed).

6   SELLER'S TITLE (S 12)

It is an implied *condition* that the seller has, or will have at the time when property in the goods is to be transferred, a right to sell the goods: s 12(1).

In the ordinary way the seller satisfies this condition if he has title to the goods at the moment when property is to pass to the buyer. (In this statutory code 'title' and 'property' are both used in different contexts to mean the same thing, ownership.) But the condition is broken if the seller, although he owns the goods, can be stopped by a third party from selling them: the right to transfer ownership is essential.

> *Niblett v Confectioners Materials 1921*
> A seller sold condensed milk in tins labelled with the name 'Nissly'. When the goods arrived in the UK the well known company Nestlé took legal action to have them detained as infringing the Nestlé trademark. The buyers were obliged to remove the labels from the tins in order to have them released from the customs warehouse in which they were held at the instance of Nestlé.
>
> *Held:* as Nestlé could have obtained an injunction to prevent the sale of the goods, the seller was in breach of the implied condition that he had a 'right to sell'.

If the seller delivers goods to the buyer without having the right to sell, there is a total failure of consideration, and the buyer does not obtain the ownership of the goods which is the essential basis of the contract. If the buyer has then to give up the goods to the real owner he may recover the entire price from the seller, without any allowance for the use of the goods meanwhile: *Rowland v Divall 1923*.

The seller also gives implied *warranties* that the buyer shall have quiet possession of the goods and that the goods are free of any encumbrance or challenge by a third party (unless disclosed to the buyer when the contract is made): s 12(2).

Exclusion of s 12

Although the seller cannot contract out of these terms by stipulating that they shall not apply, he can achieve a rather similar result by undertaking to transfer only such title as he (or some third party from whom he acquired the goods) may have (or have had). This stipulation puts the buyer on notice that the seller is uncertain of title. Furthermore, the seller must disclose to the buyer any charges or encumbrances of which the seller knows. But if the buyer is prepared to buy the goods on that basis he gets what he bargained for, and there is no breach of contract if the seller's title is imperfect.

Activity 3

A and B are in dispute over which of them owns some corn which is in A's possession. A sells the corn to C (who is unaware of the dispute) for £1,000. The dispute is then resolved in favour of B, who obtains possession of the corn from C. By that time its value has fallen to £800. Advise C as to his legal position.

7   DESCRIPTION OF THE GOODS (S 13)

In a contract for sale of goods by description, a *condition* is implied that the goods will correspond to the description. If a description is applied to the goods by the contract, it is a sale by description even though the buyer may have inspected the goods.

> *Beale v Taylor 1967*
> The defendant advertised a Triumph as a 'Herald convertible, white, 1961'. The plaintiff came to inspect the car and subsequently bought it. After buying the car he found that only the back half corresponded with the description. It had been welded to a front half which was part of an earlier Herald 948 model. The defendant relied on the buyer's inspection and argued that it was not a sale by description.
>
> *Held:* the advertisement described the car as a 1961 Herald, and this formed part of the contract description. It was a sale by description in spite of the buyer's pre-contract inspection.

If the buyer asked for the goods by stating his requirements and the seller then supplies them to those requirements that is also a sale by description. However if the buyer makes it clear that he is buying goods because of their unique qualities, and that no other item will meet his requirements, the sale is not a sale by description: *Harlingdon & Leinster Ltd v Christopher Hill Fine Art Ltd 1989*.

Where the sale is by sample as well as by description, the bulk must correspond to the sample *and* the description.

Compliance with the description must be complete and exact.

> *Arcos v E and A Ronaasen and Son 1933*
> The contract was for half-inch wooden staves. Some of the staves delivered by the seller were thicker than the measurements described.
>
> *Held:* The buyer was entitled to reject the consignment.

'Description' is widely interpreted to include ingredients, age, date of shipment, packing, quantity, and so on.

> *Re Moore & Co and Landauer & Co 1921*
> The buyers agreed to buy 3,000 tins of Australian canned fruit packed in cases of 30 tins. The correct total quantity was delivered, but it was found that half the goods were packed in cases of 24 tins.
>
> *Held:* although there was no difference in value there had been a breach of s 13 and the buyers were entitled to reject.

In this case it did not matter that there was no effect on the value of the goods. The decision has been criticised as being unduly technical, for example by Lord Diplock in the *Ashington Piggeries* case described later in this chapter: 'The "description" by which unascertained goods are sold is, in my view, confined to those words in the contract which were intended by the parties to identify the kind of goods which were to be supplied. It is open to the parties to use a description as broad or as narrow as they choose. But ultimately the test is whether the buyer could fairly and reasonably refuse to accept the physical goods offered to him on the grounds that their failure to correspond with what was said about them makes them goods of a different kind from those he had agreed to buy.'

If the seller uses a false description he may also commit an offence punishable under the Trade Descriptions Act 1968.

8 SALE BY SAMPLE (S 15)

In a sale by sample there are implied *conditions* that:

(a) the bulk corresponds in quality with the sample;

(b) the buyer shall have a reasonable opportunity of comparing the bulk with the sample; and

(c) the goods are free of any defect rendering them unsatisfactory which would not be apparent on a reasonable examination of the sample.

Activity 4

There is a contract for the sale of '200 cases of 1958 Bordeaux wine'. If the seller were to supply wine made in 1959, is it likely that he could rely on Lord Diplock's remarks in the *Ashington Piggeries* case to force the buyer to proceed with the purchase? Give reasons for your answer.

9 SATISFACTORY QUALITY (S 14 (2))

There is an implied condition that goods supplied under a contract are of satisfactory quality. This *condition* applies only to goods sold 'in the course of a business'; the seller must be carrying on a business or profession and make the sale in connection with that activity. Goods sold privately by a seller who is not selling in the course of a business therefore fall outside the scope of this section.

The condition applies to all 'goods supplied under the contract': not only to the goods themselves therefore but also to the packaging in which they are sold and also to any instructions provided for the use of the goods.

The condition that the goods supplied under the contract are of satisfactory quality is excluded if the buyer's attention is drawn to defects before the contract is made or the buyer examines the goods before the contract is made, and that examination ought to reveal the defects.

Under the original s 14(2), there was an implied conditions of merchantable quality. Under the Sale and Supply of Goods Act 1994, which came into force on 3 January 1995, the term 'merchantable' was replaced with the term 'satisfactory' designed to extend the law to cover more minor but niggling defects which cause consumer dissatisfaction. Satisfactory quality is met if the goods 'meet the standard that a reasonable person would regard as satisfactory, taking account of any description of the goods, the price (if relevant) and all other relevant circumstances'. The Act lists some of the attributes which are to be taken into account in deciding whether the goods are of satisfactory quality, including fitness for the purpose, appearance and finish, freedom from minor defects, safety and durability.

In *Rogers v Parish (Scarborough) Ltd 1987* the Court of Appeal criticised the practice of looking to case law to provide a suitable definition of satisfactory (at that time merchantable) quality and insisted that the statutory definition should be applied consistently and in isolation from decided cases: 'Goods are of satisfactory quality if they meet the standard that a reasonable person would regard as satisfactory, taking account of any description of the goods, the price (if relevant) and all the other relevant circumstances' s 14(2A).

The Act (s 14(2B)) identified factors which may in appropriate cases be aspects of the quality of goods.

(a) *Fitness for all the purposes for which goods of the kind in question are commonly supplied*. Under the old law, goods could be of merchantable quality if they were fit for one of their common purposes (as for example in *Aswan Engineering Establishment Co v Lupdine Ltd 1987*).

(b) *Appearance and finish*. This is one of the significant changes in the underlying law. Previously goods with superficial damage but which operated properly could be of merchantable quality. This aspect is likely to affect such matters as sales of new motor cars, an area in which there was much dissatisfaction with the old law.

(c) *Freedom from minor defects*. A series of minor defects could, under existing case law, render goods of unmerchantable quality (as for example in *Rogers v Parish 1987*).

(d) *Safety*. This is a new aspect, as there is no clear case law on this.

(e) *Durability*. Under the old law, it was generally accepted that goods had to be of merchantable quality only at the time of sale, although a later defect could be held to be evidence of unmerchantability at the date of sale (as for example in *Bristol Tramways v Fiat Motors 1910*). This aspect suggests that goods will have to remain of satisfactory quality for a period which could be expected by a reasonable person.

Activity 5

P sells an expensive new pen to Q. Q finds that it can only be made to write with difficulty. P claims that the pen is of satisfactory quality, because it can write and because its casing is perfect so that it can be used as a status symbol (as expensive pens sometimes are used). Consider whether P's claim is likely to be accepted by the courts.

---

10 FITNESS FOR PURPOSE (S 14(3))

This *condition* applies only to goods sold 'in the course of business'.

Where the buyer expressly or by implication makes known to the seller any particular purpose for which the goods are bought, it is an implied condition that the goods supplied under the contract are reasonably fit for that purpose (whether or not that is the common purpose of such goods), unless the circumstances show that the buyer does not rely, or that it is unreasonable for him to rely, on the skill or judgment of the seller.

A buyer may specify the 'particular purpose' quite broadly without listing all possible uses within that particular purpose. Thus where a substance is commonly used as fertiliser or as animal feedstuff it is sufficient to specify the latter without naming each kind of animal to which it might be fed.

Ashington Piggeries v Christopher Hill 1972

B gave S a recipe for mink food and requested that S should mix the food in accordance with the recipe and supply it to B. S told B that they had never supplied mink food before although they were manufacturers of animal foodstuffs. One of the ingredients was herring meal which had been stored in a chemical which created a poisonous substance damaging to all animals but particularly damaging to mink. As a result many of the mink died.

Held: because the poison affected all animals the food was unfit for its disclosed purpose since B relied on S's skill and judgement to the extent that S was an animal food manufacturer and should not have supplied a generally harmful food. If the poison had only affected mink then B's skill and judgement demonstrated by its supply of a recipe would have made it unreasonable to rely on S's skill or judgement.

If the goods have only one obvious purpose, the buyer by implication makes known his purpose merely by asking for the goods.

Priest v Last 1903

A customer at a chemist's shop asked for a hot water bottle and was told, in answer to a question, that it would withstand hot water but should not be filled with boiling water. It burst after only five days in use.

Held: if there is only one purpose, that particular purpose is disclosed by buying the goods. Because it was not an effective hot water bottle, there was a breach of s 14(3). (This was followed by *Frost v Aylesbury Dairy Co 1905*: in the purchase of milk supplied to a domestic address the buyer discloses his purpose, which is human consumption.)

There are two further variations on the interpretation of 'particular purpose'. Where goods are required for a particular purpose which is *not obvious* to the seller or where they are required for a *particular* purpose known to the seller but there is some peculiarity about that purpose, the buyer must make clear to the seller the particular purpose or the peculiarity involved.

Manchester Liners v Rea 1922

The defendant supplied coal for a particular ship. The coal was unsuitable for that ship but would have been suitable for other ships.

Held: coal merchants knew well enough that ships differed in their types and requirements. If a merchant undertook to supply coal for a particular ship, he must supply coal suitable for that ship.

Griffiths v Peter Conway Ltd 1939

The plaintiff contracted dermatitis from a Harris Tweed coat purchased from the defendants. She had an unusually sensitive skin and the coat would not have harmed a normal person.

Held: the plaintiff's sensitive skin rendered the required use so special that she had not made known the particular purpose for which the coat was to be used.

Even partial reliance of the buyer on the seller's skill or judgement makes the latter subject to the condition.

,Cammell Laird v Manganese Bronze & Brass Co 1934

Shipbuilders ordered a ship's propeller to be manufactured by a specialist contractor. The buyers specified the materials and certain dimensions but left other details to the seller's judgement. The propeller was unsuitable due to defects in a matter not covered by the specification.

Held: partial reliance on the seller's skill and judgement is sufficient to bring the condition into operation as regards matters left to the seller to determine.

Activity 6

R buys a filing cabinet from S, who runs an office furniture shop. R tells S that he will use the cabinet to store land certificates issued by the Land Registry, and asks S whether the cabinet is of the right size for such certificates. S replies that he does not know how large land certificates are, but R goes ahead and buys the cabinet. If the cabinet proved to be too small, why could R not claim that S had breached the condition of reasonable fitness?

---

11 PASSING OF PROPERTY AND RISK

In determining when property in goods passes the following general principles apply.

(a) No property can pass in goods which are unascertained and not yet identified as the goods to be sold under the contract: s 16.

(b) The property in specific or ascertained goods is transferred to the buyer at the time when the parties *intend* it to be transferred. Their intention may be deduced from the terms of the contract, the conduct of the parties and the circumstances of the case: s 17.

(c) Unless a different intention appears (and the parties can agree upon whatever terms they like) the rules of s 18 are applied to ascertain what their intention is on the passing of property to the buyer.

Many contracts for the supply of goods contain a clause stating that title to the goods remains with the seller until the contract price is paid. Such 'retention of title' or *'Romalpa'* clauses are a common example of the s 17 rule that title to specific goods passes when the parties so intend.

11.1 Passing of property: the s 18 rules

Rule 1. If the contract is unconditional and the goods are specific or identified, property passes when the contract is made. It is immaterial that the seller has not yet delivered the goods or that the buyer has not yet paid the price. However, the seller may, and often does, stipulate that property shall not pass until the price is paid. If the seller insists on retaining the goods or documents relating to them (such as the registration book of a car which has been sold) until the price is paid then it will readily be inferred that he intended (and the buyer agreed) that property would not pass on making the contract, but only on payment of the price.

Rule 2. If, under a contract for sale of specific goods, the seller is bound to do something to put the goods into a deliverable state, property does not pass until the seller has done what is required of him and the buyer has notice of this.

Underwood v Burgh Castle Brick and Cement Syndicate 1922
The plaintiffs entered into a contract for the sale of a condensing engine to be loaded onto a railway wagon. At the time of making the contract the engine, which weighed over 30 tons, was embedded in cement foundations at a factory. It was expected that it would take the sellers about two weeks to dismantle it. In loading it into the railway wagon the sellers broke part of the machine. The buyers refused to accept it.

Held: property had not passed when the contract was made, because the engine was not in such a condition that the defendants had to take delivery of it. At the time of the damage the engine was still in the sellers' ownership and so at their risk. The buyers were entitled to reject it in its damaged state and to refuse to pay the price.

Rule 3. Where there is a contract for the sale of specific goods in a deliverable state but the seller is bound to weigh, measure or test them to fix the price, property passes when he has done so and the buyer has notice of this. The rule does not apply when it is the buyer who must take this action.

Rule 4. When goods are delivered to the buyer on approval, that is on sale or return terms, the property passes to the buyer when:

(a) he signifies to the seller that he approves, or indicates approval by dealing with them; or

(b) he retains the goods beyond the time fixed for their return without giving notice of rejection or, if no time has been fixed, if he retains them beyond a reasonable time.

Rule 5. When there is a contract for the sale of unascertained or future goods by description, and goods of that description and in a deliverable state are unconditionally appropriated to the contract by the seller with the assent of the buyer, or by the buyer with the assent of the seller, the property then passes to the buyer.

Such assent may be express or implied and given before or after the appropriation is made. For example, if the buyer orders goods to be supplied from the seller's stock he gives implied assent to the seller to make an appropriation from his stock.

To bring rule 5 into operation, something more definite is required than merely selecting or setting aside goods for delivery to the buyer. The act must be irrevocable, for example where the seller sets aside goods and also informs the buyer that they are ready for collection.

Delivery of goods to the buyer, or to a carrier for transmission to the buyer, without reserving to the seller a right of disposal, is an unconditional appropriation which brings rule 5 into operation. However, delivery to a carrier does not pass the property if identical goods destined to be sent to different buyers are mixed and need to be counted or sorted by the carrier.

Healey v Howlett & Sons 1917
The defendant ordered 20 boxes of mackerel from the plaintiff. 190 boxes were despatched, instructions being given to railway officials to set aside 20 for the defendant and the rest for two other buyers. The train was delayed before this was done and by the time the officials were ready to set them aside the fish had deteriorated badly.

Held: neither property nor risk had passed before the boxes were set aside.

Rule 5 only applies to appropriation of goods in a deliverable state.

Philip Head & Sons v Showfronts 1970
The parties entered into a contract for supply and laying of carpet at the buyer's premises. A roll of carpet was delivered but it was stolen before it could be laid.

Held: the carpet was deliverable to the buyer when laid and not before. It was the seller's property when stolen. The risk of loss remained with him.

Activity 7

On Monday, a contract is made for the sale of goods which are unascertained at that time. On Tuesday, the seller takes goods from stock and decides that these are the goods to be supplied to the buyer. However, the goods must first be packed. This is done on

Wednesday and the buyer is notified on Thursday that this has been done and that the goods are ready for collection. Identify the day on which property in the goods passes to the buyer.

The Sale of Goods (Amendment) Act 1995 is now in force. It deals with the passing of ownership in goods which are unascertained in the sense that they have not been set aside for the buyer but are nevertheless to come from an ascertained source – 'I will buy 20 boxes of goods out of the stock of 60 boxes being transported to Doncaster by train.' If there is no appropriation of a particular 20 boxes to the buyer, the ownership remains with the seller and if the seller goes insolvent, the goods are available for sale by the relevant insolvency practitioner. This is particularly unfortunate where the buyer has made a whole or partial pre-payment. The goods do not belong to him and he cannot recover the pre-payment but only some form of dividend in the insolvency which may be worthless.

12 NEMO DAT QUOD NON HABET

The general rule is that only the owner, or an agent acting with his authority, can transfer the title in goods to a buyer. This is expressed in the Latin maxim *nemo dat quod non habet*: no one can give what he does not have. To the general rule there are a number of *exceptions* to protect an honest buyer against loss.

Agency (s 21). If an ordinary agent sells goods without actual or apparent authority, there is usually no transfer of title to the buyer. But a mercantile agent, that is an agent whose business is selling goods for others, may have possession of goods (or documents of title to them) with the owner's consent. He can then sell them, in the ordinary course of his business, to a buyer who buys in good faith and without notice that the agent had no authority to sell (or was exceeding his authority). The buyer acquires title to the goods: s 21.

Estoppel. If, by his conduct, the true owner leads the buyer to believe that the person who makes the sale owns the goods, the true owner is prevented (estopped) from denying the seller's authority to sell. Merely to put goods in the possession of another is not to represent that he is the owner.

Market overt (s 22). This longstanding exception to the *nemo dat* rule was abolished by the Sale of Goods (Amendment) Act 1994.

Sale under voidable title (s 23). A person may acquire goods under a contract which is voidable, say for misrepresentation. He then has title to the goods until the contract is avoided. If, before the sale to him is avoided, he re-sells to a person who buys in good faith and without notice of his defective title, that buyer obtains a good title to the goods. Normally the first contract of sale is not avoided until the person entitled to avoid it communicates his decision to the other party but if that party has disappeared other evidence of intention to avoid the first sale, such as reporting the matter to the police, will suffice: *Car & Universal Finance Co v Caldwell 1965*.

Re-sale by seller in possession (s 24). If a seller, or a mercantile agent acting for him, continues in possession of the goods (or documents of title to them) after a sale, and he makes a delivery of them to a person who receives them in good faith and without notice of the previous sale, the transaction takes effect as if the seller were authorised for that purpose.

Suppose that A sells specific goods to B and B, to whom the ownership of the goods passes, immediately leaves them in A's possession until B can collect them. A by mistake then re-sells the goods and delivers them to C, who is unaware of the previous sale to B. C gets good title to the goods; B's only remedy is to sue A. But if A does not actually deliver the goods to C, B has the better right.

Re-sale by a buyer in possession (s 25). The seller may permit the buyer to take possession of the goods before ownership has passed to the buyer, as when the seller makes delivery but retains title until the price is paid. If the buyer then makes a re-sale or other disposition in the normal course of business as mercantile agent, with actual delivery or transfer of the goods (or documents of title), to a person who takes them in good faith and without notice of the original seller's rights, title passes to that person as if the buyer had acted as a mercantile agent. This applies even if the buyer has a voidable title which is actually avoided (say by notifying police of the buyer's lack of title).

> *Newtons of Wembley v Williams 1965*
> X purchased a car and paid the price by cheque. The seller stipulated that title to the car should not pass until the cheque was cleared, but allowed X to take possession of the car. The cheque was dishonoured and the sellers informed the police and thereby avoided the sale to X in the only way available to them. But X sold the car for cash in an established secondhand car market to Y who took delivery forthwith.
>
> *Held:* Y acquired good title since X was a buyer in possession with the seller's consent and the re-sale in the market was a disposition in the ordinary course of business of a mercantile agent. The loss must fall on the original seller if he could not recover from X.

To be a buyer in possession, the person must have obtained possession of the goods or documents of title to goods *with the seller's consent.* It is immaterial that the seller withdraws consent after the buyer has obtained possession, and that the latter obtains possession after contracting to sell to the innocent purchaser. He is a buyer in possession provided he obtains possession before delivering possession to the innocent purchaser: *Cahn v Pockett's Bristol Channel Steam Packet Co 1899.*

However, s 25 does not allow good title to be given to an innocent purchaser from a buyer in possession if the latter had obtained possession from a 'seller' not entitled to sell, that is, a thief: *National Mutual General Insurance Association Ltd v Jones 1988.*

The sale of a motor vehicle acquired under hire purchase. By the Hire Purchase Act 1964 a private (but not a trade) purchaser of a motor vehicle sold by a hirer under a hire purchase agreement or a buyer under a conditional sale agreement obtains good title (even though the seller had none) if the purchaser takes the vehicle in good faith and without notice that it was only let on hire purchase. The innocent buyer's purchase may be an ordinary sale or a hire purchase or conditional sale agreement. If there are intermediaries who are not private purchasers, the protection is available only to the first private purchaser. For example, A, who has a car under a hire purchase agreement, purports to sell it to B, a car dealer, who sells it to C, a private purchaser. B does not obtain title but C does. This is so even if B is a car dealer buying a vehicle for private, not business, purposes: *Stevenson v Beverley-Bentinck 1976.*

Activity 8

R buys a car and pays with a fraudulent cheque. The seller is unable to communicate with him, but informs the police and the AA of the fraud. R resells the car to J. Does J get good title to the car?

Special powers of sale. The court may order goods to be sold. Various persons, such as pawnbrokers, unpaid sellers, hotel keepers and bailees (such as dry cleaners) in possession of abandoned goods for which charges are owing, have specific powers of sale.

Activity 9

Peter sells a car bearing the distinctive registration number DAWN 10 to Dawn Smith, who tells her friend Dawn Jones that she has just bought this car. The car is still with Peter when Dawn Jones calls on him, and attempts to buy the same car. Peter confuses the two Dawns, accepts Dawn Jones's cash and allows her to take the car away. When Dawn Smith claims the car from her, Dawn Jones relies on Section 24 of the Sale of Goods Act 1979 to retain the car.

Consider whether the car belongs to Dawn Jones or Dawn Smith.

13 DELIVERY

Unless otherwise agreed, the seller is entitled to receive the price before delivering the goods to the buyer, but he must deliver them as soon as the price is paid: s 28. The parties may agree on whatever delivery arrangements may suit them. But unless otherwise agreed the following rules apply.

(a) *Method.* Delivery is the voluntary transfer of possession from one person to another (s 61). It may be by physical transfer of possession, or of the means of control (such as the key of a warehouse) or by arranging that a third party who has the goods acknowledges ('attorns') to the buyer that he holds them on his behalf, or by delivery of a document of title to the goods.

(b) *Place.* Delivery is to be made at the seller's place of business or, if he has none, at his residence, unless the goods are specific and, to the knowledge of both parties when the contract is made, the goods are at some other place. Delivery is, in those circumstances, to be at that other place.

(c) *Time.* If no time is agreed, delivery is to be made within a reasonable time and at a reasonable hour: s 29(5).

(d) *Expense.* The seller bears the expense of putting the goods into a deliverable state (for example by packing or bagging them).

Delivery by instalment

Unless otherwise agreed the buyer is not obliged to accept delivery by instalments: s 30(1). He may reject a delivery of part only of the goods.

If the contract does provide for delivery by instalments with separate payment for each instalment, the contract is *severable or divisible.* If one or more instalments under a severable contract are defective, this may amount to repudiation of the entire contract or it may merely give a right to claim compensation for the defective deliveries only. It depends on the ratio of defective to sound deliveries and the likelihood or otherwise that future instalments will also be defective.

If the seller delivers the wrong quantity the buyer may reject the whole quantity, but if he accepts what is delivered he must pay at the contract rate for the quantity accepted. When the seller delivers too much the buyer may also accept the correct quantity and reject the rest: s 30.

If the seller delivers the contract goods mixed with other goods the buyer may reject the whole or accept the contract goods and reject others: s 30.

Where the contract requires that the goods be moved in the course of delivery:

(a) delivery to a carrier for transmission to the buyer is deemed to be delivery to the buyer unless the contrary intention appears, as when the seller consigns the goods to himself or his agent at their destination: s 32;

(b) the seller must make a reasonable arrangement with the carrier and (if the goods are sent by sea) give the buyer notice in time to permit the buyer to arrange insurance: s 32;

(c) the buyer must bear the risk of any deterioration necessarily incidental to the course of transit: s 33.

14 ACCEPTANCE AND REJECTION

Acceptance of goods or part of them (unless the contract is severable), deprives the buyer of his right to treat the contract as discharged by breach of condition (for example, as to the quality of the goods) on the part of the seller. But he may claim damages.

The buyer is not deemed to have accepted the goods until he has had a reasonable opportunity of examining them for the purpose of ascertaining whether they are in conformity with the contract: s 34. The buyer is deemed to have accepted the goods in the following circumstances (s 35, as amended by Sale and Supply of Goods Act 1994).

(a) When he intimates to the seller that he has accepted them, provided that he has had a reasonable opportunity of ascertaining whether they are in conformity with the contract;

(b) When the goods have been delivered to the buyer and he does any act in relation to them which is inconsistent with the ownership of the seller, for example, using or reselling them;

(c) When after the lapse of a reasonable time he retains the goods without intimating to the seller that he has rejected them. In determining whether a reasonable time has elapsed, one factor is whether the buyer has been afforded a reasonable opportunity of examination, for example by use. In the case of *Bernstein v Pamsons Motors 1987*, a buyer whose new car was neither of merchantable quality nor fit for the purpose, but who had used the car for three weeks and 140 miles, was unable to rescind the contract. Such a case might be decided differently under the revised legislation.

Where the seller has breached a condition the buyer may treat the contract as repudiated and hence reject the goods. The buyer does not have to return the goods to the seller – he merely has to inform the seller of his rejection: s 36.

The buyer loses his right to reject goods if:

(a) he waives the breached condition;

(b) he elects to treat the breach of condition as a breach of warranty;

(c) he has accepted the goods (in a contract which is not severable); or

(d) he is unable to return the goods because, for example, he has sold them on to a buyer who keeps them.

Activity 10

The parties to a contract for the sale of non-perishable goods agree that the goods shall be delivered to the buyer's premises 'during normal business hours'. The seller then states that the only time of day that the goods can be delivered is 10 pm and that the goods must be accepted or rejected immediately on delivery. At that time a caretaker will be present to receive the goods, but he is not competent to inspect them. In what ways has the seller failed to meet his legal obligations?

15 THE PARTIES' REMEDIES

As with any other contract, one for sale of goods may be breached. Aside from the usual common law remedies (damages, action for the price, and so on) the parties have rights peculiar to this type of contract. They are categorised as:

(a) the seller's remedies against the goods;

(b) the seller's remedies against the buyer;

(c) the buyer's remedies against the seller.

The remedies which are against goods are described as ' real remedies'; all others are called ' personal remedies'.

15.1 The seller's remedies against the goods

Ownership of goods often passes to the buyer before they are delivered to the buyer in exchange for the price. If the buyer then defaults, for example by failing to pay the price when due, the seller is given rights against the goods in his possession or under his control although those goods are now owned by the buyer. It is usually more satisfactory to him to retain the goods than merely to sue a buyer, who may well be insolvent, for breach of contract.

These rights are given only to an 'unpaid seller' (s 38). He is unpaid if either:

(a) the whole of the price has not been paid or tendered to him; or

(b) he has received a bill of exchange and the bill has been dishonoured.

An unpaid seller of goods which are now the property of the buyer has the following statutory rights in respect of the goods (s 39):

(a) a *lien* on the goods so long as they are in his possession;

(b) a right of stoppage *in transitu* if the buyer is insolvent and the goods are in the hands of a carrier;

(c) a right of *resale* in certain circumstances.

Lien

Definition

Lien: the seller's right to retain the goods in his possession until the price is paid or tendered (s 41).

The unpaid seller's right of lien applies:

(a) where the goods are sold without any stipulation as to credit;

(b) where they have been sold on credit terms but the credit period has expired; or

(c) where the buyer becomes insolvent.

Even if part of the goods have been delivered to the buyer, the unpaid seller has a lien on the rest unless part delivery indicates his agreement to give up his lien altogether: s 42.

The unpaid seller loses his lien when he delivers the goods to a carrier or warehouseman for transmission to the buyer (unless the seller reserves a right of disposal), or when the buyer or his agent lawfully obtains possession of the goods, or when the seller waives his lien: s 43.

Lien merely gives a right to retain possession until the price is paid. It does not rescind the contract, deprive the buyer of his ownership nor entitle the seller to re-sell the goods.

Stoppage in transitu

The right of stoppage *in transitu* (s 44-45) exists when the buyer becomes insolvent. He is insolvent if he has ceased to pay his debts in the ordinary course of business or cannot pay his debts as they fall due: it is not necessary to wait until he becomes bankrupt.

While goods are in transit, neither seller nor buyer has possession of the goods since they are in the possession of a carrier. The unpaid seller may stop the goods in transit by issuing an order to the carrier. The goods cease to be in transit and the seller's right of stoppage ends:

(a) on delivery to the buyer or his agent (whether at the appointed destination or before);

(b) if the carrier acknowledges to the buyer or his agent that the goods (arrived at their original destination) are now held on behalf of the buyer. It is immaterial that the buyer may have indicated to the carrier that the goods are to be taken on to a further destination; or

(c) if the carrier wrongfully refuses to make delivery to the buyer or his agent.

But if the buyer refuses to accept the goods which remain in the possession of the carrier, they are still in transit.

Activity 11

A seller of goods consigns them to a carrier for transmission to the buyer, thereby ending his lien. Why is the seller's lien not automatically replaced by a right of stoppage *in transitu* at that point?

Right of resale

As between the unpaid seller and the buyer of the goods, the seller has a *right of resale*:

(a) if the goods are of a perishable nature;

(b) if the seller gives notice to the buyer of his intention to re-sell and the buyer fails within a reasonable time to pay or tender the price; or

(c) If the seller reserves a right of resale under the contract.

If the seller does not, by resale, recover the full amount of his loss he may sue the buyer for damages for breach of contract: s 48. On a sale in these circumstances the second buyer gets good title to the goods.

15.2 Retention of title clauses

Many commercial contracts now contain a retention of title clause, often known as a *Romalpa* clause after the case discussed below. Under such a clause, possession may pass to the buyer but ownership does not pass until the price is paid.

Aluminium Industrie Vaassen BV v Romalpa Ltd 1976
Romalpa purchased aluminium foil on terms that the stock of foil (and any proceeds of sale) should be the property of the Dutch supplier until the company had paid to the supplier all that it owed. Romalpa got into financial difficulties and a receiver was appointed. The receiver found that the company still held aluminium foil and proceeds of selling other stocks of foil, and had not paid its debt to the supplier. The receiver applied to the court to determine whether or not the foil and the cash were assets of the company under his control as receiver.

Held: the conditions of sale were valid. The relevant assets, although in the possession of the company, did not belong to it. The receiver could not deal with these assets since his authority under the floating charge was restricted to assets of the company.

The extent to which a *Romalpa* clause protects an unpaid seller depends to a great extent on the wording of the actual clause. A retention of title clause may be effective even though goods are resold or incorporated into the buyer's products so as to lose their identity *if* it expressly states that they can be used in these ways before title has passed: *Clough Mill Ltd v Martin 1985.*

Unless the clause expressly retains title even after resale or incorporation, the supplier is not entitled to a proportionate part of the sale proceeds of the manufactured product: *Borden (UK) Ltd v Scottish Timber Products Ltd 1979.* Where there is no express provision, resale or incorporation is conversion of the supplier's property but a third party will still get good title.

If the buyer resells the goods when there is an express provision allowing resale before title passes, the proceeds of sale are held by the buyer as trustee for the supplier.

A reservation of title clause can cover, besides the price of the goods specifically subject of the particular contract of sale, other debts due to the seller under unrelated contracts.

Armour and Carron Co Ltd v Thyssen Edelstahlwerke AG 1990
The defendants transferred possession in steel strip to a buyer under a contract of sale. The buyer agreed that it would not acquire the property (ownership) until *all* amounts due to the defendant had been paid. The plaintiffs were appointed receivers of the assets of the buyer; the steel strip had not been paid for. The buyer argued that the clause was an attempt to create a security over moveable property and that it was therefore void.

Held: it was not possible to create a security over goods which you did not own. Under Sale of Goods Act s 19(1) 'where there is a contract for the sale of specific goods … the seller may … reserve the right to disposal of the goods until certain conditions are fulfilled'. The defendant had reserved this right until fulfilment of the condition that *all* the buyer's debts had been paid, including those due under other contracts. They therefore remained owners of the steel strip.

Registrable charges

The buyer may seek to demonstrate that a retention clause creates a *charge* which should be registered under s 396 Companies Act 1985. This would render the clause inoperative if no such registration had taken place, as failure to register such a charge causes it to be void. However, in cases such as *Romalpa* and *Armour* this claim cannot succeed, as s 396 can only apply to charges over the property of the buyer, and the goods do not belong to the buyer.

15.3 The seller's remedies against the buyer

The seller has two possible remedies against the buyer personally.

(a) He may bring an *action for the price* if:

    (i) the ownership of the goods has passed to the buyer and he wrongfully neglects or refuses to pay the price according to the terms of the contract; or

    (ii) the price is payable on a certain day (regardless of delivery) and the buyer wrongfully neglects or refuses to pay it.

(b) The seller may *sue for damages for non-acceptance* if the buyer wrongfully refuses or neglects to accept and pay for the goods. In this case the claim may include any expense incurred by the seller (for example in storing the goods) caused by the buyer's failure to take delivery after being requested to do so.

When the seller claims damages, the first head of the rule in *Hadley v Baxendale* applies. If there is an available market for this type of goods, the measure of damages is usually the difference between the contract price and the market price on the day when the goods should have been accepted.

Activity 12

Some nuts and bolts are sold to Z Ltd subject to a retention of title clause, the full text of which is as follows.

'Property in the goods shall not pass to the buyer until the buyer has paid for the goods in full'.

Before paying for the nuts and bolts, Z Ltd incorporates them into electric motors which are sold. If Z Ltd fails to pay for the nuts and bolts, what remedy might the supplier seek?

15.4 The buyer's remedies against the seller

If the seller is in *breach of a condition* of the contract, the buyer may reject the goods unless he has lost his right to do so by accepting the goods or part of them. In addition he may claim damages.

If the buyer has paid the price and the consideration has failed entirely, for example if the seller has no title or delivers goods which the buyer is entitled to reject, the buyer may sue to recover the price: s 54.

If there is a *breach of a warranty* by the seller, or if the buyer is obliged (or prefers) to deal with a breach of a condition by a claim for damages, the buyer may either reduce the amount paid to the seller by an allowance for the breach or sue for damages. The amount of damages is determined on principles similar to those of the seller's claim against the buyer.

It is open to the buyer to base his claim on any circumstances within the general scope of these rules.

Mason v Burningham 1949
The plaintiff had been sold a typewriter which turned out to be stolen property. She had to return it to the owner. In addition to the price paid she claimed damages for breach of implied warranty of quiet enjoyment including her expenditure in having the typewriter overhauled.

Held: damages should be awarded as claimed.

A buyer may also claim damages for non-delivery, calculated on the same principles as described earlier when a seller claims damages. This claim may be made if the seller either fails to deliver altogether or delivers goods which the buyer is entitled to, and does, reject.

The buyer's claim for damages for loss of profit or liability for damages arising on that contract is not affected by a resale by him, unless it can be shown that the parties to the original sale contemplated that there would be a resale.

Williams v Agius 1914
There was a contract for the sale of coal at 16s 3d [81p] per ton. The buyers resold at 19s 6d [97p] per ton. The market price at the date for delivery was 23s 6d [£1.17]. per ton. The sellers failed to deliver. The sellers contended that the buyer's actual loss was the difference between the contract price (16s.3d) and the resale price (19s.6d) per ton only.

Held: the buyers should be awarded damages of 7s 3d [36p] per ton, the full difference between the market price and the contract price; the resale contract should be ignored.

In an action for breach of contract to deliver specific or ascertained goods, the court may order specific performance or delivery of the goods. But it will only do so if damages would be an inadequate remedy: s 51.

Activity 13

Why, in a case such as *Williams v Agius 1914*, might the buyer/reseller's loss (for which he would need to be compensated) be the difference between the full market price (23s 6d per ton in that case) and the originally agreed price (16s.3d per ton)?

16 THE SUPPLY OF GOODS AND SERVICES ACT 1982

The Supply of Goods and Services Act 1982 (SGSA 1982) applies to certain contracts which do not fall within the definition of a sale of goods even though they do involve a transfer of ownership. The types of transaction which are covered by the Act include:

(a) *contracts of exchange or barter:* these are not contracts of sale of goods because there is no money consideration involved;

(b) *contracts of repair:* although some goods are supplied (for example spare parts) the substance of the contract is the provision of services (see below);

(c) *contracts of hire:* these are not contracts for the sale of goods because they contain no provision for ownership to pass to the hirer;

(d) *collateral contracts to the sale of goods :* for example, where a person buys a car and receives a free set of seat covers as part of a special deal, the purchase of the car is governed by the Sale of Goods Act 1979 but the seat covers, for which consideration was given by buying the car, are part of a collateral contract governed by the Supply of Goods and Services Act 1982.

The Act specifically does not cover contracts of apprenticeship or employment (s 12).

If the main purpose of a contract is, for example, the provision of skilled labour, whilst an ancillary object is the transfer of ownership of goods, the contract is one governed by the 1982 Act.

The general effect of the Act is to provide safeguards similar to those provided by the Sale of Goods Act in respect of contracts for sale of goods. Where the supply of goods is a part of the transaction, ss 2-5 of the 1982 Act imply certain terms relating to the goods. The terms implied relate to the goods supplied and are similar to those of the Sale of Goods Act 1979, dealing with strict liability regarding:

(a) title, freedom from encumbrances and quiet possession (s 2);

(b) description (s 3);

(c) satisfactory quality and fitness for purpose (s 4);

(d) sample (s 5).

Under the Unfair Contract Terms Act 1977, clauses purporting to exclude or restrict liability under these headings are subject to the same rules as similar exclusion clauses in sale of goods contracts.

Where the contract is wholly or substantially for the provision of services, the 1982 Act implies a number of further terms.

(a) Where the supplier of the service is acting in the course of a business, there are implied terms that he will carry out the service with reasonable care and skill (s 13) and within a reasonable time (s 14).

(b) Where the consideration is not determined by the contract, there is an implied term that the party contracting with the supplier will pay a reasonable charge (s 15).

These terms are implied whether there is a supply of goods or not. But they are *not* conditions of strict liability, and may be excluded so long as such exclusion complies with the reasonableness requirement of the Unfair Contract Terms Act 1977: s 16 SGSA 1982.

Activity 14

Robinson v Graves 1935 concerned a contract to paint a portrait. *Marcel (Furriers) Ltd v Tapper 1953* concerned a contract for the supply of a mink jacket of a special style made to the customer's requirements. In both cases materials were worked on by skilled persons, but in one case it was held that there was a sale of goods and in the other case it was held that there was a supply of services. In which case do you think it was held that there was a sale of goods?

Chapter roundup

- Contracts for the sale of goods are subject to the Sale of Goods Act 1979 as amended by the Sale and Supply of Goods Act 1994. In considering such contracts, we must distinguish between existing and future goods, and between specific and unascertained goods.

- If the price for goods is not determined by the contract then a reasonable price must be paid.

- The Sale of Goods Act 1979 implies several terms into contracts for the sale of goods, and the Unfair Contract Terms Act 1977 limits the extent to which these implied terms may be overridden.

- If time is not of the essence, it may be made so. Performance must be tendered at a reasonable time.

- There is an implied condition that the seller of goods has a right to sell, but the seller may put the buyer on notice that his title may be defective.

- In a sale by description, the goods must match the description given. In a sale by sample, the bulk must correspond to the sample.

- Goods are of satisfactory quality if they meet the standard that a reasonable person would regard as satisfactory.

- If the seller of goods knows the purpose for which the goods are being bought, it is normally an implied condition that the goods are reasonably fit for that purpose.

- The property in goods passes when the parties intend that it shall pass. Where such intention is not otherwise made clear, the rules of s 18 Sale of Goods Act 1979 apply to fix the time. Goods are generally at the buyer's risk from the time that property passes.

Chapter roundup *continued*

- A person not owning goods cannot in general transfer title to a buyer. However, there are several exceptions to protect an innocent buyer.

- Goods must be delivered as agreed, but there are rules which apply in the absence of agreement.

- A buyer must be given an opportunity to inspect and if necessary reject goods, but once he has accepted the goods, either explicitly or by conduct, he cannot later reject them.

- An unpaid seller of goods may be able to retrieve the goods even if title has passed to the buyer. He may also attempt to protect his position by retaining title until he has been paid. Failing such remedies, the seller may sue the buyer. If the seller breaches a condition of the contract, the buyer may reject the goods. The buyer may also sue the seller for breaches of conditions or warranties.

- The Sale of Goods Act 1979 applies only to sales of goods. The Supply of Goods and Services Act 1982 makes similar provisions for contracts outside the scope of the 1979 Act.

Quick quiz

1   What topics are covered by statutory conditions implied (as part of the contract) by the Sale of Goods Act 1979?

2   What is the implied condition as to the seller's right to sell the goods?

3   What is a sale of goods by description and what is implied in such a sale?

4   When are defects of quality not a breach of the condition of satisfactory quality?

5   What is satisfactory quality?

6   In what circumstances is it an implied condition that the goods shall be fit for the purpose for which they are bought?

7   State (in outline) the statutory rules which determine when property in goods passes. Do these rules apply to every sale of goods?

8   Give three exceptions to the rule *nemo dat quod non habet*.

9   What is a severable contract?

10 When is a buyer deemed to have accepted goods?

11 What are the seller's remedies if he is not paid?

12 What is a retention of title clause?

13 What are the buyer's remedies for breach of contract?

14 What terms are implied into a contract which is wholly or substantially for the provision of services?

Solutions to activities

1   This is not a contract for the sale of goods because there is no agreement to transfer ownership of the car until B exercises the option to buy.

2   No: there would have been a single contract to sell petrol and coins for cash.

3   C may recover the entire price (£1,000) from the seller, A, because C did not receive ownership of the corn and the depreciation in value is irrelevant.

4   No: although 1959 is very close to 1958, the exact year is crucial for wine.

5   P's argument would fail because, although the pen can be made to write with difficulty, this is not the standard of quality expected from an expensive pen.

6   S made it clear that he did not have the skill or judgement on which R sought to rely.

7   Property passes on Thursday under Rule 2 of s 18 Sale of Goods Act 1979.

8   No: This is a case of sale under voidable title and the seller has rescinded the contract by taking all reasonable steps.

9   The car belongs to Dawn Smith because Dawn Jones has attempted to purchase the car while having notice of the previous sale and acting in bad faith. Section 24 does not apply.

10 Ten pm is not during normal business hours, and the seller has not given the buyer a reasonable opportunity to inspect the goods.

11 The buyer may not become insolvent, or the carrier may be the buyer's agent.

12 The seller may bring an action for the price. The retention of title clause does not mention incorporation into Z Ltd's products, so it cannot be relied upon in this case.

13 The buyer/reseller might have to buy coal from other suppliers at the market price (23s 6d per ton) in order to fulfil the contract for resale. The loss on that transaction of 23s 6d – 19s.6d = 4s. per ton would have to be added to the lost profit of 3s 3d per ton.

14 *Marcel (Furriers) Ltd v Tapper 1953.*

Further question practice

Now try the following practice questions at the end of this text

Multiple choice questions: **38 and 39**

Exam style question: **10**

Chapter 11

CONSUMER CREDIT

Introduction

The Consumer Credit Act 1974 was passed to protect consumers by introducing a new concept, that of 'truth in lending'. The Act applies to any defined lending transactions to individuals, not to companies, and its main provisions govern lending up to and including £15,000. As an example of its scope, all lending institutions regulated by the Act must inform borrowers of all charges connected with regulated lending, and the rate of interest must be calculated and quoted in a similar way. These are the twin phenomena of the Total Charge for Credit and the Annual Percentage Rate.

Typical problems encountered before the Act were inaccurate advertising, canvassing and the charging of extortionate rates of interest by lenders. The Act is a complex piece of legislation and seeks to regulate transactions (those which are not exempt, such as mortgages of land) including hire purchase agreements, conditional sale transactions, credit sales and personal loans.

Statutory references in this chapter are to the Consumer Credit Act 1974 unless otherwise noted.

Your objectives

After completing this chapter you should:

(a) understand the features of the different forms of consumer credit agreement;

(b) know which agreements are regulated by the Consumer Credit Act 1974;

(c) know how regulated agreements are classified;

(d) know how debtors under regulated agreements are protected;

(e) understand the extent to which a connected lender may be liable along with a supplier of goods;

(f) know the ways in which an agreement may be terminated;

(g) know the extent to which the courts may intervene in extortionate credit bargains;

(h) know how advertising and canvassing for consumer credit are restricted;

(i) understand the legal status of credit card transactions.

1 FORMS OF CONSUMER CREDIT

Consumer credit takes a variety of forms. The simplest form is a loan to a customer which he may use to purchase whatever goods or services he requires. But the creditor often prefers to supply goods himself to the consumer on hire purchase terms so that the goods remain the creditor's property until the consumer has paid the price including credit charges, and can be recovered if the debtor defaults. It is a common business practice for a trader to sell his goods to a finance company so that the latter, in providing credit to a customer of the trader, can do so under a hire purchase or related transaction. There are also other special forms of credit transaction such as those involving bank credit cards, shop budget accounts, loans by pawnbrokers on the security of chattels deposited with them, and so on.

1.1 Hire purchase

There are two elements in a hire purchase transaction.

(a) Goods are bailed (or delivered) to the possession of the hirer, for his use, by the creditor who has purchased the goods from the dealer.

(b) The hirer has an option to purchase the goods when he has completed payment of a number of instalments which represent the cash price plus a charge for credit.

The legal effect of a hire purchase agreement is that the hirer is *not* a buyer in possession of goods, the property in which has not yet passed to him. He has an option to buy the goods but he is not bound to exercise that option. He does not yet own the goods nor can he pass ownership to another person by an unauthorised sale. This protects the owner of the goods from losing title to them: the hirer is not legally competent to deprive him of it (with an exception under the Hire Purchase Act 1964 limited to motor vehicles).

The same conditions and warranties (in substance) are implied by law in a hire purchase agreement as in a sale of goods: Supply of Goods (Implied Terms) Act 1973. There are the same restrictions on contracting out of these terms by the use of exclusion clauses as apply to agreements for the sale of goods: s 6 Unfair Contract Terms Act 1977.

1.2 Conditional sale

The conditional sale agreement was developed as a means of avoiding the controls applied to hire purchase agreements. But it no longer has this effect since the same rules apply to either type of agreement. The essential features of a conditional sale agreement are as follows.

(a) The buyer agrees to buy goods from the creditor, who purchased them from the dealer, and to pay the price by instalments.

(b) The buyer obtains immediate possession but the transfer of ownership is postponed until he has paid all the instalments.

(c) He is not a buyer or person who has agreed to buy goods for the purposes of Sale of Goods Act 1979 and so he cannot transfer ownership (which he has not yet obtained) to another person.

The Sale of Goods Act 1979 applies to such agreements.

1.3 Credit sale

A credit sale agreement is an agreement under which ownership as well as possession is transferred to the buyer by the creditor without delay, but the price is payable by instalments. The buyer is free to sell before the price has been paid. Such a sale is subject to regulation (to protect the buyer) under the Consumer Credit Act 1974.

1.4 Consumer hire

A consumer hire agreement is one for the bailment or hiring of goods which fulfils the following four conditions under s 15.

(a) It is not a hire purchase agreement.

(b) It is capable of lasting more than three months.

(c) It does not require the hirer to pay more than £15,000.

(d) The hirer is not a corporate body.

Because there is no element of credit a consumer hire agreement is *not* a consumer credit agreement.

Activity 1

In which one of a hire purchase agreement, a conditional sale agreement and a credit sale agreement can the consumer pay all the instalments required yet still not acquire ownership of the goods?

---

2 WHAT IS A REGULATED AGREEMENT?

The Consumer Credit Act 1974 (CCA) regulates the provision of credit. 'Credit' includes a cash loan and any other form of financial benefit including hire purchase, conditional sale and credit sale agreements. As noted above, consumer hire agreements are *not* covered.

Except in respect of extortionate credit bargains (which are discussed later in this chapter) the CCA only applies to *regulated agreements*. These are agreements meeting the following conditions set out in ss 8-9.

(a) *Individuals* (not companies) obtain credit. The use of the phrase *consumer credit* here is rather misleading since a sole trader or partnership obtaining credit for commercial purposes is protected by the 1974 Act.

(b) *Credit not exceeding £15,000* is provided. The amount of credit given is not the total price paid by the debtor, but rather that total less any initial payment paid when the agreement is made and any charges for credit. If, for example, the debtor is to pay £16,500 in total (of which £500 is paid on signing the agreement), and £1,000 in interest charges, the credit given is £15,000 (£16,500 less £500 less £1,000) and so the agreement is regulated by the 1974 Act.

(c) The agreement is not *exempt*. The CCA does not apply (s 16) to certain transactions, for example, building society loans for the purchase of land, running account credit which is *settled in full* (as with American Express cards), credit sale agreements for *less than £50* or agreements where the creditor does not act in the course of a *business*.

3 THE CLASSIFICATION OF REGULATED AGREEMENTS

The 1974 Act uses an elaborate classification of consumer credit agreements to apply rules selectively to some types but not others. Small and non-commercial agreements, for example, are not subject to all the rules. What follows applies generally both to agreements for lending money and to agreements for the supply of goods under hire purchase and related types of agreement. References to 'debtor' and 'creditor' are to the hirer and the owner of goods let under a hire purchase agreement respectively. A regulated agreement is one covered by the Act.

To understand the Act we need to look at how regulated agreements are classified. This means analysing:

(a) the type of credit;

(b) the nature of the credit; and

(c) the relationship of the parties to the agreement.

3.1 The type of credit

There are two types of credit, identified by s 10 of the Act.

(a) In *running account credit*, also known as a revolving credit, the debtor does not have to apply for further amounts of credit after making the original credit agreement but automatically has the right to further credit, although there is usually a credit limit. Common examples are bank overdrafts and shop or credit card agreements.

(b) *Fixed sum credit* is a once-only credit, such as a single loan. If the creditor later agrees to make a further loan there are deemed to be two fixed-sum credits, since the debtor had no automatic right to receive further credit.

3.2 The nature of the credit

A distinction is made as to the nature of credit in s 11 between an agreement whereby the creditor exercises some control over the use of his finance and one where he has no such control.

(a) *Restricted use credit* (RUC) is seen in agreements whereby

   (i)   the creditor pays the funds direct to a supplier;

   (ii) the debtor receives a credit token (such as a credit card) which may only be used in transactions with those suppliers who have agreed to take it; or

   (iii) the creditor also acts as supplier.

(b) *Unrestricted use credit* (UUC) is the residual category where the creditor merely supplies funds and the debtor can use them in any way he sees fit.

3.3 The relationship of the parties to the agreement

Many of the more important provisions of the Act depend on the relationship between the parties to the agreement: that is, between the debtor, the creditor (the provider of finance and owner of goods) and the supplier (the provider of or dealer in the goods).

(a) In a *debtor-creditor (D-C) agreement* the persons who supply the finance and the goods respectively are entirely separate. Thus the use of an overdrawn current account at a bank to purchase a hi-fi from a shop is a debtor-creditor agreement.

(b) In a *debtor-creditor-supplier (D-C-S) agreement*, there are arrangements whereby the creditor and supplier of goods are linked: s 12. An arrangement whereby a car sales agency provides credit via its linked finance house is such an agreement; so too is a credit card transaction where, although creditor and supplier are different persons, a business arrangement exists between them that the supplier will accept the creditor's card produced by the buyer.

It is important to distinguish the two types of agreement above in order to see how rights are protected under the Act. In particular a creditor is jointly and severally liable with the supplier for misrepresentations made by the supplier (s 56) or for breach of contract by the supplier (s 75) in a D-C-S agreement.

A *linked transaction* is one which is subsidiary to but in some way connected with the main credit transaction: s 19. It is thus automatically terminated if the main transaction is cancelled.

Activity 2

George borrows £5,000 from his bank as a loan of a fixed amount at 2% over base rate for an unspecified purpose. He uses the money to buy double glazing for his house.
(a) Is there a regulated credit agreement?
(b) Has RUC or UUC been provided?
(c) Is the bank liable for misrepresentations by the double glazing company?

---

4   THE PROTECTION OF DEBTORS

We have seen that the main object of the 1974 Act is the protection of individual debtors. The way in which it does this can be analysed into protection given *before* the agreement is made, *at the time* the agreement is made and *after* the agreement has been made.

4.1   Protection of the debtor before the agreement is made

It often happens that a 'negotiator' is involved in the 'antecedent negotiations' of a consumer credit agreement. This can happen in two ways.

(a) A person buying, say, a motor car and wishing to finance it by a hire purchase agreement will obtain the car from a dealer. The dealer will arrange the finance on behalf of the purchaser through a credit institution. In effect, the car dealer, acting as negotiator, is a credit broker.

(b) A person buys goods from a shop and pays by credit card.

In these cases s 56 provides of the Act that the 'negotiator' (the car dealer or the shop) is the agent of the creditor. This has two effects. The creditor is liable for any misrepresentations made by the negotiator as though he had made them himself, and any money paid by the debtor to the negotiator will be regarded as having been received by the creditor.

Two further rules protect the debtor who has not yet entered into a binding regulated agreement.

(a) A debtor is not bound by any prior agreement to enter into a regulated agreement, such as an option (s 59). Without this protection, the detailed rules covering regulated agreements could be circumvented by a prior promise to enter into obligations.

(b) The debtor may withdraw from the agreement at any time before all the formalities are completed by giving notice to the creditor, the negotiator or the creditor's agent (s 57). Thus he may withdraw up to the time when the agreement is fully executed.

4.2 Protection of the debtor at the time the agreement is made

To protect the debtor at the time the agreement is being made the Act lays down detailed requirements as to the formalities of execution and the provision of copies.

Formalities of execution

The agreement must be in writing and its form (printed) and content are prescribed by regulations to ensure that the debtor is made aware of his rights and obligations, particularly his rights of cancellation and termination. The terms of the agreement must be complete and legible and all necessary insertion of particulars in blank spaces must be made before the debtor signs the agreement. Signature must be made in the 'signature box'.

The debtor must be supplied with all 'relevant information' relating to the agreement, including the cash price, the deposit paid, the timing and number of instalments, the total charge for credit (TCC) and the annual percentage rate (APR).

Failure to comply with the required formalities in making a consumer credit agreement makes it an improperly executed agreement. It can still be enforced by the debtor but the creditor will find it either difficult or impossible to enforce. It is:

(a) *unenforceable* by the creditor (s 127) if it did not contain the basic terms when the debtor signed it or the requirements for copies (and notices for a cancellable agreement) were not met (see below);

(b) *difficult to enforce* in other circumstances: for example, court orders will be required and security and repossession will be more difficult to enforce (ss 65 and 113).

The provision of copies

When the agreement is sent or presented to the debtor for his signature, he must be provided with a copy (which he may keep) of the agreement and of any document (such as conditions of sale of goods) referred to in the agreement. If, unusually, the creditor signs at the same time, this will be the only copy the debtor receives. If, as is common practice, the agreement has to be signed by the creditor or some other person, such as a guarantor, after the debtor has signed, the debtor is entitled within seven days of the agreement becoming completely executed (being signed by all parties) to receive a *second copy* of the executed agreement and all documents referred to in it.

Activity 3

What types of insertions in blank spaces might an unscrupulous creditor try to make after a debtor has signed an agreement, were it not for the law against doing so?

4.3 Protection of the debtor after the agreement has been made: cancellable agreements

Even after the agreement has been made and the provisions as to formalities and copies have been met the debtor is protected to a limited extent by virtue of the fact that certain agreements are cancellable.

A cancellable agreement is one (other than most agreements for loans made in land transactions to which alternative safeguards apply) made in the following circumstances.

(a) There have been *oral representations*, for example statements concerning the terms of the loan or the quality of the goods, made in the presence of the debtor by or on behalf of the person with whom the debtor negotiates before the agreement is made.

(b) The agreement is signed by the debtor *elsewhere than at the place of business of the creditor, supplier of the goods or other negotiator: s 67*.

This rather involved definition is designed to protect the debtor who may have been persuaded to enter into the agreement by a sales representative or other agent, usually in the course of a visit to the debtor's house. In such cases the debtor has a limited opportunity to cancel the agreement even after he has signed it. But if the debtor goes to the creditor's office to sign the agreement that is treated as a deliberate act, no longer influenced by salesmanship, and the debtor has no right of cancellation.

Notice and cooling off

The debtor must be given written notice of his right to cancel a cancellable agreement. If he is entitled, as he usually is, to receive a second copy of the agreement when executed, it suffices to send him by post that copy which must include a statement of his rights. If, however, he is not entitled to a second copy of the agreement (because debtor and creditor sign together), he must be sent by post a separate notice of his right of cancellation within the same period of seven days after the agreement is made.

On receiving notice of his right of cancellation the debtor has a five day 'cooling off' period in which he may exercise it. If he decides to cancel he must give notice in writing to the appropriate person (designated in the notice of his cancellation rights). It takes effect as soon as it is posted.

If the procedures for notification of rights of cancellation are not observed, the creditor may not enforce the agreement against the debtor without obtaining the leave of the court.

The effect of cancellation

The effect of cancelling an agreement depends in part on the particular circumstances. In a D-C-S agreement for restricted use credit (such as a hire purchase agreement):

(a) the debtor is no longer bound to make payments under the agreement and may recover any payments made (or goods which he has supplied in part exchange: in some circumstances he may have their value instead);

(b) any goods supplied to the debtor may be collected from him at his address by the creditor; while waiting for recovery the debtor must for 21 days take reasonable care of the goods and he has a lien on them for any money or goods (see (a) above) to be returned to him.

Where there is simply a D-C agreement for unrestricted use credit (such as a cash loan), cancellation means that the debtor must repay that amount of the loan already received with interest. The agreement continues in force in relation to repayment of the debt and interest (including terms relating to timing and method), although if he repays the loan either within one month of cancellation or before the date of the first instalment due the debtor will not have to repay interest. Cancellation of an unrestricted use credit agreement has no effect on a linked transaction unless it is also a D-C-S agreement.

Activity 4

S signs a credit agreement on 4 May. The notice of her right of cancellation is posted to her on 7 May and she receives it on 9 May. She posts a notice of cancellation on 13 May and it is received on 16 May. Is her notice of cancellation effective?

5   LENDERS' LIABILITY

We have seen above that a creditor may be jointly liable with a supplier where there have been misrepresentations and/or a breach of contract. We shall now look at this in a little more detail.

5.1   Misrepresentation in antecedent negotiations: s 56

The negotiator in a regulated agreement who takes part in antecedent negotiations with the debtor is a deemed agent of the creditor or owner of the goods. A negotiator is defined by s 56 as:

(a) the creditor or owner (no agency arises);

(b) the dealer in case of an HP, conditional sale or credit sale agreement; or

(c) the supplier in the case of any other D-C-S agreement, such as a credit card transactions.

The term 'antecedent negotiations' means negotiations, such as advertisements, direct communication and other dealings, which take place either before the agreement is made (say in a hire purchase agreement) or before an individual transaction under an agreement takes place (say a particular purchase under an ongoing credit card agreement).

An example may clarify the protection offered by these provisions. A enters into a hire purchase agreement with B (the supplier) and C (the creditor) following antecedent negotiations by B. It later transpires that B made misrepresentations. A is entitled to rescind the entire agreement for credit against C and to rescind the agreement for the hire of goods against B.

It is only rarely that a debtor will have to rely on the supplier's agency under s 56 in order to make a claim against the creditor as principal. Usually he will simply sue the supplier, but alternatively he can make use of the connected lender's liability under s 75.

5.2   Connected lender liability: s 75

In a D-C-S agreement there are two primary contracts: one between the debtor and the supplier (for the goods) and another between the debtor and the creditor (for the credit). Under normal principles of contract law only the parties to a contract can enforce it or be liable under it. However in D-C-S agreements the debtor is entitled to claim for breach of contract and/or misrepresentation against the creditor *provided* he also has such a claim against the supplier: s 75. Hence if A pays B for a holiday using the credit card supplied by C, and B fails to supply the holiday (and is therefore in breach), A may claim for breach of contract against C. This right is of most help to consumers when the supplier becomes insolvent and cannot provide compensation.

Note that an important limitation on s 75 is that it applies only to transactions valued between £100 and £30,000. Transactions of less than £100 are protected only by s 56. By far the most important application of s 75 is to credit card (*not* debit card) agreements.

Where the creditor himself contracts with the debtor to supply goods or services, and where there is a conditional sale, credit sale or hire purchase agreement, with the creditor first purchasing the goods from the supplier, there is no need for ss 56 or 75. The creditor is himself liable for breach of implied terms as to title, description, quality and so on, and for misrepresentation.

Activity 5

A buys goods costing £90 from B using a credit card provided by C. B made no representations about the goods, but they have proved to be unsatisfactory and A wishes to sue for breach of contract. Does A have any claim against C?

---

6 TERMINATION OF CREDIT AGREEMENTS

Once it has come into operation, an agreement may be terminated before it is fully performed.

6.1 Debtor's election to pay off credit

No provision in a consumer credit agreement may prevent the debtor from paying off the entire amount of credit early. He will obtain a rebate of the interest which he is required to pay under the agreement but which is not yet due. He may either give notice of his intention to repay or merely pay the balance less the rebate. In the latter case the notice immediately takes effect (although some future date may be specified on which it is to take effect).

6.2 Debtor's election to terminate

The debtor has a statutory right (which cannot be excluded by the agreement) to terminate a hire purchase or conditional sale agreement at any time if he pays an amount which raises his aggregate payments to half of the total price plus the whole of any installation charge: s 100.

Suppose, for example, that the total price is £100 and the installation charge £10. The debtor has paid instalments of £30 in all plus the installation charge, and owes an instalment of £10. The debtor may terminate the agreement and must raise the aggregate of his payment to £60 (half of £100 plus £10). As he has paid £40 already his liability on giving notice of termination is to pay a further £20. If he had paid instalments of £50 in aggregate plus the installation charge and owed £10 as an overdue instalment he would be liable to pay that £10 since (although he has already paid half the total price) it is a payment due at the time of termination.

If the debtor considers that the above formula produces an excessive amount, he may apply to the court to order a reduction. The debtor must of course permit the creditor to retake possession of the goods. If the debtor has not taken reasonable care of the goods while in his possession, the creditor is entitled (in addition to the sums payable as described above) to recover compensation for the damage to his goods caused by the debtor's failure to take care of them.

6.3   Creditor's right to terminate

By s 98 the creditor is allowed to terminate the agreement if the debtor is in breach of one of the contract's terms other than that relating to repayment. For example, he may terminate where the debtor made misrepresentations, where the debtor has become insolvent or where the goods are destroyed. The creditor usually then has the right to repossess the goods and the debtor must pay up to half of the price. Seven days' notice must be given.

If the creditor is entitled to terminate the agreement by reason of the debtor's failure to maintain the agreed payments, the creditor must first serve on the debtor a *'default notice'* which specifies the default alleged, requires it to be remedied (if remediable) or demands compensation (if irremediable) and specifies a period of not less than seven days in which action is to be taken as required. This gives the debtor time to apply to the court if he decides to do so: s 87.

Repossession of goods

If the debtor is in breach of a hire purchase or conditional sale agreement and he has paid at least one third of the total price for the goods (plus the whole of any installation charges) the goods are then *'protected goods'* which the creditor may only repossess from the debtor after obtaining an order of the court: s 90.

If the creditor recovers possession of protected goods without a court order, the regulated agreement is terminated and the debtor is released from all liability under the agreement: he may even recover all sums he has paid under it: s 91.

Activity 6

D obtained credit of £3,000 under a hire purchase agreement, falsely representing that he is a homeowner. When the creditor discovers the facts, he decides to repossess the goods and terminate the agreement. At that time D has paid £1,300 and is not in arrears. How should the creditor proceed, and what is the most he can hope to obtain?

7   EXTORTIONATE CREDIT BARGAINS

Unlike the rest of the 1974 Act there is no £15,000 limit on the application of the Act to an extortionate credit bargain: s 137.

This part of the CCA gives the court the power to re-open and make appropriate orders in relation to a credit agreement made on terms which the court finds 'grossly exorbitant' or 'contrary to ordinary principles of fair dealing'. It is intended to apply, for example, to moneylending at very high rates of interest. However, the rate of interest is not the only factor considered by the court: *Ketley v Scott 1981*. The courts also look at 'other relevant circumstances': s 138. These circumstances include the debtor's age and business experience, the degree of sales pressure and the extent of explanations. If it does decide to reopen an agreement the court has wide powers to relieve the debtor of having to make payments beyond what is 'fairly due and reasonable': s 139.

The extortionate credit bargains provision can be used in one of two ways: as a separate action in itself or as a defence to an action brought by the creditor to enforce the agreement.

8 CONSUMER CREDIT LICENSING, ADVERTISING AND CANVASSING

Part III of the CCA relates to persons conducting a business dealing with regulated agreements. The aim of these provisions is to establish a system of licensing for:

(a) consumer credit businesses and consumer hire businesses; and

(b) ancillary businesses.

Category (a) above includes not only finance companies, but also any retailer who sells his goods on credit sale, conditional sale or hire purchase. Category (b) includes such businesses as credit brokerage, debt collecting and operating a credit reference agency. It follows that the retailer who arranges finance for his customer through a finance house is included, because he is in effect acting as a credit broker. All these businesses must be licensed under a system operated by the Director General of Fair Trading (DGFT). Anyone carrying on such a business without a licence commits an offence.

The DGFT has powers to vary, suspend, renew and withdraw licences. A regulated agreement made by an unlicensed business or through the agency of an unlicensed credit broker will generally be unenforceable against the customer. Similarly, any agreement for the services of an unlicensed ancillary business will be unenforceable against the client.

8.1 Advertising consumer credit

Regulations made under the Act control advertisements aimed at providing credit or goods on hire to non-business customers. The objective of these regulations is to ensure that consumers have a fair impression of the product offered and a means of comparison between different products.

Warnings as to the consequences of giving security for regulated agreements are also required. For example, it is compulsory when advertising home mortgages to include the warning 'Your home may be at risk if you do not keep up repayments on a mortgage or other loan secured on it.'

8.2 Canvassing consumer credit

'Canvassing' is 'orally soliciting an individual to enter into a credit agreement'. This is permitted if it occurs on the trade premises of either the debtor or the creditor (s 48) but it is greatly restricted off trade premises.

Canvassing off trade premises by making representations to induce a customer to make a regulated agreement arises when the canvasser:

(a) makes oral representations during a visit by the canvasser for that purpose;

(b) makes that visit to somewhere other than the business premises of the canvasser, creditor, supplier or consumer; and

(c) does not make that visit in response to a request made on a previous occasion.

The controls on canvassing off trade premises are as follows.

(a) Canvassing D-C agreements off trade premises is an offence: s 49. It is an offence even if made in response to a request unless that request is in writing and signed.

(b) Canvassing other regulated agreements off trade premises can only be done under a licence expressly authorising such activity: s 23.

One important exception relates to overdrafts on current accounts where the canvasser is the creditor or an employee of the creditor. Such an activity is not banned nor does it require a special licence.

Activity 7

A supplier of credit in D-C agreements sends L a leaflet about credit and a card for her to reply on. The card already has her name and address printed on it. It says 'Please tick the box below and post the card back to us, and a representative will call at your home to discuss credit facilities'. L returns the card and a representative calls. L decides not to take any credit. Has an offence been committed?

9 CREDIT CARDS

The use of a credit card involves three parties and three transactions between them.

(a) On producing his card to a supplier for goods and/or services, the cardholder can obtain what he requires without paying for it immediately.

(b) The supplier recovers from the credit card company the price of the goods or services less a discount which is the credit card company's profit margin.

(c) At monthly intervals the credit card company sends to the cardholder a monthly statement. The cardholder may either settle interest free within 25 days or he may pay interest on the balance owing after 25 days. He is required to pay a minimum of 5% or £5 whichever is the lesser.

Payment by credit card is *not* a conditional payment, unlike payment by cheque where the drawer of the cheque is not discharged from his debt until the cheque has been honoured. As soon as a buyer completes and signs a valid credit card voucher which is accepted by the supplier, the buyer's obligations to the supplier are complete: *Re Charge Card Services Ltd 1988*.

A credit limit is set for each card holder, the limit usually being well below £15,000. Hence the card issued to an individual is subject to regulation by the Consumer Credit Act 1974. In the terminology used in the Act a credit card is a 'credit token' used in a debtor-creditor-supplier agreement.

Activity 8

When a credit card is used in a shop, there are three parties: the cardholder, the shop and the credit card company. There are three contracts, one between each pair of these parties. Briefly describe each of these three contracts.

Chapter roundup

- Consumer credit arises in simple loans and overdrafts, in credit card transactions, in revolving credit arrangements and in hire purchase, conditional sale and credit sale agreements.

- Agreements regulated under the Consumer Credit Act 1974 are non-exempt agreements to provide credit of up to £15,000 to individuals.

- Credit may be running account or fixed sum, and it may be restricted use or unrestricted use.

- Agreements may be debtor-creditor agreements or debtor-creditor-supplier agreements, and there may be linked transactions.

- A debtor is protected before an agreement is made in that a negotiator may be treated as the creditor's agent, agreements to enter into regulated agreements are not binding and the debtor may withdraw at any time before completion of the formalities.

- The formalities of execution protect the debtor at the time of making an agreement.

- Some agreements are cancellable by the debtor even after they have been made. The debtor may recover payments made, but must give up goods supplied.

- A creditor may be liable for misrepresentations in antecedent negotiations. Where connected lender liability arises and the debtor could sue the supplier for misrepresentation or breach of contract, he may also sue the lender.

- An agreement may be terminated by the debtor's election to pay off credit, by the debtor's election to terminate or (in certain circumstances) by the creditor.

- The courts can make orders in respect of extortionate credit bargains.

- Consumer credit businesses and ancillary businesses must be licensed by the Director General of Fair Trading. Advertisements for consumer credit are regulated, and canvassing consumer credit is subject to strict controls.

- In a credit card transaction, the buyer obtains goods or services from the supplier in return for a signed credit card slip. The only subsequent transactions are between the supplier and the credit card company (which pays the supplier), and between the credit card company and the buyer (who pays the company).

Quick quiz

1 What is (a) a hire purchase agreement and (b) a conditional sale?

2 To what transactions does the Consumer Credit Act 1974 apply?

3 What is the difference between a debtor-creditor and a debtor-creditor-supplier consumer credit agreement?

4 What form must a regulated agreement take?

5 When must a debtor be given a copy of the agreement?

6 What is a cancellable regulated agreement?

7 How long after signing the agreement may a debtor in a cancellable agreement cancel?

8   What is connected lender liability?

9   What limit is placed on the amount to be paid by a hirer who terminates a hire purchase agreement before completing payment of the agreed instalments?

10 What is a default notice and what must it contain?

11 What are protected goods?

12 How may the court regulate (a) extortionate credit bargains and (b) consumer credit transactions?

13 What restrictions are contained in CCA relating to advertising and canvassing of consumer credit?

Solutions to activities

1   A hire purchase agreement.

2   (a) Yes

    (b) UUC

    (c) No

3   The rate of interest and the levels of penalties for defaults are two obvious examples.

4   Yes: 13 May is within five days of 9 May.

5   No: s 75 does not apply to transactions of less than £100, and s 56 only applies if misrepresentations are made.

6   He should seek a court order. He may obtain the goods plus a further £200 (£3,000/2 – £1,300).

7   Yes: L did not sign the request for a visit.

8   The shop contracts with the cardholder to supply goods in exchange for an authorisation to the credit card company to debit the cardholder's account.

    The credit card company contracts with the shop to pay the amounts due on sales less a fee charged by the credit card company.

    The cardholder contracts with the credit card company to pay amounts debited to his account.

Further question practice

Now try the following practice questions at the end of this text

Multiple choice questions: **40 to 44**

Chapter 12

CONSUMER PROTECTION

Introduction

The Fair Trading Act 1973 (FTA) created the post of Director General of Fair Trading (DGFT). The DGFT heads the Office of Fair Trading (OFT) and has overall supervision of consumer protection. The OFT is divided into two sections dealing respectively with consumer affairs and competition. Competition is the subject of Chapter 13; in this chapter we will describe various aspects of consumer affairs.

Your objectives

After completing this chapter you should:

(a) understand the role of the Director General of Fair Trading;

(b) know what constitutes a trade description and how an offence may be committed by giving one;

(c) know how statements about services, accommodation and facilities may constitute offences;

(d) know how statements about prices may constitute offences;

(e) appreciate the extent to which a consumer may sue and recover damages for negligence;

(f) understand the scope of actions for product liability.

1 CONSUMER PROTECTION

The FTA gave the DGFT a number of different functions, as follows:

(a) to identify and eliminate harmful practices;

(b) to take direct action against individual traders;

(c) to promote codes of practice.

1.1 Harmful practices

The DGFT has a general duty to keep under review commercial activities carried on in the UK, in order to establish whether the interests of consumers are suffering in any way. The OFT collates information (mainly provided by local trading standards departments) and investigates and reports on matters of public concern.

The FTA established the Consumer Protection Advisory Committee (CPAC). This is a body consisting of up to 15 members with experience in consumer affairs. The DGFT may refer to the CPAC any consumer trade practice, and will do so where the practice appears to have the effect of misleading or otherwise harming consumers. If the CPAC reports adversely on the practice, the DGFT can recommend to the Secretary of State that an order under s 22 for the control or prevention of practices which adversely affect the consumer's interest be made: s 17.

The Secretary of State may make orders under s 22 FTA to prevent or control consumer trade practices, infringement of which is an offence. Such orders expressly do not affect civil rights: s 26. Defences are available similar to those under the Trade Descriptions Act 1968 (see below).

1.2 Persistent offenders

The DGFT also has wide powers in respect of individual traders. Where it appears that a trader is persistently in breach of the law in such a way as to harm the interests of consumers, the DGFT will try to obtain an undertaking from the trader as to his conduct in the future: s 34(1). If that fails, he can institute proceedings in the Restrictive Practices Court: s 35. Breach of an order issued by the Restrictive Practices Court constitutes contempt and may lead to fines or imprisonment.

Persistent offenders are identified by local authority trading standards officers, who may report them to the DGFT. Cases usually concern traders who have continued to defy the law despite warnings from the local authority in question.

1.3 Codes of practice

Codes of practice for particular trades can be classified into four groups.

(a) *Codes of practice carrying the DGFT's endorsement.* The DGFT is responsible under FTA for promoting codes of practice amongst traders. After negotiations between him and the relevant trade association a list of rules of conduct is drawn up, the objects being to promote a high standard of trade practice and to protect the consumer's interests. These codes are purely voluntary in that they are not enforced by the courts, but the OFT monitors their operation and the trade associations themselves try to ensure that the standards are adhered to by their members. Common features in these codes would be an agreement not to limit legal liability except in special, stated circumstances (and obviously within the limits of the Unfair Contract Terms Act 1977), a set standard of care, a disciplinary procedure for members, and agreed procedures such as arbitration for the settlement of disputes.

(b) *Enforceable codes of practice.* A code of practice which is enforceable by means of sanctions falling short of legal proceedings is known as an enforceable code. It will set down codes of conduct which can be enforced against people engaged in a certain trade or business, even though they are not members of the relevant trade body. The British Code of Advertising Practice is an example.

(c) *Statutory codes of practice.* Codes which are drawn up with the involvement of government departments and the approval of the relevant minister may be given legal status. The Highway Code is an example.

(d) *Other codes of practice.* Because of the aura of respectability imparted to a trade which has an association and a code of practice, many commercial areas have acquired codes of practice which have no status at all and afford neither legal nor practical assistance.

Activity 1

Give some examples of trade practices (not involving collusion with other traders) which might be harmful.

2 TRADE DESCRIPTIONS

The law relating to trade descriptions is contained in the Trade Descriptions Act 1968 (TDA) which replaced and considerably extended the provisions of earlier Merchandise Marks Acts, and in the Consumer Protection Act 1987 (CPA).

A consumer seeking a *civil* remedy for a false trade description will need to rely on the Misrepresentation Act 1967 or the Sale of Goods Act 1979. This is because the TDA defines *criminal* offences, and 'a contract for the supply of goods shall not be void or unenforceable by reason only of a contravention of this Act': s 35. However, the criminal court has power to order an offender to pay compensation to his victim.

There are three principal offences created by the legislation.

(a) Applying a *false* trade description to *goods* and supplying or offering to supply any such goods: s 1 TDA (a *strict liability* offence).

(b) Making false statements relating to *services, accommodation or facilities:* s 14 TDA.

(c) Making misleading statements as to the price of goods: s 20 CPA.

Private individuals are not within the scope of the Act; these activities only constitute an offence if they occur *in the course of a trade or business.*

Davies v Sumner 1984
The defendant was a self-employed courier who used his car almost exclusively in connection with his business as a courier. After one year of ownership following which the car had covered 118,000 miles, he sold it in part exchange for a replacement vehicle. The odometer had gone right round the clock, thus presenting a false reading.

Held: the sale transaction was incidental to the business and it was not made in the course of the business. It was outside the scope of s 1 TDA.

This case can be contrasted with another.

Havering London Borough v Stevenson 1970
The defendant ran a car hire business. In accordance with his usual practice, he sold a hire car when it was of no further use to the business. A false description was given as to the mileage of the vehicle.

Held: the false description was made in the course of a trade or business.

2.1 False trade descriptions

A *trade description* (s 2 TDA) is any indication, direct or indirect, of any of the following.

(a) Quantity, size or gauge of goods;

(b) Method of manufacture, production, processing or reconditioning;

(c) Composition;

(d) Fitness for purpose, strength, performance, behaviour or accuracy.

> *Sherratt v Geralds The American Jewellers Ltd 1970*
> A 'diver's watch', which was described as 'waterproof', filled with water when immersed in a bowl of water for an hour.
>
> *Held:* this was a false trade description in breach of the Act.

(e) Any physical characteristics not included in the preceding paragraphs;

(f) Testing by any person and the results of testing;

(g) Approval by any person or conformity with a type approved by any person;

(h) Place or date of manufacture, production, processing or reconditioning;

(i) Person by whom manufactured, produced, processed or reconditioned;

(j) Other history, including previous ownership or use. For example, this would cover the kind of claim often made by car dealers, 'only one previous owner'.

A trade description is regarded as false in this context if it is false to a material degree (s 3(1)) and relates in some way to the sale and supply of goods.

> *R v Ford Motor Co Ltd 1974*
> The defendants supplied a dealer with a new Ford Cortina which had been damaged at the factory in a collision, and then repaired.
>
> *Held:* it was not false to describe the car as 'new' since to a material extent this was true: the car had been perfectly repaired. The repairs were not intended to conceal defects but to restore the car to sound condition.

False trade descriptions need not necessarily be made by the seller: a buyer can commit the offence. The statement might be made deliberately, recklessly or entirely innocently: the offence is the same.

> *Fletcher v Budgen 1974*
> A car dealer negotiating to buy a Fiat 500 informed the owner that it could not be repaired and was only fit for scrap. The owner sold it to the dealer for £2. The dealer repaired it and advertised it for sale for £136.
>
> *Held:* the dealer was guilty of an offence.

Odometer readings

The motor trade industry has featured in a number of cases under the TDA, particularly in respect of the mileage and condition of used cars. It was held in *Norman v Bennett 1974* that a disclaimer as to the accuracy of the odometer given equal prominence as the figure on the odometer is a valid defence. But the disclaimer must be reasonable under the Unfair Contract Terms Act 1977 and its terms must be as 'bold, precise and compelling' as the claim itself. A supplier who has deliberately made a false statement cannot issue a disclaimer in relation to it: *R v Southwood 1987*.

Activity 2

Which one or more of the following might be a false trade description?
(a) As used by the United States Army
(b) Worthy of your serious consideration

(c) Has won a Design Council award

(d) Functions at room temperature

2.2 Services, accommodation and facilities

With regard to services, accommodation and facilities, s 14 TDA makes it an offence to make false statements deliberately or recklessly. The statement in question must be false 'to a material degree'. Under s 14, an element of knowledge or recklessness (*mens rea* – literally 'guilty mind') is required. Recklessness will be established even though the falsity was due to lack of thought rather than actual dishonesty. The situation here differs from the situation with regard to *goods*: false statements with regard to goods are normally an offence whether or not they were made deliberately and/or recklessly.

The subject matter to which s 14 TDA applies is the provision of services, accommodation and facilities as well as their nature and the time at which, manner in which or persons by whom they are to be provided. The location and amenities of any accommodation provided are covered, as are any claims as to the services, accommodation or facilities having been approved or examined by any person.

2.3 Misleading prices

It is an offence to make misleading statements as to price: ss 20 and 21 CPA. Such misleading statement might be any of the following.

(a) That the price is less than it really is.

(b) That the price applied depends on facts which are not in fact the case.

(c) That the price covers matters for which an additional charge will actually be made.

(d) That the price is expected to rise, fall or stay the same, when in fact the trader has no such expectation.

(e) Price comparisons.

There are other ways in which a price description may be misleading. For example, it may be an offence to indicate a price which fails to state that VAT will be added: *Richards v Westminster Motors Ltd 1975*.

The protection afforded by s 20 only operates in favour of consumers and only when the price indication is made in the course of a business. Although the protection applies to accommodation, it only affects the sale or leasing of property if it is a new house.

The prices code

A code of practice has been issued under s 25 CPA giving practical advice to retailers as to what exactly constitutes a misleading price indication. It deals mainly with some difficult issues such as price comparisons and seasonal sales.

2.4 Defences under trade descriptions legislation

Under s 24 TDA it is a general defence for a person to prove *both* of the following.

(a) The commission of the offence was due to:

(i) a mistake;

(ii) reliance on information supplied to the defendant;

(iii) the act or default of another person; or

(iv) an accident or some other cause beyond his control.

(b) He took all reasonable precautions and exercised all due diligence to avoid the commission of such an offence by himself or any person under his control.

The reasonableness of precautions is often closely scrutinised; they must be more than a token gesture.

A specific defence is available to a supplier of goods. He has a defence under s 24(3) if he can show that he did not know and could not reasonably have found out:

(a) that the goods did not conform to the description; or

(b) that the description had been applied to the goods.

Activity 3

A boiler is advertised at a price of '£1,200 including installation'. In fact, only delivery and fixing the boiler to the wall are included, and an extra charge is made for connecting gas and water pipes. Consider whether an offence has been committed.

3 PRODUCT LIABILITY

A person who suffers injury or loss in connection with defective or dangerous goods may have remedies in contract, in tort or under Part I of the Consumer Protection Act 1987.

3.1 Contract

If he is the purchaser he can probably recover damages from the vendor for breach of the statutory implied conditions of quality imposed by the Sale of Goods Act 1979. If he deals as consumer he cannot be deprived of these safeguards; in any other case an attempt to exclude or restrict them is void unless it satisfies a test of reasonableness: Unfair Contract Terms Act 1977.

3.2 Tort

If he suffers personal injury or damage to property by a defective product he may be able to recover damages for *negligence* from the manufacturer under the law of tort. Any attempt to exclude liability for personal injury or death due to negligence is void, and exemption from other liability is usually subject to a test of reasonableness: Unfair Contract Terms Act 1977. Negligence is covered fully in Chapter 15.

To succeed in an action for negligence, the plaintiff must show three things.

(a) *The existence of a duty of care by the defendant.* A manufacturer's liability for physical damage or injury to users of his products has been well established since the case of *Donoghue v Stevenson 1932.* In this celebrated case, the House of Lords ruled that a person might owe a duty of care to another with whom he had no contractual relationship at all. The law of negligence applies in product liability cases such as *Donoghue v Stevenson* itself where physical injury or damage results from a failure to take proper precautions. However if the consumer/user has a reasonable opportunity of avoiding the injury by intermediate inspection or by routine precautions, there is no duty to a plaintiff who could have avoided it by these means.

(b) *A breach of that duty by the defendant.* The standard of care when a duty of care exists is that which is reasonable. This requires that the person concerned should do what a reasonable man 'guided upon those considerations which ordinarily regulate the conduct of human affairs' would do, and abstain from doing what a reasonable man would not.

(c) *Injury or damage* (or in some cases financial loss) *suffered by the plaintiff as a foreseeable consequence* of the breach. For a claim to succeed, the third element must be proved. In deciding whether a claim should be allowed, the court will consider whether the breach of duty of care gave rise to the harm (a question of fact) and whether the harm was too remote from the breach (a question of law).

Activity 4

M bought a new fridge. The fridge bore a conspicuous notice that the instruction booklet should be read in full before the fridge was used. The booklet stated that the fridge should be left for three hours before being turned on, so that the refrigerant could settle. M ignored the notice and the booklet and turned the fridge on immediately. There was a small explosion, damaging her kitchen. Advise M as to whether she would be able to sue the manufacturer for negligence?

3.3   Consumer Protection Act 1987

Part I of the Consumer Protection Act 1987 deals with liability for defective products. It covers strict liability for death, personal injury and damage to consumer property. It was brought into force in March 1988 to implement a European Community Directive. For the consumer the Act has the advantage that he does not have to prove negligence, nor that there was any privity of contract between him and the person he is suing. In other words the Act imposes strict civil liability, and this liability cannot be excluded by any disclaimer.

Claims for losses caused by defects in a product may be brought against any of the following.

(a) The manufacturer of the end-product;

(b) The manufacturer of a defective component (although he has a defence if he can show that he followed the instructions or specifications of the manufacturer of the end-product);

(c) An importer into the EC (the principle behind this is that anybody responsible who is outside the EC may be much more difficult to find);

(d) An 'own-brander';

(e) A supplier, who is usually a retailer.

Because of the potential liability of the parties above, it is usual for a supplier only to be liable if he will not disclose the identity of the importer or manufacturer.

The burden of proof is on the consumer to prove that:

(a) the product contained a defect;

(b) he suffered damage;

(c) the damage resulted from the defect; and

(d) the defendant was either the producer or some other person listed above.

'Defective' product

A product will be found to be unsafe where it is not as safe as it is reasonable to expect. This standard of relative safety requires a court to take into account all circumstances surrounding the product-the way it is advertised, the time at which it was supplied, its anticipated normal use, the provision of instructions for use, even its likely misuse-in establishing the standard required. The benefit to society and the cost of making the product safer can also be considered.

Scope of the Act

Consumers and other users (such as the donee of an electric iron received as a gift), but not business users, can claim compensation for *death, personal injury or damage to other property* (*not* to the product itself or for economic loss, that is loss caused by the product not working). There is unlimited liability but the following limitations apply.

(a) A claim must be brought within three years of the fault becoming apparent.

(b) No claim may be brought more than ten years after the original supply.

(c) Where the claim is for damage to property, it must not be business property which is damaged and the amount of the damage must be more than £275.

Defences

The defendant in a case under this Act has six possible defences.

(a) The product complied with mandatory statutory or EC standards;

(b) The product was not at any time supplied to another;

(c) The supply was otherwise than in the course of a business;

(d) The defect did not exist in the product when originally supplied;

(e) 'Development risk' – the state of knowledge at the time of manufacture and supply was such that no manufacturer could have been expected to detect the fault. The inclusion of this defence in the Act means that many victims of drugs which had damaging side-effects may be left without a remedy. The defence was kept so as not to discourage medical research;

(f) The defect was wholly attributable to the design of a subsequent product into which the product in question was incorporated.

Although liability under the Act to a person who has suffered damage cannot be excluded or limited by any contract term or by a notice, parties other than the person damaged who are in the chain of distribution are free to adjust the liabilities between themselves, subject to any common law or statutory controls, such as the Unfair Contract Terms 1977.

Activity 5

A gas cooker is made by A Ltd. A Ltd uses gas valves made by B Ltd to A Ltd's specification. A Ltd sells the cooker to C (Retailers) Ltd, which sells it to D, a private individual. The cooker explodes because the gas valve, although correctly made to A Ltd's specification, had been fitted wrongly. C (Retailers) Ltd are unable to identify the manufacturer. Consider whether D may claim under Part 1 of the Consumer Protection Act 1987.

---

4   CONSUMER SAFETY

It is an offence punishable under criminal law to supply consumer goods which fail to comply with a general safety requirement: Part II Consumer Protection Act 1987. This requires that goods must be reasonably safe, bearing in mind the manner in which and the purposes for which they are marketed, any instructions or warnings provided with them, any published safety standards and the existence of any means by which it would have been reasonable to make the product safer.

The general safety requirement applies to all consumer goods except for a defined list of items, each of which is covered by its own more specific legislation (thus food falls under the Food Safety Act 1990) or which falls into a special category (tobacco, which 'could raise particular problems').

The Department of Trade and Industry is empowered to make safety regulations under the Act. Contravention of such regulations is a criminal offence. Examples include the following.

(a) Cooking Utensils (Safety) Regulations 1972/1957. These govern the proportion of lead permitted in kitchen utensils used for cooking food.

(b) Electrical Equipment (Safety) Regulations 1975/1366. These require that various items of electrical equipment shall comply with appropriate British Standards.

(c) Pencil and Graphic Instruments Safety Regulations 1974/226. These control the maximum amounts of arsenic, cadmium, chromium, mercury, antimony, lead and barium permitted in pencils, pens, brushes, crayons and chalk.

The general safety requirement and the safety regulations are again enforced by trading standards officers, who have a system of notices which are served on offenders. The General Product Safety Regulations 1994 came into effect in October 1994 and are relevant to all suppliers of consumer products. These regulations impose a general safety requirement on all products to be placed on the market by producers or to be sold, offered for sale of possessed by distributors. The two safety requirements (that is the new regulations and Part II CPA 1987) are not identical.

The key provision of the new regulations is section 7. This states that no products should be placed on the market unless it is a 'safe product'. This is a product which, under normal or reasonably foreseeable conditions of use, presents no, or minimal, risk. This must be consistent with a high degree of protection for users' health and safety. Four factors will be taken into account.

(a) The characteristics of the product, for example packaging and instructions for assembly.

(b) The effect of the product on other products.

(c) The presentation of the product, for example labelling and instructions for use.

(d) The categories of consumer (for example children) at serious risk.

Chapter roundup

- The Director General of Fair Trading works to eliminate harmful practices, seeks assurances from persistent offenders and promotes codes of practice. Some codes of practice have the force of law, but many do not.

- Practically all statements of fact about goods can be trade descriptions. Applying false trade descriptions to goods which are supplied or offered for supply is an offence.

- It is an offence to make false statements about services, accommodation or facilities deliberately or recklessly.

- It is an offence to make misleading statements as to price.

- Defences under trade descriptions legislation are mostly based on mistake or the actions of other people. They are only available if the defendant took all reasonable precautions and exercised all due diligence.

Chapter roundup *continued*

- A consumer suffering loss or injury may seek damages for breach of conditions implied by the Sale of Goods Act 1979, or he may sue for the tort of negligence. Alternatively he may claim against both the manufacturer and the supplier under Part I of the Consumer Protection Act 1987.

- It is a crime to supply consumer goods which fail to comply with a general safety requirement.

Quick quiz

1 What is the function of the Consumer Protection Advisory Committee?

2 How must a disclaimer be displayed so as to provide a valid defence under the TDA?

3 What limitations are there on the offence of making false statements relating to services, accommodation and facilities?

4 What are the general defences available in a case under TDA?

5 What must a plaintiff prove in a claim under Part I of CPA?

6 What defences are available to an action under Part I of CPA?

Solutions to activities

1 Refusing to supply certain goods unless other goods are also bought.

Refusing to supply certain customers because they also deal with other suppliers.

Using sales staff not qualified to advise customers about special risks.

No doubt you can think of other examples.

2 (a), (c) and (d).

3 A misleading statement as to price has been made under s 20 CPA 1987 because the statement indicates that the price covers matters (that is installation) for which an additional charge is actually made.

4 M would probably fail in bringing an action in negligence against the manufacturer because it is she who has failed to take reasonable precautions.

5 D would be able to sue C (Retailers) Ltd because they as the supplier have failed to identify the manufacturer (A Ltd).

Further question practice

Now try the following practice questions at the end of this text

Multiple choice questions: **45 and 46**

Exam style question: **11**

Chapter 13

COMPETITION LAW

Introduction

The bodies which have control over UK competition policy are the Director General of Fair Trading (DGFT), the Monopolies and Mergers Commission (MMC) and the Secretary of State for Trade and Industry. Duties are imposed on them in the main by the Fair Trading Act 1973 (FTA) and the Competition Act 1980. Competition law is also regulated by Articles 85 and 86 of the Treaty of Rome.

Your objectives

After completing this chapter you should:

(a) understand the main object of UK competition law;

(b) know which monopolies and mergers may be investigated, and how action may be taken;

(c) know what constitutes an anti-competitive practice, and how such practices may be investigated;

(d) know how action may be taken against restrictive trade practices;

(e) know which agreements must be registered under the Restrictive Trade Practices Act 1976;

(f) know which restrictive trade practices may be allowed to continue;

(g) be aware of the restrictions on resale price maintenance;

(h) know the restrictions imposed by Articles 85 and 86 of the Treaty of Rome.

1 UK COMPETITION LAW

The role of the Director General of Fair Trading in competition law is as follows.

(a) He can report on *monopolies and mergers* to the Secretary of State for Trade and Industry, who may refer cases to the MMC.

(b) He may undertake initial investigations into any alleged *anti-competitive practices*.

(c) He has responsibility for registration of arrangements designed to fix prices or other *restrictive trade practices*.

(d) He can attempt to get *undertakings* from persons under investigation as to their future conduct and he then monitors that conduct.

1.1 The public interest

For the most part the object of UK competition law is to protect the public interest. For instance the MMC in its investigations has to address the following factors under s 84 FTA.

(a) The maintenance and promotion of effective competition between UK suppliers;

(b) The promotion of customers' interests with regard to quality, price and choice of goods and services;

(c) The maintenance and promotion of a balanced distribution of industry and employment in the UK;

(d) The promotion of competition in exports;

(e) The use of competition to achieve the opening of markets to new entrants, the development of new products and techniques and the promotion of cost reduction.

Activity 1

In an industry in which there are many independent suppliers, how could the interests of small customers be adversely affected by the existence of one large customer buying 70% of the total quantity produced?

2 MONOPOLIES AND MERGERS

It is generally supposed that monopolies and large mergers of business organisations tend to operate against the public interest. A major part of UK competition law therefore concerns the regulation of monopolies and mergers.

2.1 Monopolies

A monopoly situation exists under ss 6-7 FTA if 25% or more of the goods or services of a particular kind supplied in the UK are supplied either *by* a single person or *to* a single person. For this purpose members of an interconnected group of companies are regarded as a single person. The definition also covers cases where two or more otherwise unconnected persons or companies voluntarily or involuntarily act in such a way as to prevent or restrict the operation of a free market in the goods or services in question.

Three elements must be defined when a monopoly reference is made to the MMC.

(a) *The market:* 25% of the market for books is very much larger than 25% of the market for detective novels, so a careful definition of the market is required.

(b) *The geographical area:* if a firm confines itself to one part of the UK but has more than 25% of the market in that area then a monopoly effectively exists.

(c) *Forms of supply:* the same goods and services can be supplied in a number of different ways. For instance, a firm may have 25% of the market for home deliveries of milk but only 2% for milk sold over the counter.

2.2 Mergers

The FTA is also concerned with *mergers* of such magnitude that they may pose a threat to free competition. In s 64 of the Act a definition is given of the circumstances which may lead to a merger being referred to the MMC. Broadly, a qualifying merger is one which:

(a) leads to two or more enterprises ceasing to be distinct, that is they come under common ownership or control;

(b) leads to an enterprise ceasing to be carried on at all under arrangements designed to prevent competition between enterprises; or

(c) leads to assets being taken over with a value equal to or greater than a defined amount (currently £30m), and leads to a more than 25% dominance.

There are special provisions in ss 57-62 of the Act concerning newspaper mergers. Broadly speaking any newspaper merger or takeover may be referred.

2.3 The Monopolies and Mergers Commission

Only the Secretary of State for Trade and Industry may refer a merger to the MMC; the DGFT has an advisory role only. The MMC is an independent advisory body with no executive powers. When a monopoly or merger is referred to it for consideration, it must advise the Government whether it believes that the public interest will be harmed.

An adverse report by the MMC is not binding on the Government. But the Government will usually obtain suitable undertakings from the persons concerned and will ensure that they are complied with. The Secretary of State for Trade and Industry makes the final decision; he has extensive powers to place conditions on the takeover or merger, and may even prohibit it.

3 ANTI-COMPETITIVE PRACTICES

The Competition Act 1980 (CA) regulates the control of anti-competitive practices (ACPs) as opposed to monopolies, mergers, restrictive trade practices and resale price maintenance. The DGFT is primarily responsible for investigations into ACPs. An ACP is defined by s 2 of the CA as a course of conduct which restricts, distorts or prevents competition in the production or acquisition of goods or in the supply of goods and services in the UK.

Unless it is also a monopolist, a firm with a turnover below £5 million is exempted from ACP legislation; the object is to prevent large firms from abusing their power, rather than to prevent new firms breaking into a market.

3.1 Types of anti-competitive practice

Most acts aimed at *resale price maintenance* are illegal under other legislation, covered later in this chapter. Generally *restrictive trade practices* are also regulated elsewhere, but there may also be an ACP here if one firm engages in a series of registrable restrictive trade practices, since this would be a 'course of conduct'. Neither monopolies nor mergers are in themselves ACPs, either because there is no 'course of conduct' or because they do not set out to restrict, distort or prevent competition.

ACPs include discriminatory pricing, forcing customers to buy entire product ranges rather than individual items and refusals to supply.

Activity 2

X Ltd obtains a patent on a new product. This gives the company a monopoly for 20 years. While this might be anti-competitive, why is it in the public interest to grant such monopolies?

3.2 ACP investigations

It is in the DGFT's sole discretion as to whether or not to investigate an ACP, and broadly speaking at any stage he may decide that the purpose is better served by obtaining and monitoring undertakings from firms that such practices shall be given up. Once he has investigated, he publishes a report and may refer the case to the MMC which in turn submits a report to Parliament. The Secretary of State may then make an order to restrict the ACP or to remedy its effect.

3.3 Other provisions of the Competition Act 1980

The Act also provides for a form of investigation into the activities of nationalised industries and certain other bodies: ss 10 and 11. The Secretary of State may require the MMC to investigate, for example, whether such a body is abusing a monopoly position.

Monopoly pricing is also covered by the CA (s 13) which allows the Secretary of State to refer any specified price to the DGFT. The price must be of major public concern: that is, of general economic importance and likely to have a significant effect on consumers.

4   RESTRICTIVE TRADE PRACTICES

The Restrictive Trade Practices Act 1976 (RTPA) requires that arrangements designed to fix prices or to regulate supplies of goods must be registered with the DGFT who has a duty to take proceedings before the Restrictive Practices Court. Unless it is then shown that the arrangements are in the public interest they are declared void. There can be heavy fines for infringement of these rules. The DGFT also has the duty to enforce orders made by the Court; breach of such orders is punishable as contempt of court.

The RTPA applies to agreements made between two or more persons carrying on business within the UK either in the production or supply of goods or in the supply of services. All agreements must be registered with the DGFT if they contain restrictions in respect of:

(a) prices to be charged, quoted or paid for goods or services;

(b) prices to be recommended or suggested as the prices to be charged or quoted;

(c) the terms or conditions subject to which goods or services are to be supplied or obtained;

(d) the quantities or descriptions of goods, or the scale or extent of services, to be supplied or obtained;

(e) the processes of manufacture of goods, or the form or manner in which services are to be supplied or obtained; or

(f) the person or classes of person to whom goods or services are to be supplied or from whom they are to be obtained.

The Act also extends to *information agreements*, defined as agreements between two or more persons carrying on business within the UK under which the parties exchange information with each other on the matters described above. The information so exchanged may relate to past activities, not just to future intentions.

Certain agreements are exempt from registration. These cover such areas as patents, distribution rights and agriculture and forestry matters.

If a registrable agreement is not registered it is void. A third party who suffers loss by the operation of a void restrictive agreement, for example a customer who has paid higher prices for goods than would have been charged if the suppliers had been competing, may sue for damages. The Director General may apply to the court for an injunction to restrain arrangements operated in contravention of these rules.

Activity 3

Some manufacturers of domestic fuse boards agree that they will only supply one electrician in each town. Is this a registrable trade practice? Why?

4.1 The Restrictive Practices Court

The Restrictive Practices Court is presided over by a High Court judge. Its members include both judges and laymen. Laymen are chosen for their knowledge or experience in industry, commerce or public affairs (s 3(1) Restrictive Practices Court Act 1976).

The DGFT applies to the Court for a declaration as to whether a restriction contained in a registered agreement is contrary to the public interest. If the Court decides that it is, the agreement is declared void in respect of that restriction (s 2(1) RTPA). The DGFT may then request an order from the Court prohibiting the parties from continuing in the agreement or making a new agreement to similar effect.

RTP gateways

The parties to the agreement must try to satisfy the Court that the restriction is not contrary to the public interest. To do so they must show that one or more of a number of 'gateways' applies (s 10), for example that the restriction is reasonably necessary to protect the public against injury or that the removal of the restriction would deny to the public specific and substantial benefits or advantages.

5 RESALE PRICE MAINTENANCE

The Resale Prices Act 1976 (RPA) consolidated the law relating to resale price maintenance. The Act declares void collective agreements between suppliers or dealers and manufacturers for the enforcement of price maintenance arrangements.

They are prohibited from imposing conditions for the maintenance of minimum prices at which goods are to be resold, and are also prohibited from enforcing such prices by withholding supplies from dealers who do not comply with them. However, it is still open to an *individual* supplier to recommend a minimum price for his goods, and there are exceptions to the rules on withholding supplies, as where buyers have premises or after sales services which are unsatisfactory.

Classes of goods may be exempted from the Act if to do so will be in the public interest. The only classes actually exempted are books and ethical and proprietary drugs.

Activity 4

Until recently the Net Book Agreement imposed retail price maintenance on all books sold subject to its terms. Why might the agreement be argued to be in the public interest, and why might it be argued to be against the public interest?

6 EUROPEAN COMMUNITY COMPETITION LAW

Anti-competitive practices which affect only the trader within one member state of the European Community (the EC) are subject only to national legislation. However, where such practices may affect trade *between* member states, the EC rules on competition come into force. These prohibit 'all agreements between undertakings, decisions by associations of undertakings and concerted practices which may affect trade between member states and which have as their object or effect the prevention, restriction or distortion of competition within the EC'.

6.1 Restrictions on undertakings: Articles 85 and 86

Articles 85 and 86 of the Treaty of Rome are designed to prevent the economies of specific states from enjoying particular advantages arising from the practices of business or the policies of national governments. Both Articles refer to 'undertakings' to cover any body or person engaged in commercial activities. Proceedings for infringement are brought by the Commission subject to control by the Court of Justice, but in any proceedings before them national courts may declare that an infringement has taken place. This will normally have the effect, if the infringement is embodied in a provision in a contract, that the provision will be void.

Article 85: restrictive agreements, decisions and concerted practices

Article 85 prohibits all agreements between undertakings, decisions of associations of undertakings and concerted practices which affect trade between member states and prevent, restrict or distort competition. Any such agreement or decision is void. Any agreement may, however, be justified (subject to certain conditions) and the prohibition be declared to be inapplicable if the agreement contributes to improving production or distribution or promotes technical or economic progress, while allowing consumers a fair share of the resulting benefit. But the power to make such declarations is vested in the Commission, not the national courts.

Individual agreements which do not pose any serious threat of distorting competition (such as agreements restricting the rights of a transferee or user of intellectual property rights) may be exempted on application by the parties to the Commission, and there is a general exemption for certain agreements such as those for exclusive distributorships or exclusive purchasing, agreements relating to research and development up to the stage of industrial exploitation and motor vehicle distribution and servicing agreements. The Commission has issued a notice stating which agreements of a *co-operative* kind are regarded as not distorting competition, for example joint activities such as sharing market research reports, sharing financial consultancy and advice, and sharing production facilities and advertising.

Agreement is not limited to legally binding contracts: any consensual arrangement is covered so long as it is between undertakings which are *separate economic entities*: thus arrangements between a principal and his agent or between a parent company and its subsidiary are outside the Article.

Decision is not limited to decisions which are legally binding on the members of the association: any decision, including a decision to recommend a particular practice by its members, is within the article.

Concerted practice embraces activities involving contact between the parties (falling far short of legally binding agreements), but the contact may derive from the practice itself, such as where a number of companies in a trade each adhere to a traditional periodical price notification system, which enables each company to learn of the prices of competitors swiftly and concurrently. But generally merely adjusting to the practices of competitors, such as raising or lowering prices in response to competitors' price movements, is not a concerted practice.

Activity 5

Give some examples of agreements which would affect trade between member states and which would therefore be likely to be void under Article 85.

Article 86: abuse of dominant position

Any abuse by one or more undertakings of a dominant position within the EC or in a substantial part of it is prohibited so far as it affects trade between member states; the list of particular abuses is similar to that set out in Article 85. Where a group of interrelated companies is involved, their conduct jointly may infringe Article 86.

An undertaking will enjoy a *dominant position* where it has power 'which enables it to hinder the maintenance of effective competition in the relevant market by allowing it to behave to an appreciable extent independently of its competitors and customers and ultimately of consumers'. Whether a dominant position is enjoyed depends upon the definition of the market in which the undertaking operates and the undertaking's overall power in respect of that market. A dominant position itself is not reprehensible: only an abuse of it is an infringement.

Chapter roundup

- The Director General of Fair Trading reports on monopolies and mergers, investigates anti-competitive practices, registers restrictive trade practices and seeks undertakings from persons as to their future conduct. The Monopolies and Mergers Commission and the Secretary of State for Trade and Industry may become involved in particular cases.

- The main objective of UK competition law is to protect the public interest.

- A monopoly generally exists when one person has a market share of 25% or more, either as seller or as buyer. The Secretary of State may refer such monopolies, and any mergers meeting certain criteria, to the Monopolies and Mergers Commission.

Chapter roundup *continued*

- Anti-competitive practices are regulated under the Competition Act 1980. The Director General of Fair Trading may investigate and report on such practices, and the Secretary of State may make orders in relation to them.

- Restrictive trade practices must in general be registered. They may be challenged before the Restrictive Practices Court, which will only allow such a practice to continue if one or more of the recognised gateways applies.

- Resale price maintenance is in general forbidden, but there are exceptions for books and for drugs.

- Under Article 85 of the Treaty of Rome, restrictive agreements, decisions of associations of undertakings and concerted practices are void if they affect trade between member states, they cannot be justified and they are not exempt. Under Article 86, abuses of dominant positions are forbidden.

Quick quiz

1   What is the role of the Secretary of State for Trade and Industry in UK competition law?
2   Define a monopoly.
3   What kinds of merger are affected by FTA?
4   How does the Competition Act 1980 define an anti-competitive practice?
5   List five types of agreement required to be registered under the Restrictive Trade Practices Act 1976.
6   What is an information agreement?
7   How may the provisions of the Resale Prices Act 1976 be enforced?
8   What is a concerted practice for the purposes of Article 85?
9   What is a dominant position under Article 86? Will such a position automatically be regarded as an infringement?

Solutions to activities

1   The large customer could enforce a precise product specification to suit his purposes, and could demand substantial discounts, leading the suppliers to raise the price to other customers.

2   Without the possibility of obtaining patents, many companies would not invest in research and development.

3   Yes: it restricts the persons to whom goods are to be supplied.

4   The agreement sustained small and specialist bookshops, but it also kept the prices of some titles artificially high.

5   Agreements to supply at different prices in different states.

    Agreements not to sell to certain states.

    You may be able to think of other examples.

Further question practice

Now try the following practice questions at the end of this text

Multiple choice questions: **47 to 50**

Chapter 14

TORT

Introduction

There is no entirely satisfactory definition of tort. The principle is that the law gives various rights to persons, such as the right of a person in possession of land to occupy it without interference or invasion by trespassers. When such a right is infringed the wrongdoer is liable in tort.

There is therefore a duty imposed by law to respect the legal rights of others. When a tort is committed the remedy is an action at common law for unliquidated damages, which represent such compensation as the court may see fit to award. The principles of tort are based on rights, the related duty to respect them and compensation for infringement.

Tort is distinguished from other legal wrongs.

(a) A *crime* is an offence prohibited by law. The state prosecutes the offender and punishment is by fine or imprisonment. A tort is a civil wrong and the person wronged sues in a civil court for compensation (or for an injunction against repetition).

(b) *Breach of contract* and *breach of trust* are civil wrongs. It must be shown that the defendant was subject to the obligations of a contract or a trust and did not perform or observe those obligations. In tort no previous transaction or relationship need exist: the parties may be complete strangers.

Your objectives

After completing this chapter you should:

(a) understand the significance of both wrong and damage;

(b) know how damage is assessed for remoteness;

(c) appreciate when an employer may be responsible for a tort committed by an employee;

(d) know the rule in *Rylands v Fletcher*;

(e) know the main defences to an action in tort;

(f) appreciate the effect of contributory negligence;

(g) know the main remedies for torts, and the types of damages which may be awarded.

1 WRONG AND DAMAGE DISTINGUISHED

When a plaintiff sues in tort claiming damages as compensation for loss he must normally prove his loss. But the necessary basis of his claim is that he has suffered a wrong. If there is no wrong *(injuria)* for which the law gives a remedy, no amount of damage *(damnum)* caused by the defendant can make him liable. *Damnum sine injuria* (loss not caused by wrong) is not actionable.

In some torts it is necessary to establish both wrong and loss resulting from it; this is the rule in the tort of negligence. But in other cases, for example, trespass or libel, it suffices to prove that a legal wrong has been done and damages (possibly nominal in amount) may be recovered without proof of any loss *(injuria sine damno)*. Substantial damages may be awarded where the loss is serious, but difficult to quantify in money terms, as in cases of damage to reputation by defamation.

1.1 Motive

In tort, unlike crime, it is not usually necessary to prove anything about the defendant's state of mind. A good motive will not excuse a tortious act and a bad motive *(malice)* will not turn an innocent act into a tortious one. (There are a few exceptions such as the tort of *malicious prosecution* where there must be evidence of malice.)

Mayor of Bradford v Pickles 1895
P wished the Bradford Corporation to buy his land, adjoining the corporation's water reservoir, at a very high price. He sank a shaft on his land to divert the flow of subterranean water through it (as he was legally entitled to do). As a result less water flowed into the reservoir and it was discoloured. The corporation sued for an injunction, a court order to P to desist.

Held: the action must fail. P was exercising his rights as a landowner and was not infringing any rights of the corporation. It was immaterial that the corporation had suffered loss and that P's express motive was to inflict loss.

Activity 1

Tony plants trees in his garden. The roots remain on his land, but the trees soak up water from Peter's garden next door, thereby causing Peter's plants to wither. Is there *injuria*? Is there *damnum*?

---

2 REMOTENESS OF DAMAGE

When a person commits a tort with the intention of causing loss or harm which in fact results from the wrongful act, that loss or harm can never be too remote a consequence. Damages will be awarded for it.

If the sequence of cause and effect includes a new act (called a *novus actus interveniens*) of a third party or of the plaintiff, it may terminate the defendant's liability at that point: further consequences are too remote and he is not required to pay compensation for them. But where the intervening act is that of a third party who could be expected to behave as he did in the situation arising from the defendant's original wrongful act, the intervening act does not break the chain.

Scott v Shepherd 1773
A threw a lighted firework cracker into a crowded market. It landed on the stall of B who threw it away. It then landed on the stall of C who threw it away and it then hit D in the face and blinded him in one eye. D sued A.

Held: there was no break in the chain of causation from A's intentional wrongful act and he was liable to D.

2.1 Reasonable foresight

If the intervening act is that of the plaintiff himself and he acts unreasonably, for example, by taking an avoidable and foreseeable risk of injury to himself, that breaks the chain (or if it does not it may reduce his claim for loss because of his contributory negligence).

When there is a sequence of physical cause and effect without human intervention, the ultimate loss is too remote (so that damages cannot be recovered for it) unless it could have been reasonably foreseen that some loss of that kind might occur as a consequence of the wrong.

The Wagon Mound 1961

A ship (the *Wagon Mound*) was taking on furnace oil in Sydney harbour. By negligence oil was spilled onto the water and it drifted to a wharf 200 yards away where welding equipment was being used to repair another ship. The owner of the wharf at first stopped work because of the fire risk but later resumed working because he was advised that sparks from a welding torch were unlikely to set fire to furnace oil. Safety precautions were taken. A spark fell onto a piece of cotton waste floating in the oil and this served as a wick, thereby starting a fire which caused damage to the wharf. The owners of the wharf sued the charterers of the *Wagon Mound*, basing their claim on an earlier decision that damage caused by a direct and uninterrupted sequence of physical events is never too remote even though it could not reasonably be foreseen.

Held: the claim must fail. The earlier decision was overruled and the reasonable foresight test was laid down. Pollution was the foreseeable risk: fire was not. This was a decision of the Privy Council on appeal from Australia and as such only a persuasive precedent for English courts. But as it was a decision of the most senior English judges it is always applied in cases where the claim is for negligence.

Hughes v Lord Advocate 1963

Workmen left lighted paraffin lamps as a warning sign of an open manhole in the street. Two small boys took one of the lamps as a light and went down the manhole. As they clambered out the lamp fell into the hole and caused an explosion in which the boys were injured. Evidence was given that a fire might have been foreseen but an explosion was improbable.

Held: the defendants were liable for negligence in leaving the lamps where they did. A risk of fire was foreseeable and the explosion must be regarded as 'an unexpected manifestation of the apprehended physical dangers'. It was not (as it was in the *Wagon Mound* case) damage of an entirely different kind.

Doughty v Turner Manufacturing Co 1964

An asbestos cement lid accidentally fell into a cauldron of sodium cyanide at a temperature of 800 degrees Centigrade. The intense heat caused a chemical change in the asbestos lid as a result of which there was an explosion. The plaintiff was injured by the eruption of molten liquid. The chemical reaction leading to the explosion was previously unknown to science.

Held: a splash of sodium cyanide was foreseeable but a violent explosion was not. The result was unforeseeable and therefore too remote.

In cases of physical injury which is more serious than would normally be expected because the plaintiff proves to be abnormally vulnerable, the defendant is liable for the full amount of injury done. This is the thin skull principle: if A taps B on the head and cracks B's skull because it is abnormally thin, A is liable for the fracture.

Smith v Leech Braine & Co 1962
A workman was near a tank of molten zinc in which metal articles were dipped to galvanise them. One article was allowed to slip and the workman was burnt on the lip by a drop of molten zinc. The burn activated latent cancer from which he died three years later. His widow sued for damages.

Held: damages for a fatal accident would be awarded. Some physical injury (the burn on the lip) was a foreseeable consequence. The defendants must accept liability for the much more serious physical injury (cancer) caused by their negligence.

If the plaintiff suffers avoidable loss because his lack of resources prevents him from taking costly measures to reduce his loss, he may still recover damages for it: *Martindale v Duncan 1973*.

Activity 2

A factory owner noticed that a machine was not running smoothly. She had heard of similar cases in which the increased vibration had led to small parts flying off and causing minor injuries, so she warned the workers to check that all such parts were secure and instructed them to carry on using the machine. The motor disintegrated and part of it broke through the casing and badly injured a worker, who then sued the factory owner. Why would the factory owner be unlikely to be able to rely on either The *Wagon Mound 1961* or *Doughty v Turner Manufacturing Co 1964* in her defence?

---

3 VICARIOUS LIABILITY

Definition

Tortfeasor: a person who commits a tort.

A tortfeasor is always liable for his wrong. Others may be jointly and severally liable with him under the principle of vicarious liability. If, for example, a partner commits a tort either with the authority of the other partners or in the ordinary course of the firm's business, the other partners are liable with him.

The most important application of the principle of vicarious liability is to the relationship of employer and employee. It is often not worthwhile to sue the employee for damages since he is unable to pay them. The employer however has greater resources and may also have insurance cover.

To make the employer liable for a tort of the employee it is necessary that:

(a) there is the relationship between them of employer and employee; and

(b) the employee's tort is committed in the course of his employment.

3.1 Employment relationship

It is usually clear enough whether an employment relationship exists because of the formalities it involves (such as PAYE). Sometimes, however, it can be unclear whether a person is an employee and certain tests are applied by the courts in such circumstances to assess whether the employer has *control* over the way the employee performs his duties, whether the employer is *integrated* into the organisation and the *economic reality* of the situation.

3.2 The course of employment

The employer is only liable for the employee's torts committed in the course of employment. Broadly the test here is whether the employee was doing the work for which he was employed. If so the employer is liable even in the following circumstances.

(a) The employee disobeys orders as to how he shall do his work.

Limpus v London General Omnibus Co 1862
The driver of an omnibus intentionally drove across in front of another omnibus and caused it to overturn. The bus company resisted liability on the ground that it had forbidden its drivers to obstruct other buses.

Held: the driver was nonetheless acting in the course of his employment.

Beard v London General Omnibus Co 1900
The same employer forbade bus conductors to drive buses. A bus conductor caused an accident while reversing a bus.

Held: the employer's instructions served to demarcate the limits of the conductor's duties. He was not, when driving, doing the job for which he was employed and so the employers were not liable.

General Engineering Services Ltd v Kingston and St Andrew Corporation 1988
Firemen were involved in a 'go-slow' policy in support of a pay claim and therefore took longer to reach a fire at the plaintiff's premises. The premises were destroyed as a result.

Held: the employees were not employed to proceed to a fire as slowly as possible, thus their conduct amounted to an 'unauthorised act'.

(b) While engaged on his duties, the employee does something for his own convenience.

Century Insurance v Northern Ireland Road Transport Board 1942
A driver of a petrol tanker lorry was discharging petrol at a garage. While waiting he lit a cigarette and threw away the lighted match. There was an explosion.

Held: the employer was liable since the driver was, at the time of his negligent act, in the course of his employment.

If the employer allows the employee to use the employer's vehicle for the employee's own affairs, the employer is not liable for any accident which may occur. There is the same result when a driver disobeys orders by giving a lift to a passenger who is injured.

Twine v Bean's Express 1946
In this case there was a notice in the driver's part of the van that the firm's drivers were forbidden to give lifts. The passenger was killed in an accident.

Held: the passenger was a trespasser and in offering a lift the driver was not acting in the course of his employment.

Rose v Plenty 1976
The driver of a milk float disobeyed orders by taking a 13 year old boy round with him to help the driver in his deliveries. The boy was injured by the driver's negligence.

Held: the driver was acting in the course of his employment. The boy was not a mere passenger but was assisting in delivering milk.

If the employee, acting in the course of his employment, *defrauds* a third party for his own advantage the employer is still vicariously liable.

Lloyd v Grace Smith & Co 1912
L was interviewed by a managing clerk employed by a firm of solicitors and agreed on his advice to sell property with a view to reinvesting the money. She signed two documents by which (unknown to her) the property was transferred to the clerk who misappropriated the proceeds.

Held: the employers were liable. It was no defence that acting in the course of his employment the employee benefited himself and not them.

Activity 3

A research chemist employed by a drug company works in a laboratory in which, for safety reasons, all experiments involving the application of heat are forbidden. The chemist tries a reaction in which heat is spontaneously generated, and an explosion results, injuring other employees. Discuss whether the chemist acted in the course of his employment.

3.3   Independent contractors

A person who has work done not by his employee but by an independent contractor, such as a freelance plumber used by a builder, is vicariously liable for torts of the contractor in the following circumstances.

(a) The operation creates a hazard for users of the highway, as in repair of a structure adjoining or overhanging a pavement or road.

(b) The operation is exceptionally risky.

> *Honeywill & Stein v Larkin Bros 1934*
> Decorators who had redecorated the interior of a cinema brought in a photographer to take pictures of their work. The photographer's magnesium flare set fire to the cinema.
>
> *Held:* in commissioning an inherently risky operation through a contractor the decorators were liable for his negligence in causing the fire.

(c) The duty is personal. For example, an employer has a common law duty to his employees to take reasonable care in providing safe plant and a safe working system. If he employs a contractor he remains liable for any negligence of the latter in his work.

(d) There is negligence in selecting a contractor who is not competent to do the work entrusted to him.

(e) The operation is one for which there is strict liability (see below).

4   STRICT LIABILITY

In many torts the defendant is liable because he acted intentionally or at least negligently. He may escape liability if he shows that he acted with reasonable care. That is essentially the position in the tort of negligence itself. But there are also torts which result from breach of an absolute duty: the defendant is liable even though he took reasonable care.

The outstanding example of a tort of strict liability is the rule in *Rylands v Fletcher*.

'Where a person who, for his own purposes, brings and keeps on land in his occupation anything likely to do mischief if it escapes, he must keep it in at his peril, and if he fails to do so he is liable for all damage naturally accruing from the escape.'

Rylands v Fletcher 1868

F employed competent contractors to construct a reservoir to store water for his mill. In their work the contractors uncovered old mine workings which appeared to be blocked with earth. They did no more to seal them off and it was accepted at the trial that there was no want of reasonable care on their part. When the reservoir was filled, the water burst through the workings and flooded the mine of R on adjoining land.

Held: F was liable, and the principle quoted above was laid down.

Activity 4

A is the owner of a piece of land, and he knows that natural gas tends to accumulate in caverns under the land. Building works by A cause one of the caverns holding this gas to fracture, and the resulting escape of gas causes a fire on B's adjoining land. Why could B not sue A under the rule in *Rylands v Fletcher*?

5 DEFENCES TO AN ACTION IN TORT

In an action in tort the defendant may be able to rely on a defence applicable to the specific tort – such as justification in an action for defamation, or that he took reasonable care in an action for negligence. But those particular defences are not available in every tort action. There are, however, general defences which may be pleaded in any action in tort. Of these general defences the most important is consent.

5.1 Consent

Volenti non fit injuria (no wrong is done to a person who consents to it) is the maxim which describes consent as a defence in tort (sometimes abbreviated merely to *volenti*). It must however be true consent, which is more than mere knowledge of a risk, and also a consent which is *freely given*.

In some cases the plaintiff expressly consents to what would otherwise be a wrong. For example a hospital patient awaiting a surgical operation is asked to give his written consent to the operation. But more often the consent is merely the voluntary acceptance of a risk of injury.

ICI v Shatwell 1965

Two experienced shotfirers were working in a quarry. Statutory rules imposed on them (not their employer) a duty to ensure that all persons nearby had taken cover before a dangerous test was carried out. As their electric cable was too short they decided to carry out the test without taking cover before doing so. There was a premature explosion and both were injured. They sued the employer.

Held: they had consented to the risk. The employer was not liable since it had not been negligent nor had it committed or permitted a breach of statutory duty over safety procedures. The injured men were trained for their work and properly left to carry out safety procedures of which they were well aware.

Consent in taking a normal risk may be implied. A competitor in a boxing contest or a rugby match gives an implied consent to the risks incidental to the sports played fairly in accordance with its rules, even if the actual injury is exceptional. In the same way a spectator at a motor race or an employee engaged on inherently dangerous work, such as a test pilot of experimental aircraft or a steeplejack, is deemed to accept the inherent risks. But an employee, by accepting a job or continuing in it, does not consent to abnormal or unnecessary risks created by his employer merely because the employee is aware of them.

Smith v Baker & Sons 1891

S was put to work by B (his employer) in a position where heavy stones were swung over his head on a crane. Both S and B were aware of the risk. S was injured by a falling stone.

Held: S could recover damages. In working in circumstances of known risk he was not deemed to consent to the risk of the employer's negligence. This principle has been developed in later cases to impose on the employer a common law duty to provide a safe working system.

In other circumstances it has to be decided on the facts how far knowledge implies consent.

Morris v Murray 1990

The plaintiff and defendant spent all afternoon drinking together with another man. Despite the fact that the weather was poor, the two decided to go flying in a plane owned by the defendant, who piloted it. He took off downwind and uphill; in such conditions a different runway into the wind should have been used. The plane crashed, killing the defendant and severely injuring the plaintiff, who sued the defendant's estate. His administrators claimed *volenti non fit injuria* and/or contributory negligence on the part of the plaintiff.

Held: right from the beginning the drunken escapade was fraught with danger and, although drunk, the plaintiff knew what he was doing. It was very foreseeable that such an escapade would end tragically and so, by embarking on the flight, the plaintiff had implicitly waived his rights in the event of injury consequent on the deceased's failure to fly with reasonable care.

Kirkham v Chief constable of Greater Manchester 1990

The deceased had hanged himself while in custody and his estate sued the police for negligence for failing to inform the prison authorities of the deceased's suicidal tendencies, contrary to official procedure.

Held: the defendants could not plead the defence of *volenti non fit injuria* because the plaintiff was suffering from a mental illness at the time of the suicide and therefore was not capable of consenting.

Rescue cases

A person who accepts a risk in order to effect a rescue does not lose his rights against the defendant if he is injured since his consent to the risk was constrained and not freely given. But the principle only applies when the risk is taken in order to safeguard others from the probability of injury for which the defendant is responsible.

Haynes v Harwood & Son 1935

The defendant's driver left his horse-drawn van unattended in a street. The horses bolted and a policeman (the plaintiff) ran out of the nearby police station to stop the horses since there was risk of injury to persons, including children, in the crowded street. He suffered injury in taking this action. The defendant pleaded *volenti*.

Held: the policeman (for the reasons given above) had not forfeited his claim by exposing himself to the risk.

Cutler v United Dairies 1933

The horse attached to an unattended horse-drawn van bolted into an empty field. The driver called for help and a spectator who responded was injured.

Held: the spectator had consented to the risk. He was not impelled by the need to save others from danger. His claim was barred by his consent.

Activity 5

A petrol tanker is supplying petrol to a filling station next to a busy road. A small fire starts on the forecourt, and a bystander picks up a fire extinguisher and goes to put it out. Because some petrol has been spilled, there is an explosion and the bystander is injured. If the bystander were to sue the petrol company, could the company plead *volenti non fit injuria*?

5.2   Unavoidable accident

Accident is a defence only if it could not have been foreseen nor avoided by any reasonable care of the defendant.

> *Stanley v Powell 1891*
> A member of a shooting party fired at a pheasant. A pellet glanced off a tree and injured a beater (the plaintiff).

> *Held:* the defendant was not liable for the reasons given above.

5.3   Act of God

Act of God, which is an unforeseeable catastrophe, is a special type of unavoidable accident. This defence is rarely available.

5.4   Statutory authority

If a statute requires that something be done, there is no liability in doing it unless it is done negligently. If a statute merely permits an action it must be done in the manner least likely to cause harm and there is liability in tort, for nuisance, if it is done in some other way.

5.5   Act of State

If a person causes damage or loss in the course of his duties for the State, he may claim Act of State. But it is not a defence in any case where the plaintiff is a British subject or the subject of a friendly foreign power.

> *Buron v Denman 1848*
> D was captain of a British warship who had a general duty to suppress the slave trade. He set fire to a Spanish ship carrying slaves and released them. The Crown later ratified his act.

> *Held:* neither D nor the Crown was liable.

5.6   Necessity

An act which causes damage may be intentional. If this is so, the defence of *necessity* may be raised, provided:

(a) that the act was reasonable (such as shooting a dog to prevent it worrying sheep), and

(b) either the act was done to prevent a greater evil or it was done to defend the realm.

5.7 Mistake

An intentional act done out of *mistake* may occasionally be defensible if it was reasonable. Such a case may be where a person makes a citizen's arrest in the reasonable and sincere belief that the plaintiff committed a crime.

5.8 Self defence

Similarly, *self defence* is a valid defence if the defendant acted to preserve himself, his family or his property, so long as the act was reasonable and in keeping with the nature of the threat. But if a blow is struck in response to mere verbal attack, there is no defence.

Activity 6

A lorry is carrying mirrors, stood upright and with the whole cargo being covered by a tarpaulin. The tarpaulin breaks free, exposing one of the mirrors. The sun is reflected off this mirror into the eyes of the driver of another vehicle, which then crashes injuring a pedestrian. If the lorry owner is sued by the pedestrian, which defence should he put forward?

6   CONTRIBUTORY NEGLIGENCE

If the damage suffered as a result of negligence was partly caused by contributory negligence of the plaintiff his claim is proportionately reduced: Law Reform (Contributory Negligence) Act 1945.

The defendant need not prove that the plaintiff owed him a duty of care. It is sufficient if part of the damage was due to the plaintiff's failure to take reasonable precautions to avoid a risk which he could foresee. If a motorcyclist, injured in a crash caused by the negligence of another driver, suffers avoidable hurt by failure to wear a crash helmet (which is compulsory), that is contributory negligence (*O'Connell v Jackson 1971*), which will reduce damages by 15% if injury would have been less had the helmet been worn and 25% if it would not have happened at all: *Froom v Butcher 1976*. So too is failure of a front seat passenger in a car to use a seat belt. The test of contributory negligence is what caused the damage, not what caused the accident.

There is however a standard of reasonableness. Mere failure to take a possible precaution or even thoughtlessness or inattention are not contributory negligence, unless there is a failure to do what a prudent person should do to avoid or reduce a foreseeable risk. If the plaintiff is a workman working at a monotonous task or in factory noise which may dull his concentration, due allowance is made in determining whether he is guilty of contributory negligence. A child of any age may be guilty of contributory negligence, but in deciding whether he has been negligent the standard of reasonable behaviour is adjusted to take account of his inexperience.

> *Yachuk v Oliver Blais 1949*
> A boy of nine bought petrol from a garage stating falsely that his mother's car had run out of petrol down the road. It was supplied in an open margarine tub. The boy (and his friend of seven who accompanied him) wished in fact to play Red Indians. They set fire to the petrol and the elder was badly burnt. The garage pleaded contributory negligence by the boys.

Held: the garage was negligent in selling the petrol in this way. There was no evidence that the boys realised the danger of what they did and so it was not a case of contributory negligence.

7 REMEDIES IN TORT

7.1 Damages

The amount of damages is based on the principle of compensating the plaintiff for his financial loss and not of punishing the defendant for his wrong. But there are several categories of damages related to the circumstances.

(a) *Ordinary (compensatory) damages* are assessed by the court as compensation for losses which cannot be positively proved or ascertained, and depend on the court's view of the nature of the plaintiff's injury.

(b) *Special damages* are those which can be positively proved, such as damage to clothing or cars.

(c) *Exemplary damages* or *aggravated damages* are intended to punish the defendant for his act, and to deter him and others from a similar course of action in the future. These damages are only rarely awarded. In *Rookes v Barnard 1964* the House of Lords ruled that exemplary damages could only be awarded for torts where statute permits, where the defendant calculated to make more money from the tort than he would have to pay in damages (as is sometimes the situation in newspaper libel cases), or where a government official acts oppressively, arbitrarily or unconstitutionally.

(d) *Nominal damages* are given where the plaintiff has suffered injury but has suffered no real damage (as in trespass to land without damage to that land).

7.2 Injunction

Injunction is an equitable remedy given by the court which requires an individual to refrain from doing a certain act, or orders him to do a certain act. There are two types of injunction.

(a) An *interlocutory injunction* is awarded before the hearing of an action so as to preserve the status quo. The plaintiff enters into an undertaking to pay the defendant for any loss arising out of the granting of the injunction.

(b) A *perpetual injunction* is granted after the full hearing and continues until revoked by the court.

Activity 7

A factory has its own electrical generator. The building containing the generator is left unlocked so as to allow rapid access in the event of fire, but there is a notice on the door which reads (in full): 'High voltage. Trained electricians only'. A child of ten is negligently allowed by his parents to play near the building. The child enters the building, suffers an electric shock and is injured. To what extent could the building's owner plead contributory negligence to reduce damages payable to the child?

Chapter roundup

- A tort is a civil wrong arising from a general duty rather than from a contractual relationship.

- If a plaintiff has suffered damage but no legal wrong has been done, he will not succeed in his action. If a legal wrong has been done but no damage has been suffered, damages may be awarded in some cases, but they may be only nominal.

- In most torts, the plaintiff need not show that the defendant acted maliciously, only that he acted voluntarily.

- Damages will only be awarded for loss which is not too remote from the actions of the defendant. Chains of causation may be broken by the actions of others, or may become too tenuous when the consequences go beyond what could reasonably have been foreseen. However, the thin skull principle may allow damages to be awarded for unexpected damage.

- An employer is liable for torts committed by his employees in the course of their employment. An employee may be acting in the course of his employment even if he disobeys his employer's orders. Vicarious liability can also arise for the torts of independent contractors.

- The rule in *Rylands v Fletcher* defines a tort of strict liability, in which reasonable care is no defence. It covers the escape of anything brought onto the defendant's land and likely to do mischief if it escapes, but it does not cover things naturally on the land.

- Consent of the plaintiff is usually a defence to an action in tort, but someone who acts to save others does not consent to the risk involved in the rescue. Other defences include unavoidable accident, act of God, statutory authority, act of State, necessity, mistake and self defence.

- The main remedies for torts are damages (which are generally intended to compensate rather than to punish) and injunctions. Damages may be reduced to take account of contributory negligence by the plaintiff.

Quick quiz

1 What is a tort? How is it different from other legal wrongs?

2 Distinguish wrong from damage, and identify the factors which must be present for there to be liability in tort.

3 How may remoteness of damage affect a claim in tort?

4 What two factors must be present for an employer's vicarious liability to be established?

5 When is a person liable for the torts of his independent contractor?

6 What is the rule in *Rylands v Fletcher*?

7 What is the meaning and significance of the defence *volenti non fit injuria*?

8 When will the defence of necessity be effective?

9 What happens if the court finds that there was contributory negligence on the part of the plaintiff?

10 Describe the different types of damages which may be awarded.

Solutions to activities

1 There is *damnum* but no *injuria*.

2 It was reasonably foreseeable that the part of the machine would break loose. The harm caused by large parts is of the same type as that caused by smaller parts.

3 The company would not be able to plead this defence because the bystander acted as a rescuer to prevent injury to other persons.

4 A did not bring the gas onto his land.

5 No: the bystander acted to prevent injury to persons.

6 Unavoidable accident.

7 Not at all: the parents' negligence is irrelevant, and the child was too young to understand the risk.

Further question practice

Now try the following practice questions at the end of this text

Multiple choice questions: **51 to 55**

Exam style question: **12**

Chapter 15

NEGLIGENCE

Introduction

As we saw in the previous chapter, many torts may be committed by mere carelessness rather than intentionally. In modern times the law has developed a tort of *negligence,* which is liability for a failure to take proper care to avoid inflicting foreseeable injury. It has become the most important and far-reaching of modern torts.

To succeed in an action for negligence the plaintiff must prove the following three things.

(a) The defendant owed him a *duty of care* to avoid causing injury to persons or property.

(b) There was a *breach* of that duty by the defendant.

(c) In *consequence* the plaintiff suffered injury, damage or (in some cases) financial loss.

Your objectives

After completing this chapter you should:

(a) know what must be proved in an action for negligence;

(b) understand the extent to which a duty of care may be owed;

(c) know the extent to which nervous shock is actionable;

(d) understand what constitutes reasonable care;

(e) appreciate when *res ipsa loquitur* may be invoked;

(f) know the main cases on negligent misstatement.

1 DUTY OF CARE

In the famed case of *Donoghue v Stevenson* the House of Lords ruled that a person might owe a duty of care to another with whom he had no contractual relationship at all.

> *Donoghue v Stevenson 1932*
>
> A purchased from a retailer a bottle of ginger beer for consumption by A's companion B. The bottle was opaque so that its contents were not visible. B drank part of the contents of the bottle and topped up her glass with the rest. As she poured it out the remains of a decomposed snail emerged from the bottle. B became seriously ill. She sued C, the manufacturer, who argued that as there was no contract between himself and B he owed her no duty of care and so was not liable to her.
>
> *Held:* C was liable to B. Every person owes a duty of care to his 'neighbour', to 'persons so closely and directly affected by my act that I ought reasonably to have them in contemplation as being so affected'. In supplying polluted ginger beer in an opaque bottle the manufacturer must be held to contemplate that the person who drank the contents of the bottle would be affected by the consequences of the manufacturer's failure to take care to supply his product in a clean bottle.

This narrow doctrine has been much refined in later cases. For any duty of care to exist, three points must be proved (as stated in *Anns v London Borough of Merton 1977*).

(a) There must be a sufficient relationship of proximity or neighbourhood between the parties (defendant and plaintiff).

(b) The defendant should be able reasonably to foresee that carelessness on his part may damage the plaintiff.

(c) The law should allow that duty to result in liability. In particular, liability for the acts of independent third parties has been restricted.

The comments made in *Anns* suggest that objective foreseeability leads automatically to a duty of care and that a defendant who satisfies the foresight test is therefore liable unless there are reasons (such as public policy) why he should not be liable. In *Murphy v Brentwood DC 1990*, a case with facts similar to *Anns*, the House of Lords seems to have overruled its own decision on the earlier case, and the test of liability has been tightened, both by this case and by the *Caparo* case (see below). The *Murphy* case suggests that a duty of care will be based upon proximity, a principle similar to that in *Donoghue v Stevenson* itself.

The decision in *Caparo Industries plc v Dickman 1990* has also cast doubt on whether a single general principle of negligence can provide a practical test which may apply to every situation. In particular, the concepts of foreseeability or 'neighbourhood' are little more than convenient labels to attach to different specific situations before the court which, on detailed examination, it recognises as giving rise to a duty of care.

In any given case, if a reasonable man could have foreseen the consequences then a duty of care may be owed; whether it has actually arisen or not depends on the facts. The duty may be restricted or ignored completely in the following circumstances.

(a) A person is not normally liable for the acts of third parties unless they were under his control. In an employment relationship, where there is control by the employer, the latter normally has vicarious liability for the acts of his servants done in the course of their employment.

(b) Certain persons involved in judicial process are immune from all civil action, particularly judges, lawyers and jurors during a trial. Arbitrators are immune when they act in that capacity, as are valuers acting as arbitrators or quasi-arbitrators.

(c) A person may be liable for omission, such as where an accountant carelessly leaves out part of his report, but a duty of care rarely arises from an obligation to take positive action which has not been taken.

Activity 1

Consider the reasons why a barrister acting as an advocate in legal proceedings should be immune from being sued in negligence.

There is generally no duty to take care to prevent third parties from doing damage: mere foreseeability of damage is not enough.

Perl v Camden LBC 1983
Thieves entered an empty house owned by the defendant and broke through from there into the adjacent property, stealing a number of valuable items.

Held: because there was no special relationship by which the house owner could control the acts of the thieves, no duty of care arose to the plaintiffs.

But if the defendant is in control of third parties he has a duty of care in the exercise of that control.

Home Office v Dorset Yacht Club 1970
DY's property was damaged by a number of boys who escaped at night from a Borstal institution. The escape was due to lack of care by the guards for whom the Home Office was responsible.

Held: the Home Office was vicariously liable for the negligence of its staff as it owed a duty of care to persons whose property it could be foreseen might be damaged if the boys escaped.

1.1   Economic loss

One of the most uncertain areas in the law on negligence is how far and in what circumstances there is liability for financial (usually called 'economic') loss, if it is not the direct consequence of physical damage caused by negligence. The most common example of economic loss is where a person who has suffered physical damage makes a claim for loss of business profits while the damage is put right.

But in the last 20 years successful claims have been made for loss of profits both in cases where the root cause was physical damage and in cases where no actual physical damage occurred at all.

Ross v Caunters 1980
A solicitor gave negligent advice to a testator and drew up a will carelessly. A gift to the plaintiff (an intended beneficiary) failed as a result.

Held: the solicitor owed a duty of care to beneficiaries since it was reasonably foreseeable that they would be damaged by negligent advice. The beneficiary could therefore sue for loss since he was actually in mind when the solicitor drew up the will.

If the courts can identify a special relationship 'akin to contract' between plaintiff and defendant, a claim for loss of profits may succeed. This case is generally regarded as exceptional.

Junior Books v Veitchi Co Ltd 1983
The defendants were sub-contractors engaged to lay a floor in the plaintiff's factory. Their contract was with the main contractor, not with the plaintiff. The

floor was defective and had to be replaced (pure economic loss, as the only damage was to the product itself).

Held: the defendants owed the plaintiffs a duty of care. They were not producing goods for an unknown consumer; they were working for a particular person whose identity was known and who was relying on their skill and judgement as flooring contractors.

The special nature of the *Junior Books* case has been stressed in subsequent decisions, which have reverted to the award of damages for economic loss only where that loss is attached to physical loss.

Muirhead v Industrial Tank Specialities Ltd 1986
The plaintiffs, wholesale fish merchants, purchased lobsters in the summer with the intention of selling them at Christmas when prices were higher. The pumps which they purchased to oxygenate the water were inadequate. The lobsters died.

Held: the death of the lobsters was reasonably foreseeable and this loss was recoverable. The additional losses were purely economic and were not recoverable.

Activity 2

As a security measure, A installs lights outside his house. The house of B, his neighbour, is thereby illuminated, and B expresses his gratitude to A for choosing a security measure which benefits both of them. A later removes the lights without warning B, and the night after he does so B's house is burgled. Could B sue A?

1.2   'Nervous shock'

The plaintiff may claim compensation for nervous shock caused by the defendant's negligent act. Typically the plaintiff has suffered a reaction when they have witnessed an accident in which a close relative is injured. Compensation will not be awarded for mere grief or distress: the plaintiff must prove a definite and identifiable psychiatric illness.

Nervous shock is dealt with separately from ordinary physical damage because it has been perceived as a potential area for a vast litigation and therefore particular rules have developed. A duty of care is not owed to everyone who may in fact be affected by the defendant's act.

There is a duty of care not to cause nervous shock by putting a person in fear of his own safety *Dulieu v White & Sons 1901*, or in fear for the safety of his children *Hanbrook v Stoke Bros 1925*, or by making him an actual witness to an act of negligence by which he suffers nervous shock such as seeing his house on fire: *Attia v British Gas plc 1987*.

A person suffering nervous shock may have a claim if they can show that there was a sufficiently close relationship between themselves and the primary victim and that they either saw the accident with their unaided senses or came upon the 'immediate aftermath'.

McLoughlin v O'Brien 1982
The plaintiff was called to the hospital where her husband and children were receiving emergency treatment shortly after an accident caused by the defendant. She was informed that her daughter had died. She suffered nervous shock.

Held: it was reasonably foreseeable that the plaintiff would be affected. She had a close relationship with the primary victims and came upon the immediate aftermath. Therefore she could recover damages.

It appears then that a distinction can be drawn between those who have a close family tie to the victim and a mere bystander. There is also a distinction between those who witness an event and are proximate to the accident in terms of time and space and those who are told of the accident or witness it via simultaneous television broadcast.

Alcock & Others v Chief Constable of South Yorkshire Police 1991

This case involves the Hillsborough disaster when 95 people were killed and another 400 injured due to being crushed in crowded stands. Various relatives of the victims, who had proved various psychiatric illnesses as a result of learning of the tragedy, being at the ground or witnessing it on television, brought an action against the defendants in negligence.

Held: the plaintiffs' claim must fail either because they could not establish a sufficient degree of kinship to make it reasonably foreseeable that psychiatric illness would result, or because they witnessed the accident via simultaneous (or recorded) broadcasts and therefore were not sufficiently proximate in time and space.

Vernon v Bosley 1997

Two young children were passengers in a car driven by the defendant, their nanny, when it went off the road and crashed into the river. The plaintiff, their father, did not see the accident but was called to the scene and witnessed the unsuccessful attempt to rescue the children. The plaintiff suffered nervous shock.

Held: the plaintiff could recover damages from the defendant.

The Piper Alpha disaster in the North Sea produced further developments in this area. The issue was whether a duty of care was owed to a mere bystander who witnessed a horrific accident with his own unaided senses and subsequently suffered nervous shock.

McFarlane v E E Caledonia Ltd 1994

The plaintiff, an employee of the defendants, stood and witnessed the massive explosions on the oil rig in which 164 men were killed, before being evacuated by helicopter. As a result he suffered psychiatric illness and sued the defendants in negligence.

Held: No duty of care was owed in these circumstances. The plaintiff had not been in fear for his own safety nor had he been in actual danger. He had no close relationship with the primary victims and had taken no active part in rescue operations. As a mere bystander he had no claim.

It is established then that a person who suffers nervous shock as a result of participating in the rescue of injured victims in an accident would be owed a duty of care.

Chadwick v British Railways Board 1967

A serious train crash occurred as a result of the negligence of the train driver. The plaintiff attended the scene and over a prolonged period of time helped in the rescue work. As a result he suffered nervous shock.

Held: A duty of care was held to rescuers and as nervous shock was foreseeable in the circumstances. The defendants were liable.

Activity 3

S and her daughter, A, visit the local fair owned by C. A has a ride on the big wheel. S watches in horror as the carriage in which A is riding becomes disconnected due to rust and decay and plummets to the ground. S suffers nervous shock. Consider whether S could sue C in negligence.

2   BREACH OF DUTY OF CARE

The standard of reasonable care requires that the person concerned should do what a reasonable man 'guided upon those considerations which ordinarily regulate the conduct of human affairs' would do and abstain from doing what a reasonable man would not do. The standard of 'a reasonable man' is not that of an average man: for instance, the standard of a 'reasonable' car driver is a very high standard indeed, and would not be lowered for a learner driver. The rule has been developed as follows.

(a) In considering what precautions should be taken or foresight applied, the test is one of knowledge and general practice existing at the time, not hindsight or subsequent change of practice.

> *Roe v Minister of Health 1954*
> A doctor gave a patient an injection, taking all the precautions required at that time. The drug was contaminated and the patient became paralysed. At the time of the trial seven years later medical practice had been improved to avoid the risk of undetected contamination (through an invisible crack in a glass tube).
>
> *Held:* the proper test was normal practice based on the state of medical knowledge at the time. The doctor was not at fault in failing to anticipate later developments.

(b) A person who professes to have a particular skill, for example in a profession, is required to use the skill which he purports to have. But an error of judgement is not automatically a case of negligence: *Whitehouse v Jordan 1981*.

(c) In deciding what is reasonable care the balance must be struck between advantage and risk. The driver of a fire engine may exceed the normal prudent speed on his way to a fire but not on the way back.

(d) If A owes a duty of care to B and A knows that B is unusually vulnerable, a higher standard of care is expected. For example, B might be a child, an inexperienced employee given risky work to do or a person with a thin skull.

> *Paris v Stepney Borough Council 1951*
> P was employed by K on vehicle maintenance. P had already lost the sight of one eye. He was hammering metal. It was not the normal practice to issue protective goggles to men employed on this work since the risk of eye injury was small. A chip of metal flew into P's eye and blinded him.
>
> *Held:* although industrial practice did not require the use of goggles by workers with normal sight, a higher standard of care was owed to P because an injury to his remaining good eye would blind him. S had failed to maintain a proper standard of care in relation to P.

Activity 4

An accountant advises a client to use a well known tax avoidance scheme. At the time when he does so, the Inland Revenue is challenging the scheme in the courts. In a test case, the High Court has found in favour of the Inland Revenue but the Court of Appeal has found in favour of the taxpayer, and an Inland Revenue appeal to the House of Lords is pending. If the Inland Revenue succeed, any taxpayer who has used the scheme will be substantially worse off than if he had not used the scheme. If the Inland Revenue were to succeed in the House of Lords and the client were to sue the accountant, would the accountant be able to rely on *Roe v Minister of Health 1954* in his defence?

2.1 Res ipsa loquitur

It rests on the plaintiff to show both that the defendant owed him a duty of reasonable care and that the defendant failed in that duty. If the plaintiff does not know how the accident happened it may be difficult to demonstrate that it resulted from failure to take proper care. In some circumstances the plaintiff may argue that the facts speak for themselves *(res ipsa loquitur)*: that want of care is the only possible explanation for what happened and negligence on the part of the defendant must be presumed.

To rely on this principle the plaintiff must first show that the thing which caused the injury was under the management and control of the defendant and that the accident was such as would not occur if those in control used proper care.

> *Scott v London & St Katharine Docks Co 1865*
> S was passing in front of the defendant's warehouse. Six bags of sugar fell on him.

> *Held:* in the absence of explanation it must be presumed that the fall of the bags of sugar was due to want of care on the part of the defendants.

3   CONSEQUENTIAL HARM

A claim for compensation for negligence will not succeed if damage or loss is not proved. In deciding whether a claim should be allowed, the court considers whether the breach of duty gave rise to the harm and whether the harm was too remote from the breach.

A person will only be compensated if he has suffered actual loss, injury, damage or harm as a consequence of another's actions. The claim will not be proved if:

(a) the plaintiff followed a course of action regardless of the acts of the defendant;

(b) a third party is the actual cause of harm;

(c) a complicated series of events takes place such that no one act was the cause of all the harm; or

(d) an intervening act by the plaintiff or a third party breaks the chain of causation *(novus actus interveniens)*.

Having decided whether harm arose from a breach of duty, the court will finally look at whether the harm which occurred was reasonably foreseeable. The legal issues were discussed in the previous chapter.

Activity 5

E left her horse in a paddock surrounded by a high fence and with only one gate, but the horse got out of the paddock and injured J. E claims that she had shut the gate securely, but J claims that she had not disturbed the gate. It is certain that no other person was involved. What principle of the law of negligence might J try to rely on in suing E?

4   NEGLIGENT MISSTATEMENT

There is a duty of care not to cause economic loss by negligent misstatement, but the duty exists only where the person who makes the statement foresees that it may be relied on. There must therefore be a *special relationship*. To establish such a special relationship the person who makes the statement:

(a) *must do so in some professional or expert capacity which makes it likely that others will rely on what he says.* This is the position of an accountant providing information or advice in a professional capacity (or indeed of any other person professing special knowledge, skill and care), but the principle was recently extended to a friendly relationship with business overtones.

> *Chaudry v Prabhakar 1989*
> A friend of the plaintiff undertook (as a favour) to find a suitable car for her to buy; the plaintiff stipulated that any such car should not have been involved in an accident. The friend (who knew more about cars than the plaintiff did) failed to enquire of the owner of a car (which had, to the friend's knowledge, a straightened or replaced bonnet) whether it had been in an accident. In fact the car had been in a serious accident and it was unroadworthy and worthless. The plaintiff sued the friend for £5,500.
>
> *Held:* the friend owed a duty to take such care as was reasonable in the circumstances and had broken that duty; there had been a voluntary assumption of responsibility against the background of a business transaction; hence the friend was liable for the plaintiff's loss.

(b) *must foresee that it is likely to be relied on by another person.*

> *Hedley Byrne v Heller & Partners 1964*
> HB were advertising agents acting for a new client, E. If E failed to pay bills for advertising arranged by HB then HB would have to pay the advertising charges. HB through its bank requested information from E's bank (HP) on the financial position of E. HP returned non-committal replies which were held to be a negligent misstatement of E's financial resources. In replying HP expressly disclaimed legal responsibility.
>
> *Held:* there is a duty of care to avoid causing financial loss by negligent misstatement where there is a 'special relationship'. HP were guilty of negligence having breached the duty of care but escaped liability by reason of their disclaimer.

The House of Lords in this case adopted Lord Denning's tests of a special relationship laid down in *Candler v Crane Christmas 1951*:

> *a special relationship is one where the defendant gives advice or information and the plaintiff relies on that advice. The defendant should realise that his words will be relied on either by the person he is addressing or by a third party.*

It is almost certain that advice given on a social occasion cannot give rise to a duty of care, unless the person giving it realised (or should have realised) that it was going to be relied upon.

The principle of liability for negligent misstatement has been refined in the area of professional negligence to take account of the test of *reasonable foresight* being present to create a duty of care.

> *JEB Fasteners Ltd v Marks, Bloom & Co 1982*
> The defendants, a firm of accountants, prepared an audited set of accounts showing stock valued at £23,080. It had been purchased for £11,000, but was nevertheless described as being valued 'at the lower of cost and net realisable value'. Hence profit was inflated. The auditors knew there were liquidity problems and that the company was seeking outside finance. The plaintiffs were shown the accounts; they doubted the stock figure but took over the company

for a nominal amount nevertheless, since by that means they could obtain the services of the company's two directors. At no time did the defendants tell the plaintiffs that stock was inflated. With the investment's failure, the plaintiffs sued the defendants claiming that:

(a) the accounts had been prepared negligently;

(b) they had relied on those accounts;

(c) they would not have invested had they been aware of the company's true position; and

(d) MB owed a duty of care to all persons whom they could reasonably foresee would rely on the accounts.

Held: The defendants owed a duty of care (d) and had been negligent in preparing the accounts (a). But even though the plaintiffs had relied on the accounts (b), they would not have acted differently if the true position had been known (c), since they had really wanted the directors, not the company. Hence the accountants were not the cause of the consequential harm and were not liable.

This case implied that an auditor should reasonably foresee that he has a legal duty of care to a stranger. The decision was confirmed in *Twomax Ltd and Goode v Dickson, McFarlane & Robinson 1983*, where the auditors had to pay damages to three investors who purchased shares on the strength of accounts which had been negligently audited.

Activity 6

At a party, A asks B, a friend of his and a solicitor, about a dispute which he is having with his neighbour. B suggests that A comes to her office for a chat about it the next day. He does so, and B gives him some advice without charge. He acts upon that advice, and in consequence loses his right to sue his neighbour. Discuss whether A could sue B.

4.1   The *Caparo* decision

The *Caparo* decision has made considerable changes to the tort of negligence as a whole, and the negligence of professionals in particular.

Caparo Industries plc v Dickman and Others 1990
In March 1984 C purchased 100,000 Fidelity shares in the open market. On 12 June 1984, the date on which the accounts were published, they purchased a further 50,000 shares. Relying on information in the accounts, which showed a profit of £1,300,000, further shares were acquired. On 25 October C announced that they owned or had received acceptances amounting to 91.8% of the issued shares and subsequently acquired the balance. C claimed against the directors and the auditors because the accounts should have shown a loss of £460,000. The plaintiffs argued that the auditors owed a duty of care to investors and potential investors in respect of the audit. They should have been aware that in March 1984 a press release stating that profits would fall significantly had made Fidelity vulnerable to a takeover bid and that bidders might well rely upon the accounts.

Held: the auditors' duty did not extend to potential investors nor to existing shareholders increasing their stakes. It was a duty owed to the body of shareholders as whole.

In the *Caparo* case the House of Lords decided that there were two very different situations facing a person giving professional advice:

(a) preparing advice or information in the knowledge that a particular person was contemplating a transaction and was expecting to receive the advice or information in order to decide whether or not to proceed with the transaction (a special relationship); and

(b) preparing a statement (such as an audit report) for more or less general circulation which could foreseeably be relied upon by persons unknown to the professional for a variety of different purposes.

In *MacNaughton (James) Papers Group Ltd v Hicks Anderson & Co 1991*, it was stated that, in the absence of some general principle establishing a duty of care, it was necessary to examine each case in the light of the concepts of foreseeability, proximity and fairness. The absence of a general principle establishing a duty of care was now acknowledged by the courts, so the court had to consider whether it was fair, just and reasonable for a legal duty of care to arise in the particular circumstances of each case. Lord Justice Neill set out the matters to be taken into account in considering this as follows.

(a) The purpose for which the statement was made;

(b) The purpose for which the statement was communicated;

(c) The relationship between the maker of the statement, the recipient and any relevant third party;

(d) The size of any class to which the recipient belonged;

(e) The state of knowledge of the maker;

(f) Any reliance by the recipient.

In spite of the decision in the *Caparo* case, it is still possible for professional advisers to owe a duty of care to an individual. The directors and financial advisors of the target company in a contested takeover bid have been held to owe a duty of care to a known takeover bidder in respect of financial statements and other documents prepared for the purpose of contesting the bid: *Morgan Crucible Co plc v Hill Samuel Bank Ltd and others 1990*.

> *Galoo Ltd and Others v Bright Graham Murray and Another 1994*
> A firm had advanced loans to and purchased shares in G Ltd. A claim was made against the defendants who were auditors for G Ltd during the relevant years.
>
> *Held:* No duty of care was owed to the plaintiffs by the defendants because it was not foreseeable that the particular accounts would be relied upon for the purpose used.

Activity 7

An electrical engineer writes a book for general publication on the safe use of electricity. The advice given is generally sound, but there are certain circumstances in which precautions not mentioned in the book should be taken. Consider whether someone who suffers injury through not taking these precautions could sue the author in negligence.

Chapter roundup

- Negligence is causing loss by failing to take reasonable care when there is a duty to do so. A duty of care is owed to persons whom it could be reasonably be foreseen would be affected by the defendant's carelessness.

- The plaintiff may be expected to have taken reasonable and expected precautions, and defendants are not liable for the actions of third parties not under their control.

- Liability for economic loss is limited to cases in which there is a special relationship between the plaintiff and the defendant.

Chapter roundup *continued*

- Nervous shock is not generally actionable except by persons in fear of their own safety, witnesses actually present and relatives who learn of an accident immediately afterwards.

- The standard of reasonable care varies with the expertise of the defendant and with the circumstances, but later improvements in methods are not taken into account.

- Where there is no explanation for how an accident happened but want of care is the only possible explanation, the doctrine of *res ipsa loquitur* may be invoked.

- Damages are only recoverable for the consequences of the defendant's actions. The actions of third parties, or the actions of the plaintiff uninfluenced by the defendant's actions, may break the chain of causation and prevent damages from being awarded.

- Negligent misstatements by experts are actionable, but there is uncertainty about how widely a duty of care is owed. The most important recent case is *Caparo Industries plc v Dickman and Others 1990*.

Quick quiz

1   What is required to establish a valid claim for negligence?
2   How far has liability for want of care been restricted by developments in case law?
3   To what extent are damages recoverable for nervous shock.
4   Explain the significance of *res ipsa loquitur*.
5   How is a special relationship established in a case of negligent professional advice?
6   Describe the two ways in which professionals give advice, only one of which gives rise to a special relationship.

Solutions to activities

1   It is for public policy reasons that barristers may not be sued in negligence. If every unsuccessful litigant sued his barrister this would effectively lead to a retrial and excessive litigation which would be detrimental to the legal system and justice.
2   No: A is not responsible for the actions of third parties.
3   S could claim damages for nervous shock because she witnessed the accident with her own unaided senses and has a sufficiently close relationship (mother and child) with the primary victim, A.
4   No: the accountant knew (or at least should have known) of the risk.
5   J could sue E for negligence and rely on the principle of *res ipsa loquitur*. The horse was under the control and management of E and the facts speak for themselves.
6   A could sue B for negligent misstatement because B is giving advice in the capacity of solicitor (rather than friend) in a formal business context.
7   An action for negligent misstatement in these circumstances would fail due to the absence of a special relationship between the author and injured party.

Further question practice

Now try the following practice questions at the end of this text

Multiple choice questions: **56 to 59**
Exam style question: **13**

Chapter 16

OTHER TORTS

Introduction

In the last chapter we looked at the specific tort of negligence, which is particularly relevant to businesses. There are numerous torts, for example, trespass and false imprisonment. This chapter concentrates on three other specific torts: conversion, nuisance and defamation.

These three torts deal with a person's right to enjoy goods, property, land and reputation without adverse interference from another. Once again it is monetary compensation in the form of damages which is the usual remedy available.

Your objectives

After completing this chapter you should:

(a) know what constitutes conversion;

(b) know what constitutes a private nuisance;

(c) know what makes a statement defamatory;

(d) be able to distinguish between libel and slander;

(e) know what defences may be put forward to an action for defamation.

1 CONVERSION

Definition

Conversion: any action in connection with goods which denies or is inconsistent with the plaintiff's title.

Oakley v Lister 1931
O, a demolition contractor, agreed under a particular contract to dispose of 8,000 tons of hardcore from a runway. He rented some land on a farm to store the material pending its disposal. He had sold half of it when the freehold of the farm was purchased by L. L claimed that he had bought all that was on the land and removed some of the hardcore. He forbade O from removing any more of it, threatening him with an action for trespass. O contracted to sell the remaining 4,000 tons to a third party, who withdrew on hearing of L's claims. O claimed conversion.

Held: O was a lawful tenant and the owner of the material. L was asserting rights inconsistent with O's ownership of the goods. He had to pay in damages for conversion.

To maintain an action for conversion the plaintiff must be the owner and either have the goods in his possession or be entitled to immediate possession. A person who has possession but not ownership cannot sue for conversion. A refusal to return goods to the owner on demand is a form of conversion. If there is no prejudice to the owner's rights of possession and enjoyment, there is no conversion.

Fouldes v Willoughby 1841
F had put his horses on W's ferry boat but a dispute arose over the charges. W asked F to remove his horses and when F refused W put the horses ashore. F sued W for conversion.

Held: this was not conversion since W's action in putting the horses ashore in no way disputed F's ownership.

The normal remedy for conversion is damages. The value of the goods is usually determined as at the date of conversion, but in a case of wrongful detention the defendant may be ordered to return the goods.

2 NUISANCE

Nuisance may be of two types, public and private.

2.1 Private nuisance

Definition

Private nuisance: unlawful interference with the plaintiff's use of his property or with his health and comfort or convenience.

Private nuisance often takes the form of emitting noise, smell or vibration: it is essentially an indirect form of interference. If A throws garden rubbish over the fence into B's garden that is trespass; if A burns his rubbish by a series of smoky bonfires which causes real discomfort to B that may be private nuisance.

In private nuisance cases it is often necessary to strike a balance between the convenience and interests of two parties. The following factors may enter into the decision.

(a) If the activity causes significant damage to property it will generally be restrained as private nuisance. If it merely causes discomfort the advantages and disadvantages may be balanced to determine whether the activity complained of is so unreasonable as to amount to nuisance.

(b) Causing intentional discomfort to a neighbour is very likely to be restrained as unreasonable.

Christie v Davey 1893
C and D occupied adjoining semi-detached houses with a common party wall. D objected to the sounds of C's activities as a music teacher. He made very loud noises, for example banging metal trays to annoy C.

Held: C's music lessons were a reasonable use of her house; D's deliberate racket made purely to annoy was unreasonable. D was restrained from this conduct.

Where the plaintiff can establish actual damage to land or property, he is not normally required to show an additional element of interference: *St Helens Smelting Co v Tipping 1865.*

Where there is no element of physical damage, and the alleged nuisance consists of interference with the occupier's comfort and convenience, it is for the courts to balance the conflicting interests of plaintiff and defendant. The test has been stated to be whether the interference is an 'inconvenience materially interfering with the ordinary comfort physically of human existence, not merely according to elegant or dainty modes and habits of living, but according to plain and sober and simple notions among the English people': *Walter v Selfe 1851.*

Halsey v Esso Petroleum Co Ltd 1961
The defendant operated an oil depot. The plaintiff lived nearby. Acid damaged clothing hanging out to dry in his garden and the paintwork of his car parked on the highway. Noise from the depot's boilers and from oil tankers arriving and departing during the night interfered with his sleep.

Held: the defendants were liable for private nuisance for the damage to clothes and the noise from the depot. (They were also liable for *public* nuisance for the damage to the motor vehicle and the noise of the oil tankers.)

Defences

Defences to an action for private nuisance include the following.

(a) The right to commit private nuisance may be acquired by *prescription*. The defendant must show that the actions causing the nuisance have been carried on for 20 years.

(b) The defendant may plead that an activity which causes interference is authorised by *statute*. He must demonstrate that the interference is inevitable and that he has not been negligent. Negligence here means behaviour without reasonable regard and care for the interests of other persons.

Allen v Gulf Oil Refining Ltd 1981
The plaintiffs alleged that noise, smell and vibrations from an oil refinery caused a nuisance. The Gulf Oil Refining Act 1965 (a private act of Parliament) authorised the defendants to make compulsory purchases of land for the construction of a refinery, but did not authorise the construction or use of the refinery.

Held: construction and operation of the refinery were impliedly authorised by statute.

(c) *Consent* may be a defence to an action.

(d) *Act of God* is a possible defence.

(e) *Act of a third party* may constitute a defence.

(f) 'Coming to the nuisance', a claim that the plaintiff acquired land with knowledge of an existing nuisance, is no defence: *Sturges v Bridgman 1879*. It would be unreasonable to expect someone not to purchase a property because a neighbour is committing an actionable nuisance.

Remedies

Three remedies are available to a victim of private nuisance.

(a) *Damages:* this will be calculated on the same basis as an award of damages for other torts.

(b) *Injunction:* This is an equitable remedy and therefore discretionary: *Miller v Jackson 1977*. In spite of this the courts will usually grant an injunction where the nuisance is continuing.

(c) *Abatement:* This can be defined as removal of the nuisance by the victim. This is, as might be expected, not a remedy encouraged by the law. Notice must usually be given to the wrongdoer, except where there is an emergency or where the nuisance can be removed without entering the wrongdoer's land, for example to remove tree roots and branches: *Lemmon v Webb 1895*.

2.2   Public nuisance

Definition

> *Public nuisance:* 'any nuisance which materially affects the reasonable comfort and convenience of life of a class of Her Majesty's subjects.'

The sphere of the nuisance may be described generally as the neighbourhood; but the question of whether the local community within that sphere comprises a sufficient number of persons to constitute a class of the public is a question of fact in each case': *Attorney-General v PYA Quarries 1957*. An action for public nuisance is conceptually different from an action for private nuisance, even though the two may arise from the same conduct: *Halsey v Esso Petroleum Co Ltd 1961*.

Public nuisance is essentially a criminal act for which the person at fault may be prosecuted. A criminal action ensues, involving either prosecution or an action by the Attorney-General on behalf of the public. A plaintiff who wishes to commence an action in *tort* for public nuisance must show that he has suffered 'particular damage' beyond the damage sustained by the general public.

Examples of public nuisance include the following.

(a) *Obstruction of the highway.* The public has a right of passage along the highway. Interference with this right by means of obstruction constitutes public nuisance. The test is one of whether the defendant's action is unreasonable: *Dymond v Pearce 1972*.

(b) *Danger to the highway.* This may take the form of an obstruction which is dangerous, for example an unlit spiked barrier: *Clark v Chambers 1878*. It may also take the form of danger from buildings or premises adjoining the highway. 'If owing to want of repair, premises on a highway become dangerous and therefore a nuisance, and a passer by or neighbouring owner suffers damage by their collapse, the occupier, or the owner if he has undertaken the duty of repair, is answerable whether he knew or ought to have known of the danger or not': *Wringe v Cohen 1940*.

Activity 1

M holds loud parties in his house, annoying his neighbour J. Consider whether J is likely to succeed in an action for nuisance:
(a) if parties are held twice a year;
(b) if parties are held once a week.

2.3 Trespass to land

Definition

Trespass to land: unauthorised interference with a person's possession of land.

Trespass to land is committed by deliberately coming onto the plaintiff's land, even if the defendant did not realise that he was trespassing. The plaintiff may sue even if no damage has been done, but only nominal damages will be awarded unless damage is proved. The plaintiff may also seek an injunction to prevent repetition of the trespass.

3 DEFAMATION

Definition

Defamation: a defamatory statement is that it *damages the reputation* of the person defamed, and lowers his standing in society, causing him to be shunned or avoided or making imputations which are damaging to him in his profession, business or occupation.

Defamation, then, involves the publishing of a statement which has the effect of causing 'right-minded persons' to think less of the person or to avoid him. If a person makes a statement which is defamatory, he may be liable to the person he has defamed, unless one of a number of recognised defences is available. If a High Court judge allows, it is possible to bring a criminal prosecution for a particularly offensive statement. In general, however, the remedy for defamation is a *civil action* to recover damages. Less often an injunction, which is a prohibition against the repetition of a defamatory statement, may be obtained.

3.1 Libel and slander

There are two distinct forms of defamatory statement.

(a) A *libel* is typically made in writing, but it includes other statements made in a form which is likely to be disseminated widely or continuously, such as a film made for public exhibition (both sound and visual effects may be libellous), a programme broadcast by radio or television, a play (s 4 Theatres Act 1968) and effigies.

> *Yousoupoff v MGM Pictures Ltd 1934*
> A film was produced in England depicting the rape of a lady by Rasputin, and his subsequent murder. The lady had been romantically linked with one of his murderers. The plaintiff, who was married to one of Rasputin's murderers, alleged that people thought she was the lady who had been raped.

Held: a talking film, even where the defamation is only in pictures, is libellous. Hence the plaintiff did not have to show special damage to obtain her damages.

(b) A *slander* is typically spoken, or in some other transitory form, such as a gesture.

The distinction between these forms is important, since slander cannot be a crime, whereas libel may be. In addition, many actions for slander will only produce a remedy if 'special loss' is proved by the plaintiff, whereas libel is actionable *per se*.

A person may sue without proof of damage if a slander:

(a) casts aspersions on his integrity or competence in his profession;

(b) alleges that he has committed a crime punishable by imprisonment (*Gray v Jones 1939*);

(c) imputes unchastity to a woman (Slander of Women Act 1891); or

(d) imputes that he suffers from venereal disease.

'Special loss' must be proved in any other case of alleged slander to gain a remedy. This may be easier for a business client to prove; telling a supplier that his customer is a crook may lead to the latter losing a contract and so incurring special expense in loss of profit or in finding another supplier. But mental suffering and social ostracism leading to loss of habitual hospitality have been seen as special losses for individuals.

Each occasion on which a statement is made can be a separate case of defamation: there may be liability for a defamatory statement each time it is made, by whomever it is made. The defence of 'privilege' (as described later) is sometimes available to a person (such as a newspaper reporter) who repeats what was said by someone else; but in principle it is no defence to assert that the statement is only a repetition and not an original statement.

Activity 2

A club runs a gaming machine for the amusement of its members without the necessary licence. The authorities discover this, and one of the members of the club is accused (falsely) of having informed the authorities. Why is this accusation not defamatory?

3.2   An action for defamation

To succeed in an action for defamation, the plaintiff must show the following.

(a) That the statement complained of was *defamatory*.

It is the *sense of the statement, as reasonably understood by those to whom it was communicated*, which determines whether it is defamatory. In other words, it does not have to be shown that the defendant intended to damage the plaintiff's reputation or even that he was aware of its defamatory nature. The statement must be both *false* and *capable of being construed in a defamatory way*. It is up to the judge to decide whether a statement can be defamatory (question of law). The jury decides whether it was (question of fact).

(b) That the statement was *understood* to refer to him (the plaintiff).

On this issue also, the deciding factor is not what was *intended* by the person who makes the statement, but what was *understood* by the persons to whom the statement was made.

Hulton v Jones 1910
A newspaper published a humorous article describing the peccadilloes, while on holiday in France, of a churchwarden from Peckham, giving the fictitious name (it was thought) of Artemus Jones. However there was a *real*

Artemus Jones (a barrister who did *not* live in Peckham and who was *not* a churchwarden). He sued the newspaper, producing evidence from some of his acquaintances that they had understood the rather distinctive name to refer to him. The newspaper's defence was that it did not even know of the plaintiff's existence.

Held: the article must be taken to refer to the plaintiff since it had been understood in that sense. It was defamatory because it alleged sexual misconduct.

(c) That the statement was *published* so that third parties became aware of its contents.

For a statement to be defamatory, it must have been published. This means that some person other than the plaintiff, the defendant and the defendant's spouse must have knowledge of its contents. There is no case for defamation if the only way in which the statement is published is the action of the plaintiff himself – in showing a third party a defamatory letter which was addressed to hem alone.

3.2 Defences to an action for defamation

Consent

It is a defence that the plaintiff gave his *consent*, possibly only by implication, to the publication of a defamatory statement about himself: *Cookson v Harewood 1932*. This sounds unlikely, but, for example, the subject of a defamatory statement made at a company meeting may fail to object to it, thereby consenting to its publication in the minutes of that meeting.

Justification

Justification is a defence; the defendant must show that the statement was true in all *material* particulars. Defamation cannot be committed by telling the truth.

Fair comment

For the defence of *fair comment* to succeed, it must be shown that the statement was a fair comment on a matter of public interest which, insofar as it gave facts, was accurate, and that the defendant was not actuated by malice (improper motive) in making the statement.

Privilege

It is a defence that the statement was protected by *privilege,* which may be absolute or qualified. This is the most important defence in practice. The difference between absolute and qualified privilege is that absolute privilege remains available as a defence despite any evidence of malice on the part of the person who makes the statement. It enables members of Parliament, for example, to make statements with the deliberate intention of causing prejudice to the person about whom the statement is made.

Absolute privilege is given to enable a person to make statements *in the public interest*, without fear of personal liability. It extends to:

(a) statements made in Parliament and papers laid before Parliament;

(b) statements made by judges, juries, witnesses, counsel or parties in judicial proceedings and contemporary newspaper reports of those proceedings and other fair and accurate reports of those proceedings, such as the Law Reports;

(c) communications between high officers of state, in the course of their official duties;

(d) statements between solicitor and client, in some cases. (In others, only qualified privilege is given.)

Activity 3

If justification is pleaded as a defence to an action for defamation but the defence fails, the court may award aggravated damages. Why should this be so?

The defence of *qualified privilege* evolved through case law. It was extended to newspapers (subject to certain conditions) by the Defamation Act 1952.

Qualified privilege is applicable to a statement made *without* malice or improper intent, being a statement made:

(a) by a person who has an interest or a social, moral or legal duty to make the statement;

(b) to a person who has a corresponding interest or duty to receive the statement.

Qualified privilege has been held to apply to:

(a) references to prospective employers or credit agencies: *London Association for the Protection of Trade v Greenlands 1916*;

(b) statements in protection of one's private interests: *Osborn v Thos Boulter 1930*;

(c) statements made by way of complaint to a proper authority;

(d) professional communications between solicitor and client.

(e) fair and accurate reports of Parliamentary proceedings;

If a statement to which qualified privilege might otherwise apply is made in circumstances which give it wider circulation than is necessary to protect the common interest, malice may be inferred, and the privilege will be lost.

Activity 4

J is planning to bring an action for nuisance against her neighbour. She is discussing this with her solicitor in a wine bar, and she utters the words 'I think Mrs Smith next door to me is running a brothel'. Her words are overheard by someone who knows both her and Mrs Smith. If J were to be sued for defamation, would she be able to claim qualified privilege?

Chapter roundup

- Conversion is any action in connection with goods which denies or is inconsistent with the plaintiff's title. The plaintiff must be the owner and must have possession or be entitled to immediate possession.

- Private nuisance is unlawful interference with the plaintiff's use of his property or with his health and comfort or convenience. An injunction and/or damages may be awarded.

- A defamatory statement is one which damages the reputation of the plaintiff. In general, defamatory statements in permanent form or in radio or television broadcasts are libel and actionable without proof of special loss, whereas defamatory statements in transient form are slander.

- Defences to an action for defamation include consent, justification, fair comment and privilege (which may be absolute or qualified).

Quick quiz

1 What is conversion?
2 How is private nuisance distinguished from public nuisance?
3 What is the effect of a defamatory statement?
4 When may a person gain a remedy for slander without proof of damage?
5 What defences are there to an action for defamation?

Solutions to activities

1 J must be able to prove that M is unlawfully interfering with his enjoyment of his own land by holding loud parties. Annoyance may not be sufficient. An occasional party held twice a year would be reasonable on M's part. Parties held once a week could be unreasonable as to amount to private nuisance particularly if M holds them intentionally to annoy J.

2 The member is being accused of upholding the law, which does not damage his reputation.

3 The defamatory statement will have been given added publicity in the course of the trial.

4 No: she gave unnecessary publicity to the allegation.

Further question practice

Now try the following practice questions at the end of this text

Multiple choice questions: **60 and 61**

Chapter 17

THE NATURE OF A COMPANY

Introduction

Chapters 17 to 26 deal with company law. Many students feel that they are simply having to memorise a list of rules, but the subject will be more interesting if you keep an eye on the newspapers and try to apply your knowledge to real life situations.

This chapter defines the nature of a company. A company is a separate legal person in its own right, distinct from its owners, and much of what follows derives from this principle.

Your objectives

After completing this chapter you should:

(a) understand the separate legal personality of companies;

(b) know when a company may be identified with its members;

(c) be able to contrast a company with a partnership;

(d) know how a company may be liable in tort and crime;

(e) understand how public and private companies differ;

(f) understand the relationship between holding and subsidiary companies.

1   THE COMPANY AS A LEGAL ENTITY

The word 'company' is generally used to describe a company formed by *registration* under the Companies Act 1985. This is the main piece of legislation on companies, and all statutory references in the remainder of this book are to this Act (as amended by later legislation) unless otherwise stated.

Definition

Corporate body: a legal entity or person that exists distinct from its members.

A company has a number of characteristics in consequence of being a legal entity separate from its members.

Limited liability. The company is liable without limit for its own debts. However it obtains its capital from and distributes its profits to its members. It may be – and usually is – formed on the basis of limited liability of its members. In that case they cannot be required to contribute (if the company becomes insolvent) more than the amount outstanding (if any) on their shares.

Transferable shares. The interest of members as proprietors of the company is a form of property (measured in 'shares') which they can transfer to another person subject to any restriction imposed by the constitution of the company.

Perpetual succession. A change of membership or the death of a member is not a change in the company itself because, as a separate person, it continues unaffected by changes among its members.

Assets, rights and liabilities. The assets and liabilities, rights and obligations incidental to the company's activities are assets of the company and not of its members.

The distinction between a company and its members as different legal persons was authoritatively established by the House of Lords in 1897.

> *Salomon v Salomon Ltd 1897*
> For 30 years S carried on business as sole trader. In 1892 he decided to form a registered company to which he transferred the business as a going concern. Soon after the company was formed it suffered losses. The company failed and went into liquidation. It then had £6,000 of assets left but owed £7,000 to its unsecured trade creditors and £10,000 to S under a debenture. If the secured debenture originally issued to S was valid, he would take the all remaining assets. The other creditors however argued that the security given by the debenture was invalid because 'the company was Mr Salomon in another form'.
>
> *Held:* the company has a legal existence and it is impossible to deny the validity of the transaction (the purchase of the business and the issue of the debenture) into which it has entered.

2   THE VEIL OF INCORPORATION

The veil of incorporation means merely that a company is to be distinguished as a separate person from its members. Exceptions are made (called *lifting the veil of incorporation*) in some specific situations.

2.1 Lifting the veil by statute to enforce the law

If, when a company is wound up, it appears that its business has been carried on with intent to defraud creditors or others the court may decide that the persons (usually the directors) who were knowingly parties to the fraud shall be personally responsible for debts and other liabilities of the company: s 213 Insolvency Act 1986. This is a restraint on directors who might otherwise permit their company to continue trading fraudulently when they know that it can no longer pay its debts. Even in the absence of fraud, s 214 Insolvency Act 1986 (wrongful trading) may apply.

A *public* company must, under s 117, obtain a certificate from the Registrar before it may commence to trade. Failure to do so leads to personal liability for the directors for any loss or damage suffered by a third party to a transaction entered into by the company in contravention of s 117.

A company is identified by its name which distinguishes it from other companies. Every company is required to *exhibit its name in its correct form* outside every place of business, on its seal (if it has one) and on its business letters and other documents such as bills of exchange. If the rule is broken an officer of the company responsible for the default may be fined and, as regards business documents, he is personally liable to the creditor if the company fails to pay the debt: s 349.

Activity 1

In *Macaura v Northern Assurance Co Ltd 1925*, M insured (in his own name) some timber which he had sold to a company of which he was the sole owner. When the timber was destroyed by fire, the insurance company was found to be not liable to pay for the loss. Why do you think this was?

2.2 Identification of a company and its members

The courts may ignore the distinction between a company and its members and managers if the latter use that distinction to evade their legal obligations or to conceal their criminal activities.

Gilford Motor Co Ltd v Horne 1933

H (the defendant) had been employed by the plaintiff company under a contract which forbade him after leaving its service to solicit its customers. After the termination of his employment H formed a company of which his wife and an employee were the sole directors and shareholders. H managed the company and used it to evade the covenant by which he himself was prevented from soliciting customers of G.

Held: an injunction requiring observance of the covenant would be made both against H and the company which he had formed as a 'a mere cloak or sham'.

Re H and Others 1996

Three company directors were charged with excise duty evasion. Between them they held 75% of the shares in two family companies. HM Customs & Excise had applied for orders to restrain the defendants from dealing with their property, and to appoint a receiver to manage it.

The defendants claimed that the assets of the family companies should not be treated as their assets for these purposes.

Held: the defendants had used the companies as a facade to conceal their criminal activities and the court could lift the corporate veil to treat the assets of the company as the assets of the defendants.

Evasion of liabilities

The veil of incorporation may also be lifted where directors themselves ignore the separate legal personality of two companies and transfer assets from one to the other in disregard of their duties in order to avoid a contingent liability.

Creasey v Breachwood Motors Ltd 1992
Breachwood Welwyn Ltd ('W') had dismissed the plaintiff from his position as manager in 1988. He issued a writ against W alleging wrongful dismissal. W then ceased to trade and transferred its assets to the defendants. The plaintiff obtained judgment against Welwyn which by then had no assets. Welwyn was dissolved in 1991.

Held: where a company with a contingent liability (in this case to the plaintiff), transfers its assets to another company which continues its business under the same trade name, then the court would lift the veil of incorporation in order to allow the plaintiff to proceed against the new company.

Evasion of taxation

The court may lift the veil of incorporation where it is being used to conceal the nationality of the company.

Unit Construction Co Ltd v Bullock 1960
Three companies, wholly owned by a UK company, were registered in Kenya. Although the companies' constitutions required board meetings to be held in Kenya, all three were in fact managed entirely by the holding company.

Held: the companies were resident in the UK and liable to UK tax. The Kenyan connection was a sham, the question being not where they ought to have been managed, but where they were managed.

Quasi-partnership

An application to wind up a company on the 'just and equitable' ground under s 122(1)(g) Insolvency Act 1986 may involve the court piercing the veil to reveal the company as a quasi-partnership. This may happen where individuals who have operated contentedly as a company for years fall out, and one seeks to remove the other: the courts are willing in such cases to consider the central relationship between directors rather than to look at the 'bare bones' of the company.

Ebrahimi v Westbourne Galleries Ltd 1973
The plaintiff and N carried on business together for 25 years, originally as partners and for the last ten years through a company in which each originally had 500 shares. They were the first directors and shared the profits as directors' remuneration; no dividends were paid. When N's son joined the business he became a third director and the plaintiff and N each transferred 100 shares to him. Eventually there were disputes. N and his son used their voting control in general meeting (600 votes against 400) to remove the plaintiff from his directorship under the power of removal given by s 303 Companies Act 1985 (removal by ordinary resolution).

Held: the company should be wound up. N and his son were within their legal rights in removing the plaintiff from his directorship, but the past relationship made it 'unjust or inequitable' to insist on legal rights and the court could intervene on equitable principles to order liquidation.

2.3 Groups of companies

A holding company must ordinarily produce group accounts in which the profits or losses, assets and liabilities of subsidiary companies are consolidated or treated as if they belonged to the holding company.

There is no general rule that commercial activities of a subsidiary are to be treated as acts of the holding company merely because of the relationship of holding company and subsidiary. But the companies may be so identified if either one is in fact acting as agent or trustee of the other. In the past the courts have been willing to treat a group of companies as a single economic entity where they were involved in carrying on what amounted to a single business.

> *DHN Food Distributors Ltd v Tower Hamlets LBC 1976*
> DHN carried on business as grocers from premises owned by a subsidiary of DHN. The subsidiary itself had no business activities. Both companies had the same directors. The local authority (the defendant) acquired the premises compulsorily but refused to pay compensation for disturbance of the business since the subsidiary which owned the premises did not also carry on the business.
>
> *Held:* holding company and subsidiary should be regarded as an 'economic entity'. Accordingly there was a valid claim for disturbance since ownership of the premises and business activity were in the hands of a single group.

However, in *Woolfson v Strathclyde Regional Council 1978* the House of Lords upheld a decision of the Scottish courts, on similar facts, in which they had refused to follow *DHN*. That approach was also disapproved of in *Adams v Cape Industries plc 1990* in which the Court of Appeal stated that, except in cases where the working of a particular statute or contract requires it, the principle of *Salomon* could not be disregarded merely because justice so requires.

A final blow to the single entity approach was struck in the more recent case of *Re Polly Peck International 1996*. There the judge felt unable to identify the companies as a single entity as this would create an additional exception to *Salomon*. The judge commented that the law normally looks for the legal substance of a transaction and not its economic substance, if different.

If a subsidiary becomes insolvent the holding company will not be liable for its debts unless it guaranteed them. A mere 'comfort letter' indicating an intention to pay is not binding.

3 COMPANIES AND PARTNERSHIPS

The owners of a small business have a choice whether to trade as a partnership or as a company but some professions, including solicitors, do not permit their members to practise as companies. The choice is often determined by the amount of tax likely to be paid under one alternative or the other. There are however a number of other factors of comparison.

The essential features of a partnership are as follows.

(a) A partnership is the relation which subsists between persons carrying on a business in common with a view of profit: s 1 Partnership Act 1890. A partnership is *not a separate entity*: it is merely the partners as a group working in a particular relationship with each other.

(b) Every partner is *liable without limit* for the debts of the partnership. It is possible to register a limited partnership in which some (but not all) partners have limited liability. But the limited partners may not take part in the management of the business: Limited Partnerships Act 1907. This exception is little used and is of no importance.

(c) Since partnership is a personal relationship *it ends on a change in the personnel* of the partnership.

(d) The *assets and liabilities belong to the partners* in a partnership. But they own the assets as 'partnership property' to be used in the firm's business.

(e) A partnership, unlike a company, cannot create a floating charge over its assets (such as stock in trade or book debts) as security for a loan.

Activity 2

In *Daimler Co Ltd v Continental Tyre and Rubber Co 1916*, heard when the UK and Germany were at war, the defendant was a UK company largely owned by Germans. The plaintiff was held not to be required to pay a debt to the defendant, because the defendant should be treated as an enemy alien. What did the court have to do to ignore the fact that the defendant was a UK company?

---

4 A COMPANY'S LIABILITY IN TORT AND CRIME

A company can have civil liability in tort for wrongs done by its officers and employees acting on its behalf in its business. This is a normal application of the principle of vicarious liability.

There is more uncertainty about the liability of a company for a crime committed in the course of its business activity. In general there can never be liability for a crime unless the person responsible for the criminal act did it with the necessary knowledge, intent or other mental condition (called *mens rea*: guilty mind). A company has no mind of its own.

It has been held that when a crime is committed by a senior employee of a company (not necessarily a director) he may be treated as the *directing mind and will* of the company which is then itself guilty of crime. This principle only applies to officers of senior status.

On 8 December 1994 *OLL Ltd* became the first company in English legal history to be convicted of homicide. The company was fined £60,000 and its managing director sentenced to three years' imprisonment, the first director to be given a custodial sentence for a manslaughter conviction arising from the operation of a business. The sentences followed the deaths of four teenagers in the Lyme Bar canoe trip disaster on 22 March 1994.

The conviction marks the first time a company has been successfully prosecuted for this offence. Previous attempts, most notably in the case brought against the P&O shipping line as a result of the Zeebrugge ferry tragedy, failed. The problem is that in crimes such as manslaughter a particular state of mind (that is recklessness) is required. A company obviously cannot have a reckless mind since it has no mind as such. However, if, as in the OLL case, the company's directors or senior management operate recklessly, there is no reason why the company should not be convicted.

The OLL case is likely to be confined to small companies. In larger companies it will be difficult to ascertain that the company's 'brain', that is senior management, was actually involved with or cognisant of the reckless conduct leading to death.

This decision is a logical extension of the *Salomon* principle. It is accepted that companies can 'do things', including committing crimes.

Where there is strict liability for a criminal offence a company may be convicted of it since the accused's state of mind (*mens rea*) is irrelevant to liability for such an offence: *Mousell Bros Ltd v London & North-Western Railway Co 1917*.

5 PUBLIC AND PRIVATE COMPANIES

A public company is a company registered as such under the Companies Acts with the Registrar of Companies. Any company not registered as public is a private company: s 1(3). A public company may be one which was originally incorporated as a public company or one which re-registered as a public company having been previously a private company.

A public company is such because the Registrar of Companies (referred to as 'the registrar' in the remainder of this text) has issued a certificate that the company has been registered or re-registered as a public company.

5.1 Differences between private and public companies

The more important differences between public and private companies imposed by law relate to the following factors.

(a) *Directors*. A public company must have at least two directors but a private company needs only one: s 282. The rules on loans to directors are much more stringent in their application to public companies and their subsidiaries than to private companies: s 330. A public company, except by ordinary resolution with special notice, may not appoint a director aged over 70: s 293.

(b) *Members*. A public company must have at least two members. A private company need only have one. There is no upper limit on the number of members of either public or private companies.

(c) *Capital*. The main differences are:

(i) minimum amount of £50,000 for a public company, no minimum for a private company;

(ii) a public company may raise capital from the general body of investors by offering its shares or debentures to the public; a private company is prohibited from doing so.

(d) *Dealings in shares*. In practice only a public company can obtain a Stock Exchange or other investment exchange listing for its shares. Not all public companies however are listed. There are additional rules of company law relating to listed securities.

(e) *Accounts*

(i) A public company has seven months from the end of its accounting reference period in which to produce its statutory audited accounts. The period for a private company is ten months: s 244(1).

(ii) A private company, if qualified by its size, may have partial exemption from various accounting provisions. These remissions are not available to a public company or to its subsidiaries (even if they are private companies): ss 246, 248 and 250.

(f) *Commencement of business*. A private company can commence business as soon as it is incorporated. A public company if incorporated as such must first obtain a certificate from the registrar who must be satisfied that the company has allotted at least £50,000 of its share capital, paid up as to at least a quarter of its nominal value and the whole of any premium: s 372.

(g) *Identification as public or private:*

    (i) the word 'limited' or 'Ltd' in the name denotes a private company; 'public limited company' or 'plc' must appear at the end of the name of a public company: s 25;

    (ii) the *memorandum of association* of a public company must include a clause describing it as a public company. Nothing of this kind is prescribed for a private company.

Activity 3

In what ways do the rules which differ between public and private companies give extra protection to investors in public companies? Why should such extra protection be given?

6 HOLDING AND SUBSIDIARY COMPANIES

A company will be the *subsidiary company* of another company, its *holding company*, if:

(a) the latter holds the majority of the voting rights in the former;

(b) the latter is a member of the former and in addition has the right by voting control to remove or appoint a majority of its board of directors; or

(c) the latter is a member of the former and controls a majority of the voting rights, pursuant to an agreement with other members or shareholders; or

(d) the former is a subsidiary of a company which is itself a subsidiary of the latter company: s 736 (1).

A company (A) is a *wholly-owned subsidiary* of another company (B) if it has no other members except B and its wholly-owned subsidiaries, or persons acting on B's or B's subsidiaries' behalf: s 736 (2).

The importance of the holding and subsidiary company relationship is recognised in company law in a number of rules.

(a) A holding company must generally prepare *group accounts* in which the financial situation of holding and subsidiary companies is consolidated as if they were one person: s 227.

(b) A subsidiary may not ordinarily be a member of its holding company or give financial assistance for the purchase of the shares of its holding company: s 23 and s 151(1).

(c) Since directors of a holding company can control its subsidiary some rules designed to regulate the dealings of a public company with its directors also apply to its subsidiaries even if they are private companies, particularly loans to directors: s 330.

Activity 4

A Ltd holds 60% of the shares in B Ltd, which holds 60% of the shares in C Ltd. A Ltd thus effectively holds 60% × 60% = 36% of C Ltd. Consider whether C Ltd is a subsidiary of A Ltd. Give reasons for your answer.

Chapter roundup

- A company is a legal entity separate from its members. It owns its own assets and has its own liabilities.

- A company may nonetheless be identified with its members in certain cases, generally to prevent the abuse of separate legal personality.

- A partnership is not an entity distinct from its members, and partners have unlimited liability for the firm's debts.

- A company can be vicariously liable for the torts of its employees. It may also be guilty of crimes committed by sufficiently senior employees.

- Public companies may, unlike private companies, offer their shares and securities to the general public. Correspondingly, they are subject to special restrictions.

- A group of companies comprises a holding company and one or more subsidiary companies. The control exercised by the holding company and its ownership of the subsidiaries is recognised in company law.

Quick quiz

1 What is meant by 'perpetual succession'?
2 What is the significance of *Salomon's* case?
3 In what circumstances does statute draw aside the veil of incorporation?
4 For what other reasons have the court identified a company with its members (excluding group companies)?
5 What is the 'economic entity' test applied to groups of companies?
6 State three differences between a partnership and a registered company.
7 Is a company liable for a tort or a crime committed by one of its employees?
8 State three differences between a public and a private company.
9 In what circumstances is one company a subsidiary of another?
10 Name three particular requirements made of groups by the Companies Acts.

Solutions to activities

1 M did not have an insurable interest because the timber belonged to the company and not to him.
2 The court had to lift the veil of incorporation to determine the owners' nationality.
3 The need for two directors may make it difficult for a single dishonest director to defraud investors.

A public company must produce accounts more quickly than a private company.

A public company must raise substantial capital before it may trade. It must therefore ensure that many investors (or a few wealthy investors) accept that it is reputable.

The extra protection is needed because capital may be raised from investors who have no prior contact with or knowledge of the company.

4 Yes: C Ltd is a subsidiary of B Ltd, which is in turn a subsidiary of A Ltd.

Further question practice

Now try the following practice questions at the end of this text

Multiple choice questions: **62 to 66**
Exam style question: **14**

Chapter 18

FORMATION OF A COMPANY

Introduction

This chapter deals with company formation. The most important topic is the section on the documents which must be submitted to the Registrar of Companies in order to form a limited company. The discussion of documents is developed more fully in Chapter 20.

In the previous chapter you were introduced to the idea that more stringent rules apply to public companies than private companies. This is true right from the start, with regard to commencement of business.

Your objectives

After completing this chapter you should:

(a) understand in outline the role of the promoters of a new company and the position of pre-incorporation contracts;

(b) know how registration of a new company is secured;

(c) know what conditions a public company must satisfy before starting business;

(d) know how a company makes contracts.

1 PROMOTERS AND PRE-INCORPORATION CONTRACTS

Definition

Promoter: the person who forms a company.

A company cannot form itself. It needs a promoter to undertake the task.

If the promoter is to be the owner of the company, it does not matter if he obtains some personal advantage from the process of forming a company. If, however, anyone else buys some or all of the shares, the promoter is in a *fiduciary* position to the company and must disclose any advantage he will gain to an independent board of directors or to existing and prospective members. If he makes proper disclosure, the promoter may retain his profit, unless he is accountable to the company under some other principle.

A promoter can recover his expenses, by agreement, from the company. If, however, he enters into a contract before the company incorporates but purportedly on its behalf, he and not the company is personally liable on it: s 36(4). The company cannot retrospectively ratify the contract; the solution is to enter into a new contract on the same terms as the old one.

2 REGISTRATION PROCEDURES

A company is formed by the issue of a certificate of registration by the registrar. The certificate identifies the company by its name and serial number at the registry and states (if it be so) that it is limited and (if necessary) that it is a public company.

To obtain the certificate of incorporation it is necessary to deliver to the registrar prescribed documents (see below) bearing the name of the proposed company.

The documents to be delivered to the registrar are as follows.

(a) A *memorandum of association* This is normally signed by at least two subscribers. However, in the case of single member private companies it is possible for only the one member to subscribe to the memorandum. The signature(s) must be dated and witnessed. Each subscriber agrees to subscribe for at least one share: s 1(1).

(b) *Articles of association* signed by the same subscribers, dated and witnessed. Alternatively the memorandum of a company limited by shares may be endorsed 'registered without articles of association'. The statutory Table A articles then become the company's articles in their entirety.

(c) A statement in the prescribed form (known as *Form 10*) giving the particulars of the first director(s) and secretary and of the first address of the registered office. The persons named as directors and secretary must sign the form to record their consent to act in this capacity. When the company is incorporated they are deemed to be appointed: ss 10 and 13.

(d) A statutory declaration *(Form 12)* by a solicitor engaged in the formation of the company or by one of the persons named as director or secretary that the requirements of the Companies Act in respect of registration have been complied with: s 12(3).

A registration fee is payable (currently £20).

The registrar considers whether the documents are formally in order and whether the objects specified in the memorandum appear to be lawful, since a company may only be registered if it has a lawful purpose: s 1. If he is satisfied, he gives the company a 'registered number' (s 705), issues a certificate of incorporation and publishes a notice in the London Gazette that it has been issued: ss 13 and 711.

2.1 Companies 'off the shelf'

Because the registration of a new company can be a lengthy business, it is often easiest for people wishing to operate as a company to purchase one 'off the shelf'. This is possible by contacting enterprises specialising in registering a stock of companies ready for sale when a person comes along who needs the advantages of incorporation.

Activity 1

'Off the shelf' companies cannot exist on the shelf, waiting to be bought, unless all the usual formalities of registration have already been complied with. What changes are the buyers of an off the shelf company likely to make immediately on purchase?

3 COMMENCEMENT OF BUSINESS

A *private company* may do business and exercise its borrowing powers from the date of its incorporation. It is normal practice to hold a first meeting of the directors at which the chairman, secretary and sometimes the auditors are appointed, shares are allotted to raise capital, authority is given to open a bank account and any other initial commercial arrangements are made. A return of allotments should be made to the registrar: s 88.

Within the first nine months of its existence the company should give notice to the registrar of the accounting reference date on which its annual accounts will be made up: s 224. If no such notice is given within the prescribed period, companies are deemed to have an accounting reference date of the last day of the month in which the anniversary of incorporation falls.

A new *public company* may not do business or exercise any borrowing powers unless it has obtained a trading certificate from the registrar: s 117.

To obtain a trading certificate a public company makes application on Form 117 signed by a director or by the secretary with a statutory declaration made by the director or secretary which states:

(a) that the nominal value of the allotted share capital is not less than £50,000;

(b) the amount paid up on the allotted share capital, which must be at least one quarter of the nominal value and the entire premium if any: s 101;

(c) particulars of preliminary expenses and payments or benefits to promoters.

The registrar must notify receipt of Form 117 in the Gazette and may accept the declaration without investigation and issue a trading certificate which is conclusive evidence that the company is entitled to do business and to exercise its borrowing powers.

4 COMPANY CONTRACTS

There is no special form of company contract – the same rules requiring use of written or sealed documents apply to companies as to individuals: s 36. The company must of course enter into contracts through agents. Its articles of assiciation delepate wide powers to its directors and they may in turn permit employees to make commercial contracts under their general or specific authorisation.

A director, secretary or other authorised officer of a company may authenticate a document on the company's behalf: s 41. Provided the signature is made in this way and in the course of the company's business, that person's signature is treated as that of the company: *UBAF Ltd v European American Banking Corporation 1984.*

Activity 2

What key principle of company law is reflected in the fact that a company can make contracts in the same ways as an individual can (albeit through agents)?

Chapter roundup

- A company is formed by its promoters. They have a fiduciary duty to the company.
- A company cannot be a party to a pre-incorporation contract, but such a contract can be replaced by a new contract which the company is a party to.
- Several documents must be submitted in order to obtain a registration certificate for a new company.
- A private company may commence business without further formality, but a public company must obtain a trading certificate.
- A company may make contracts in the same way as an individual, although it must do so through agents such as its directors.

Quick quiz

1 Define a promoter.
2 To whom should a promoter disclose any personal advantage which he obtains from the promotion?
3 If a company (a) acts on a pre-incorporation contract or (b) negotiates modifications of its terms, how in each case does that action affect the company's liability (if any) under the contract?
4 State the statutory rule on an agent's liability on pre-incorporation contracts.
5 Describe the documents which must be delivered to the registrar to form a company limited by shares.
6 How may a new enterprise avoid the complexities of registration?

Solutions to activities

1 The buyers are likely to change the company's name and its directors.
2 Separate legal personality.

Further question practice

Now try the following practice questions at the end of this text

Multiple choice questions:	**67 to 69**
Exam style question:	**15**

Chapter 19

PUBLICITY

Introduction

You should by now understand what is meant by limited liability and the advantage this affords to members. One reason that sole traders and partnerships do not choose to become limited companies is the requirement to make available to the public certain details about the company whether in the form of registers or annual accounts and audit.

Throughout these chapters on company law you will meet references to a company's obligation to publicise certain decisions, so it is important to understand at this stage how and why this should be done.

Your objectives

After completing this chapter you should:

(a) know the main sources of information about a company;

(b) know what information is available from the Companies Registry;

(c) know the required scope of accounting records;

(d) know the contents of and rights of access to the statutory registers;

(e) know how a company's annual report and accounts must be prepared and circulated;

(f) understand how auditors are appointed and removed from office;

(g) know the duties and powers of auditors.

1 ACCOUNTABILITY

1.1 Public accountability

It is a basic principle of company law that the advantages of trading through a separate corporate body (especially if its members have limited liability for its debts) should be matched by requiring the company to provide information about itself which is available to the public. Anyone who is interested in a company, typically because he intends to do business with it and perhaps to give it credit, can thus find out who owns and manages it and what its financial position was at the date of its latest accounts.

The basic sources of information about a UK company are as follows.

(a) Its *file at the Companies Registry* (situated in Cardiff but with a search room in London) in which the registrar holds all documents delivered to him by the company for filing. Any members of the public may inspect the file (called 'making a search') on payment of a small fee and obtain copies of the documents in it.

(b) The *registers and other documents* which the company is required to hold at its registered office (or in some cases at a different address of which notice is given to the registrar). Here too there are statutory rights of inspection.

(c) The *London Gazette* (published two or three times a week by HMSO) in which the company itself or the registrar is required to publish certain notices.

Constructive notice

Until 1989, the availability of information from the company's file at the registry was matched by a general principle of 'constructive' or 'deemed' notice. Because a member of the public had the opportunity of inspecting documents on the file he was treated in law as if he had done so. However, s 711A now provides as follows.

'A person shall not be taken to have notice of any matter merely because of its being disclosed in any document kept by the registrar of companies (and thus available for inspection) or made available by the company for inspection.'

Two specific exceptions to this are provided.

(a) Section 416 retains the presumption that any person who is taking a charge over the company's property has notice of any item requiring registration in the charges register, which is in fact disclosed in the register when the charge is created.

(b) Certain land charges registered at Companies House are deemed to comprise actual notice.

However, there is a general duty to make reasonable enquiries and failure to do so means that a person may still be treated as having notice: s 711A(2).

1.2 Internal accountability

A different aspect of the requirement that information must be given exists within a company. The management of the company is in the hands of the directors and they must be accountable to the members.

(a) The members have a statutory right to receive a copy of the annual accounts, together with the auditors' and directors' reports: s 238.

(b) Various transactions and interests of the directors must be disclosed in the accounts or entered in a register or other documents which members may inspect.

(c) Any loans to directors and transactions with the company in which they have a material interest must be disclosed in the accounts: s 232.

(d) There is a register of directors' interests in shares or debentures: s 325.

(e) In some cases, such as long-term service agreements or compensation for loss of office, disclosure to members is merely the first step and the transaction is terminable or void unless the members then approve it in general meeting: ss 319 and 312.

Activity 1

P receives and reads a copy of the Companies Registry file on X Ltd. In legal proceedings relating to subsequent events, he claims that he should not be treated as having had notice of the contents of the file. Why is he misinterpreting s 711A?

2 THE COMPANIES REGISTRY AND THE DTI

In its memorandum of association a company must state whether its registered office is to be situated in England (which includes Wales) or in Scotland: s 2. If in England its file is held at the Companies Registry at Cardiff and microfiche copies of the file contents are available for inspection in London. If the registered office is in Scotland the company's file is at the registry at Edinburgh.

Anyone is allowed to inspect a copy of documents held by the registrar or, if these are illegible or unavailable, the document itself: s 709(1). A person may demand the certificate of incorporation and a certified copy of any other document.

2.1 Contents of the registry file

On first incorporation the company's file includes a copy of its certificate of incorporation and the original documents presented to secure its incorporation. Every document delivered to the registrar in compliance with company law is added to the file.

If a company has been in existence for some time the file is likely to include each year's annual accounts and return, copies of special, extraordinary and some ordinary resolutions passed in general meeting, a copy of the altered memorandum or articles of association if they have been altered and notices of various events such as the appointment of a receiver or liquidator, a change of directors, secretary, auditors or address of registered office. If a company issues a prospectus, a signed copy with all annexed documents is delivered for filing. Even this list is not exhaustive.

2.2 The London Gazette

The registrar is required to give notice in the *London Gazette* of the receipt of any of the following documents (s 711 (1)):

(a) various resolutions, statements, notices and reports;

(b) a notice of change of directors;

(c) an annual return or annual accounts;

(d) a notice of change of address of the registered office;

(e) a court order for compulsory winding up or dissolution of a company or the liquidator's return of the final meeting in liquidation.

He also gives notice of the issue of a certificate of incorporation and the receipt of Form 117 for a trading certificate. He adds to the file a copy of any certificate of re-registration, for example a private company re-registered as a public company, which he may issue.

2.3 Company forms

All standard documents required to be delivered to the registry must be 'in the prescribed form'. These are printed forms in standard A4 size prescribed by statutory regulation (The Companies (Forms) Regulations 1979) so that the lay-out, content and size of the forms is uniform. Companies obtain their own supplies from specialist commercial law stationers.

Activity 2

What is the purpose of giving notice of certain documents in the *London Gazette*, when the complete file on any company is available for inspection?

3 COMPANY RECORDS AND REGISTERS

3.1 Contents of accounting records

A company is required by s 221 to keep accounting records sufficient to show and explain the company's transactions. At any time, it should be possible:

(a) to determine with reasonable accuracy the company's financial position; and

(b) to ascertain that any balance sheet or profit and loss account prepared is done so in accordance with the Act.

Accounting records may be kept in the form of bound books or in any other manner decided by the directors: s 722. If another method is used (such as loose-leaf binders or computer records) added precautions must be taken to prevent falsification: s 723; the company and its officers may be fined if they default in this respect.

Accounting records should be kept at the company's registered office or at some other place thought fit by the directors. Where accounting records are kept outside the UK, say by a branch of a UK company, accounts and returns must be made every six months to the UK.

Accounting records should be open to inspection by the company's officers: s 222. They have a right of inspection of all records, although the court has no statutory power to compel a company to allow its accounting records to be inspected. Note particularly that a *shareholder* is not given the right to inspect accounting records although the Articles of Association, the directors or an ordinary resolution may confer the right.

3.2 Registers

The statutory registers which a company must keep (with the relevant sections) are:

(a) the register of members: s 352;

(b)* the register of directors and secretaries: s 288;

(c) the register of directors' interests in shares and debentures of the company: s 325;

(d)* the register of charges: s 411;

(e)* minutes of general meetings of the company: s 382;

(f) minutes of directors' and managers' meetings: s 382;

(g) (if the company is a public company) the register of substantial interests in shares (3% or more of the nominal value of any class of shares): s 211.

Those items which are marked * must be kept at the registered office. The others may be kept at the registered office or at certain other places. Items (c) and (g) serve to amplify the register of members and therefore must be kept at the same place as that register.

Companies with debentures issued nearly always keep a register of debenture-holders, but there is no statutory compulsion to do so. If a register of debentureholders is maintained, it should not be held outside England and Wales, and should be kept at the registered office. If it is not kept there, the registrar should be informed of its whereabouts: s 190.

The *register of members* lists the company's shareholders.

The *register of charges* contains details of charges affecting the company property or undertaking, and should provide brief descriptions of property charged, the amount of the charge and the name of the person entitled to the charge. Any person may inspect the charges register; members and creditors may inspect free of charge.

In addition to keeping a register of charges, a company must also keep copies of every instrument creating a charge at its registered office: s 411. Any member or creditor may inspect the copies and register without a fee; others may inspect the register for such a fee as may be prescribed.

Activity 3

If shareholders in a company have no right to inspect accounting records, how can they tell whether the company is doing well or badly?

The *register of directors and secretaries* must contain the following details in respect of a director who is an individual: s 288:

(a) present and former forenames and surnames;

(b) residential address;

(c) nationality;

(d) business occupation;

(e) particulars of other current and former directorships held in the last five years;

(f) date of birth.

Where a director is a corporation, details must be shown of its name and registered or principal office. Similar details must also be shown regarding the company secretary. The register must include shadow directors as well as normal directors.

The register must be open to inspection by a member (free of charge) or by any other person (for a fee).

The *register of directors' interests in shares and debentures* must be maintained by the company (s 324), showing details of holdings as notified by directors under s 325 and Schedule 13 para 14. It must also enter details of rights granted to directors, irrespective of whether the directors notify the company.

3.3 Annual return

Every company must make an annual return to the registrar under ss 363-364A, giving the following information.

(a) The address of the registered office of the company: s 364.

(b) The address (if not the registered office) at which either the register of members or any register of debentureholders is kept: s 364.

(c) The type of company it is and its principal business activities: s 364.

(d) The total number of issued shares of the company up to the date on which the return was made up, and their aggregate nominal value: s 364A.

(e) In respect of each class of shares, the nature of that class and the total number of issued shares to the date of the making up of the return, and their nominal value: s 364A.

(f) The names and addresses of members of the company at the date of the return, and those who have ceased to be members since the last return. This list should be indexed or alphabetical: s 364A.

(g) The number of shares of each class held by members at the return date, along with details of shares of each class transferred since the date to which the last return was made up and the dates on which the transfers were registered: s 364A.

(h) If (f) and (g) have been fully covered in either of the preceding two returns, only changes in membership and share transfers need be noted: s 364A.

(i) Where a private company has elected to dispense with the laying of accounts and reports before the company in general meeting under s 252, or to dispense with the holding of the AGM under s 366A, this fact should be stated: s 364.

(j) Names and addresses of the directors and secretary and, in the case of each indexed director, his nationality, date of birth, previous occupation and other directorships: s 364

Activity 4

Why might a prospective investor in a company want to know about previous directorships held by the directors?

---

4 ACCOUNTS AND AUDIT

4.1 Annual accounts

The directors must, in respect of each accounting reference period of the company:

(a) prepare a balance sheet and profit and loss account (s 226);

(b) lay before the company in general meeting accounts for the period: s 241 (with exceptions as described below); and

(c) deliver to the registrar a copy of those accounts: s 242.

The accounts must be made up to a date which falls within the period seven days before or after the end of the accounting reference period: s 223. The accounting reference period is fixed to begin on the day after the expiry of the previous period and to end on the company's chosen accounting reference date: s 224.

The company's board of directors must approve the annual accounts and this approval must be signified by a director's signature on the balance sheet: s 233.

When copies are circulated the name of the director who signs must be stated.

A company is required to lay its accounts and the directors' and auditors' reports before members in general meeting (unless it is a private company which has dispensed with this requirement under s 252 by an elective resolution): s 241. It must deliver a copy to the registrar within a maximum period reckoned from the date to which the accounts are made up: s 242. The permitted interval between the end of the accounting period and the issue of accounts is seven months for a public company and ten months for a private company.

There are certain reliefs and special provisions relating to:

(a) *the first accounts of a company following its incorporation:* broadly the first accounts may cover any period of 6-18 months: thereafter the accounts follow the normal annual cycle: s 224;

(b) *small or medium sized companies* need not deliver to the registrar full accounts but only abbreviated versions: s 246. The size limits for small and medium sized companies are based on turnover, assets and number of employees.

The accounts must be audited and the auditor's report must be attached to the copies issued to members, delivered to the registrar or published. But a company which is 'dormant' may exclude this requirement: ss 235, 233 and 250. The accounts must also be accompanied by a directors' report giving information on a number of prescribed matters: s 234. It must contain a balanced review of the development of the business of the company (and any subsidiary undertakings) during the financial year and at the end of it, and must state the directors' recommendations on the application, retention and distribution of profits: s 234(1). The report must be formally approved by the board and signed by a director or the secretary: s 234A.

Circulation of accounts

Each member and debentureholder is entitled to be sent a copy of the annual accounts, together with the directors' and auditor's reports, at least 21 days before the meeting before which they shall be laid: s 238(1). Anyone else entitled to receive notice of a general meeting, including the company's auditor, should also be sent a copy. At any other time any member or debentureholder is entitled to a copy free of charge within seven days of requesting it: s 239(1).

A listed public company may prepare a summary financial statement (SFS) to be circulated to members instead of the full accounts, provided its constitution allows: s 251(1). The summary may be sent:

(a) to any member who has expressly agreed to receive any such a statement; and

(b) to any member who has failed to respond to a notice from the company enquiring whether the member wishes to receive a summary.

Adoption of accounts by members

The accounts must be laid before members in general meeting. It is usual to deal with the accounts at each year's Annual General Meeting. But it is not obligatory to do so: the accounts may be considered at an Extraordinary General Meeting.

When the accounts are laid before a general meeting it is usual to propose a resolution that they be 'adopted' or approved. This gives the members present an opportunity to ask pertinent questions and to make criticisms or suggestions. The approval of the accounts is regarded as a vote of confidence in the directors. If, however, the accounts are not 'adopted' they are still the accounts and their validity is not affected. But to reject the accounts is an expression of members' lack of confidence in the directors.

Activity 5

Why should public companies be required to file their accounts more quickly than private companies, given that public companies are likely to be larger and to have more work to do in preparing accounts?

4.2 The auditor

Every company (except a dormant private company and certain small companies) must appoint an auditor (s 384) who must be a member of a recognised supervisory body (s 25 CA 1989) and not be a member of or connected with the management of the company: s 27 CA 1989. Corporate bodies are allowed to act as auditors.

The appointment of auditors

The first auditor of a new company is appointed by the *directors* to hold office until the conclusion of the first general meeting at which the accounts are considered: s 385. The directors or the company in general meeting may also appoint an auditor to fill a casual vacancy: s 388.

In the ordinary way the *members* appoint the auditor at each general meeting at which the accounts are considered, to hold office until the next such meeting, that is to audit and report on the accounts to be prepared for that subsequent meeting.

If the members fail to appoint an auditor at the general meeting at which the accounts are considered, the company must, within seven days of the meeting, give notice to the Secretary of State who has power to appoint an auditor: s 387.

A *dormant private company* may be exempted from the requirement to appoint an auditor and have an audit if it passes a special resolution to this effect: ss 388A and 250. A company is dormant if there has been no significant accounting transaction apart from the issue of subscriber shares.

Certain small companies are exempt from the annual audit requirement (as from August 1994). Companies with a turnover of no more than £90,000 and a balance sheet total of no more than £1.4 million are totally exempt. Companies with a turnover of between £90,000 and £350,000 and a balance sheet total of not more than £1.4 million may replace the audit with a *compilation report* prepared by a reporting accountant. The exceptions do not apply to public, banking or insurance companies, group companies and statute-regulated companies.

Whoever appoints the auditor has power to fix his remuneration for the period of his appointment. It is usual when the auditor is appointed by the general meeting to leave it to the directors to fix his remuneration by agreement. Such remuneration must be disclosed in a note to the accounts: s 390A.

The termination of an auditor's appointment

A company may remove an auditor from office before the expiry of his appointment by passing an ordinary resolution in general meeting: s 391. Special notice to the company is required: s 391A.

An auditor may *resign* his appointment by giving notice in writing to the company delivered to the registered office: s 392. Alternatively he may simply decline to offer himself for re-election.

In his notice of resignation or on ceasing to hold office for any reason (s 394) the auditor must deposit at the company's registered office either:

(a) a statement that there are no circumstances connected with his resignation which he considers should be brought to the notice of members or creditors of the company; or

(b) a statement disclosing what those circumstances are.

On receiving the auditor's notice of resignation the company must send a copy of it to the registrar. If the auditor's notice contains a statement of circumstances the company must also (unless the court holds it to be defamatory) send a copy to every person entitled to receive a copy of the accounts: s 392(3). Section 394(3)(a) contains similar requirements where the statement of circumstances is not in connection with an auditor's resignation.

An auditor who includes in his statement of resignation a statement of the circumstances connected with it has the following additional rights:

(a) to circulate (through the company) to members a statement of reasonable length of the reasons for his resignation (unless it is defamatory);

(b) to requisition an Extraordinary General Meeting at which he will explain his reasons;

(c) to attend and speak at any meeting at which his resignation or the appointment of his successor is to be considered: s 392A.

Changes of auditor

Whenever a resolution is to be proposed at a general meeting for the appointment of an auditor who is not the auditor who was appointed on the last occasion (however the change may arise), or if it is a resolution for the removal of an auditor before the expiry of his year of office, 28 days' special notice must be given to the company, and the company must notify its members and the auditor concerned. This serves to bring to the notice of members and the auditor any changes of auditors: s 391A.

Duties and powers of auditors

The statutory duty of an auditor is to report to the members as to whether or not the accounts give a true and fair view and have been properly prepared in accordance with the Companies Act: s 235. To fulfil this duty, the auditor must carry out such investigations as are necessary to form an opinion as to whether:

(a) proper accounting records have been kept and proper returns adequate for the audit have been received from branches;

(b) the accounts are in agreement with the records: s 237; and

(c) the information given in the directors' report is consistent with the accounts: s 235(3).

If the auditor is satisfied on these matters they need not be mentioned in the report.

The auditor's report must be read before any general meeting at which the accounts are considered and must be open to inspection by members. The auditor may also attend any meeting after resigning at which his successor is appointed and also the meeting at which his office would have expired.

Auditors have wide statutory powers to enable them to obtain whatever information they may require for the purpose of their audit. In particular they may inspect books and records and call on officers of the company for information or explanations: s 389A. It is a crime for an officer of a company to make a false statement to an auditor if it is misleading, false or deceptive in a material particular and is made knowingly or recklessly (with indifference as to its truth): s 389A(2).

Activity 6

When an auditor ceases to hold office, he *must* deposit a statement under s 394. What could go wrong if he were merely permitted to deposit a statement?

Chapter roundup

- Companies must disclose information about themselves to the public so that other persons doing business with them can assess their financial position.

- With only two exceptions, persons are not deemed to be aware of information merely because it is disclosed at the Companies Registry.

- The file on a company at the Companies Registry includes its memorandum and articles, annual reports and accounts, the names of the directors, copies of certain resolutions and some other information. The receipt of certain documents is published in the *London Gazette*.

- A company's accounting records must enable the company's financial position to be determined at any time. They may be inspected by a company's officers, but not by its members.

- A company must keep several statutory registers, and some of them must be kept at the registered office. In most cases both the members and the public have a right of access.

- Annual accounts, accompanied by a directors' report, must be prepared and circulated. The accounts are approved by the directors, and they may be adopted by the members in general meeting. Listed public companies may circulate summary financial statements.

- The members of a company appoint an auditor who must report on the annual report and accounts. There are rules on the termination of an auditor's appointment designed to make it difficult to get rid of an auditor before he makes an adverse report.

Quick quiz

1 What are the main sources of information about a company's affairs provided by law?

2 When is a person deemed to have notice of certain items on file at the registry?

3 Where is a company's file held and what might it contain?

4 List three documents in respect of which the registrar gives notice of receipt in the *London Gazette*.

5 What must a company's accounting records make it possible to do?

6 Name six registers which may be held by a company (including relevant section numbers of the Companies Act) and state where they must be held.

7 Who may inspect copies of an instrument creating a charge?

8 What details about directors must the register of directors contain?

9 Who adopts a company's accounts?

10 What interval is allowed after the end of the period covered by accounts for laying the accounts before a general meeting and delivering a copy to the registry?

11 What reports must be attached to the accounts?

12 Who may be sent a listed public company's summary financial statement?

13 By whom may auditors be appointed (a) in normal circumstances and (b) in special circumstances?

14 What is the procedure by which an auditor may resign his appointment? By what means may he bring to the notice of members a disagreement between him and the directors?

15 On what matters does an auditor need to form an opinion when preparing his audit report?

Solutions to activities

1 Section 711A covers cases where someone did not in fact have notice. P did have notice.

2 Changes in a company's file need to be publicised, so that interested parties do not have to check the whole file for changes every few weeks.

3 They receive the company's annual report and accounts.

4 Directors might have been associated with either successful companies or failed companies.

5 Public companies can offer shares to the general public, so available information should be as up to date as possible.

6 He could resign without making any comment, leaving the members unaware of difficulties.

Further question practice

Now try the following practice questions at the end of this text

Multiple choice questions: **70 to 74**

Exam style question: **16**

Chapter 20

MEMORANDUM AND ARTICLES

Introduction

In Chapter 18 on company formation you learned that, in order to register a company, a memorandum of association and articles of association must be submitted to the Registrar of Companies. This chapter explains what is meant by these terms.

It is important to distinguish the function of each. The memorandum defines what the company is and the articles set out the internal rules.

You should make sure that you know what the compulsory clauses in the memorandum are, and that you appreciate that many legal questions can be solved by consulting a company's articles of association. Finally you should understand that the memorandum and articles together form a contract binding the members and company in specific ways.

Your objectives

After completing this chapter you should:

(a) know the contents of a company's memorandum;

(b) know the rules on the names of companies;

(c) understand the importance of a company's registered office;

(d) know how a typical modern objects clause is drafted;

(e) understand the distinction between objects and powers;

(f) understand the doctrine of *ultra vires*, and how it is severely limited by statute;

(g) know the function of a company's articles;

(h) know how a company's articles may be altered;

(i) understand the extent to which the memorandum and articles create contractual relations.

1 PURPOSE AND CONTENTS OF THE MEMORANDUM

The purpose of the memorandum and articles of association (for short 'the memorandum' and 'the articles') is to define what the company is and how its business and affairs are to be conducted. The memorandum sets out the basic elements. The articles are mainly internal rules.

For historical reasons these are two separate documents. If there is any inconsistency between them the memorandum prevails.

The original memorandum must be presented to the registrar to obtain registration of the new company. It is usually signed by at least two persons (the subscribers) who agree to become the first members. In the case of single member private companies, however, it is now possible for only one member to subscribe to the memorandum of association. Whenever the memorandum is altered a copy of the complete altered text must be delivered to the registrar for filing: s 18.

1.1 Contents of the memorandum

The memorandum of a private company limited by shares is required by s 2 to state:

(a) the *name* of the company;

(b) whether the *registered office* is to be situated in England and Wales, or Scotland;

(c) the *objects* of the company;

(d) the *limited liability* of members;

(e) the *authorised share capital* and how it is divided into shares.

The items on this list are referred to in this chapter as 'compulsory clauses'.

The memorandum of a public company contains the above particulars and also a sixth statement (placed second in order) that the company is a public company: s 1(3).

Every memorandum must also end with a *declaration of association* by which the subscribers state their wish to form the company. Each subscriber must, opposite his signature, state the number of shares (in practice always one share only) which he agrees to take.

2 THE COMPANY NAME

The name of the company serves to identify it and to distinguish it from any other company. For this reason, and to control the use of company names which might mislead the public, the registrar has statutory powers of control over the choice of names.

The choice of name (whether the first name or a name adopted by change of name later) of a limited company must conform to ss 25 to 31, as follows.

(a) The name must *end* with the word(s):

    (i) *public limited company* (abbreviated plc) if it is a public company; or

    (ii) *limited* (or *Ltd*) if it is a private limited company.

(b) No company may have a name which is the same as that of any existing company appearing in the statutory index at the registry. For this purpose two names are treated as 'the same' in spite of minor or non-essential differences; for instance the word 'the' as the first word in the name is ignored. 'John Smith Limited' is treated the same as 'John Smith & Company Ltd': s 26(3).

(c) No company may have a name the use of which would in the registrar's opinion be a criminal offence or which he considers offensive: s 26(1).

(d) No company may have a name which in the registrar's opinion suggests a connection with the government or a local authority or which is subject to control (unless of course its use is officially approved): s 26(2). Words such as 'International' or 'British' are only sanctioned if the size of the company matches its pretensions. A name which suggests some professional expertise such as 'optician' will only be permitted if the appropriate representative association has been consulted and raises no objection.

EXAMPLE: AN OFFENSIVE AND MISLEADING NAME

A member of an extreme right-wing organisation decides to set up a limited company which will sell Nazi memorabilia. He chooses the name 'Hitler Was Right (International)'. There are possible problems with registering this name: the word 'limited' is omitted, 'Hitler Was Right' is offensive, and 'International' is potentially misleading.

2.1 Change of name

A company may change its name by passing a special resolution and obtaining the registrar's certificate of incorporation that he has registered the company under a new name: s 28. The certificate makes the change effective from when it is issued, though the company is still the same legal entity as before.

The registrar can compel a company to change its name (within such time as he may allow) if:

(a) the name is the same as or in the registrar's opinion too like the name of another company which was or should have been on the register when the name was adopted, or if misleading information or assurances were given to secure registration: s 28; or

(b) the company's name gives so misleading an indication of its activities as to be likely to cause harm to the public: s 32.

Activity 1

A supplier is proposing to sell goods on credit to ABC Ltd, which he knows is owned by very wealthy individuals, well able to pay any debts. Why should the supplier pay attention to the (compulsory) 'Ltd' in the company's name?

2.2 Passing-off action

Any person may seek an injunction to restrain a company from using a name (even if duly registered) which suggests that the latter company is carrying on the business of the complainant or is otherwise connected with it (a *passing-off* action). But the complaint will not succeed if the complainant lays claim to the exclusive use of a word which has a general use.

2.3 Display of company names and other particulars

A company must:

(a) paint or affix outside every office or place of business its name in a conspicuous position and in easily legible letters. Failure to do so is punishable by fining the company and its officers in default: s 348;

(b) engrave on its seal (if it has one) its name in legible letters: s 350;

(c) mention its name in legible characters on all business letters and official publications and other communications, bills of exchange, orders for money or goods issued by the company, invoices, receipts and letters of credit: s 349.

On its business letters, invoices and order forms a company must state in legible letters the following particulars required by s 351.

(a) The company's place of registration, that is either England and Wales or Scotland.

(b) The address of its registered office. It is not sufficient to state the registered office address; it must be *identified* as the registered office address.

(c) Its registered number.

2.4 Business names other than the corporate name

Most companies trade under their own registered names. But a company may prefer to use some other name. If it does so it must:

(a) state its registered name and its address on all business letters, invoices, receipts, written orders for goods or services and written demands for payment of debts;

(b) display its name and address in a prominent position in any business premises to which its customers and suppliers have access;

(c) on request from any person with whom it does business give notice of its name and address.

Activity 2

In *Aerators Ltd v Tollit 1902* the plaintiff took action to prevent the formation of another company with a name which included the word 'aerators'. Why did the plaintiff's passing-off action fail?

3 REGISTERED OFFICE

The memorandum does not state the address of the registered office but only that it will be situate in England and Wales. This fixes the domicile of the company which, unlike other matters comprised in the memorandum, is unalterable.

The first address of the registered office is given in the documents presented to secure incorporation.

At any time thereafter the directors may alter the address of the registered office. But the new address, like the old, must be within the country specified in the memorandum. The registered office need not have any close connection with the company. Some companies arrange with their accountants or solicitors to make the latter's office premises the registered office of the company.

If the address of the registered office is changed, notice of the new address must be given to the registrar and the change takes effect after the registration: s 287(3). Documents may still be served on the company at the former address for a further 14 days.

The importance of the registered office is that:

(a) if a legal document, such as a notice or writ to commence legal proceedings, has to be served on a company this may be done by delivering it at the registered office or by sending it by post (preferably recorded delivery) to that office: s 725. The company cannot then deny that it has received the document;

(b) various registers and other documents are held either at the registered office or in some cases at another address.

4   OBJECTS

4.1   Nature of objects

The objects clause sets out the 'aims' and 'purposes' of the company. It is usually very broadly drafted, so that the company's actions cannot be challenged as outside its objects. A clause ending as follows is not uncommon.

'to carry on any other business, trade or enterprise which may be advantageously carried out, in the opinion of the directors, in connection with or ancillary to the general business of the company'.

Objects and powers

Also contained in the objects clause will be a list of permissible transactions (or express powers). These may include powers to lease and construct buildings, employ and remunerate staff, sub-contract work and so on. The most common and most important express powers are to borrow funds, to give security by creating charges over property, and to give guarantees.

The list of express powers may be long and detailed. This is to avoid the uncertainty caused by the fact that some powers to enter into transactions in the pursuit of the company's objects may only be *implied*. The danger here is that powers can only be implied to *further* the objects. Hence any action which does not promote the objects and is not an express power may not be effective as an implied power.

Independent objects

It is common practice to include a statement in the objects clause of the memorandum stating that each 'object' or 'power' should be construed as stating a separate object. This is done to avoid the interpretation of a clause as an express power to be exercised only in support of main objects.

Object as a 'general commercial company'

It is now possible to register a company with objects which merely state that the company's object is to 'carry on business as a general commercial company': s 3A. The legislation specifically states that this means that:

(a) the object of the company is to carry on any trade or business whatsoever; and

(b) the company has power to do all such things as are incidental or conducive to the carrying on of any trade or business by it.

4.1   Alteration of objects

A company may by special resolution alter its objects (s 4(1)).

Section 5 provides a procedure for a dissenting minority to apply to the court to modify an otherwise valid alteration of the objects clause. The conditions are that:

(a) application to the court must be made within 21 days from the passing of the special resolution to alter the objects; and

(b) the applicants must hold in aggregate at least 15% of the issued share capital or 15% of any class of shares. They must not originally have voted in favour of the alteration or consented to it.

Once such an objection is made the alternative which was approved can only come into effect insofar as the court allows: s 4(2). The court can arrange for the parties to come to an agreement (s 5(4)) as it can, say, order the company to buy the dissenting minority's shares: s 5(5).

Activity 3

A company is set up with the object of making and selling computers, and with the power to borrow or lend money. Why would the directors not be empowered to run a moneylending business?

4.2 Ultra vires

Since a company's capacity to contract is defined in its objects clause it has always followed that, however widely this is drawn, some acts would be beyond its capacity. The Latin term for this is *ultra vires*; in principle, the law would not allow such an act to be legally enforceable because of lack of capacity. However, this doctrine's effect is now severely restricted by legislation.

A company's contractual capacity as it affects third parties

Section 35(1) Companies Act 1985 (as amended) provides as follows.

> The validity of an act done by a company shall not be called into question on the ground of lack of capacity by reason of anything in the company's memorandum.

Note that neither the company nor a third party can plead *ultra vires* to escape their obligations, since the section operates in favour of both parties.

Section 35A(1) Companies Act 1985 provides as follows.

> In favour of a person dealing with a company in good faith, the power of the board of directors to bind the company, or authorise others to do so, shall be deemed to be free of any limitation under the company's constitution.

There are a number of points to note about s 35A(1).

(a) The section applies in favour of the *person dealing* with the company.

(b) In contrast with s 35(1), good faith is required. It is up to the company to prove lack of good faith in the third party, however, and this may turn out to be quite difficult.

(c) The section covers not only acts beyond the capacity of the company, but acts beyond any limitation under the company's constitution. This includes not only the memorandum and articles, but also resolutions of the members and other agreements made by them.

The combined effect of the above legislation (enacted in 1989) is to abolish the effect of the *ultra vires* rule in relation to acts done between a company and third parties, unless the third party acts in bad faith *and* the directors acted outside their authority. In future almost all such acts will be capable of validation, at the instance of either party.

A company's contractual capacity as it affects members

The effect of the *ultra vires* rule continues to operate *internally* between the company and its members.

Section 35(2) provides that as follows.

A member of a company may bring proceedings to restrain the doing of an action which, but for subsection (1) would be beyond the company's capacity; but no such proceedings shall lie in respect of an act to be done in fulfilment of a legal obligation arising from a previous act of the company.

This means that a member can gain an injunction to restrain an *ultra vires* act before it is done but, after the event, there will be no right to challenge the action.

The directors have a duty (to the company) to ensure that the assets of the company are not used for *ultra vires* purposes. If they have breached this duty, the situation is dealt with by s 35(3).

It remains the duty of the directors to observe any limitations on their powers flowing from the company's memorandum; and an action by the directors which but for subsection 35(1) would be beyond the company's capacity, may only be ratified by the company by special resolution. A resolution ratifying such action shall not affect any liability incurred by the directors or any other person; relief from any such liability must be agreed to separately by special resolution.

4.3 Protection of the company in contracts with directors

Sections 35 and 35A could be used to validate questionable transactions between the directors and the company. Section 322A deals with this situation, providing as follows.

Where a company enters into a transaction to which the parties include:

(a) a director of the company or its holding company; or

(b) a person connected with such a director or a company with whom such a director is associated;

and the board of directors, in connection with the transaction, exceed any limitation on their powers under the company's constitution, the transaction is voidable at the instance of the company.

The section also provides that, whether or not the transaction is avoided, the persons covered by the section (and any director who authorised the transaction) is liable to account to the company for profit made or loss and damage caused. The transaction will not be voidable if it is ratified by ordinary or special resolution (depending on circumstances), where third party rights intervene, or if restitution can no longer be made.

Activity 4

The directors of H Ltd must, under the company's articles of association, obtain the permission of the members before selling any land belonging to the company. J, an outsider, knows this and knows that no such permission has been obtained. She contracts to buy some land from the company for half of its market value, acting in collusion with the directors. Before completion, the members discover what has happened and take legal action to stop the sale going ahead.
Consider whether J could rely on s 35A(1).

---

5 ARTICLES OF ASSOCIATION

The articles of association deal mainly with the internal conduct of the company's affairs – the issue and transfer of shares; alterations of capital structure; calling general meetings and how they are to be conducted (including members' voting rights); appointment, powers and proceedings of directors; dividends; accounts and the issue of notices. If the company has more than one class of shares the rights of a class and the procedure for varying them is usually set out in the articles.

The memorandum differs from the articles in that it deals with the constitution of the company mainly as it affects outsiders. In cases of conflict the memorandum prevails over the articles. It is possible to alter the standard clauses of the memorandum (with one exception, namely the clause specifying country of origin) but special restrictions and procedures make it less easy to do so. The articles, however, may as a general rule be altered simply by passing a special resolution. Clauses which could be included in the articles may be placed in the memorandum in order to make it more difficult to alter them.

5.1 Table A articles

A company limited by shares may have its own full-length special articles, or it may adopt all or any part of the statutory standard model articles (known as Table A) made under s 8. Private companies usually have a short form of articles which state that Table A is to apply subject only to a few exclusions or modifications deemed desirable for the company.

As regards form, the articles must be printed and divided into numbered paragraphs: s 7(3). The first articles presented to obtain registration of a new company are signed by the subscribers to the memorandum, dated and witnessed. But if new or altered articles are adopted later the copy of the text to be delivered to the registrar need not be signed.

Whenever any alteration is made to the articles a copy of the altered articles must be delivered to the registrar within 15 days, together with a signed copy of the special resolution by which the alteration is made: ss 18 and 380.

6 ALTERATION OF THE ARTICLES

A company has a statutory power to alter its articles by special resolution: s 9(1). This means that if a special resolution is properly moved and carried at a general meeting by a 75% majority of votes cast, the alteration is valid and binding on all members of the company.

Alteration of the articles is restricted by the following principles.

(a) The alteration is void if it conflicts with the Companies Act or with the memorandum.

(b) In various circumstances, such as to protect a minority (s 459) or in approving an alteration of the objects clause (s 5(5)), the court may order that an alteration be made or, alternatively, that an existing article shall not be altered. The leave of the court is then required if the relevant article is later to be altered to vary it from the terms approved by the court.

(c) A member may not be compelled by alteration of the articles to subscribe for additional shares or to accept increased liability for the shares which he holds unless he has given his consent: s 16.

(d) An alteration of the articles which varies the rights attached to a class of shares may only be made if the correct variation procedure has been followed to obtain the consent of the class (s 125). A 15% minority may apply to the court to cancel the variation under s 127.

(e) An alteration may be void if the majority who approve it are not acting *bona fide* in what they deem to be the interests of the company as a whole (see below).

(f) A person whose contract is contained in the articles cannot obtain an injunction to prevent the articles being altered, but he may be entitled to damages for breach of contract.

Activity 5

R holds 10% of the shares in C Ltd. A special resolution is voted for by all the other shareholders (R voting against) to alter the articles so as to make each member liable to contribute an extra £10 per share. R is told that, as his holding is less than 15%, he must accept this. Is this true? Why?

7 THE MEMORANDUM AND ARTICLES AS CONTRACTS

A company's memorandum and articles bind, under s 14:

(a) members to company;

(b) company to members (but see below);

(c) members to members; but not

(d) company to third parties.

The members are deemed to have separately covenanted to observe the articles and memorandum. The principle that only rights and obligations of members are covered by s 14 applies when a member seeks to rely on the articles in support of a claim made as an outsider.

Eley v Positive Government Security Life Assurance Co 1876
E, a solicitor, drafted the original articles and included a provision that the company must always employ him as its solicitor. E became a member of the company some months after its incorporation. He later sued the company for breach of contract in not employing him as a solicitor. The case turned partly on technical points which no longer arise since the law (the Statute of Frauds) has been changed.

Held: E could not rely on the article since it was a contract between the company and its members and he was not asserting any claim as a member.

Section 14 gives to the memorandum and articles the effect of a contract made between (a) the company and (b) its members individually. It can also impose a contract on the members in their dealings with each other as illustrated by the case below.

Rayfield v Hands 1958
The articles required that (a) every director should be a shareholder and (b) the directors must purchase the shares of any member who gave them notice of his wish to dispose of them. The directors, however, denied that a member could enforce the obligation on them to acquire his shares.

Held: there was 'a contract ... between a member and member-directors in relation to their holdings of the company's shares in its article' and the directors were bound by it.

Activity 6

In *Beattie v ECF Beattie Ltd 1938* the articles provided that disputes between the company and its members should be submitted to arbitration. B, the managing director, was sued by the company to recover money improperly paid to him. Although B was a member, why could he not insist that the dispute be submitted to arbitration?

Chapter roundup

- A company's memorandum states basic facts such as the company's name and its objects.

- A company's name must not be the same as that of any existing company, and it must not be inappropriate in certain ways. The use of a name likely to be confused with one already in use may be restrained by a passing-off action. A company's name must be displayed so that outsiders know who they are doing business with.

- A company must have a registered office, at which documents may be served on it.

- A company's objects are set out in its memorandum. It is the modern practice to state the objects in very broad terms, so that advantage may be taken of any commercial opportunity. The powers of a company, if not stated to be independent objects, may only be exercised in furtherance of the company's objects.

- A company's objects may be altered by special resolution of the members, but a dissenting minority may have a right to object.

- Even if an act of a company is outside the scope of its objects and therefore *ultra vires*, its validity cannot usually be called into question. However, the company may have a remedy when the directors contract with the company in excess of their powers.

- A company's articles of association set out its detailed constitution. A company may adopt a standard set of articles (Table A), or it may write its own articles. The articles may be changed by special resolution, but certain changes require the consent of the members directly affected.

- A company's memorandum and articles create contractual relations affecting the members, but only in their capacity as members.

Quick quiz

1 What are the compulsory clauses of a public company's memorandum (in correct order)?

2 To what do the signatories to the memorandum commit themselves?

3 On what grounds may the registrar refuse to register a company name?

4 What is the procedure for voluntary change of name by a registered company?

5 On what grounds may the registrar order a company to change its name?

6 What particulars must appear on the letterhead of a company which carries on a trade?

7 What is a 'business name' and what requirements apply to a company if it uses such a name?

8 May a company change the address of its registered office?

9 Describe the general content of a modern objects clause.

10 Who may object to an alteration of the objects clause?

11 Can a member of the company challenge an *ultra vires* action of the company after it has been done?

12 How is a company protected in respect of transactions entered into by the company with its directors beyond the limits of the latter's authority?

13 Is a company limited by shares obliged to adopt Table A in force at the time of the company's formation as its articles?

14 How may a company alter its articles?

15 What is the result if a company alters its articles so that in their altered form the articles conflict with (a) the Acts or (b) the memorandum or (c) a separate contract with another person?

16 May an alteration of the articles deprive a member of rights accrued under the articles before alteration? May it impose new obligations on him?

17 To what extent are the articles a contract between the company and its members?

Solutions to activities

1 The shareholders are not liable for the company's debts (beyond any amount unpaid on their shares). Their wealth is therefore not available to the company's creditors.

2 'Aerators' is a word in general use.

3 The power is restricted to use in connection with the company's object.

4 No: J has not acted in good faith.

5 No: a member may not be compelled to accept increased liability for his shares.

6 He was being sued as managing director, not as a member.

Further question practice

Now try the following practice questions at the end of this text

Multiple choice questions: 75 to 79

Exam style question: 17

Chapter 21

SHARE CAPITAL AND DIVIDENDS

Introduction

A company's capital is the funds it has available for use in the business and represents its assets. Some, if not all, of a company's capital is provided by its members subscribing for shares. That is the subject of this chapter.

Share capital is elaborately regulated by law; in particular there are special rules relating to maintenance of capital in order to protect the 'creditors' buffer'.

Capital provided by lenders is dealt with in Chapter 22.

Your objectives

After completing this chapter you should:

(a) know what different amounts of share capital may be stated;

(b) know how shares are allotted;

(c) know what consideration for shares is acceptable;

(d) understand rights issues and bonus issues;

(e) know the difference between ordinary shares and preference shares;

(f) know how class rights may be varied;

(g) know how shares are transferred and how transfers may be restricted;

(h) understand the significance of share certificates;

(i) understand the concept of maintenance of capital;

(j) know how a company is prevented from reducing its capital except in restricted circumstances;

(k) know the powers of directors in relation to dividends;

(l) know what profits may be distributed and the consequences of paying excessive dividends.

1   TYPES OF CAPITAL

The term 'capital' is used in several senses.

(a) *Authorised share capital* is the total amount of share capital which the company is authorised to issue by the capital clause of its memorandum. This total must be divided into shares of fixed amount (called the *nominal* or *par* value of the shares). It can be increased as prescribed in the articles (usually an ordinary resolution suffices).

(b) *Issued share capital* (or allotted share capital) is the nominal value of the shares which have been allotted and issued to members. A company need not issue all its share capital at once. If it retains part this is *unissued* share capital.

(c) *Called up share capital* is the aggregate amount of calls for money or other consideration which members are required to pay (or have paid in applying for shares): s 737. If, for example, a company has issued 70 £1 (nominal) shares, has received 25p per share on application and has called on members for a second 25p, its *called up* share capital is £35 (50p per share). When the members pay the call the *paid up* share capital is then £35 also. Capital not yet called is *uncalled capital*.

2   ALLOTMENT OF SHARES

The allotment of shares is a form of contract. The intending shareholder applies to the company for shares. This is an offer which the company accepts by allotting shares to him.

2.1   Procedure for allotment of shares

The allotment of shares of a private company is a simple and immediate matter.

Public companies listed on The Stock Exchange usually follow a two-stage procedure.

(a) They first issue a renounceable *allotment letter* (or similar document) which the original allottee may for a limited period (up to six weeks) transfer to another person by signing a form of renunciation (included in the letter) and delivering it to the transferee. The original allottee or the ultimate renouncee, sends in the allotment letter with a completed application for registration of the shares in his name. No entry is made in the register of members when the allotment letter is first issued.

(b) On receipt of the *application for registration* the company enters the name of the applicant in the register of members and delivers a return of allotments to the registrar made up to show who is then on the register. The applicant becomes a member by *entry on the register* and receives a share certificate from the company.

Except where renounceable allotment letters are issued, the name of the allottee is usually entered in the register soon after, and as a direct consequence of, the allotment of shares to him. He then becomes a member: s 22.

Subscribers to the memorandum become members of the company as soon as it is incorporated and their names should be entered in the register of members without any decision to allot shares to them.

2.2 Directors' powers to allot shares

It is long established practice to delegate to the board of directors (as part of their general management functions) the decision on the terms of the contract of allotment and the power to allot shares. The directors may only exercise the power of allotment if they are properly authorised to do so, either by the articles or by ordinary resolution passed in general meeting.

Section 80 requires of a public company that the authority to allot shall be given until a specified date and for a specified period of not more than five years. A private company may confer authority to allot shares for an *indefinite* period, or for a fixed period longer than five years.

Activity 1

Z Ltd has an authorised share capital of 20,000 £2 shares. It issues 60% of these shares, but only calls upon members to pay 70% of the nominal value, in three equal annual instalments. All members pay the amounts required on time. Calculate the company's paid up share capital after the second instalment has been paid.

2.3 Pre-emption rights: s 89

If a company proposes to allot shares described as 'equity securities' wholly for cash it has a statutory obligation (subject to certain exceptions) to offer those shares to holders of similar shares in proportion to their holdings: s 89.

The offer must be made in writing in the same manner as a notice of a general meeting is sent to members. It must specify a period of not less than 21 days during which the offer may be accepted. If not accepted within that period the offer is deemed to be declined: s 90.

Equity securities subject to the rules just explained are broadly ordinary shares whenever issued for cash. But subscribers' shares, preference shares, bonus issues and shares allotted under an employees' share scheme are exempt from these restrictions which would be inappropriate to them: s 94.

Equity securities which have been offered to members in this way but are not accepted may then be allotted on the same (or less favourable) terms to non-members.

A *private* company may by its memorandum or articles permanently exclude these rules so that there is no statutory right of first refusal: s 91.

Any company may, by special resolution, resolve that the statutory right of first refusal shall not apply: s 95. For public companies, the period of disapplication is limited to five years.

2.4 Consideration for shares

Every share has a nominal value and may not be allotted at a discount. In allotting shares every company is required to obtain in money or money's worth consideration of a value at least equal to the nominal value of the shares: s 100. To issue shares 'at par' is to obtain equal value, say, £1 for a £1 share. If shares are allotted at a discount on their nominal value the allottee must nonetheless pay the full nominal value with interest at the appropriate rate (5%).

The no-discount rule only requires that, in allotting its shares, a company shall not fix a price which is less than the nominal value of the shares. It may leave part of that price to be paid at some later time by whoever then holds the shares.

2.5 Payment for shares

The price for the shares may be paid in money or 'money's worth', including goodwill and know-how: s 99. It need not be paid in cash and the company may agree to accept a 'non-cash' consideration of sufficient value. For instance, a company may issue shares in payment of the price agreed in the purchase of a property. The allotment of shares as a bonus issue is for full consideration since reserves, which are shareholders' funds, are converted into fixed capital and used to pay for the shares: s 99(4).

Private companies

A private company may allot shares for inadequate consideration by acceptance of goods or services at an over-value. This loophole has been allowed to exist because in some cases it is very much a matter of opinion whether an asset is or is not of a stated value.

EXAMPLE: VALUING A PRIVATE COMPANY

K and M have sold their business and the assets used in it to a newly incorporated private company at a price of £56,300. The price was paid by the allotment of £20,000 in shares and the balance in cash and debentures. The company goes into liquidation and the liquidator, S, contends that the value of the business was overstated by about £18,000. S contends that K and M should be treated as having failed to provide adequate consideration for their shares, so that he could recover their excess value. However K and M argue that the business was valued by an expert at £56,300.

The courts would not overrule the directors in their valuations of the business as it appeared reasonable and honest.

Public companies

The more stringent rules which apply to *public companies* regarding consideration and payment are as follows.

(a) Future services are not to be accepted as consideration: s 99(2).

(b) The company must, at the time of allotment, receive at least one quarter of the nominal value of the shares and the *whole* of any premium.

(c) Non-cash consideration may not be accepted as payment for shares if an undertaking contained in such consideration is to be, or may be, performed more than five years after the allotment: s 102.

(d) Any non-cash consideration accepted must be independently valued (except when shares are being issued in return for shares in a company being taken over): s 103.

(e) Within two years of receiving its certificate under s 117, a public company may not receive a transfer of non-cash assets from a subscriber to the memorandum, unless its value as consideration is less then 10% of the issued nominal share capital and it has been independently valued and agreed by an ordinary resolution: s 104.

2.6   Allotment of shares at a premium

A company may be able to obtain consideration for new shares in excess of their nominal value. The excess, called 'share premium', must be credited to a share premium account (s 130) to which certain restrictions apply.

2.7   Return of allotments

Within one month of allotting shares, a company must deliver to the registrar a return of allotments in the prescribed form showing what shares have been allotted, to whom and for what consideration: s 88.

2.8   Rights and bonus issues

A *rights issue* is an allotment (or the offer of it by renounceable allotment letter) of additional shares made to existing members. If the members do not wish to subscribe for additional shares under a rights issue they may be able to sell their rights to other persons and so obtain the value of the option.

A *bonus issue* is more correctly but less often called a *capitalisation issue* (also called a *scrip issue*). The articles of a company usually give it power to apply its reserves (including its undistributed profits) to pay up unissued shares and then to allot these shares as a bonus issue to members.

Activity 2

How might existing members of a company be unfairly treated if pre-emption rights did not exist, even assuming that all new shares were issued for their full market value?

---

3   THE NATURE OF SHARES AND TYPES OF SHARE

A share is a form of property, carrying rights and obligations. It is by its nature *transferable*. A member who holds one or more shares is by that fact a shareholder.

If no differences between shares are expressed it is assumed that all shares have the same rights. It is unnecessary to classify them as *ordinary shares* since there are no others. But there is no objection to doing so.

A company may at its option attach special rights to different shares, for example as regards dividends, return of capital, voting or, less often, the right to appoint a director. Any share which has different rights from others is grouped with the other shares carrying identical rights to form a class in distinction from shares with different rights included in another class.

The most common classes of share capital with different rights are *preference shares* and *ordinary shares*; there may also be ordinary shares with voting rights and ordinary shares (often distinguished as 'A' ordinary shares) without voting rights.

The essential characteristic of any *preference share* is that it carries a prior right to receive an annual dividend of fixed amount, say a 6% dividend. There are no other *implied* differences between preference and ordinary shares, though there are often express differences between them. For example, preference shares may carry a priority right to return of capital.

Activity 3

J Ltd has some £1 8% preference shares and some £1 ordinary shares in issue. Nothing is stated about the rights attaching to the preference shares. A holds 100 preference shares and 500 ordinary shares. In years 1 and 2 no dividend is paid. In year 3 a 9% dividend is declared on the ordinary shares.
Calculate how much A will receive in year 3.

4 VARIATIONS OF CLASS RIGHTS

The holders of issued shares have vested rights which can only be varied by the company with the consent of all the holders or with such consent of a majority as is specified in the articles.

The usual procedure for variation of class rights requires that an *extraordinary resolution* (giving approval) shall be passed by a *three-quarters majority* cast either:

(a) at a *separate meeting* of the class, or

(b) by *written consent*: s 125(2).

4.1 Minority appeals to the court

Whenever class rights are varied under a procedure contained in the memorandum or articles a minority of holders of shares of the class may apply to the court to have the variation cancelled: s 127. The objectors together must:

(a) hold not less than 15% of the issued shares of the class in question;

(b) not themselves have consented to or voted in favour of the variation; and

(c) apply to the court within 21 days of the consent being given by the class: s 127 (2) and (3).

The court can either approve the variation as made or cancel it as 'unfairly prejudicial': s 127 (4). It cannot, however, modify the terms of the variation or approve it subject to conditions. To establish that a variation, although approved by a three-quarters majority of the class, is 'unfairly prejudicial' to the class, it must generally be shown that the majority who voted in favour were seeking some advantage to themselves as members of a different class instead of considering the interests of the class in which they were then voting.

5 THE TRANSFER OF SHARES

To obtain transfer of the legal ownership of shares two conditions must be satisfied.

(a) A 'proper instrument of transfer' must be delivered to the company which may not enter the transfer in its register until this is done: s 183(1).

(b) If, as is general practice with private companies, the articles give to the directors power to refuse to register a transfer and the directors exercise their power in proper way, the contractual restriction imposed by the articles operates to prevent a transfer of legal ownership.

It is standard practice in unlisted companies nowadays to use the stock transfer form authorised for general use by the Stock Transfer Act 1963: s 1. This can be used to transfer fully paid shares irrespective of any provision in the articles requiring some other form and must be signed but not sealed: s 2 Stock Transfer Act 1963. Transactions on The Stock Exchange are effected using sold transfer and bought transfer forms.

5.1 Transfer procedures in unlisted companies

The unlisted company transfer procedure is that the registered holder (the 'seller') completes and signs the stock transfer form and delivers it with his share certificate to the transferee (the 'buyer') who completes the transfer and pays stamp duty before delivering it together with the seller's share certificate to the company for registration. The buyer becomes the holder and legal owner of the shares only when his name is entered in the register of members: s 22. The company issues to him a new share certificate within two months (s 185) and cancels the old one.

5.2 Transfer procedure for Stock Exchange transactions

The sequence of action for a transfer of shares listed on the Stock Exchange is as follows.

(a) A shareholder, acting through a stockbroker, agrees to sell shares at a specified price.

(b) The broker sends a 'TALISMAN *Sold* transfer' to his client, who signs the transfer and returns it to the broker with his share certificate. The shareholder thereby sells his shares to SEPON (Stock Exchange Pool Nominees Ltd).

(c) The broker sends the documents in to the Centre, which *certifies* the transfer and returns it for presentation to the company, to effect the transfer to SEPON.

(d) The share transfer is registered by the company, with SEPON as the transferee. Each listed company maintains a running SEPON account for this purpose.

(e) At the end of each account period SEPON issues 'TALISMAN *Bought* transfers' to the ultimate purchasers, and these transfers are presented to the company for registration in the names of the buyers. Thus SEPON sells the shares to the new investor.

This sequence still applies, but the account system was replaced in July 1994 by a system of *rolling settlement* called CREST , whereby transactions become due for settlement five business days after dealing. (Prior to 26 June 1995, the period was ten days.)

Activity 4

In *Re Holders Investment Trust Ltd 1971*, a scheme to substitute unsecured loan stock for preference shares was voted through by the holders of the vast majority of the preference shares, because they (as holders of 52% of the ordinary shares) would benefit overall. On what ground do you think the court forbade the change in preference shareholders' rights?

5.3 Restrictions on transfer of shares

Although it is no longer legally necessary to do so the articles of private companies usually provide that the directors may refuse to register a transfer of any share, whether fully or partly paid. The articles of a public company may impose this restriction but the company cannot have a Stock Exchange listing for its shares if the transfer of fully paid shares is restricted.

If the directors have a power under the articles to refuse a transfer they should exercise that power properly. Otherwise the transfer must be registered and the court may order rectification of the register for that purpose.

(a) To exercise their power the directors must consider the transfer and take an active decision to refuse to register it.

(b) The directors in reaching their decision must act *bona fide* in what they consider to be the interest of the company. But the court is reluctant to intervene.

(c) The articles should either authorise the directors to refuse in their absolute discretion to register a transfer, or specify grounds of refusal.

(d) The power of refusal must be exercised within a reasonable time from the receipt of the transfer. A company is required to give notice of any refusal within two months: s 183(5).

In the recent case of *Popely v Planarrive Ltd 1996* the court reinforced the rule that they would uphold provisions in a company's articles giving directors the right to refuse share transfers, provided they act *bona fide* within their powers. The fact that the directors are ill-disposed towards the transferee is irrelevant.

The articles may also restrict the right of transfer of shares by giving to members a right of first refusal of the shares which other members may wish to transfer. Any such rights are strictly construed. A member who wishes to accept such shares must observe the terms of the articles; a member wishing to sell shares will not be permitted to evade his obligation to make the offer.

6 SHARE CERTIFICATES

Within two months of allotting shares or receiving a transfer a company must have ready for delivery a certificate of the shares allotted or transferred (unless the transfer is rejected). This is a formal written declaration that the person named is entered in the register as the holder of the shares specified: s 185. A company listed on The Stock Exchange has the shorter time limit of 14 days.

A share certificate is not a document of title but is *prima facie* evidence of ownership: s 186. The company therefore requires the holder to surrender his certificate for cancellation when he transfers all or any of his shares.

If a company issues a share certificate which is incorrect it is *estopped* from denying that it is correct but only against a person who has relied upon it and thereby suffered loss: *Re Bahia & San Francisco Railway Co 1868*.

6.1 Share warrants

If authorised by its articles, a company limited by shares may issue share warrants which are negotiable instruments transferable by delivery: s 188. A warrant entitles its bearer to shares specified therein and allows him to transfer those shares by delivery of the warrant. On the issue of a share warrant the company removes the name of the registered holder from its register of members. He (or the person to whom the warrant may be transferred) is then only a member to the extent that the articles may provide. The company does not know who has the warrant. The bearer may subsequently surrender it for cancellation and the company must then enter the bearer's name in the register as a member: s 355.

Activity 5

In *Re Hackney Pavilion Ltd 1924*, a company's two directors were unable to agree on whether to register a share transfer, and neither had a casting vote. How would this situation be resolved?

7   MAINTENANCE OF CAPITAL

The capital which a limited company obtains from its members as consideration for their shares (and its right to call for payment of the balance (if any) still owing on its shares) is sometimes called 'the creditors' buffer'. No one can prevent an unsuccessful company from losing all or part of its capital by trading at a loss. But insofar as subscribed capital remains in the hands of the company it must be held for the payment of the company's debts and may not be returned to members (except under procedures which safeguard the interest of creditors). That is the price which members of a limited company are required to pay for the protection of limited liability. They cannot be compelled to pay more than the amount due on their shares but they cannot recover what they or their predecessors have subscribed for the shares unless the company's debts have been paid.

7.1   Share premium account

A company which obtains for its shares a consideration in excess of their nominal value must transfer the excess to a share premium account: s 130.

The permitted uses of share premium are:

(a) to make an issue of fully paid bonus shares;

(b) to make an authorised reduction of capital. Such reductions are strictly controlled;

(c) to pay capital expenses, such as the preliminary expenses of forming the company;

(d) to pay a discount on the issue of shares or debentures;

(e) to pay a premium (if any) on the redemption of debentures: s 130(2).

Private companies (but not public companies) may also use a share premium account in purchasing or redeeming their own shares out of capital. This procedure is strictly controlled.

7.2   Redemption or purchase by a company of its own shares

There is a general prohibition against any voluntary acquisition by a company of its own shares, though there is no objection to accepting a gift: s 143.

The prohibition is subject to exceptions. A company may:

(a) purchase its own shares in compliance with an order of the court;

(b) issue redeemable shares and then redeem them (out of distributable profits or the proceeds of a new issue);

(c) purchase its own shares under certain specified procedures; and

(d) forfeit or accept the surrender of its shares.

7.3   Purchase of own shares

Companies are allowed to purchase shares provided certain safeguards are followed. A limited company may now *purchase its own shares* (whether issued as redeemable or irredeemable):

(a) out of profits or the proceeds of an issue of new shares; or

(b) if it is a *private company*, out of capital.

For redemption or purchase of shares out of capital there is a long and involved procedure which includes the following steps.

(a) A statutory declaration must be made by the directors (supported by a report of the auditors) to the effect that after the payment is made the company will be able to pay its debts and to carry on its business for at least a year to come: s 173; these must also be delivered to the registrar: s 195.

(b) Shareholders must approve the payment by passing a *special resolution*. In this decision any vendor of shares may not use the votes attached to the shares which he is to sell to the company: s 173.

(c) A member who did not vote for the resolution and a creditor (for any amount) may within five weeks apply to the court to cancel the resolution (which may not be implemented until the five weeks have elapsed): s 176.

(d) A notice must be placed in the *London Gazette* and in an appropriate national newspaper, or every creditor must be informed: s 175.

If the company goes into insolvent liquidation within a year of making a payment out of capital the persons who received the payment and the directors who authorised it may have to make it good to the company.

Activity 6

Why are elaborate precautions not needed when a company buys its own shares out of profits or the proceeds of an issue of new shares?

7.4   Financial assistance for purchase of own shares

Giving financial assistance to a third party to enable him to buy the company's shares can take many forms. Hence it is difficult to prohibit altogether or to regulate. The relevant rules (ss 151-158) comprise:

(a) a general prohibition;

(b) a procedure by which a private company may give such assistance;

(c) a complex set of definitions and exceptions intended to determine which transactions are or are not prohibited.

Subject to exceptions it is not lawful for a company to give any financial assistance for the purpose of the acquisition of shares either of the company or of its holding company or to discharge liabilities incurred in making the acquisition. The prohibition applies to assistance given either directly or indirectly, before or after, or at the time of the acquisition. 'Financial assistance' is elaborately defined to mean a loan, a guarantee or indemnity or security, purchase of such rights from a third party and 'any other financial assistance given by a company which reduces to a material extent, its net assets': s 152.

Two main tests have to be applied to any suspect transaction.

(a) What was its *purpose*? It is not objectionable if its principal purpose was not to give financial assistance for the purchase of the shares nor if it was an incidental part of some larger purpose of the company: s 153(1)(a).

(b) What was the state of mind of the directors in approving the transaction? Did they act in *good faith* in what they deemed to be the interests of the company and not of a third party?: s 153 (1)(b).

A private company may give financial assistance for the acquisition of its own shares or the shares of its holding company, subject to the following conditions of ss 155-158.

(a) The financial assistance given must not reduce the net assets of the company or, if it does, the financial assistance is to be provided out of distributable profits.

(b) There must be a statutory declaration of solvency by the directors of the company (with a report by the auditors) of the same type as is prescribed when a private company purchases its own shares by a payment out of capital.

(c) A special resolution must be passed to approve the transaction. Normally this is a resolution of the company which gives the assistance. But if that company is a wholly owned subsidiary which assists the acquisition of shares of its holding company the members of the latter company must pass the resolution.

(d) A right to apply to the court is given to members holding at least 10% of the issued shares (or of a class of shares). To permit them to exercise this right there is a four week delay in the implementation of the resolution.

Three other specific exceptions are made. A company is not prohibited from entering into any of the following transactions: s 153(4).

(a) Making a loan, if lending is part of its ordinary business and the loan is made in the ordinary course of its business. This exception is restricted to money-lending companies, but it would permit a bank to make a loan to a customer on standard terms even though he then used the money to invest in shares of the bank;

(b) Providing money in good faith and in the best interests of the company for the purpose of an employees' share scheme or for other share transactions by *bona fide* employees or connected persons;

(c) Making loans to persons (other than directors) employed in good faith by the company with a view to those persons acquiring fully paid shares in the company or its holding company to be held by them as beneficial owners.

7.5   Loss of capital in a public company

If the net assets of a public company are half or less of the amount of its called up share capital there must be an extraordinary general meeting: s 142. The duty to call the meeting arises as soon as any of the directors comes to know of the problem. When the directors' duty arises they must issue a notice to convene a meeting within 28 days of becoming aware of the need to do so. The meeting must be convened for a date within 56 days of their coming to know the relevant facts. The purpose of this procedure is to enable shareholders to consider 'whether any, and if so what, measures should be taken to deal with the situation'.

Activity 7

A borrows money to buy shares in a manufacturing company, which is a public company and is not her employer. The loan is for five years, but the lender may demand early repayment. The lender does so, because he is concerned that A may soon become unable to pay her debts. The lender suggests that A asks the company to guarantee the loan, in return for which he will not demand early repayment. He says that the use made of the loan is immaterial, because the purchase of shares has already been made. Would the company be allowed to give the guarantee? Give reasons for your answer.

8 DIVIDENDS

8.1 Payment of dividends

Dividends may only be paid by a company out of profits available for the purpose: s 263. The power to declare a dividend is given by the articles which usually follow the model of Table A.

(a) The company in general meeting may declare dividends but no dividend may exceed the amount recommended by the directors: Table A Article 102.

(b) The directors may declare such interim dividends as they consider justified: Article 103.

(c) Dividends are normally declared payable on the paid up amount of share capital. For example, a £1 share which is fully paid will carry entitlement to twice as much dividend as a £1 share 50p paid: Article 104.

(d) A dividend may be paid otherwise than in cash: Article 105. Without such a provision, payment must be in cash.

(e) Dividends may be paid by cheque or warrant sent through the post to the shareholder at his registered address: Article 106. If shares are held jointly payment of dividend is made to the first-named joint holder on the register.

A shareholder (including a preference shareholder) is not entitled to a dividend unless it is declared in accordance with the procedure prescribed by the articles and the declared date for payment has arrived.

8.2 Distributable profits

The profits which may be distributed as dividend are 'accumulated realised profits, so far as not previously utilised by distribution or capitalisation, less accumulated realised losses, so far as not previously written off in a reduction or reorganisation of capital duly made': s 263(3).

The word 'accumulated' requires that any losses of previous years must be included in reckoning the current distributable surplus.

8.3 Dividends of public companies – the full net worth test

The above rules on distributable profits apply to all companies, private or public. A public company is subject to an additional rule which may diminish but cannot increase its distributable profit as determined under the above rules.

A public company may only make a distribution if its net assets are, at the time, not less than the aggregate of its called-up share capital and undistributable reserves. The dividend which it may pay is limited to such amount as will leave its net assets at not less than that aggregate amount: s 264(1).

Undistributable reserves are defined in s 264(3) as:

(a) share premium account;

(b) capital redemption reserve;

(c) any *surplus* of accumulated unrealised profits over accumulated unrealised losses (known as a revaluation reserve);

(d) any reserve which the company is prohibited from distributing by statute or by its memorandum or articles.

8.4 Relevant accounts

The question of whether a company has profits from which to pay a dividend is determined by reference to its 'relevant accounts' which are generally the latest audited annual accounts: s 270. Relevant accounts must be properly prepared in accordance with the requirements of the Companies Acts. If the auditor has qualified his report on the accounts he must also state in writing whether, in his opinion, the subject matter of his qualification (if it relates to statutory accounting requirements) is material in determining whether the dividend may be paid: s 271.

8.5 Infringement of dividend rules

Any member of a company may apply to the court for an injunction to restrain the company from paying an unlawful dividend. A resolution passed in general meeting to approve it is invalid and does not relieve the directors of their liability.

The company is entitled to recover an unlawful distribution from its members if at the time of receipt they knew or had reasonable grounds for knowing that it was unlawful: s 277. If only part of the dividend is unlawful if it exceeds the distributable profits by a margin, it is only the excess which is recoverable. If a member knowingly receives an improperly paid dividend a derivative action cannot be brought by him against the directors.

The directors are liable to make good to the company the amount unlawfully distributed as dividend if they caused an unlawful dividend:

(a) if they recommend or declare a dividend which they know is paid out of capital;

(b) if without preparing any accounts they declare or recommend a dividend which proves to be paid out of capital;

(c) if they make some mistake of law or interpretation of the memorandum or articles which leads them to recommend or declare an unlawful dividend. But in such cases the directors may well be entitled to relief under s 727 (acts performed 'honestly and reasonably').

The directors may however honestly rely (in declaring or recommending a dividend) on proper accounts which disclose an apparent distributable profit out of which the dividend can properly be paid. They are not liable if it later appears that the assumptions or estimates used in preparing the accounts, although reasonable at the time, were in fact unsound.

Activity 8

In year 1 H Ltd suffers a realised loss of £1,000. In year 2 it has a realised profit of £9,000 and pays dividends totalling £4,700. In year 3 it suffers a realised loss of £500.
What total dividend could be paid at the start of year 4? How is this calculated?

Chapter roundup

- Every company has an authorised share capital, an issued share capital, a called up share capital and a paid up share capital. All of these amounts may differ.

- Shares may be allotted to investors immediately on application, or alternatively renounceable allotment letters may be issued. The directors normally have power to allot shares, but in a public company

Chapter roundup *continued*

they may not be given authority to allot for more than five years at a time. Existing members have pre-emption rights in relation to ordinary shares issued wholly for cash unless these rights have been disapplied.

- The consideration for shares need not be cash, but some forms of consideration are excluded or subject to special restrictions in the case of public companies.

- Shares may be allotted at a premium. A return of allotments must be made. Shares may be issued in rights issues and bonus issues.

- Shares may have different rights attaching to them. The most common distinction is between ordinary shares and preference shares. Preference shareholders have certain standard rights in comparison to ordinary shareholders unless the contrary is stated.

- Class rights may be varied, but a minority may have a right of objection to the court.

- There are standard procedures for the transfer of shares. The directors of a company may be given the power to refuse to register a transfer, but they must exercise such a power properly.

- A share certificate is *prima facie* evidence of ownership of shares, and a company may be estopped from denying its correctness.

- The paid up capital of a limited company is the investment of the members to which the creditors may have recourse if need be. Its reduction is therefore carefully controlled. Shares may be issued as redeemable and then redeemed, and shares may be purchased, but only in such a way as to maintain the company's capital. A private company may purchase its own shares out of capital subject to certain safeguards designed to ensure the company's continued solvency. The giving of financial assistance by a company for the purchase of its own shares is severely restricted. If a public company suffers a severe loss of capital the members must consider the situation.

- The directors of a company determine what dividends, if any, are to be declared. The members have no right to insist on the payment of a dividend.

- Dividends may only be paid out of accumulated realised profits less accumulated realised losses. Public companies are subject to a further restriction, the full net worth test. The permissible level of dividend payments is determined by reference to the 'relevant accounts'. Excessive dividends may in certain cases be recovered from the members or from the directors.

Quick quiz

1   Distinguish between authorised, issued and called up share capital.

2   Describe the procedure by which a person who holds a renouncable allotment letter may (a) transfer his rights and (b) obtain registration of his shares in his name.

3   What are the statutory rules under which directors may be authorised to allot shares?

4   In respect of which share issues must a company give to its members a right of first refusal? When may this be disapplied by (a) a private and (b) a public company?

5   What statutory rules apply to the issue of shares of a public company in relation to the consideration given for the shares?

6 What is a return of allotments?

7 What is (a) a rights issue and (b) a bonus issue?

8 What is the main way in which preference shares differ from ordinary shares?

9 What is the usual procedure for obtaining the consent of holders of a class of shares to variation of their class rights?

10 What statutory right of objection exists in favour of the minority of a class who have been outvoted at a class meeting held to approve a variation of class rights?

11 To what principles should directors conform if they wish to make a valid refusal of a share transfer?

12 What is the legal significance of a share certificate?

13 In what ways may funds standing to the credit of the share premium account be used?

14 What are the exceptions to the general rule that a company may not acquire its own shares?

15 What resources may (a) a public company and (b) a private company use to purchase its own shares?

16 Give examples of transactions expressly excepted from the prohibition on giving 'financial assistance' for the purchase of the company's shares.

17 By what procedure may a private company lawfully give financial assistance for the purchase of its own shares or the shares of its holding company?

18 What are the duties of the directors of a public company whose assets fall to half or less of its called up share capital?

19 What is the Table A procedure for declaration of (a) an interim dividend and (b) a final dividend?

20 What profits may lawfully be distributed as dividends?

21 What rule may prevent a public company from distributing as dividend profits which a private company might lawfully distribute?

22 What are 'relevant accounts' and what is their significance?

23 What is the position of the directors if, after *payment of a dividend*, it is discovered that they have recommended or declared a dividend which is not covered by sufficient distributable profits?

Solutions to activities

1 $20,000 \times £2 \times 60\% \times 70\% \times 2/3 = £11,200$.

2 A new member could obtain control of the company if enough shares were issued to him.

3 $100 \times 8\% \times 3 + 500 \times £1 \times 9\% = £69$.

4 The holders of the vast majority of the preference shares sought an advantage as members of a different class (the ordinary shareholders).

5 The directors did not take an active decision to refuse to register and therefore the company would be forced to register.

6 There is no reduction of non-distributable capital.

7 No: assistance after the acquisition of shares is forbidden.

8 $£(-1,000 + 9,000 - 4,700 - 500) = £2,800$.

Further question practice

Now try the following practice questions at the end of this text

Multiple choice questions: **80 to 84**

Exam style question: **18**

Chapter 22

LOAN CAPITAL AND CHARGES

Introduction

In the previous chapter we looked at aspects of share capital. You should be aware that capital is also provided by lenders who provide loan capital by taking debentures or debenture stock.

Loan capital is less closely regulated than share capital. Furthermore, it will become apparent in this chapter that the interests and position of a provider of loan capital are very different from those of a shareholder.

Your objectives

After completing this chapter you should:

(a) know what powers a company has to borrow money;

(b) know what a debenture is, and understand the role of a debenture trust deed;

(c) be able to distinguish between fixed and floating charges;

(d) know the rules on the priority of charges and on the registration of charges;

(e) know the ways in which debentureholders may enforce a company's obligations to them.

1   BORROWING

A company whose objects are to carry on a trade or business has an implied power to borrow for purposes incidental to the trade or business. The objects clause, however, nearly always contains an express power to borrow. It is usual not to impose any maximum amount on the company's capacity to borrow (though it is possible to do so). In delegating the company's power to borrow to the directors it is usual, and essential in the case of a company whose shares are listed on The Stock Exchange, to impose a maximum limit on the borrowing arranged by directors.

If there is a power to borrow there is also a power to create charges over the company's assets as security for the loan: *Re Patent File Co 1870*.

A public company initially incorporated as such cannot borrow money until it has obtained a certificate under s 117. Only a public company may offer its debentures to the public and any such offer is a prospectus; if it seeks a listing on The Stock Exchange then the rules on listing particulars must be followed.

2   DEBENTURES

Any document which states the terms on which a company has borrowed money is a debenture (a written acknowledgement of a debt): s 744. It may create a charge over the company's assets as security for the loan. However, a document relating to an unsecured loan is also a debenture in company law (though often called an unsecured loan note in the business world to distinguish it from a secured debenture).

2.1   Debenture trust deeds

A company may create a *debenture trust deed*. It is usually a long and elaborate legal document whose main elements are as follows.

(a) A trustee for prospective debentureholders is appointed.

(b) The nominal amount of the debenture stock is defined, which is the maximum amount which may be raised then or later. The date or period of payment is specified, as is the rate of interest and interest payment dates.

(c) If the debenture stock is secured the deed creates a charge or charges over the assets of the company (and often of its subsidiaries which are parties to the deed for that purpose).

(d) The trustee is authorised to enforce the security in case of default and, in particular, to appoint a receiver with suitable powers of management.

(e) The company enters into various covenants, for instance to keep its assets fully insured or to limit its total borrowings; breach is a default by the company.

(f) There are provisions for a register of debentureholders, transfer of stock, issue of stock certificates, and meetings of debentureholders at which extraordinary resolutions passed by a three-quarters majority are decisions binding on all debentureholders.

2.2   Comparison of shares and debentures

There are important differences between shares and debentures.

(a) A shareholder is a proprietor or owner but a debentureholder is a *creditor* of the company. As a member a shareholder may vote at general meetings; a debentureholder has no such right, though exceptionally he may have votes if the Articles and the deed allow.

(b) In the event of liquidation debentures, like other debts, must be repaid in full before anything is distributed to shareholders.

(c) Interest at the agreed rate must be paid on debentures even if it is necessary to pay out capital in doing so. A shareholder only receives dividends if they can be paid out of distributable profits and the company decides to declare a dividend.

(d) A company has no statutory restriction on redeeming or purchasing its debentures (unless prohibited by the terms of the debenture). It may usually re-issue debentures which have been redeemed. There are elaborate rules to regulate the redemption or purchase by a company of its own shares.

Activity 1

A company offers 10% preference shares and 7% debentures to investors. Ignoring tax considerations and the repayment of capital, why might an investor prefer the debentures?

---

3 CHARGES

A charge over a company's assets gives to the creditor (called the 'chargee') a prior claim (over other creditors) to payment of his debt out of those assets. Charges are of two kinds.

(a) *Fixed or specific charges* attach to the relevant asset as soon as the charge is created. A fixed charge is best suited to fixed assets which the company is likely to retain for a long period.

(b) *Floating charges* do not attach to the relevant assets until the charges crystallise.

A floating charge attaches to all the company's assets of the relevant description at the time of crystallisation, so it may be given over current assets. A floating charge over 'the undertaking and assets' of a company (the most common type) applies to fixed assets as well as to current assets.

EXAMPLE: TYPES OF CHARGE

B plc obtained a substantial loan from A plc on 1 January 1997. The loan is secured by the following charges which are set out in the bank's standard form of debenture document and which were registered at Companies House on 18 January 1997.

(a) A charge over the company's freehold land. The company is not free to sell, lease or in any way deal with the land without A's express permission.

(b) A charge over the company's book debts now and from time to time owing to the company. The company shall immediately pay all moneys received in respect of such debts into the company's bank account and the company may not otherwise deal with the book debts without A's express permission.

(c) A charge over all the company's other assets and undertaking. The company may deal freely with these in the ordinary course of business.

Charge (a) is clearly a fixed charge because the company is not free to deal with the land, and it is a charge over a specific piece of property.

Similarly, charge (b) is a fixed charge because the company is not free to deal with the debts.

Charge (c), however, is a floating charge because the company may carry on business and deal with the assets.

Crystallisation of a floating charge means that it is converted into a fixed charge on the assets owned by the company at the time of crystallisation. Events causing crystallisation are:

(a) the liquidation of the company;

(b) cessation of the company's business;

(c) active intervention by the chargee, generally by way of either appointing a receiver over the assets of the company subject to the security or exercising a power of sale;

(d) if the charge contract so provides, when notice is given by the chargee that the charge is converted into a fixed charge;

(e) automatically on the occurrence of some specified event, without notice from the chargee, if the charge contract so provides;

(f) the crystallisation of another floating charge if it causes the company to cease business.

3.1 Priority of charges

If different charges over the same property are given to different creditors it is necessary to determine their priority. Leaving aside the question of registration, the main points in connection with the priority of any charges are as follows.

(a) Legal charges (legal mortgages of land or of shares) rank according to the order of creation.

(b) An equitable charge (any charge other than a legal mortgage of land or of shares) created before a legal charge will only take priority over the latter if, when the latter was created, the legal chargee had notice of the equitable charge.

(c) A legal charge created before an equitable one has priority.

(d) Two equitable charges take priority over each other according to the time of creation.

It is always possible to vary these rules by agreement of both creditors.

If a floating charge is created and a fixed charge over the same property is created later, the fixed charge will rank first since it attached to the property at the time of creation but the floating charge attaches at the time of *crystallisation*.

4 REGISTRATION OF CHARGES

If a company creates a fixed or floating charge over its assets the charge should usually be registered within 21 days of its creation: s 398(1). It is primarily the duty of the company to register the charge but particulars may also be delivered by another person interested in the charge: s 398(1). The registrar files the particulars in the 'companies charges register' which he maintains (s 397) and notes the date of delivery. He then sends copies of the particulars and of the note of the date of registration delivered to the company and chargee: s 398(5).

4.1 The effect of non-delivery

Non-delivery within 21 days results in the charge being void against an administrator, liquidator or person acquiring an interest in the charged property.

(a) The charge will be void even if insolvency proceedings or the acquisition of an interest in the property occur *within* the 21 days prescribed for delivery, if the particulars are not in fact delivered during this period: s 399(1).

(b) Creditors who subsequently take security over property and duly register their charge within 21 days will take precedence over a previous unregistered charge. This will be the case even if the later chargee had *actual notice* of the previous unregistered charge (unless the later charge was expressed as being subject to the earlier charge).

Non-delivery of a charge means that the sum secured by it is payable forthwith on demand, even if the sum so secured is also the subject of other security: s 407(1).

Late delivery of particulars

If the charge is not registered within 21 days, it is possible to perfect it by late delivery under s 400(1), so that it will not be void against an administrator, liquidator or acquirer of an interest if insolvency proceedings on the acquisition of an interest happens *after* registration. If it occurs on the same day then there is a rebuttable presumption that the relevant event happened first.

Activity 2

On 1 January, a company mortgages its factory to A as security for a £50,000 loan. On 1 February the same factory is mortgaged to B as security for a £40,000 loan. On 1 March C takes a floating charge over all the company's assets as security for a £60,000 loan, and on 1 April D takes a floating charge over all the company's assets as security for a £20,000 loan. All charges are registered within 21 days of creation, except that C's charge is not registered.

On 1 August, the company goes into liquidation. The factory is worth £120,000 and the company's other assets are worth £12,000. The company has no other liabilities. How much do each of A, B, C and D receive? Why is this so?

---

5 DEBENTUREHOLDERS' REMEDIES

Any debentureholder is a creditor of the company with the normal remedies of an unsecured creditor. He could:

(a) sue the company for debt and seize its property if his judgment for debt is unsatisfied;

(b) present a petition to the court for the compulsory liquidation of the company;

(c) present a petition to the court for an administration order.

A *secured* debentureholder (or the trustee of a debenture trust deed on behalf of secured debentureholders) may enforce the security. He may:

(a) take possession of the asset subject to the charge if he has a legal charge (if he has an equitable charge he may only take possession if the contract allows);

(b) sell it (provided the debenture is executed as a deed);

(c) apply to the court for its transfer to his ownership by foreclosure order (rarely used and only available to a legal chargee);

(d) appoint a receiver of it.

6 RECEIVERS

The debenture (or debenture trust deed) usually gives power to the debentureholders (or their trustee) to appoint a receiver in specified circumstances of default by the company. The debenture also provides that the receiver, when appointed:

(a) shall have suitable powers of management and disposal of the assets under his charge; and

(b) shall be an agent of the company and not of the debentureholders by whom he is appointed. The purpose of this stipulation is to safeguard the debenture-holders against liability for any wrongful act of the receiver.

A receiver may be appointed under a fixed or a floating charge. He takes control of the assets subject to the charge as a means of enforcing the security for the benefit of the secured creditor by or for whom the receiver is appointed.

6.1 Administrative receivers

A receiver who is appointed under a floating charge extending over the whole or substantially the whole of the company's property is called an *administrative receiver*. He is in charge of the company's business and therefore he has to manage it, and he must be a qualified insolvency practitioner.

An administrative receiver is automatically given a long list of statutory powers, unless the debenture provides to the contrary. These include powers:

(a) to borrow money and give security;

(b) to carry on the business of the company;

(c) to sell the company's property;

(d) to transfer the business of the company (or part of it) to a subsidiary.

Unless appointed by the court, the receiver is an agent of the company unless or until it goes into liquidation. As agent:

(a) he is personally liable on contracts made in the course of his duties as receiver;

(b) he is entitled to an indemnity for that liability out of the company's assets; and

(c) he can bind the company by his acts.

An administrative receiver is also liable on employment contracts, adoption of which does not require any formal act. Once the contracts have been adopted, for example by continuing to pay wages, regardless of any disclaimer, such contracts have a first charge on the company's assets: *Powdrill & Another v Watson & Another 1994*, better known as the *Paramount* case. However, the Insolvency Act 1994 restricts liability to certain 'qualifying liabilities' such as wages and salaries, sickness and holiday pay and pension contributions.

The function of a receiver is to manage or to realise the assets which are the security with a view to paying out of those assets what is due to the debentureholders whom he represents (plus the expenses, including his own remuneration). If he is able to discharge these debts he vacates his office of receiver and the directors resume full control.

Activity 3

A lender to a company takes a fixed legal charge over the company's only premises and a floating charge over the company's assets and undertaking. The company defaults at a time when its premises are worth much less than the debt but the company's inventory is very valuable. How should the lender proceed?

Chapter roundup

- Companies generally have powers to borrow and to create charges over assets.

- A debenture is a written acknowledgement of a debt. An issue of debentures may be accompanied by a debenture trust deed, appointing a trustee to look after the interests of the debentureholders and imposing constraints on the issuing company.

- A debentureholder is a creditor of the company, and the company must pay interest and repay capital on the due dates. A shareholder has no automatic right to the payment of dividends, and share capital is normally only repaid on a liquidation.

- A company may create fixed or floating charges over its assets as security for money borrowed. A fixed charge is given over specific assets, whereas a floating charge attaches to whatever assets of a given class the company has at the time of crystallisation.

- Charges must be registered within 21 days of their creation. There are rules on the priority of charges, and late registration may cause a charge to lose its priority.

- Debentureholders have the usual remedies of any creditor if amounts owing to them are not paid on time. Secured debentureholders may take and sell the assets they have a charge over, or they may appoint a receiver.

Quick quiz

1 State three matters on which a debenture trust deed normally makes provision.

2 Compare the legal position of a debentureholder and a shareholder.

3 What are the characteristics of a floating charge?

4 In what circumstances does a floating charge crystallise and what is the effect of its doing so?

5 In what circumstances will a fixed charge created later than a floating charge take priority over the floating charge?

6 What is the effect of non-delivery of particulars of a charge?

7 What remedies are available to (a) a secured and (b) an unsecured debentureholder?

Solutions to activities

1 Interest must be paid on time even if the company makes a loss. Dividends need not be paid, even if the company makes a profit.

2 A receives £50,000 and B receives £40,000 because A has the first fixed charge on the factory and B the second. D's charge than takes priority over C's unregistered charge and therefore D receives £20,000 and C receives what is left (£22,000).

3 The lender should appoint a receiver under the floating charge to sell as much of the inventory as is needed to pay the debt.

Further question practice

Now try the following practice questions at the end of this text

Multiple choice questions: **85 to 89**

Exam style question: **19**

Chapter 23

DIRECTORS

Introduction

In Chapter 17, the idea of a company as an abstract legal person was discussed. As an abstract person, a company cannot manage itself. Company law therefore requires that every company must have one or more directors.

Since directors are in control of the assets of another person (the company) they are subject to an elaborate code of rules. These rules derive mainly from statute and case law, but recently the Cadbury Code has started to have an influence on directors of listed companies.

Your objectives

After completing this chapter you should:

(a) understand the role of directors;

(b) know how directors may be appointed;

(c) know the rules on the disclosure of directors' shareholdings

(d) know the other required disclosures concerning directors;

(e) know how a director's term of office may come to an end;

(f) know when a person may be disqualified from being a director;

(g) understand the fiduciary position of directors;

(h) know the extent of directors' duty of care;

(i) know the restrictions on directors' interests in company contracts and on loans to directors;

(j) know the extent of directors' powers and the rules on board meetings;

(k) understand the position of a managing director;

(l) know how members can control directors;

(m) know what is meant by corporate governance;

(n) understand the position of outsiders when directors exceed their actual authority;

(o) understand the role of the company secretary.

1   WHO AND WHAT IS A DIRECTOR?

Any person who occupies the position of a director is treated as such: s 741. The test is one of function. Any person (except a professional adviser) by whose directions the board is accustomed to act (but who is not officially a director) is called a *shadow director*. A person appointed by a director to attend board meetings and vote on his behalf is an *alternate director*. A director who merely sits on the board, with no additional management duties, is a *non-executive director*. If the articles provide for it, a *managing director* may be appointed.

Every company must have at least one director, and for a public company, the minimum is two: s 282. There is no statutory maximum.

2   APPOINTMENT OF DIRECTORS

The documents delivered to the registrar to form a company include a form giving particulars of the first directors and signed by them to signify their consent: s 13(5). On the formation of the company those persons become the first directors.

Once a company has been formed any appointment of directors in addition to or in replacement of previous directors is made as the articles provide. Most companies follow Table A in providing for co-option of new members by existing directors and election of directors in general meeting. Table A also provides (Articles 73 – 80) for *rotation* (retirement and re-election) of directors. However, the articles may exclude retirement by rotation or permit some person, such as the holding company or a major shareholder, to appoint one, several or all directors. It is a matter of choosing whichever procedure is convenient.

2.1   Register of directors and secretaries

A company must keep at its registered office, where any person may inspect it, a register of its directors and secretaries showing:

(a) the name of each director/secretary;

(b) his address;

(c) his nationality;

(d) his date of birth;

(e) particulars of his business occupation and other directorships.

Items (c), (d) and (e) above apply only to directors, not to the company secretary.

3   DIRECTORS AS SHAREHOLDERS

There is no general rule that a director must be a shareholder nor any rule which prohibits him from being one. The articles may however require that each director shall be the registered holder of a specified number of shares (called 'qualification shares').

If a director does hold shares or debentures, he is required to give notice to the company and the company must enter the information in a register of directors' interests which is kept with the register of members (normally at the registered office) and is similarly open to public inspection.

4   DISCLOSURES CONCERNING DIRECTORS

4.1   Loans to directors

A company may not (subject to exceptions) enter into a loan or similar transaction with a director of the company or of its holding company nor (in the case of a public company or its subsidiary) with a person connected with such a director. If any such loan (whether prohibited or permitted) existed during the year prescribed particulars must be included (subject to limited exceptions) in the annual accounts for the year: s 232.

4.2   Directors' interests in contracts

There are similar requirements for disclosure in the annual accounts of transactions in which a director had a material interest either directly or indirectly (for example through another company): Sch 6 para 1. The other directors may decide whether a director's interest is 'material' (and so requires disclosure).

A company must make available for inspection by members a copy or particulars (if there is no written service agreement) of contracts of employment between the company or a subsidiary with a director of the company: s 318.

There are two exceptions to the general rule (s 319).

(a) If the service contract requires the director to work wholly or mainly outside the UK only brief particulars (the director's name and the duration of the contract) need to be given.

(b) If the contract will expire or if the company can terminate it without compensation within a year, no copy or particulars need be kept available for members' inspection.

More detailed rules now apply to listed companies.

The copy or particulars must be available either at the registered office, or at the principal place of business in England.

Prescribed particulars of directors' emoluments must be given in the accounts and also particulars of any compensation for loss of office and directors' pensions: Sch 5.

5   THE TERMINATION OF DIRECTORSHIPS

A director may always vacate his office by resignation (Table A Article 81 provides for resignation by notice in writing given to the company) or by not offering himself for re-election when his previous term of office ends under the rotation rules. Obviously office is also vacated on the death of a director or on the dissolution of the company. In addition there are statutory provisions for removal from office and for disqualification.

The articles may provide for the removal of a director from office. But if the director also has a service agreement he may still be entitled to compensation for its breach by his dismissal.

In addition to any provisions of the articles for removal of directors, a director may be removed from office by ordinary resolution of the members (passed by a simple majority) of which special notice to the company has been given by the person proposing it: s 303. On receipt of the special notice the company must send a copy to the director who may require that a memorandum of reasonable length shall (unless it is defamatory) be issued to members; he also has a right to address the meeting at which the resolution is considered: s 304.

This statutory power of removal overrides the articles and any service agreement (but the director may claim damages for breach of the agreement). The power is, however, limited in its effect in two ways.

(a) A member who gives special notice to remove a director cannot insist on the inclusion of his resolution in the notice of a meeting unless he qualifies by representing members who either have one-twentieth of the voting rights or are at least 100 members on whose shares an average of at least £100 has been paid up: s 376.

(b) A director may be irremovable if he has weighted voting rights and can prevent the resolution from being passed.

Retirement of directors

A director of a public company is deemed to retire at the end of the AGM following his 70th birthday: s 293(3). This rule is disapplied if the articles permit him to continue or if his continued appointment is approved by the general meeting. It is the duty of directors to disclose their ages to the company for the purposes of this rule: s 294.

Activity 1

In *Bushell v Faith 1969*, the company had three members who were also the directors and each held 100 shares. On a resolution to remove a director, that director was to have three votes per share while other members were to have one vote per share. Could a director prevent a resolution to remove him from being put forward? Could he prevent it from being passed?

---

6   DISQUALIFICATION OF DIRECTORS

Table A Article 81 provides that a director must vacate office:

(a) if he is disqualified by the Act or any rule of law (for example, if he ceases to be the registered holder of qualification shares);

(b) if he becomes bankrupt or enters into an arrangement with his creditors;

(c) if he becomes of unsound mind;

(d) if he resigns by notice in writing;

(e) if he is absent for a period of six consecutive months from board meetings held during that period without obtaining leave of absence and the other directors resolve that he shall on that account vacate office.

6.1   Statutory disqualification of directors

The Company Directors Disqualification Act 1986 (CDDA) provides that a court may disqualify any person from being without leave of the court a director (including a shadow director), liquidator, administrator, receiver or manager of a company's property or in any way directly or indirectly being concerned or taking part in the promotion, formation or management of a company: s 1. The terms of the disqualification order are thus very wide. They have been held to include acting as a consultant to a company.

The court may make an order on any of the following grounds.

(a) *Where a person is convicted of an indictable offence in connection with the promotion, formation, management or liquidation of a company or with the receivership or management of a company's property:* s 2. An indictable offence is an offence which may be tried at a crown court; it is therefore a serious offence. It need not actually have been tried on indictment (at the crown court) but if it was, the maximum period for which the court can disqualify is 15 years compared with only five years if the offence was dealt with summarily (at the magistrates court): s 5. Either the court which convicted the person or the court with jurisdiction in regard to the insolvency (if there is one) may make the disqualification order.

(b) *Where it appears that a person has been persistently in default in relation to provisions of company legislation* requiring any return, account or other document to be filed with, delivered or sent, or notice of any matter to be given to the registrar of companies: s 3. Three defaults in five years are conclusive evidence of persistent default. The maximum period of disqualification under this section is five years.

(c) *Where it appears in the course of the winding up of a company that a person has been guilty of fraudulent trading* (the person does not actually have to have been convicted of fraudulent trading) or has otherwise been guilty, while an officer or liquidator of the company or receiver or manager of its property, of any fraud in relation to the company or of any breach of his duty as such officer, etc: s 4. The maximum period of disqualification under this section is 15 years. The first case to be brought under this section was *Re Samuel Sherman plc 1991*. The director of a public company had committed a number of persistent and deliberate breaches of important statutory provisions. The period of disqualification chosen was five years, the top of the 'minimum bracket' (see below).

(d) *Where the Secretary of State acting on a report made by the inspectors or from information or documents obtained under the Companies Act, applies to the court* for an order believing it to be expedient in the public interest. If the court is satisfied that the person's conduct in relation to the company makes that person unfit to be concerned in the management of a company then it may make a disqualification order: s 8. Again the maximum is 15 years.

(e) *Where a director has participated in wrongful trading:* s 10. Maximum 15 years.

The court must make an order where it is satisfied:

(a) that a person has been a director of a company which has at any time become insolvent (whether while he was a director or subsequently); and

(b) that his conduct as a director of that company makes him unfit to be concerned in the management of a company: s 6 CDDA.

In such cases disqualification is mandatory, and the fact that alternative remedies are available will not justify refusing to disqualify (*Secretary of State for Trade and Industry v Gray 1994*).

Almost 5,000 directors had been disqualified under the CDDA by Spring 1996. There has been considerable litigation on disqualification, most of it concerned with s 6.

> *Re Firedart, Official Receiver v Fairall 1994.*
> F, one of four directors, ran a company. Amongst other things, he failed to ensure that the company kept proper accounts, allowed it to trade whilst insolvent and authorised unjustified payments to himself and his wife.
>
> *Held:* F was unfit under s 6 and was disqualified for six years.

The judge stressed the importance of proper accounting records, stating that directors who do not keep proper accounts must expect to be considered unfit.

More recently in *Re Continental Assurance Co of London plc 1996* a director was disqualified for failing to read the company's accounts.

In *Secretary of State for Trade and Industry v Gray 1994* the Court of Appeal held that, in appropriate circumstances, the past conduct of a director could determine his disqualification even if he would no longer constitute a threat to the public if allowed to continue in management. This emphasises that there is a penal element to disqualification as well as it being a means of protecting the public.

In *Re living Images Ltd 1996*. the judge stated that the test was whether the director's conduct had fallen below the standards of 'probity and competence' suitable for directors when viewed cumulatively and taking account of any extenuating circumstances.

In *Re Sevenoaks Stationers (Retail) Ltd 1991* the Court of appeal laid down certain disqualification brackets. The appropriate period of disqualification which should be imposed where a director had been found unfit to be concerned in the management of a company was a minimum of two to five years if the conduct was, in relative terms, not very serious, six to ten years if the conduct was serious but did not merit the maximum penalty and over ten years only in particularly serious cases.

In *Secretary of State for Trade and Industry v Arif and Others 1996* it was decided that a company director who had not been able to act as such for some two and a half years while disqualification proceedings were pending could not have that period set off against the disqualification period the Court finally decided on.

The Act makes it clear that the court in assessing 'unfitness' may take into account the director's conduct in relation to other companies. Administrators, receivers and liquidators all have a statutory duty to report to the DTI on directors of companies in whose affairs they have become involved, where they believe the conditions in s 6 for a disqualification order have been satisfied: s 7. It will then be up to the Secretary of State to decide whether to apply to the court for an order, but if he does decide to apply he must do so within two years of the date on which the company became insolvent. The minimum period of disqualification under the section is two years and the maximum five years: *Re Eurostern Maritime Ltd 1987*. The court will also take mismanagement of foreign companies into account.

There is a register of disqualification orders which is open to public inspection: s 18. A court may in particular cases grant exemption from a disqualification order. In addition to this register the company's register of directors and secretary will facilitate the tracing of a director's connection with companies which are known to have been mismanaged since the register must (as a result of a change made in 1981) include particulars of directorships of other companies held in the previous five years.

Increasing numbers of directors are being disqualified, particularly on the grounds of wrongful trading, a matter which is provoking some concern.

Activity 2

S was a director of a company which, a month after her resignation, became insolvent. She was also responsible for wrongful trading while a director of another company. Consider whether she would be disqualified from being a director, if a court considered the matter.

7 FIDUCIARY DUTIES OF DIRECTORS

Directors are said to hold a fiduciary position (a position in which they must serve faithfully) since they make contracts as agents of the company and have control of its property.

The directors owe a fiduciary duty to the company to exercise their powers *bona fide* in what they honestly consider to be the interests of the company: *Re Smith & Fawcett Ltd 1942*. The effect of this rule is seen in cases on gifts made to persons not employed by the company.

> *Re W & M Roith Ltd 1967*
> The controlling shareholder and director wished to make provision for his widow, but did not want to leave her shares. His service agreement therefore provided her with a pension for life on his death.
>
> *Held:* the object of this was to benefit the widow, not the company, and hence could be rescinded.

In exercising the powers given to them by the articles the directors have a fiduciary duty not only to act *bona fide* but also only to use their powers for a proper purpose.

The directors owe a fiduciary duty to avoid a conflict of duty and personal interest. It is unnecessary to show that the company has been prejudiced in any way by the conflict of interest.

A director may not obtain any personal advantage from his position of director without the consent of the company for whatever gain or profit he has obtained.

> *Industrial Development Consultants Ltd v Cooley 1972*
> C was managing director of the company which provided consultancy services to gas boards. A gas board declined to award a contract to the company but C realised that he personally might be able to obtain it. He told the board of his company that he was ill and persuaded them to release him from his service agreement. On ceasing to be a director of the company C obtained the contract. The company sued him to recover the profits of the contract.
>
> *Held:* C was accountable for his profit.

Activity 3

In *Regal (Hastings) Ltd v Gulliver 1942*, the company had an investment opportunity, but insufficient capital. It formed a subsidiary and subscribed some of the necessary capital, while the directors and others subscribed the rest. The result was that the directors made a substantial profit, and the company had lost nothing because it could not have made the investment without their help. However, the directors still had to account to the company for their profit. Which of the above rules on directors' duties was applied?

---

8 DIRECTORS' DUTY OF CARE

Directors have a common law duty of care to show reasonable competence. A director is expected to show the degree of skill which may reasonably be expected from a person of his knowledge and experience: the standard set is personal to the director.

In the absence of ground for suspicion and subject to normal business practice, he is entitled to leave the routine conduct of the business in the hands of its management and may trust them, accepting the information and explanation which they provide, if they appear to be honest and competent.

8.1 Company's action against negligent directors

The company may recover damages from its directors for loss caused by their negligence. But something more than imprudence or want of care must be shown. It must be shown to be a case of gross negligence.

9 DIRECTORS' DEALINGS WITH THEIR COMPANY

There are several statutory rules forbidding or restricting transactions affecting or involving directors.

9.1 Directors' interests in company contracts

A director shall always 'declare the nature of his interest', direct or indirect, in a contract or proposed contract with the company: s 317. The disclosure must be made to the first meeting of the directors at which the contract is considered or (if later) the first meeting held after the director becomes interested in the contract.

The requirement to declare his interest at a meeting of the company directors also applies in the case of a sole director: *Re Neptune (Vehicle Washing Equipment) Ltd 1995*. In this case it was held that it was especially important for a sole director to consider any conflict of interest and, furthermore, that the word 'meeting' did not exclude sole directors. Compliance with s 317 could be achieved by either holding a meeting alone or with, say, a company secretary. Any declaration must be minuted.

The shareholders' approval is required for any contract or arrangement by which the company buys from or sells to a director of the company or of its holding company or a person connected with any such director property which exceeds £100,000 in value or (if less) exceeds 10% of the company's net assets (subject to a minimum of £2,000 value): s 320.

A company must disclose in the annual report and accounts any contract or arrangement with the company (or a subsidiary) in which a director, directly or through a connected person, has an interest which is material. The other directors may decide that a director's interest in a contract is not material for disclosure. But contracts of a value not exceeding £1,000 or (if greater) not exceeding 1% of the company's assets (subject to a maximum of £5,000) are exempt from this disclosure requirement: s 232 and Sch 6.

If a director's service contract extends for longer than five years and under its terms the company either cannot terminate by notice or can only terminate it in specified circumstances (s 319(6)), the company can in fact terminate it at any time with reasonable notice. However, such a contract will only be valid if it is first approved by an ordinary resolution: it cannot later be ratified.

9.2 Loans to directors (ss 330-338)

Every company is prohibited by s 330 from:

(a) making a loan to a director of the company or of its holding company;

(b) guaranteeing or giving security for a loan to any such director;

(c) taking an assignment of a loan which, if made originally by the company, would have been contrary to (a) and (b);

(d) providing a benefit to another person as part of an arrangement by which that person enters into a transaction forbidden to the company itself by rules (a), (b) or (c).

There are the following general exceptions to these rules.

(a) A company may make a loan or give a guarantee or security in respect of a loan to a director which is also its holding company: s 336.

(b) A company may fund a director to enable him to perform his duties provided that the money is approved in general meeting before or afterwards; if it is made available before approval is obtained, it must be approved at or before the next AGM and must be repaid within six months of that AGM if not so approved: s 337.

(c) A money-lending company may advance money to a director, provided it is done in the normal course of business and the terms are not more favourable than the company would normally allow: s 338.

(d) A company may make a loan of up to £5,000: s 334.

(e) Group members may lend to each other: s 333.

(f) A holding company may make loans to directors of its subsidiaries, provided they are not directors of, nor connected to directors of, the holding company.

Relevant companies

There are more stringent rules for 'relevant companies' which include any public company and any private company which is a member of a group which includes a public company. The same basic rules apply to relevant companies as to other companies. In addition:

(a) the exceptions described in (b) and (c) above are limited to a maximum of £10,000 and £100,000 respectively, although a bank is only restricted to the £100,000 limit if the loan is to buy a residence: s 338;

(b) there are restrictions on indirect means of enabling a director to obtain goods or services on credit;

(c) a company transaction with a third party who is connected with one of its directors is subject to the same rules as apply to its transactions with a director himself.

Activity 4

A company is to buy from a director a piece of land worth £3,500. The company's net assets are worth £80,000. The other directors consider that the director's interest is material. Must the shareholders approve the contract? Must the contract be disclosed in the annual report and accounts?

---

10 DIRECTORS' POWERS

The powers of the directors are defined by the articles. It is usual (Table A Article 70) to authorise the directors 'to manage the business of the company' and 'to exercise all the powers of the company'. They may then take any decision which is within the capacity (as defined by the objects clause) of the company unless either the Act or the articles themselves require that the decision shall be taken by the members in general meeting.

10.1 Board meetings

The articles confer powers on the directors collectively and not upon individual directors (unless appointed as managing directors). The directors should therefore exercise their powers by holding board meetings at which collective decisions are taken.

The articles usually leave the directors free to decide when and how board meetings shall be held. No period of notice is prescribed by law nor need a notice of a board meeting disclose the business to be transacted. Any member of the board may call, or require the secretary to call, a meeting. Reasonable notice should be given to all members sufficient to enable them to attend unless the articles (Table A Article 88) provide that directors who are abroad are not entitled to receive notice.

Minutes must be kept of the proceedings of board meetings and when signed by the chairman are evidence of those proceedings. The directors (and also the auditors for the purpose of their audit) have a right to inspect the minute book. No one else has the right of inspection nor need the minute book be kept at any particular place: s 382.

The directors are usually authorised by the articles (Table A Article 72) to delegate any of their powers to a *committee* of the board or to a *single director* either for a specific transaction or as managing director.

10.2 Managing and other working directors

If the articles provide for it (as they usually do) the board may appoint one or more directors to be managing directors. In his dealings with outsiders the managing director has apparent authority as agent of the company to make business contracts. No other director, even if he works full time, has that *apparent* authority as a director, though if he is employed as a manager he may have apparent authority at a slightly lower level. The managing director's *actual* authority is whatever the board gives him, and the board may change the limits of that authority, if necessary breaching his service agreement to do so.

11 MEMBERS' CONTROL OF DIRECTORS

The members of a company appoint the directors and may remove them from office under s 303. They can also, by altering the articles, re-allocate powers between the board and the general meeting. The members therefore have some control over the directors. But the directors are not agents of the members who can be instructed by the members in general meeting as to how they should exercise their powers.

Salmon v Quin and Axtens Ltd 1909
The articles provided that certain transactions should require the approval of both the two joint managing directors. One of them dissented from a resolution which the board wished to pass. The company in general meeting passed an ordinary resolution to 'ratify' the board resolution.

Held: this was 'an attempt to alter the terms of the contract (the articles) between the parties by a simple resolution instead of by a special resolution'. The general meeting could not override a veto given to a managing director by the articles.

John Shaw & Sons (Salford) Ltd v Shaw 1935
In exercise of their general management powers given by the articles the directors began legal proceedings in the name of the company. The defendants,

who were shareholders and directors convened an EGM to pass a resolution that the action against them should be discontinued. The board challenged this decision.

Held: the general body of shareholders 'cannot themselves usurp the powers which by the articles are vested in the directors'. The resolution passed by the EGM was therefore invalid.

Activity 5

In *Holdsworth & Co v Caddies 1955* a managing director had a service agreement under which his duties related to several companies in a group. The board confined his duties to one subsidiary. Were they entitled to do so?

12 CORPORATE GOVERNANCE

Definition

Corporate governance: the accountability of those who control and manage large public companies to do so for the benefit of the shareholders.

The Report of the Committee on the Financial Aspects of Corporate Governance (the Cadbury Report) was published on 1 December 1992. It defines corporate governance as the system by which companies are directed and controlled, and identifies the three elements of governance as the board of directors, the shareholders and the auditors.

The Cadbury report, with its accompanying Code of Best Practice ('the Code') seeks to clarify and redress the balance between the respective roles and responsibilities of the directors, the shareholders and the auditors. The directors are responsible for corporate governance, the shareholders must see that an appropriate governance structure is in place and the auditors must provide an external and objective check.

The Code itself covers the role and structure of the board of directors, the appointment and independence of non-executive directors, the determination of the executive directors' remuneration and the financial reporting and controls to be exercised by the board.

All Stock Exchange listed companies must now comply with the Code, although it is applicable to many companies, whether public or private.

13 LIABILITY OF THE COMPANY FOR UNAUTHORISED ACTS OF DIRECTORS

The powers given to 'directors' by the articles are only vested in persons who *are* directors. If they have not been properly appointed or if they have ceased to be directors they do not have the directors' powers under the articles. But a person who deals with a company through persons who appear to be and who act as directors can usually enforce the contract. It is provided that the acts of a director or manager are valid notwithstanding any defect that may afterwards be discovered in his appointment or qualification: s 285 and Article 92. But to bring this statutory rule into operation there must be an appointment which is later found to be defective. It does not extend to a case where no appointment at all is made or the 'director' has ceased to be a director.

13.1 The 'indoor management' rule

The articles may reserve to the company in general meeting power to authorise certain transactions or impose on the directors some rule of procedure such as fixing a quorum of two or more for board meetings. The rule in *Turquand's* case is that the outsider who deals with the directors (or apparent directors):

(a) is deemed to be aware of the requirements or restrictions imposed by the articles; but

(b) is entitled to assume (unless he knows or should suspect the contrary) that these internal rules have been observed.

> *Royal British Bank v Turquand 1856*
>
> Under the articles the directors could only borrow for the company such amounts as might be authorised by ordinary resolution passed in general meeting. A resolution was passed but it was defective since it did not specify the amount which the directors might borrow. The directors issued to the bank a debenture for £2,000 believing that they had authority to do so. The bank did not know of the defective terms of the resolution and had no legal right to inspect it since no copy of an ordinary resolution (of this type) is filed at the registry. The company went into liquidation and the liquidator (Turquand) argued that the company had no obligation to repay the loan since the loan contract (debentures) had been made without the authority required by the articles (of which the bank must be deemed to be aware – the doctrine of constructive notice of a company's basic public documents).
>
> *Held:* the bank must be deemed to be aware that the directors needed authority to borrow but it was also entitled to assume that authority had been properly given since the bank had no means of discovering whether a valid resolution had been passed.

13.2 Turquand's case and the Companies Act 1989

The status of the rule in *Turquand's* case is questionable in the light of the amendments made to the Companies Act 1985 by the Companies Act 1989. The new ss 711A, 35(1), 35A and 35B all impact on this position. Section 711A abolishes the doctrine of constructive notice as it applies to documents held by the registrar, or made available to the company for inspection. This strikes out a basic premise of *Turquand's* case. However, s 711A(2) specifically provides that the abolition does *not* affect the question of whether a person is affected by notice of any matter by reason of a failure to make such enquiries as ought reasonably to be made: that is, a person is deemed to have constructive notice if he did not bother to make reasonable enquiries.

The combined effect of the new provisions certainly overlaps with the rule in *Turquand's* case. An *ultra vires* act is now almost always validated. In relation to *intra vires* actions beyond the delegated powers of directors, it is clear that s 35A covers very similar situations to *Turquand's* case, and that it applies in some situations where *Turquand's* case does not.

Activity 6

How might the outcome in *Turquand's* case have differed if the bank had been a member of the debtor company?

13.3 Agency by holding out

Holding out is a basic rule of the law of agency: if the principal (the company) holds out a person as its authorised agent it is estopped (against a person who has relied on the representation) from denying that he is its authorised agent and so is bound by a contract entered into by him on the company's behalf.

This situation usually results from the board of directors permitting a director to behave as if he were a managing director duly appointed when in fact he is not. As explained above a managing director does, by virtue of his position, have apparent authority to make commercial contracts for the company. If the board allows a director to enter into contracts, being aware of his dealings and taking no steps to disown him, the company will usually be bound: *Freeman & Lockyer v Buckhurst Park Properties (Mangal) Ltd 1964*.

14 THE COMPANY SECRETARY

Every company must have a secretary and a sole director must not also be the secretary. The directors of a public company must take all reasonable steps to ensure that the secretary is suitably qualified for his post by his knowledge and experience. Under s 286, a public company secretary may be anyone who:

(a) was the secretary or his assistant on 22 December 1980; or

(b) has been a public company secretary for at least three out of the five years previous to appointment; or

(c) is a member of the Institute of Chartered Secretaries and Administrators or of one of several accountancy bodies; or

(d) is a barrister, advocate or solicitor in the UK; or

(e) is a person who, by virtue of holding or having held any other position or being a member of any other body, appears to the directors to be capable.

The Act does not define the general duties of a company secretary since these will vary according to the size of the company and of its headquarters. The standard minimum duties of the secretary are:

(a) to make the arrangements incidental to meetings of the board of directors. The secretary usually convenes the meetings (Table A Article 88), issues the agenda (if any), collects or prepares the papers for submission to each meeting, attends the meeting, drafts the minutes and communicates decisions taken to the staff of the company or to outsiders, for instance a refusal of the directors to approve the transfer of shares;

(b) to maintain the register of members (unless this work is contracted out to professional registrars), to enter in transfers of shares and to prepare share certificates for issue to members. The secretary also keeps the other statutory registers and prepares the notices, returns and other documents which must be delivered to the registrar.

14.1 The secretary as agent

It is a general principle of agency law that if a person is employed in a capacity in which he does certain things for his principal he has *apparent* authority to bind his principal by such actions on his behalf, unless the principal has denied him that authority and the other party has notice of the restriction. In 1971 the Court of Appeal applied this principle and recognised that it is a normal function of a company secretary to enter into contracts connected with the administration of the company.

Panorama Developments (Guildford) Ltd v Fidelis Furnishing Fabrics Ltd 1971
B, the secretary of a company, ordered cars from a car hire firm, representing that they were required to meet the company's customers at London Airport. Instead he used the cars for his own purposes. The bill was not paid, so the car hire firm claimed payment from B's company.

Held: B's company was liable, for he had apparent authority to make contracts such as the present one, which were concerned with the administrative side of its business. The decision recognises the general nature of a company secretary's duties. The court also said that, if the issue had arisen, it might not have treated the secretary as having apparent authority to make *commercial* contracts such as buying or selling trade goods, since that is not a normal duty of the company secretary.

The Cadbury Report stated that the company secretary also has an important role in corporate governance.

The report states that the secretary has a key role in ensuring that board procedures are observed and regularly reviewed.

The point was also made that the company secretary may be seen as a source of guidance on the responsibilities of the board and its chairman under the new regulations, and on the implementation of the Code of Best Practice laid down in the report.

Activity 7

Would a company secretary ordering office stationery be likely to be treated as acting with apparent authority in a plumbing company? Why?
Why might the position differ if the company traded as a stationer?

Chapter roundup

- A director is a person who takes part in making decisions by attending board meetings, whether or not he is called a director. Directors may also be employees of their company, with contracts of employment. A private (but not a public) company may have only one director, but a sole director may not also be the company secretary.

- Directors are generally elected by the members. Table A provides for the rotation of directors.

- Directors need not be members unless the articles require them to be, but they may be members. Any shareholdings must be disclosed in a register of directors' interests.

- Loans to directors, directors' interests in contracts and the terms of directors' service contracts must all be disclosed.

- A director may resign. He may also be removed from office, either in accordance with the articles or by an ordinary resolution of the members.

- A director may be required by the articles to vacate office in certain circumstances. Any person may be disqualified from being a director under the Company Directors Disqualification Act 1986.

Chapter roundup *continued*

- A director holds a fiduciary position, and must act in the best interests of his company. If he makes a personal profit from his position he may be required to account for it to the company.

- A director has a duty of care, and is expected to show the degree of skill which may reasonably be expected from a person of his knowledge and experience.

- A director must declare any interest he has in a contract with the company, and such interests may have to be disclosed in the annual report and accounts. There are severe restrictions on loans by companies to their directors.

- Directors have the power to manage their company. This power is exercised in board meetings. A managing director has apparent authority to make contracts for the company on his own.

- The members of a company cannot tell the directors how to exercise their powers, but they can remove the directors.

- The acts of an irregularly appointed director are valid. Under the indoor management rule, an outsider is entitled to assume that internal formalities required by a company's articles have been observed. However, this rule is now less important than it was because of legislation contained in the Companies Act 1989.

- If a director is allowed to represent that he is a managing director, he may come to have the apparent authority of a managing director.

- Every company must have a company secretary, and the secretary of a public company must be appropriately qualified. The secretary is effectively the company's chief administrative officer. He has apparent

Quick quiz

1 What is meant by the expressions (a) 'shadow director' and (b) 'alternate director'

2 What are the rules about the number of directors?

3 What particulars must be entered in (a) the register of directors and secretary and (b) the register of directors' interests, and where must each be kept?

4 What information is available to members concerning the terms of employment of directors?

5 What are the practical limitations on the members' statutory powers to remove a director from office?

6 Give the grounds, included in the Table A model articles, for disqualification of a director from continuing to hold office in the company.

7 Upon what grounds *may* a director be disqualified by a court order from holding office? When *must* the court disqualify him?

8 What are the main elements of a director's fiduciary duty?

9 What standard of competence is expected of directors?

10 What are the disclosure requirements of a director in relation to a contract of the company in which he has an interest?

11 What are the main exceptions to the general rule against a company making a loan to one of its directors?

12 What is the standard (Table A) formula by which the powers of the directors are defined?

13 What are the rules on notice to call a board meeting?

14 In what respect is it material to a person dealing with a company that he reasonably believes that the company representative is a managing director?

15 Are members in general meeting allowed to exercise powers which under the articles are delegated to the directors?

16 What is 'corporate governance'?

17 State the rule in *Turquand's* case.

18 Who may be appointed secretary of a public company?

19 State the standard minimum duties of a company secretary.

Solutions to activities

1 A resolution to remove a director could be put forward against his wishes, but he could prevent it from being passed (by 300 votes to 200).

2 S might be disqualified, but she need not be (unless her conduct while a director of the insolvent company makes her unfit to be concerned in the management of a company).

3 The rule that directors must not obtain any personal advantage or profit from their position.

4 The shareholders need not approve the contract, but it must be disclosed in the annual report and accounts.

5 Yes: the board may change the limits of his authority despite the consequent breach of his contract.

6 The bank would have known that the required resolution had not been passed, so it would probably have lost its right to repayment of the loan.

7 Yes, because the contract is connected with the administration of the company. If the company traded as a stationer, the contract might be a commercial contract outside the company secretary's apparent authority.

Further question practice

Now try the following practice questions at the end of this text

Multiple choice questions: **90 to 94**

Exam style question: **20**

Chapter 24

MEETINGS

Introduction

In the previous chapter we considered who has the right to manage and the obligations which such a right carries with it. In this chapter we go on to consider one of the *procedures* by which companies are managed and controlled, namely meetings.

General meetings afford members a measure of protection of their investment in the company, as many transactions cannot be entered into without a resolution of the company in general meeting. You will already have come across the terms 'ordinary resolution', 'special resolution' and 'extraordinary resolution', as we have mentioned them where relevant in earlier chapters. It is important that you are quite clear about when the different types of resolution are used.

Your objectives

After completing this chapter you should:

(a) understand the difference between annual and extraordinary general meetings;

(b) know how a meeting may be validly convened;

(c) know when special notice of a resolution is required, and how it is given;

(d) know how a resolution may be requisitioned;

(e) know what must be stated in the notice convening a meeting;

(f) be aware of the rules on proxies;

(g) be able to distinguish between ordinary, extraordinary and special resolutions;

(h) know the rules governing elective and written resolutions;

(i) know how votes are conducted, and appreciate the effect of the assent principle;

(j) understand the special rules applying to single member private companies.

1 TYPES OF MEETING

Although the management of a company is in the hands of the directors, the decisions which affect the existence of the company, its structure and scope, are reserved to the members in general meeting.

There are two kinds of general meeting of members of a company, annual general meetings (AGMs) and extraordinary general meetings (EGMs).

1.1 Annual general meetings

The rules are as follows.

(a) Every company must hold an AGM in each (calendar) year: s 366.

(b) S 366A allows a private company to dispense with the holding of an AGM by the passing of an elective resolution. An election has effect for the year in which it is made and subsequent years. In any such year affected by the resolution any member, by notice to the company not later than three months before the end of the year, may require the holding of an AGM in that year.

(c) Not more than 15 months may elapse between meetings. But provided that the first AGM is held within 18 months of incorporation, the company need not hold it in the year of incorporation or in the following year: s 366.

(d) If a default is made, the Department of Trade and Industry on application of any member may call the AGM and give whatever directions are necessary, even to modify the articles or fix a quorum of one. In this case the company may resolve that this meeting also constitutes the AGM of the year in which it is held: s 367.

(e) A notice convening an AGM must be in writing and in accordance with the articles. At least 21 days' notice should be given; shorter notice is valid only if all members entitled to attend agree: s 369.

(f) The notice must specify the meeting as an AGM: s 369.

It is usual, but not obligatory, to transact at an AGM the 'ordinary business' of the company if so described in the articles.

1.2 Extraordinary general meetings

The *directors* have power to convene an EGM whenever they see fit: Table A Article 37.

The directors may be required to convene an EGM by *requisition of the members*. The rules (s 368) are as follows.

(a) The requisitionists must hold at least 10% of the paid up share capital carrying voting rights.

(b) They must deposit at the registered office a signed requisition stating the objects of the meeting, that is the resolutions which they intend to propose.

(c) If the directors fail within 21 days of the deposit of the requisition to convene the meeting, any reasonable expenses of the requisitionists in convening the meeting are then payable by the company and recoverable from the directors.

(d) The date for which an EGM on requisition of the members is called must be within 28 days of the issuing of the notice.

Activity 1

Give some examples of events which might lead to an EGM, bearing in mind that the ordinary management of a company is entrusted to the directors and not the members.

---

2 CONVENING A MEETING

A meeting cannot make valid and binding decisions until it has been properly convened.

(a) The meeting must be called by the board of directors or other competent person or authority. If, however, there is some irregularity in the board meeting which convenes a general meeting and the members in general meeting nonetheless pass the resolutions proposed, this may be taken as a waiver of irregularity.

(b) The notice must be issued to members in advance of the meeting so as to give them 14 days' notice of the meeting (21 days if a special resolution is to be proposed). The members may agree to waive this requirement.

(c) The notice must be sent to every member (or other person) entitled to receive it, but it need not be sent to a member whose only shares do not give him a right to attend and vote (as is often the position of preference shareholders), nor need it usually be sent to a joint holder of voting shares who is not the first named holder on the register. If, however, the business to be done must by law be disclosed to all members (for example proposals to pay compensation to directors for loss of office requiring approval under s 312) then notice of it must be sent even to members who are not entitled to vote on it).

(d) The notice must include any information reasonably necessary to enable shareholders to know in advance what is to be done.

2.1 Special notice of a resolution

Special notice must be given *to the company* of the intention to propose a resolution:

(a) to remove an auditor or to change the auditor: s 391A;

(b) to reappoint a director aged more than 70 where the age limit applies: s 293;

(c) to remove a director from office or to appoint a replacement after removal: s 303.

When special notice is given under s 379 the sequence is as follows.

(a) The member gives special notice of his intention to the company at least 28 days before the date of the meeting at which he intends to move his resolution. If, however, the company calls the meeting for a date less than 28 days after receiving the special notice that notice is deemed to have been properly given.

(b) On receiving special notice the company may be obliged under s 376 to include the resolution in the AGM notice which it issues. But in other circumstances the company (the directors) may refuse to include it in their notice. If the company gives notice to members of the resolution it does so by a 21 day notice to them.

(c) If special notice is received of intention to propose a resolution for the removal from office of a director (under s 303(2)) or to change the auditor (under s 391A) the company must forthwith send a copy to the director or auditor so that he may exercise his statutory right to defend himself by issuing a memorandum and/or addressing the meeting in person.

2.2 Requisitioning a resolution

It usually rests with the directors to decide what resolutions shall be included in the notice of a meeting. But (apart from the requisition of an EGM) members can take the initiative if they represent at least 5% of the voting rights or are at least 100 members holding shares on which there has been paid up an average per member of at least £100: s 376. These members may, under s 377:

(a) by requisition delivered at least six weeks in advance of an AGM require the company to give notice to members of a resolution which they wish to move;

(b) by requisition delivered at least one week in advance of an AGM or EGM require the company to circulate to members a statement not exceeding 1,000 words in length (unless the court declares it to be defamatory).

In either case, the requisitionists must bear the incidental costs unless the company otherwise resolves. The company need not comply if the court is satisfied that the procedure is being used to obtain needless publicity for defamatory material.

2.3 Content of notices

The notice of a general meeting must give the date, time and place of the meeting, and an AGM or a special or extraordinary resolution must be described as such. Information must be given of the business of the meeting sufficient to enable members (in deciding whether to attend or to appoint proxies) to understand what will be done at the meeting.

In issuing the notice of an AGM it is standard practice merely to list the items of routine business to be transacted, such as the declaration of dividends, the election of directors and the appointment of auditors and fixing of their remuneration.

Non-routine business may be transacted equally validly at an AGM or at an EGM. In either case its nature makes it necessary to set out in the notice convening the meeting the full text of the relevant resolution.

Activity 2

D, a shareholder in Q Ltd, wishes to include a resolution in the notice of an AGM about to be sent to members. The directors do not wish to include his resolution. He holds 4% of the votes, but his paid up share capital is £15,000. Can he force the inclusion of his resolution? Why not?

3   PROXIES

Any member of a company which has a share capital, if he is entitled to attend and vote at a general or class meeting of the company, has a statutory right (s 372) to appoint an agent (called a proxy) to attend and vote for him. The rules are as follows.

(a) A meeting of a *private* company may only appoint one proxy who may, however, speak at the meeting.

(b) A member of a *public* company (who may be a nominee of two or more beneficial owners of the shares whose voting intentions conflict) may appoint more than one proxy but his proxy has no statutory right to speak at the meeting (this is to prevent the use of professional advocates at large meetings).

(c) The proxy need not himself be a member of the company.

(d) Whether it is a private or a public company the proxy may vote on a poll but not on a show of hands.

The articles may vary condition (a) for private companies. Both public and private company articles may vary condition (d): proxies voting on a show of hands.

4 TYPES OF RESOLUTION

A meeting reaches a decision by passing a resolution. There are five kinds of resolution.

(a) An *ordinary resolution*: is carried by a simple majority of votes cast (over 50%).

(b) An *extraordinary resolution* is carried by a 75% majority of votes cast.

(c) A *special resolution* is carried by a 75% majority of votes cast.

> Twenty-one days' notice is required for a meeting at which a special resolution is to be put forward, but only 14 days' notice is required if only ordinary and extraordinary resolutions are to be put forward.

(d) An *elective resolution* may be passed by a private company:

    (i)   to confer authority to issue shares indefinitely or for a fixed period which may exceed five years: s 80A;

    (ii) to dispense with the laying of accounts before a general meeting, unless a member or the auditors require it: s 252;

    (iii) to dispense with holding an AGM unless a member requires it: s 366A;

    (iv) to reduce the 95% majority needed to consent to short notice under ss 369(4) or 378(3), to a figure of not less than 90%;

    (v) to dispense with the annual appointment of auditors (so that the incumbent auditors are automatically reappointed): s 386.

> To pass such a resolution, *all* the members entitled to attend and vote must agree: s 379A. Twenty-one days' notice is required and the resolution must be registered within 15 days. An elective resolution may be revoked by ordinary resolution (s 379A(3)) but this must also be registered: s 380(4).

(e) A *written resolution* is available to private companies. Anything that a private company could do by a resolution of a general meeting or a class meeting may be done by a written resolution. All members entitled to attend and vote must sign the resolution (s 381A(1)). Note the following restrictions.

    (i)   A written resolution cannot be used to remove a director or auditor from office, since such persons have a right to speak *at a meeting*.

    (ii) A written resolution must be sent to the auditors at the same time as or before it is sent to the shareholders. However, under the new s 381(B) auditors will no longer be able to object to written resolutions. In addition, if the company's officers fail to send the auditors a copy the resolution will remain valid, although they may be liable to a fine.

> S 381(c) provides that written resolutions may be used notwithstanding any provision in a company's articles.

A signed copy of every special and extraordinary resolution (and equivalent decisions by unanimous consent of members) must be delivered to the registrar for filing. Some ordinary resolutions, particularly those relating to share capital, have to be delivered for filing, but many do not.

Activity 3

Distinguish special resolutions from resolutions requiring special notice.

4.1 Voting and polls

The rights of members to vote and the number of votes to which they are entitled in respect of their shares are fixed by the articles. One vote per share is normal but some shares, for instance preference shares, may carry no voting rights in normal circumstances. To shorten the proceedings at meetings the procedure is as follows.

(a) *Voting on a show of hands*. On putting a resolution to the vote the chairman calls for a show of hands. One vote may be given by each member present in person: proxies do not vote. The chairman declares the result. Unless a poll is then demanded, the chairman's declaration (duly recorded in the minutes) is conclusive.

(b) *Voting on a poll*. If a real test of voting strength is required a poll may be demanded. The result of the previous show of hands is then disregarded. On a poll every member and also proxies representing absent members may cast the full number of votes to which they are entitled. A poll need not be held forthwith but may be postponed so that arrangements to hold it can be made.

A poll may be demanded as provided by the articles, but in any case:

(a) by not less than five members;

(b) by member(s) representing not less than one tenth of the total voting rights;

(c) by member(s) holding shares which represent not less than one tenth of the paid-up capital.

5 THE ASSENT PRINCIPLE

The purpose of holding general meetings with all the formality which they entail is to give each member the opportunity of voting (in person or by proxy) on the resolutions before the meeting. If the meeting is not properly convened and conducted its purported decisions are not binding on any member who disagrees with and challenges them. His right to do so exists whether he was absent from the meeting or attended it but was in the minority. But this is a protection given to a dissenting member. If every member in fact agrees it would be pointless and wrong to allow any non-member to dispute the validity of the unanimous decision purely on the grounds that unanimity was achieved in some informal way. Accordingly a unanimous decision of the members is often treated as a substitute for a formal decision in general meeting properly convened and held, and is equally binding.

6 SINGLE MEMBER PRIVATE COMPANIES

Since 1992, a private company can be formed and operate with only one member. One effect of the new regulations is that, following s 382B, if the sole member takes any decision that could have been taken in general meeting, that member shall (unless it is a written resolution) provide the company with a written record of it. This allows the sole member to conduct members' business informally without notice or minutes.

Filing requirements still apply, for example, in the case of alteration of articles. Furthermore, the single member company must hold an annual general meeting unless it has opted out by elective resolution.

Single member companies may conduct business by written resolution, provided they follow the formalities of s 381A.

Chapter roundup

- Major decisions affecting a company are taken by the members in general meeting. Every company must hold AGMs, except for private companies which have decided not to by elective resolution. EGMs may be called by the directors or requisitioned by a sufficiently large number of the members.

Chapter roundup *continued*

- A meeting must be properly convened. Certain resolutions can only be included in the agenda if special notice has been given to the company. The directors can exclude a resolution unless a sufficiently large number of the members force its inclusion.

- Any member entitled to attend and vote may send a proxy to the meeting instead.

- Resolutions may be ordinary, extraordinary or special. A private company may also pass an elective resolution or a written resolution.

- Voting is normally by a show of hands, although a poll may be demanded.

- Under the assent principle, a unanimous but informal decision of the members may be treated as a substitute for a formal decision in general meeting.

Quick quiz

1   What are (a) the intervals and (b) the period of notice fixed by law for an AGM?

2   How may an EGM be convened?

3   List the routine items of business of an AGM for which it is unnecessary to include a detailed description in the notice.

4   State the rules on proxies.

5   Describe the types of resolution which may be passed at a general meeting and the requirements applicable to each.

6   For what purposes may a private company use an elective resolution?

7   Describe the procedure for taking a vote at a company general meeting.

8   Who may demand a poll?

9   What is the assent principle?

Solutions to activities _____

1   The directors might all die or otherwise become incapable of acting.

   It might become impossible for the company to carry on its business, because of (say) a fire or a change in the law.

   You can probably think of other examples.

2   No: he does not hold 5% of the votes.

3   A special resolution is passed by a 75% majority, and needs 21 days' notice *to the members*.

   Special notice of a resolution (which may be an ordinary resolution) is given *to the company* at least 28 days before the relevant meeting.

Further question practice _____

Now try the following practice questions at the end of this text

Multiple choice questions: **95 to 99**

Exam style question: **21**

Chapter 25

SHAREHOLDERS

Introduction

In the previous chapter we looked at one means of protecting members: the company general meeting. However, meetings mainly serve to protect the *majority* of members; in this chapter we see how minority shareholders are protected.

Firstly, however, we consider how a person becomes and ceases to be a member and the details that must be shown in the register of members.

Your objectives

After completing this chapter you should:

(a) understand how persons become and cease to be members of companies;

(b) know the contents of a register of members;

(c) know how the position of a beneficiary of a trust which owns shares may be protected;

(d) know what interests in shares must be notified;

(e) know how the principle of majority rule is restricted in order to protect minorities;

(f) be aware of the powers of the DTI to investigate companies.

1 BECOMING A MEMBER

A member of a company is a person who has agreed to be a member and whose name has been entered in the register of members: s 22(2). Entry in the register is essential. Mere delivery to the company of a transfer does not make the transferor a member.

Subscribers to the memorandum are deemed to have agreed to become members of the company. The subscribers are liable to pay an amount equal to the nominal value of their shares unless the company waives its rights against them by allotting all the authorised share capital to other persons.

2 CEASING TO BE A MEMBER

A member ceases to be a member if:

(a) he transfers all his shares to another person and the transfer is registered;

(b) he dies;

(c) he becomes bankrupt and his shares are registered in the name of his trustee;

(d) he is a minor who repudiates his shares;

(e) he is the trustee of a bankrupt member and disclaims his shares;

(f) the company forfeits or accepts the surrender of shares or sells them under a lien;

(g) the company is dissolved and ceases to exist.

3 THE REGISTER OF MEMBERS

Every company must, under s 352, keep a register of members and enter in it:

(a) the name and address of each member and the class (if more than one) to which he belongs, unless this is indicated in the particulars of his shareholding;

(b) if the company has a share capital, the number of shares held by each member. In addition:

(i) if the shares have distinguishing numbers, the member's shares must be identified in the register by those numbers; and

(ii) if the company has more than one class of shares, the member's shares must be distinguished by their class, such as preference or ordinary shares;

(c) the date on which each member became and eventually the date on which he ceased to be a member. The company must preserve entries relating to former members for 20 years from the date of their ceasing to be a member: s 352(6).

Any member of the company can inspect the register of members of a company without charge; a member of the public has the right of inspection but must pay a fee.

3.1 Location of register

To make the right of inspection effective, the company is required to hold its register of members either at its registered office or at any other place at which the work of making up the register is done. But if the register of members is kept elsewhere than at the registered office:

(a) notice of the place at which the register is held must be sent to the registrar (and notice of any change of that address). It must also be shown in the annual return; and

(b) the alternative address at which the register is kept must be within the same country as the registered office.

Activity 1

J sells all her shares in a company to S. The contract for the sale is made on Monday, S pays J on Wednesday and the transfer is registered on Friday. Which of the two is a member on Thursday?
Why is this the case?

---

4 SHARES HELD ON TRUST

An English company is forbidden to make any note on its register of a trust relating to its shares. The company deals with the registered holder as the legal owner of his shares and is not concerned with the fact that he may hold the shares as nominee or trustee: s 360.

4.1 Stop notices

If a beneficiary gives notice to an English company that he has an interest in shares registered in the name of another person, the company will return the notice stating that it is not permitted to accept it. The beneficiary may however protect his interests by serving a *stop notice*. Thereafter the company may not register a transfer of the shares to which the stop notice relates without giving written notice to the person who has served the stop notice on the company. After giving notice the company must wait for 14 days before registering the transfer, and during that time the beneficiary can, if he wishes, apply to the court for an injunction to prohibit the transfer.

5 SUBSTANTIAL SHAREHOLDINGS

Any person who acquires a notifiable interest in voting shares of a public company must give notice (with prescribed particulars) to the company of his interest: s 198. Thereafter so long as his interest is above the minimum he must give similar notice of all changes: s 202. The company on receiving the information must enter it in a register of interests in shares which is open to public inspection: s 211.

A person has a notifiable interest when he is interested in at least 3% of the shares: ss 198201. Disclosure must be made to the company within two days: s 202. A person has an interest even if shares are held in someone else's name: thus substantial investors cannot conceal themselves by using nominees to hold their shares.

The company may (and on the requisition of 10% or more (in share value) of its members, must) call on anyone (not necessarily a member) to declare whether he has a notifiable interest: s 212 and s 214.

Activity 2

On 1 June L buys 500 shares in a company with 50,000 shares in issue. On 4 June she buys a further 400 shares, on 12 June she buys a further 700 shares and on 20 June she buys a further 2,000 shares. By what date must she disclose her interest to the company? Why?

6 MINORITY PROTECTION

6.1 The rule in *Foss v Harbottle*

Ultimate control of a company rests with its members voting in general meeting since (among other things) the directors are required to lay annual accounts before a general meeting and may be removed from office by a simple majority of votes. But if the directors hold a majority of the voting shares or represent a majority shareholder the minority has no remedy unless the rules of minority protection apply.

Foss v Harbottle 1853
A shareholder (Foss) sued the directors of the company alleging that the directors had defrauded the company by selling land to it at an inflated price. The company was by this time in a state of disorganisation and efforts to call the directors to account at a general meeting had failed.

Held: the action must be dismissed since:

(a) the company as a person separate from its members is the only proper plaintiff in an action to protect its rights or property; and

(b) the company in general meeting must decide whether or not to bring such legal proceedings.

6.2 Common law rules

Case law recognises a number of limitations to the principle of majority control (the rule in *Foss v Harbottle*) and in those cases permits a minority to bring legal proceedings. The decisions are not entirely consistent but the principles are generally summarised as follows.

(a) No majority vote can be effective to sanction an act of the company which is illegal. Illegal decisions taken in general meeting are not binding because a majority of members cannot decide that the company shall break the law. If they attempt to do so any member may apply to the court for a declaration that the decision is void and (if necessary) for an injunction to restrain the company from acting on the decision.

(b) If the law or the company's articles require that a special procedure shall be observed, say alteration of the articles by special resolution, the majority must observe that procedure and their decision is invalid if they do not do so.

Where a majority merely disregards procedure or restrictions imposed by the articles of the company it is less certain that a minority can enforce due compliance by action in the courts. The courts have sometimes been inclined to treat these situations as mere internal matters which a majority of members should be free to regulate as they see fit. The cases below illustrate the two different judicial approaches:

Edwards v Halliwell 1950

A trade union (subject to rules of company law on this point) had rules (equivalent to articles) by which members' contributions were fixed at a specific rate which could only be increased if so decided by a twothirds majority of votes cast in a members' ballot. A meeting decided, without holding a ballot of members, to increase the rate of subscriptions.

Held: the decision was invalid since it conflicted with the rules, and the members who brought the action were entitled to a declaration that it was void. In *Salmon v Quin & Axtens* the court said that the articles were a contract and the minority was entitled to have the company's affairs managed in accordance with that contract.

Macdougall v Gardiner 1875

The articles provided that a poll must be held if demanded at the meeting by at least five members. But when five members demanded a poll the chairman refused to comply. One of the members sued for a declaration that the resolutions passed on a show of hands were invalid.

Held: the court would not intervene in a mere 'irregularity' of internal procedure which could be regularised by a majority approving it. This doctrine has been much criticised. It is unlikely to be extended or even perhaps applied in modern cases.

A minority may also apply to the court for a remedy if a meeting is convened by a notice which does not, as the articles usually require (Table A Article 38), disclose in sufficient detail 'the general nature of the business' to be done: *Kaye v Croydon Tramways* and *Baillie v Oriental Telephone Co*. But a mere technical irregularity of procedure in convening a meeting may not suffice to invalidate its decisions.

Bentley-Stevens v Jones 1974

A director complained that he had not been given notice of a board meeting held to convene a general meeting at which a resolution was duly passed to remove him from office. In all other respects the correct procedure had been observed.

Held: the members of the company could waive any irregularity in convening the general meeting and the court would not intervene.

If the directors exercise powers given to them by the articles for an improper purpose a member may challenge them in the courts. But the court is likely to remit the matter back to the company in general meeting for decision by majority vote: *Bamford v Bamford 1970*.

(c) If the company under majority control deprives a member of his individual rights of membership, he may sue the company to enforce his rights.

Pender v Lushington 1877

The articles gave members one vote for each ten shares held by them but subject to a maximum of 100 votes for each member. A company which was a large shareholder transferred shares to the plaintiff to increase its voting power. At the meeting the chairman rejected the plaintiff's votes. The plaintiff sued and the company relied on the argument that only the company itself could object to an irregularity of voting procedure.

Held: the plaintiff's votes were a 'right of property' which he was entitled to protect by proceedings against the company.

The principle of *Pender's* case is restricted to protection of personal rights of membership. A member cannot sue merely to have the voting procedure of the articles observed (*Macdougall's* case above) since that is not sufficiently personal to him. But if he is denied his right to vote or to receive the dividend due to him (*Wood v Odessa Waterworks Co 1889*) he can sue the company.

(d) If those who control the company use their control to defraud it (or possibly to act oppressively towards a minority) the minority may bring legal proceedings against the fraudulent (or oppressive) majority. Otherwise a wrong would be without remedy since the majority would prevent the company from taking action.

The exception to the rule in *Foss v Harbottle* over fraud by a controlling majority is to protect the company by a member's action since the company cannot protect itself. It must be shown that:

(i)   what was taken belonged to the company;

   (1)   it passed to those against whom the claim is made; and

   (2)   those who appropriated the company's property are in control of the company.

To divert away from the company profitable contracts which it was about to make is to deprive it of its property (for the purposes of this rule).

Cook v Deeks 1916
The directors, who were also controlling shareholders, negotiated a contract in the name of the company. They took the contract for themselves and passed a resolution in general meeting declaring that the company had no interest in the contract. A minority shareholder sued them as trustees for the company of the benefit of the contract.

Held: the contract 'belonged in equity to the company' and the directors could not, by passing a resolution in general meeting, bind the company to approving this action of defrauding it.

But merely to prevent the company from trading (so as to benefit a competitor) is not to deprive it of property:

SCWS v Meyer 1959
Minority shareholders held 3,900 shares in a company formed by SCWS, which held the remaining 4,000. Three of the directors were SCWS's nominees, the remaining two being the minority. Following a dispute between the two sides SCWS proceeded to cut off supplies to the company, it being its sole supplier. From shares being worth about £6 they became virtually valueless.

Held: the petitioners succeeded only under s 459 (unfair prejudice). SCWS were ordered to pay them a fair price to buy them out.

If the property of the company passes to a third party that may be negligence – it is not fraud. But if it passes to those who are controlling shareholders, that is equivalent to 'fraud' even though no dishonesty is shown.

Pavlides v Jensen 1956
The plaintiff, a minority shareholder, alleged that the directors who represented the controlling shareholder, had negligently sold the principal asset, a mine worth £1m (in his opinion) to a third party for a mere £182,000.

Held: there could be no fraud unless the controlling shareholder benefited. Merely to allege negligence was not enough to justify a minority action to protect the company's rights. The company in general meeting must decide whether to hold the directors liable for mismanagement or alternatively it could exonerate them. The judge described the directors as 'an amiable bunch of lunatics' – they were not fraudsters.

Daniels v Daniels 1977
The company was controlled by its two directors, husband and wife. It bought land for £4,250 (probate value) from the estate of a deceased person and later resold it at the same price to the lady director. She resold it for

£120,000. A minority shareholder sued the directors but did not allege fraud. Objection was raised that a member could not sue the directors on the company's behalf for negligence (*Pavlides'* case above) but only for fraud.

Held: the circumstances required investigation and a member might sue the directors and controlling shareholders for negligence if one of them secured benefit from the company by reason of it.

In particular those directors who are also managers of the company's business are able to control the flow of information to the full board and to a general meeting. If the information is inaccurate or incomplete it may result in a wrong decision by the independent majority. This was the main issue in the case below:

Prudential Assurance Co Ltd v Newman Industries Ltd (No 2) 1982
The company had purchased property in which the chairman and vicechairman had a disclosed interest. The transaction had been approved by the board and later by a general meeting. But it was alleged that this approval had been procured by the supply of inaccurate information by the two directors, who were also minority shareholders (through another company which they controlled). The High Court took the view that this was a case of 'wrongdoer control' and that 'the justice of the case' required that a remedy should be given by way of exception to the principle in *Foss v Harbottle*. The two directors appealed against the decision but in the meantime the company 'adopted' the case against them – so that the company itself was seeking its own remedy. Many of the original allegations were not in the end substantiated.

Held: (by the Court of Appeal) that the principles applied by the High Court (Vinelott J) were incorrect, but it was no longer necessary to consider whether an exception should be made to the *Foss v Harbottle* principle in view of the company's 'adoption' of the case.

In the *Newman Industries* case the Court of Appeal did discuss (but only as an *obiter dictum*) what should be done in such situations. It did not think that a minority should be allowed to institute proceedings on the basis of allegations which it had yet to substantiate. 'It may well be all right' however for the court to adjourn any such action so that the minority may put their allegations before the members at a general meeting for a decision on the course to be taken.

The *Newman Industries* decision was tested in a more recent case. The issue was whether, as a matter of law, a shareholder in a company was entitled to recover damages for the diminution of the value of his shareholding, where such diminution is the result of loss inflicted on the company by the defendants breach of contract.

George Fischer (Great Britain) Ltd v Multi-Construction Ltd 1995
F Ltd was a holding company and ran its business through a number of wholly owned subsidiaries. F Ltd contracted with the defendants for the design and construction of a warehouse and distribution centre, which was to be occupied by one of its subsidiaries as a storage and distribution centre for the metal and plastic pipes. The defendants sub-contracted with a third party, 'Dexion' for the design and installation of three cranes inside the warehouse. The cranes had a design defect and as a result F Ltd incurred additional operating costs of £262,000, and lost sales amounting to £229,000. The issue in the Court of Appeal was whether F Ltd, as a shareholder in the subsidiaries, could sue for losses incurred by those subsidiaries. Dexion relied on the case of *Prudential v Newman Industries* on the basis that it was the company that should be the proper plaintiff for the loss in value of its shares, and not the individual shareholder.

Held: the claim by F Ltd was not too remote and a £1 loss to the subsidiary companies was treated as also being a £1 loss to F Ltd. As a 100% shareholder in each of the three subsidiaries, F Ltd was entitled to claim damages representing losses which it indirectly suffered as a result of the diminution of the value of its shares in the subsidiaries, or for the loss of its profits resulting from the diminution in the subsidiaries' profits.

The *George Fischer* case was distinguishable from the *Prudential* case mainly on the grounds that this was a claim for breach of contract, while *Prudential* was a decision on conspiracy.

A minority may have a remedy for fraud by the majority even if the minority only holds nonvoting shares. The cases below are also interesting as examples of 'fraud' in the sense of discrimination against the minority rather than misappropriation of company property.

Eastmanco (Kilner House) Ltd v Greater London Council 1982
The GLC planned to sell a block of flats by granting long leases to individual tenants. For management purposes a company was formed in which the GLC originally owned all the shares. As each flat was sold the GLC transferred one share to the tenant but the share was not to carry voting rights until all the flats (and shares) had been disposed of – so that the GLC would retain control up to that point. Following the election of a new GLC in May 1981 the GLC decided not to complete the planned disposal of the flats. It convened a general meeting of the company at which a resolution was passed (on GLC votes only) by which the directors were instructed to discontinue the legal proceedings which they had begun on behalf of the company against the GLC for breach of contract. An individual tenant then applied to the court to be substituted as plaintiff to continue the action. She was a shareholder but had no vote.

Held: although a shareholder (the GLC) may as a general rule cast his votes to promote his own interests, he is not entitled to vote so as to stultify the purpose for which the company was formed and deprive other members of their existing prospects of obtaining votes.

Clemens v Clemens Bros Ltd 1976
A and B (who were aunt and niece) held 55% and 45% respectively of the shares with voting rights. A proposed to vote in favour of ordinary resolutions to increase the authorised share capital and to approve the allotment of new shares to or for the benefit of employees of the company. No more shares would be allotted to A or B but the effect of the scheme would be to reduce B's shareholding from 45% to 24.5% with the object of depriving B of her power to block a special resolution to alter the articles as A desired. B sought a declaration that A could not use her votes in this way.

Held: it would be equitable to restrain A from using her votes to deprive B of her 'negative control' (her ability to block an alteration of the articles to which B objected).

In *Barrett v Duckett 1995* the Court of Appeal ruled that in order for a shareholder to sue on behalf of the company, in a situation of 'wrongdoer control', the shareholder must bring the action *bona fide* for the company's benefit for wrongs to the company for which no other remedy was available. In this case an alternative remedy (liquidation) was available and so the shareholder could not bring a claim. However there may have been a remedy under s 459 (see later in this chapter).

The case law explained above is not entirely consistent and is further confused by an overlap (in *Daniels'* case, for example) between the restrictions placed on majority control and the liability of directors (who are or represent the controlling shareholders) for misuse of their powers. Owing to changes in the statutory code the dissatisfied minority is now more likely to apply to the court for relief under ss 459–461 than to attempt to sue the majority under common law rules. The court can give authority for legal proceedings and it will be simpler to proceed on that statutory basis.

There are also procedural intricacies in bringing a minority shareholders' action.

(a) The plaintiff may bring a *derivative* action on behalf of the company to enforce its rights or recover its property. Any benefit obtained will accrue to the company since the claim is derived from and made on behalf of the company. The court is prepared to order the company to pay the plaintiff's legal costs (and may do so even if he fails in his action). In the *Newman Industries* case the action was at first a derivative one but subsequently was adopted by the whole company.

(b) The plaintiff usually combines a derivative action with a *representative* action – he asserts that he sues on behalf of all other shareholders (except the defendants). He may however combine this form of action with a personal claim for damages provided that he can show that he has suffered actual loss.

(c) In the *Newman Industries* case the plaintiff combined a derivative action with a personal claim for damages for the loss which it was alleged the plaintiff had suffered.

The matter is further confused by the practice, even in a derivative action, of making the company a defendant, so that any order made by the court may be binding on it. If this were not done the controlling shareholders might continue to use their control of the company to avoid some of the consequences of a court decision against them.

Activity 3

A Ltd has three directors. D, B and C. Together they own 85% of the shares in the company. They agree to sell a plot of land to W for £50,000 which is what they honestly believe it to be worth. They do not, however, have the land professionally valued until later when it is shown to be worth nearer £100,000. E and J are two minority shareholders who are considering bringing an action against the directors and the company.

Advise E and J whether they are likely to be successful.

6.3 Statutory rules

Any member may now apply to the court for relief under s 459 on the grounds that the company's affairs are being or have been conducted in a manner which is unfairly prejudicial to the interests of the members generally or of some part of the members. Application may also be made in respect of a particular act or omission which has been or will be prejudicial. It is not necessary to show that there has been bad faith or even an intention to discriminate against the minority. But the complaint must be based on prejudice to the member as a member and not, for example, as an employee or as an unpaid creditor.

In *quasi-partnerships* 'interests of the members' can include the expectation that a member would continue to participate in management so it is unfairly prejudicial for the other members to ignore that expectation and expel him: *Re a Company 1986*.

Re Bird Precision Bellows Ltd 1985
A minority with 26% of the shares suspected the MD of this 'quasi-partnership' company of concealing bribes paid to secure contracts. When the DTI refused to investigate the minority was removed from the board. They claimed unfair prejudice under s 459.

Held: the claim was allowed as it was a quasi-partnership. (Hence today *Ebrahimi* could claim under s 459 and not have to see the company wound up, nor wait for relief till then.)

Whatever the basis of the petition the court will take account of the surrounding circumstances and conduct of the parties.

Re R A Noble & Sons (Clothing) Ltd 1983
B had provided the capital but left the management in the hands of N, the other director, on the understanding that N would consult B on major company matters. N did not do so and B confined himself to enquiries to N on social occasions; he accepted N's vague assurances that all was well. The petition followed from a breakdown of the relationship.

Held: B's exclusion from discussion of company management questions was largely the result of his own lack of interest. His petition was dismissed.

Re Jermyn Street Turkish Baths Ltd 1971
The petitioners were the executors of a deceased member who had been a guarantor of the company's overdraft. At the time of his death the company was in poor financial shape. The controlling shareholder, who took over at this point, pulled the company round and among other things paid off the overdraft. The value of the deceased's shareholding increased. The complaint was that the controlling shareholder had allotted more shares to herself and had also taken most of the profits as commission (under a pre-agreed formula) so that no dividends were paid.

Held: on balance there had been no 'oppression' (and presumably would be no 'unfair prejudice' under the current formula). The petition was dismissed.

Re a Company 1983
The petitioners' grievance was the directors' refusal to put forward a scheme of reconstruction or a proposal to purchase their shares (by the company). The directors were preoccupied with plans for diversification of the business.

Held: the directors' duty was to manage the company to its advantage as they saw it. It was not a case of 'unfair prejudice'.

Re London School of Electronics Ltd 1985
The other shareholders had removed the petitioner from his directorship after he had alleged that they were diverting business from the company to themselves. He then set up a rival business and took part of the company's connection with him.

Held: he had a right to relief even though he did not have 'clean hands'. The majority had to buy out the minority without any discount for the fact that his were minority shares and therefore of less value.

Re McGuinness and Another 1988
Disputes arose among board members after one company had taken over another. The petitioners, who included the MD and a minority shareholder, requisitioned on 4 November an EGM to consider a resolution to remove two directors and appoint others, including one of the petitioners. The board notified them on 23 November that the EGM would be held in seven months' time.

Held: this was not a breach of s 368 but was unfairly prejudicial to the minority and hence a s 459 claim succeeded. The court ordered an earlier meeting. Note that the company did not have a 1985 set of Table A articles and hence were not constrained by Article 37 to hold the EGM within eight weeks; nor had s 368 yet been amended to impose the new 28-day limit, which effectively solves the problem.

When a petition is successful the court may make whatever order it deems fit –

though the petitioner is required in presenting his petition to state what relief he seeks. It may include, under s 461:

(a) an order regulating the future conduct of the company's affairs: for example, that a controlling shareholder shall conform to the decisions taken at board meetings (*Re H R Harmer Ltd 1958*);

(b) an authorisation to any person to bring legal proceedings on behalf of the company. The company is then responsible for the legal costs;

(c) an order requiring the company to refrain from doing or continuing an act complained of;

(d) provision for the purchase of shares of the minority by either the controlling shareholder or the company;

(e) inclusion in the memorandum or articles of provisions which may only be altered or removed thereafter by leave of the court.

Two recent cases have considered the scope of s 459 and the availability of the rare remedy of requiring the majority to sell to the minority.

> *Re Brenfield Squash Racquets club Ltd 1996*
> Eighty-six per cent of the shares in Brenfield were held by FMR Ltd and 14% by S and his family. S was appointed Managing Director of the company and the remaining directors were nominated by FMR. The nominees failed to distinguish between the affairs of FMR and the company, treating the company's assets as available for FMR's benefit.
>
> Relations between the directors broke down and S was replaced by M as Managing Director, and eventually removed from the board.
>
> *Held:* s 459 had been made out. The new MD had deliberately set out to conceal information from S and to remove him from his company position. FMR was ordered to sell its share to the minority.

However, in *Re a company 1996* the same remedy was refused. The judge said that the order was rare and would not be available in this case as the applicant was 85 and had not played a recent part in the company's affairs. The action was thus struck out as the majority had offered to buy out the minority's shares, thus giving him all the relief he could expect from a successful petition.

6.4 Investigations by the Department of Trade and Industry

The Department of Trade and Industry (the DTI) has statutory power to appoint an inspector to investigate the affairs or ownership of a company (ss 431–432, 442-443).

The DTI must appoint inspectors if a court so orders. In addition, it may appoint inspectors to investigate the affairs of a company:

(a) if the company itself applies: s 431;

(b) if application is made by members who are not less than 200 in number or who hold at least one tenth of the issued shares (or, if the company has no share capital, by at least one fifth of the members). The applicants may be required to produce evidence to show good reasons for their application and to give security (not exceeding £5,000) for the costs of the investigation: s 431;

(c) if the DTI considers that the affairs of the company have been conducted in a fraudulent or unlawful manner (or that it was formed for a fraudulent or unlawful purpose) or in a manner unfairly prejudicial to some part of its members or that members have not been given all the information with respect to its affairs which they might reasonably expect: s 432.

Activity 4

The controlling shareholders of a company resolve to replace the directors with new directors who will work to increase efficiency by reducing the number of employees. John, a minority shareholder and senior employee, is made redundant by the new directors. Could he apply for relief under s 349. Why?

Chapter roundup

- A person becomes a member of a company by being entered in the register of members. He ceases to be a member when he dies, when the company ceases to exist or when all of his shares are registered in the name of another person.

- The shareholdings of all members are recorded in the register of members. No notice of a trust may be included in the register, but the position of a beneficiary may be protected by serving a stop notice on the company.

- Any person interested in at least 3% of a company's shares must notify the company.

- In general, majority rule prevails, but this principle is restricted to protect minorities. There are several common law restrictions, and under statute law any member may apply for relief if the company's affairs are conducted in a way which is unfairly prejudicial to some or all of the members.

- The Department of Trade and Industry may appoint inspectors to investigate a company.

Quick quiz

1 In what ways may a person (a) become and (b) cease to be a member of a company?

2 What particulars must be entered in a register of members and where must the register be kept?

3 Who may inspect a register of members?

4 In what circumstances (if any) is a company affected by notice from a third party of his interest in shares registered in a name not his own?

5 Describe briefly the methods by which a person who has an interest in shares registered in another person's name may be required to disclose his interest. To which shares do the rules relate and to whom is the disclosure to be made?

6 What is the rule in *Foss v Harbottle*?

7 State the main exceptions to the principle of majority control.

8 On what grounds may a shareholder obtain a statutory remedy against a controlling majority?

9 When may the DTI appoint inspectors to investigate a company's affairs?

Solutions to activities

1   J (she is on the register on Thursday).

2   $50,000 \times 3\% = 1,500$ shares, so L must disclose her interest by 14 June (two days after 12 June).

3   The type of action open to E and J would be a derivative action, that is one brought by E or J on behalf of the company, with the directors as defendants. However, they would be unlikely to succeed. The facts of this case resemble those of *Pavlides v Jensen 1956*. In this case it was held that mere negligence did not justify a minority action to protect the company's rights. Thus, in the absence of fraud, the sale could legitimately be approved by a majority of the shareholders.

4   No: he would be applying as an employee and not as a member.

Further question practice

Now try the following practice questions at the end of this text

Multiple choice questions: **100 to 104**

Exam style question: **22**

Chapter 26

LIQUIDATIONS AND OTHER INSOLVENCY PROCEDURES

Introduction

This chapter completes your studies of company law with an insight into liquidations and other insolvency procedures.

Liquidations and receiverships have been in the news all too frequently in recent years, and you will enhance your understanding of a potentially dry and technical topic by relating it to real life events.

Liquidation is expensive and unconstructive; alternatives have therefore been put forward in the form of administration and voluntary arrangements.

Your objectives

After completing this chapter you should:

(a) know how a company may come to be dissolved;

(b) understand the effects of a decision to liquidate a company;

(c) know the grounds for compulsory liquidation;

(d) be able to distinguish between a members' and a creditors' voluntary liquidation;

(e) know how each type of liquidation proceeds;

(f) understand the role of a liquidation committee;

(g) understand the position of contributories;

(h) know the powers and duties of liquidators;

(i) understand the effects of an administration order and the position of an administrator;

(j) understand when and how a voluntary arrangement may be made.

Statutory references in this chapter are to the Insolvency Act 1986 unless otherwise stated. 'CA' denotes the Companies Act 1985.

1   METHODS OF DISSOLUTION

Dissolution occurs when a company's name is removed from the register. At this point it ceases to exist. There are a number of ways in which this may be done.

(a) By the registrar, under s 652 CA, if it appears to him that the company is defunct;

(b) By order of the court under s 427(3)(d) CA following a scheme of arrangement under s 425: no winding up is necessary as the company is transferring its business;

(c) By Act of Parliament (very rarely used);

(d) By cancellation of registration on application for judicial review by the Attorney-General. This may be invoked if the registrar has erroneously registered a company with illegal objects: *R v Registrar of Companies (ex p Attorney General) 1980*;

(e) On application by the official receiver for early dissolution: s 202;

(f) On completion of a compulsory liquidation;

(g) On completion of a voluntary liquidation.

2   LIQUIDATIONS

Most dissolutions follow liquidation or 'winding up' (the terms are used synonymously). The assets are realised, debts are paid out of the proceeds, and any surplus amounts are returned to members.

Liquidation begins with a formal decision to liquidate. If the members in general meeting resolve to wind up the company, that is a *voluntary* liquidation. This may be either a members' or a creditors' voluntary liquidation, depending on whether the directors believe that the company will or will not be able to pay its debts in full.

A company may also be obliged to wind up by a *compulsory* liquidation, ordered by the court on a petition usually presented by a creditor or a member.

Whether liquidation is voluntary or compulsory it is in the hands of the liquidator (or joint liquidators), who takes over control of the company from its directors. Liquidators' actions are valid even if the appointment or qualifications are defective. No further share dealings or changes in membership will be permitted (unless the court sanctions a rectification or other change); and all invoices, orders, letters and other company documents must state prominently that the company is in liquidation.

Activity 1

What is the point of requiring that all documents state that a company is in liquidation, given that the members and creditors are likely to be aware of that fact?

3 COMPULSORY LIQUIDATION

A petition is presented to the Chancery Division of the High Court (or, if the company has an issued and paid up share capital not exceeding £120,000 in the county court of the district in which the registered office is situated): s 117. The petition will specify the ground for compulsory winding up and be presented (usually) either by a creditor or by a member (called a 'contributory' in the context of liquidation). The standard grounds for compulsory liquidation are listed in s 122.

(a) The company has by special resolution resolved that it should be wound up by the court.

(b) The company, incorporated as a public company, has failed within a year to obtain a trading certificate.

(c) The number of members of a public company has been reduced to below two. This used to apply to private companies, but single member private companies are now allowed.

(d) The company has not commenced its business within a year of incorporation or has suspended its business for a year.

(e) The company is unable to pay its debts: s 122(1)(f). This is the most common ground.

(f) The court considers that it is just and equitable to wind up the company: s 122(1)(g). This ground may be used by a dissatisfied member.

3.1 Company unable to pay its debts

A creditor who petitions on the grounds of the company's insolvency may rely on any of three situations to show that the company is unable to pay its debts: s 123.

(a) A creditor (or creditors) to whom the company owes more than £750 serves on the company at its registered office a written demand for payment and the company neglects, within the ensuing 21 clear days, either to pay the debt or to offer reasonable security for it.

(b) A creditor obtains judgment against the company for debt, and attempts to enforce the judgment but is unable to obtain payment because no assets of the company have been found and seized.

(c) A creditor satisfies the court that, taking into account the contingent and prospective liabilities of the company, it is unable to pay its debts. The creditor may be able to show this:

(i)   by proof that the company is not able to pay its debts as they fall due: the *commercial insolvency test*; or

(ii) by proof that the company's assets are less than its liabilities: the *balance sheet test*.

At the hearing other creditors of the company may oppose the petition. If so, the court is likely to decide in favour of those to whom the larger amount is owing. But the court may also consider the reasons for the differences between the creditors.

3.2 The just and equitable ground

Orders have been made for liquidation on the just and equitable ground in the following situations.

(a) The substratum of the company has gone: the main object of the company can no longer be achieved.

(b) The company was formed for an illegal or fraudulent purpose or there is a complete deadlock in the management of its affairs.

(c) The understandings between members or directors which were the basis of the association have been unfairly breached by lawful action.

(d) The directors deliberately withheld information so that the shareholders have no confidence in the company's management.

Activity 2

In *Re a Company (No 003729 of 1982) 1984*, the petitioner for compulsory liquidation had demanded a sum due under a contract from the company. The company had disputed the amount due, and had only paid part of the sum demanded. The petitioner therefore claimed that the company had neglected to pay a debt. Why do you think the petitioner failed?

3.3 Proceedings for compulsory liquidation

When a petition is presented to the court a copy is delivered to the company in case it objects. It is advertised so that other creditors may intervene if they wish.

If the petition is presented by a member (a contributory) he must show (in addition to suitable grounds for compulsory liquidation) that the company is *solvent* or, alternatively, refuses to supply information of its financial position, and that he has been a registered shareholder for at least six of the 18 months up to the date of his petition.

Once the court has received a petition, it may appoint a provisional liquidator: s 135. The Official Receiver is usually appointed, and his powers are conferred by the court. These usually extend to taking control of the company's property and applying for a special manager to be appointed (ss 144 and 177).

3.4 Effects of an order for compulsory liquidation

The effects of the order, which may be made some time after a provisional liquidator is appointed, are as follows.

(a) The Official Receiver (an official of the DTI whose duties relate mainly to bankruptcy of individuals) becomes liquidator: s 136.

(b) The liquidation is deemed to have commenced at the time (possibly several months earlier) when the petition was first presented. If compulsory liquidation follows voluntary liquidation already in progress liquidation runs from the commencement of the voluntary liquidation: s 129.

(c) Any disposition of the company's property and any transfer of its shares subsequent to the commencement of liquidation is void unless the court orders otherwise: s 127. The court will decide whether to validate a disposition made under s 127.

(d) Any legal proceedings in progress against the company are halted (and none may thereafter begin) unless the court gives leave. Any seizure of the company's assets after commencement of liquidation is void: ss 130 and 128.

(e) The employees of the company are automatically dismissed. The provisional liquidator assumes the powers of management previously held by the directors.

(f) Any floating charge crystallises.

The assets of the company may remain the company's legal property but under the liquidator's control – unless the court vests the assets in the liquidator. The business of the company may continue but it is the liquidator's duty to continue it with a view only to realisation, for instance by sale as a going concern.

Within 21 days of the making of the order for winding up (or of the appointment of a provisional liquidator) a *statement of affairs* must be delivered to the liquidator verified by one or more directors and by the secretary. The statement shows the assets and liabilities of the company and includes a list of creditors with particulars of any security which creditors may hold and how long it has been held: s 131.

Meetings of contributories and creditors

The Official Receiver has 12 weeks to decide whether or not to convene separate meetings of creditors and contributories. The purpose of these meetings would be to provide the creditors and contributories with the opportunity to appoint their own nominee as permanent liquidator to replace the official receiver, and a liquidation committee as their representative to work with the liquidator. (In cases of conflict, the creditors' nominee takes precedence over the members' nominee.) If the Official Receiver believes there is little interest and that the creditors will be unlikely to appoint a liquidator he can dispense with a meeting, informing the court, the creditors and the contributories of the decision. He must then call a meeting if at least 25% in value of the creditors require him to do so: s 136.

If the creditors do hold a meeting and appoint their own nominee he automatically becomes liquidator subject to a right of objection to the court: s 139. Any person appointed to act as liquidator must be a qualified insolvency practitioner.

At any time after a winding up order is made, the Official Receiver may ask the Secretary of State to appoint a liquidator. Similarly, he may request an appointment if the creditors and members fail to appoint a liquidator: s 137.

3.5   Completion of compulsory liquidation

When the liquidator completes his task he reports to the DTI, which examines his accounts. He may apply to the court for an order for dissolution of the company. The order is sent to the registrar who gives notice of it in the *London Gazette* and dissolves the company: s 205.

Activity 3

Following an order for compulsory liquidation of a company with debts of £120,000, meetings of the creditors and contributories are held. The creditors nominate P as liquidator, whereas the contributories nominate S. P claims that he can realise the company's assets within a month for £100,000, whereas S claims that she can run the business and sell it as a going concern for £140,000 within six months. If nobody reconsiders his or her position, who will be appointed liquidator? Why is this?

---

4   VOLUNTARY LIQUIDATION

There are two types of voluntary liquidation, a members' voluntary liquidation (where the company is solvent) and a creditors' voluntary liquidation (where the company is insolvent and the members resolve to liquidate in consultation with creditors).

4.1   Members' voluntary liquidation

The type of resolution to be passed varies with the circumstances of the case: s 84. A company may by *extraordinary* resolution resolve to wind up because it cannot, by reason of its liabilities, continue its business. This enables an insolvent company to go into liquidation on a 14 day notice. A company may, by *special* resolution (giving no reasons), resolve to wind up.

The winding up commences on the passing of the resolution. A liquidator is usually appointed by the same resolution (or a second resolution passed at the same time).

Declaration of solvency

A voluntary winding up is a members' voluntary winding up *only* if the directors make and deliver to the registrar a declaration of solvency: s 89. This is a statutory declaration that the directors have made full enquiry into the affairs of the company and are of the opinion that it will be able to pay its debts, together with interest (at the rate applicable under s 189(4)) on those debts, in full, within a specified period not exceeding 12 months. If the liquidator later concludes that the company will be unable to pay its debts he must call a meeting of creditors and lay before them a statement of assets and liabilities: s 95.

The liquidator calls special and annual general meetings of contributories to whom he reports. Within three months after each anniversary of the commencement of the winding up the liquidator must call a meeting and lay before it an account of his transactions during the year: s 93. When the liquidation is complete the liquidator calls a meeting to lay before it his final accounts: s 94.

After holding the final meeting the liquidator sends a copy of his accounts to the registrar who dissolves the company three months later by removing its name from the register: s 201.

4.2 Creditors' voluntary liquidation

If no declaration of solvency is made and delivered to the registrar the liquidation proceeds as a creditors' voluntary liquidation even if in the end the company pays its debts in full: s 96.

To commence a creditors' voluntary liquidation the directors convene a general meeting of members to pass an extraordinary resolution. They must also convene a meeting of creditors (s 98), giving at least seven days' notice of this meeting. The notice must be advertised in the *London Gazette* and two local newspapers. The notice must either:

(a) give the name and address of a qualified insolvency practitioner to whom the creditors can apply before the meeting for information about the company; *or*

(b) state a place in the locality of the company's principal place of business where, on the two business days before the meeting, a list of creditors can be inspected.

The meeting of members is held first and its business is to resolve to wind up, to appoint a liquidator and to nominate up to five representatives to be members of the liquidation committee.

The creditors' meeting should preferably be convened on the same day at a later time than the members' meeting, or on the next day, but in any event within 14 days of it. One of the directors presides at the creditors' meeting and lays before it a full statement of the company's affairs and a list of creditors with the amounts owing to them. The meeting may (if the creditors so wish) nominate a liquidator and up to five representatives to be members of the liquidation committee. If the creditors nominate a different person to be liquidator, their choice prevails over the nomination by the members.

4.3   The effect of voluntary winding up

Unlike a compulsory winding up, there is no automatic stay of legal proceedings against the company and the employees are not automatically dismissed.

Activity 4

Why do the creditors of a company ordinarily have no role in a members' voluntary liquidation?

5   LIQUIDATION COMMITTEE

A liquidation committee may be appointed in a compulsory liquidation and in a creditors' voluntary liquidation. It usually comprises an equal number of representatives of members and of creditors (in a creditors' voluntary liquidation it is limited to a maximum of five from each side). The committee meets once a month unless otherwise agreed and may be summoned at any time by the liquidator or by a member of the committee: Sch 8.

The general function of the committee is to work with the liquidator, to supervise his accounts, to approve the exercise of certain of his statutory powers and to fix his remuneration. Like the liquidator himself members of the committee are in a fiduciary position and may not secure unauthorised personal advantages, for example by purchase of the company's assets.

6   CONTRIBUTORIES

Shareholders and past shareholders are called *contributories*. A contributory may have to contribute funds to meet a company's debts if the shares which he holds or previously held are partly paid or if it is found that the rules on consideration have been breached in the allotment of the shares as fully paid.

If it is necessary to make calls on contributories the liquidator draws up an 'A' List of contributories who were members at the commencement of the winding up and a 'B' List of contributories who were members within the year preceding the commencement of winding up. A B List contributory has liability limited by the following principles.

(a) He is only liable to pay what is due on the shares which he previously held and only so much of the amount due on those shares as the present holder (an A List contributory) is unable to pay.

(b) He can only be required to contribute (within the limits stated in (a) above) in order to pay those debts of the company incurred before he ceased to be a member which are still owing.

No contributory who ceased to be a member more than a year before the commencement of liquidation can be liable.

7 POWERS OF LIQUIDATORS

In order to perform his function satisfactorily, the liquidator is given certain powers, contained in Sch 4. His basic function is to obtain and realise the company's assets to pay off its debts.

All liquidators may, with the relevant sanctions:

(a) pay any class of creditors in full;

(b) make compromises or arrangements with creditors;

(c) compromise any debt or questions relating to assets;

(d) take security;

(e) bring or defend legal proceedings (without sanction in a voluntary liquidation): s 167;

(f) carry on the business in a way beneficial to the winding-up (without sanction in a voluntary liquidation).

His subsidiary powers, given to enable him to perform the above, include selling assets, giving receipts (often under seal), receiving dividends, drawing bills of exchange, raising money, appointing agents and doing any other necessary things.

8 DUTIES OF LIQUIDATORS

Given the wide-ranging powers invested in a liquidator, he has certain duties.

(a) He must exercise his discretion personally. Although he may delegate clerical tasks and those which he cannot perform personally (for which he can appoint agents), a liquidator cannot delegate his duty to use his judgement, even to the court. However, if it is in the interest of the company's creditors and contributories, and in any case if the nature of the business requires it, a liquidator may ask the court to appoint a manager with special skills.

(b) He stands in a fiduciary relationship to the company, its creditors and contributories.

(c) He must co-operate with the official receiver.

(d) He must notify the liquidation committee of (i) dispositions to a connected person, and (ii) all matters of concern.

A liquidator must keep *records of proceedings*. He must keep a record of all receipts and payments and, if the company continues trading, a trading account should be kept. An account must be submitted to the Secretary of State every 12 months, the first one being accompanied by a summary statement of affairs and an explanation of why assets referred to therein have not been disposed of. A final account must be submitted within 14 days of leaving office. On request, creditors and contributories are entitled to free copies of accounts, and the Secretary of State may order them to be audited.

A liquidator must *act quickly* in carrying out his duties, and not delay for lack of obvious funds.

Liquidators must *keep minutes* of the proceedings and resolutions of creditors', contributories' and liquidation committee meetings.

After six months of voluntary liquidation, the liquidator must pay the balance of funds not required for day-to-day running of the liquidation into a special account at the Bank of England (the Insolvency Services Account). Money received in a compulsory liquidation must be paid into this account immediately, unless the liquidator has express authority from the DTI to operate a local bank account.

The registrar is entitled to receive reports on a voluntary liquidation at the end of 12 months and every six months thereafter.

Activity 5

J Ltd is in liquidation with debts of £70,000. The company has one asset, a building. Tony would pay £100,000 for the building, but he refuses to deal with a company in liquidation. The building is therefore sold to a company owned by the liquidator for £90,000, and then re-sold to Tony for £100,000. All the creditors of J Ltd are paid in full. What duty, if any, has the liquidator breached?

---

9   ALTERNATIVES TO LIQUIDATION

Winding up a company is a fairly drastic step involving the cessation of trading, the disposal of assets and the final dissolution of the company. There are alternatives to liquidation when a company is insolvent to some degree.

(a) *Administration:* under this procedure a moratorium is imposed by the court on creditors' actions against the company while an insolvency practitioner attempts to solve the problem.

(b) *Voluntary arrangement with creditors:* by means of this the company itself, under the supervision of an insolvency practitioner, arranges with creditors for a way of sorting out the problems surrounding it.

10   ADMINISTRATION ORDERS

If a company is not yet in liquidation but is already, or is likely to become, unable to pay its debts the company itself, its directors, or any of its creditors, including unsecured creditors, may present a petition to the court to make an administration order in respect of the company: s 9(1). The broad effect of such an order is to put an insolvency practitioner in control of the company with a defined programme, and meanwhile to insulate it from pressure by creditors. The administration order provides an alternative for the unsecured creditor to suing for the debt in the courts or petitioning for winding up. For the secured creditor it is an alternative to both these solutions and to putting in a receiver.

Effectively the secured creditors have a right of veto over the making of an administration order. This is because anyone petitioning for an administration order must give notice of the fact to anyone who is entitled to put in a receiver or to anyone who has actually put one in. The secured creditor on receiving the notice can then appoint a receiver. If he does, an administration order cannot be made. If a receiver is already in place and the secured creditor does not consent to that receiver stepping down, then again an administration order cannot be made. On the other hand once an administration order is made it is no longer possible for a creditor to appoint a receiver.

Once a winding up resolution has been passed or the court has ordered the company to be wound up, an administration order can no longer be made. On the other hand once an administration order has been made it will no longer be possible to petition the court for a winding up order.

10.1 The petition for administration

The first step is to present a petition to the court for an administration order: s 9. In order to make an order the court must be satisfied that:

(a) the company is or is likely to become unable to pay its debts; and

(b) the making of an administration order is likely to achieve one or more of:

    (i)   the survival of the company and its undertaking as a going concern;

    (ii) the approval of a voluntary arrangement;

    (iii) the sanctioning of a scheme of arrangement under s 425 CA;

    (iv) a more advantageous realisation of the company's assets than would be effected in a liquidation.

The effect of the administration *petition* is to impose a standstill on any move:

(a) for voluntary liquidation;

(b) for seizure of the company's goods in execution of a judgment for debt;

(c) to re-possess goods obtained on hire purchase, rental or retention of title arrangements;

(d) for the institution of any legal proceedings against the company.

It does not, however, prevent the presentation of a petition for compulsory liquidation, though no *order* may be made while the petition for an administration order is pending, nor does it prevent a receiver from being appointed.

Activity 6

A petition for an administration order is made on 1 August, and the order is made on 15 August.
(a) Could a receiver have been appointed on 8 August?
(b) Could a petition for compulsory liquidation have been presented on 8 August?

10.2 The administration order

If the administration order is made, the above temporary measures become permanent; in addition no petition may be presented for compulsory liquidation nor may any administrative receiver be appointed: s 11. Other effects of an administration order are as follows.

(a) In addition to the powers given to a receiver an administrator may challenge past transactions of the company with a view to having them reversed by court order.

(b) An administrator may, with the sanction of the court or with the charge-holder's agreement, sell property of the company subject to a fixed charge: s 11. He may also sell property subject to a floating charge and in this case the charge is then transferred to the proceeds of sale: s 15.

(c) A supplier of goods on hire purchase or retention of title terms may not, unless the administrator consents or the court gives leave, re-possess those goods: s 11(3). The powers of sale described in (b) extend to goods in this category: s 15(2).

(d) The administrator acts as the company's agent (s 14), but he does not have statutory liability on contracts. A person dealing with an administrator in good faith is entitled to assume that he is acting within his powers: s 14(6).

(e) As regards contracts, the administrator can be prevented by injunction from refusing to carry on with a contract made by the company.

(f) Under the Insolvency Act 1994, the administrator's liability under employment contracts is restricted to certain qualifying liabilities, as for administrative receivers. This was discussed in Chapter 22.

10.3 The administrator

The court appoints an insolvency practitioner to be the administrator of the company; in that capacity he has all the statutory powers of an administrative receiver. In addition he may remove any director from office, appoint directors and call meetings of creditors and of members: s 14. With the approval of the court he may also dispose of, free of encumbrance, property of the company until then subject to a charge and also property in its possession under a hire purchase, rental or retention of title agreement. But if he does so, a sum equal to the market value of the property (the net proceeds topped up if necessary) must be applied in repayment of the previously secured debt, or in meeting the claims of the persons whose goods have been sold: s 15.

The order must be publicised.

(a) All company correspondence and documentation must bear the administrator's name and state that an order has been made: s 12.

(b) The administrator must give notice to the company (immediately), to the registrar (within 14 days) and to the creditors (within 28 days): s 21.

An administrator is entitled to receive a statement of affairs. Within three months (or such longer time as the court may allow) he must produce and circulate a statement of his proposals for implementing the purpose of the administration order. Copies go to the creditors; members receive copies or a notice is published to inform them where they may apply for a copy. The administrator next calls a meeting of creditors, on 14 days' notice, to consider and, if thought fit, approve his proposals. He then reports to the court on the result of the meeting. If the proposals have been approved, the administration order will continue in force so that they may be implemented. If the proposals have not been approved the court is likely to discharge the order: s 24(5).

In approving the administrator's proposals, the creditors' meeting may resolve to appoint a creditors' committee to work with the administrator: s 26. They may modify his proposals, but only if he agrees to each change: s 24.

Activity 7

An administrator of a company with three factories proposes to close and sell one factory and to buy new equipment for the two remaining factories. The creditors are generally in favour of the proposed sale, but will not under any circumstances agree to spending money on new equipment. The administrator will not agree to the sale unless new equipment is to be bought. What is the likely outcome?

---

11 VOLUNTARY ARRANGEMENTS

The insolvency of a company may of itself increase its debts and/or reduce its resources. An insolvent company may cease to trade, it may default on its commercial contracts because its suppliers will no longer do business with it, or it may dismiss its employees who are thereby entitled to redundancy payments. Hence it can be in the interest of creditors to accept a compromise with a company rather than insist on its adopting formal insolvency procedure. They are particularly likely to agree to do so if there is a prospect of selling the company's business as a going concern or of pulling it back into solvency by reorganisation or improved management.

A *voluntary arrangement* is either a composition (part payment) in satisfaction of a company's debts or a scheme of arrangement of its affairs: s 1(1). A scheme of arrangement might, for example, be an agreed postponement or rescheduling of payment of debts pending reorganisation or sale of the business.

The initiative in proposing a voluntary arrangement may be taken either:

(a) by the directors, if the company is neither already in liquidation nor subject to an administration order; or

(b) by a liquidator or administrator in office at the time.

In either case the initiative proceeds under the guidance of an insolvency practitioner (called 'the nominee' at this stage) but in case (a) the company is not formally insolvent. The nominee holds separate meetings of members and of creditors and lays before them his proposals for a voluntary arrangement.

If both meetings approve it, the voluntary arrangement becomes binding on the company and on all creditors concerned: s 5. But there are safeguards which significantly limit the possibility of effecting a binding arrangement.

(a) Any secured or preferential creditor whose rights are affected by the arrangement is not bound by the scheme unless he has expressly consented to it: s 4.

(b) Any creditor or member of the company may raise objections to the scheme before the court by showing either (i) that it is unfairly prejudicial (it discriminates against him) or (ii) that there has been a material irregularity in relation to one or other of the meetings: s 6. If the court upholds such an objection, it may revoke or suspend the arrangement or order that revised proposals shall be submitted to further meetings for approval.

If the company is in liquidation or is subject to an administration order when the arrangement is approved, the court may make a suitable order to terminate or suspend those proceedings. An insolvency practitioner, now called a supervisor, implements the arrangement. He may be, but need not be, the same practitioner who was nominee at the initial stage.

Activity 8

A company has debts of £100,000 (all unsecured) and assets which could be sold to raise £30,000. There are at present 20,000 ordinary shares in issue. If the company can overcome its temporary difficulties, it is likely to prosper. Two possible voluntary arrangements have been suggested.

(a) The debts could be exchanged for £80,000 unsecured debentures carrying no interest, repayable in five years' time.

(b) The debts could be exchanged for 20,000 ordinary shares. No dividends would be paid on any shares for five years.

If, in five years' time, the company is likely to have assets of £180,000 and no liabilities (except the unsecured debentures if issued), which arrangement are the creditors likely to prefer? Why might they prefer the other arrangement?

Chapter roundup

- When a company is dissolved, it is removed from the register and ceases to exist. This can happen in several ways, but the most common way is liquidation. In a liquidation, a company's assets are disposed of, its debts are paid so far as possible and any surplus is paid to the members.

- A compulsory liquidation may be petitioned for on any of several grounds, but the most common ground is that the company is unable to pay its debts. A provisional liquidator (usually the Official Receiver) is appointed on the presentation of a petition and, if the court is satisfied, an order for winding up is granted. A statement of affairs is prepared and meetings of contributories and creditors may be held in order to appoint a replacement liquidator. The liquidator reports to the DTI on the completion of his work.

- If a company is solvent, it may go into members' voluntary liquidation. The liquidator holds meetings of contributories, and prepares final accounts once he has finished his work.

- A creditors' voluntary liquidation is also instigated by the members, but a meeting of the creditors must also be held. The creditors may nominate a liquidator and their choice prevails over the members' choice. A liquidation committee may be appointed to work with the liquidator.

- In any liquidation, contributories may be called upon to provide funds to meet the company's debts if they hold partly paid shares or if they disposed of such shares within the year preceding the commencement of the winding up.

- A liquidator may pay and compromise debts, and may conduct legal proceedings. He stands in a fiduciary relationship to the company, and he must exercise his discretion personally and keep records.

- If a company is in temporary difficulty, it, its directors or any of its creditors may apply for an administration order. Once an administration order has been made, a receiver cannot be appointed and the court cannot be petitioned for a winding up order. The administrator then has time to devise a scheme to save the company from insolvency.

- It may benefit creditors and members to enter into a voluntary arrangement under which debts are paid in part or exchanged for shares or securities, rather than putting the company into liquidation.

Quick quiz

1 Describe how a company may be dissolved.

2 Give three grounds on which an order may be made by the court for compulsory liquidation of a company.

3 What grounds may be asserted in a creditor's petition to establish that the company is unable to pay its debts?

4 What is the result likely to be if other creditors oppose a creditor's petition for compulsory liquidation?

5 Give two examples of circumstances which can provide 'just and equitable' grounds for compulsory winding up.

6 What are the effects of an order for compulsory liquidation on those who have dealings with the company?

7 What meetings are called by the Official Receiver and for what purposes?

8 What type of resolution is passed to put a company into voluntary liquidation?

9 What is a liquidation committee? When is it appointed? What does it do?

10 In what circumstances and within what limits may a previous holder of shares be liable to contribute towards the payment of the company's debts even though he has transferred his shares to some other person before the company goes into liquidation?

11 What are the main powers of liquidators?

12 How far may a liquidator delegate his duties?

13 What accounting records must a liquidator keep? To whom must he submit records?

14 How do liquidations, receiverships and administrations interact?

15 What is the effect of an administration order once made?

16 How may a secured creditor ensure that he is not affected by a company's voluntary arrangement?

Solutions to activities

1 Persons with no previous dealings with the company need to be warned before they make contracts with the company.

2 The company had not neglected to pay: it was deliberately disputing the amount due.

3 P: the creditors' choice prevails.

4 It is expected that all creditors will be paid in full, so there is no need for them to interfere.

5 He has breached his fiduciary duty to the company by making a profit from his position.

6 (a) Yes: the petition for an administration order does not prevent a receiver from being appointed.

(b) Yes: the petition for an administration order does not prevent a petition for compulsory liquidation, although an order may not be granted.

7 The court will discharge the administration order.

8 The creditors are likely to prefer (b), giving them wealth of £180,000 × 20,000/40,000 = £90,000 in five years' time. They might prefer (a) if they doubted the accuracy of the forecast of assets.

Further question practice

Now try the following practice questions at the end of this text

Multiple choice questions:

105 to 109

GLOSSARY

ACAS Advisory, Conciliation and Arbitration Service.

Acceptance A positive act by a person accepting an offer so as to bring a contact into effect.

Accord and satisfaction Agreement and consideration.

Actus reus Guilty act. One of the two requirements normally present in a crime, the other being *mens rea*.

Ad idem Of the same (mind or intention). A requirement for a valid contract.

Administration order A court order made in relation to a company in financial difficulties, which insulates it from further pressure from creditors.

Administrative receiver A person defined by the Insolvency Act 1986 under a *floating charge* to manage or realise the assets which are the security with a view to paying out of those assets what is due to the debentureholders whom he represents.

Administrative tribunals Special 'courts' set up to settle disputes.

Administrator Insolvency practitioner appointed by the court to look after the affairs of the company whilst an administration order is in force.

Agent A person authorised to act for another (the principal) and bring that other into legal relations with a third party.

Allotment of shares The allocation to a person of a certain number of shares under a contract of allotment. The intending shareholder applies to the company for shares. This is an offer which the company accepts by allocating shares to him.

Annual general meeting (AGM) Every company is required to hold a meeting of each its members each (calendar) year, at intervals of not more than 15 months, at which it is usual, but not obligatory to transact the 'ordinary business' of the company. Such business may include consideration of the accounts, declaration of a dividend and appointment of auditors. Private companies may dispense with such meetings if they pass an *elective resolution*.

Anticipatory breach Renunciation by party to a contract of his contractual obligations before the date for performance.

Anti-competitive practice A course of conduct which restricts, distorts or prevents competition in the production or acquisition of goods, or the supply of goods and services.

Appeal A request to a higher court by a person dissatisfied with a decision of a lower court that the previous decision be reviewed.

Arbitration A means of settling a dispute outside the courts.

Articles of association Rules governing the internal conduct of a company's affairs, such as appointment, powers and proceedings of directors, alteration of capital structure, dividends and so on. Limited companies may draft their own articles or adopt a model format provided by *Table A* of the Companies (Tables A – F) Regulations 1985.

Assignment Transfer of rights and liabilities.

Auction A type of contract for the sale of property.

Auditor A person appointed by the company in general meeting to report whether the accounts reflect a true and fair view of the company's affairs.

Bill The draft of a proposed statute.

Bill of exchange A type of order to pay money.

Bona fide In good faith

Bonus issue A bonus issue is made when a company applies its reserves to paying up unissued shares which are then allotted to members. Bonus shares are a substitute for additional dividends which might otherwise be paid.

Business name A name used by a company other than the registered one.

Bye-law Type of delegated legislation.

Call A demand made by a company upon a member to pay an amount outstanding on his partly-paid shares. The power of the directors to make calls is defined by the articles.

Called up share capital The aggregate amount of calls for money or other consideration which members are required to pay (or have paid) in applying for shares.

Capacity The ability or power of a person to enter into legal relationships or carry out legal acts.

Capital clause A clause appearing in the memorandum of association of a company which specifies the amount of share capital and its division into shares of a fixed amount.

Capital redemption reserve A reserve created by a company to maintain its capital structure when it carries out a purchase of its own shares. A transfer is made to the reserve from the proceeds of a fresh issue and distributable profits. The sum must be equal to the amount of the capital redeemed.

Capitalisation The conversion of profits into capital by the issue of bonus shares.

Care, duty of The care owed by one person to another which, if broken, may give rise to an action for negligence.

Case stated A particular form of appeal.

Caveat emptor Let the buyer beware.

Certificate of incorporation A certificate issued by the Registrar of Companies on the registration of a company. The certificate is conclusive evidence that the company has been registered and that all the requirement of the Companies Act in respect of registration have been complied with.

Certorari A prerogative order.

Chancery division A division of the High Court.

Charge An encumbrance upon an asset which gives the holder certain rights over the asset. In particular a charge gives to the creator a prior claim over other creditors for payment of his debt out of the asset.

Charterparty A contract between the shipowner and the charterer whereby a ship is hired for a period of time or for a particular voyage.

Class rights Rights attaching to particular types of shares. They are usually specified in the articles.

Codification The replacement of common law rules by statute which embodies those rules.

Collective agreement An agreement between a trade union and an employer.

Commercial court A specialised court.

Common law The body of legal rules developed by the common law courts and now embodied in legal decisions.

Compensation for loss of office A sum paid by a director when he ceases to hold office. If a director has a service contract he may be entitled to compensation for its breach by his dismissal as provided by the Companies Act 1985. The Companies Act provides that such compensation must be approved by the company in general meeting and disclosed in the accounts.

Compulsory liquidation A liquidation ordered by the Chancery Division of the High Court, initiated by a petition, usually from a creditor or contributory.

Concert party Several persons acting in concert who control a significant part of a company's share capital. Where the joint holding is more than 3% of equity shares in a public company, this holding must be disclosed.

Condition Term vital to a contract. Breach of a condition destroys the basis of the contract.

Condition precedent Specific type of contract term which prevents the contract from coming into operation unless the condition is satisfied.

Condition subsequent Specific type of contract term by which the contract is discharged on the later happening of an event.

Connected person With regard to directors' loans and substantial property transactions, this includes the director's spouse or child under 18, a company in which the director and connected persons own one fifth or more of the equity share capital.

Consideration That which is given, promised or done by a party to a contract.

Consolidation The passing of an act to 'tidy up the law'.

Constructive dismissal Serious breach of contract by an employer which forces an employee to leave.

Constructive notice A person may be deemed in law to know of a certain matter regardless of whether he has actual knowledge of it. In the case of companies this applies to some of the details in company registers, for example the register of charges.

Constructive trust So called because a trust relationship is construed regardless of the wishes or intentions of the parties concerned. Specifically directors are held to be constructive trustees of corporate property. If they misappropriate the property, they are liable to account to the company for any profit and compensate the company for any loss.

Continuous employment Period of unbroken employment required for certain statutory rights to be available to the employee.

Contract An agreement which the law will recognise and enforce.

Contributory A person liable to contribute to the assets of a company in a winding up. This includes present and certain past members, personal representatives of deceased members and trustees of bankrupt members.

Control test Test used by the courts to determine whether a contract of employment exists.

Council on Tribunals Statutory body which overseas the workings of administrative tribunals.

Counsel's opinion The advice of a barrister on a specialised or difficult point of law which may be obtained by a solicitor before advising his or her client on whether or not to proceed with his or her action.

Counterclaim When court proceedings are begun by the plaintiff serving details of his claim upon the defendant, the defendant may reply with a counterclaim alleging that he or she is the injured party. For example, he or she may allege that he or she did not pay for the goods because they were defective.

County court Inferior civil court.

Court of Appeal Appeal court divided into two divisions.

Court of protection Specialised court within the Chancery Division of the High Court which deals with the estates of mentally disordered persons.

Covenant A clause in a deed whereby a person promises to do, or refrain from doing, a specific act.

CRE Commission for Racial Equality.

CREST A paperless system of share transfer due to replace TALISMAN in 1996.

Crystallisation A *floating charge* is converted into a *fixed charge*, for example on liquidation or if the contract so provides.

Cumulative preference share A type of *preference share* where dividends which are not paid in one year are payable the following year.

Custom Unwritten law which formed the basis of common law.

Damages The sum claimed or awarded in a civil action in compensation for the loss or injury suffered by the plaintiff.

De facto As a matter of fact, disregarding questions of right or title.

De jure As a matter of law.

Debenture A written acknowledgement of a debt.

Debenture trust deed A deed made in connection with a series of separate registered debentures. The deed appoints a trustee to represent the interests of the holders, defines the nominal amount of the debenture stock and specifies the date of repayment, the interest rate and the rights of the trustee to enforce the security.

Decision Secondary source of EC law.

Defendant The person against whom a civil action is brought or who is prosecuted for a criminal offence.

Delegated legislation Rules of law made by subordinate bodies to whom the power to do so has been given by statute.

Derivative action A remedy available to a minority shareholder to redress a wrong done to the company. Such an action is brought where those who have committed the offence control the company, and thus, under *Foss v Harbottle* could prevent it from taking action. Any benefit obtained will accrue to the company since the claim is derived from and made on behalf of the company.

Directive Secondary source of EC law.

Director A person who takes part in making decisions and managing a company's affairs.

Director General of Fair Trading the head of the Office of Fair Trading who is responsible for administering the Fair Trading Act 1973, the Consumer Credit Act 1974 and the Restrictive Trade Practices Act 1976.

Dismissal Termination by an employer of a contract of employment.

Dissolution (of a company). Occurs when a company's name is removed from the register.

Dividend A distribution of profits to members made in proportion to their shareholdings.

Divisional court A court in the High Court.

Enabling act A statute which establishes a framework within which some subordinate body, often a minister, is 'enabled' or empowered to fill in the details by delegated legislation.

Entire contract Contract in which the consideration on both sides is indivisible.

EOC Equal Opportunities Commission.

Equity A source of English law consisting of those rules which emerged from the Court of Chancery.

Equity share A share which gives the holder the right to participate in the company's surplus profit and capital. There is no limit to the size of the dividend which may be paid except the size of the profit itself. In a winding up the holder is entitled to a repayment of the nominal value plus a share of surplus assets. The term equity share embraces ordinary shares but it can also include a *preference share* when the terms of issue include either the right to an additional dividend or the right to surplus assets in a winding up.

Estoppel If a person, by his words or conduct, leads another to believe that a certain state of affairs exists and that other alters his or her position to his or her detriment in reliance on that belief, the first person is estopped (prevented) from claiming later that a different state of affairs existed. Thus if a principal, by honouring contracts made by his or her agent, induces a third party to believe that the agent possesses certain authority, the principal will be bound by later contracts of a similar nature made by the agent even if they are unauthorised.

Exclusion clause Contract clause purporting to exclude or restrict liability.

Ex gratia By way of favour or gift.

Ex parte Of the one part or one side.

Executed That which takes place at the present time.

Executory That which is to take place at some future time.

Expressio unius est exclusio alterius To state one thing is to exclude others.

Extraordinary resolution A resolution requiring a 75% majority at a general meeting of which 14 days' notice has been given. An extraordinary resolution is required, for example, to put the company into creditors' voluntary liquidation.

Fixed charge A *charge* attaching to a particular asset on creation. The asset in question is usually a fixed asset, which the company is likely to retain for a long period. If the company defaults in payment of the debt the holder can realise the asset to meet the debt. Fixed charges rank first in order of priority in a liquidation.

Floating charge A *charge* on a class of assets of a company, present and future which changes in the ordinary course of the company's business. Until the holders enforce the charge the company may carry on business and deal with the assets charged. It attaches to the assets only on *crystallisation*.

Fraud Using misrepresentation to obtain an unjust advantage in the knowledge that it is untrue, without belief in its truth or recklessly, not caring whether it be true or false.

Fraud on the minority Discrimination by the majority shareholders against the minority. The minority may have a remedy at common law.

Fraudulent trading Carrying on business and incurring debts when there is to the knowledge of the directors no reasonable prospect that these debts will be repaid, that is with intent to defraud the creditors. Persons so acting may be liable for the debts of the company as the court may decide.

Freedom of contract Principle that parties may contract on the terms which they choose.

Frustration Discharge of contract by some outside event which makes further performance impossible in the form anticipated.

Fundamental breach Doctrine developed by the courts as a protection against unreasonable exemption clauses in contracts.

Gazette An official publication from HMSO in which certain notices must be inserted as prescribed by statute, for example the appointment of a liquidator.

General commercial company An *objects* clause of a company implying that it can carry on any trade or business whatsoever. This clause may now be used as a result of the reforms of the Companies Act 1989.

Good faith Fair and open action without any attempt to deceive or take advantage of knowledge of which the other party is unaware.

Guarantee A promise to answer for the debt or default of another.

Habeas corpus You have the body.

High Court Civil court with extensive jurisdiction.

Holding company A company which controls another, its *subsidiary* by holding the majority of its voting rights, being a member of it and having the power to appoint or remove a majority of the board of directors.

HSC Health and Safety Commission.

HSE Health and Safety Executive.

Implied term Term deemed to form part of a contract even though not expressly mentioned by the parties.

In personam An action *in personam* is one seeking relief against a particular person.

In rem An action *in rem* is one brought in respect of property.

Indemnity Security against or compensation for loss.

Independent contractor Self-employed person.

Indoor management rule The principle which states that the outsider who deals with the directors (or apparent directors) is aware of the requirements or restrictions imposed by the articles but is entitled to assume, unless he knows or should suspect the contrary, that these internal rules have been observed. This is also known as the rule in *Turquand's* case.

Industrial tribunals Local tribunal dealing with disputes between employer and employee.

Injunction An order of the court directing a person not to carry out a certain act.

Inns of Court There are four such Inns – Grays, Lincoln's, Middle Temple and Inner Temple – which intending barristers must join and which have the exclusive privilege of conferring the status of barrister.

Insider dealing A person who has been knowingly connected with the company in the previous six months uses unpublished price sensitive information to make a profit or avoid a loss on a recognised stock exchange or through an off-market dealer. This is a criminal offence under Part V Criminal Justice Act 1993.

Insolvency The inability to pay creditors in full after realising all the assets of a business.

Insolvency practitioner Persons acting as a liquidator, administrative receiver, administrator or supervisor of a voluntary arrangement must be insolvency practitioners, authorised by the professional body to which they belong or by the DTI.

Integration test Test used by the courts to determine whether a contract of employment exists.

Intention to create legal relations Element necessary for an agreement to become a legally binding contract.

Interpretation clause Most statutes and statutory instruments include a clause, either at the beginning or the end, which defines the meaning to be given to words or phrases used in the enactment.

Investment company A company which has given notice to the registrar of companies that the business of the company consists of spreading investment risks of members. The distinction between investment and ordinary companies is important because the former have special rules on profits available for distribution.

Invitation to treat Indication that a person is prepared to receive offers with a view to entering into a binding contract.

Issue at a discount An issue of company securities at less than their nominal value. Debentures may be issued at a discount but shares may not, according to the Companies Act 1985.

Issue at a premium An issue of a share at more than its nominal value. There are special rules laid down by the Companies Act governing the treatment of the premium.

Issued share capital The *nominal value* of the shares which a company has issued.

Judgment The sentence or order of the court.

Judgment debts Money due by reason of a decision of the court.

Judicial review Application to the High Court for relief from a wrongful act.

Justice of the Peace A magistrate, normally without legal qualifications, appointed by the Lord Chancellor to adjudicate in a Magistrates' Court.

Law Commission Two Commissions were set up in 1965, for England and Wales and for Scotland, as permanent bodies charged with the task of keeping the law under review and proposing reforms where necessary. There are five full-time Commissioners, a High Court judge as chairman and four other legal practitioners or academic lawyers. Normal practice is to publish a working paper first to invite comment and then a final report, often with a draft bill included which embodies the proposed reforms.

Law Lords The name given to the ten life peers or Lords of Appeal in Ordinary who, together with the Lord Chancellor and any other peers who have held high judicial office, sit in the House of Lords as the final court of appeal. In practice, five will normally sit.

Law Merchant Early mercantile customs.

Law Reports The principal reports of decided cases

Law Society The statutory body governing the solicitors' branch of the legal profession.

Leapfrog procedure Procedure by which appeal from the High Court may go directly to the House of Lords.

Legal aid A statutory scheme administered by the Law Society for assisting applicants with the cost of legal proceedings, either in whole or in part. It may cover preliminary legal advice or it may extend to the actual court proceedings. The applicant must show that he or she cannot afford to proceed because his or her disposable capital and disposable income are below prescribed amounts. In civil actions he or she must also show that he or she has an arguable case whilst in criminal prosecutions the charge must be serious or complex.

Legal person A human being (natural person) or a corporate body (artificial person) having rights and duties recognised by law.

Lien A right to retain possession of property until a debt has been paid.

Lifting the veil (of incorporation) A company is normally to be treated as a separate legal person from its members. 'Lifting the veil' means that the company is identified with its members or directors or that a group of companies is to be treated as a single commercial entity. An example of this is to prevent fraud.

Limitation of actions By statute, proceedings must be commenced within a certain period of time from the date when the action could first have been brought.

Limited liability Limitation of the liability of members to contribute to the assets of a business in the event of a winding up.

Liquidated damages Fixed sum agreed by parties to a contract and payable in the event of a breach.

Liquidation The winding up of a company. Assets are realised and debts paid off. Any surplus is returned to the members.

Liquidator A person who organises a company's liquidation or winding up. His task is to take control of the company's assets with a view to their realisation and the payment of all debts of the company and distribution of any surplus to members.

Listed Quoted on a recognised stock exchange.

Loan capital A form of business finance which means that the lender is a creditor of the business either short term (for example, a bank overdraft) or long term (for example, a debenture redeemable in five years' time). Loan creditors are not the same as members and have no voting rights.

Maintenance of capital A principle whereby creditors are protected. This involves preventing companies from making payments out of capital and thus depleting their assets.

Mandamus We command.

Market purchase A purchase by a company of its own shares under the normal market arrangements of a recognised investment exchange.

Medium sized company A private company which in both the current and preceding year complies with at least two of the three conditions listed below.

(a) Turnover is not more than £11.2m

(b) Gross assets are not more than £5.6m

(c) Monthly average employees are not more than 250.

Member Shareholder of a company.

Memorandum of association Together with the *articles of association*, this defines what the company is and how its affairs are to be conducted. It gives details of the companies name, objects, capital and registered office.

Mens rea Guilty mind.

Merger an amalgamation of companies, usually effected by a take-over bid.

Minimum number of members A public company must be formed with two members. The Companies Act provides that if a public company carries on business without at least two members for more than six months, the remaining member who is aware of this is jointly and severally liable with the company for the company's debts. A *private* company, however, may now be formed and operate with only one member.

Minor A person under the age of eighteen.

Minutes A written, indexed record of the business transacted and decisions taken at a meeting. Company law requires minutes to be kept of all company meetings. Minutes of general meetings should be available for inspection by members.

Misrepresentation False statement made with the object of inducing the other party to enter into a contract.

Monopolies and Mergers commission An independent advisory body which advises the government on monopolies and mergers.

Monopoly A situation where 25% of goods or services of a particular kind in the UK are supplied to or by a single person.

Multiple test Test used by the courts to determine whether a contract of employment exists.

National insurance State insurance scheme funded by deductions from earnings which provides for benefits to be paid in the event of unemployment, sickness, invalidity, industrial injuries etc.

Natural justice The principles of natural justice are designed to ensure that courts, tribunals and public authorities follow a fair and proper procedure. The two main rules are that no one shall be a judge in his own cause, that is that a person shall not take a part in making a decision in which he or she has a personal interest, and that both parties shall have a right to be heard. In addition, there must be no inexcusable delay, reasons should be given for a decision, and justice should be seen to be done. A party injured by a failure to observe these principles may seek relief, normally by way of judicial review in the High Court.

Natural person A human being with rights and duties recognised by the law as opposed to an artificial person such as a corporate body.

Negligence This may refer to the way in which an act is carried out, that is carelessly, or to the tort which arises when a person breaches a legal duty of care that is owed to another, thereby causing loss to that other.

Negotiability Quality possessed by certain documents representing claims to money which may be transferred by delivery (and in some cases endorsement).

Negotiable instrument A document which is negotiable, for example a bill of exchange or a cheque.

Nominal damages Category of damages which may be awarded in tort.

Nominee shareholder A person whose name appears on a company's register of members but who in fact holds the shares for somebody else. This is important in connection with *concert parties*.

Novation Transaction whereby a creditor agrees to release an existing debtor and substitute a new one in his or her place.

Obiter dictum Something said by the way.

Objects clause A clause in a company's memorandum of association which sets out the 'aims' and 'purposes' of the company.

Offer Express or implied statement of the terms on which the maker is willing to be contractually bound.

Order in Council A form of delegated legislation.

Ordinary resolution A resolution carried by a simple majority of votes cast. Where no other resolution is specified, 'resolution' means an ordinary resolution.

Ordinary share A share which gives the holder the right to participate in the company's surplus profit and capital. The dividend is payable only when preference dividends, including arrears, have been paid.

Oversea company A company incorporated outside Great Britain which establishes a place of business in Great Britain.

Partnership The relation which subsists between persons carrying on a business in common with a view of profit. Every partner is liable without limit for the debts of the partnership. In the absence of any written agreement, matters such as profit sharing are determined by the Partnership Act 1890.

Passing off Carrying on a business in a manner which is likely to mislead the public. This normally relates to using a name which is similar to that of another business.

Past consideration Something already done at the time that a contractual promise is made.

Penalty clause Clause in a contract providing for a specific sum to be payable in the event of a subsequent breach.

Per sey itself.

Perpetual succession The principle by which a change in the membership of a company or the death of a member is not a change in the company itself. A company is a separate legal person which continues unaffected by changes among its members.

Plaintiff he person who complains or brings an action asking the court for relief.

Poll A method of voting whereby each person entitled to vote does so in writing, indicating the number of votes which he is casting in proportion to his shareholding.

Possession Actual physical control over property with the intention of maintaining that control.

Power of attorney An authority in the form of a deed which enables one person to act on behalf of another, if necessary by deed and, for example, convey property.

Pre-emption rights The right of shareholders to be offered new shares issued by the company in proportion to their existing holdings of that class of shares.

Pre-incorporation contract A contract purported to be made by a company or its agent before the company has received its certificate of incorporation. An agent may be made personally liable on such a contract which will be unenforceable against the company.

Precedent A previous court decision.

Preference shares A share which carries a prior right to receive an annual dividend of a fixed amount. There are no other *implied* differences between preference and ordinary shares but there may be express differences, for example preference shares may carry a priority right to return of capital. Unless otherwise stated, preference shares are assumed to be *cumulative*.

Premium The amount by which the payment for a share exceeds its nominal value. The Companies Act lays down detailed rules regarding the treatment of a premium and a *share premium account.*

Prerogative order An order made by the High Court.

Presumption A rule of evidence.

Prima facie At first sight or on first impressions.

Private company A company which may not offer shares to the public, and which has not been registered as a public company.

Privity of contract The relation between two contracting parties which allows either to sue the other for breach.

Pro rata In proportion to the value.

Prohibition A type of court order.

Promise Voluntary understanding by one person to another to perform or abstain from performing a certain act.

Promoter Person who undertakes to form a company by making the appropriate business preparations.

Prospectus A notice, circular, advertisement or other invitation offering to the public for subscription or purchase any shares or debentures of a company.

Proxy A person appointed by a shareholder to vote on behalf of that shareholder at a company meeting.

Public company A company registered as such under the Companies Act. The principal distinction between public and private companies is that only the former may offer shares to the public.

Purchase of own shares A company may, subject to detailed rules, purchase its own shares. A private company may finance the purchase out of capital but this is closely regulated.

Quantum meruit As much as he has deserved.

Quasi contract Resembling a contract but not really a contract.

Quasi loan A payment to a third party on a director's behalf with the company being indemnified later by the director.

Quasi partnership A small, usually private company, where the relationship between the directors is essentially like that of a partnership. The courts have taken into account the existence of such quasi-partnerships when applying the law.

Queen's Bench Division Division of the High Court.

Quorum Minimum number required to be present for a valid meeting to take place.

Quoted company Company whose securities are listed on a stock exchange.

Ratification Subsequent validation by the members of a decision which the company did not take in general meeting at the appropriate time.

Ratio decidendi The reason for the decision.

Re In the matter of.

Receiver Person who takes control of the assets of a company subject to a charge as a means of enforcing the security for the benefit of the secured creditors by or for whom he was appointed.

Rectification An equitable remedy.

Reduction of capital A diminution of the share capital of a company, for example to reflect a loss in the value of its assets. The scheme needs to be approved by the court to ensure that the creditors are not adversely affected.

Registered office A business address to which all communication with a company must be sent.

Registration Process by which a company comes into being. Certain documents must be filed with the Registrar of Companies and a Certificate of Incorporation must be issued.

Regulation A secondary source of EC law.

Remoteness of damage Relationship between a wrongful act and the resulting damage which determines whether or not compensation may be recovered. Different principles apply in contract and in tort.

Repudiation Rejection or renunciation.

Rescission The act of repudiation of a contract. An equitable remedy.

Restitutio in integrum Restoring to the original position.

Restraint of trade Restriction upon a trade or business which is *prima facie* void at common law.

Restrictive Practices Court A special court with High Court status.

Restrictive Trade Practices An arrangement designed to fix prices or regulate the supply of goods.

Royal Assent Final stage in the process by which a Bill becomes an Act.

Sale of goods A contract whereby the seller transfers or agrees to transfer the property in goods for a money consideration called the price.

Secretary An officer of a company appointed to carry out general administrative duties. Every company must have a secretary and a sole director must not also be the secretary.

Securities Company shares and debentures.

Shadow director A person in accordance with whose instructions other directors re accustomed to act.

Share A member's stake in a company's share capital.

Share premium account An account into which an excess of payment for a share over its nominal value cannot be placed.

Show of hands Method of voting in which each member has only one vote, shown by raising his hand, regardless of the size of his shareholding. This contrasts with a *poll*.

Small claim A claim not exceeding £1,000 may be brought within the quicker, cheaper and more informal arbitration procedure within the county court.

Small company Company which complies with two out of the three conditions below in two successive years.

    (a) Turnover does not exceed £2.8m

    (b) Gross assets do not exceed £1.4m

    (c) Monthly average employees do not exceed 50.

Special resolution Resolution requiring a 75% majority of votes cast and 21 days' notice. A special resolution is required for major changes in the company, such as alteration of the name or articles.

Specific performance: A type of court order.

Standard form contract Contract where the terms are drawn up by the stronger party

Standard of proof The extent to which the court must be satisfied by the evidence presented.

Statute-barred Inability to pursue an action because proceedings were not started within the period prescribed by statute.

Statutory instrument Form of delegated legislation.

Subject to contract Qualified acceptance pending making of a more formal agreement.

Subpoena Under penalty (for refusal).

Subsidiary company A company under the control of another company, its holding company.

Substantial property transaction An arrangement by which the company buys from or sells to a director of the company or of its holding company property which exceeds £100,000 in value or (if less) 10% of the company's net assets subject to a minimum of £2,000. The shareholders' approval is required.

Summons Generally an order to appear before a court but used particularly of the document which begins County Court proceedings and of the order to appear before a Magistrates' Court when the accused is not arrested.

Supreme Court of Judicature Established by the Judicature Acts 1873-75, it consists of the Court of Appeal and the High Court.

Table A A model form of *articles* for a company limited by shares set out in the Companies (Tables A – F) Regulations 1985.

TALISMAN The computerised share transfer system operated by the Stock Exchange. The system operates by the transfer of shares to a company called Sepon Ltd, owned by the Stock Exchange. Transfer to the ultimate buyer occurs at the end of each two or three week period called an 'account'. To be replaced by CREST in 1996.

Tender Offer, particularly of goods or money.

Title Legal right to possession or ownership of property.

Tort A wrongful act.

Trade union An organisation of employees formed to regulate relations between employer and employees.

Trust An arrangement by which the legal owner of a property has an obligation to administer it for the benefit of the beneficiary who has an equitable interest in it.

Uberrimae fidei Of utmost good faith.

Ultra vires Beyond their powers. In company law this term is used in connection with transactions which are outside the scope of the objects clause and therefore, in principle at least, unenforceable.

Unenforceable Not actionable in a court

Unfair dismissal Termination of a contract of employment in breach of certain statutory rights given to the employee.

Unfair prejudice to members Treating any part of the membership of a company unfavourably. A member may apply to the court for relief under the Companies Act.

Vicarious liability Liability for the wrongful acts of another.

Void Having no legal effect.

Voidable Capable of being rendered void at the option of one of the parties, but valid until the option is exercised.

Voluntary liquidation A liquidation decided upon by the members in general meeting.

Waive Give up a claim or right, such as the right to receive notice.

Warranty Minor term in a contract.

Winding up A process by which a company ceases to exist, otherwise known as a liquidation.

Writ A written command.

Wrongful dismissal Breach of contract of employment by the employer without justification and without appropriate notice.

Wrongful trading The term used where directors of an insolvent company knew or should have known that there was no reasonable prospect that the company could have avoided insolvency and did not take sufficient steps to minimise the potential loss to the creditors.

MULTIPLE CHOICE QUESTIONS

Chapter 1

1   Which of the following is *not* a maxim of equity?

   A   He who seeks equity must do equity

   B   Equity must prevail

   C   He who comes to equity must come with clean hands

   D   Equality is equity

   A   B   C   D

2   Before a High Court judge is required to apply a previous decision to the case actually before him, he must

   1   decide whether the decision is binding or merely persuasive

   2   distinguish the *obiter dicta* from the *ratio decidendi* and apply the former in his reasoning

   3   determine that the material facts of the two cases are similar

   4   be convinced that the decision was made by a court of higher status than the county court or magistrates' court

   A   1 and 3 only

   B   2 and 4 only

   C   1, 2 and 3 only

   D   1, 3 and 4 only

   A   B   C   D

3   The Court of Appeal is bound by the previous decisions of

   A   the House of Lords only

   B   the House of Lords and a Divisional Court of the High Court only

   C   the House of Lords and the Court of Appeal only

   D   the House of Lords, the Court of Appeal and a Divisional Court of the High Court only

   A   B   C   D

4   Delegated legislation is drawn up under powers conferred by the full Parliament in acts. Which of the following statements concerning delegated legislation are true?

   1   The power to make such legislation may be delegated to local authorities

   2   Ministerial powers are exercised by Order in Council, a common form of delegated legislation

   3   All delegated legislation must be laid before Parliament

   4   Legislation laid before Parliament for 40 days without a negative resolution being passed in respect of it automatically comes into force

A   1 and 4 only
B   2 and 3 only
C   1, 2 and 4 only
D   1, 3 and 4 only

A B C D

5   Which of the following presumptions are 'canons of statutory interpretation'?

1   An act of Parliament applies only to England and Wales unless otherwise stated

2   An act of Parliament does not have retrospective effect

3   For a criminal offence to be committed, there must be intention on the part of the accused

4   An Act of Parliament does not repeal a previous act

A   1 and 3 only
B   2 and 4 only
C   1, 2 and 4 only
D   2, 3 and 4 only

A B C D

Chapter 2

6   The criminal law aims

A   to compensate injured parties
B   to recover property which has been taken from the true owner
C   to enforce legal obligations
D   to penalise wrongdoers

A B C D

7   One of the following actions lies outside the jurisdiction of the county court. Which one?

A   A debt action for £3,500
B   A claim of £15,000 for negligent advice given by a solicitor
C   An uncontested divorce
D   A dispute over the probate of a will where the deceased's estate is valued at £18,000

A B C D

8   An order by the High Court to a court or other body to carryout a public duty is an order of

A   specific performance
B   *habeas corpus*
C   *certiorari*
D   *mandamus*

A B C D

9 What is a 'reversed' judgment?

A A dissenting judgment given in the Court of Appeal

B A judgment contained in a precedent which is subsequently found to be wrong

C A judgment which is contradicted on appeal

D A judgment which contradicts previous precedents

A B C D

Chapter 3

10 The UK joined the European Community in:

A 1957

B 1971

C 1973

D 1986

E 1960

A B C D E

11 Qualified majority voting in the Council of Ministers means that:

A each member state has only one vote

B each member state has a right of veto

C all member states must vote the same way on each issue

D there must be a majority vote

E voting is weighted according to the size of the member state

A B C D E

12 Which of the following correctly describes the principle of direct effect:

A that EC legislation must arise from and out of the Treaties

B that EC legislation overrides national legislation

C that EC legislation applies without further national legislation

D that EC legislation applies in a national court of a member state and may be enforced by individuals

E that a directive does not have direct applicability

A B C D E

13 Regulations differ from directives in that:

A Regulations are directly applicable in all states and also have direct effect

B Regulations are proposed by the Commission

C Regulations are equivalent to Treaty provisions

D Regulations have vertical direct effect

E Directives have direct applicability

A B C D E

Chapter 4

14 Which one of the following is not an administrative tribunal?

A   An industrial tribunal

B   An administrative enquiry

C   The Advisory, Conciliation and Arbitration Service

D   The Employment Appeals Tribunal

A B C D

15 In which one of the following circumstances may the parties to an arbitration agreement *not* apply to the High Court?

A   When both parties agreed in writing not to appeal against an arbitrator's award

B   When one party institutes legal proceedings in breach of the arbitration agreement

C   When both parties agreed to appeal on a preliminary point of law

D   When the High court is satisfied that an appeal on a preliminary point of law could substantially affect the rights of the parties

A B C D

Chapter 5

16 To be a fully binding agreement, which of the following attributes must *always* be demonstrated by a contract?

1   Offer and acceptance

2   Intention to create legal relations

3   Consideration

4   Full capacity of each party to contract

5   Legality

6   Writing

A   Attributes 1, 2 and 3 only

B   Attributes 2, 4 and 5 only

C   Attributes 1, 2, 4 and 6 only

D   Attributes 1, 3, 4 and 5 only

A B C D

17 Tim offered to sell a stereo system to Neil for £200 on 2 September saying that the offer would stay open for a week. Neil told his brother that he would like to accept Tim's offer and, unknown to Neil, his brother told Tim of this on 3 September. On 4 September Tim, with his lodger present, sold the stereo to Ingrid. The lodger informed Neil of this fact on the same day. On 5 September Neil delivered a letter of acceptance to Tim. Is Tim in breach of contract?

A   No: Neil delayed beyond a reasonable time and so the offer had lapsed by the time Tim sold to Ingrid

B   No: Neil was told by a reliable informant of Tim's effective revocation before Neil accepted the offer

C   Yes: Tim agreed to keep the offer open and failed to do so

D   Yes: Tim was reliably informed of Neil's acceptance on 3 September so his sale to Ingrid on 4 September is breach of contract

A B C D

18 Maud goes into a shop and sees a price label for £20 on an ironing-board. She takes the board to the checkout but the till operator tells her that the label is misprinted and should read £30. Maud maintains that she only has to pay £20. How would you describe the price on the price label in terms of contract law.

A   An offer
B   A tender
C   An invitation to treat
D   An acceptance

A B C D

19 Consideration
1   must be of adequate and sufficient value
2   must move from the promisee
3   must never be past
4   must be given in every binding agreement
5   may be performance of an existing obligation

A   1 only
B   2 only
C   2, 3 and 4 only
D   3, 4 and 5 only

A B C D

20 Miranda owes Emma £500 for her wedding dress. Emma, because she is in need of cash, agrees to accept £400 in full settlement of the debt, but she later claims the full amount. Will she succeed?

A   No: Miranda's payment is full consideration for Emma's promise to waive her rights

B   No: she is estopped from retracting her promise

C   Yes: her waiver was not entirely voluntary

D   Yes: she had no intention that Miranda should act on the waiver and so the doctrine of promissory estoppel does not apply

A B C D

Chapter 6

21 Which of the following statements concerning contractual terms are true?

1   Terms are usually classified as either conditions or warranties, but some terms may be unclassifiable in this way

2   If a condition in a contract is not fulfilled the whole contract is said to be discharged by breach

3   If a warranty in a contract is not fulfilled the whole contract is said to be discharged by breach, but either party may elect to continue with his performance

4   Terms which are implied into a contract by law are always contractual conditions

A   1 and 2 only

B   3 and 4 only

C   1, 2 and 4 only

D   All of them

A B C D

22 Which of the following methods is *not* an effective way to determine the price in a contract in which the details are incomplete?

A   A clause stating it to be 'on usual hire purchase terms'

B   Price to be set at that ruling in the market on the day of delivery

C   An arbitrator to set the price

D   Price to be set by course of dealing between the parties

A B C D

23   A term may be implied into a contract

1   by statute

2   by trade practice unless an express term overrides it

3   by the court to provide for events not contemplated by the parties

4   by the court to give effect to a term which the parties had agreed upon but failed to express because it was obvious

5   by the court to override an express term which is contrary to normal custom

A   2 and 3 only
B   1, 2 and 4 only
C   1, 4 and 5 only
D   1, 3, 4 and 5 only

A B C D

24   Wincey purchases a nylon and polyester electric blanket from Sleeptight Ltd by mail order. The contract contains the following clauses purporting to exclude Sleeptight's liability.

1   'We accept no liability for death or personal injury caused by this product except where our negligence is proved'

2   'The limit of our liability for loss or damage caused by this product is that of the enclosed Customer Guarantee'

3   'We accept no liability for breach of Section 14 Sale of Goods Act 1979'

4   'The product supplied under this contract satisfies the description applied to it by the catalogue and no liability attaches to the company if this is not so'

5   'Any defect in the company's title to sell the product is not to affect the validity of this contract'

Which of these exclusion clauses will be void if Wincey is (1) a consumer and (2) a business customer?

(1) *Consumer*	(2) *Business customer*
A 1, 3 and 5 only	1 and 5 only
B 3, 4 and 5 only	5 only
C 2, 3, 4 and 5 only	5 only
D All of them	1 and 5 only

A B C D

25 What is the effect of the *'contra proferentem'* rule?

A A person who signs a written contract is deemed to have notice of and accepted the terms contained in it in the absence of misinformation as to their meaning

B A person who seeks to enforce an exclusion clause in a consumer contract must show that it is reasonable

C The working of an exclusion clause will generally, in the absence of absolute clarity, be construed against the party seeking to rely on it

D The court acts on the presumption that an exclusion clause was not intended to work against the main purpose of the contract

A B C D

Chapter 7

26 A court will declare a clause in an employment contract *prima facie* in restraint of trade and void where it is intended to protect

A an employer's customers from being poached by an ex-employee's or a current employee's business

B an employer from competition from an ex-employee

C an employer's trade secrets from being disclosed

D an employer's patents and trade marks from infringement

A B C D

27 How is the 'blue pencil test of deletion' applied by the courts?

A A restraint of trade is deleted if it does not protect a legitimate interest

B A contract containing a clause in restraint of trade is deleted where the restraint is unreasonable between the parties

C A restraint of trade is tested to ensure that it is reasonable from the standpoint of the community

D Words are deleted in a restraint of trade where it is shown that the intention was not to impose such a wide restriction

A B C D

28 Timid Sales Co Ltd requested the Bully Beef Delivery Co Ltd to deliver a quantity of corned beef to their premises in Ludlow. Many previous such orders had been made and satisfied, but on this occasion the van-driver on arrival insisted that Mr Meek, Timid's managing director, sign an agreement increasing the delivery charge by 50%. Mr Meek refused to do so at which the van-driver stated that he would not unload the van and amicable business relations would not continue. Desperate to fulfil sales in order to continue in business, Mr meek signed. Timid Sales Co Ltd now wish to repudiate the agreement. Will it succeed?

A Yes: the contract is unenforceable since the van-driver could not have had authority for such claims

B Yes: The contract is void for misrepresentation

C Yes: the contract is violable for duress

D No: a company as an artificial person cannot be subject to illegitimate pressure and so the contract is binding.

A B C D

29 A misrepresentation is

1 a statement of fact which proves to be untrue

2 a statement of law which proves to be untrue

3 made by one party to the other before the contract is formed in order to induce the latter to enter into the contract

4 made by one party before the contract though the other was not aware of it

5 a statement which affects the plaintiff's judgement

A 2 and 4 only

B 1, 3 and 5 only

C 1,2,3 and 5 only

D All of them

A B C D

Chapter 8

30 Part payment of the contract price may *not* be recovered in exchange for incomplete performance where

A one party has prevented complete performance

B the work has been substantially completed

C part of the work agreed under a fixed sum contract has been completed

D part of the work agreed under a contract payable by instalment has been completed

31 Davina engages Rupert as interior decorator and designer to do up her flat in South Kensington. The contract is for a fixed sum of £7,500. Within the allotted time Rupert informs Davina that the work is completed. On inspection Davina finds that the doorbell does not chime and an aspidistra she requested has not be supplied. Must she pay Rupert?

A Yes: though she may retain the purchase price of the aspidistra and amount for repair of the chimes

B Yes: the contract has been substantially performed and the full £7,500 must be paid

C No: the failures in performance constitute anticipatory breach

D No: performance must be complete, entire and exact so nothing is payable until the defects are put right

A B C D

32 A contract may be discharged on the grounds of personal incapacity to perform a contract of personal service where

1 an employee's ill-health prevents him from performing his duties

2 an employee dies

3 an employee is sent to prison for six months

4 an employee who is a foreign national is called up for military service

5 an employee is a national of a country on whom the UK declares war

A 2 only

B 1, 2 and 4 only

C 2, 3 and 5 only

D 1, 2, 3 and 4 only

A B C D

33 Where there has been anticipatory breach of contract the injured party is entitled to sue

A after a reasonable time

B only from the moment the other party actually breaches a contractual condition

C from the moment the other party indicates that he does not intend to be bound

D from the moment the injured party has fulfilled his obligations but the other party indicates that he does not intend to be bound

A B C D

Chapter 9

34 Andrew approaches Trading Post & Co and tells them that he is acting as agent on behalf of Petronella. Relying on his assurance, Trading Post & Co sell goods to Andrew on credit but the account is never settled. Petronella has never heard of Andrew and disputes the claim. Who is liable and on what ground?

A Andrew the claim – because he acted outside his actual and apparent authority as agent and so is personally bound

B Andrew the claim – because his principal is non-existent

C Petronella claim – because she is estopped from denying the validity of Andrew's acts on her behalf

D Petronella claim – because as a dislosed principal she is bound

A B C D

35 Alice, a book-keeper, agrees to act as Peregrine's agent in managing his portfolio of investments. In which of the following situations *must* she perform the task described herself?

A Peregrine asks her to write up his ledgers in return for remuneration of £5 an hour

B Peregrine asks her to sell £500 of shares in a company listed on The Stock Exchange

C Peregrine asks her as a favour to complete a stock transfer form for him

D Peregrine asks her to acquire shares in a public company on which he has inside information for a fee of £50

A B C D

36 Which one of the following is *not* a consequence of an agent accepting a bribe?

A The agent may be dismissed by the principal at the latter's option

B The principal may recover the amount of the bribe from the agent

C The principal may refuse to pay the agent his agreed remuneration

D The principal may repudiate the contract with the third party, but may not sue him to recover damages for any loss

A B C D

37 Which of the following does *not* describe the legal position following ratification by a principal of his agent's contract?

  A The principal may sue the third party on the contract

  B The agent is no longer liable for exceeding his authority

  C The principal is liable to pay the agent reasonable remuneration

  D The agent may be sued by the third party on the contract

A B C D

Chapter 10

38 George owns a used car sales business in Petty France. He currently possesses a range of motors including two Citroen 2CVs, one red and one beige, both of which have a retail price of £2,000. Clotilde contacts him and agrees to purchase the next day a 2CV from him for £2,000. Under the Sale of Goods Act 1979, the 2CV in the contracts would be classified as

  A specific goods

  B existing unascertained goods

  C existing ascertained goods

  D future goods

A B C D

39 The rule that only an owner or his agent may transfer title in goods to a buyer is expressed by the Latin maxim

  A *caveat emptor*

  B *delegatus non potest delegare*

  C *nemo dat quod non habet*

  D *volenti non fit injuria*

A B C D

Chapter 11

40 Doreen enters into an agreement with Michael to buy a Ford Escort XR3 for £7,500. She takes the car with her having paid a 20% deposit, and agrees to pay the remainder in 12 monthly instalments of £550. They agree that Doreen is to be treated as the car's owner only on payment of the final instalment. This transaction is a

  A conditional sale agreement

  B hire purchase agreement

  C credit sale agreement

  D consumer hire agreement

A B C D

NOTES

41 What is the APR (annual percentage rate)?

A The rate per annum at which simple interest on a credit agreement is calculated

B The rate per annum which equals the present value of all repayments of credit under the agreement

C The rate per annum which equals the present value of all credit and the total charge for credit repayments under the agreement

D The rate per annum such that the sum of the present values of all repayments of credit and the total charge for credit equals the sum of the present values of all credits when calculated at that rate

A B C D

42 Which of the following statements regarding cancellation of a debtor-creditor agreement for unrestricted-use credit are true?

1 The debtors must repay the amount of the loan so far received

2 Repayments of the loan must be made in accordance with the terms as to timing and method set out in the cancelled agreement

3 Repayment of the loan on giving notice of cancellation can be made without paying any interest

4 Repayment of the loan before the first instalment was due can be made without paying any interest

A All of them
B 1, 2 and 3 only
C 1 and 4 only
D 1 only

A B C D

43 A hire purchase agreement provides that the creditor shall be entitled to terminate the agreement in the event of the debtor becoming insolvent. Before the period of the contract has expired, the debtor becomes insolvent. The creditor is not entitled to terminate the agreement unless

A he obtains a court order
B he serves a default notice
C he gives the debtor seven days' notice in prescribed form
D at least one-third of the total price has been paid

A B C D

44 To which of the following areas does the Consumer Credit Act 1974 apply even though credit given is greater than £15,000?

    A Charge cards
    B Extortionate credit bargains and liability of creditor for supplier's misrepresentations and/or breach of contract
    C Extortionate credit bargains, charge cards and agreements with companies
    D Liability for supplier's misrepresentations and breach, and agreement with companies

A B C D

Chapter 12

45 Which of the following statutes contain the law relating to trade descriptions?

    1 Trade Descriptions Act 1968
    2 Consumer Protection Act 1987
    3 Fair Trading Act 1973
    4 Supply of Goods and Services Act 1982

    A 1 3, and 4 only
    B 1 and 3 only
    C 1 and 2 only
    D All of them

A B C D

46 Which of the following is not a function of the Director General of Fair Trading?

    1 To identify and eliminate harmful practices
    2 To take direct action against individual traders
    3 To promote codes of practice
    4 To act as arbitrator between traders

    A 1 3, and 4 only
    B 1, 2 and 3 only
    C 1 and 3 only
    D All of them

A B C D

Chapter 13

47 Which of the following are within the remit of the Director General of Fair Trading?

    1 Reporting on monopolies and mergers
    2 Undertaking investigations into anti-competitive practices
    3 Registering restrictive trade practices

    A 1 and 3 only
    B 2 and 3 only
    C 1 and 2 only
    D All of them

A B C D

48 Which of the following represents a monopoly?

1 30% of the cabbages in the UK are supplied by the Healthy Veg Co

2 20% of the market for tights is satisfied by a single manufacturer

3 35% of the market for apples in the South East is supplied by a producer in Kent

4 Paul's company purchases 50% of the bricks manufactured in the UK

A 1, 2 and 3
B 2, 3 and 4
C 1, 3 and 4
D All of them

A B C D

49 Which articles of the Treaty of Rome are concerned with competition?

A Articles 35 and 36
B Articles 45 and 46
C Articles 65 and 66
D Articles 85 and 86

A B C D

50 Which of the following restrictions, if contained in an agreement, would constitute a registerable restrictive trade practice?

1 Prices to be charged

2 Prices to be recommended

3 Quantities to be supplied

4 The classes of person to whom they are to be supplied

A 1, 2 and 3
B 1, 3 and 4
C 2 and 3 only
D All of them

A B C D

Chapter 14

51 In tort the rule that there must be a relationship of cause and effect between the wrong *(injuria)* and the damage *(damnum)* means that

A a person will be liable for loss rising out of his wrongful action or omission if *damnum* is not too remote from *injuria*

B a person who commits an *injuria* with the intention of causing *damnum* will only be liable if the latter is to remote

C a person will never be liable for *damnum* arising out of another person's intervention in his *injuria* so as to break the chain of causation

D a person can never be vicariously liable for another person's *injuria* when the *damnum* is not its immediate effect

A B C D

52 Since the decision in *The Wagon Mound 1961* the test for the recoverability of damages in general tort is that

A the loss or damage was reasonably foreseeable by the defendant only

B the loss or damage was reasonably foreseeable by both plaintiff and defendant

C the loss or damage was the direct and natural consequence of the defendant's breach of duty

D the loss or damage caused by something under the defendant's control was of a kind which would not have been suffered but for the defendant's negligence

A B C D

53 Which of the following requirements must be satisfied before an employer will be vicariously liable for the torts of his employee?

1 The employee must have a written employment contract with the employer at the time of the tort

2 A contract of service must exist between employee and employer

3 The employee must, at the time of the tort, be carrying out the work for which he was employed

4 If the employee is doing the work for which he was employed at the time it is immaterial if he disobeys orders as to how he shall do it

A 1 and 3 only
B 2 and 4 only
C 2, 3 and 4 only
D All of them

A B C D

54 Which one of the following statements is not true of the defence in tort known as *volenti non fit injuria* (consent)?

A True consent must be freely given and be more than a mere knowledge of risk

B An employee, by accepting or continuing in a job, consents to abnormal risks created by his employer if he is aware of them

C Consent to a known risk maybe implied even if the actual consequences of taking the risk are exceptional

D This defence could be raised against an action in tort brought by a patient against a surgeon

A B C D

55 Chris leaves his horse-drawn dray-cart in the street while he delivers beer to a free-house. The horse bolts and Neil, a passer-by, is badly injured when he successfully manages to restrain it. What is the consequence of these events?

A Neil can sue Chris in tort only if he can show that his rescue prevented other persons for being injured

B Neil can sue Chris in tort on the basis that the need for his rescue was created by Chris

C Chris can raise *volenti non fit injuria* as a defence against a claim by Neil

D Chris can raise Neil's contributory negligence as a defence against any claim by Neil.

A B C D

Chapter 15

56 Which of the following elements must be present for a duty of care to exist?

1 There must be a sufficient relationship of proximity between defendant and plaintiff

2 It must be reasonable that the defendant should foresee that damage might arise from his carelessness

3 The plaintiff must have acted in good faith and without carelessness

4 It must be just and reasonable for the law to impose liability

A B C D

57 Below are four circumstances in which Virginia, a writer, suffers nervous shock

1   Virginia is trapped in her flat during a fire downstairs caused by the negligence of Margaret

2   Virginia returns from shopping to find her flat on fire, an event caused by Douglas's negligence

3   Virginia is working at her desk when she hears an accident in the road outside. She moves outside and sees the aftermath of a collision between a bus and an unknown cyclist

4   Virginia leaves the only copy of a manuscript on which she has worked for two years with her publisher. She later learns that the manuscript has been destroyed in a fire at the publisher's offices caused by Dennis, a cleaner.

In which of these cases will Virginia receive damages for nervous shock?

A   1 and 2 only
B   3 and 4 only
C   1, 2 and 3 only
D   All of them

A B C D

58 In order to show that there exists a duty of care not to cause financial loss by negligent misstatement, the plaintiff must show that

1   the person making the statement did so in an expert capacity of which the plaintiff was aware

2   the context in which the statement was made was such as to make it likely that the plaintiff would rely on it

3   in making the statement the defendant foresaw that it would be relied upon by the plaintiff

4   the plaintiff had actually relied on the statement

A   1 and 2 only
B   1, 2 and 3 only
C   2, 3 and 4 only
D   All of them

A B C D

59 In order to rely on the maxim of *res ipsa loquitur* it is necessary for the plaintiff in a negligence action to show only that

A it was reasonably foreseeable that the way in which the defendant controlled the thing which caused the injury would result in injury to the plaintiff

B the plaintiff could not reasonably have foreseen that the injury would occur in the way it did

C the thing which caused the injury was under the defendant's management and control and the defendant had not used proper care

D the thing which cause the injury was beyond the management or control of the defendant

A B C D

Chapter 16

60 What is the difference between public nuisance and private nuisance?

	Private nuisance	Public nuisance
A	Unlawful interference with a person's use of his property	A crime
B	A tort of strict liability	A crime
C	A tort of statutory authority	A tort only actionable by the State
D	Unlawful interference with any person's health and comfort	A tort only actionable by the State

A B C D

61 In the tort of defamation, which one of the following persons may not be libelled?

A An individual

B A company

C A special register trade union

D A partnership

A B C D

Chapter 17

62 The case of *Salomon v Salomon 1897* established which important principle of company law?

A   A company and its members are separate legal persons

B   A director cannot take a decision to employ himself and later make a claim against the company as an employee

C   When a company is wound up, directors who knowingly carried on the business with intent to defraud creditors may be made personally liable for the company's liabilities

D   The sale of a business to a company owned by the vendor of the business will be a legal nullity if the sale made no change in the business's commercial position.

A B C D

63 The minimum authorised share capital of a public limited company is

A   £12,500

B   £50,000

C   £100,000

D   £500,000

A B C D

64 Mr Bayleaf is a gardener who is also sole owner and major creditor of Pressedflower Ltd, a company which sells preserved rare flowers. He has sold to the company the entire crop of rare orchids raised on his large country estate. Being a prudent man, he insures the orchids on his land, the policy being issued with Mr Bayleaf named as the person insured. Two weeks later the entire crop is eaten by a horde of giant locusts. He claims under his policy, but the insurance company denies liability, despite the fact that the policy specifically includes a clause covering destruction by locusts or other pests. Is Mr Bayleaf's claim valid?

A   Yes: he has an insurable interest in the orchids

B   No: he has no insurable interest in the orchids

C   Yes: although he has no insurable interest in the orchids, he does have one in the debt which would be adversely affected by damage to company property

D   Yes: although he has no insurable interest in the orchids, he does have one in the price of his shares, which would be adversely affected by damage to company property.

A B C D

65   Which of the following is not a situation in which
      the court will 'lift the veil of incorporation'?

      A   Where the members or managers are using the
          veil to evade their legal obligations
      B   Where the directors are in breach of the
          regulations governing the giving of financial
          assistance for the purchase of the company's
          own shares
      C   Where the true nationality of the company is
          being concealed
      D   Where it is suspected that the company is
          controlled by enemy aliens during wartime.

      A   B   C   D

66   What is the minimum number of directors which a
      private company is required to have?

      A   One
      B   Two
      C   Four
      D   Seven

      A   B   C   D

Chapter 18

67   Section 36(4) Companies Act 1985 governs the
      positions of the parties to a pre-incorporation
      contract. It will *not* apply where

      A   no action whatsoever has been taken to begin
          the formation of the company, and both parties
          are aware of this
      B   no action whatsoever has been taken to begin
          the formation of a company, even if one of the
          parties is not aware of this
      C   where there is an implied 'agreement to the
          contrary'
      D   where there is an express 'agreement to the
          contrary'

      A   B   C   D

68   Prior to registration a number of documents must be
      delivered to the registrar. Which one of the following
      is *not* essential at this stage?

      A   The memorandum of association
      B   A statement on the prescribed form of the first
          director(s), secretary and address of the
          registered office
      C   A declaration on the prescribed form that the
          requirements of the Companies Act in respect
          of registration have been complied with
      D   A statement on the prescribed form of the dates
          of the company's accounting year

      A   B   C   D

69 How many persons must sign the original memorandum of a company?

    A One
    B Two
    C Four
    D Seven

A B C D

Chapter 19

70 The annual accounts of a company must be made up to

    A the date of the end of the accounting reference period always
    B a date falling within seven days before or after the end of the accounting reference period
    C a date falling within ten days before or after the end of the accounting reference period
    D a date falling within five days before or after the end of the accounting reference period

A B C D

71 A small or medium-sized company

    A need not deliver a copy of its accounts to the registrar at all
    B need not deliver full accounts to the registrar
    C need not circulate its accounts to its members
    D need not have its accounts audited

A B C D

72 In the general meeting of Bowen plc, the members of the company reject the accounts when they are laid before them. The result of this is that

    A the accounts are still valid and need not be altered
    B the accounts are declared invalid and must be prepared again and re-submitted to a general meeting
    C the accounts remain *prima facie* valid, but must be redrawn by the auditors and resubmitted to a general meeting
    D the accounts remain *prima facie* valid, but must be re-drawn by different auditors and re-submitted to a general meeting

A B C D

73 Who is entitled (apart from the registrar where appropriate) to receive a copy of a company's statutory accounts?

    A Every member of the company
    B Every member of the company and every debentureholder only
    C Members who hold voting shares only
    D All members without charge and all other members of the public on payment of a fee

A B C D

74 Auditors may be appointed by
A the general meeting only
B the general meeting and the directors only
C the general meeting, directors or the DTI only
D the general meeting, directors, DTI or the companies court

A B C D

Chapter 20

75 If a company's name is to be altered, what method must be used?
A Special resolution
B Extraordinary resolution
C Ordinary resolution with special notice
D Ordinary resolution

A B C D

76 What is an *ultra vires* action?
A An illegal act for which a company cannot be given capacity
B An act beyond the directors' power, for which the company has the capacity but the directors do not have the authority
C An act beyond the company's capacity to contract as defined by its objects clause
D An act which is beyond the established commercial activities of the company

A B C D

77 Which of the following persons are *not* contractually bound to one another by the memorandum and articles?
A Members to company
B Company to members
C Members to members
D Company to third parties

A B C D

78 Where the Companies Act permits a company to do something if its articles authorise it, but there is no provision actually made in the articles of the company on the matter, what is the position?
A Since the Act overrides any conflict with a company's articles, the company can exercise the statutory power
B The company can exercise the statutory power, but must alter its articles to include the necessary power *before* exercising the statutory power
C The company can exercise the statutory power, but must alter its articles to include the power within six months
D The company can exercise the statutory power but must alter its articles to include the power within 12 months

A B C D

79 Boris has been appointed as managing director under a service agreement which will expire in three years' time.

The company proposes to alter its articles to confer on its holding company power to remove any director from office. It further proposes to exercise the power to remove Boris from the board, thus automatically also removing him from his position as managing director. What can Boris, who does not want to be removed, do to protect his position?

A Boris can apply to the court under s 459 for an injunction restraining the company from making the alteration

B Boris cannot restrain the company from making the alteration, but may obtain an order for specific performance of his service contract as managing director

C Boris cannot restrain the company either from making the alteration or from removing him from the board, but can claim damages for breach of contract

D Boris has no remedy; the alteration of the articles and the exercise of the new power are unfettered by his service contract as managing director, so no claim for an injunction or damages can arise

A B C D

Chapter 21

80 The term 'authorised share capital' is best defined as:

A the total amount of share capital which the company is authorised to issue by the capital clause of its memorandum

B the total mount of share capital which the board of directors may from time to time decide to issue

C the total amount of shares which have been allotted to members

D the aggregate amount of shares which have been fully paid up

A B C D

81 If a company wishes to increase the amount of its authorised share capital, what type of resolution is required by the standard form Table A articles?

A Ordinary resolution

B Extraordinary resolution

C Ordinary resolution with special notice

D Special resolution

A B C D

82 Before offering shares to the public, a company allots £6,000 (nominal) shares as fully paid to Uhura and Sulu for services given in the formation of the company. In fact no such services have been given. Eighteen months later the company goes into liquidation, and the liquidator, Mr Klingon, contends that £6,000 is due on the shares as no consideration had been given. What is the legal position?

A Uhura and Sulu have no liability on the shares, since the due process of allotment has been properly completed and this is valid and conclusive

B Uhura and Sulu have no liability on the shares since the allotment is a nullity and they therefore do not hold them in the first place

C Uhura and Sulu are liable on the grounds given by Mr Klingon

D Uhura and Sulu are in principle liable but need not pay anything in practice since the shares are now worthless, and they cannot be compelled to subscribe for shares at an over-value

A B C D

83 Thunderbird Ltd, a company which sells aeroplanes, lends £250,000 to Stingray Ltd, to allow Stingray to purchase shares of Thunderbird from shareholders who are also directors of Thunderbird. Thunderbird later goes into liquidation, and the liquidator seeks to recover the money from the directors of Thunderbird. Can he do so?

A No: all companies selling goods have a power incidental to that business to lend money

B Yes: all such transactions are unlawful

C No: this is an ordinary business loan

D Yes: the transaction is *prima facie* invalid, and does not fall into any of the relevant exceptions to the general rule

A B C D

84 What is the minimum percentage of the issued shares (or class of share) that must be held by members who wish to apply to the court to object to a private company giving financial assistance for the acquisition of its own shares?

A 5%

B 10%

C 15%

D 30%

A B C D

Chapter 22

85 Which of the following elements might be contained in a debenture trust deed?

1. The appointment of a trustee for prospective debenture stockholders
2. A definition of the nominal amount of debenture stock
3. The date or period of repayment
4. The rate of interest
5. A register of debenture stockholders
6. Provisions for meetings of debenture stockholders

A 1, 2, 3, 4 and 6 only
B 1, 2, 5 and 6 only
C 2, 3 and 4 only
D 1, 3 and 4 only

A B C D

86 Shares and debentures have much in common. Which one of the following is *untrue* of the two forms of capital?

A Both are transferable company securities
B An offer of either to the public is a prospectus under the Financial Services Act 1986
C The procedure for the transfer of registered shares and debentures is the same
D The holders of both are proprietors of the company

A B C D

87 Which one of the following is an *incorrect* statement of the relationship between ordinary shares and debentures?

A Debentures do not confer voting rights, whilst ordinary shares do
B The company's duty is to pay interest on debentures, and to pay dividends on ordinary shares
C Interest paid on debentures is deducted from pre-tax profits, share dividends are paid from net profits
D A debentureholder takes priority over a member in liquidation

A B C D

88 In which of the following situations will 'crystallisation' of a floating charge occur?

1. Liquidation of the company
2. Disposal by the company of the charged asset
3. Cessation of the company's business
4. After the giving of notice by the chargee if the contract so provides
5. The appointment of an administrative receiver

A 1, 3, 4 and 5 only
B 1, 2, 3 and 5 only
C 2 and 5 only
D 1 and 5 only

A B C D

89 Section 396 requires registration for nine types of fixed and floating charge. What is the maximum time allowed for such registration?

A 21 days
B 28 days
C 1 month
D 3 months

A B C D

Chapter 23

90 Mr Flay and Mr Swelter are first directors of a company. They quarrel, and Mr Swelter forges an entry in the board minutes to record the appointment of Mr Steerpike as a director. Messrs Swelter and Steerpike then purport to co-opt Mr Fluke as a director. No general meeting is held within the time allowed for the first AGM at which Messrs Flay and Swelter should have retired and offered themselves for re-election, so they both cease to be directors. At a board meeting, Messrs Swelter and Steerpike purport to allot shares to Mr Fluke, but this is later challenged by Mr Flay, arguing that neither Mr Swelter or Mr Steerpike were at the time directors, so they had no power to allot shares. Will Mr Flay's claim to rectify the register of members succeed?

A No: the acts of a director are (by statute) valid notwithstanding the defects which have occurred here

B No: although the fraud in the appointment of Mr Steerpike invalidates his position, Mr Swelter is covered by statute and his acts are taken as valid

C Yes: the statute validates only the acts of those appointed defectively – here (being fraudulent) there is no appointment of Mr Steerpike, and Mr Swelter's appointment, though valid, has expired

D No: although Mr Swelter and Mr Steerpike's actions are invalid, Mr Fluke is a third party who had no way of knowing this, so he is protected in his transactions

A B C D

91 The articles of a company contain a power to appoint a managing director, but this is never done. One of the directors, to the knowledge (but without the *express* authority) of the remainder of the board, acts as if he were managing director in arranging a contract. Later, the company refuses to honour the contract. Is the company bound by the contract?

A No. The director had no apparent or actual authority

B No. The director may have had apparent authority, but he had no actual authority

C Yes. The director had actual authority, and this is the crucial thing

D Yes. The director had apparent authority, the company had acquiesced to this, and this is enough to bind it

A B C D

92 If a claimant is to succeed in a claim under the principle of 'holding out', which of the following elements must he show to have taken place?

1 A representation was made to him that the agent had the authority to enter into the contract on behalf of the company

2 The representation was made by a person with actual authority to manage the company's business

3 He relied on the representation

4 There is nothing in the memorandum or articles to prevent the agent from being given valid authority to enter into the contract on the company's behalf

A 1 and 4 only

B 1, 2 and 3 only

C All of them

D 1 and 3 only

A B C D

93 Mr Machiavelli is managing director of a company which has just failed to win a large contract. Feigning a rare disease, he persuades the company to release him from his service agreement. Now that he is no longer a director, he feels free to attempt to obtain the contract for himself, which he successfully does. Is he accountable for his profit when the company sues him?

A Yes: he is accountable in this situation

B No, since he is no longer a director and therefore no longer owes any duty

C No, since the company could not have obtained the contract anyway and therefore lost nothing

D No, since the company chose to release him from his service agreement and therefore from his obligations to it

A B C D

94 If a director fails to give notice of an interest in a
    contract made with the company as required by s
    317, the contract is
    A automatically void
    B voidable by the company
    C voidable by either party   A B C D
    D valid, but the director may be held to account
       for his profit

Chapter 24

95 What is the maximum period that may elapse
    between one AGM and the next?
    A 12 months
    B 15 months
    C 18 months   A B C D
    D 20 months

96 When members requisition an EGM, the date set for
    it to take place must be within
    A 28 days
    B 1 calendar month
    C 8 weeks   A B C D
    D 3 months

97 The right of a member to appoint a proxy is
    A statutory
    B conferred by the articles
    C at the chairman's discretion   A B C D
    D at the board's discretion

98 What proportion of votes cast is required to pass a
    special resolution?
    A A simple majority
    B A two-thirds majority
    C A three-quarters majority   A B C D
    D A 95% majority

99 A special resolution is put to the vote on a show of
    hands. The chairman declares '6 for and 23 against,
    but there are 200 voting for the resolution by proxy
    and I declare the resolution carried.' Is this valid?
    A Yes: proxy votes are as valid as the votes of the
       members present
    B No: the votes of members present take precedence
       over proxy votes
    C No: proxies may vote on a poll, but not a show   A B C D
       of hands
    D Yes: since (had there be a poll) it is self-evident
       what the result *would* have been, the voting
       will stand.

Chapter 25

100 In an action brought on the grounds of fraud on the minority, it must be shown that

  A those who appropriated the company's property are in control of the company

  B those who appropriated the company's property held sufficient voting rights to exert a 'significant influence' over the company's affairs

  C those who are bringing the action hold at least 5% of the voting rights

  D those who are bringing the action hold at least 5% of the voting rights and have suffered a personal loss in their capacity as members

A B C D

101 From decided case law, in which of the following situations can an action for fraud on the minority *not* be brought?

  A Where profitable contracts have been diverted away from the company to the directors, but the general meeting has ratified this action

  B Where the directors have caused the company to sell the property at a price lower than valuation to a third party

  C Where the property has passed to the directors, but there is no evidence of dishonesty

  D Where the minority attempting to bring the complaint hold only non-noting shares and could therefore not have influenced the decision

A B C D

102 Where the complaint is of the exclusion of a 'partner' from participation in the management of a quasi-partnership, it is necessary to show that there had been

  1 bad faith

  2 an intention to discriminate

  3 prejudice to a member as a member

  4 prejudice to a member as a member or as an employee

  5 prejudice to a member as a member or as an unpaid creditor

  A 1, 2 and 4 only

  B 2, 3 and 4 only

  C 2 and 4 only

  D 3 only

A B C D

103 Remedies for a successful petition for unfair prejudice are given by s 461. Which of the following are included?

1   An order regulating the future conduct of the company's affairs

2   An authorisation to any person to bring legal proceedings on behalf of the company

3   An order to restrain the company from a particular course of action

4   Inclusion in the memorandum of provisions which may only be altered thereafter by leave of the court

5   Inclusion in the articles of provisions which may only be altered thereafter by leave of the court

A   1, 3 and 4
B   1, 2 and 5
C   All of them
D   3 only

A B C D

104 Where the court orders the purchase of the share of a dissentient minority which of the following is *not* the case?

A   The court decides the fair price
B   The basis of the valuations is the worth of the shares before the majority's actions diminished it
C   an allowance must be made for the fact that the shares are only a minority (and therefore a non-controlling) holding
D   Such a purchase may be ordered to be made by the company or the controlling shareholder

A B C D

Chapter 26

105 In which of the following ways can dissolution of a company be made to occur?

1   By order of the court, without a winding-up, under s 427(3)(d) Companies Act 1985

2   By act of Parliament

3   By cancellation of registration on application for judicial review by the Attorney-General

4   On application by the Official Receiver for early dissolution

A   1 and 2 only
B   3 and 4 only
C   2, 3 and 4 only
D   All of them

A B C D

106 A liquidator's actions are

    A valid even if his appointment or his qualifications are defective

    B valid if his appointment is defective, but not if his qualifications are defective

    C invalid if his appointment is defective, but not merely because his qualifications are defective

    D invalid if there is a defect in either his appointment or his qualifications

A B C D

107 What is the minimum amount which must be owed (and unpaid) to creditors to enable them to petition the court to wind up a company on the grounds that it is unable to pay its debts?

    A £500

    B £750

    C £1,000

    D £1,500

A B C D

108 In which of the following situations have orders for compulsory winding up under the 'just and equitable' ground been made?

    1 The main object of the company can no longer be achieved

    2 The company was formed for an illegal or fraudulent purpose

    3 There is a complete deadlock in the management of the company's affairs

    4 The understandings between members or directors have been unfairly breached by lawful action

    5 The directors have deliberately withheld information so that the shareholders have no confidence in the company's management

    A 1 and 5 only

    B 2, 3 and 4 only

    C 1, 2, 3 and 5 only

    D All of them

A B C D

109 A creditors' voluntary winding up not commenced as a members' voluntary winding up is begun by passing

    A a special resolution only

    B an extraordinary resolution only

    C an ordinary resolution with special notice only

    D a resolution of the appropriate type, which will vary according to the circumstances of each case

A B C D

EXAM STYLE QUESTIONS

Chapter 1

1 EQUITY AND THE COMMON LAW

Explain from the historical viewpoint the origin and development of the relationship between equity and the common law.

Chapter 2

2 COURTS

Watt, a manufacturer of electrical heaters, markets a new model which, contrary to safety regulations, has faulty wiring. Purchase buys one of these heaters from Sellors, a retailer. When Purchase uses the heater he is badly burned and some of the clothing of his wife, Vera, is destroyed. A criminal prosecution is now pending and both Purchase and his wife are seeking compensation.

You are required to explain:

(a) briefly, the grounds upon which Purchase and his wife may bring actions;

(b) the persons against whom these actions will be brought;

(c) the court(s) in which the civil actions will be brought and the provisions which exist for appeal;

(d) the court(s) which will deal with the criminal prosecution and the provisions which exist for appeal.

Chapter 3

3 EC LAW

Article 189 of the Treaty of Rome provides that 'in order to carry out their task the Council and the Commission shall, in accordance with the provisions of this Treaty, make regulations, issue directives, take decisions, make recommendations or deliver opinions'.

Explain the effect of regulations, directives and decisions. What do you understand by the terms 'directly applicable' and 'direct effect'?

Chapter 4

4 ARBITRATION AND TRIBUNALS

Explain the nature and significance of arbitration and tribunals as a means of settling legal disputes.

What are the advantages of using this means of settling disputes over the ordinary courts?

Chapter 5

5 NOTICE IN WRITING

(a) To what extent is it correct to say that an acceptance is effective only when it has been communicated to the offeror by the offeree?

(b) Seller Ltd wrote to Buyer Ltd on 1 February 1995 offering to sell various items of plant and machinery for £20,000. The letter included the following statement.

'Notice in writing of your acceptance of this offer must be received by the sales director by 14 February 1995.'

Buyer Ltd decided to accept the offer and posted its acceptance on 8 February 1995. In addition, the managing director of Buyer Ltd telephoned Seller Ltd and asked to speak to the sales director. Unfortunately, he was out of the office, so a message was left with his secretary confirming Buyer Ltd's acceptance of the offer.

Buyer Ltd has since discovered that Seller Ltd's sales director never received the letter of acceptance, and that the secretary forgot to inform him of the telephone call. Consequently, the plant and machinery has been sold to Exe Ltd.

Explain whether Seller Ltd may be held liable for breach of contract.

Chapter 6

6 FREEDOM

It is difficult to exclude or limit liability when entering a contract.

In what ways has freedom to contract in this respect been restricted by:

(a) the courts;

(b) the Unfair Contract Terms Act 1977.

Chapter 7

7 REMEDIES FOR MISREPRESENTATION

D wishes to purchase a new computing system for his office. D wants it to run a particular spreadsheet and E, the computer salesman, assures him that the proposed system is capable of running the spreadsheet, believing this to be the case. Ten days later D signs a contract for the purchase of the system which makes no mention of the spreadsheet. During that period E discovered that the system was not capable of running the spreadsheet, but he had forgotten that he had discussed it with D and he did not mention it further.

D paid £500 for the system. When he tried to operate the spreadsheet software all his data held on disk was corrupted. Over £3,000 worth of information was lost.

Advise D of any remedies he may have in the law of contract for misrepresentation.

(Note: your answer should not include discussion of possible remedies under the Sale of Goods Act 1979.)

Chapter 8

8 FRUSTRATION

Laggard agreed to make and supply to Abel a piece of machinery by a certain date and in accordance with certain specifications. Delivery was late and the specifications were not followed.

Laggard pleads that the delay was caused by a shortage of labour. An outbreak of food poisoning at his works canteen had led to many employees being ill and this had then been followed by a strike. He also pleads that new safety regulations had made the machines more expensive to manufacture and that he had been obliged to economise by using cheaper materials.

Explain any remedies which may be available to Abel.

Chapter 9

9 UNDISCLOSED PRINCIPAL

(a) Explain how the doctrine of the undisclosed principal forms an exception to the general rule of privity of contract.

(b) Principal Ltd is a manufacturer of machine tools for industry. Agent Ltd is the company's sole agent for the UK. In November 1995 Agent Ltd accepted an order from TZ plc for 5,000 tools to be delivered on 1 January 1996. This was in breach of the agreement between Principal Ltd and Agent Ltd, which specified that no single sale should exceed 3,000 tools.

Explain whether these facts may give rise to any liability on the part of Principal Ltd or Agent Ltd.

Chapter 10

10 ARTHUR

Arthur is extremely interested in cycling. He recently saw an advertisement in a local newspaper placed there by Cycle Mania Shops Ltd, advertising for sale a second-hand mountain bicycle and stating that it was 'in excellent condition and the latest model'. Arthur visited the shop and was shown the bicycle. The salesman confirmed that it was only three months old, was the latest model, had hardly been used and was in excellent condition.

Arthur purchased the bicycle. Eight weeks after taking delivery of it he discovered that it had had a major repair to its frame following an accident. He has also discovered that it is not the latest model.

Arthur now wishes to return the cycle and recover the money he paid for it.

Advise him as to his rights, if any, under the Sale of Goods Act 1979.

Chapter 12

11 CONSUMER PROTECTION

Frances and her husband James invited their friends Neil and Hannah to dinner at their home. The first item on the menu was prawn cocktail, which Frances had prepared earlier in the day. She had bought the frozen prawns from Greg's Grocers, a local retailer, who in turn had bought them from Special Seafoods Ltd.

As a result of eating the prawn cocktails, all four were violently ill for a number of weeks. James was sick on the Oriental rug which was ruined as a result. Neil's new silk shirt was also ruined.

The doctor informed them that they were suffering from a rare form of food poisoning caused by a bacteria unknown in this country and thought to be caused by defrosting prawns and then re-freezing them.

Discuss whether James, Neil and Hannah could claim compensation for the injuries and loss that they have suffered.

Chapter 14

12 VICARIOUS LIABILITY

To what extent is an employer liable for wrongful acts committed by those who work for him?

Chapter 15

13 SPENDER

Spender is a customer of the Barland Bank. He asks Masters, the branch manager, for a statement of his account and Masters instructs Penn, a bank clerk, to provide this statement. Penn does so carelessly and misleads Spender into believing that his financial position is much better than is actually the case.

In reliance upon this, Spender embarks upon a financial transaction and suffers loss when he is obliged to withdraw through shortage of funds.

Advise Spender as to

(a) the grounds upon which he may seek to obtain compensation;

(b) against whom his claim may be made.

Chapter 17

14 PUBLIC AND PRIVATE COMPANIES

What are the differences between the requirements for being a private and a public limited company? In what circumstances would you advise a client to register a company as a public limited company?

Chapter 18

15 XYZ PLC

The Board of XYZ plc is considering the registration of a new private company limited by shares, in order to pursue a business outside the normal scope of XYZ plc's activities. The Board wishes to call the new subsidiary company 'Tee Ltd'.

Write a memorandum to the Board listing, and where appropriate stating the purpose of, the documents which have be to be submitted to the Registrar of companies in order to form a new company limited by shares.

Chapter 19

16 AUDITORS

(a) How may a company remove an auditor from office before the expiration of his term of office?

(b) What can, and what must, the auditor do when he leaves office for any reason?

(c) What statutory duty does the auditor owe to the company he is auditing? What can the company do if it believes the auditor has been negligent in his duties to the company?

Guidance notes

1   Part (a) should be a straightforward statement of fact.

2   In part (b) it is important to distinguish

   (i)   between the general rules relating to any auditor, and the specific rules that relate to auditors who are resigning or being removed other than at the annual general meeting; and

   (ii) between what the auditor must do on departure from office, and what he has the power to do.

3   In part (c) we are not concerned with the individual shareholder, but the company. You should not therefore write all you know about the *Caparo* and *James McNaughton* cases.

Chapter 20

17 ARTICLES OF ASSOCIATION

(a) To what extent is it correct to say that a company's articles of association form a contract between the members and the company?

(b) The Articles of Association of Retailer Ltd include the following provisions.

Article 1: K is to be the company's managing director for life at a salary of £50,000 per annum plus such annual bonus as shall be agreed by the company in general meeting.

Article 2: Any member who wishes to sell his shares must offer them to the directors who will purchase them at the price determined by the auditors.

Explain whether the Articles may be relied upon

(i) by K to obtain compensation in the event of the company dismissing him; and

(ii) by L if the board should refuse to purchase her shares in the company.

Chapter 21

18 H Ltd

H Ltd is a manufacturing company and controls all the shares in S Ltd. The latter company has the same board of directors as H Ltd and was incorporated to provide retail outlets for H Ltd's products. The board has resolved to withdraw from retailing, and to find a buyer for H Ltd's shares in S Ltd. The employees of S Ltd have been informed of this decision and have submitted the following proposal to the board.

First, the employees will incorporate a new company, B Ltd, to facilitate a 'buy-out'. Secondly, S Ltd will be asked to provide financial assistance to B Ltd, either by lending the necessary funds direct, or by agreeing to allow its assets to be used as security for a bank loan.

The board has agreed to consider this proposal at its next meeting and has asked you as the company's management accountant to provide certain background information.

You are required to prepare a report for the directors explaining:

(a) the extent to which the law permits S Ltd to provide financial assistance by either of the above methods; and

(b) the procedure which must be followed.

Chapter 22

19 DEBENTURES

Explain the following in connection with debentures.

(a) The differences between shares and debentures

(b) The rules concerning the priority of charges

(c) How secured creditors can enforce their security against the company

Chapter 23

20 SHAREHOLDER CONTROL

You are required to explain:

(a) the extent to which the law seeks to enable shareholders to exercise control over their company's board of directors;

(b) whether the law achieves that objective.

Chapter 24

21 GLAD

Glad Ltd, a company regulated by Table A, has a paid up issued share capital of 30,000 £1 shares. There are three director shareholders (Tom, Dick, and Harry) who each hold 9,500 shares. The remaining 1,500 shares are held by Len.

The directors wish to appoint Bill as managing director. Bill is prepared to invest £10,000 in the company by way of shares on condition that the company changes its name to Sorry Ltd. In order to permit this investment it will be necessary to increase the company's share capital and to give the directors authority to issue shares. The directors wish that this authority shall be for an indefinite period.

Time is of the essence. Tom, a director, approaches you on behalf of the board. He has heard of the written resolution procedure and the short notice procedure. He believes that these may be a help in the speedy resolution of these issues.

Tom raises the following questions with you.

(a) What is the written resolution procedure? Can any company matter be dealt with by this procedure?

(b) What is the short notice procedure?

(c) If the company calls a general meeting to give effect to the above proposals, what kind of resolutions will have to be passed and how much notice will each resolution require?

(d) Would the company be able to dispense with holding a general meeting and use either the written resolution procedure or short notice procedure if Len objected?

Chapter 25

22 FOSS V HARBOTTLE

You are required to discuss the statutory and common law exceptions to the rule in *Foss v Harbottle 1843* which allow a minority shareholder to bring a legal action to redress a wrong which has been done to the company of which he is a member.

SOLUTIONS TO
MULTIPLE CHOICE QUESTIONS

Chapter 1

1 **B** 'Equity must prevail' is the rule used by judges when there is a conflict between equity and common law. It is derived from a decision by the King in the *Earl of Oxford's case 1615*. The other phrases are statements of principles or 'equitable maxims' which are used to decide whether a person who seeks an equitable remedy should be granted it.

2 **A** A High Court judge sitting alone is only compelled to follow a previous decision if it is binding on him and if the material facts are similar. To do this he must follow the *ratio decidendi*, not the *obiter dicta* (hence option 2 is incorrect). He is only bound by it if it was made by a court of higher status than the High Court – option 4 is incorrect because it includes the decisions of a High Court which in fact are not binding on the future decisions of a High Court.

3 **C** The Court of Appeal is of higher status than a Divisional Court but ranks below the House of Lords – hence it is bound by the latter but not by the former. It is also bound by its own decisions: *Young v Bristol Aeroplane Co 1940*.

4 **A** Parliament may delegate the power to make legislation to local authorities, who thereby are allowed to make bye-laws (option 1). If it is so provided in the enabling act, delegated legislation may have to go through the 40-day 'laying-before' procedures without a resolution against it before it comes into force (option 4). Option 2 is incorrect since ministerial powers are exercised by statutory instrument; Orders in Council are an emergency, not a common, measure. Option 3 is incorrect because unless its act provides otherwise, much delegated legislation is never seen by Parliament.

5 **D** Although an Act may rebut these presumptions by express words, they apply in the absence of any express provision to the contrary. Option 1 is incorrect since in fact the complete opposite is true – an Act applies to the whole of the UK unless it is specially expressed to exclude some part of it.

Chapter 2

6 **D** Punishment is a central tenet of the criminal law, as is the suppression of crime and the protection of society. The aims expressed in Distractors A to C are in fact among those of the civil law.

7 **B** The County Court only has jurisdiction in tort (negligent advice) for claims up to £15,000. Although the cause in Key B is within it scope, the amount of the claim means that it must be heard in the Queens' Bench division of the High Court. The county court has jurisdiction in contract up to £5,000 (Distractor A) and in undefended matrimonial cases (Distractor C). Its jurisdiction over probate matters goes up to £30,000 (Distractor D).

8 **D** *Mandamus* literally means 'we command', and such an order requires the court or other body to carryout a public duty – such as a tribunal being ordered to hear an appeal which it previously refused to do. An order of specific performance (Distractor A) is an equitable remedy *in personam*, given by any court, that the person ordered should do something which he had previously promised to do. The *habeas corpus* order requires the release of a person wrongfully detained (Distractor B). A *certiorari* order (Distractor C) orders a court or tribunal which has taken some action to submit the record of its proceedings to the High Court for review.

9   C   A reversed judgment, as described in Key C, must be distinguished from an overruled one, as described in Distractor B. The former affects the outcome of the actual case while the latter merely affects the standing of the precedent. Distractor A simply describes a minority dissenting judgment while Distractor D describes the judgment which actually overrules the overruled judgment.

Chapter 3

10   C

11   E   Larger states have more votes than smaller states, but the five largest states cannot win a vote against the other seven states combined.

12   D

13   A   Regulations are directly applicable in all states and have direct effect, while directives are not directly applicable, but only apply to those states to which they are addressed.

Chapter 4

14   D   The Employment Appeals Tribunal, despite its name, is in fact a full court with status equal to the High Court.

15   A   Although the right of appeal against an arbitrator's decision or award can be quite limited, the three Distractors B, C and D all describe circumstances in which the Arbitration Act 1979 allows one or both parties to appeal to the court. The parties are allowed, however, to exclude the right to appeal against an arbitrator's award.

Chapter 5

16   B   The intention to create legal relations, whether it is express or implied is an essential element of any valid contract, as is legality and capacity (without which it may be void, voidable or unenforceable). Note that where a minor who otherwise has limited contractual capacity, enters into a contract for necessaries or a service contract he is treated for that purpose as having full capacity. Offer and acceptance (attribute 1) are not required in reward cases, cross-offers and collateral contracts, whilst consideration (attribute 3) is not required where the contract is made by deed. Many contracts have no requirement for writing (attribute 6).

17   B   Revocation of an offer may be communicated by a reliable informant (*Dickinson v Dodds 1876*) but communication of acceptance of an offer may only be made by a person actually authorised to do so (*Powell v Lee 1908*). Hence Neil's brother's purported acceptance for Neil is invalid (Distractor D), but the lodger's communication of revocation to Neil is valid since his presence at the deal makes him a reliable informant (Key B). Tim's promise to keep the offer open was not supported by a separate option agreement and so he was free to sell before such time as he received acceptance (Distractor C). Since the offer was expressed to be kept open for a week, there is no question that Neil failed to accept within a reasonable time so that the offer lapsed (Distractor A).

18 C That a price label, or even a display of goods, is an invitation to the customer to make an offer which the shop may then choose to accept was established in *Fisher v Bell 1961* (among other cases). It is an invitation to treat (Key C).

19 B Consideration need only be sufficient – it need not be adequate: *Thoman v Thomas 1842* (option 1). It can be past consideration in limited cirumstances, such as to support a bill of exchange (option 3). It need not be given in a contract by deed (option 4). Performance of an existing obligation (option 5) cannot support a new contract because there is no extra obligation *(Stilk v Myrick 1809)*. Hence only option 2 is correct – as consideration is the price of a promise, it must be paid the by the person who seeks to enforce it: *Tweddle v Atkinson 1861*.

20 D A promise to waive an existing right given for no consideration is not binding, and Miranda's payment of less than is due is not consideration for Emma's promise: *Foakes v Beer 1884* (Distractor A). Emma would only be estopped from retracting her waiver if she had made it with the intention that Miranda should place reliance on it and Miranda then did so (Distractor B). In fact she made the promise because she needed cash. The fact that her waiver was not entirely voluntary (Distractor C) is irrelevant since this is only an issue if promissory estoppel is claimed: *D & C Builders v Rees 1966*. Hence, because she has received no consideration and she is not affected by promissory estoppel, Emma may claim the £100 balance (Key D).

Chapter 6

21 A Most contractual terms in business agreements are identified as being either conditions or warranties (option 1) – the importance of the distinction being that failure to fulfil the former (option 2) leads to the whole contract being at an end (discharged by breach) whilst breach of warranty leads only to a claim for damages, not to discharge (option 3). An unclassified term as mentioned in option 1 is one which cannot be identified as either a condition or warranty until the effects of failure to fulfil it are known and assessed. Option 4 is incorrect since statute often implies warranties as well as conditions (for example Sale of Goods Act 1979).

22 A Although a legally binding contract must be complete in its terms it is possible to look outside its express terms in order to fix a price so long as the method fixed is not uncertain (as in *Scammell v Ouston 1941*).

23 B Statute can imply a term either by overriding an express term (for example the Sale of Goods Act 1979) or by providing a term which applies unless overridden (for example the Partnership Act 1890). The latter method is also the way in which custom and trade practice imply terms. In order to give 'business efficacy' to an agreement which is only deficient because the parties have failed to provide expressly for something because it was so obvious, the court may also imply terms *(The Moorcock 1889)*. But the court will no imply a term to provide for events not contemplated at the time of agreement (option 3), to contradict an express term (option 5) nor to remedy a defective agreement.

24 C You should have spotted that option 1 merely reiterates s 2(1) Unfair Contract Terms Act 1977 (UCTA) – an exclusion clause relating to death or personal injury is only void if it attempts to exclude liability arising *from negligence*. Where Wincey deals as a consumer, all the other clauses are void; a customer guarantee cannot limit liability for loss or damage (s 5 UCTA); the terms as to merchantable quality and fitness for purpose (s 14 Sale of Goods Act 1979 (SGA) cannot be excluded and the product must comply with its description (s 13 SGA) by virtue of ss 6 and 7 UCTA. No supplier may exclude liability where he supplies goods to which he has no title (term implied by s 12 SGA): s 6(1) UCTA. But where Wincey does not deal as a consumer as defined by s 12 UCTA then only the exclusion clause as to title is void.

25 C Literally this phrase translated means 'against he who is relying'. Anything ambiguous in an exclusion clause is interpreted against the person who is seeking to rely on it. The rules stated in Distractors A and D are true but do not refer to *contra proferentem*. Distractor B is now wholly true since in many consumer contracts an exclusion clause is rendered void by UCTA 1977. In most standard term contracts the person imposing the exclusion clause must show reasonableness in order that a term restricting liability for breach or claiming entitlement to render substantially different or no performance should be binding (s 3 UCTA 1877).

Chapter 7

26 B Although such clauses may be justified, they will be declared *prima facie* void where their only aim is to protect the employer from competition brought about by its employee leaving and setting up in a similar business. Employees should be given the right to exercise their personal skills acquired in the employer's service (*Morris v Saxelby 1916*). But an employer is entitled to protect his customer list (Distractor A) provided the employee in question had close contact with customers (*Fitch v Dewes 1921*), and also to protect its trade secrets (Distractor C); (*Forster & Sons v Suggett 1918*). In both cases the employer is simply trying to protect his business's 'assets' from 'theft' or dilution. Patents and trade-marks are identifiable intangible assets of a business and their protection from infringement is enforced by law as well as by individual contract clauses (Distractor D).

27 D The 'blue pencil test' is a device used by the court to delete words which impose too wide a restraint into an agreement which is otherwise reasonable (*Home Counties Dairies v Skilton 1970* – words 'or other dairy produce' deleted so that only a restriction from selling milk remained on a milkman). Distractors A, B and C all relate to the tests which the court applies to see whether an actual restraint of trade may be justified.

28 C The events described amount to economic duress to which, following *The Atlantic Baron 1979*, a company may be subject (Distractor D). Mr Meeks' refusal to sign was overcome by the van driver's threats to such an extent that his consent was invalidated; the facts are based on the recent case of *Atlas Express Ltd v Kafco (Exporters and Distributors) Ltd 1989*. From the facts as given no misrepresentation was made (Distractor B). A contract entered into outside an agent's authority is void, not unenforceable (Distractor A).

29 B A misrepresentation must also, by definition, be a representation – it must be one of fact (not law, intention, opinion or 'sales talk'), its existence must be known to the other party, the other party must have allowed it to affect this judgement and he must have been unaware of its untruth. The misrepresentation must have been intended to induce the other party to enter into a contract and it must have actually done so – he must rely on it.

Chapter 8

30   C   Where the agreement states that a fixed sum is to be payable this will become due only when precise, exact and complete performance has been rendered. Failure in this respect will not entitle the person to part payment (Key C). Where one party prevents complete performance (Distractor A) the other may claim part payment by way of quantum meruit *(Planche v Colburn 1831)*. A divisible contract (where payment is to be made by instalments) requires that separate payment be made for each tranche or work (Distractor D). The doctrine of substantial performance (Distractor B) states that where work has been completed but a small number of deficiencies remain the contractor is entitled to payment less a deduction (or retention) to cover the cost of the outstanding work *(Hoenig v Isaacs 1952)*.

31   A   Although the contract has been substantially performed, complete performance has not yet been rendered; nevertheless, Davina must pay over most of the £7,500 to Rupert. There is no question of Rupert's minor failings constituting anticipatory breach (Distractor C) since by definition this occurs before the time of performance arrives; in this case the time of performance is already past.

32   D   Because frustration of a contract of personal service, such as an employment contract, occurs when the person is incapable of performance, this will clearly arise where the employee is too ill to work *(Condor v Barron Knights 1966)*, dead, in prison (or Borstal – *FC Shepherd & Co Ltd v Jerrom 1986*) or absent on military service (either in the UK or abroad). But the contract of employment is not frustrated by the outbreak of war (option 5); it is instead rendered void since no person can continue to have contractual relations with an enemy alien.

33   C   Anticipatory breach or repudiation occurs when one party, expressly or by implication, indicates that he does not intend to be bound by an agreement. The injured party is entitled to sue immediately, though he may elect to allow the contract to continue until there is actual breach *(Hochster v De La Tour 1853)*. Because the right to sue is instantaneous, the injured party need not complete his obligations nor wait a reasonable time in order to effect his intentions.

Chapter 9

34   B   Although Petronella exists as a person she is non-existent as a principal since she has never heard of Andrew, who has obviously plucked her name from the air. An agent who contracts on behalf of a non-existent principal is himself personally liable. There is no question of Petronella being bound by estoppel (Distractor C) since in this case it is the 'agent' who holds himself out as agent, not the principal: *Armagas v Mundogas, the Ocean Frost 1986*.

35   A   In Key A Alice must perform this agreed task since she has agreed to act as an agent for reward. It is a contractual obligation. In Distractor B Alice will have to delegate her authority to a stockbroker since as a book-keeper only she cannot sell shares directly in the Stock Exchange. In Distractor C she acts as an unpaid agent and has no duty to perform the task. In Distractor D Peregrine is asking Alice to insider deal and no agent has to perform an illegal task, personally or otherwise.

36 **D** The statement in Key D is incorrect since, although the principal may repudiate the contract with the third party, he may sue either the agent or the third party for damages for loss: *Mahesan v Malaysian Government Officers' Co-operative Housing Society 1978*.

37 **D** The agent no longer has any liability to the third party. The principal may sue or be sued by the third party.

Chapter 10

38 **B** Because George has two 2CVs in stock it can be said that the goods in the contract of sale are existing, but since Clotilde does not state whether it is the red or the beige car she wants the goods are as yet unascertained (Key B). Specific goods (Distractor A) are identified immediately as the goods to be sold; ascertained goods (Distractor C) are those which are identified as the relevant goods *after* the contract is made. Future goods (Distractor D) either do not exist or the seller does not own them when the contract is made.

39 **C** This is a phrase much loved by examiners which you should be able to recognise instantly. Literally translated it means 'no-one gives what he does not have'. The other options, though wrong, should also be learnt:

Caveat emptora – 'let buyer beware'

delegatus non potest delegare – 'a person to whom a duty is delegated may not himself delegate it'

volenti non dit injuria – 'to he who is willing no wrong may be done'.

Chapter 11

40 **A** A conditional sale agreement must be distinguished from hire purchase (bailment with an option to buy), credit sale (immediate transfer of ownership and possession with the price payable by instalments) and consumer hire (involving the transfer of possession only, not ownership).

41 **D** The APR is defined by regulations made under s 20 CCA.

42 **A** These rules are set out in ss 69-73 of the act.

43 **C** By s 98 CCA the creditor must serve seven days' notice on the debtor in the form prescribed by the Consumer Credit (Enforcement, Default and Termination Notices) Regulations 1983.

44 **B** Sections 137-140 CCA on extortionate credit bargains applies to all credit agreements, not just to those regulated by the Act. By s 75 CCA a creditor is liable for a supplier's misrepresentation or breach of contract in a debtor-creditor-supplier agreement where credit given ranges between £100 and £30,000.

Chapter 12

45 **C**

46 **B**

Chapter 13

47	D	All these functions are undertaken by the Director General of Fair Trading under the provisions of the Fair Trading Act 1973, the Competition Act 2980 and the Restrictive Trade Practices Act 1976.

48 C Generally a monopoly exists when one person has a market share of 25% or more. In option 1 30% of the product is being supplied by a single supplier. This fulfils the criteria for a monopoly. In option 2 only 20% of the market is supplied by a single supplier and therefore a monopoly has not yet been reached. In option 3 an effective monopoly exists in the South East as over 25% of the market in the South East is supplied by a single supplier. In option 4, a monopoly is created because more than 25% of the bricks supplied in the UK are supplied *to* a single person.

49 D Article 85(1) prohibits restrictive agreements, decisions and concerted practices if they affect trade between member states. Article 86 prohibits the abuse of a dominant position.

50 D They are all capable of being the subject of a restrictive trade practice and will be declared void unless it can be shown that they are in the public interest.

Chapter 14

51 A Key A describes the test of remoteness of damage which is applied when damage arises at some distance down a chain of cause and effect from the wrong. Distractor B is incorrect because if a person commits a wrong intentionally to cause damage then he is liable however remote the damage actually is from the wrong. Distractor C is incorrect since a wrongdoer *may* still be liable for damage arising from his wrong, even though a third party has intervened, if that third party could have been *expected* to intervene in that way. Distractor D is wrong because it contradicts the doctrine of vicarious liability which applies whether or not damage was remote from the wrong.

52 A *The Wagon Mound 1961* set the precedent for how far down a chain of cause and effect without human intervention the court is prepared to go before the injury is judged too remote from the loss. If the injury is reasonably foreseeable by the defendant at the beginning then damages will be recoverable.

53 C Vicarious liability, to be a valid basis for seeking compensation, requires that an employment relationship should exist and that the employee, at the time, should be acting in the course of his employment (even if he is disobedient in the course of his employment). It is not a requirement that there should be a written contract of employment – a contract of service may exist simply on the facts (option 1).

54 B Even though an employee knows of abnormal risks created by the employer and does his job as requested he is not deemed thereby to have consented to them *(Smith v Baker & sons 1891)* and so consent may not be raised as a defence.

55 A This question is based on the situations in *Haynes v Harwood & Son 1935* and *Cutler v United Dairies 1933*. In the former case the fact that people were in danger prevented the claim of *volenti* from being used; in the latter it could be used because only property, not people, were threatened.

Chapter 15

56 D The elements in options 1, 2 and 4 are the formulation of the tort of negligence as recently adopted in *Caparo v Dickman and Others 1989*. If these are present then there is a right of action for the tort of negligence, whatever the actions of the plaintiff (but the mount of the claim may be reduced if there was contributory negligence on his part): option 3.

57 A In option 1 Virginia is in immediate fear for her own safety while in option 2 she is an actual witness to the destruction of her flat. In both cases there is a clear duty to her owed by Margaret and Douglas respectively not to cause her nervous shock by their actions.

In option 3 she cannot claim for nervous shock because she was not a person likely to be affected (*Bourhill v Young 1943*). In option 4 Dennis could not know that such an important document might be destroyed – again Virginia is too remote from the cause of the problem.

58 D Options 3 and 4 are developed from *Hedley Byrne v Heller & Partners 1964*: options 1 and 2 develop earlier case-law.

59 C Key C describes completely the basis of the doctrine of *res ipsa loquitur* as seen in *Scott v London & St Katherine's Docks Co 1865*. There is no question of reasonable foreseeability.

Chapter 16

60 A The definition of private nuisance in A and D are correct, as are those of public nuisance in A and B. Only Key A is wholly correct therefore.

61 D A partnership (Key D), being an unincorporated body made up of individuals, has no corporate identity to be protected from defamation.

Chapter 17

62 A Option B is untrue; a director can do this (and has: *Lee v Lee's Air Framing 1961*). Option C is a true statement, but is governed by s 213 Insolvency Act 1986, not *Salomon's* case. Option D is untrue – this is essentially what Mr Saloman had done, and the transaction was valid.

63 B The requirement derives from ss 11 and 118.

64 B The facts here are parallel with those of *Macaura v Northern Assurance Co 1925*, where the product in question was timber destroyed by fire. Options C and D were specially excluded by the judgment. There is no insurable interest since the property belongs to the company, not Mr Bayleaf; following *Salomon v Salomon 1897*, it is clear that the company is a legal 'person' entirely separate from its owners or creditors.

65 B The relevant authorities are, respectively: *Gilford Motor Co Ltd v Horne 1933*, *Re FG films Ltd 1953*, and *Daimler Co Ltd v Continental Tyre and Rubber Co Ltd 1916*.

66 A A *public* company must have two directors, a *private* company needs only one (s 282).

Chapter 18

67 D Section 36(4) provides that 'subject to any agreement to the contrary, the contract shall have effect as a contract entered into by the person purporting to act for the company or as agent for it, and he shall be personally liable on the contract accordingly'. *Phonogram Ltd v Lane 1981* makes it clear that options A and B are not fatal to the application of the section, despite the fact that it refers to a contract, which 'purports to be made by the company'. The knowledge (or lack of it) which either party had concerning the stage of formation reached is not relevant. The case also states that any 'agreement to the contrary' must be express, not merely implied (ruling out option C).

68 D The dates of the accounting year are, in practice, often decided after incorporation to maximise any benefit to the company's trading position. If they are not notified within the prescribed period, however, an accounting year end of 31 March will be imposed, which may prove inconvenient.

69 B The provision here is s 1.

Chapter 19

70 B This is governed by s 224.

71 B Again, the provisions are to allow a greater degree of confidentiality.

72 A Options B to D are nothing more than smoke screens. Whatever the general meeting says about the accounts, they remain the accounts. The effect of rejecting them is to give a symbolic vote of no confidence in the directors; it has no effect whatsoever on the validity of the accounts.

73 B The matter is covered by s 240.

74 C The DTI may do so when the members have failed to appoint auditors at the general meeting where the accounts are considered, and the company has fulfilled its statutory obligation to inform the DTI within seven days: s 384(5).

Chapter 20

75 A

76 C It is important to remember that an illegal act is not properly regarded as an example of *ultra vires* (it could never have been made *intra vires* by inclusion in the objects clause in the first place). Option B is an abuse of directors' powers but, since the company has the capacity, the act is not *ultra vires* the company. Option D is simply wrong – there is no objection to the development of a company's business activities, as long as any development is covered by the objects clause.

77 D The contractual effect of the articles is established by s 14. It is important to remember that the principle applies to members only insofar as they are affected *in their capacity as members*. If the question is confined to members in their personal capacity, it is not subject to the rule (see *Hickman v Kent or Romney Marsh Sheepbreeders Association 1915* and *Beattie v Beattie 1938*). As regards third parties, the contractual effect of the articles can be a little difficult to unravel. In *Eley v Positive Government Security Life Assurance Co 1876*, a third party who was also a member failed in his claim (since he was not asserting any right as a member); in *Re new British Iron Co ex parte Beckwith 1898*, it was held that if an outsider makes a contract with a company and that contract makes no provision on a particular point (but the articles do), then the contract may be deemed to incorporate the articles to *that extent*. Thus the articles are clearly not a contract with a non-member, but may supply a missing term on a separate contract.

78 B Option A is of itself true, but there is nothing in the articles in this situation with which the Act can be in conflict. Options C and D are both simply untrue.

79 C This question reflects the facts of *Southern Foundries v Shirlaw 1940*. Boris' remedy lies in a straightforward action for breach of contract, since his service contract specifies a term of appointment. If there had been no such term, *no* liability for damages would arise if 'reasonable notice of termination' is given. Boris cannot restrain the alteration of the articles or the exercise of the new power.

Chapter 21

80 A It is important to keep the concepts of authorised and issued capital separate; the latter is the nominal value of the shares which have been *actually* allotted and issued to members. Not all the authorised share capital need be so issued.

81 A The model articles of Table A only prescribe an ordinary resolution, but the company is free to employ articles specifying a different type of resolution should it wish to do so.

82 C The facts here are parallel with *Re Eddystone Marine Insurance Co 1893*. The liquidator's claim must be upheld; even if any services had in fact been given, they would be past consideration and hence treated as being of no value.

83 D Option A is true, but this does not mean that the relevant rules (ss 151-158) are excluded. The general prohibition remains, and is not overridden by a subordinate power to lend money. Option B is too sweeping a statement – not *all* such transactions are forbidden. The 'ordinary business loan' of option C is an exception, but applies only to companies whose ordinary business is lending money. The facts are taken from *Steen v Law 1964*.

84 B

Chapter 22

85 A A debenture trust deed is a long and elaborate legal document, so this list is by no means exhaustive.

86 D A shareholder is a proprietor or owner of the company. A debenture holder is a *creditor* of the company.

87 B The company has a duty to pay interest on the debentures based on the contract under which they were formed. There is, however, no *necessity* for the company to pay a dividend to ordinary shareholders; a decision not to do so is within the company's discretion. Option B is therefore incorrect. Options A and C are self-explanatory. Option D is true, since a debentureholder (whether or not secured by a charge over the company assets) is a creditor of the company (not a member) and therefore takes precedence in a liquidation.

88 A The charge does not attach to the assets until crystallisation; indeed, it is merely a charge on a class of assets, present and future, the assets contained in each class change from time to time. It follows therefore that until the charge is enforced the company may carry on its business in the class of assets charged (*Re Yorkshire Woolcombers Association 1903*). Number 2 is therefore untrue, Number 4 is established by *Re Brightlife Ltd 1987*.

89 A

Chapter 23

90 C These are the facts of *Morris v Kanssen 1946*. By statute (s 285) it is provided that the acts of a director or manager are valid notwithstanding any defect that may afterwards be discovered in his appointment or qualification (so there is a whiff of truth about option A). However, to bring the rule into operation there must be an appointment which is later found to be defective. It does not extend to a case where there has been no appointment at all or where the 'director' has simply ceased to hold office. Neither Steerpike nor Swelter are covered by statute, therefore. Mr Fluke cannot rely on the principle of *Mahony v East Holyford Mining Co 1875* (as option D suggests) since he is himself an insider who has access to the records and therefore the opportunity to discover the true position.

91 D The facts of this case come from *Freeman & Lockyer v Buckhurst Park Properties (Mangal) Ltd 1964*. A managing director has apparent authority to act in this way, and since the board has acquiesced to one of their number acting as though he were a managing director, the company is bound.

92 C These propositions also come from *Freeman & Lockyer v Buckhurst Park Properties (Mangal) Ltd 1964*.

93 A The facts are parallel with *IDC v Cooley 1972*, which illustrates the very strict nature of the controls on directors.

94 B This proposition is derived from dicta of Lord Denning in *Hely-Hutchinson v Brayhead 1968*

Chapter 24

95 B In addition, an AGM must be held each calendar year (with the exception of the first AGM after incorporation, which must be held within eight months, but need not be in the first year or the following year after incorporation).

96 C Article 37 requires that such a meeting be held within eight weeks of the requisition.

97 A The right to appoint a proxy is given by s 372.

98 C

99 C These are the facts of *Re Caratal (New) Mines 1902*. On the chairman's own figures there was no majority on the show of hands. Proxies may vote on a poll, not on a show of hands, and no poll had been held.

Chapter 25

100 A The test is control, not 'significant influence'. Options C and D are both incorrect, since a single member can bring the action.

101 B Option A was the case in *Cook v Deeks 1916*. Option B (held *not* to be a fraud on the minority since there could be no offence unless the controlling shareholder benefited) is from *Pavlides v Jensen 1956*. Option C is *Daniels v Daniels 1977*, Option D is derived from *Eastmanco (Kilner House) Ltd v GLC 1982*.

102 D Statements 1 and 2 are not necessary elements *(Re R A Noble and Sons (clothing) Ltd 1983)*. The prejudice must be to a member as a member, not as an employee *(Elder v Elder & Watson Ltd 1952)* or as an unpaid creditor *(Re Balador Silk Ltd 1965)*.

103 C

104 C No such allowance need be made: *Re Bird Precision Bellows Ltd 1985*. The authority for Option B is *Scottish Co-operative Wholesale Society v Meyer 1958*.

Chapter 26

105 D Other methods include dissolution by the registrar under s 652 Companies Act 1985 if it appears to him that the company is defunct, and on the completion of a voluntary or compulsory liquidation.

106 A This is laid down by s 232 IA.

107 B The relevant authority is s 123 IA.

108 D The authorities for these propositions are, respectively: *Re German Date Coffee Co 1882*, *Re Yenidje Tobacco Co Ltd 1916* (for propositions 2 and 3), *Ebrahimi v Westbourne Galleries Ltd 1973*, and *Lock v John Blackwood Ltd 1924*.

109 B This time period is required by s 98 IA.

SOLUTIONS TO EXAM STYLE QUESTIONS

Chapter 1

1 EQUITY AND THE COMMON LAW

Common law

The common law of England has its roots in custom. After the Norman conquest, Royal Commissioners toured the country, settling disputes on the basis of local custom. When sitting in the court at Westminster, these local rules hardened into principles of law, which were applied uniformly throughout the country. The system developed into a rigid series of procedural rules. To bring a case, it was necessary to issue a writ in the correct form; if this was not done, the case failed. It was to relieve the harshness of the common law that equity was developed.

Equity

Where there was no procedure designed to cover a person's grievance, that person would often petition the King. The case would then be investigated by the Chancellor, who would impose a just solution without regard for technicalities and procedural points. The system developed its own rules of procedure (less rigid than those of the common law) and introduced new rights (such as the trust concept) and new remedies (such as the decree of specific performance).

The relationship between the two

The two systems ran in parallel. The common law was the primary system, but equity would intervene to ensure a fair result if necessary. At first highly arbitrary in its application, the appointment of experienced common-law men as Chancellors ensured that a more regular and consistent body of equity rules emerged. However, because the systems of common law and equity were developed and administered separately, there were often conflicts between the two, with equity sometimes reversing a common law ruling. To some extent the conflict was resolved in the *Earl of Oxford's Case 1615*, where it was held that equity would prevail where the systems were in conflict.

Although the supremacy of equity was established, the two systems continued to be administered by two separate courts. The common law was administered by the royal courts and equity by the Court of Chancery. This caused problems; a plaintiff could begin a case in one system only to discover that the action should have been heard in the other court, and would thus have to bring the case again. This dual system was ended by the Judicature Acts 1873-5; both systems may now be applied in the same court.

Today the historical reasons behind the development of the two systems are still apparent in the relationship between them. The common law rules are applied automatically, whereas equitable principles are applied at the court's discretion in those cases where the strict application of the common law will not give the fairest result.

Chapter 2

2 COURTS

(a) Purchase has rights in contract. The sale contract will include implied conditions as to the satisfactory quality and the fitness for its purpose of the electrical heater (Sale of Goods Act 1979 s 14). These terms cannot be excluded in a consumer contract (Unfair Contract Terms Act 1977). Vera may not sue in contract, as there is no contractual relationship between her and Sellors.

Both Purchase and Vera may also have an action in tort for negligence. The principles of *Donoghue v Stevenson 1932* state that a duty of care is owed to those who may foreseeably suffer harm from one's negligence; here the purchaser of faulty goods and his family.

There may also be scope for a strict liability action under the Consumer Protection Act 1987, under which Purchase and Vera, as consumers and users of the defective goods, may claim for the physical injury to Purchase and the damage to Vera's clothes.

(b) Purchase can bring an action in contract against Sellors, for breach of the terms in the contract of sale which they have made. Vera is not a party to the contract, so she cannot bring an action under it.

Both Purchase and Vera can bring an action in tort against Watt for his negligence in manufacturing the faulty heater, although this does depend on the foreseeability of injury to them. They may also bring actions against both supplier and manufacturer under the 1987 Act. Here they do not need to prove negligence. Such an action will only be necessary if Sellor does not disclose the identity of Watt.

(c) Depending on the size of the claim in contract or tort, the civil court of first hearing is the county court or High Court. Criteria are laid down for determining where proceedings are to be commenced and tried and where judgements are to be enforced. In particular, actions in respect of *personal injuries* are to be commenced in a county court unless the claim is worth £50,000 or more. Actions in contract and tort worth less than £25,000 must normally be tried in a county court and those worth £50,000 or more must normally be tried in the High Court, with those in between going either way, subject to:

(i) the 'financial substance' of the action;

(ii) whether questions of public interest are raised;

(iii) the complexity of the facts, the legal issues, remedies or procedures involved; and

(iv) whether transfer is likely to result in a more speedy trial.

These criteria may also be used to transfer an action worth less than £25,000 to the High Court or an action worth over £50,000 to the county court. If the claim is for less than £3,000 it may be referred to arbitration in the Small Claims Court.

The High Court has three divisions; the Queen's Bench Division deals with most common law matters. Appeals from either court may be made to the Civil Division of the Court of Appeal. The legal arguments and evidence will be reviewed by a panel of judges (usually three) who decide by majority. From this court, an appeal may be made (with the leave of the court) to the House of Lords. Five Law Lords will review the case and again will decide by a majority. There is no appeal from the House of Lords.

(d) The first criminal court is the magistrates' court which hears cases which are either triable summarily (ie without a jury) or are each way offences where the defendant has chosen trial in this court. The case is heard by a panel of magistrates, who are usually lay persons, or by a stipendiary magistrate. More serious cases (triable on indictment or where the defendant has elected for crown court trial) are first heard by a judge and jury in a Crown Court. Cases may be referred to the Crown Court from the magistrates' court where the powers of sentencing of the latter are considered insufficient (a maximum of a £5,000 fine or six months imprisonment). There is a right of appeal to the Crown Court from a magistrates' court. There is also a right of appeal from the Crown Court to the Criminal Division of the Court of Appeal. Again the case is heard by three judges. With leave, a further appeal may be made to the House of Lords. The majority decision prevails; there is no further court of appeal.

Chapter 3

3   EC LAW

Regulations

Regulations (unless expressed to the contrary) have effect as law throughout the European Community as soon as they are made. Direct law-making of this type is generally restricted to matters within the basic aims of the Treaty of Rome such as the establishment of a single unrestricted market in the EC territory in manufactured goods. For example, certain types of agreement which would restrict competition are prohibited by regulations, and infringement of the regulations is punished by fines imposed in Brussels. There is no need in such cases to enact any UK act of Parliament since the regulation is already legally binding.

Directives

Directives are statements of principle to which the member states must, by their national law-making process, adapt their own law. For example, the several directives on company law require that British, French, German, etc company law shall conform to certain principles, such as the law on prospectuses now contained in the Financial Services Act 1986. If they do conform to that extent, they may still differ in other respects.

Although directives are mainly statements of principle to be absorbed into national law by a national law-making process, it is sometimes permissible for an EC national in court proceedings to rely on the principles of a Directive: *Van Duyn v Home Office 1974.*

Decisions

Decisions are taken in Brussels to implement such objectives as the Common Agricultural Policy. A decision is immediately binding on the government or person to whom it is addressed. As a source of law, decisions are less important than regulations or directives.

Direct applicability

If law is made in Brussels with immediate legal effect in the EC area, it is said to be 'directly applicable' so that no national law-making is needed to introduce it into national law. A self-executing regulation is directly applicable. A directive, on the other hand, is not directly applicable except when a court is willing to recognise (usually as a result of guidance by the European Court of Justice) that some principle of the directive should already be in operation as a statement of principle.

Direct effect

EC law has 'direct effect' when an individual person can rely on it to establish rights or obligations. To that extent, direct effect and direct application overlap. But a regulation, for example, may be directly applicable without also having direct effect in terms of rights and obligations of citizens.

Chapter 4

4   ARBITRATION AND TRIBUNALS

Arbitration

Arbitration is settlement of a dispute by an independent person usually chosen by the parties themselves. A dispute may be referred to arbitration by the agreement of the parties, by statute or by court order. They are usually governed by the rules set out in the Arbitration Acts 1950 to 1979.

The arbitrator is usually an expert in the field of dispute, appointed by the parties or by some agreed third person (or in some cases by the court). The procedure is less formal than in the courts, but the parties are bound by the ordinary rules of evidence (subject to agreement to the contrary), including discovery of documents and evidence on oath.

The arbitrator's decision on the dispute is final. Furthermore the 1979 Act restricted the right of appeal to preliminary points of law, but only where either the court gives leave or the parties agree. The right may be excluded by agreement. The arbitrator is usually not required to give reasons for his decision. If either party, in breach of an agreement, seeks to institute proceedings in court in respect of the dispute, the court will usually grant an application to stay those proceedings pending the arbitration. The arbitration decision may be enforced in the same manner as a court decision.

Tribunals

Administrative tribunals are specialist courts established by statute to deal with disputes between individuals or between individuals and government agencies. They are specialised in jurisdiction. For example, disputes regarding a refusal of social security benefits are settled in the Social Security appeals tribunal; this consists of a chairman (usually a lawyer) and two other persons drawn from a panel of employer and employee representatives. There are other tribunals to deal with issues of:

(a) property valuation – *the Lands tribunal;*

(b) setting of rents – *the Rent tribunal;*

(c) mental health review – *the mental health review tribunal;*

(d) employment – *industrial tribunals; and*

(e) town and country planning – *administrative enquiries.*

The working of tribunals is subject to the supervision of the Council on Tribunals. There is also usually a right of appeal from the decision of the tribunal to the court on a point of law. The High Court may also review the workings of the tribunals to prevent abuses of natural justice or procedure.

Advantages

The advantages of *arbitration* over court procedure are many. Commercial disputes are often commercially sensitive; arbitration is relatively private as the press and the public do not have a right to attend the proceedings. Furthermore the parties may choose the arbitrator; in this way they can ensure the decision is made by one with expert knowledge in the field, which may be desirable in highly technical matters. It is also possible to modify the rules of procedure and evidence which may assist in making the proceedings quicker and cheaper than a court action. For these reasons arbitration clauses are popular in business contracts. However the use of arbitration clauses in consumer contracts is restricted by the Consumer Arbitration Agreements Act 1988, as the Small Claims Court may prove an even speedier and cheaper forum for smaller claims.

The advantages of *tribunals* lie largely in their informality. They are not subject to the strict rules of evidence and procedure, and are thus usually quicker and cheaper than a court action. They also develop specialist knowledge as a consequence of their specialised jurisdictions. However this specialisation and informality may lead to the impression of bias or injustice, something which the court's supervisory jurisdiction attempts to prevent.

Chapter 5

5 NOTICE IN WRITING

Tutorial note. Part (a) of this question is pretty straightforward and you should have been looking to 'bank' some easy marks here. In part (b), it is important to note that, where the offeror specifies 'notice in writing', he is effectively opting out of the postal rule.

(a) An offer must be legally accepted before a contract can be said to exist. Acceptance may be defined as 'a positive act by a person to whom an offer has been made which, if unconditional, brings a binding contract into effect.'

Acceptance must be communicated

As a general rule, in order to be effective, acceptance must be communicated to the offeror. The onus is on the offeree to show that his acceptance has been properly made and communicated.

What constitutes acceptance

Acceptance must be a positive act. It can be communicated by means of express words or by action or inferred from conduct: *Brogden v Metropolitan Railway Co 1877*. Passive inaction by the offeree will not be sufficient to constitute acceptance: *Felthouse v Bingley 1862*. For example, a recipient of unsolicited goods will not be considered to have accepted the offer of those goods simply by failing to return them to the sender (Unsolicited Goods and Services Act 1971).

Although acceptance must be communicated, the means of communication can vary unless clearly stipulated by the offeror in making the offer. Thus in *Yates Building Co v R J Pulleyn & Sons (York) 1975*, despite the offer calling for acceptance by registered or recorded delivery letter, acceptance by means of an ordinary letter was held to be valid since the offeror had not sufficiently clearly stipulated that only the means stated would constitute acceptance.

Exceptions to the rule that acceptance must be communicated

There are certain exceptions to the general rule that acceptance is effective only when communicated by the offeree to the offeror.

Waiver of need for acceptance

First, the offeror may dispense with, or waive, the need for acceptance to be communicated (though acceptance is still required to be a positive act). Instead, he may either expressly or impliedly indicate that performance of the offeree's side of the bargain will be sufficient. In *Carlill v Carbolic Smoke Ball Co 1893* acceptance by conduct was sufficient and it was held that there was no need for the plaintiff to communicate her intention to the offeror to accept the offer by using the celebrated smoke balls.

The postal rule

Secondly, as a result of the judgment in *Adams v Linsell 1818*, acceptance by posted letter is regarded as effective upon posting (provided it is properly addressed and stamped) and not upon receipt by the addressee. The fact that the acceptance may subsequently be lost or destroyed will not invalidate the acceptance: *Household Fire and Carriage Accident Insurance Co v Grant 1879*. The scope of this exception is limited: it applies only to ordinary post and not to instantaneous means of communication such as telephone, fax or telex: *Entores v Miles Far Eastern Corporation 1955*. Nor will it apply where the offer clearly excludes postal acceptance or where such acceptance was clearly not in the contemplation of the parties. Furthermore the offeree must be able to show that the letter was actually posted.

Apart from these two established exceptions, positive acceptance is required and must be communicated to the offeror in order to be valid.

(b) The general rule, as noted in part (a), is that acceptance of an offer must be communicated to the offeror in order to be effective.

In this case, the offer – though made by letter – stipulates that acceptance must be communicated by 'notice of writing' and 'received' by the sales director. The effect of this wording, as in Holwell Securities v Hughes 1974, is to exclude the postal rule developed in *Adams v Lindsell 1818*, which otherwise would have meant that Buyer Ltd's posting of its acceptance on 8 February would have been effective.

The effect of the wording in the offer is that posting of acceptance will not suffice, but rather that it must be communicated to the sales director. On the strength of the letter from Buyer Ltd which was not received, therefore, there can be no liability on the part of Seller Ltd.

This would appear to be the case also in respect of the telephone call. If the message had been passed on, it would still not have been sufficient according to the offer terms, as it was not 'notice in writing' (unless the reasoning in *Yates Building Co v Pulleyn & Sons 1975* could be applied) even though it might have:

(i) put the sales director on notice that written acceptance could be expected; or

(ii) put the director of Buyer Ltd on notice that his letter had not been received. This would not be enough to impose liability on Seller Ltd.

Furthermore, the offer states that notice of acceptance must be received by the sales director. It is likely that, in these circumstances, only he according to the offer terms, as it was not 'notice in writing' (unless the reasoning in Yates Built is submitted that, for these reasons, Seller Ltd is not liable to Buyer Ltd for breach of contract.

Chapter 6

6 FREEDOM

(a) If a party to a contract wishes to introduce a clause into his contracts expressly excluding or limiting his liability, he must ensure that the clause is incorporated into the contracts in accordance with common law rules.

Notice of the exemption clause given to other party

The other party must be aware of the clauses at the time when the contract is made, that is when each party enters into the agreement. Notice of the clause given afterwards will not suffice: *Olley v Marlborough Court 1949*. If the existence of the clause is indicated at the time of the contract being made, this may be adequate notice (for example, the contract is 'subject to conditions' which are printed in a separate document: *Thompson v LMS Railway 1930*). Merely including a disclaimer on, for example, a receipt given later, is not: *Chapelton v Barry UDC 1940*.

It can be difficult to ascertain exactly when the contract is formed, but any reference to conditions which is received too late for the conditions to be included as contractual terms will not be held as incorporated into the contract: *Thornton v Shoe Lane Parking 1972*. This means that the party seeking to introduce the clause should ensure that such a clause is not introduced subsequent to the making of the contract.

Previous dealings with the other party

If the party introducing the clause has previously dealt with the other party on the basis of the contract including the clause, he may be able to show incorporation by this past use: *Spurling v Bradshaw 1956*. However in a consumer contract (where there have not been 'consistent' dealings) he will have to show that the customers were actually aware of and had agreed to the clause: *Hollier v Rambler Motors 1972*.

Clause included in contract signed by the other party

In a written signed contract it is usually considered that the person signing is bound by the terms of that contract *(L'Estrange v Graucob 1934)* although this will not be the case if that person has been given a misleading explanation of the terms: *Curtis v Chemical Cleaning Co 1951*.

Even if incorporation is shown, it is then a question of interpretation as to whether the clause is drawn widely enough to cover the type of liability alleged: *Photo Productions v Securicor Transport 1980*.

(b) There are also statutory limitations on exclusion clauses in consumer contracts imposed by the Unfair Contract Terms Act 1977. In general the Act applies to clauses inserted into agreements by commercial concerns or businesses.

Exclusion of liability for breach of contract

In a contract for the provision of services to the consumer, a term excluding liability for certain breaches of contract is void except insofar as it is subject to a test of reasonableness (s 3 of the Act). This attacks those clauses which purport to allow either no performance or a performance substantially different from that agreed, or which exclude liability for breach or fundamental breach.

Exclusion of liability for negligence

The Act also controls the use of clauses which attempt to exclude liability for negligence. A clause which excludes liability for death or personal injury caused by negligence is void. Exclusion from liability for other types of damage is permitted only as far as the clause is reasonable (s 2).

Test of reasonableness

There is also a test of reasonableness applied to clauses designed to exclude liability for misrepresentations. 'Reasonableness' is considered in s 11 of the Act. The clause must be fair and reasonable in all the circumstances which were or ought to have been known by the parties when the contract was made: *Walker v Boyle 1981*. There are some guidelines as to factors in the Act; these are the resources of the contracting party to meet liability if it arises and the extent to which he could insure himself against it. It will be for the party seeking to rely on the clause to show that the clause is reasonable.

Chapter 7

7 REMEDIES FOR MISREPRESENTATION

Contracts are often preceded by negotiation. Various statements may then be made, only some of which will be incorporated in the final contract; these represent the substance, or 'terms', of the contract.

Other statements, however, can still have a legal effect, that is they can still give rise to a legal remedy. This happens where one party makes an untrue statement which induces another party to enter a contract. Obviously, this is only possible where the statement is made before or at the time that the contract is formed.

What is a representation?

The statement must be one of fact not of law. Neither must it be a statement of opinion (*Bisset v Wilkinson 1927*), though if a person expresses an opinion he does not hold, then he is making an untrue statement of fact: *Edgington v Fitzmaurice 1885*. Complete silence, where the facts are suppressed, cannot be a misrepresentation, but a partial non-disclosure which misleads can be: *R v Kylsant 1931*.

If a person makes a statement which is true at the time but which, before the contract is concluded, he knows subsequently to have become false, he must inform the other party or be guilty of a misrepresentation: *With v O'Flanagan 1936*.

Inducement to contract

To be actionable the misrepresentation must induce the other party to enter into the contract. Whether it does so is a question of fact, but where a false statement is made, if the innocent party makes his own inquiries and relies on these, then the misrepresentation cannot be said to induce the contract. The innocent party is not obliged to make such inquiries however: *Redgrave v Hurd 1881*.

Types of misrepresentation

Misrepresentation can be fraudulent, negligent or innocent according to the state of mind of the party making the statement; this is important because the type of misrepresentation affects the remedy.

Someone who knowingly states something that is false makes a *fraudulent* misrepresentation; and if he makes the statement without belief in its truth or if he is reckless as to its truth, the result is the same: *Derry v Peek 1889*. In these circumstances the contract will be 'voidable', the victim of the misrepresentation having a right to 'rescind' (or 'avoid') the contract; that is, to bring his and the other party's obligations under the contract to an end.

Normally rescission involves both parties being restored to their original positions, each of them having to give back whatever he has received under the contract. This is called 'restitution' and will only be granted if *'restitutio in integrum'* is possible – the parties must be able to be returned to their pre-contract positions. A victim of fraud, though, will only have this obligation if he himself sues for rescission. If he is sued by the other party for refusing to carry out the contract, he can plead fraud as a defence and refuse to return what he received under the contract.

The right to rescind can be lost if the party who has been misled initially continues with, or 'affirms', the contract: rescission is an equitable remedy, so the court has a discretion to refuse it where there has been unreasonable delay in seeking rescission. The victim of fraudulent misrepresentation may also sue for damages in the tort of 'deceit'. He is not suing for breach of contract, of course, because the false statement was not a contractual term.

Negligent misrepresentation is the second category for which a legal remedy can be sought. It exists under two sorts of liability – tortious: *Hedley Byrne v Heller & Partners 1964* and statutory (s2(1) Misrepresentation Act 1967).

Negligence in tort can give rise to misrepresentation if there is a 'special relationship' between the parties or if one party is an 'expert' who makes a careless misstatement inducing the contract: *Esso Petroleum v Mardon 1976*. The remedy is rescission and/or damages.

A defence to the statutory charge exists if the misrepresenting person can prove 'that he had reasonable grounds to believe ... that the facts represented were true'.

A party who is misled by an *innocent* misrepresentation may also rescind the contract. As for damages, he has no right to these, though s 2(2) of the Misrepresentation Act gives the court a discretion to award damages instead of rescission. S 2(2) even allows the court to refuse rescission for negligent misrepresentation and to award damages on their own 'where it would be equitable to do so'.

Advice to D

In the case in question, E's statement is a statement of fact. It induces D to enter into the contract.

There is no fraudulent misrepresentation, as the misrepresentation is not made knowingly, without belief in its truth or recklessly. It is therefore either negligent or innocent. If it is held that the salesman made the statement in the belief that it is true and with reasonable grounds for the belief, the misrepresentation will be innocent. However, if D can show that there is a 'special relationship', by which E has some special knowledge or skill relevant to the advice contained in his misrepresentation and knows that D will rely on that advice having asked for it, then the misrepresentation becomes negligent: *Esso Petroleum Co Ltd v Mardon 1976*. This will entitle D to look for rescission and damages (as opposed to mere rescission if the misrepresentation is innocent). A computer salesman could reasonably be expected to know about the software capability of systems he sells, and so it is likely that the court would infer the existence of a special relationship.

Chapter 8

8 FRUSTRATION

Review of circumstances

At first sight it would appear that Abel may have an action for breach of contract against Laggard. Laggard fulfils his contract but he does so imperfectly, with late delivery of substandard products. Breach of these contractual specifications is a breach of both an express term of the contract and of s 13 Sale of Goods Act 1979 (goods to correspond with contract description). Partial performance is not full performance *(Moore v Landauer 1921)* and, as a general rule, time is of the essence in commercial contracts: *Elmdore v Keech 1969*.

Frustration

It would appear then that Abel has access to all the usual remedies for breach of contract. However Laggard may be able to show that the contract has actually become impossible to perform and thus has been discharged by frustration, and not by breach. The essence of this doctrine is that the underlying fundamental assumptions of the parties when making the contract have not materialised and thus the contract is now fundamentally different in its nature. A contract is also discharged by frustration if the parties assumed that certain underlying conditions would continue and those assumptions prove to be false.

Being an exception to the general rule that parties are bound by their contractual promises, the doctrine is limited in scope and Laggard will have to show that the events preventing performance are sufficient to amount to frustration.

Labour issues

The shortage of labour due to illness and the strike may be sufficient to frustrate the contract, if Laggard can demonstrate that the contract relied heavily on personal skills exercised by the absent members of the workforce: *Condor v Barron Knights 1966*. He would have to show that it was not possible to make up the lost time in some way. However if Laggard has diverted workers away from Abel's work to fulfil other contracts this positive choice will mean that he cannot plead frustration on this ground: *Maritime National Fish v Ocean Trawlers 1935*.

Laggard may claim that the strike interrupted performance in such a way that it prevented performance. The test to be applied is whether the interruption is such that the contract can no longer be performed in the way envisaged by the parties: *Jackson v Union Marine Insurance 1874*.

The strike may well be regarded as an event which was within Laggard's power to avoid, and thus be declared not relevant to the issue of frustration.

Added expenses

Laggard may also point to the new regulations and the consequent added expense as causing frustration. A change in the law rendering performance impossible will certainly be a frustrating event: *Re Shipton, Anderson & Co 1915*. The important point here is impossibility; if Laggard is still capable of performing the contract in some other way there is no frustration (*Tsakiroglou v Noblee Thorl 1962*) even if the alternative involves him in additional expense: *Davis Contractors v Fareham UDC 1956*.

Effect of frustration

Laggard is likely to fail in his plea of frustration, and Abel will seek damages to compensate him for his losses. However, if Laggard succeeds, the terms of the contract may provide for a solution in the event of subsequent impossibility. If they do not do so, the Law Reform (Frustrated Contracts) Act 1943 will apply to determine the respective rights and obligations of the parties. Money paid by Abel to Laggard must be repaid by Laggard, although the court may allow Laggard to retain or recover expenses incurred up to the time of discharge (up to the amount due from Laggard at the time of frustration). The court may also order Abel to pay Laggard the value of the benefit received under the contract, that is the machinery.

Chapter 9

9 UNDISCLOSED PRINCIPAL

(a) In the law of contract, there is a general rule of privity of contract. The doctrine states that only a person who is a party to a contract has enforceable rights or obligations under it. A leading case on the matter is *Dunlop v Selfridge*. A consequence of the doctrine is that only a party to a contract may sue or be sued on the contract. The CIMA *Terminology of Business and Company Law* defines privity of contract as:

> 'the relation between two parties to a contract which allows either to sue for a breach of that contract. Third parties who are not privy to the contract even though they may receive benefits under it have no right of action save in certain exceptional instances.'

One of these exceptional instances arises in the law of agency. In normal circumstances, the agent discloses to the third party with whom he contracts that he (the agent) is acting for a principal whose identity is also disclosed. The contract, when made, is between the principal and the third party. The agent has no liability under the contract and no right to enforce it. However, if a person enters into a contract apparently as a principal on his own behalf, but in fact as an agent on behalf of a principal, the doctrine of the undisclosed principal applies to determine the positions of the parties.

The doctrine of the undisclosed principal states that, provided that the agent acts within the scope of his authority, it is possible to put forward evidence which shows that the undisclosed principal is a party to the transaction. As a result, he may sue or be sued on the contract made between the agent and the third party.

The undisclosed principal will usually intervene and enforce the contact on his own behalf against the other party, since it really is his own contact and not that of the agent. Until such time as the principal takes this action, the agent himself may sue the third party (since up to that point he is treated as the other party to the contract). It should be noted that the undisclosed principal only has a right to intervene in contracts made by his agent where the agent was legally authorised to enter into the contract in the first place. He cannot ratify an unauthorised act of the agent: *Keighley, Maxsted & Co v Durant 1900*. The undisclosed principal is also prevented from taking over a contract in the following circumstances.

(i) Where agency is expressly denied by the contract terms: *United Kingdom Mutual SS Insurance Association v Nevill 1887*;

(ii) Where agency is implicitly denied by the contract terms: *Humbel v Hunter 1848*;

(iii) Where the agent expressly denies in making the contract that a principal is involved (this is a case of misrepresentation);

(iv) Where the identity of the principal is material to the third party: *Said v Butt 1920*.

If the contract is not performed as agreed, the third party may sue the agent or the principal. He must elect for one or the other within a reasonable period of time after he has discovered the facts and may not sue both the principal and the agent: *Chestertons v Barone 1987*.

(b) A contract made by an agent is binding on the principal and the other party if the agent was acting within the limits of the authority set by his principal. The other party cannot always know the exact limits of the authority of the agent and so he is legally entitled to rely on the agent's apparent authority. This apparent authority, or ostensible authority, may exceed the actual authority which has been given to the agent by the principal. As a result the principal may incur liability on a contract even when his instructions have not been followed.

Apparent authority is sometimes called ostensible authority. It is the authority which an agent appears to have to a third party. A contract made within the scope of such authority will bind the principal even though the agent was not following his instructions'. It may arise in the following circumstances.

(i) Where a person allows another, who is not his agent, to appear as if he is: *Barrett v Deere 1828*;

(ii) Where a principal allows his agent to give the impression that he has more extensive authority than is really the case: *Todd v Robinson 1825*;

(iii) Where, following termination of the agency agreement, the principal allows his former agent to continue to appear as his agent: *Drew v Nunn 1879*.

Other situations where the agent has a greater authority than that which is expressly set are as follows.

(i) Where the agent has been appointed to act in a particular capacity, he has authority to make those contracts which are necessarily or normally incidental to the agent's activities.

(ii) Where the agent is operating in a particular market, he may have 'implied customer authority to act in a way customary in that market: *Dingle v Hare 1859*.

(iii) Where an agent occupies a particular position, he may have authority to do things which are normal practice for someone in that position: *Howard v Sheward 1866*.

It should be noted that the agent cannot contravene the principal's express instructions by claiming that he had implied authority for acting as he did, but the third party is nonetheless entitled to assume that, unless he has notice to the contrary, the agent has authority to enter into the contact: *Watteau v Fenwick 1893*.

In the case in hand, it will be necessary to examine whether Agent Ltd has authority in any of the above categories. If he does, it will be likely that the courts will hold Principal Ltd as bound by the contract to sell 5,000 tools. It will have to be shown that TZ plc knew nothing of the restriction to 3,000 tools. Principal Ltd may, if required to pay damages to TZ plc (for example because he is unable to satisfy the order), recover compensation from Agent Ltd. Agent Ltd may also be liable to TZ plc for breach of warranty of authority.

Chapter 10

10 ARTHUR

There are two separate issues to be considered here. Firstly, the advertisement and the salesman have both described the mountain bicycle as 'the latest model'. It is not the latest model. Secondly, although the salesman has confirmed that the bicycle is 'in excellent condition', Arthur has discovered that it has had a major repair.

Section 13

Section 13 of the Sale of Goods Act 1979 applies to all sales and is not limited to sales made in the course of a business. S 13(1) provides that 'where there is a contract for the sale of goods by description, there is an implied condition that the goods correspond with the description.'

The term 'description' is widely interpreted by the courts and includes attributes such as ingredients, age, date of shipment, packing and quantity. In *Varley v Whipp 1900*, the seller advertised a 'second hand self-binder reaping machine' describing it as 'new the previous year' and 'hardly used at all'. The buyer bought it without seeing it. When it arrived he found that it was very much more than a year old and rejected it. The seller sued for the price. It was held that this was a sale by description and the machine did not correspond with the description given. This was a breach of condition which entitled the buyer to reject the goods.

It should be noted that if a description is applied to the goods by the contract, it does not matter whether or not the buyer inspects the goods. There is a sale by description even if the buyer does inspect the goods: *Beale v Taylor 1967*. If a contract contains the phrase 'bought as seen' or similar (as for example at an auction) then the sale is expressly not one by description: *Cavendish-Woodhouse Ltd v Manley 1984*. If there is no reliance at all by the buyer on the description, the description is not influential on the sale in any way and there is therefore no sale by description: *Harlington & Leinster Enterprises v Christopher Hull Fine Art 1990*.

Section 14(2)

Under s 14 SGA 1979, where the seller sells goods in the course of a business, there is an implied condition that the goods supplied under the contract are of satisfactory quality.

Under s 14(2A), goods meet the requirement of satisfactory quality if they 'meet the standard that a reasonable person would regard as satisfactory, taking account of any description of the goods, the price (if relevant) and all other relevant circumstances'. The Act lists some of the attributes which are to be taken into account in deciding whether the goods are of satisfactory quality, including fitness for the purpose, appearance and finish, freedom from minor defects, safety and durability.

There are two exceptions to this: the condition does not apply

(a) as regards defects specifically drawn to the buyer's attention before the contract is made; or

(b) if the buyer examines the goods before the contract is made, as regards defects which that examination ought to reveal.

The condition applies to goods sold in the course of a business. The meaning of the term satisfactory quality will probably, like the term merchantable quality before it, be subject to much debate. The definition also applies to second-hand goods, which are required to be of satisfactory quality. It is apparent, however, that a buyer cannot expect second-hand goods, of a lower price, to be of the same quality as new goods of a higher price: *Bartlett v Sydney Marcus Ltd 1965*.

Acceptance

Even if there is a breach of s 13 or s 14(2), the seller may argue that the buyer has accepted the goods. This means that the buyer is unable to exercise a remedy of *rejecting* the goods and reclaiming the purchase price but must instead treat the breach of condition as a breach of warranty and sue for damages for breach of contract. Under ss 34 and 35, the buyer is deemed to have accepted the goods in the following circumstances.

(a) When he intimates to the seller that he has accepted them, provided that he has had a reasonable opportunity of ascertaining whether they are in conformity with the contract: s 35(1);

(b) When the goods have been delivered to the buyer and he does any act in relation to them which is inconsistent with the ownership of the seller, for example, using or reselling them: s 35(1);

(c) When after the lapse of a reasonable time he retains the goods without intimating to the seller that he has rejected them: s 35(4). In determining whether a reasonable time has elapsed, one factor is whether they buyer has been afforded a reasonable opportunity of examination, for example by use: s 35(5). In the case of *Bernstein v Pamsons Motors 1987*, a buyer whose new car was neither of merchantable quality nor fit for the purpose, but who had used the car for three weeks and 140 miles, was unable to rescind the contract. Such a case might be decided differently under the revised legislation.

Arthur and s 13

The mountain bicycle was described as 'in excellent condition' and 'the latest model' by the salesman. It transpires that it is arguably not in excellent condition (because of the repair) and that it is not the latest model. This should support a conclusion that there has been a breach of s 13.

Arthur and s 14(2)

It is not clear whether the major repair to the frame has actually caused Arthur any problems; that is whether the mountain bicycle is no longer fit for the purpose. (If, for example, the repair was a substandard one, a breach would be likely.) It is not possible on the facts to determine whether there is a breach.

Acceptance by Arthur

It is likely that the lapse of a period of eight weeks will be deemed to constitute acceptance of the goods by Arthur. This is by no means clear-cut, though, especially in the light of the revised legalisation and its probable effect on cases such as *Bernstein*. His remedy will therefore be to sue for damages. He will probably be unable to return the goods and claim a full refund.

Chapter 12

11 CONSUMER PROTECTION

James, Neil and Hannah could bring an action against the producer of the prawns, Special Seafoods Ltd under the Consumer Protection Act (CPA) 1987. The essence of the Act is stated in s 2(1) CPA 1987: the producer of a defective product is liable for damage caused by that product. Liability is 'strict' and therefore there is no need for the plaintiff to prove that the defendant was negligent or at fault.

A producer will only be liable if it can be shown that its product was defective in some way. Defect is defined in Section 3(1): 'there is a defect if the safety of the product is not such as persons generally are entitled to expect.' This standard is an objective one. It is not what the actual consumer in question expects from the product but what 'persons generally' expect. This test will ultimately be answered by the court which is required to take into account the following guidelines in Section 3(2). These are:

(a) the way in which the goods are sold, and purpose;

(b) instructions or warnings;

(c) what might reasonably be done with the product

(d) the time the product was supplied

The plaintiffs in this case must be able to show that the prawns were defective and that this caused their illness.

Once a defect has been established the producer will be liable for damage caused wholly or partly by that defect. It is essential for the claimant to prove damage. The definition of damage is found in Section 5 CPA 1987. There is liability for death, personal injury and damage to property. However, there are certain limitations under the statute which apply to claims relating to damage to *property*. If compensation is being sought for damage to property caused by a defect in the product then there can be *no claim* for:

(a) damage to actual product or product supplied with defective product in it;

(b) damage to property not ordinarily intended for private use, occupation or consumption;

(c) damage to property not exceeding £275.

The object of this last limitation is to cut out small claims.

The plaintiffs will be able to claim compensation for the illness and any consequential loss arising from it. James will be entitled to compensation for the oriental rug provided that its value is more than £275. The same applies to Neil's silk shirt.

Once a plaintiff is able to satisfy all the requirements outlined above then they will have a good chance of success under the CPA 1987. It is then open for the producer to defend themselves on the grounds of one of the statutory defences stated in Section 4 of the Act. Special Seafoods may argue the 'state of the art' defence in relation to the unknown bacteria. This is the most controversial of the defences. The producer may argue that the state of scientific and technical knowledge was not such that a reasonable producer of products of the same description might be expected to have discovered the defect. If such a defence did succeed than this would defeat the claims of each of the plaintiffs.

Chapter 14

12 VICARIOUS LIABILITY

As a general rule, the person who is liable for the consequences of a wrongful act is the person who performs that act (the tortfeasor). In some circumstances the law recognises that there is another person who stands in such a position of authority in respect of the wrongdoer that he or she should share the responsibility for that wrong. This is the principle of vicarious liability. It is particularly important when considering the responsibility of an employer for the torts of his employee; the person suffering damage may prefer to seek damages from the wealthy employer rather than from the individual worker.

Employer/employee relationship

There must be the required employer-employee relationship to establish such vicarious liability. The distinction between the contract of service (of the employee) and the contract for services (of the independent contractor) is not always clear. A number of tests have been developed in the courts.

In *Mersey Docks and Harbour Board v Coggins & Griffiths 1947*, the test was the degree of control exercised by the 'employer' over the manner in which the 'employee' performed his duties. In *Cassidy v Minister of Health 1951*, this test was modified; where the employee was so skilled that detailed supervision was impossible, did the employer appoint and assign duties to that person? There is also the equipment test: did the 'employee' provide his own tools and equipment? If so the worker is more likely to be an independent contractor. By applying some or all of these tests the courts will decide on whether there is the necessary employer-employee relationship.

The course of employment

It must also be shown that the wrong was committed in the course of employment. The employer will be liable even if the employee carries out his job in a way which is contrary to his employer's instructions. Where a bus driver obstructed another vehicle, thereby causing an accident, he was still engaged in his duties as a driver even though he had been expressly forbidden to obstruct other vehicles, and so the employer was liable: *Limpus v London Omnibus Co 1862*. In contrast, where a conductor drove a bus he was acting outside the ambit of his job and the employer was not liable: *Beard v London Omnibus Co 1900*.

Actions by the employee for his own convenience may nonetheless be in the course of employment. A petrol tank driver carelessly disposing of a match while making a delivery was still within his employment (*Century Insurance v N Ireland Road Transport Board 1942*) whereas a petrol pump attendant who quarrelled with and assaulted a customer was not: *Warren v Henleys 1944*. An employer is liable if the employee defrauds a third party for his own gain in the course of his work: *Lloyd v Grace Smith 1912*.

The law is full of narrow distinctions in this area. This may be illustrated further by the various 'unauthorised passenger' cases. The usual position is that a person picked up by an employee who has been forbidden to give lifts is a trespasser and the employer is not liable for any harm done to him: *Twine v Bean's Express 1946*. This is in contrast to those cases where the passenger is a fellow employee or is giving assistance in the job: *Rose v Plenty 1976*.

The importance of the employer-employee relationship to vicarious liability is highlighted by the relatively limited scope of liability for the torts of an independent contractor. For a person other than the independent contractor to be liable the job must be exceptionally risky, or create a hazard for users of the highway, or the duty must be a personal one. There may be liability for the negligent choice of an incompetent contractor. There is also liability if the operation is one where strict liability is imposed.

Chapter 15

13 SPENDER

(a) There is a tort of negligence, which, briefly, consists of causing loss by failure to take reasonable care when there is a duty to do so. Most torts are wrongful acts. There can also be liability for a failure to act. To succeed in an action for negligence, the plaintiff must prove three things.

(i)   The defendant owed him (the plaintiff) a duty of care.

(ii) There was a breach of that duty by the defendant.

(iii) In consequence the plaintiff suffered injury, damage or, in some cases, financial loss.

The duty of care is owed to neighbours. This includes 'persons so closely and directly affected by my act that I ought reasonably to have them in contemplation as being so affected': *Donoghue v Stevenson 1932*. This has been developed in subsequent cases, so that it is now often said that there must be a special relationship. This means that the person making the statement must do so in some professional or expert capacity which makes it likely that others will rely on what has been said *(Esso Petroleum Co Ltd v Mardon 1976)* and that he or she must foresee that it is likely to be relied upon by another person: *Hedley Byrne v Heller & Partners 1964*. In this latter case, Hedley Byrne, an advertising agency, requested financial information about a client from the client's bankers, Heller & Partners. The bankers made non-committal replies which were held to be negligent misstatements of the client's resources. It was held that they had breached the duty of care.

Lord Denning laid down a test of a special relationship in *Chandler v Crane Christmas*. 'A special relationship is one where the defendant gives advice or information and the plaintiff relies on that advice. The defendant should realise that his words will be relied upon either by the person he is addressing or by a third party.'

Spender

Spender may therefore seek to obtain compensation by means of an action for breach of contract, perhaps by claiming that there has been a breach of s 13 SGSA and that the service was not carried out with reasonable care and skill. Alternatively, he may commence an action for negligence against the bank, claiming that the bank owed him a duty of care and that it was in breach of that duty.

(b) The contract which is embodied in the banker-customer relationship is a contract between the customer and the bank. This may sound obvious, but it means that in any action for breach of contract, Spender will make a claim against Barland Bank rather than against any of its employees.

A claim in negligence is usually brought by the injured party against the person who, it is claimed, has committed the tort. However in certain circumstances, notably the employer-employee relationship, the principle of vicarious liability can apply. It is often not worthwhile to sue the employer for damages since he may be of limited financial means. The employer usually has greater resources and may also have insurance cover. Two conditions must be satisfied for the employer to be liable for a tort of the employee. Firstly there must actually be the relationship between them of employer and employee. Secondly, the employee's tort must have been committed in the course of his employment. The first is usually fairly clear-cut. The second considers whether the employee was actually doing the work for which he was employed (compare *Limpus v London General Omnibus Co 1862* and *Beard v London General Omnibus Co 1900*).

This means that Spender would, under normal circumstances, claim against Penn, but that he could also rely on the principle of vicarious liability and bring a negligence action against Barland Bank. There is also a third possible person against whom a claim in negligence could be made. Penn's branch manager, Masters, instructed Penn to prepare and issue the information and so it may be possible to bring an action against Masters and attempt to show that he was negligent in allowing the statement to be issued.

Chapter 17

14   PUBLIC AND PRIVATE COMPANIES

Section 1(3) CA 1985 defines and specifies the requirements for being a public company, and provides that any company which is not a public company is a private company. The definition of 'public' company is a company, the memorandum of which states that it is to be a public company and which has also complied with the statutory requirements. These requirements relate to the following matters.

(a) *Membership and name:* the company must have at least two members and two directors. Its name must end with the words 'public limited company' (plc).

(b) *Capital.* The main differences between public and private companies are:

    (i)   minimum amount of £50,000 for a public company, no minimum for a private company;

    (ii) a public company may raise capital from the general body of investors by offering its shares or debentures to the public; a private company is prohibited from doing so. In practice only a public company can obtain a Stock Exchange or other investment exchange listing for its shares.

(c) *Registrar's certificate:* a public company may not do business or exercise any borrowing powers unless the Registrar has issued it a certificate of compliance with the statutory requirements. He must be satisfied that the company's allotted share capital is not less than the 'authorised minimum' (see (b) above). The company must have submitted a statutory declaration, signed by a director or the secretary, stating:

    (i)   compliance with 'authorised minimum' requirements;

    (ii) the amount paid up on allotted share capital;

    (iii) the amount of preliminary expenses of the company and the recipients of those expenses;

    (iv) payments or benefits given to any promoter and the consideration for them.

(d) *Payment for shares:* a public company may not allot shares unless they are allotted as paid up to at least one quarter of the nominal value plus any premium: nor may it allot partly or wholly for a non-cash consideration which may be performed more than five years after the allotment. In addition, it may not accept an undertaking for future performance of services as payment for shares or of a share premium.

(e) *Directors.* A public company must have at least two directors but a private company only one. A public company, except by ordinary resolution with special notice, may not appoint a director aged over 70: s 293.

(f) *Accounts*

   (i)   A public company has seven months from the end of its accounting reference period in which to produce its statutory audited accounts. The period for a private company is ten months.

   (ii) A private company, if qualified by its size, may have partial exemption from various accounting provisions.

   (iii) A listed public company may prepare a summary financial statement to be sent to members instead of full accounts in certain circumstances.

   (iv) The members of a private company may elect to dispense with the laying of accounts and reports before a general meeting: s 252.

Why register as a public limited company?

A company will need to register as a public company if it wishes to 'go public' and have a share issue quoted on The Stock Exchange.

It may also wish to register as a public company if it wishes to offer shares to the public, including any section of the public, however selected. The reason may be simply to extend the range of investors in the company. For instance, it may offer shares on the Alternative Investment Market, or under the Enterprise Investment Scheme.

Chapter 18

15 XYZ plc

Internal Memorandum

To: Board of Directors, XYZ plc

From: Company Secretary   Date: 1 January

Subject: Company formation

In order to form a company limited by shares it is necessary to submit the following documents to the Registrar of Companies.

i)   A memorandum of association. This contains the name and domicile of the company, its liability (e.g. limited) and capital and sets out the scope of its business by listing its objects and powers. It must be signed by at least two subscribers, dated and witnessed. Each subscriber must agree to subscribe for at least one share.

ii) The articles of association. This document sets out how the business affairs of the company are to be carried out. The document must be signed by the same subscribers, dated and witnessed. If the company's internal conduct is to be governed by the statutory Table A Articles set out in the Companies Act with no variations, then instead of submitting the document, the memorandum can be submitted endorsed 'registered without articles of association'. The Table A articles would then apply.

iii) A statement in the prescribed form giving particulars of the company's first directors and secretary and giving the address of the company's registered office. This is known as Form 10. The persons named as directors and secretary must sign the form to indicate their consent to act in these capacities and are then deemed to be appointed on incorporation.

iv) A statutory declaration. This is Form 12 and is given either by a solicitor involved in the company's formation or by one of the persons named as director or secretary. The declaration to be sworn is that all requirements of the Companies Act with respect to the company's registration have been complied with.

v) A fee for registration. This is currently £20.

Provided the documents are in order and lawful the Registrar of Companies will then issue a Certificate of Incorporation which gives the name, description and serial number of the company.

Chapter 19

16 AUDITORS

(a) An auditor may be removed from office before the expiry of his appointment by passing an ordinary resolution in general meeting: s 391. Special notice is required: s 391A.

(b) On ceasing to hold office for any reason (s 394) the auditor must deposit at the company's registered office either:

  (i) a statement that there are no circumstances connected with his departure which he considers should be brought to the notice of members or of creditors of the company, or

  (ii) a statement disclosing what those circumstances are.

This provision is intended to deal with the situation where the auditor is unhappy with the state of the company's affairs, but merely declines to seek further appointment and therefore avoids making his suspicions known.

In the case of resignation, the statement shall be deposited along with the notice of resignation; in the case of failure to seek re-appointment, it shall be deposited not less than 14 days before the time allowed for next appointing auditors; in any other case, the time limit is 14 days after ceasing to hold office: s 394(2).

If the auditor's notice contains a statement of circumstances the company must (unless the court holds it to be defamatory) send a copy to every person entitled to receive a copy of the accounts: s 394(3)(a). In all cases, a copy of the notice must be sent to the registrar.

An auditor who has been removed retains the right conferred by s 390 in relation to any general meeting of the company at which his term of office would have expired or at which it was proposed to fill the vacancy caused by his departure from office, namely to:

  (i) receive all notices of, and other communications relating to, a general meeting which a member of the company is entitled to receive;

  (ii) attend a general meeting of the company; and

  (iii) be heard at a general meeting which he attends on any part of the business of the meeting which concerns him as auditor.

If an auditor is to be removed, he can require the company to send to members a statement of circumstances prior to the meeting at which his removal is proposed. A resigning auditor can likewise require a statement of circumstances to be sent to members, prior to any general meeting at which his term of office would have expired or at which the vacancy is to be filled, or prior to an extraordinary general meeting which he has exercised his right to convene.

(c) The statutory duty of auditors is to report to the members whether the accounts give a true and fair view and have been properly prepared in accordance with the Companies Act: s 235. To fulfil this duty, the auditors must carry out such investigations as are necessary to form an opinion as to whether:

(i) proper accounting records have been kept and proper returns adequate for the audit have been received from branches;

(ii) the accounts are in agreement with the records: s 237; and

(iii) the information given in the directors' report is consistent with the accounts: s 235(3).

As in other breaches of a contractual duty, the remedy against an auditor who fails to discharge his duty is to be sued for any loss that results from the breach. An example can be found in *Re London and General Bank 1895*, where the auditors had breached their duty to report the true financial position of the company to the members. They had mentioned that possible difficulties might arise over some securities, but this was not sufficient to relieve them of liability for a dividend erroneously paid after they had reported.

Obviously the removal of auditors who are in breach of their duty is also an option.

Chapter 20

17 ARTICLES OF ASSOCIATION

(a) Section 14 provides that, once registered, a company's articles of association (and memorandum) bind a company to its members, the members to the company and members to members. Members are deemed to have separately covenanted with each other and the company to observe the provisions of the articles.

However, the binding effect is limited to the rights and obligations contained in the company's constitution which affect members in their capacity as members, for example, the right to receive notice of meetings, voting rights *(Pender v Lushington 1877)* and rights to receive dividends. Thus in *Hickman v Kent and Romney Marsh Sheepbreeders Association 1915*, an article which provided that disputes between the company and its members should be referred to arbitration was held to be binding on a member whose court action was stayed as a result. However, a similar provision was not binding in a dispute with a director in his capacity as director *(Beattie v ECF Beattie Ltd 1938)*. (It is often difficult to identify whether the rights and obligations which are sought to be enforced belong to the member *qua* member or in some other capacity *(cf Salmon v Quinn & Axtens 1909)*.

If a contract makes no express provision on a particular point but the articles do cover it, then the contract will be deemed to include the articles to that extent. An example would be where services are provided without agreement as to their remuneration. In *Re New British Iron Co ex part Beckwith 1898*, a contract between a director and the company was silent as to the remuneration payable but the articles provided that the directors should be paid £1,000 per annum. Here it was held that, although the directors could not enforce the articles under s 14, since they were asserting a claim *qua* directors not *qua* members, they could refer to the articles in order to establish the amount payable under their separate contracts. Equally a contract may expressly incorporate provisions in the articles, in which case, likewise, the articles will be upheld (subject always to the company's right to alter its articles) but not directly by virtue of the s 14 contract.

Section 14 binds members to members also. Thus in *Rayfield v Hands 1958*, where the articles provided that every director should be a member and that the directors must purchase the shares of any member who gave notice of his wish to dispose of them, there was held to be a contract between a member and the member-directors in relation to their holdings of the company's shares in its articles. The directors were thus bound by the provision.

(b) (i)   In such circumstances, K would be seeking to assert his right to receive compensation in his capacity as managing director and not in his capacity as a member of Retailer Ltd. The circumstances are similar to the case of *Eley v Positive Government Security Life Assurance Company 1876*. In this case the articles provided that Eley should be appointed as solicitor for life. It was held that the article was not enforceable by Eley against the company under s 14 since this statutory contract bound members to the company (and vice versa) only in their capacity as members. Eley was effectively making a claim as an outsider.

If K's contract expressly incorporates Article 1 then he has a contractual right to sue the company for breach of contract and for compensation based on the level of remuneration set out in that article. If his contract is silent on the matter, the courts, following the *Beckwith* case, are likely to imply the article into his service contract in order to ascertain the proper amount of remuneration. Either way, K should proceed against the company on the basis of his own contract for services and not s 14.

(ii)   The right which L is asserting affects her as a member of the company but the obligation on the directors, pursuant to Article 2, it can be argued, affects them as directors. In such a case, s 14 does not operate to create a contract between members and directors.

There is not an additional requirement in the Article that the directors must also be shareholders as there was in the case of *Rayfield v Hands* where an otherwise similar article was held to be enforceable by the member. There is no general rule that a director must also be a shareholder and it is unclear whether the courts would follow *Rayfield v Hands* on these slightly different facts. If the case was followed, L would be able to enforce her rights.

Chapter 21

18   H LTD

Report

To: The Board of Directors

From: A N Accountant   Date: 21 May 19X1

Subject: Financial assistance for purchase of own shares

(a) There is a general prohibition in s 151 against the provision by a company of financial assistance for the purchase of its own shares or for the purchase of shares in its holding company. 'Financial assistance' is very widely and comprehensively defined, to cover both direct and indirect methods. The situation described in the question is covered by the prohibition, whether the financial assistance comes directly in the form of a loan, or indirectly by allowing assets to be used as a security for a bank loan.

However, there are some exceptions to the general rule. S 153 applies two main tests to any suspect transaction.

(i) The principal purpose in giving assistance was not for the purpose of acquiring shares, or if it was for acquiring shares that purpose was an incidental part of some larger purpose of the company;

(ii) The assistance was given in good faith in the interests of the company.

While the second of these tests is satisfied, since the scheme aimed to cause minimum disruption to the company's trading, the first is not because the scheme's sole purpose was the giving of financial assistance. However, because S Ltd is a private company, it may be able to give such assistance, provided the company's net assets are not thereby reduced and provided certain requirements (part (b)) are met.

The facts of this case are not dissimilar to *Brady v Brady 1988* where assistance was provided for a management buy-out which would prevent the company from going into liquidation.

(b) A private company may give financial assistance for the acquisition of its own shares or the shares of its holding company, subject to the following conditions: ss 155-158.

(i) The financial assistance given *must not reduce the net assets* of the company or, if it does, the financial assistance is to be provided out of distributable profits.

(ii) There must be a *statutory declaration of solvency* by the directors (with a report by the auditors), stating that the company will be able to pay its debts in full over the following year after providing the financial assistance.

(iii) A *special resolution* must be passed to approve the transaction. Normally this is a resolution of the company which gives the assistance. However, if that company is a wholly owned subsidiary which assists the acquisition of shares of its holding company the members of the latter company must pass the resolution.

(iv) A *right to apply to the court* is given to members holding at least 10% of the issued shares (or of a class of shares). To permit them to exercise this right there is a four week standstill on the implementation of the resolution.

(v) The assistance must be given within eight weeks of the passing of the resolution.

Signed: A N Accountant

Chapter 22

19 DEBENTURES

(a) The major differences between shares and debentures are as follows.

(i) A shareholder is an owner or member of the company whereas a debentureholder is a creditor of the company.

(ii) A shareholder is entitled to vote at company meetings but a debentureholder has no such right (subject to the terms of the company's articles and debenture).

(iii) A shareholder becomes a member of the company when his name is entered on the register of members (s 22) which is a compulsory register; a debenture holder becomes a creditor of the company on completion of the debenture and a register of debentureholders, though usually kept, is not compulsory.

(iv) Unless the terms of the debenture impose restrictions, a company is entitled to redeem or purchase its debentures and can usually re-issue debentures which have been redeemed. With regard to shares, however, a company is subject to elaborate and stringent rules regulating the redemption or purchase of its own shares. Unlike debentures, shares cannot be issued at a discount.

(v) Interest must be paid to debentureholders regardless of a company's profits (it can be paid out of capital) whereas dividends will only be paid to shareholders if they can be funded by distributable profits and the company decides to declare a dividend.

(vi) On a liquidation, debentures must be repaid in full before anything is distributed to shareholders.

(b) Where there are insufficient assets in a company to satisfy all debts secured by charges it becomes necessary to determine their order of priority.

The basic principles are as follows.

(i) Legal changes rank according to their order of creation, the earliest taking priority.

(ii) Equitable changes also rank in order of creation, but an equitable change will only rank in priority to a later legal charge if the legal chargee had notice of the equitable charge.

(iii) A legal charge has priority over a later equitable charge.

(iv) A floating charge becomes a fixed charge upon crystallisation and, if crystallised at the time a later fixed charge is created, will rank in priority to it, but if not crystallised at that time will rank behind it.

These basic principles are subject to:

(i) any agreement reached between creditors and

(ii) to the system of registration which effectively provides notice to subsequent buyers or chargees of the existence of registered charges, whether legal or equitable.

Failure to register a registrable charge within 21 days of creation means that it will be void against an administrator or liquidator or purchaser and can be ignored by a subsequent chargee. If particulars are not delivered within the statutory period, a creditor who subsequently takes security over the company's property, and duly registers his charge, will take precedence over the previous unregistered charge, even if he had actual notice of it (unless expressed to be subject to it).

A floating charge will often contain a prohibition against the company creating any later fixed charges which would otherwise take priority. If the company breaches such a prohibition, the later chargee will take priority unless he had actual notice of the prohibition. Constructive notice, on the basis that filed particulars refer to the prohibition, will not in itself be sufficient to prejudice the fixed chargee: *Wilson v Kelland 1910*.

(c) Any debentureholder is a creditor who has the normal remedies of an unsecured creditor. These include:

(i) suing the company for debt and seizing its property if his judgment for debt is unsatisfied;

(ii) presenting a petition to the court for the compulsory liquidation of the company;

(iii) presenting a petition to the court for an administration order, ie a temporary reprieve.

A *secured* debentureholder (or the trustee of a debenture trust deed on behalf of secured debentureholders) may enforce the security. He may:

(i) take possession of the asset subject to the charge if he has a legal charge (if he has an equitable charge he may only take possession if the contract allows);

(ii)   sell it (provided the debenture is executed as a deed);

(iii) apply to the court for its transfer to his ownership by foreclosure order (rarely used and only available to a legal charge);

(iv) appoint a receiver of it (the usual first step).

The secured creditor may need an order of the court in some circumstances to enforce these remedies.

Chapter 23

20 SHAREHOLDER CONTROL

(a) *Directors' powers*

As a general rule, a company's directors are charged with managing the company's affairs on a day-to-day basis and are authorised to exercise all the powers of the company (Art 70, Table A): *John Shaw & Sons (Salford) Ltd v Shaw 1935*. They can take any decisions which are within the capacity of the company (as defined by the memorandum of association) unless a decision falls to be taken by the members in general meeting in accordance with either statutory provision or the company's articles of association.

Role of general meeting

They are many instances where the law seeks to hand power to the members in general meeting. For example, a 75% majority of votes cast in general meeting is required in the following circumstances:

(i)   to bring about an alteration of the company's articles (s 9);

(ii)   a reduction in share capital (s 135);

(iii) a change of name (s 28); or

(iv) an alteration of the objects clause (s 4).

The company in general meeting is also empowered to sanction any breach by the directors of the company's memorandum or articles.

Removal of directors

The shareholders also have the ultimate power of removing a director by passing an ordinary resolution (s 303) requiring only a simple majority. This power of removal – and the threat of removal – are perhaps the most effective means of exercising 'control' over the directors permitted by law. Shareholders also appoint the directors.

Directors' duties

The directors also owe certain 'duties' to the company and, in the event of breach of those duties can be sued in legal proceedings – by the company itself or, in certain cirumstances, by individual shareholders. broadly speaking, they owe a duty to the company to be honest, reasonably competent and not to seek personal advantage.

(b) However, the directors are not 'agents' of the members and it is only in defined circumstances (whether defined by the memorandum or articles or statutory provisions as mentioned above) that they can be directed by the company in general meeting.

Thus in *Salmon v Quin and Axtens Ltd 1909* the company's articles gave a power of veto to each of two joint managing directors in respect of certain transactions. When one of them dissented from a relevant resolution, the company in general meeting passed an ordinary resolution to 'ratify' the board resolution. The court held that the members could not override a provision in the articles by ordinary resolution alone. In *John Shaw & Sons (Salford) Ltd v*

Shaw 1935 the court said that the shareholders 'cannot themselves usurp the powers which by the articles are vested in the directors'.

However the *Salmon* case also illustrated that articles could give individual members a right of veto over certain specific decisions.

In practice, the effectiveness of the common provisions outlined in (a) above may be limited. In private companies this is often because the directors and shareholders are the same and so questions of the division of power between them are not relevant. In public companies, it will happen for the following reasons.

(i) There will be such a large number of shareholders who are widely dispersed and many of whom might not take a very active interest in the decisions taken by the company. This means that their ability to unite as a significant controlling force is much diminished.

(ii) A large proportion of the shares are held by institutional investors who are likely to be represented at board level and whose interests might be quite different from those of individual members.

In practice, therefore, it might be said that power rests with the board, particularly in the case of public companies, to a greater extent than an analysis of the various legal provisions empowering the shareholders might suggest.

Chapter 24

21 GLAD

(a) The written resolution procedure (s 381(A)) is a procedure available to private companies to pass resolutions without the need to call and hold a meeting nor to give prior notice. It requires the signature by or on behalf of all members who, at the date of the resolution, would be entitled to attend and vote at general meetings, to one or more documents, but if more than one then they must all accurately state the terms of the resolution. The date of the resolution is taken to be the date on which it is signed by or on behalf of the last member to sign.

A copy of any written resolution must be sent to the company's auditor.

Any company matter normally dealt with by resolution of the company in general meeting (whether ordinary, special or extraordinary) or by resolution of a meeting of a class of members of the company can be dealt with by this procedure save for the removal of a director or auditor before the expiration of his period of office (Sch 15 A) since both have a right to speak at a meeting.

(b) The short notice procedure (s 369) is one which enables a private limited company to call meetings without the need to comply with the usual rules for giving at least 21 days' notice in the case of an annual general meeting, and at least 14 days' notice (unless the business of the meeting requires longer notice) in the case of an extraordinary general meeting.

A company can call an annual general meeting at short notice provided all members agree, that is all members entitled to attend and vote at such meeting.

A company can call an extraordinary general meeting at short notice provided members together holding at least 95% in nominal value of the shares giving a right to attend and vote at such a meeting agree to it. A private company is entitled, furthermore, to pass an elective resolution (in accordance with s 379A) reducing the percentage in this case from 95% to not below 90%. The agreement to the short notice need not be in writing, although normally the practice is to append a formal waiver of the usual notice period to the notice of the meeting and obtain the members' signatures to it.

(c) If the company calls a general meeting to give effect to these proposals, the type of resolution and notice required in respect of each one is as follows.

   (i)   To elect Bill as managing director, an ordinary resolution for which 21 clear days' notice of the meeting at which it is to be considered is required (Art 38 Table A).

   (ii) To change the company's name to Sorry Ltd, a special resolution is required for which 21 clear days' notice is required (s 28).

   (iii) To increase the company's share capital, an ordinary resolution for which 14 days' notice is required (Arts 32 and 38).

   (iv) To authorise the directors to issue shares for an indefinite period, an elective resolution (s 80) with 21 clear days' notice is required and the consent of all members.

(d) If Len objects then the written resolution procedure cannot be used since it requires the agreement of all members (who would be entitled to attend and vote at the meeting which it replaces).

   However, the short notice procedure will still be available provided the other members agree, since the agreement of members holding only 95% in nominal value of the shares carrying the right to attend and vote is required. Len's holding is 5% and so the remaining members hold the necessary 95% to consent to this procedure being used.

Chapter 25

22   FOSS V HARBOTTLE

Ultimate control of a company rests with its members voting in general meeting since (among other things) the directors are required to lay annual accounts before a general meeting and may be removed from office by a simple majority of votes. But if the directors hold a majority of the voting shares or represent a majority shareholding the minority has no remedy unless the rules of minority protection apply. In *Foss v Harbottle 1843*, a shareholder (Foss) sued the directors of the company alleging that the directors had defrauded the company by selling land to it at an inflated price. The company was by this time in a state of disorganisation and efforts to call the directors to account at a general meeting had failed. It was held that the action must be dismissed since:

(a) the company as a person separate from its members is the only proper plaintiff in an action to protect its rights or property; and

(b) the company in general meeting must decide whether to bring such legal proceedings.

In laying down the general principles of procedure the court did nonetheless recognise that 'the claims of justice' must prevail over 'technical rules'. The protection of a minority in various situations is provided by making exceptions to *Foss v Harbottle* or defining its scope so that it is not applied where fairness requires a different solution.

(a) No majority vote can be effective to sanction an act of the company which is illegal.

   Such decisions taken in general meeting are not binding because a majority of members cannot decide that the company shall exceed its power or break the law. If they attempt to do so any member may apply to the court for a declaration that the decision is void and (if necessary) for an injunction to restrain the company from acting on the decision. The same used to be true of an *ultra vires* act, but the case law on this subject has been overruled by the provisions of the Companies Act 1989 allowing ratification of *ultra vires* actions.

(b) Where a majority merely disregards procedure or restrictions imposed by the articles of the company it is less certain that a minority can enforce due compliance by action in the courts. The courts have sometimes been inclined to treat these situations as mere internal matters which a majority of members should be free to regulate as they see fit. The cases below illustrate the two different judicial approaches.

In *Edwards v Halliwell 1950*, a trade union (subject to rules of company law on this point) had rules (equivalent to articles) by which members' contributions were fixed at a specific rate which could only be increased if so decided by a two-thirds majority of votes cast in a members' ballot. A meeting decided, without holding a ballot of members, to increase the rate of subscriptions. It was held the decision was invalid since it conflicted with the rules and the members who brought the action were entitled to a declaration that it was void. In *Salmon v Quin & Axtens 1909* the courts said that the articles were a contract and the minority was entitled to have the company's affairs managed in accordance with that contract.

In *Macdougall v Gardiner 1875*, however, the articles provided that a poll must be held if demanded at the meeting by at least five members. But when five members demanded a poll the chairman refused to comply. One of the members sued for a declaration that the resolutions passed on a show of hands were invalid. Here it was held that the court would not intervene in a mere 'irregularity' of internal procedure which could be regularised by a majority approving it. This doctrine has been much criticised. It is unlikely to be extended or even perhaps applied in modern cases.

A minority may also apply to the court for a remedy if a meeting is convened by a notice which does not, as the articles usually require (Table A Art 38), disclose in sufficient detail 'the general nature of the business' to be done: *Kaye v Croydon Tramways* and *Baillie v Oriental Telephone Co*. But a mere technical irregularity of procedure in convening a meeting may not suffice to invalidate its decisions. In *Bentley-Stevens v Jones 1974*, a director complained that he had not been given notice of a board meeting held to convene a general meeting at which a resolution was duly passed to remove him from office. In all other respects the correct procedure had been observed. It was held that the members of the company could waive any irregularity in convening the general meeting and the court would not intervene.

If the directors exercise powers given to them by the articles for an improper purpose a member may challenge them in the courts. But the court is likely to remit the matter back to the company in general meeting for decision by majority vote: *Bamford v Bamford 1970*.

(c) Where a member can show that there has been a fraud by the controlling majority, he may bring an action to protect the company (since the company cannot protect itself). It must be shown that:

(i)   what was taken belonged to the company;

(ii) it passed to those against whom the claim is made; and

(iii) those who appropriated the company's property are in control of the company.

To divert away from the company profitable contracts which it was about to make is to deprive it of its 'property' (for the purposes of this rule). In *Cook v Deeks 1916*, the directors who were also controlling shareholders negotiated a contract in the name of the company. They took the contract for themselves and passed a resolution in general meeting declaring that the company had no interest in the contract. A minority shareholder sued them as trustees for the company of the benefit of the contract. It was held that the contract 'belonged in equity to the company' and the directors could not, by passing a resolution in general meeting, bind the company to approving this action of defrauding it.

But merely to prevent the company from trading (so as to benefit a competitor) is not to deprive it of property. In *Scottish Cooperative Wholesale Society v Meyer 1959*, minority shareholders held 3,900 shares in a company formed by SCWS, which held the remaining 4,000. Three of the directors were SCWS's nominees, the remaining two being the minority. Following a dispute between the two sides SCWS proceeded to cut off supplies to the company, it being its sole supplier. From shares being worth about £6 they became virtually valueless. It was held that the petitioners succeeded only under s 459 (unfair prejudice). SCWS were ordered to pay them a fair price to buy them out.

(d) It is possible for a member to bring a 'derivative action'. This is an action taken out in his own name, and those of other shareholders, asserting the company's rights to recover property belonging to it. The action needs to demonstrate that those controlling the company have prevented the general meeting (or the company) from taking a particular course of action which is in the company's commercial interests: *Prudential Assurance Co v Newman Industries Ltd 1982*.

(e) A member may sue the company to enforce his personal rights against it. This is a different kind of minority action. In the other cases the majority is usually seeking to protect the company (and their interests in it) against others. In protecting his personal rights the member is protecting himself against the company. In *Pender v Lushington 1877*, the articles gave members one vote for each ten shares held by them but subject to a maximum of 100 votes for each member. A company which was a large shareholder transferred shares to the plaintiff to increase its voting power. At the meeting the chairman rejected the plaintiff's votes. The plaintiff sued and the company relied on the argument that only the company itself could object to an irregularity of voting procedure. It was held that the plaintiff's votes were a 'right of property' which he was entitled to protect by proceedings against the company.

The principle of Pender's case is restricted to protection of personal rights of membership. A member cannot sue merely to have the voting procedure of the articles observed (Macdougall's case above) since that is not sufficiently personal to him. But if he is denied his right to vote or to receive the dividend due to him *(Wood v Odessa Waterworks Co 1889)* he can sue the company.

(f) Any member may now apply to the court for relief under s 461 against *unfair prejudice* caused by the general conduct of the affairs of the company over a period, or by some specific act or omission, actual or proposed, of the company or done on its behalf: s 459. In addition to members a transferee, a personal representative of a deceased member or a trustee of a bankrupt member may apply. The Secretary of State may also make such a petition under s 460. The court has a wide discretion in making its order.

In addition, under s 122 Insolvency Act 1986 a single member may petition the court to wind up a company on the grounds that it is just and equitable to do so. In bringing the petition a member is not confined to matters that affect him as a member. What constitutes just and equitable grounds for winding up has been defined by case law prior to the Insolvency Act 1986. Examples include the breakdown in the relationship between the members of a quasi-partnership company leading to the exclusion of one or more members from the management of the company's business: *Ebrahimi v Westbourne Galleries Ltd 1973*.

INDEX OF TOPICS

For cases and statutes, please refer to the list at the front of this text.

Index of topics

For cases and statutes, please refer to the list at the front of this text.

For cases and statutes, please refer to the list at the front of this text.

For cases and statutes, please refer to the list at the front of this text.

For cases and statutes, please refer to the list at the front of this text.

For cases and statutes, please refer to the list at the front of this text.

For cases and statutes, please refer to the list at the front of this text.

ORDER FORM

To order your BUSINESS BASICS books, ring our credit card hotline on 0181-740 2211. Alternatively, send this page to our Freepost address or fax it to us on 0181-740 1184.

To: BPP Publishing Ltd, FREEPOST, London W12 8BR   **Tel: 0181-740 2211**
Fax: 0181-740 1184

Forenames (Mr / Ms): _____

Surname: _____

Address: _____

Post code: _____   Date of exam (month/year): _____

Please send me the following books:

	Price	Quantity	Total
Accounting	£13.95	....	....
Human Resource Management	£13.95	....	....
Law	£13.95	....	....
Organisational Behaviour	£13.95	....	....
Economics	£13.95	....	....
Information Technology	£13.95	....	....
Marketing	£13.95	....	....
Quantitative Methods	£13.95	....	....

Please include postage:

UK: £3.00 for first plus £2.00 for each extra   ....

Europe (inc ROI): £5.00 for first plus £4.00 for each extra   ....

Rest of the World: £8.00 for first plus £6.00 for each extra   ....

Total

I enclose a cheque for £ _____ **or charge to Access/Visa/Switch**

Card number ☐☐☐☐ ☐☐☐☐ ☐☐☐☐ ☐☐☐☐ ☐☐☐☐

Start date (Switch only) _____   Expiry date _____

Issue number (Switch only) _____

Signature _____